Succeeding in Business™ with Microsoft® Excel® 2010:
A Problem-Solving Approach

*"With knowledge comes opportunity,
with opportunity comes success."*
— Anonymous

Debra Gross
The Ohio State University

Frank Akaiwa
Indiana University

Karleen Nordquist
Smarthinking, Inc.

COURSE TECHNOLOGY
CENGAGE Learning™

Australia • Brazil • Japan • Korea • Mexico • Singapore • Spain • United Kingdom • United States

COURSE TECHNOLOGY
CENGAGE Learning

Succeeding in Business™ with Microsoft®
Excel® 2010: A Problem-Solving Approach
   Debra Gross, Frank Akaiwa, Karleen Nordquist

Vice President, Publisher: Nicole Jones Pinard

Executive Editor: Marie L. Lee

Senior Product Manager: Kathy Finnegan

Product Manager: Leigh Hefferon

Associate Product Manager: Julia Leroux-Lindsey

Editorial Assistant: Jacqueline Lacaire

Senior Marketing Manager: Ryan DeGrote

Marketing Coordinator: Kristen Panciocco

Developmental Editor: Jane Pedicini

Senior Content Project Manager: Jennifer Goguen McGrail

Composition: Value Chain International

Art Director: GEX Publishing Service

Text Designer: Tim Blackburn

Cover Designer: GEX Publishing Services

Cover Illustration: GEX Publishing Services

Copy Editor: Suzanne Huizenga

Proofreader: Kathy Orrino

Indexer: Sharon Hilgenberg

For product information and technology assistance, contact us at
Cengage Learning Customer & Sales Support, 1-800-354-9706

For permission to use material from this text or product, submit all requests online at **cengage.com/permissions**
Further permissions questions can be emailed to
permissionrequest@cengage.com

Library of Congress Control Number: 2010931063

International Edition:
ISBN-13: 978-0-538-47323-1
ISBN-10: 0-538-47323-1

Cengage Learning International Offices

Asia
www.cengageasia.com
tel: (65) 6410 1200

Australia/New Zealand
www.cengage.com.au
tel: (61) 3 9685 4111

Brazil
www.cengage.com.br
tel: (55) 11 3665 9900

India
www.cengage.com.co.in
tel: (91) 11 4364 1111

Latin America
www.cengage.com.mx
tel: (52) 55 1500 6000

UK/Europe/Middle East/Africa
www.cengage.com.co.uk
tel: (44) 0 1264 332 424

Represented in Canada by
Nelson Education, Ltd.
Tel: (416) 752 9100 / (800) 668 0671
www.nelson.com

Cengage Learning is a leading provider of customized learning solutions with office locations around the globe, including Singapore, the United Kingdom, Australia, Mexico, Brazil, and Japan. Locate your local office at: **www.cengage.com/global**

For product information: **www.cenage.com/international**
Visit your local office: **www.cengage.com/global**
Visit our corporate website: **www.cengage.com**

Printed in the United States of America
1 2 3 4 5 6 7 14 13 12 11 10

Brief
Contents

Table of **Contents**

Chapter 5: Retrieving Data for Computation, Analysis, and Reference   290

Chapter 8: Using Data Tables and Excel Scenarios for What-If Analysis   500

Preface

THE SUCCEEDING IN BUSINESS™ SERIES

Because you're ready for more.

Increasingly students are coming into the classroom with stronger computer skills. As a result, they are ready to move beyond "point and click" skills and learn to use these tools in a way that will assist them in the business world.

You've told us you and your students want more: more of a business focus, more realistic case problems, more emphasis on application of software skills and more problem-solving. For this reason, we created the **Succeeding in Business Series.**

The **Succeeding in Business Series** is the first of its kind designed to prepare the technology-savvy student for life after college. In the business world, your students' ability to use available tools to analyze data and solve problems is one of the most important factors in determining their success. The books in this series engage students who have mastered basic computer and applications skills by challenging them to think critically and find effective solutions to realistic business problems.

We're excited about the new classroom opportunities this new approach affords, and we hope you are too. We look forward to hearing about your successes!

The Succeeding in Business Team
www.cengage.com/ct/succeeding
course.succeeding@cengage.com

The Succeeding in Business Instructor Resources

A unique approach requires unique instructor support; and we have you covered. We take the next step in providing you with outstanding Instructor Resources—developed by educators and experts and tested through our rigorous Quality Assurance process. Whether you use one resource or all the resources provided, our goal is to make the teaching and learning experience in your classroom the best it can be. With Course Technology's resources, you'll spend less time preparing, and more time teaching.

To access any of the items mentioned below, go to www.cengage.com/coursetechnology or contact your Course Technology Sales Representative.

Instructor's Manual
The instructor's manual offers guidance through each level of each chapter. You will find lecture notes that provide an overview of the chapter content along with background information and teaching tips. Also included are classroom activities and discussion questions that will get your students thinking about the business scenarios and decisions presented in the book.

ExamView® Test Bank

ExamView features a user-friendly testing environment that allows you to not only publish traditional paper and LAN-based tests, but also Web-deliverable exams. In addition to the traditional multiple-choice, true/false, completion, short answer, and essay, questions, the **Succeeding in Business Series** emphasizes new critical thinking questions. Like the textbook, these questions challenge your students with questions that go beyond defining key terms and focus more on the real-world decision making process they will face in business, while keeping the convenience of automatic grading for you.

Student Data Files and Solution Files

All student data files necessary to complete the hands-on portion of each level and the end-of chapter material are provided along with the solution files.

Annotated Solution Files and Rubrics

Challenging your students shouldn't make it more difficult to set grading criteria. Each student assignment in your textbook will have a correlating Annotated Solution File that highlights what to look for in your students' submissions. Grading Rubrics list these criteria in an auto-calculating table that can be customized to fit the needs of your class. Electronic file format of both of these tools offers the flexibility of online or paper-based grading. This complete grading solution will save you time and effort on grading.

PowerPoint Presentations

The PowerPoint presentations deliver visually impressive lectures filled with the business and application concepts and skills introduced in the text. Use these to engage your students in discussion regarding the content covered in each chapter. You can also distribute or post these files for your students to use as an additional study aid.

Figure Files

Every figure in the text is provided in an easy to use file format. Use these to customize your PowerPoint Presentations, create overheads, and many other ways to enhance your course.

Sample Syllabus

A sample syllabus is provided to help you get your course started. Provided in a Word document, you can use the syllabus as is or modify it for your own course.

Succeeding in Business Series Walk-Through

The Succeeding in Business approach is unique. It moves beyond point-and-click exercises to give your students more real-world problem solving skills that they can apply in business. In the following pages, step through *Succeeding in Business with Microsoft Excel 2010* to learn more about the series pedagogy, features, design, and reinforcement exercises.

Thought-provoking quotes at the beginning of each chapter set the stage for the concepts to be presented.

The Learning Objectives provide a quick reference for topics covered in the chapter.

Each chapter begins with an introduction that provides an overview of the skills and concepts students will learn.

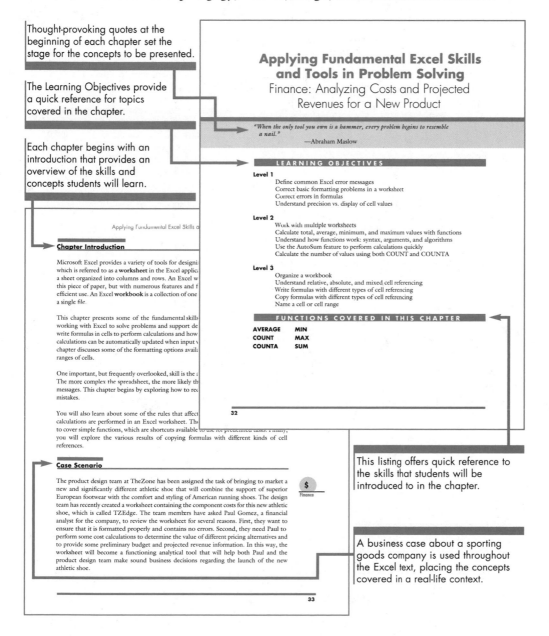

Applying Fundamental Excel Skills and Tools in Problem Solving
Finance: Analyzing Costs and Projected Revenues for a New Product

"When the only tool you own is a hammer, every problem begins to resemble a nail."
—Abraham Maslow

LEARNING OBJECTIVES

Level 1
Define common Excel error messages
Correct basic formatting problems in a worksheet
Correct errors in formulas
Understand precision vs. display of cell values

Level 2
Work with multiple worksheets
Calculate total, average, minimum, and maximum values with functions
Understand how functions work: syntax, arguments, and algorithms
Use the AutoSum feature to perform calculations quickly
Calculate the number of values using both COUNT and COUNTA

Level 3
Organize a workbook
Understand relative, absolute, and mixed cell referencing
Write formulas with different types of cell referencing
Copy formulas with different types of cell referencing
Name a cell or cell range

FUNCTIONS COVERED IN THIS CHAPTER

AVERAGE	MIN
COUNT	MAX
COUNTA	SUM

Chapter Introduction

Microsoft Excel provides a variety of tools for designi[ng] which is referred to as a **worksheet** in the Excel applic[ation] a sheet organized into columns and rows. An Excel w[orksheet] this piece of paper, but with numerous features and f[or] efficient use. An Excel **workbook** is a collection of one [or more] a single file.

This chapter presents some of the fundamental skills [for] working with Excel to solve problems and support de[cisions] write formulas in cells to perform calculations and how calculations can be automatically updated when input v[alues] chapter discusses some of the formatting options avail[able for] ranges of cells.

One important, but frequently overlooked, skill is the [ability] The more complex the spreadsheet, the more likely th[at it contains] messages. This chapter begins by exploring how to rec[ognize and correct] mistakes.

You will also learn about some of the rules that affect [how] calculations are performed in an Excel worksheet. Th[is chapter goes on] to cover simple functions, which are shortcuts available [to use for predefined tasks. Finally,] you will explore the various results of copying formulas with different kinds of cell references.

Case Scenario

The product design team at TheZone has been assigned the task of bringing to market a new and significantly different athletic shoe that will combine the support of superior European footwear with the comfort and styling of American running shoes. The design team has recently created a worksheet containing the component costs for this new athletic shoe, which is called TZEdge. The team members have asked Paul Gomez, a financial analyst for the company, to review the worksheet for several reasons. First, they want to ensure that it is formatted properly and contains no errors. Second, they need Paul to perform some cost calculations to determine the value of different pricing alternatives and to provide some preliminary budget and projected revenue information. In this way, the worksheet will become a functioning analytical tool that will help both Paul and the product design team make sound business decisions regarding the launch of the new athletic shoe.

This listing offers quick reference to the skills that students will be introduced to in the chapter.

A business case about a sporting goods company is used throughout the Excel text, placing the concepts covered in a real-life context.

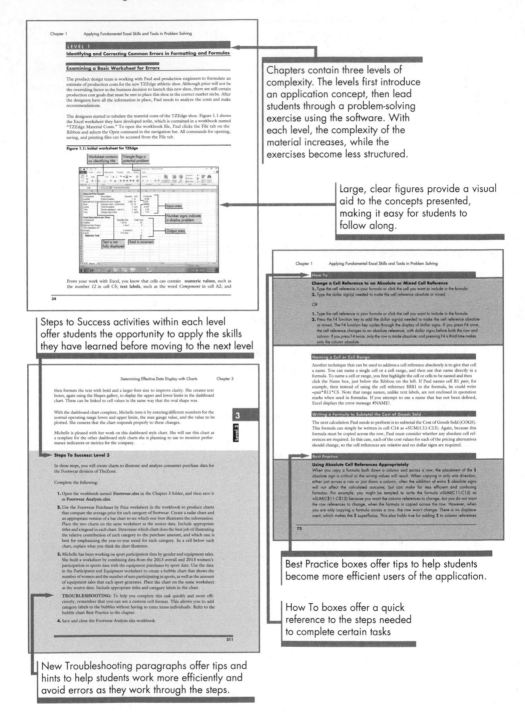

Chapters contain three levels of complexity. The levels first introduce an application concept, then lead students through a problem-solving exercise using the software. With each level, the complexity of the material increases, while the exercises become less structured.

Large, clear figures provide a visual aid to the concepts presented, making it easy for students to follow along.

Steps to Success activities within each level offer students the opportunity to apply the skills they have learned before moving to the next level

Best Practice boxes offer tips to help students become more efficient users of the application.

How To boxes offer a quick reference to the steps needed to complete certain tasks

New Troubleshooting paragraphs offer tips and hints to help students work more efficiently and avoid errors as they work through the steps.

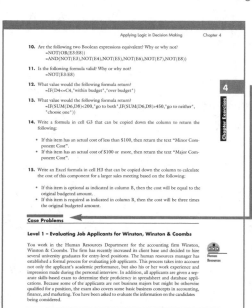

Business-focused case problems provide additional practice for the problem-solving concepts and skills presented in each level.

The Chapter Summary provides a brief review of the lessons in the chapter.

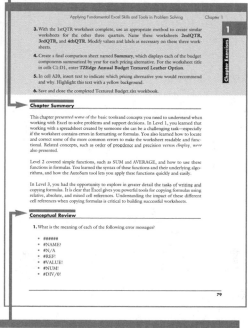

The Case scenario for the Level 3 problem builds through the text, giving students the opportunity to build a portfolio of projects.

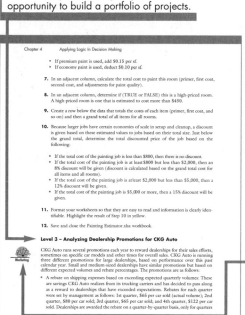

Conceptual Review questions provide a brief review of key concepts covered throughout the chapter.

Each case problem focuses on a specific business discipline, such as accounting, finance, marketing, sales, and operations management. Marginal icons representing each discipline make it easy to see which disciplines are covered in each case problem.

About the Authors

Debra Gross
Ohio State University
For the past 13 years Debra has been teaching students to use business software tools for problem solving. Prior to teaching, Debra spent 17 years in the corporate world in various aspects of capital project management and business process redesign in the food and chemical industries. She has co-authored several books and a series of case study problems. Debra currently teaches at the Ohio State University in the department of Computer Science and Engineering where she is also the Course Coordinator for several classes teaching the use of spreadsheet and databases to solve problems. Debra received her MBA from the University of Chicago Graduate School of Business in Finance and Accounting and an S.B. from MIT in Chemical Engineering.

Frank Akaiwa
Indiana University
Frank E. Akaiwa has been teaching in the Kelley School of Business at Indiana University since 1997. He holds degrees from Tennessee Technological University and Indiana University. Prior to teaching at Indiana University, Mr. Akaiwa worked as a civilian engineer for the U. S. Navy. Bringing together his engineering and operations background with his affinity for technology, Mr. Akaiwa has thoroughly enjoyed helping students learn how to apply technology to contemporary business situations. Many of the ideas and concepts presented in this textbook were developed to help students move beyond simple "point and click" usages of computer applications. The author resides in Bloomington, IN with his wife, Carolyn Cooke, their three children, Jonathon, Benjamin, and Abigail, a menagerie of animals, and a closet full of old computers.

Karleen Nordquist
Smarthinking, Inc.
Karleen Nordquist has been tutoring Accounting and Finance topics for post-secondary students through Smarthinking, Inc., since 2000. She also has over a dozen years of experience teaching information systems and business-related courses, and enjoys reading and learning about technology of all forms. Teaching and learning is in Ms. Nordquist's blood, as she comes from a family rife with educators. She also works as an accounting and information systems analyst and consultant. Ms. Nordquist has earned degrees at Minnesota State University Moorhead and the University of North Dakota. Prior to entering the teaching profession, she worked in public accounting and as an auditor.

Author Acknowledgements

Our thanks to the many people at Course Technology for helping us to make the third edition of this text such a success, including Marie L. Lee, Executive Editor; Brandi Shailer, Associate Acquisitions Editor; Leigh Hefferon, Product Manager; and our phenomenal and patient developmental editor, Jane Pedicini. We would also like to single out the following people at Course Technology in appreciation of their excellent work in support of this book: Jennifer Goguen McGrail, Senior Content Project Manager; Ryan DeGrote, Senior Marketing Manager; Kristen Panciocco, Marketing Coordinator; GreenPenQA, John Freitas, Susan Pedicini, and Susan Whalen, QA Testers; Julia Leroux-Lindsey, Associate Product Manager; and Jacqueline Lacaire, Editorial Assistant.

— **Debra Gross**
— **Frank Akaiwa**
— **Karleen Nordquist**

In addition to the wonderful Course Technology team, I would also like to thank my husband, Dan for his patience and continuing sound advice. A special thank you to my Ohio State University colleagues Katherine Reeves and Michelle Mallon, who both provided much needed assistance while I was focused on this book. I would also like to acknowledge Joshua King for his enormous help testing the chapter problems.
— **Debby**

Carolyn, you are the love of my life; thank you for your love and patience through this journey. Without your help, I never would have found the time for this project. To my children; Abigail, Benjamin, and Jonathon, thank you for allowing me to spend many nights and weekends working instead of paying attention to you. Now, it is finally your turn!
— **Frank**

I would very much like to thank Richard and Edna Nordquist and the rest of my family for all their continual love, prayers, and support.
—**Karleen**

We would like to dedicate this book to the memory of our friend and colleague, Bill Littlefield, who enjoyed teaching so much, he helped develop the Succeeding in Business series as a means of sharing his pedagogy with other teachers.

New Features in Microsoft Excel 2010

"If a man empties his purse into his head, no man can take it away from him. An investment in knowledge always pays the best interest."
—Benjamin Franklin

Introduction to Microsoft Excel 2010

Microsoft Excel 2010 includes innovative features that assist you in creating professional worksheets and performing a wide range of calculations. Some of the new features in Excel 2010 include a new File tab, which displays the new Backstage view when you click it. This new user interface provides easier access to file tasks and commands. There is a similar layout and design for the Backstage view for each of the Microsoft Office 2010 applications. They are differentiated by color with green signifying Excel.

Collaboration among Excel users has been made even easier with the ability to directly save files to a Microsoft SharePoint Server, which is a Microsoft technology solution for hosting Web sites and making workbooks available on the Internet, and to SkyDrive, which is part of Windows Live. Users can then access these files via a new Web App version of Excel 2010, which offers much of the functionality of the desktop version of Excel 2010 and allows multiple people to work together on the same file. Excel 2010 also includes many new and improved functions. Microsoft has addressed any inconsistency issues with previous versions with its new Compatibility functions category.

Starting Excel 2010

Starting Excel 2010 in Windows 7 is similar to starting the program in previous versions of Windows. If you are starting Excel for the first time, you may be prompted to register the program, which is relatively easy to do through the Internet by following the steps in the Activation Wizard.

How To

Start Excel 2010
1. Click the Start button 🔵 on the Windows taskbar.
2. Point to All Programs.
3. Click the Microsoft Office folder, and then click Microsoft Excel 2010.

OR

1. Click the Start button 🔵 on the Windows taskbar.
2. Type **ex** in the Search programs and files text box.
3. Click Microsoft Excel 2010 under Programs.

If you want the Excel program option to always appear on the Start menu, simply right-click the Microsoft Office Excel 2010 command in the Start menu, and then click Pin to Start Menu. The program moves to the upper portion of the Start menu.

Exploring the Excel Window

The default Excel window, as shown in Figure 1, contains several standard elements. In the upper-left corner is the Quick Access Toolbar, which by default contains the Save, Undo, and Redo buttons. You can customize the Quick Access Toolbar to include command buttons that you frequently use so they are easily available at all times. On the far left of the Quick Access Toolbar is the new Excel program button ▣. Clicking this button displays a menu with the standard window sizing features.

Figure 1: Initial Excel window with the Home tab displayed

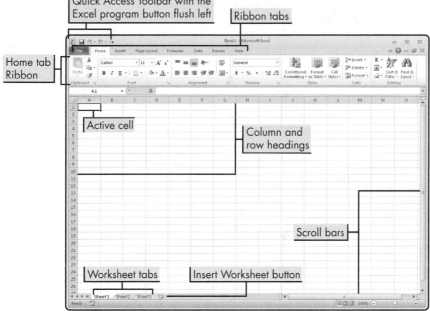

Just below the Quick Access Toolbar is the Ribbon. The Ribbon, which first appeared in Excel 2007, is here to stay. The Ribbon feature replaces menus and toolbars formerly in earlier versions of Excel and makes finding options easier than ever.

The Excel worksheet consists of cells—a **cell** being the intersection of a row and a column. Each cell is named according to the column and the row where it's located. In Figure 1, for example, the active cell is named A1 because it is located in column A, row 1. Excel 2010 supports up to 16,384 columns and 1,048,576 rows for data in a single worksheet. Column headings are labeled from A to Z, and then AA to ZZ, and then finally AAA through XFD. To move across the columns or down the rows, you can use horizontal and vertical scroll bars on the right and bottom edges of the worksheet.

Each worksheet is identified by its sheet tab. A new workbook contains three worksheets by default, as in previous versions. If you need additional worksheets, simply click the Insert Worksheet button ⬚ located to the right of the last worksheet tab.

How To

Rename a Worksheet
1. Double-click the worksheet tab.
2. Type the new name.
3. Press the Enter key.

OR

1. Right-click the worksheet tab.
2. Click Rename on the shortcut menu.
3. Type the new name.
4. Press the Enter key.

Using the File Tab in Backstage View

The File tab, located to the left of the Quick Access Toolbar, replaces the 2007 Office button. When you click the File tab, some of the features formerly found on the Office button, such as Save, Open, Print, and Close, appear in the navigation bar on the left side of the screen. There are also tabs that provide access to frequently used commands, such as Recent, New, and Help. You use the Options command to open the Excel Options dialog box, where you can customize your Excel working environment, specifying, for example, options related to formula calculations, performance, and error handling, as well as options for saving your workbooks. See Figure 2.

Also new is the way in which the File tab commands and options are displayed—that is, in the **Backstage view**. For example, when you select the New tab in the navigation bar (see Figure 2), two columns of options appear to the right side of the screen. In this case, you have the option to create a new blank workbook, select a recently used template or a sample one, or search Office.com for a specialize template. When you select an option, a preview of it appears on the right.

Opening and Closing Files in Excel 2010

Excel 2010 still uses the file format introduced in Excel 2007. You can open any file created in a previous version of Excel, and if you want, you can save files in the format associated with a previous version of Excel as well. However, if you save the file in the Excel 97–2003 format, it might not include all the functionality available in the Excel 2010 format.

Figure 2: File tab in Backstage view

Backstage view provides easy access to file-related tasks

How To

Open a File

1. Click the File tab on the Ribbon.

2. Click the Open command. The Open dialog box appears, as shown in Figure 3.

Figure 3: Open dialog box

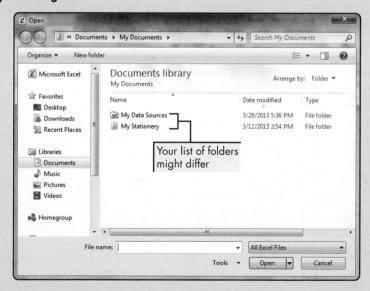

3. In the Open dialog box, navigate to the drive and folder location for the file, and then select the filename.

4. Click the Open button.

OR

1. Click the File tab on the Ribbon.

2. Click the Recent tab to display a list of workbooks that you have opened recently.

3. Click the file you want to open.

How To

Close a File

1. Click the File tab on the Ribbon.

2. Click the Close command.

3. Click the Save button. If you need to save the file before closing, a message box appears, asking if you want to save the changes you made to the file. If the file has never been saved before, clicking the Save button in the message box opens the Save As dialog box.

Saving Files in Excel 2010

The default file extension for files created in Excel 2010 consists of four characters, such as .xlsx. You can still save a file in an earlier Excel file format, but the file might not include all the functionality available in the Excel 2010 format. Table 1 lists the file extensions for the file types available in Excel, most of which you may be familiar with. For example, .xlsx is the file format for an Excel workbook. Also available are Portable Document Format (PDF) and the XML Paper Specification (XPS) options, which you use to save the content of a workbook in a format that preserves the worksheet appearance, but not the spreadsheet functionality. The OpenDocument Spreadsheet (ODS) format, which is part of the Open-Document Formats (ODFs) family, uses XML to represent electronic documents in an open, non-proprietary manner. The format is common to many office productivity suites including GoogleDocs and OpenOffice.

Table 1: Comparison of frequently used file extensions

File Type	Excel 2010
Excel workbook	.xlsx
Excel template	.xltx
Excel workbooks with macros	.xlsm
Excel templates with macros	.xltm
PDF	.pdf
XPS Document	.xps
OpenDocument Spreadsheet	.ods

Excel 2010 gives you 27 different format options for saving a file using either the File tab or the Quick Access Toolbar.

How To

Save a File

1. Click the File tab on the Ribbon.

2. Click the Save command. Excel saves the changes you have made.

3. If you are saving a file for the first time, the Save As dialog box opens.

4. Enter a filename, choose a location in which to save the file, and specify the file type (if necessary), and then click the Save button.

OR

1. Click the Save button 🖫 on the Quick Access Toolbar. Excel saves the changes you have made.

2. If you are saving a file for the first time, the Save As dialog box opens.

3. Enter a filename, choose a location in which to save the file, and specify the file type (if necessary), and then click the Save button.

Sharing Files in Excel 2010

You can use the File tab to access sharing options in Excel 2010. Options include sending a variety of formats using email, and saving directly to SharePoint and also directly to the Web on Windows Live SkyDrive, as shown in Figure 4. The Windows Live SkyDrive offers up to 25 GB of online storage space that can be shared with friends and co-workers. Microsoft Office 2010 allows you to save your files directly to your Windows Live account. Folders on the SkyDrive can be shared or kept private. There is also a public space available for anyone to share a file without having to authorize permissions.

Figure 4: Saving to Windows Live SkyDrive

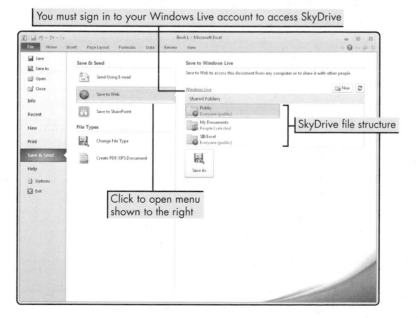

You must sign in to your Windows Live account to access SkyDrive

SkyDrive file structure

Click to open menu shown to the right

How To

Save a File to Windows Live SkyDrive
1. Click the File tab on the Ribbon.
2. Click the Save & Send tab.
3. Click Save to Web under the list of Save & Send options.
4. Click the Sign In button. If you don't have a Windows Live account, click the Sign up for Windows Live link and follow the instructions to sign up for an account.

Using the Excel Web App

The Excel Web App offers a user interface that is consistent with Excel 2010, including the appearance of the Ribbon. You can store and share files using Windows Live SkyDrive. You can set permissions to allow other users to access your files. Moreover, you can enable multiple users to allow a group to simultaneously work on the same file. All you need to do is log in to Windows Live.

Using and Customizing the Ribbon

The Ribbon allows Excel users, both experienced and novice, to find commands and features without searching through endless menus. Instead, the Ribbon organizes them into tabs and groups. Each time you launch Excel 2010, eight tabs initially appear on the Ribbon: File, Home, Insert, Page Layout, Formulas, Data, Review, and View, as described in Table 2. The Ribbon is dynamic and changes when you click a tab or as you perform various tasks. For example, if you create a chart, three additional contextual tabs appear on the Ribbon. Contextual tabs are displayed when you create or select various features, such as a chart, picture, or diagram.

Table 2: Tabs on the Ribbon in Excel

Ribbon Tab	Description
Home	Includes the most frequently used editing and formatting options, such as Cut, Copy, Paste, Font, Alignment, Number formats, Styles
Insert	Includes options for inserting objects, such as tables, pictures, charts, PivotTables, sparklines, and text boxes, as well as creating hyperlinks and inserting headers and footers
Page Layout	Includes options for changing the layout of a worksheet, such as Page Setup, Page Orientation (Portrait and Landscape), and Scale to Fit
Formulas	Includes commands for creating formulas and functions, auditing formulas, and naming ranges
Data	Includes commands for sorting and filtering data, creating outlines, and getting external data
Review	Includes features for finalizing your workbook before distributing it, such as Spelling, Thesaurus, Worksheet and Workbook Protection, and Comments
View	Includes options for changing your view of the worksheet, such as Hide, Split, Page Break Preview, Page Layout View, and Freeze Panes

On each tab, commands are organized into groups. On the Home tab, for example, you'll find a Clipboard group, which contains commands for moving and copying data and formats, and a Font group, which contains commands for enhancing font formats. Some groups also display a small arrow on the right side, called a Dialog Box Launcher. Clicking a Dialog Box Launcher opens a dialog box or task pane for the group, with the full set of features and options available for that group. For example, to see font options beyond what you see on the Home tab of the Ribbon, click the Dialog Box Launcher in the Font group, and the Format Cells dialog box opens, as shown in Figure 5.

Figure 5: Font dialog box launcher and Format Cells dialog box

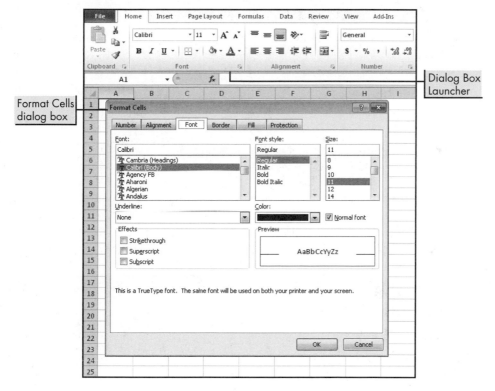

In addition to the standard tabs, Excel 2010 includes an optional Developer tab that can be added to the Ribbon. You might want to add this tab to the Ribbon if you use macros or work with XML files. To add the Developer tab to the Ribbon, open the Excel Options dialog box (click the File tab and then click the Options command), and then click the Customize Ribbon category. See Figure 6. Click the check box to the left of the Developer tab name. Click the plus sign to see the Developer-related options.

As you can see in Figure 6, you can use the Excel Options dialog box to customize the Ribbon. You can add new tabs to the Ribbon, add new groups to any tab, and rename any group or tab. You can also add or remove any command to or from a group. This level of customization will allow knowledge workers to arrange the menus and commands as they see fit. A cautious approach is advised until you are comfortable working with the default Excel 2010 Ribbon. You can easily reset any customization with the Customizations Reset feature.

Figure 6: Excel Options dialog box

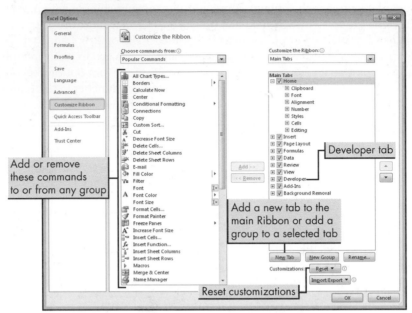

If you need more room on the screen for your worksheet, you can minimize the Ribbon so that only the tabs are displayed. The Minimize the Ribbon button is located to the left of the Help button just above the Ribbon. Once you minimize the Ribbon, the button changes to the Expand the Ribbon button so you can redisplay the Ribbon.

How To

Minimize or Redisplay the Ribbon

1. Click the Minimize the Ribbon button ⌃. Click the Expand the Ribbon button ⌄.

OR

1. Right-click any tab or right-click in an empty area on the Ribbon.
2. Click Minimize the Ribbon on the shortcut menu. Right-click the tab and then deselect Minimize the Ribbon on the shortcut menu.

OR

1. Double-click any tab to minimize or redisplay the Ribbon.

Using the Keyboard to Make Selections

You can still use the keyboard to initiate certain commands. If you press the Alt key, Excel displays KeyTips next to each command on the Quick Access Toolbar and next to each tab on the Ribbon. **KeyTips** display the access key for a particular command or tab. Figure 7 shows the KeyTips that appear when you press the Alt key. To invoke a command on the Quick Access Toolbar or to choose a tab, simply type the appropriate KeyTip. For example, press the 1 key to save the workbook or the H key to choose a command on the Home tab.

Figure 7: KeyTips on the Ribbon

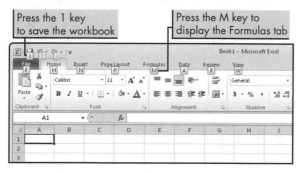

If you choose to display KeyTips for a particular tab, the tab opens and displays KeyTips for all commands for which an access key is available. For example, Figure 8 shows the KeyTips that appear on the Home tab once you have pressed the H key. To initiate a command, press the letter(s) or number, or you can press the Tab key to move from command to command.

Figure 8: KeyTips on the Home tab on the Ribbon

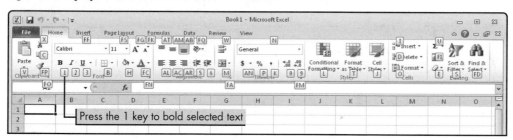

If you press the Alt key to display the KeyTips, you can then use the right and left arrow keys to move forward or back, respectively, to adjacent tabs. Once the tab you want is selected, simply press the down arrow key to move down into the options for that tab and then use the arrow keys, the Tab key, or the key combination Shift+Tab to navigate between the various options. To select a command, simply press the Enter key. For example, press the Alt key, press the P key to move to the Page Layout tab, press the down arrow key, and then move to the command you want by pressing the Tab key, the right or left arrow key, or Shift+Tab. To disable KeyTips, press the Alt key again.

If you are familiar with using shortcut keys with menus in previous versions of Excel— such as the key combination Alt, F, S to save a file—some of these shortcut keys still work if they are associated with the same letters on the KeyTips. Other keys still work, such as the F1 function key for Help and the F5 function key for Go To. However, you will need to recall these shortcut keys from previous versions from memory.

You can also use some Ctrl key combinations from Excel 2007 to activate a command. Table 3 shows Ctrl key combinations for many popular commands.

Table 3: Ctrl key combinations

Key Combination	Action
Ctrl+O	Open
Ctrl+S	Save
Ctrl+C	Copy
Ctrl+X	Cut
Ctrl+V	Paste
Ctrl+B	Bold
Ctrl+I	Italic
Ctrl+U	Underline
Ctrl+Z	Undo

Additional keyboard shortcuts can be found in the Excel Help in the Getting started with Excel 2010 section and on the Microsoft Web site at *www.microsoft.com/excel*.

Adding Commands to the Quick Access Toolbar

When you first start Excel 2010, three tools appear on the Quick Access Toolbar by default: Save, Undo, and Redo. You can customize this toolbar to add or remove commands, or to move it to a more convenient location in the program window. After adding several commands to the Quick Access Toolbar, you might choose to move it below the Ribbon. Locating the Quick Access Toolbar below the Ribbon allows you quick access to the commands.

How To

Add Commands to the Quick Access Toolbar
1. Place your mouse pointer over a command on the Ribbon and right-click.
2. Click Add to Quick Access Toolbar on the shortcut menu. The command is added to the Quick Access Toolbar.

OR

1. Click the Customize Quick Access Toolbar button ⏷ located on the right side of the toolbar.
2. If you see the command on the Quick Customize menu, then simply click the command and it will appear on the toolbar. Notice that the Save, Undo, and Redo options have a check mark in front of them indicating that they are already on the Quick Access Toolbar.

OR

1. Click the Customize Quick Access Toolbar button ⊡ located on the right side of the toolbar.
2. If you do not see the command you want on the Quick Customize menu, then click More Commands. The Excel Options dialog box opens with the Quick Access Toolbar category selected.
3. By default, the Popular Commands list appears in the Choose commands from box. If you see the command you want, double-click to move it to the list on the right side of the dialog box with the other options that are on the toolbar. If you do not see the desired command in the Popular Commands category, click the Choose commands from arrow and choose the category for the command.

How To

Remove Commands from the Quick Access Toolbar

1. Place your mouse pointer over the Quick Access Toolbar command you want to remove and right-click.
2. Click Remove from Quick Access Toolbar on the shortcut menu.

How To

Change the Location of the Quick Access Toolbar

1. Click the Customize Quick Access Toolbar button ⊡ located on the right side of the toolbar.
2. Click Show Below the Ribbon on the Quick Customize menu.

Introducing Compatibility Functions

For many years, there have been questions in the academic community about the accuracy of some Excel functions. Another issue has been the consistency of function names and definitions. Excel 2010 has updated its function library with improvements that result in better accuracy in many of the math, finance, and statistical functions. More than 50 new functions have been added to the library as a result of Microsoft's efforts to improve accuracy and consistency.

If workbooks using these new functions are opened in a previous version of Excel, the #NAME? error will result. The need to share Excel workbooks with people using previous versions of Excel has resulted in the addition of a new Compatibility Function category to the library. Compatibility functions are essentially the older versions of many of the new Excel 2010 functions. As you add functions to a worksheet, you will have the option to select the new version or the older version. Compatibility functions have a yellow caution icon in the formula AutoComplete interface, as shown in Figure 9, with the various versions of the RANK function.

Figure 9: Compatibility functions in formula AutoComplete

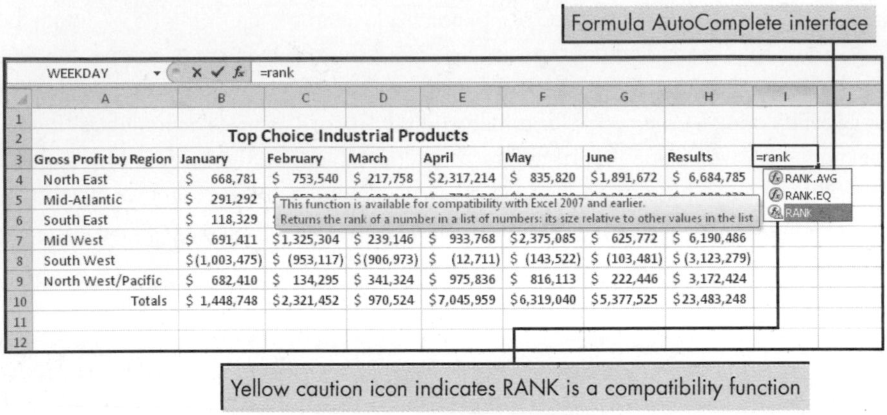

Formula AutoComplete interface

Yellow caution icon indicates RANK is a compatibility function

Thirty-eight Excel functions have been included in the Compatibility category. Many of these function name changes illustrate Microsoft's attempt to be more consistent in its naming conventions. For example, all functions that return a distribution end with .DIST. Functions that return an inverse of a distribution end with .INV. The .EXC and .INC extensions refer to exclusive and inclusive versions of the same function. You can find more information and a complete list of compatibility functions in Excel 2010 Help.

Table 4: Sample of Excel Compatibility functions

Excel 2010 Function	Compatibility Function	Description
MODE.MULT, MODE.SNGL	MODE	Returns the most common value in a data set
NORM.DIST	NORMDIST	Returns the normal cumulative distribution
NORM.INV	NORMINV	Returns the inverse of the normal cumulative distribution
NORM.S.DIST	NORMSDIST	Returns the standard normal cumulative distribution
NORM.S.INV	NORMSINV	Returns the inverse of the standard normal cumulative distribution
PERCENTILE.EXC, PERCENTILE.INC	PERCENTILE	Returns the k-th percentile of values in a range
PERCENTRANK.EXC, PERCENTRANK.INC	PERCENTRANK	Returns the percentage rank of a value in a data set
QUARTILE.EXC, QUARTILE.INC	QUARTILE	Returns the quartile of a data set
RANK.AVG, RANK.EQ	RANK	Returns the rank of a number in a list of numbers
STDEV.S	STDEV	Estimates standard deviation based on a sample
STDEV.P	STDEVP	Calculates standard deviation based on the entire population
VAR.S	VAR	Estimates variance based on a sample
VAR.P	VARP	Calculates variance based on the entire population

Getting Help

You have many options for getting help as you work in Excel 2010. If you point to most buttons and dialog box launchers, Excel displays a context-sensitive ScreenTip about the feature. To open the Excel Help dialog box, you can click the Help button ⑦ located on the right end of the Ribbon, or you can press the F1 key. A Help button appears in most dialog boxes for easy access to information.

When the Excel Help dialog box first opens, Excel tries to connect to online help at Office.com, which is a Web site maintained by Microsoft that provides access to the latest information and additional Help resources. You can easily search this site using Microsoft's default search engine, Bing, which is now part of the Excel Help window. You can still search for help using the Search box, displaying the Table of Contents, or selecting a topic in the Browse Excel 2010 support list.

How To

Use the Excel Help Dialog Box

1. Click the Help button ⑦ on the Ribbon or in a dialog box, or press the F1 key.

2. Use one of the following options to search for help:

- Type the task for which you need help in the Search box, and then click the Search button or press the Enter key.
- Click the Show Table of Contents button on the Excel Help toolbar, and then click a topic and navigate to the information you need.
- Click a topic in the Browse Excel 2010 support list, and then click additional links to navigate to the desired topic.

Chapter Summary

This chapter introduced you to some of the new features in Excel 2010. After you get comfortable with these changes, you'll find you're spending less time performing common tasks. The File tab and Quick Access Toolbar make it easy to find your frequently used commands. Having the ability to customize the Ribbon and Quick Access Toolbar means you will no longer need to search for commands within menus. If you like using the keyboard, you are still able to use keystrokes with the KeyTips and Ctrl key combinations. You can open workbooks created in a previous version of Excel; and, if necessary, you can save files in one of those versions. However, saving files in the Excel 2010 format ensures that your workbook will have the advantages of the latest features and functionality of Excel. You can now easily share your Excel files using the Save & Send options, like Windows Live SkyDrive, available on the File tab. Finally, you also can take advantage of Excel's new Compatibility functions, which offer improved accuracy. The Compatibility functions ensure backward compatibility with earlier versions of Microsoft Office.

In the chapters ahead, you will practice using these new features as you build worksheets, make calculations, and present information effectively.

Introduction to Problem Solving and Decision Making with Microsoft Excel 2010

"We are continuously faced by great opportunities brilliantly disguised as insoluble problems."
—Lee Iacocca

LEARNING OBJECTIVES

Understand concepts related to problem solving and decision making
Identify the different steps in the problem-solving process
Explain the role Excel can play in problem solving and decision making
Describe how problem solving is presented in this text

About This Book and Microsoft Excel 2010

The traditional study of computer applications has mostly involved acquiring skills related to an application's features and functions. Although this approach is important in teaching the mechanics required to perform certain tasks, it does not address *when* a particular tool is most appropriate or *how* it should best be utilized to solve a specific problem.

This book focuses on teaching how to solve problems using Microsoft Excel 2010, although the concepts and tasks presented could apply to a variety of computer applications and programming languages. Excel is widely used in business as a tool for solving problems and supporting decision making. There are two perceptions of Excel to consider: one is that Excel is the obvious extension of the desktop calculator into the personal computer; the other is that Excel is a powerful tool for the manipulation and analysis of data. Data is usually analyzed to provide support for deciding whether or not to take some course of action—a decision. Not all decisions require a spreadsheet for analysis, but many of the complexities faced in business are made simpler and easier to understand when a tool like Excel is employed properly. This book helps you learn what kinds of problems are best solved using spreadsheets and how to solve them; however, for in-depth exploration of effective decision making, further study is recommended. One of the main goals of this book is that you will "learn how to learn," becoming confident in your own ability to explore new Excel features and tools to solve problems and support your decisions.

When you work with Excel, using the correct tools can greatly increase your ability to deal with not only the immediate problem presented, but also the inevitable "what-if" analyses. One example of how an organization might perform what-if analysis is with a financial model of its business in a spreadsheet. The model summarizes various pieces of financial data to determine information such as assets, liabilities, sales, and profitability—creating a representation or model of the organization in the spreadsheet. In this example, the spreadsheet could be used to evaluate what would happen if:

- The organization cut sales prices by 5%.
- The sales volume increased by 10%.
- The organization improved its inventory turnover by 8%.
- The organization issued $1,000,000 in bonds.

Using a spreadsheet allows the organization to quickly change various inputs (think of these as independent variables in a mathematical equation) and see what happens to the outputs (think of these as dependent variables in a mathematical equation). The ability to model the potential impacts of decisions before they are made is very valuable in today's complex business environment. As a result, many organizations spend hundreds of hours building models in spreadsheets. Of course, a model is limited by the detail and quality of the data used to build it.

One benefit of spreadsheet modeling lies in the ability to quickly revise and update the data and mathematical formulas used to generate the answers or results. Consider the typewriter: It provides just as much productive value as a word-processing program until you need to revise what you are writing. Easy revision and calculation are important features of Excel, but its power as a decision-making tool is what moves it far beyond paper and pencil. What-if analysis is often a key element in the decision-making process, allowing decision makers to see the impact of changes to their businesses. This type of analysis is extremely valuable because the only sure thing in business today is that nothing will stay the same.

The Relationship Between Problem Solving and Decision Making

In his book, *Management Challenges for the 21st Century*, Peter Drucker states the following:

> The most important, and indeed the truly unique, contribution of management in the 20th century was the fifty-fold increase in the productivity of the "manual worker" in manufacturing. The most important contribution management needs to make in the 21st century is similarly to increase the productivity of "knowledge work" and the "knowledge worker." The most valuable assets of a 20th-century company were its production equipment. The most valuable asset of a 21st-century institution, whether business or non-business, will be its knowledge workers and their productivity.

Knowledge workers are those people who work with and develop knowledge. Data and information are their raw materials. Knowledge workers use this raw material to analyze a particular situation and evaluate a course of action. As a reader of this text, you are most likely a knowledge worker or trying to become one. The rise of the knowledge worker over the last century has followed a corresponding rise in the value of information in business and society. More knowledge and information are readily available now than at any other time in history.

Information Overload

How much information is created every year? According to a study by Peter Lyman and Hal Varian, researchers at the University of California, Berkeley, "Print, film, magnetic, and optical storage media produced about 5 exabytes of new information in 2002. Ninety-two percent of the new information was stored on magnetic media, mostly in hard disks." This figure was roughly double the amount of information created in 1999, the first year the pair looked at this issue, and surely is continuing to grow. The amount of information generated was so large that a new term, the exabyte (EB), was coined to describe it. An exabyte is the equivalent of 1,000,000 terabytes (TB). A TB is the equivalent of 1000 gigabytes (GB). Five EBs of information is equivalent in size to the information contained in 37,000 new libraries the size of the Library of Congress, which has the largest book collection in the world.

What is information and where does it come from? The term *information* can mean many things to different people. For the purpose of this discussion, **information** is defined as data that is organized in some meaningful way. **Data** can be words, images, numbers, or even sounds. Using data to make decisions depends on an organization's ability to collect, organize, and otherwise transform data into information that can be used to support those decisions—a process more commonly referred to as **analysis**.

The amount of information available can overwhelm or overload many decision makers as they try to determine which sets of data/information are important and which should be ignored. The result is a complex world in which decision makers can no longer rely on intuition and back-of-the-envelope calculations to make effective decisions; they need tools that support decision making and help them to solve problems.

Which Comes First: The Problem or the Decision?

You have been trained since grade school to solve problems. These problems start with simple addition and subtraction, and then move to multiplication and division. You might start by counting on your fingers and then learn to become a "human calculator" by memorizing multiplication tables. These are skills you use every day to solve simple problems, such as dividing the lunch bill and figuring out the tip. These problems result from the need to make a decision. Do you want to pick up the entire lunch tab? If not, you need to figure out what each person owes.

Decision making and problem solving are interrelated—two sides of the same coin. **Decision making** is simply making up your mind about something. A **problem** can be thought of in two ways: as an obstacle or a difficulty that prevents you from reaching some goal, or as a question to be answered. So, which comes first, the problem or the need to make a decision? It depends. You might encounter an obstacle that must be removed in order to move forward, or you might be presented with a choice that requires certain questions to be answered before you can make a decision. The complexity of the situation determines the number of problems requiring solutions and choices requiring decisions. Thus, problem solving and decision making are interrelated.

The complexity of decision making in today's business world often requires that a great deal of time be spent considering the available options and what their potential outcomes will be. To do this well, you need to learn some new skills. Specifically, you need to learn how to use applications that can support your decision making. In technical terms, this type of application is referred to as a **decision support system**, or **DSS**. Decision making utilizing computer models is part of a larger concept of decision support systems that can encompass a variety of diverse topics, such as management science, decision theory, mathematical modeling, operations management, artificial intelligence, cognitive science, psychology, and database management. This text focuses on how to use Excel as a decision support tool and shows you that a spreadsheet is far more than a sophisticated calculator; it is used extensively at the highest level of decision making.

Problem solving in Excel has a numbers-oriented, or quantitative, basis. These problems can be expressed in numerical terms. Although Excel can be a powerful tool to manipulate text, especially in lists (as you will see in a later chapter), it is strongest in *quantitative* analysis. But decisions are rarely based solely on numbers. There is a more subjective, or *qualitative*, side that is hard to put into numerical terms, but which can determine the success or failure of any implementation. Consider outsourcing as an example. Outsourcing is the action of obtaining a product, component, or service from an outside supplier instead of making or doing it in-house. The quantitative basis for such a decision revolves around comparing the costs and benefits of each alternative. The qualitative factors that need to be considered include the supplier's reputation for quality and performance, as well as how much effort would be required to integrate the supplier into the organization's business processes. Regardless of the quantitative or qualitative nature of the situation, the interrelationship of problem solving and decision making will continue.

A Problem-Solving Process

Problem solving is, of course, the process used to find a solution to a given problem. But how do you know what the problem is in the first place? As mentioned earlier, a problem can be thought of as something that keeps you from achieving your goals. Usually it is the result of some sort of stoppage or obstacle—something that gets in the way of your progress—and you need to figure out a way to deal with it.

There are probably as many problem-solving approaches as there are problems. Figure 1 illustrates a general model of a problem-solving process, consisting of three main phases— Problem Recognition, Problem Statement, and Solution—with detailed analysis activities occurring to move from one phase to the next.

Figure 1: General model of a problem-solving process

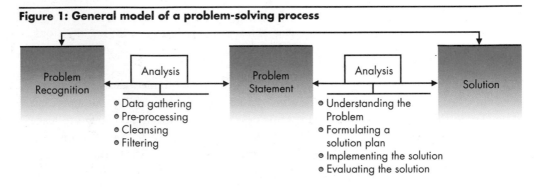

Problem Recognition

The first step in solving a problem is to recognize what the problem is or even if any problem exists. After a problem is recognized, it needs to be described and analyzed further.

How do you make sense of all the information around you when faced with a problem to solve? Every day, people are presented with information that they must process in order to function in their personal and professional lives. In the morning, you might use the weather report in the newspaper, on the radio, or on television to guide you on how to dress for the day. Should you wear a coat, add a sweater, or even carry an umbrella? You can rely on carefully calculated weather data indicating there is a 60% chance of rain that day, or you could look at the sky and decide based on your intuition and experience that it might rain. Both are equally valid strategies. After all, what is the risk? You might get wet, but eventually you'll dry out.

Some decisions carry a bit more risk and might require more thought before acting. How do you think about making a decision and what role does gathering information play in that thought process? Using the previous example, most people have all the information they need to decide how to dress for the weather, based on past experiences. They don't need to gather raw data and take surveys. Many times in business, however, people don't have enough information to make a decision. Consider the example of an airline company that is deciding whether to enter a new market. The airline executives could make the decision based on intuition and experience, but the company's investors might be more comfortable if the decision could be justified based on market research and sound analysis by industry experts. Information is required to do any such analysis.

Analyzing the Problem

As shown in Figure 2, four analysis steps are required to move from the Problem Recognition phase to the Problem Statement phase.

Figure 2: Analyzing the problem

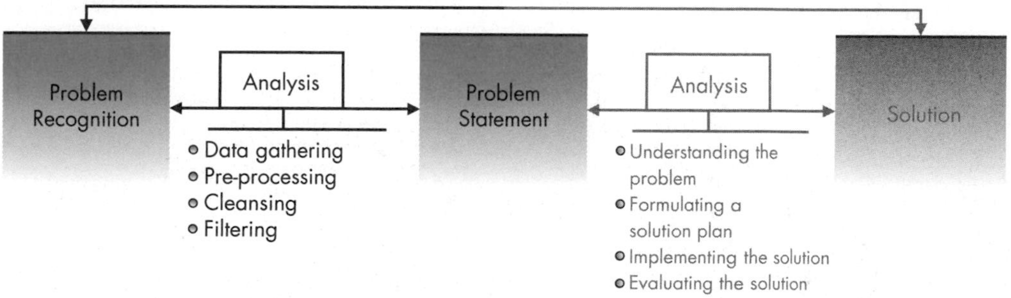

The first step in analyzing the problem is **data gathering**. Data can come from a variety of sources, such as an enterprise-wide data system or industry market analyses. After sources have been identified, credibility, reliability, and accuracy of the data should be considered. Data is rarely in exactly the right format you need and is often corrupt in some way. This brings up the next step in analysis—**pre-processing**, in which the data is manipulated into the needed format. After the format is set, you move to the **cleansing** step, in which any data corruption is identified and corrected, if possible. Corrupt data is missing some element or is incorrect in some way. Corruption can be caused by data loss due to computer problems, but is often caused by human error. The final step in analysis involves **filtering** out data that isn't useful or necessary. As you narrow your sources of data, you are beginning to transform it into information and are getting closer to being able to recognize problems that exist. After firmly establishing the problem or problems that exist, you move to the next phase of the process: articulating the problem statement.

Problem Statement

The problem statement can be similar to a typical math word problem found in early education. The key characteristic of any problem statement or word problem is that some missing piece of information is identified that is required to solve a problem or make a decision. Unlike many of the math word problems solved in school, today's business problems don't have a missing piece of information and the answer in the back of the book. The problems are real, and the answers are unknown.

When you are confident that you understand the problem and can articulate the problem statement, you're ready to move toward a solution.

Solution

As illustrated in Figure 3, most problems require a minimum of four steps to move from the problem statement to a solution: understanding the problem, formulating a solution plan, implementing the solution, and evaluating the solution.

Figure 3: Analyzing the solution

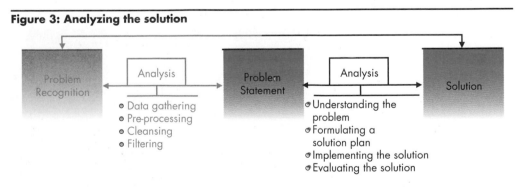

Although this process might appear to be a sequential set of tasks, it is often a reiterative process that moves back and forth through the steps. For a simple problem that you have seen many times before, these steps might require no more than a few seconds to complete; whereas more complex problems might require many hours of going back and forth formulating, implementing, and evaluating the solution.

When using Excel to solve problems, you might underestimate the time it takes to set up and use a spreadsheet model on a computer. In general, solving a problem for the first time on the computer takes at least the same amount of time as it would if you did it by hand, if not more. However, the advantage of using productivity software tools comes when dealing with more complex problems and larger amounts of data. In the same way that a lever is a tool that allows you to increase your own physical force, a spreadsheet can increase or improve your mental force. The spreadsheet can become a "thinking tool" that helps you organize and analyze data in ways that are impossible by hand. Additional benefits are gained when corrections or changes are required—and from the ability to adapt the solution to other similar problems. To reap these advantages, it is important to plan your spreadsheets to take advantage of Excel's capabilities.

Understanding the Problem

After you have recognized and defined the problem, you need to gain an understanding of what solving the problem will require. Specifically, you need to know the following:

- What data is needed and what data or information is already known?
- Is the data or information reliable and accurate?
- What is the likely range of potential solutions for the problem?
- What type of output is required—a single value, a table, a graph, and so on?

Consider a simple problem such as calculating the cost of a new computer system for the sales group in your company. It might take you no more than a moment to decide you need to list the price of each component and calculate the total price of the system. On the other hand, if you were asked to create a cost calculator in Excel for the sales group that would automatically retrieve the price, discount, and sales tax of a specific order, it might require hours of data gathering to determine which items to price, what prices to apply, what discounts are available, and by localities, what sales taxes apply. You would also need to speak with the sales personnel to determine what type of output is needed—a single value or each component—and how they would use it. Would the sales personnel be able to manipulate an Excel spreadsheet, or would they need a different type of tool in which they could enter a few items and the answer would be displayed?

Formulating a Solution Plan

After you have a better understanding of the problem and its scope, you need to begin planning how you will use Excel to reach a solution. What steps will you need to take to solve the problem? Will you be performing a numerical calculation, determining if a value meets specific criteria, organizing data in a specific format, or a combination of several of these steps?

One common mistake people make is to immediately jump to a specific implementation, often worrying about how to use a particular function or tool before determining if that is the right function or tool to use. If you are unsure at all, it is always wise to ask yourself, "How would I solve this problem without a computer?" Invariably, if you think about what you need to do and define the steps you need to take, you can better surmise how to formulate a solution plan.

When considering a spreadsheet solution, you need to determine the following:

- What mathematical, logical, or organizational processes will be required?
- Will these tasks be done multiple times and, if so, will some of the calculations require looking up specific related data?
- What type of spreadsheet design will be best? How should the inputs and outputs be arranged, or "laid out"—on a single worksheet, on multiple worksheets, organized by inputs and outputs, or organized by scenarios?
- What formulas and/or functions will be required to perform the necessary tasks?

Good planning can save you from spending many hours reworking the spreadsheet later. You must consider all of the elements required to reach a solution and the way in which these elements should be laid out. An Excel worksheet can be thought of as a "smart piece of paper." Many people use this paper like a scratch pad, filling it with seemingly random sets of calculations. This approach is inefficient and difficult to share with others. You are better off to spend some time placing your data and formulas into well-organized layouts that make it easy to refine and evolve your solution. In many ways, your worksheet reflects your understanding of the problem.

Formulating a solution plan for a simple problem, such as, adding up the cost of a new computer system, may require no more than a few seconds of "unconscious" thought. But, even for what seems to be a simple problem, you might need to develop different implementations, depending on if you are considering only one computer system or a suite of them. On the other hand, creating a cost calculator for the sales group might require many hours of work. To facilitate the solution plan for a more complex problem, first, you need to consider an overall plan, and then you can break down the larger problem into several separate, more workable parts. In the case of the sales cost calculator, you can approach this problem by breaking it into four parts: calculating the cost of the item, determining discount percentages, calculating sales tax, and setting up an appropriate display. Working each part of the problem makes what initially seems like an enormous task more manageable.

Implementing the Solution

At this point, you should understand the problem to be solved and how you are going to solve it. Now it's time to input the data, write the appropriate formulas, and configure the desired output. You need to know the following to properly implement your spreadsheet solution:

- **How to correctly write formulas and functions as well as how to use the spreadsheet tools.** For example, if a value is needed in several different formulas, it is best to enter the value in a cell on the spreadsheet and refer to that cell in each of the formulas. If the value changes, you can easily update the spreadsheet by changing the one cell instead of having to modify every formula that uses this value.
- **How to copy repeated elements required in the solution.** For example, if purchasing a computer involves the comparison of several different options, you might need to sum a single column for each option. Instead of writing a separate formula for each column, Excel provides ways for you to copy formulas that tell the program to use the same method of computation but change the values, or to keep some values the same and change others. This is one example of the tremendous advantage a spreadsheet has over a simple calculator, where each sum operation must be done separately.

Many times during the implementation process, you might find it necessary to restructure or revise your spreadsheet. This is a necessary part of finding the optimal structure for the solution to the problem. The computational power of Excel makes it easy to revise your spreadsheet, allowing you to explore a variety of alternative solutions.

Evaluating the Solution

No matter how experienced the problem solver or how simple the task, it is always wise to check the results to ensure they are correct. You should at least estimate what the expected calculated values should be and compare them with the spreadsheet solution. With more complex spreadsheets, it's advisable to manually go through the entire series of steps to verify the answer. Something as minor as a typo in a value or an incorrect formula can result in an incorrect solution. When it appears that the spreadsheet is correct, a good practice is to vary some of the inputs and ascertain that the results are updated correctly. And, finally, as illustrated in the original problem-solving model (Figure 1), the solution you arrive at can sometimes lead to the recognition of another problem, at which point the process loops back and begins again.

Problem Solving in This Book

Throughout this book, you will be presented with various problems to solve or analyses to complete using different Excel tools and features. Each chapter in this book presents three levels of problem solving with Excel. Level 1 deals with basic problems or analyses that require the application of one or more spreadsheet tools, focusing on the implementation of those tools. However, problem solving not only requires you to know *how* to use a tool, but, more important, *why* or *when* to use *which* tool. With Level 2, the problems and analyses presented increase in complexity. By the time you reach Level 3, the complexity increases further, providing you with opportunities for more advanced critical thinking and problem solving. Each level ends with a section called "Steps To Success," which provides hands-on practice of the skills and concepts presented in that level.

In the Case Problems at the end of each chapter, not only does the degree of complexity *increase*, matching how the material is presented in each level, but the structure of the problem to be solved *decreases*. Figure 4 illustrates the approach to problem solving in this text.

Figure 4: Pedagogical model for problem solving

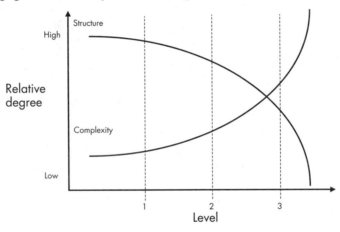

In this model, structure can be thought of as the way that various parts of a problem are held or put together. In a highly structured situation, almost all parts of the problem are defined, and it is up to you to put the last few pieces in place to reach a solution. As the amount of structure is reduced, you need to understand more of the pieces and how they fit together to reach a solution. As structure is further reduced (more missing pieces of the puzzle) and complexity is increased (more pieces to understand), the difficulty of solving the problem increases. This difficulty can be measured in the time, number of steps, and decisions required to reach a solution. The goal is to increase your problem-solving skills while moving you toward an environment that is more like the real business world you will encounter during internships and upon graduation from college.

Case Scenario

The problems to be solved and analyses to be performed in this text are presented within the context of a fictional large-scale sporting goods company named TheZone Sports Corporation, or simply TheZone. This case scenario is used to provide real-world business examples to illustrate the lessons in each chapter; it is not based on real people or events.

You will be guided through the solutions to realistic business problems that face various people working for this company. These "employees" represent a variety of business functions: accounting, finance, human resources, marketing, operations management, and sales. Context is an important factor to consider in problem solving. The following background on TheZone will give you perspective on the situations you will encounter throughout the book.

The Company

TheZone is an international sporting goods company that provides sports equipment, apparel, and footwear to thousands of retail locations primarily in the United States and Canada. Its corporate headquarters are located in Fort Collins, Colorado. The company is noted for its innovative product designs and quality. TheZone employs approximately 15,000 people working on three continents to provide the highest quality products and services possible.

The Brand

TheZone has paid particular attention to managing its brand image with an emphasis on associating the company's products with an athletic lifestyle that pushes individuals to be their best, while having fun. This philosophy is reflected in the company's motto:

Play Right: Get in TheZone.

Key Players

William Broadacre—Founder and Chairman of the Board
William Broadacre is chairman of the board of TheZone Sports Corporation, a position he has held since he founded the company in 1977. Prior to founding TheZone, William was the owner of the Broadacre Sporting Goods store in Fort Collins, Colorado. He holds a B.A. degree in business from Colorado State University and an M.B.A. from Indiana University. A sports enthusiast himself, William has been able to turn a lifelong passion for athletics into a successful and rewarding business venture.

Una Baatar—President and Chief Executive Officer
Una Baatar is president and chief executive officer (CEO) of TheZone, a position she has held since the company's founding in 1977. Like William, Una attended Colorado State University, from which she earned her B.A. degree in marketing and finance. Una is the driving force behind TheZone's successful expansion from the original sporting goods retail store into an international supplier of sports equipment, apparel, and footwear. Una's truly innovative approach to business has allowed TheZone brand name to become an icon that represents the best in sports and athletic endeavors.

Introduction

Molly Richardson—Senior Vice President and Chief Financial Officer

Molly Richardson joined TheZone in 1998 as vice president and controller. She was named senior vice president (VP) and chief financial officer (CFO) in April 2001. Prior to joining TheZone, Molly was employed by Williams Corporation, a leading national advertising firm specializing in print media, as its executive VP and CFO. She earned a B.S. degree in industrial engineering from Cornell University and also holds an M.B.A. from Ohio State University.

Company Goal: Expand the Product Line

TheZone's strength as a company lies in its design, marketing, and distribution capabilities. The company retains in-house manufacturing for some key products, such as certain shoes and skis, but has also been able to expand its product lines through acquisition. The company usually targets businesses that are struggling with manufacturing costs, but have strong product designs that will fit well within TheZone brand image. TheZone works with its manufacturing partners to bring the costs under control. From its humble beginnings over 30 years ago, TheZone has grown into an international sporting goods company with hundreds of products in the sports equipment, apparel, and footwear market segments of the industry.

How Is Excel Used at TheZone?

Employees of TheZone use Excel in the day-to-day management of business functions across the company, such as the following specific examples:

Finance

- The finance group is looking at different pricing alternatives for a new shoe being designed. This group is also using Excel to analyze projected revenues and costs/expenses for a new swimwear product, primarily to decide whether to carry the new product, and if so, to help set a pricing policy for it.

Marketing

- The marketing group uses Excel to monitor and chart both industry trends and company performance for all of its product lines.

Accounting

- The accounting group monitors accounts receivable to determine what terms should be offered to the company's customers based on payment history and credit rating. This group is also using Excel to develop a projected income statement for a new sunglasses product line.

Operations Management

- The operations management group is using Excel to monitor quality control values in an effort to identify production problems in the ski product line. This group is also looking at ways to optimize production schedules and product distribution (transportation) for other product lines.

- The sales group is using Excel to create a tool that will help the salesforce quickly price product orders. This group, along with the Marketing group, is also analyzing different marketing plans/options for the sweatshirt category of apparel products.

Sales

- The human resources group is using Excel to compile and track data about the company's employees, which can then be used to create summary reports and calculate certain information based on salary data.

Human Resources

As you progress through the chapters in this book, you will encounter these various business functions and learn how they use Excel to analyze data, solve problems, and support decision making.

Introduction

Chapter Summary

This chapter introduced you to the focus of this text—using Excel to solve problems and to support decision making. It also described the interrelationship between problem solving and decision making, and provided a general model of the problem-solving process. The three main phases of this model—Problem Recognition, Problem Statement, and Solution—involve the completion of different analysis steps to move from one phase to another. The powerful features and capabilities of Excel enable you to apply this problem-solving process in ways that are impossible by hand, providing a "thinking tool" that helps you organize and analyze the data you must manipulate to reach a solution.

The method of teaching problem solving in this book was also discussed. Each chapter is organized into three levels of problem solving with Excel, and the material presented increases in complexity from one level to the next. The Case Problems at the end of each chapter present problems that both increase in complexity and decrease in structure, providing more challenging problems for you to solve and analyses to perform as you move from level to level.

Conceptual Review

1. Define what a *knowledge worker* is and discuss the significance of the knowledge worker in today's business world.

2. Define and differentiate between the terms *information* and *data*.

3. What is the relationship between problem solving and decision making?

4. What role can Excel play in decision making?

5. Describe a time you have performed a what-if analysis.

6. Describe a situation in which having access to large amounts of information had a negative impact on your decision making.

7. Describe a situation in which having access to large amounts of information had a positive impact on your decision making.

8. Describe the general model of problem solving presented in the text. What are the three main phases and the different analysis steps involved?

9. Give an example of each of the following: a quantitative basis for making a decision and a qualitative basis for making a decision.

10. What should you consider before implementing or building a spreadsheet model?

Applying Fundamental Excel Skills and Tools in Problem Solving
Finance: Analyzing Costs and Projected Revenues for a New Product

LEARNING OBJECTIVES

Level 1

Define common Excel error messages
Correct basic formatting problems in a worksheet
Correct errors in formulas
Understand precision vs. display of cell values

Level 2

Work with multiple worksheets
Calculate total, average, minimum, and maximum values with functions
Understand how functions work: syntax, arguments, and algorithms
Use the AutoSum feature to perform calculations quickly
Calculate the number of values using both COUNT and COUNTA

Level 3

Organize a workbook
Understand relative, absolute, and mixed cell referencing
Write formulas with different types of cell referencing
Copy formulas with different types of cell referencing
Name a cell or cell range

FUNCTIONS COVERED IN THIS CHAPTER

AVERAGE	MIN
COUNT	MAX
COUNTA	SUM

Chapter Introduction

Microsoft Excel provides a variety of tools for designing and working with a spreadsheet, which is referred to as a **worksheet** in the Excel application. A paper spreadsheet is simply a sheet organized into columns and rows. An Excel worksheet is an electronic version of this piece of paper, but with numerous features and functions that facilitate its easy and efficient use. An Excel **workbook** is a collection of one or more worksheets combined into a single file.

This chapter presents some of the fundamental skills and tools you'll encounter when working with Excel to solve problems and support decision making. You'll learn how to write formulas in cells to perform calculations and how to design a workbook so that these calculations can be automatically updated when input values are changed. In addition, this chapter discusses some of the formatting options available that can be applied to cells and ranges of cells.

One important, but frequently overlooked, skill is the ability to correct spreadsheet errors. The more complex the spreadsheet, the more likely that you will encounter Excel's error messages. This chapter begins by exploring how to recognize and address these common mistakes.

You will also learn about some of the rules that affect how information is displayed and calculations are performed in an Excel worksheet. The coverage of formulas is expanded to cover simple functions, which are shortcuts available to use for predefined tasks. Finally, you will explore the various results of copying formulas with different kinds of cell references.

Case Scenario

The product design team at TheZone has been assigned the task of bringing to market a new and significantly different athletic shoe that will combine the support of superior European footwear with the comfort and styling of American running shoes. The design team has recently created a worksheet containing the component costs for this new athletic shoe, which is called TZEdge. The team members have asked Paul Gomez, a financial analyst for the company, to review the worksheet for several reasons. First, they want to ensure that it is formatted properly and contains no errors. Second, they need Paul to perform some cost calculations to determine the value of different pricing alternatives and to provide some preliminary budget and projected revenue information. In this way, the worksheet will become a functioning analytical tool that will help both Paul and the product design team make sound business decisions regarding the launch of the new athletic shoe.

Finance

Identifying and Correcting Common Errors in Formatting and Formulas

Examining a Basic Worksheet for Errors

The product design team is working with Paul and production engineers to formulate an estimate of production costs for the new TZEdge athletic shoe. Although price will not be the overriding factor in the business decision to launch this new shoe, there are still certain production cost goals that must be met to place this shoe in the correct market niche. After the designers have all the information in place, Paul needs to analyze the costs and make recommendations.

The designers started to tabulate the material costs of the TZEdge shoe. Figure 1.1 shows the Excel worksheet they have developed so far, which is contained in a workbook named "TZEdge Material Costs." To open the workbook file, Paul clicks the File tab on the Ribbon and selects the Open command in the navigation bar. All commands for opening, saving, and printing files can be accessed from the File tab.

Figure 1.1: Initial worksheet for TZEdge

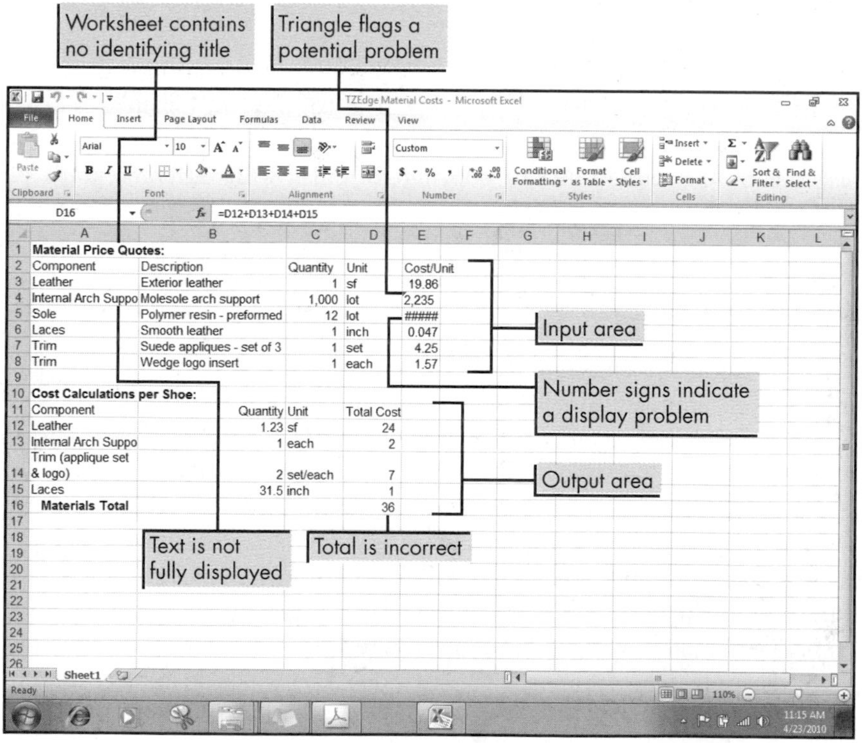

From your work with Excel, you know that cells can contain **numeric values**, such as the number *12* in cell C5; **text labels**, such as the word *Component* in cell A2; and

calculated values, such as the total *36* shown in cell D16. As you can see, the worksheet contains the cost information in the input area, cells A2 through E8, and the results of the cost calculations in the output area, cells A11 through D16. Typically, workbooks are organized so that there are distinct areas for **inputs**, the labels and values upon which the calculations are based, and **outputs**, the calculations and their results. The input and output areas can be located on the same worksheet or on separate worksheets.

As you can see in Figure 1.1, there are some obvious problems with the worksheet. For example, cell E5 contains a series of ### signs. Also, a quick look at the numbers reveals that the Materials Total does not add up to the value shown. There are other problems related to formatting and formulas as well.

Excel uses a variety of symbols to indicate specific types of errors to help you identify and resolve problems in a worksheet. Table 1.1 describes some of these error messages. To learn about these messages or any of the other tools in Excel, use the Help feature available by clicking the Help button ⊚ located in the upper-right corner of the Ribbon.

Table 1.1: Excel error messages

Error Message	Description
######	Insufficient width in cell to display numerical data, or formulas that result in negative date/time (prior to 1/1/1900)
#NAME?	Unrecognized text in a formula
#N/A	No answer
#REF!	Invalid cell reference
#VALUE!	Wrong argument type or operand
#NUM!	Invalid numeric values in a formula or function
#DIV/0!	Division by zero

Because someone else has already created the spreadsheet, the focus here is on identifying the problems and testing the solution, which sometimes leads to rethinking and reimplementing various parts of the original solution. This task might involve many basic spreadsheet skills, including worksheet and cell formatting, as well as writing simple formulas.

Correcting Formatting Problems

In addition to the contents of a cell, you can format individual cells, ranges of cells, and entire worksheets to display the information in a variety of ways. After reviewing the worksheet created by the product design team, Paul determines that the worksheet needs to be formatted to make the data easier to read. The necessary changes include modifying column widths, checking error messages, formatting numbers consistently, and including a title to identify the worksheet contents. Paul decides to look at these formatting issues first before examining the worksheet formulas.

Modifying Column Width and Row Height

The first problem to tackle is the ### signs in cell E5. As noted in Table 1.1, the series of number signs indicates that the column width is insufficient to display the complete value in the cell. A similar problem exists in cells A4, A13, and E2, where the column is not wide enough to display the text labels within these cells. Unlike with values, if there is insufficient room to display a label, the text either is displayed in a truncated format (A4 and A13) or spills over into the next cell (E2) if this cell is empty.

To correct column-width-related problems, Paul can adjust the column width using one of the following methods:

- Double-click the column dividing line (the border between each of the column letter headings) to make the column as wide as the longest entry in the column.
- Drag the column dividing line to the desired width.
- Click the Format button in the Cells group on the Home tab on the Ribbon, click Column Width on the menu, and then type the width in the Column width box. You can also open this dialog box by right-clicking a column heading, and then clicking Column Width on the shortcut menu. Column width is measured by number of characters.
- Click the Format button in the Cells group on the Home tab, and then click AutoFit Column Width on the menu to make the column as wide as the longest entry in the column.

The process for changing row height is similar to changing column width. To modify the height of a row, use one of the following techniques:

- Double-click the row dividing line, located just below the row number of the row to be modified. This makes the row as high as the tallest entry in the row.
- Drag the row dividing line to the desired height.
- Click the Format button in the Cells group on the Home tab, and then use the Row Height or AutoFit Row Height option.

Checking Error Messages

Another possible error has been flagged in cell E4. The triangle in the upper-left corner of the cell is an alert. If you select this cell, the Error Alert button appears ⬦. Clicking this button displays a menu, indicating what the problem might be. In this case, the "Number Stored as Text" message appears. The value in cell E4 was entered with an apostrophe at the beginning of the value, causing it to be treated as a text label instead of as a numeric value. This could cause problems if this cell reference is used in formulas.

Excel is somewhat inconsistent in how it handles numbers stored as text. The formula =E4+1 would correctly return the value 2236 even though cell E4 contains text and not a numerical value. However, if cell E4 were included in a SUM function, the function would ignore the value entirely and not include it in the total. It is a good idea to correct this problem by changing numbers stored as text to numbers. There are situations when you would not want to do this, however. Consider a ZIP Code such as 02139. In all likelihood, you would not include this ZIP Code in any functions or formulas for calculations, and if you changed the entry from text to a number, the leading zero would be dropped and the value displayed would be 2139. In this case, you would want the number to be stored as text.

To correct the problem in cell E4, Paul can simply select the cell and retype the number 2235, or he can choose the Convert to Number option on the menu that appears when the Error Alert button is clicked.

Best Practice

Using Commas When Entering Values

When entering a value in a cell, you can enter the value with or without commas; for example, the entry 2,235 is equivalent to the entry 2235. However, if you plan to use this value in a formula, typing commas could be problematic. If you enter the formula =2,235+B1, Excel displays a message box asking if you want to change the formula to =2235+B1. Using commas becomes even more problematic if your formula includes functions, in which a comma indicates to Excel the beginning of the next argument. The formula =SUM(2,235,B1) is interpreted as =2+235+B1 instead of =2235+B1.

Some experienced Excel users recommend never typing commas with numbers to avoid possible problems in formulas and instead using the Comma Style button 🟡 in the Number group on the Home tab and on the Mini toolbar that opens when you right-click a cell, or the options in the Format Cells dialog box, which can be opened from the Number group dialog box launcher 🔲 to display values in the desired manner. Other users prefer to enter values directly with commas so that the formatting is already done—particularly if they know these values will not be used in formulas or functions.

Formatting Numbers

Next, Paul considers the formatting of the input values. Consistent and appropriate formatting makes a worksheet easier to read and understand. In Figure 1.1, note that the Cost/Unit values in cells E3:E8 are displayed in various formats with different numbers of decimal places. To signify that the values in cells E3:E8 represent dollars, Paul wants to display a dollar sign in cell E3. He wants the values in all of these cells (E3:E8) to contain three decimal places and align on the decimal point.

To incorporate the desired formatting, Paul can apply the predefined Accounting Number Format to cell E3 using the Accounting Number Format button 🟡 in the Number group on the Home tab or on the Mini toolbar. The Mini toolbar, as well as a shortcut menu of commonly used tools, can be accessed by right-clicking the active cell. The **Accounting Number Format** is an accounting format that displays the dollar sign ($) at the left edge of the cell, commas, and two decimal places for the numeric value, with a column of values aligned on the decimal point. For cells E4:E8, Paul can apply the Comma Style mentioned earlier, which displays values with commas and two decimal places, but no dollar signs. The dollar sign is needed only for the first unit cost; repeated dollar signs can clutter a worksheet. After applying these formats, Paul uses the Increase Decimal button [icon] in the Number group on the Home tab or on the Mini toolbar to increase the decimal places displayed for cell E3 and then cells E4:E8 to three places, which provides more accurate information about the unit cost for each item.

How To

Format Numbers

1. Select the cell or cells containing the numbers you want to format.

2. Click the Number group dialog box launcher [icon] on the Home tab to display the Format Cells dialog box with, in this case, the Number tab displayed, or right-click the cell or cells and then click Format Cells on the shortcut menu. Either method opens the Format Cells dialog box with options available for formatting numbers. See Figure 1.2.

Figure 1.2: Format Cells dialog box

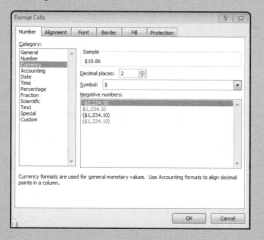

The Category box lists the available number formats. The category and other settings selected depend on which cell is active when you open the Format Cells dialog box. Note the selected Currency format in Figure 1.2; this is not to be confused with the Accounting format, which applies an accounting format. The Currency format is similar to the Accounting Number Format, except it does not align values on the decimal point, and it places the dollar sign immediately in front of the value instead of at the leftmost edge of the cell.

3. Click the number format you want, and then modify the options for the display of Decimal places, Symbol, and Negative numbers, as needed.

4. Click the OK button.

OR

1. Select the cell or cells containing the numbers you want to format.

2. Click one of the buttons in the Number group on the Home tab or the Mini toolbar to quickly apply a predefined style:

- The Accounting Number Format button $ formats numbers in an accounting format, with commas, two decimal places, values aligned on the decimal point, and the dollar sign displayed at the left edge of the cell.
- The Percent Style button % formats numbers as percentages, displayed to the nearest percent, with no decimal places.
- The Comma Style button , formats numbers with commas, two decimal places, and values aligned on the decimal point.

Note that several predefined format styles, including Currency, Long Date, Scientific, and so on, are also available from the Number Format menu that can be accessed from the Number group on the Home tab.

Best Practice

Formatting Dollar Values

Different disciplines or companies often have requirements for formatting dollar values in a spreadsheet. In accounting, for example, the preferred format is to align values on the decimal point, in a column of dollar values, and to include a dollar sign only in the first entry in the column and for any grand totals. Repeated dollar signs can clutter the worksheet and are often unnecessary.

Inserting and Aligning a Title

Another modification that will improve the format of the worksheet is to insert a title, such as "TZEdge Material Analysis," at the top to identify the worksheet's contents. To accomplish this, Paul inserts a row at the top of the worksheet and enters the title in the new row. To insert a new row, select a cell in the row just below the insertion point. Click the Insert button arrow in the Cells group on the Home tab, and then select Insert Sheet Rows. After the text is entered, additional formatting of the title, such as centering and merging it across the columns, adding a colored background, adding a border, and bolding the text, further enhances the worksheet. To merge and center the title, Paul selects the cell containing the title and the adjacent cells over which he wants to center the title and then clicks the Merge & Center button in the Alignment group on the Home tab. Changing the cell background, bolding the text, and applying a border can be accomplished using the buttons in the Font group on the Home tab.

The Alignment group also contains icon buttons for wrapping text, left/right justification of text, and placement of text (top/bottom) within the cell. The Wrap Text button automatically wraps text within the cell, and the cell height adjusts accordingly. This is a particularly useful feature when a text entry does not fit well in a cell. Additional formatting features can be accessed from the Format Cells dialog box.

Figure 1.3 shows the worksheet with the formatting problems corrected.

Figure 1.3: Worksheet after correcting formatting problems

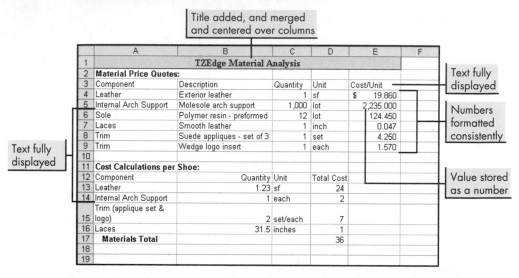

How To

Modify Cell Formatting

1. Select the cell or cells you want to format.

2. Click the Alignment group dialog box launcher on the Home tab on the Ribbon to open the Format Cells dialog box. The Alignment tab with the available options for aligning cell contents is displayed. See Figure 1.4.

Figure 1.4: Alignment options in the Format Cells dialog box

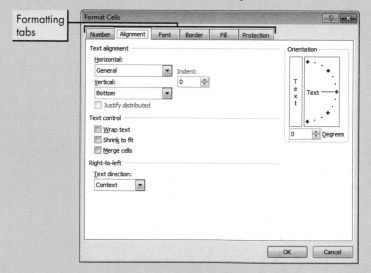

3. Click the appropriate formatting feature and select the desired format, including the following:

- Text alignment and indenting properties
- Text control
- Text direction
- Text orientation

In addition to the Alignment and Number tabs, the Format Cells dialog box offers the following tabs: Font, Border, Fill, and Protection. Each tab provides different settings that affect the display of cell contents, including font type, font style (bold, italic, and so on), and font size; border types, line styles, and border colors; and fill type, including colors and patterns. Note that some of the most common formatting options available in the Format Cells dialog box are also available on the Home tab and on the Mini toolbar.

4. Click each dialog box tab, as needed, and make the appropriate formatting changes. Alternatively, open the Format Cells dialog box directly to a specific tab using the Dialog Box Launcher in the appropriate group on the Home tab.

5. Click the OK button.

Inserting Columns

In addition to being able to insert new rows within an existing worksheet, you can also insert new columns. To insert a new column, select a cell anywhere in the column just to the right of where the new column is to be inserted. Using the Insert button arrow in the Cells group on the Home tab, select Insert Sheet Columns.

Selecting either multiple columns or multiple rows and then using the Insert Sheet Columns/Rows commands allows you to insert multiple columns or rows simultaneously. The number of columns or rows added corresponds to the number originally selected. When adding new columns or rows, be sure to clearly label the data so that it can be easily understood.

Best Practice

Documenting a Worksheet

When working in teams, with several groups, or even with different companies, it is advisable to include a title on the worksheet, the creation date, worksheet author, and any specific information about the company and/or project. Including this information on a separate documentation worksheet usually suffices for the workbook, but not if a single worksheet will be printed separately. For example, if the current worksheet were to be printed, it would be helpful to include the following information above the "TZEdge Material Analysis" title:

TheZone: TZEdge Product Design Team

November 15, 2013

Prepared by: Paul Gomez

As an alternative to including such information on the worksheet itself, you can create a custom header. In Microsoft Excel 2010, you can modify headers and footers using Page Layout view. You can also access them by clicking the Header & Footer button in the Text group on the Insert tab on the Ribbon. This places the insertion point directly in the center Header box and automatically switches you to Page Layout view. Clicking either to the left or right of the center Header box allows you to enter text in the left and right sections of the header. To include page numbering or dates, use the buttons in the Header & Footer Elements group on the Header & Footer Tools Design tab on the Ribbon, as shown in Figure 1. 5. To return to Normal view, click any cell within the worksheet (not in the header or footer), and then select the Normal button on the status bar in the lower-right corner of the window, or select the Normal button in the Workbook Views group on the View tab on the Ribbon.

Figure 1.5: Header in Page Layout view

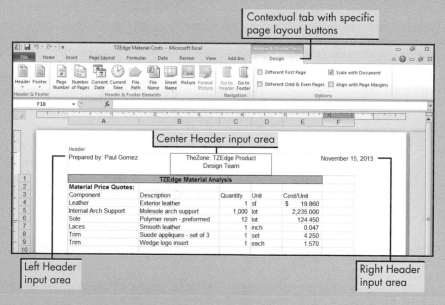

An alternate way of inputting a header or footer is via the Page Setup dialog box. One way to access this dialog box is to click the Page Setup dialog box launcher on the Page Layout tab on the Ribbon, and then select the Header/Footer tab.

Correcting Errors in Formulas

Now that the worksheet is easier to read, Paul can address any problems related to the formulas. As you know, a **formula** is an equation that performs calculations, the result of which can be either a value or a label, depending on the formula. A formula in Excel always begins with an equal sign (=) and can contain constants, cell references to previously entered values, or cell references to other calculated values. Formulas can also include one or more functions, which you'll explore later in this chapter.

One way to determine where an error might exist in a formula is to print the worksheet in two different formats: the default format, which displays the *values* in each cell, and the format that displays the *formulas* instead of the values. Figure 1.6 shows both formats for the TZEdge Material Analysis worksheet. Note that, when the formulas are displayed, the worksheet column widths and formats are modified to accommodate the display.

Figure 1.6: Comparing values with their formulas

Worksheet with values displayed

	A	B	C	D	E
1		TZEdge Material Analysis			
2	**Material Price Quotes:**				
3	Component	Description	Quantity	Unit	Cost/Unit
4	Leather	Exterior leather	1	sf	$ 19.860
5	Internal Arch Support	Molesole arch support	1,000	lot	2,235.000
6	Sole	Polymer resin - preformed	12	lot	124.450
7	Laces	Smooth leather	1	inch	0.047
8	Trim	Suede appliques - set of 3	1	set	4.250
9	Trim	Wedge logo insert	1	each	1.570
10					
11	**Cost Calculations per Shoe:**				
12	Component		Quantity	Unit	Total Cost
13	Leather		1.23	sf	24
14	Internal Arch Support		1	each	2
15	Trim (applique set & logo)		2	set/each	7
16	Laces		31.5	inches	1
17	**Materials Total**				36
18					
19					

Worksheet with formulas displayed

	A	B	C	D	E
1		TZEdge Material Analysis			
2	**Material Price Quot**				
3	Component	Description	Quantity	Unit	Cost/Unit
4	Leather	Exterior leather	1	sf	19.86
5	Internal Arch Support	Molesole arch support	1000	lot	2235
6	Sole	Polymer resin - preformed	12	lot	124.45
7	Laces	Smooth leather	1	inch	0.047
8	Trim	Suede appliques - set of 3	1	set	4.25
9	Trim	Wedge logo insert	1	each	1.57
10					
11	**Cost Calculations pe**				
12	Component		Quantity	Unit	Total Cost
13	Leather	1.23		sf	=B13*E4
14	Internal Arch Support	1		each	2.235
15	Trim (applique set & logo)	2		set/each	=E8+E9*2
16	Laces	31.5		inches	=B16*E7
17	**Materials Total**				=D13+D14+D15+D16
18					
19					

=D13+D14+D15+D16 in cell D17 displays the value 36

How To

Display Formulas in a Worksheet
1. Click the Formulas tab on the Ribbon.
2. Click the Show Formulas button 🖺 in the Formula Auditing group.

OR

1. Press and hold the Ctrl key while pressing grave accent (`) to toggle between the display of formulas and the display of values.

The information in cells A4:E9 was obtained from the vendors that the product design team dealt with when making the shoe prototype. Each of the different vendors quoted prices based on varying lot sizes: per item (each), per set, per inch, or per square foot (sf). The product design team then attempted to convert this information to a per-shoe basis.

Checking Simple Formulas for Accuracy

The formula in cell D13 calculates the cost of leather per shoe. Each shoe requires 1.23 sf of leather. According to the component prices, the premium leather being used is sold at $19.86 per square foot (cell E4). The formula in cell D13 should multiply the quantity times the price. In Excel syntax, this formula would be =B13*E4. So, this formula seems to be correct. Notice that Excel uses an asterisk (*) to represent multiplication, as opposed to the "x" or "•", which are symbols frequently used in algebraic expressions. Table 1.2 shows a list of the Excel arithmetic operators.

Table 1.2: Excel arithmetic operators

Calculation	Excel Operator	Example
Addition	+	=3+A1
Subtraction	–	=A1–A2
Multiplication	*	=A1*4
Division	/	=X4/Y4
Exponent	^	=2^8

Next, Paul looks at the formula in cell D16, which calculates the cost of laces. Laces are priced by the inch. A total of 31.5 inches is needed for each shoe. The formula =B16*E7 was entered into cell D16. This formula appears to be correct.

Using Formulas and Cell References Instead of Values

The formula in cell D14 should calculate the cost of internal arch support in the shoe. The arch supports are sold in lots of 1000 (cell C5) for a total price of $2235 (cell E5). The cost of each arch support is $2235 divided by 1000, as represented by the arithmetic formula 2235/1000. The number of arch supports in each shoe is 1 (cell B14), so the total cost should be 2235/1000*1. However, notice that the resulting value was directly typed into cell D14. Typing a value into a cell instead of entering the formula that produced the value is not a good practice when building a spreadsheet. To correct this problem, Paul replaces this value with the formula =E5/C5*B14 so that any later changes to any of these cell value inputs will be automatically reflected in the costs.

Best Practice

Using Cell References in Formulas

The formula in cell D13, =B13*E4, calculates the cost of leather. The formula contains cell references pointing to the appropriate input values. Using cell references is preferable to directly inputting values into a formula because it allows the user to easily update the spreadsheet without having to know exactly which formula or formulas contain the changed value. For example, if the price of the leather (cell E4) or the quantity required to make a shoe (cell B13) changes, the value displayed in cell D13 will automatically be recalculated. By explicitly listing data inputs, which have the potential to vary, in their own cells and referencing those cells in formulas, you can be secure in the knowledge that all calculations requiring those values will be automatically updated.

Determining Order of Precedence

Now look at the formula in cell D15, which calculates the cost of trim, including two suede applique sets and two wedge logo inserts. The formula –E8+E9*2 was entered into cell D15. On closer inspection, this formula presents a problem. If one set of appliques costs more than $4 (cell E8), certainly two would cost at least $8, plus the cost of the inserts. Yet, the value displayed in cell D15 is only 7.

The problem is related to how Excel performs calculations, specifically in the order of precedence of the various operations. In this case, Excel performs the multiplication of cell E9 by 2 before adding the value in cell E8, resulting in the incorrect value of 7. To produce the correct results, the formula should first add the value in cell E8 to the value in cell E9 and then multiply that amount by 2. This would return the correct value 11.64 for the cost of trim. To fix this problem, Paul needs to enclose the addition operation in parentheses to indicate that this should be completed first, as follows: =(E8+E9)*2. Table 1.3 describes the order of precedence rules in Excel.

Table 1.3: Order of precedence rules

Order of Precedence	Example	Resulting Value	Explanation
1. Operations in parentheses	=A1*(3+5)	If A1=2, the resulting value is 2*(3+5), or 2*8,=16	Excel first performs the addition of 3+5 even though multiplication has a higher precedence than addition, because the addition operation is enclosed in parentheses.

Table 1.3: Order of precedence rules (cont.)

Order of Precedence	Example	Resulting Value	Explanation
2. Exponentiation	=3*A1^3	If A1=2, the resulting value is 3*2^3, or 3*8,=24	Excel first performs the exponential operation of cubing A1, and then performs the multiplication.
3. Multiplication and division from left to right	=A1+B2*C3	If A1=2, B2=3, and C3=10, the resulting value is 2 +3*10, or 2+30,=32	Excel first multiplies cell B2 by cell C3, and then adds the result to cell A1.
4. Addition and subtraction from left to right	=A1–B2+C3/10	If A1=2, B2=3, and C3=10, the resulting value is 2–3 +10/10, or 2–3+1, or –1 +1,=0	Excel first divides cell C3 by 10, then subtracts B2 from cell A1, and finally adds this value to the quotient.

Understanding Precision vs. Display of Cells Values

Paul corrects the problems with the formulas in cells D14 and D15. Figure 1.7 shows the revised worksheet.

Figure 1.7: Worksheet after correcting formulas

	A	B	C	D	E	F
1		TZEdge Material Analysis				
2	Material Price Quotes:					
3	Component	Description	Quantity	Unit	Cost/Unit	
4	Leather	Exterior leather	1	sf	$ 19.860	
5	Internal Arch Support	Molesole arch support	1,000	lot	2,235.000	
6	Sole	Polymer resin - preformed	12	lot	124.450	
7	Laces	Smooth leather	1	inch	0.047	
8	Trim	Suede appliques - set of 3	1	set	4.250	
9	Trim	Wedge logo insert	1	each	1.570	
10						
11	Cost Calculations per Shoe:					
12	Component		Quantity	Unit	Total Cost	
13	Leather		1.23	sf	24	
14	Internal Arch Support		1	each	2	
15	Trim (applique set & logo)		2	set/each	12	
16	Laces		31.5	inches	1	
17	**Materials Total**				40	
18						
19						

Corrected formula for Internal Arch Support: =E5/C5*B14

Corrected formula for Trim: =(E8+E9)*2

Notice that the Materials Total value in cell D17 is still slightly off. If you manually add 24+2+12+1, the total is 39, not 40 as displayed. The formula in cell D17 is =D13+D14 +D15+D16, which appears to be correct. So, what is the problem?

Actually, there is no problem. The worksheet was originally set up to display the values in cells D13:D17 with no decimal places. This display does not change the precise values that are stored in the cells. Even though cell D14 displays the value 2, you know from the calculation 1*2235/1000 entered into that cell the actual value stored is 2.235. The discrepancy is simply the result of the display being rounded; the precise values stored in each cell are correct. To test out this theory, Paul could revise the worksheet to display five decimal places, as illustrated in Figure 1.8. By manually calculating the Materials Total cost, you can see that the result in cell D17 is correct.

Figure 1.8: Worksheet with values displaying five decimal places

	A	B	C	D	E	F
1		TZEdge Material Analysis				
2	Material Price Quotes:					
3	Component	Description	Quantity	Unit	Cost/Unit	
4	Leather	Exterior leather	1	sf	$ 19.860	
5	Internal Arch Support	Molesole arch support	1,000	lot	2,235.000	
6	Sole	Polymer resin - preformed	12	lot	124.450	
7	Laces	Smooth leather	1	inch	0.047	
8	Trim	Suede appliques - set of 3	1	set	4.250	
9	Trim	Wedge logo insert	1	each	1.570	
10						
11	Cost Calculations per Shoe:					
12	Component		Quantity	Unit	Total Cost	
13	Leather		1.23	sf	$ 24.42780	
14	Internal Arch Support		1	each	2.23500	
15	Trim (applique set & logo)		2	set/each	11.64000	
16	Laces		31.5	inches	1.48050	
17	**Materials Total**				$ 39.78330	
18						
19						

Values displayed with five decimal places show that there is no error in the formula

Excel can display values in several different formats without changing the precise value stored by the program. When Excel rounds the display, it does so by rounding any number *less than half* down to the next value and any number *half or greater* up to the next value. Remember that changing the display does not change the precise value stored; the stored value is the value used in any calculations. Table 1.4 provides examples of these format displays. These display options can be accessed from buttons in the Number group on the Home tab.

Table 1.4: Formats for displaying values

Description	Display	Actual Value Stored	Example
Display varying number of decimal places	2	2.201 (stored in cell B2)	=100*B2 results in the value 220.1
Display using percent	5%	0.05 (stored in cell B3)	=100*B3 results in the value 5
Date display	12/31/2013	41639.00 (stored in cell B4)	=B4+1 results in the value 41640, or if formatted as a date, displays 1/1/2014

In addition to changing the number of decimal places shown, you can also display a value as a percent without having to multiply by 100. A cell formatted with the Percent Style displays the % symbol following the value. When entering percentages, you can do one of the following:

- Enter the decimal equivalent, such as 0.23, and then click the Percent Style button in the Number group on the Home tab. The value in the cell is displayed as 23% and the precise value stored in the cell is 0.23.
- Format the cell as a percentage first, again using the Percent Style button, and then enter the value as either a whole number, such as 23, or as the decimal equivalent, such as .23. The value in the cell is displayed as 23% and the precise value stored in the cell is 0.23.
- Type the value, such as 23, either preceded or followed by a percent sign (%23 or 23%). The value in the cell is displayed as 23%, and the precise value stored in the cell is 0.23.

Dates are also a formatting option in Excel. Just like other values, dates can be added and subtracted in formulas. Usually when you enter a date such as 12/31/2013 or December 31, 2013, Excel automatically formats the entry as a date.

Best Practice

Working with Dates

Excel stores dates as sequential numbers beginning with January 1, 1900. For example, January 1, 2014 is the value 41640 representing the number of days since 1/1/1900. Excel stores times as decimal fractions. This enables you to perform numeric calculations on cells containing dates, such as adding or subtracting a specified number of days from a date to arrive at a new date, or determining the number of days between two given dates. The following are examples of date values used in formulas, assuming the date 1/10/2014 is stored in cell A1 and the date 1/20/2014 is stored in cell A2:

- =A1+10 produces the result 1/20/2014
- =A2–10 produces the result 1/10/2014
- =A2–A1 produces the result 10

Note that dates cannot be used directly in a formula because Excel interprets the date as a calculation. For example, if the formula =1/10/2014+10 were entered in a cell, Excel would interpret this as 1 divided by 10 divided by 2014 plus 10—instead of as the date January 10, 2014 plus 10.

Date inputs and values resulting from calculations with dates can be displayed in a variety of ways, including numeric values, dates shown with the format 1/1/2014, or dates written out as January 1, 2014. These formats are available by clicking the Number Format button arrow in the Number group. The Number Format menu contains choices for several commonly used date formats. Additional date formats are available on the Number tab of the Format Cells dialog box.

Depending on which version of Excel you are using and how your options are configured, Excel allows two-digit year inputs, but they might be interpreted differently. In Excel 2010, the default setting interprets the values 00 through 29 as dates after 1/1/2000; whereas two-digit values from 30 through 99 are interpreted as years prior to 1/1/2000. For example, Excel would interpret the date 3/2/88 as March 2, 1988, not as March 2, 2088. It is usually a good idea to enter the full four digits of the year to avoid any types of problems.

Checking Accuracy in Formula Updates

The worksheet includes a cost per unit (Cost/Unit) for a shoe sole in the "Material Price Quotes" section, but there is no corresponding value in the "Cost Calculations per Shoe" section. This cost was omitted in error. To complete the worksheet, Paul inserts a new row above the Materials Total to calculate the cost of the shoe sole. Then he enters the formula =B17*E6/C6 in cell D17 (in the newly inserted row) to calculate the quantity times the cost. Because the preformed polymer resin soles are priced by the dozen, the cost for each is $124.45/12, and one sole per shoe is required. The updated worksheet is shown in Figure 1.9. Note that Paul also formatted the values in cells D13:D18 so that they include two decimal places, are aligned on the decimal point, and include dollar signs for only the first calculated cost and the Materials Total cost. He also included cell borders to set off the Materials Total cost.

Figure 1.9: Worksheet with inserted row for sole costs

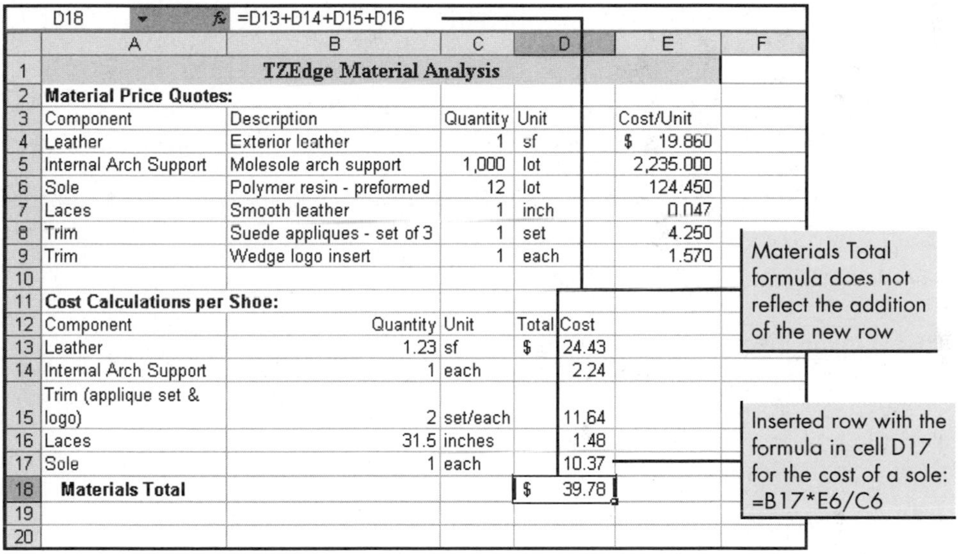

Has the Materials Total been updated accordingly to reflect the addition of the sole cost? Notice that the formula in cell D18 is still =D13+D14+D15+D16. It does not include any reference to cell D17, which now contains the cost of the sole. Paul edits cell D18 manually to include the addition of cell D17 in the total, as shown in Figure 1.10.

This is an inefficient way to update a formula, especially if you need to add several values. There is a better method to build formulas that ensures accuracy when you update or change a formula; this method is explored in the next level.

Figure 1.10: Formula modified to include new cost

	A	B	C	D	E	F
	D18		*fx* =D13+D14+D15+D16+D17			
1		TZEdge Material Analysis				
2	**Material Price Quotes:**					
3	Component	Description	Quantity	Unit	Cost/Unit	
4	Leather	Exterior leather	1	sf	$ 19.860	
5	Internal Arch Support	Molesole arch support	1,000	lot	2,235.000	
6	Sole	Polymer resin - preformed	12	lot	124.450	
7	Laces	Smooth leather	1	inch	0.047	
8	Trim	Suede appliques - set of 3	1	set	4.250	
9	Trim	Wedge logo insert	1	each	1.570	
10						
11	**Cost Calculations per Shoe:**					
12	Component		Quantity	Unit	Total Cost	
13	Leather		1.23	sf	$ 24.43	
14	Internal Arch Support		1	each	2.24	
15	Trim (applique set & logo)		2	set/each	11.64	
16	Laces		31.5	inches	1.48	
17	Sole		1	each	10.37	
18	**Materials Total**				$ 50.15	
19						
20						

Updated formula in cell D18 includes cell D17 in the calculation

Steps To Success: Level 1

The product design team has prepared another worksheet, with the assistance of the manufacturing group, listing the labor costs involved in manufacturing the TZEdge shoe. Figure 1.11 shows this worksheet.

Figure 1.11: Initial labor costs worksheet

	A	B	C	D	E
1	Description	Production Rate	Unit	$/Hour	
2	Delivery of Boxes to Product l	15	boxes/hr	10	
3	Cutting of Leather	20	shoes/hr	22.40	
4	Attachment of Appliques	30	appliques/hr	10	
5	Sewing of Logos to Leather	22.5	pieces/hr	13.1	
6	Assembly of Leather & Sole	10	shoes/hr	23	
7	Assembly of Arch Support	18.5	shoes/hr	11.66	
8					
9	Each Shoe - Manufacturing T:	Quantity /Shoe	Unit	Total Cost	
10	Delivery of Boxes to Product l	.2	boxes/shoe	#DIV/0!	
11	Cutting of Leather	1	shoe	1	
12	Attachment of Appliques	6	appliques/sh	2	
13	Assembly of Leather & Sole	1.00	shoe	######	
14	Assembly of Arch Support	1.00	shoe	0.0046	
15	Total Labor			#DIV/0!	
16					

Note the following:

- Cells A1:D7 (input area) list the different tasks that are performed in the production of the shoe and the rates at which they are performed—boxes moved per hour, pieces sewn per hour, and so on. Also listed is the labor rate to perform these tasks in dollars per hour. For example, 15 boxes can be delivered in an hour to the production line at a cost of $10 per hour.

- Cells A9:D15 (output area) show these same tasks with the specific quantities required per shoe. For example, 0.2 boxes will be delivered for each shoe. If 15 boxes can be delivered in an hour at a cost of $10, how much will it cost to deliver 0.2 boxes?

In these steps, your task is to troubleshoot this worksheet and correct any problems with formatting or formulas. Complete the following:

1. Open the workbook named **Labor.xlsx** located in the Chapter 1 folder, and then save it as **Labor Costs.xlsx**.

2. Adjust the column widths, as necessary, so that all information is fully displayed.

3. Format the values in the Production Rate and $/Hour columns with the Comma Style. In addition, format cell D2 with a dollar sign aligned at the left of the cell.

4. Address the error messages in cells B10, D10, and D15.

5. Correct the formula in cell D10 so that it accurately calculates the cost of delivering boxes for one shoe.

6. Check the formulas that were entered for each of the other manufacturing tasks to ensure they are written correctly and that the worksheet can be easily updated later if any of the inputs change (Production Rate, Unit, $/Hour, or Quantity/Shoe). Check that the formula to summarize the labor costs is correct, and modify as needed.

7. Format cells D10:D15 so that the values align on the decimal point and display two decimal places for all the values in column D. Include a dollar sign in cells D10 and D15.

8. Format cells B10:B14 with the Comma Style with two decimal places.

9. The labor cost of sewing logos onto the leather was accidentally omitted from the manufacturing tasks. There are two logos per shoe that need to be sewn on. Insert a new row just below the row containing the Attachment of Appliques and complete the data inputs/outputs to calculate the labor cost of sewing these logos.

10. Adjust the Total Labor cost accordingly.

11. Add the title **TZEdge Labor Analysis** at the top of the worksheet. Center and merge the title over the columns containing values, and format the title with a light blue background (choose from one of the different blue shades available on the color gallery).

12. Create a custom page header to contain your name, the name of the company, and today's date.

13. Save and close the Labor Costs.xlsx workbook.

LEVEL 2

Calculating and Comparing Data Using Simple Functions

Working with Multiple Worksheets

The product design team has been given the go-ahead to proceed with the project for the TZEdge shoe. The marketing group has just completed some testing with a small number of consumer focus groups. These focus groups have been extremely helpful in providing feedback to the design team. Most of the feedback has focused on two major areas: (1) the leather and styling and (2) the need for more ankle support for certain customers. As a result, the team has come up with two additional design options to consider:

- Textured leather that includes only one logo, and no appliques, for trim
- A high top design similar to the original shoe

Paul needs to compile some financial information to compare the material costs for each of these options to the original design. Refinements of the designs are expected to require several additional material components for one or more of these options. Paul needs to plan accordingly when setting up the worksheet.

The corporate Purchasing Department has also supplied some information to help price the materials for these new designs. The cost of textured leather is estimated to be approximately twice the cost of the leather currently being considered. Also, the high top design requires approximately 25% more leather and twice the lace length.

Using the information calculated in the original design, Paul sets up another worksheet in the TZEdge Material Costs workbook, listing the material costs for all three options. The costs on this new worksheet for the original option are based on the worksheet previously developed. Costs for the textured leather and high top options are based on the design requirements and cost estimates specified previously. To create the worksheet, Paul inserted a new worksheet in the existing workbook by choosing the Insert Worksheet button located to the right of the sheet tabs at the bottom of the window. Worksheets can also be inserted by clicking Insert Sheet on the Insert menu located in the Cells group on the Home tab. Figure 1.12 shows Paul's new worksheet.

Figure 1.12: Worksheet with additional design options

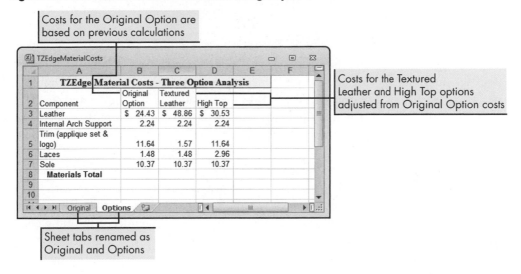

Costs for the Original Option are based on previous calculations

Costs for the Textured Leather and High Top options adjusted from Original Option costs

Sheet tabs renamed as Original and Options

When you work with multiple worksheets in a workbook, it's a good idea to rename each worksheet tab from the default labels (Sheet1, Sheet2, and so on) to assign names that better identify the worksheet contents. You can also apply color to worksheet tabs to further distinguish one worksheet from another. In this case, Paul renames the Sheet1 tab as "Original" because this worksheet contains the material analysis data for the original TZEdge shoe design; and he renames the tab for the newly inserted worksheet as "Options" because it contains the data for the three different design options.

How To

Rename and Add Color to a Worksheet Tab

1. To rename a worksheet tab, right-click the tab you want to rename, and then click Rename on the shortcut menu.

2. Type the new worksheet tab name to replace the highlighted name, and then press the Enter key or click any cell on the worksheet to continue.

3. To add color to a worksheet tab, right-click the tab, point to Tab Color on the shortcut menu, and then click a color in the gallery that opens. If you don't see the color you want, click More Colors at the bottom of the gallery, and then use the dialog box to specify a custom color.

Calculating Totals Using the SUM Function

The next step in completing the Options worksheet is to calculate the material costs for each option. Paul could simply enter the formula =B3+B4+B5+B6+B7 in cell B8 to determine the total cost of the original option. However, as you saw earlier with the Original worksheet, this method does not allow additional rows to be inserted and formulas to be recalculated automatically. Because additional material components are expected later on, this method is not recommended. A better method is to use the SUM function.

In addition to writing formulas that use constants, cell references, and operands, you can also write formulas that include one or more functions. **Functions** are predefined formulas that perform calculations. For example, the **SUM** function adds a list of values and/or cell ranges. A function is always structured beginning with the function name and an opening parenthesis mark. After the parenthesis, the function contains a list of inputs in a specific order, separated by commas. A closing parenthesis mark ends the function. The function inputs are referred to as **arguments**. Each function has its own **syntax**, which specifies the function name and order of the arguments. The syntax can be compared with the spelling of a word, where each word contains specific letters in a specific order. Changing the order of the letters can change the meaning of the word or render it meaningless, such as *two* versus *tow* versus *wto*. Similarly, changing the name of the function or the order of the arguments would change the value returned or render the formula unusable. A function always behaves in the same way, according to the rules programmed into the function. These rules are referred to as a function's **algorithm**. Later, you'll see how these rules can affect the values calculated and, therefore, how to use a particular function.

Paul needs to include a formula with a SUM function in cell B8 to total the values for the original option, which are located in cells B3 through B7. As is true with any formula, this formula begins with an equal sign followed by the appropriate equation—in this case, just the SUM function. In Excel syntax, the formula in cell B8 is =SUM(B3:B7). In a similar fashion, Paul includes the formula =SUM(C3:C7) in cell C8 and =SUM(D3:D7) in cell D8. Note the syntax used in the SUM function—two cell references separated by a colon. This is referred to as a **cell range**. Ranges can be one-dimensional along a row or column, or even a two-dimensional block such as B3:D7, which includes all cells starting in B3 and going down to row 7 and then across to column D.

Functions can also be written as part of a larger formula. For example, if Paul wanted to calculate the material cost of a pair of shoes in cell B8 instead of a single shoe, he could modify the formula to the following: =2*SUM(B3:B7).

How To

Insert a Function into a Formula

1. Enter the formula up to the point where you want to insert a function.

2. Click the Insert Function button f_x to the left of the Formula Bar to open the Insert Function dialog box, shown in Figure 1.13.

Figure 1.13: Insert Function dialog box

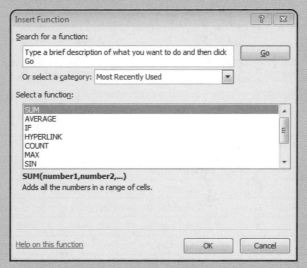

3. In the Select a function section, click the function you want (you might have to choose a category first to display the appropriate function list), and then click the OK button. The Function Arguments dialog box for that function opens.

4. Enter the appropriate arguments in the text boxes provided, and then click the OK button.

OR

1. Enter the formula up to the point where you want to insert a function.

2. Type the function name and each of the arguments required. When using cell references as arguments, you can either click the cell(s) to include the references or type the cell references. This method of using a function requires that you know the syntax of the function; however, after you type the function name and the opening parenthesis, Excel automatically displays the syntax for you as a guide. Many experienced Excel users prefer this method of entering a function because it is faster than using the Insert Function dialog box.

Calculating Quickly with AutoSum

Excel's **AutoSum** feature gives you quick access to the SUM function and other similar functions. To use this feature, you select the cell in which you want to perform the calculation, and then click the Sum button Σ in the Editing group on the Home tab. After you choose the Sum function, Excel presents a suggested range of cells to include in the calculation, based on rows or columns of numbers next to the current cell. It is important to verify that this is the range you require because the range chosen by Excel might not always be the one you want. If necessary, simply type the appropriate cell references to modify the range.

Other common functions can be accessed by clicking the Sum button arrow $\boxed{\Sigma \; \cdot}$. These include **AVERAGE**, **COUNT**, **MAX**, and **MIN**. Clicking the AutoSum button, located in the Function Library group on the Formulas tab, displays the same options on its menu.

Table 1.5 shows the Excel functions that are similar to the SUM function and simple to use. Unlike the functions presented later in this book, these functions contain only one type of argument—a number. A number can be represented by a constant, a cell reference where a value resides, or a range of cell references.

Table 1.5: Commonly used Excel functions

Function (arguments)	Description
SUM(number1,number2,...)	Calculates the sum of a list of values
AVERAGE(number1,number2,...)	Calculates the average value of a list of values
MIN(number1,number2,...)	Calculates the minimum value in a list of values
MAX(number1,number2,...)	Calculates the maximum value in a list of values
COUNT(number1,number2,...)	Determines the number of values in a list

Like the SUM function, these common functions take a list of number arguments, which can include one or more of the following:

- A range along a column; for example, B3:B7
- A range along a row; for example, B3:D3
- A two-dimensional range (also referred to as a block of cells); for example, B3:D7
- Noncontiguous cells and/or constants; for example, B3, C4, D5:D6, 6

You can obtain more detail about each of these functions by using the Help feature in Excel. You can access Help by clicking the Help icon $\boxed{?}$ or by clicking the Help on this function link in the Insert Function dialog box. It is recommended that you look at this information when you begin working with a new Excel function.

Calculating Average, Minimum, and Maximum Values

In addition to totaling the material costs for each option, Paul needs to calculate the following:

- The average cost of each material component for each of the three options. This information will give the product design team a feel for the range of costs for each component.
- The lowest component cost and the highest component cost for all three options. This information was requested by the corporate Purchasing Department so they can get an idea of the range of cost component values, and so they can prioritize their purchasing efforts accordingly.

Cell E3 will contain a formula that averages the cost of leather for the three options, as follows: =AVERAGE(B3:D3). Similar formulas will calculate the average costs of arch support, trim, and so on. The formulas =MIN(B3:D7) and =MAX(B3:D7) will determine the value of the lowest and highest cost components, respectively, for all three options. Notice that the range used in these functions is two-dimensional; it includes multiple columns and rows. The revised worksheet is shown in Figure 1.14.

Figure 1.14: Worksheet revised to include average, minimum, and maximum costs

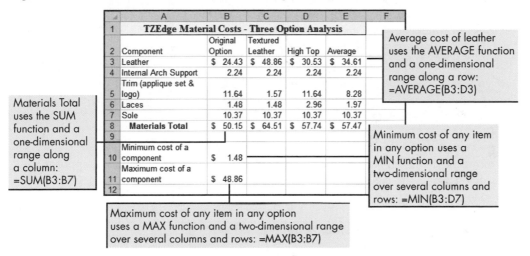

The product design team recently received some information on additional materials that will be needed to produce the shoes. For the textured leather shoe, because the material is softer than the leather in the original option, a toe support brace is needed, as well as a toe support pad to cushion it. The braces cost $1.27 each and the cushions cost $3.29 each. A back support cushion is also required for both the textured leather shoe and the high top shoe. The back support cushions are still being designed, but the purchasing group recommends using a cost of $5.00 each for the textured leather option and $6.50 each for the high top option, although these costs could change later.

Paul needs to modify the worksheet based on this new information. He inserts three rows just above the Sole component to allow for the three additional components: toe support brace, toe support pad, and back support cushion. The formulas for the totals automatically update to reflect the additional costs.

Best Practice

Inserting Rows and the Impact on Formulas
Most often when you insert rows in a list of values that is being calculated, such as with a total, Excel includes the newly inserted values and recalculates the formulas affected. Excel "senses" that the new rows are part of an existing list and either automatically includes the rows in the subsequent formulas or gives you the option to include the new rows. Also, Excel extends consistent formatting to the values in the newly inserted rows.

Depending on what values are in the list and how they are formatted, however, this might not always work as anticipated. If you think additional rows will be needed, you can avoid potential problems in one of two ways:

- Insert the new row or rows within the list of values instead of at the end of the list. This ensures that the newly inserted values are incorporated in any formulas. This method is acceptable if the values can be listed in any order. If you want to maintain a specific order, you would have to copy and paste and/or retype some of the data to obtain the order you want.
- Design your worksheet to include a blank row between the end of the list of values and the total formulas. The cell ranges you use in the formulas can include the blank row, and then whenever you insert rows, you can do so just above the blank row. This preserves the order of the values listed and ensures that all formulas are automatically updated. Because most of the commonly used functions ignore blank cells, the values generated should not be affected. When using this method, however, keep in mind that Excel might display an alert informing you that the formula refers to a blank cell. You can simply ignore this alert in this instance.

After inserting the rows, Paul enters labels in column A and the costs in the appropriate cells, leaving blank the cells for those options that do not include the three additional components. The revised worksheet is shown in Figure 1.15.

Figure 1.15: Values and formulas for revised worksheet

The worksheet on the top in Figure 1.15 displays the new values. Notice that the Materials Total cells have been updated (except the total for the original option, which does not include the new components). In addition, the minimum and maximum calculations in cells B13 and B14 have been updated as well. Because the cost of the toe support brace ($1.27) is less than any others previously entered, the value in cell B13 has been updated to show this cost.

The worksheet on the bottom in Figure 1.15 shows the new formulas. These formulas were updated automatically when the three rows were added. For example, the formula in cell B13 now reads =MIN(B3:D10); the original formula was =MIN(B3:D7). Similarly, the average calculation for the sole in cell E10 now reads =AVERAGE(B10:D10); the original formula =AVERAGE(B7:D7) was automatically updated by Excel.

The averages for the three new components must be calculated, but how should these calculations be performed? For example, to calculate the average cost of the back support cushion, should Paul average only the textured leather and high top options, because only these two options include this cushion, that is, (5+6.50)/2? Or should Paul also include the original option as $0, that is, (0+5+6.50)/3? There is no one right answer to this dilemma, but it's helpful to consider how the information will be used. Because this information will only give the purchasing group a handle on the order-of-magnitude costs of these components, it would be better to average only the values where the material is being used.

What Excel formula should be written to accomplish this? To know how to proceed, you need to understand the algorithm used by the AVERAGE function. The Help feature in Excel provides the following information about the AVERAGE function: "If a range or cell reference argument contains text, logical values, or empty cells, those values are ignored; however, cells with the value zero are included." Based on this definition, the AVERAGE function in cell E9 could be written to include all three columns, as follows: =AVERAGE(B9:D9). The advantage of including cell B9 is that if, at a later date, a back support cushion is required for the original option, a value could be entered and the average would automatically be updated. This is the method Paul chooses, so he enters the appropriate formulas in column E to calculate the averages for the three new components.

Sometimes, you would want to include a blank cell in the AVERAGE calculation because it's important for the calculation to accurately reflect the number of values being averaged. In such a case, you could simply enter the value 0 in the blank cell.

Calculating the Number of Values Using the COUNT and COUNTA Functions

A final calculation needed in the current worksheet is to determine a count of the number of material components in each option. This information is needed by the production group when they plan how much storage space is required on-site and the number of hours of material handling needed during production. Paul can enter these values just below the Materials Total in row 12. In this case, blank cells must be ignored and not counted. Fortunately, like the AVERAGE function, the COUNT function also ignores blank cells and cells with text. In cell B12, Paul enters the formula =COUNT(B3:B10). Similar formulas will count the number of components for the textured leather and high top options. Entering these formulas manually can be repetitive. In Level 3, you'll explore more efficient ways of entering similar formulas multiple times.

In cell A12, Paul wants to display the total number of components being considered for any of the three options by simply counting the component descriptions. In this case, the COUNT function will not work because it ignores cells with text. An alternative is to use the **COUNTA function**, which is similar to the COUNT function but does not ignore text cells. Paul decides to expand the formula so that it counts the number of components for each specific option as well. He enters the formula =COUNTA(A3:A10) in cell A12. The results, which are displayed in Figure 1.16, show that there are eight components in all; five components are used in the original option; eight components are used in the textured leather option; and six components are used in the high top option.

Figure 1.16: Final worksheet with formatting

	A	B	C	D	E	F
1	TZEdge Material Costs - Three Option Analysis					
2	Component	Original Option	Textured Leather	High Top	Average	
3	Leather	$ 24.43	$ 48.86	$ 30.53	$ 34.61	
4	Internal Arch Support	2.24	2.24	2.24	2.24	
5	Trim (applique set & logo)	11.64	1.57	11.64	8.28	
6	Laces	1.48	1.48	2.96	1.97	
7	Toe Support Brace		1.27		1.27	
8	Toe Support Pad		3.29		3.29	
9	Back Support Cushion		5.00	6.50	5.75	
10	Sole	10.37	10.37	10.37	10.37	
11	**Materials Total**	$ 50.15	$ 74.07	$ 64.24	$ 62.82	
12	*8*	*5*	*8*	*6*	*count*	
13	Minimum cost of a component	$ 1.27				
14	Maximum cost of a component	$ 48.86				
15						

New formulas inserted for average costs including blank cell, for example, formula in cell E7 is =AVERAGE(B7:D7)

=COUNTA(A3:A10)   =COUNT(B3:B10)

Paul also makes the following formatting changes to improve the readability of the worksheet:

- Adds the label "count" in cell E12
- Places a border around cells A12:E12 to highlight this row
- Places borders around cells A13:B14 and a border around the overall worksheet cells A2:E14
- Formats the values in cells A12:E12 with centered alignment, and bold and italic styles; highlights these cells with light gray fill

Steps To Success: Level 2

Recall that the two additional options being considered for the TZEdge shoe are as follows:

- Textured leather that includes only one logo, and no appliques, for trim
- A high top design similar to the original shoe

Now that the material analysis for the three options is in place, the labor costs must be determined. Figure 1.17 shows the labor comparison worksheet that has been developed so far; it contains the costs associated with the manufacturing tasks for one shoe produced with the original option.

The manufacturing group has been meeting to determine how the different design options will affect the number of hours and skills required to assemble the shoe. This group has provided the following information:

Figure 1.17: Labor comparison worksheet

▲	A	B	C	D	E	F
1	TZEdge Labor Cost Three Option Comparison					
2	Manufacturing Tasks Per Shoe:	Original Option	Textured Leather	High Top		
3	Delivery of Boxes to Production Line	$ 0.14				
4	Cutting of Leather	1.12				
5	Attachment of Appliques	2.03				
6	Sewing of Logos to Leather	1.16				
7	Assembly of Leather, Sole	2.25				
8	Assembly of Arch Support	0.63				
9	Total Labor					
10						

Textured Leather
- The textured leather is actually easier to work with compared with the original option. The group estimates it will take about 10% less time to assemble the leather and sole.
- The group also estimates that it will take about three-quarters of the time to assemble the arch support as compared with the original option.
- Because there are no appliques on the textured leather, there is no cost for attaching them. Therefore, the cell calculating the attachment of appliques can be left blank.
- The cutting of the leather will take approximately the same time as for the original option.
- Only one logo needs to be sewn on, so the cost for this is approximately half the amount as that of the original option.
- The cost for delivering boxes is the same as the original option.

High Top
- The high top shoes require additional leather. The group estimates it will take about 25% more time to assemble the leather and sole compared with the original option.

- Since these shoes require more leather, the costs to deliver boxes will increase by $.03 per box.
- All other manufacturing costs remain the same as those for the original option.

Now, you need to finish the worksheet to determine the manufacturing costs of the textured leather and high top options.

Complete the following:

1. Open the workbook named **Comparison.xlsx** located in the Chapter 1 folder, and then save it as **Labor Comparison.xlsx**.

2. Complete columns C and D for the textured leather and high top options based on the data provided for the original option and the information provided by the manufacturing group.

3. Calculate the total labor cost for each option.

4. Format all the values in the worksheet with two decimal places and dollar signs displayed in the first row and total row only.

5. In row 11, below the option totals, calculate the number of tasks in each option and the number of possible tasks based on the list in column A. Format these values in bold and italic, and insert the label **# Tasks** (also in bold and italic) in cell E11.

6. In cell E3, calculate the minimum cost of the box delivery task for the three options. Use the label **Min. Cost** as the column heading. Calculate the minimum cost for each of the other manufacturing tasks and for the total labor.

7. In cell F3, calculate the maximum cost of the box delivery task for the three options. Use the label **Max. Cost** as the column heading. Calculate the maximum cost for each of the other manufacturing tasks and for the total labor.

8. Several rows below the totals, in column B, calculate the average labor cost of all manufacturing tasks for all three options combined. Blank cells should not be included in the average. Place the label "Average" to the left of the calculation.

9. The data for the toe support brace, toe support pad, and back support cushion was omitted in error from the worksheet. The manufacturing group advises to include $1.05 in labor costs to assemble these three items for the textured leather option, and to include $.75 in labor costs to assemble these three items for the high top option. Insert a row above the "Assembly of Leather, Sole" task and include the necessary values and the label **Leather Support Assembly**. (Recall that the original option does not include these items.) Check all your formulas to ensure they are updated correctly, based on the newly inserted values.

10. Save and close the Labor Comparison.xlsx workbook.

LEVEL 3

Analyzing Cell References When Writing and Copying Formulas

Creating a Budget Workbook

The task of compiling material and labor costs for the TZEdge shoe is now complete. The next step for Paul is to set up a preliminary budget for each quarter of the first year of production and a combined summary. For now, Paul will produce this information for only the original option of the TZEdge shoe. He also will create budgets for three different selling price alternatives: low priced, medium priced, and high priced. Table 1.6 provides the estimated sales volumes for each of these pricing alternatives in each quarter and the associated shoe prices. The expenses such as material costs and labor costs per shoe will be constant in each alternative and in each quarter, though the volumes will vary.

Table 1.6: Shoe prices and estimated sales volumes

		1stQTR	2ndQTR	3rdQTR	4thQTR
Alternative:	$/Pair	#Pairs	#Pairs	#Pairs	#Pairs
Low Priced	200	1000	1500	1700	2500
Medium Priced	225	750	1000	1100	1600
High Priced	250	350	450	480	750

From his earlier analysis of material and labor costs and with new information provided, Paul knows the following about the original option:

- Material costs total $50.15 per shoe.
- Labor costs total $7.33 per shoe.
- Overhead costs are calculated as 25% of the direct labor costs.
- Selling expense is calculated at $10 per pair of shoes, or $5 per shoe.

Organizing the Workbook

With the necessary information in hand, how should Paul organize the new budget workbook he needs to create? Consider the Options worksheet created earlier (Figure 1.16). In this worksheet, all the inputs and outputs for the three design options are displayed on the same worksheet. This layout is easy to read and implement because there are a limited number of options and relatively simple calculations. But what if each design option had a completely different set of data inputs, or the values of the inputs varied from option to option? In such a case, it might be easier to create separate worksheets for each design option, or put all the inputs together on one worksheet and the outputs together on another.

For the budget workbook, Paul needs to organize data for four quarters with each quarter containing data for the three different pricing alternatives. If he placed all the data on one worksheet, it would contain 12 separate sets of calculations and inputs. Although this is possible, such an organization would make the worksheet cumbersome to manipulate. Figure 1.18 illustrates and compares several possible ways to organize the budget workbook.

Note the following:

- The first organization places all the inputs on one worksheet and all the outputs on another. This is a simple organization but, again, might be difficult to work with and could cause confusion, because it would be difficult to ascertain which set of inputs are associated with a particular output.
- The second organization is by quarter. The inputs and outputs are placed on a single worksheet with each worksheet containing all three pricing alternatives for a specific quarter.
- The third organization is by pricing alternative. The inputs and outputs are placed on a single worksheet with each worksheet containing all four quarters for a specific pricing alternative.

Figure 1.18: Possible workbook designs

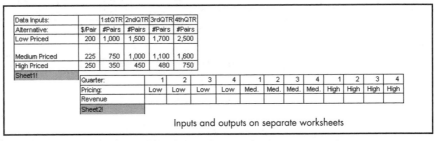

Inputs and outputs on separate worksheets

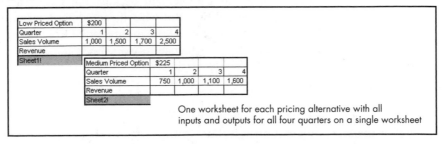

One worksheet for each quarter with all inputs and outputs for all three pricing alternatives on a single worksheet

One worksheet for each pricing alternative with all inputs and outputs for all four quarters on a single worksheet

Paul could also create 12 separate worksheets—one for each pricing alternative for each quarter.

Which workbook organization should Paul choose? That depends on what he wants to emphasize and compare, and what elements are most likely to change. Because management is probably most interested in the financial ramifications in each quarter, Paul decides to organize the worksheets by quarter. In this way, a single sheet will contain both the inputs and outputs associated with a specific time frame. The worksheets will be named 1stQTR, 2ndQTR, 3rdQTR, and 4thQTR. After entering the information for each of the four quarters, Paul can easily combine the data into a summary on a separate sheet named Summary.

To accomplish this task, Paul will complete the first quarter worksheet by typing in all of the data inputs and calculations for that quarter. After Paul completes the first quarter calculations, he will select the entire worksheet and then copy it to three new worksheets, making the appropriate changes to the data inputs for each quarter as needed. The structure of this 1stQTR worksheet is shown in Figure 1.19. Labels and values list the revenue and expense items down the column, and the volume values for each of the three pricing alternatives are listed across the row. Also, some of the inputs needed in all four quarters are listed at the top of the worksheet in cells B1:B2.

Figure 1.19: First quarter budget

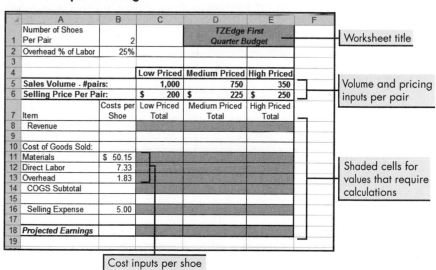

Cost inputs per shoe

Notice that cell B13 already contains the formula that calculates the unit cost of overhead for the original option. Because overhead is given as 25% of direct labor (cell B2), the formula in cell B13 multiplies the labor expense $7.33 (cell B12) by 25%. In Excel syntax, this formula is =B12*B2. Note that cell B2 can be used directly in the formula because it has been formatted as a percentage; the precise value stored is still 0.25. To clarify the work remaining to be done in the worksheet, the cells in which formulas need to be entered are shaded.

Understanding Relative Cell Referencing

Paul needs to create the necessary formulas to calculate revenues and expenses for the original option of the TZEdge shoe. The costs of material and labor on a per-shoe basis are taken from the analyses done earlier. Paul needs to adjust these values later to multiply them by 2 because sales volumes are based on pairs of shoes.

Revenue can be calculated as sales volume times selling price. The formula =C5*C6 is entered in cell C8. Rather than create similar formulas in cells D8 and E8, wouldn't it be convenient if there was a way to tell Excel to use the same formula, but with a different set of data? In fact, Excel has the ability to change a formula *relative* to the location of the original formula. This allows you to use a "general" formula over and over again, but with a different set of numbers. To do this, you use a feature called **relative cell referencing**.

When you copy a formula from one cell to another, Excel automatically alters the new formula relative to where it is being copied. For example, if you enter the formula =C5*C6 in cell C8 and then copy it to cell D8, a displacement of 1 column and 0 rows, the formula is rewritten adding 1 column and 0 rows to each relative cell reference. There are two of these references in this formula: the first is C5 and the second is C6. If you add 1 column to C, it becomes column D. If you add 0 rows to 5, it remains 5, resulting in the cell reference D5. In a similar manner, the cell reference C6 is changed to D6. The new formula is now =D5*D6, which is the formula needed in this case. This process is illustrated in Figure 1.20.

Figure 1.20: Copying formulas with relative cell references

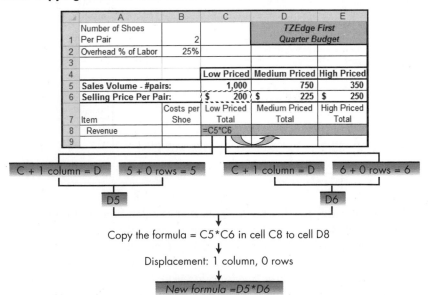

What about formulas that contain functions or constants? An example of this might be a formula to calculate the average sales volume and average selling price. If the formula =AVERAGE(C5:E5) were placed in cell F5, what would the resulting formula be if it was copied to cell F6? Here, the displacement is 0 columns and 1 row, resulting in a new formula in cell F6, =AVERAGE(C6:E6).

What happens when you copy formulas from one worksheet to another? Consider what would result if the formula =C5*C6 were copied from cell C8 on Sheet1! to cell E11 on Sheet2!. What is the displacement in this case? Because no sheet name is specified in the cell references, when the formula is copied, it would refer to cells on Sheet2! instead of Sheet1!. Which cells would it reference on Sheet2!? Here is the process:

- The displacement from C8 to E11 is 2 columns and 3 rows.
- Take the cell reference C5 and add 2 columns, 3 rows: this results in the new reference E8.
- Take the cell reference C6 and add 2 columns, 3 rows: this results in the new reference E9.
- When these elements are put together, the resulting formula is =E8*E9. Because this formula was copied to another worksheet, it now references these cells on the new sheet.

Best Practice

Avoiding #REF! Errors When Copying Formulas
Formulas can be copied in the opposite directions, back up columns, and farther to the left on rows. For example, the formula =D9*C7 could be copied from cell E9 into cell C8. In this case, the displacement is minus 2 columns and minus 1 row, resulting in the formula =B8*A6. However, you need to be careful that the resulting formulas contain only valid references.

Consider that you have just copied the formula =A2+C3 from cell C4 to cell B3, a displacement of minus one row and minus one column. Instead of displaying a value in cell B3, the cell contains the #REF! error. This error message has resulted because it is not possible to displace a reference in column A minus one column. In edit mode, Excel displays the resulting formula as =#REF!+B2.

Paul enters the formula =C5*C6 in cell C8 and copies it, using the fill handle, to cells D8 and E8. When copying formulas, you can use the copy/paste techniques, but it is easier to use the fill handle if you are copying to adjacent cells. The fill handle is a small square in the lower-right corner of a selected cell or cells that you drag to copy the contents of the selected cell or cells. The current worksheet is shown in Figure 1.21.

Figure 1.21: Revenue formulas filled across

	A	B	C	D	E	F
1	Number of Shoes Per Pair	2		TZEdge First Quarter Budget		
2	Overhead % of Labor	25%				
3						
4			Low Priced	Medium Priced	High Priced	
5	Sales Volume - #pairs:		1,000	750	350	
6	Selling Price Per Pair:		$ 200	$ 225	$ 250	
7	Item	Costs per Shoe	Low Priced Total	Medium Priced Total	High Priced Total	
8	Revenue		$ 200,000	$ 168,750	$ 87,500	
9						
10	Cost of Goods Sold:					
11	Materials	$ 50.15				
12	Direct Labor	7.33				
13	Overhead	1.83				
14	COGS Subtotal					
15						
16	Selling Expense	5.00				
17						
18	Projected Earnings					
19						
20						

=C5*C6   =D5*D6   =E5*E6

How To

Copy Formulas Using the Fill Handle
1. Select the cell or cells containing the formula(s) that you want to copy.
2. Place the pointer on the lower-right corner of the selected cell(s) until it changes to a ➕, which indicates it is positioned over the fill handle.
3. Press and hold down the left mouse button, and then drag the mouse down or across, as necessary, into one or more adjacent cells. This automatically copies the formula(s) into the adjacent cells indicated.

When you want to copy a formula down a column that is adjacent to another column of equal length, double-click ➕ to automatically copy the formula down into the corresponding cells.

Understanding Absolute and Mixed Cell Referencing

Next, Paul needs to calculate the total cost of materials. This calculation multiplies the number of shoes per pair, times the materials cost per shoe, times the sales volume. For the low-priced alternative, the formula Paul enters in cell C11 is =B1*B11*C5. As with the revenue calculation, it would save time if this formula could be copied from cell C11 across row 11, varying the sales volume for each corresponding pricing alternative. In fact, it would be ideal to copy this same formula down column C, substituting the cost of labor and then the cost of overhead for the cost of materials. As currently written, if the formula =B1*B11*C5 were copied from cell C11 to cell D11, a displacement of 1 column and

0 rows, the resulting formula would be =C1*C11*D5. Not only would the cell reference for the sales volume change, but the references for the number of shoes per pair and the materials cost per shoe would change as well. This would not work—cell C1 is blank and cell C11 contains the value just calculated for the materials cost per shoe for the low-priced alternative.

What you want Excel to do in such a case is to vary some of the values, but not others. For some operands, you want nothing to change; for others, only the row should change; and for still others, only the column should change. Can this be done? The answer is yes. In addition to relative cell references, Excel allows you to indicate that a cell reference (both column and row) or even a part of a cell reference (column or row) can remain unchanged when copying. This is called **absolute cell referencing**. The syntax used by Excel to indicate that a cell reference is absolute is a dollar sign ($) placed before the column letter, before the row number, or both. A cell reference that has only one $ is referred to as a **mixed cell reference**. Mixed referencing is common when you need to copy a formula both down a column and across the row at the same time.

Paul needs to apply absolute and mixed cell referencing to the formula he enters in cell C11, =B1*B11*C5, as illustrated in Figure 1.22.

Consider the first operand, the number of shoes per pair. Does this value change when the formula is copied down the column to calculate the total cost of labor or overhead? No, this value remains the same; specifically, you want to tell Excel, "Don't change the row of the cell reference when copying the formula down." Does this value change when the formula is copied across the row to calculate the total materials cost of the medium-priced alternative? Again, this value remains the same; specifically, you want to tell Excel, "Don't change the column of the cell reference when copying the formula across." To convey this in Excel syntax, you write the cell reference as $B$1. The first $ indicates that the column is absolute, the second $ indicates that the row is absolute.

The second operand in the formula =$B$1*B11*C5 is B11. How should this operand behave when it is copied down the column? B11 represents the cost of materials per shoe, and indeed this value should change relatively to reflect the cost of labor per shoe, and then the cost of overhead per shoe, when the formula is copied down the column. The row in cell reference B11 is therefore *relative*. What about the column reference; should that vary when the cost of materials per shoe in the formulas is copied across the row for the medium-priced alternative and the high-priced alternative? The cost of materials does not change; it remains the same regardless of which pricing alternative is being considered. So, the reference B11 must be changed to the *mixed* reference $B11, making the column absolute but allowing the row to change relatively.

Figure 1.22: Using absolute and mixed cell referencing

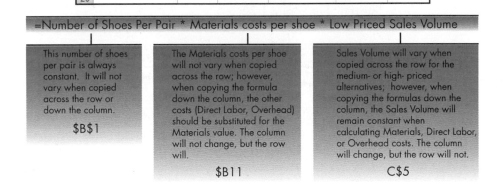

=B1*B11*C5 ⟶ $B$1*$B11*C$5

=Number of Shoes Per Pair * Materials costs per shoe * Low Priced Sales Volume

This number of shoes per pair is always constant. It will not vary when copied across the row or down the column.

$B$1

The Materials costs per shoe will not vary when copied across the row; however, when copying the formula down the column, the other costs (Direct Labor, Overhead) should be substituted for the Materials value. The column will not change, but the row will.

$B11

Sales Volume will vary when copied across the row for the medium- or high- priced alternatives; however, when copying the formulas down the column, the Sales Volume will remain constant when calculating Materials, Direct Labor, or Overhead costs. The column will change, but the row will not.

C$5

The third operand in the formula =$B$1*$B11*C5 is C5. How should this operand behave when it is copied down the column? C5 represents the sales volume for the low-priced alternative. Does this volume change depending on the expense item? No, it remains the same whether you are calculating materials costs, labor costs, or overhead. Therefore, the row must be absolute. What about when this formula is copied across the row to determine the cost of materials for the medium-priced and high-priced alternatives? Here, the sales volume varies relative to the column. So, the reference C5 must be changed to the mixed reference C$5.

To have the formula for the total cost of materials for the low-priced alternative work correctly across all three alternatives and for each of the cost components, Paul writes the formula =$B$1*$B11*C$5 in cell C11 and uses the fill handle to copy it down the column and then across the row. Figure 1.23 shows the current worksheet values and their corresponding formulas.

Figure 1.23: First quarter budget values and formulas displayed

	A	B	C	D	E	F
1	Number of Shoes Per Pair	2		TZEdge First Quarter Budget		
2	Overhead % of Labor	25%				
3						
4			Low Priced	Medium Priced	High Priced	
5	Sales Volume - #pairs:		1,000	750	350	
6	Selling Price Per Pair:		$ 200	$ 225	$ 250	
7	Item	Costs per Shoe	Low Priced Total	Medium Priced Total	High Priced Total	
8	Revenue		$ 200,000	$ 168,750	$ 87,500	
9						
10	Cost of Goods Sold:					
11	Materials	$ 50.15	100,300	75,225	35,105	
12	Direct Labor	7.33	14,660	10,995	5,131	
13	Overhead	1.83	3,665	2,749	1,283	
14	COGS Subtotal					
15						
16	Selling Expense	5.00				
17						
18	Projected Earnings					
19						
20						

First quarter Materials cost for the Low Priced alternative is $100,300 using the formula =$B$1*$B11*C$5 in cell C11; this formula was copied down the column and across the row into cells C11:E13

	A	B	C	D	E	F
1	Number of Shoes Per Pair	2		TZEdge First Quarter Budget		
2	Overhead % of	=0.25				
3						
4			Low Priced	Medium Priced	High Priced	
5	Sales Volume - #pairs:		1000	750	350	
6	Selling Price Per Pair:		200	225	250	
7	Item	Costs per Shoe	Low Priced Total	Medium Priced Total	High Priced Total	
8	Revenue		=C5*C6	=D5*D6	=E5*E6	
9						
10	Cost of Goods Sold:					
11	Materials	=50.15	=$B$1*$B11*C$5	=$B$1*$B11*D$5	=$B$1*$B11*E$5	
12	Direct Labor	7.33	=$B$1*$B12*C$5	=$B$1*$B12*D$5	=$B$1*$B12*E$5	
13	Overhead	=B2*B12	=$B$1*$B13*C$5	=$B$1*$B13*D$5	=$B$1*$B13*E$5	
14	COGS Subtotal					
15						
16	Selling Expense	5				
17						
18	Projected Earnings					
19						
20						

What would happen to the formulas if Paul needed to insert a row at the top of the worksheet to include a title? Now, the number of shoes per pair would be in cell B2 instead of cell B1. Would Paul need to rewrite the formulas, especially the ones that reference cell B1 absolutely? What happens to formulas with relative and absolute cell referencing when rows or columns are inserted into a worksheet? All references that are affected by the insertion adjust accordingly, whether they are relative or absolute. This also applies when deleting rows, columns, or cells, except when a deleted cell is directly referenced by a formula.

How To

Change a Cell Reference to an Absolute or Mixed Cell Reference

1. Type the cell reference in your formula or click the cell you want to include in the formula.

2. Type the dollar sign(s) needed to make the cell reference absolute or mixed.

OR

1. Type the cell reference in your formula or click the cell you want to include in the formula.

2. Press the F4 function key to add the dollar sign(s) needed to make the cell reference absolute or mixed. The F4 function key cycles through the display of dollar signs. If you press F4 once, the cell reference changes to an absolute reference, with dollar signs before both the row and column. If you press F4 twice, only the row is made absolute; and pressing F4 a third time makes only the column absolute.

Naming a Cell or Cell Range

Another technique that can be used to address a cell reference absolutely is to give that cell a name. You can name a single cell or a cell range, and then use that name directly in a formula. To name a cell or range, you first highlight the cell or cells to be named and then click the Name box, just below the Ribbon on the left. If Paul names cell B1 *pair*, for example, then instead of using the cell reference $B$1 in the formula, he could write =pair*B11*C5. Note that range names, unlike text labels, are not enclosed in quotation marks when used in formulas. If you attempt to use a name that has not been defined, Excel displays the error message #NAME!.

Writing a Formula to Subtotal the Cost of Goods Sold

The next calculation Paul needs to perform is to subtotal the Cost of Goods Sold (COGS). This formula can simply be written in cell C14 as =SUM(C11:C13). Again, because this formula must be copied across the row, Paul must consider whether any absolute cell references are required. In this case, each of the cost values for each of the pricing alternatives should change, so the cell references are *relative* and no dollar signs are required.

Best Practice

Using Absolute Cell References Appropriately

When you copy a formula both down a column and across a row, the placement of the $ absolute sign is critical or the wrong values will result. When copying in only one direction, either just across a row or just down a column, often the addition of extra $ absolute signs will not affect the calculated outcome, but can make for less efficient and confusing formulas. For example, you might be tempted to write the formula =SUM(C11:C13) as =SUM(C$11:C$13) because you want the column references to change, but you do not want the row references to change, when the formula is copied across the row. However, when you are only copying a formula across a row, the row won't change. There is no displacement, which makes the $ superfluous. This also holds true for adding $ to column references when a formula is only being copied down the column. As a matter of good formula writing technique and to maintain the efficiency of your worksheets, you should minimize the number of $ absolute signs in your formulas and include them only when necessary.

Writing a Formula to Calculate Selling Expense

Before calculating the projected earnings, Paul needs to determine the selling expense. Again, he needs to calculate the cost per pair—in this case, by multiplying the selling expense by both the number of shoes per pair and the sales volume for the associated pricing alternative. This is the same formula used for all of the COGS expenses. So, the formula can be copied from any one of the COGS expense formulas, such as the formula in cell C11, into cells C16:E16. Because cells C11 and C16 are not contiguous, the fill handle cannot be used to copy the formula. To complete this task, you will need to use the copy and paste features.

How To

Copy Formulas into Noncontiguous Cells
1. Select the cell or cells being copied.
2. Use the Copy button 📋 in the Clipboard group on the Home tab to copy the cell contents to the Clipboard.
3. Click the cell or cells where you want to copy this content.
4. Click in the top, leftmost cell of the range to which you want to copy. Use the Paste button in the Clipboard group to paste the contents into the desired cell(s), or simply press the Enter key.

Another method is to use the shortcut keys Ctrl+C and Ctrl+V instead of clicking the Copy and Paste buttons. Shortcut keys exist for many of the frequently used commands and are indicated in parentheses in the helpful ScreenTips that appear when you hover over many tools and commands.

Note that the Paste Options button 📋 (Ctrl) ▾ may appear when you have completed pasting. Clicking its button arrow opens a menu containing buttons that allow you to copy with or without formatting, values only, and a host of other options. These options will be discussed in Chapter 2.

Writing a Formula to Calculate Projected Earnings

Paul is now ready to determine if the original TZEdge shoe is estimated to earn any profit in the first quarter of sales. Because this worksheet is intended to provide only a rough idea of the profitability of this venture, Paul has not included any detailed accounting terminology or taken into account investment costs, which are unknown, or taxes. The term "projected earnings" for the purposes of this analysis is defined as revenue minus COGS minus selling expense. Paul writes the following formula in cell C18 to represent projected earnings for the low-priced alternative: =C8–C14–C16. This formula can then be copied across the row into cells D18 and E18. Because each of the values changes relatively, no absolute cell referencing is required in the formula. The finished first quarter budget worksheet is shown in Figure 1.24.

Figure 1.24: Finished first quarter budget

	A	B	C	D	E	F
1	Number of Shoes Per Pair	2		TZEdge First Quarter Budget		
2	Overhead % of Labor	25%				
3						
4			Low Priced	Medium Priced	High Priced	
5	Sales Volume - #pairs:		1,000	750	350	
6	Selling Price Per Pair:		$ 200	$ 225	$ 250	
7	Item	Costs per Shoe	Low Priced Total	Medium Priced Total	High Priced Total	
8	Revenue		$ 200,000	$ 168,750	$ 87,500	
9						
10	Cost of Goods Sold:					
11	Materials	$ 50.15	100,300	75,225	35,105	
12	Direct Labor	7.33	14,660	10,995	5,131	
13	Overhead	1.83	3,665	2,749	1,283	
14	COGS Subtotal		118,625	88,969	41,519	
15						
16	Selling Expense	5.00	10,000	7,500	3,500	
17						
18	*Projected Earnings*		$ 71,375	$ 72,281	$ 42,481	
19						
20						

Completing the Budget Workbook

To complete the budget workbook, Paul needs to create similar worksheets for the second, third, and fourth quarters, as well as a summary worksheet showing the annual budget. To do so, he simply copies the 1stQTR worksheet and pastes it to the other worksheets, naming each worksheet appropriately and modifying the worksheet titles.

How To

Copy a Worksheet

You can choose from the following methods to copy an entire worksheet:

Use the sheet selector box:

1. Select the entire worksheet using the sheet selector box in the upper-left corner of the worksheet (above row 1 and to the left of column A).
2. After the sheet is selected, click the Copy button 📋 in the Clipboard group on the Home tab, or right-click the selection and click Copy on the shortcut menu, or press Ctrl+C.
3. Select the worksheet where the data will be copied to, and, if necessary, select cell A1.
4. Click the Paste button 📋 in the Clipboard group on the Home tab, or right-click the selection and click Paste on the shortcut menu, or press Ctrl+V.

OR

Use the Sheet tab menu:

1. Right-click the sheet tab of the sheet to be copied.

2. Click Move or Copy on the shortcut menu. The Move or Copy dialog box opens. You can also open this dialog box by clicking the Format button in the Cells group on the Home tab, and then selecting Move or Copy Sheet on the menu.

3. Indicate the desired location of the copied sheet. To specify that you want to copy rather than move it, click the Create a copy check box.

4. Click the OK button.

Because none of the cell references used in the 1stQTR worksheet refers to a particular worksheet, the formulas adjust relative to the new worksheet when copied. Paul then substitutes the appropriate sales volumes, which were listed in Table 1.6, in each of the corresponding quarters on the remaining worksheets. The revenue and expense values are updated automatically.

To create the summary worksheet, Paul can copy any one of the quarterly budgets to a separate worksheet and then name that worksheet Summary. In each cell where he wants to aggregate the four quarter values, he can write a formula to add the corresponding values from quarter 1 plus quarter 2 plus quarter 3 plus quarter 4. Starting in cell Summary!C8, Paul could write the following formula either by entering the formula directly or clicking the appropriate worksheets and cells:

```
=1stQTR!C8+2ndQTR!C8+3rdQTR!C8+4thQTR!C8
```

Paul could also use the SUM function and then select all four worksheets simultaneously and click cell C8 in one of them. The formula would be =SUM('1stQTR:4thQTR'!C8).

Notice the syntax used for referencing cells on worksheets other than where the formula is being written. First is the sheet name, followed by an exclamation point (!), then the usual column letter, and finally, the row number. A sheet name is only needed in a formula that includes a cell reference located in another worksheet. For example, if you were writing a formula in cell Summary!Z100 to add the contents of cell A1 in the active worksheet (Summary) to cell B2 on the 1stQtr worksheet, you would write: =A1+1st Qtr!B2. Be aware that when using sheet names containing spaces or hyphens, you must enclose them in single quotation marks. For example, if the sheet name were 1st Qtr, the formula would be: =A1+'1st Qtr'!B2.

When working with multiple worksheets, as soon as one cell contains the correct formula, you can simply copy the formula into all other cells to calculate their corresponding values. When the cell references in the formula contain a sheet name, the copied cell references still refer back to the corresponding worksheets. Paul uses this method to add the sales volume values for each of the three pricing alternatives.

The final summary sheet is shown in Figure 1.25. Based on the projected earnings calculated, it appears that the low-priced alternative is the best option, at least regarding profits generated for the original shoe design. The volume seems to more than make up for the lower selling price per pair of shoes.

Figure 1.25: Annual budget summary

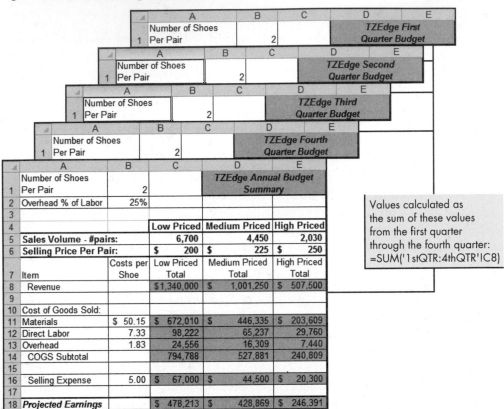

Values calculated as the sum of these values from the first quarter through the fourth quarter: =SUM('1stQTR:4thQTR'!C8)

Working with Multiple Worksheets Simultaneously

An alternative to working on a single worksheet and copying it once it's completed is to select multiple worksheets simultaneously. This is especially useful if you have multiple, almost identical, worksheets and want to modify common elements on all, such as the overhead percentage in all four quarters of the TZEdge budget file. This technique also works for creating multidimensional formulas, such as adding cell C8 on all of the quarter worksheets.

To edit the overhead costs in the 1stQtr through Summary worksheets simultaneously, complete the following steps:

- Click the first sheet tab and then hold down the Shift key and click the Summary worksheet tab. With the assumption that the 1stQtr, 2ndQtr, 3rdQtr, 4thQtr, and Summary worksheets are all adjacent to each other, all four will be selected. In cases where nonadjacent worksheets must be selected, use the Ctrl key instead of the Shift key and click each desired sheet individually.

- Once the desired worksheets are selected, type the new value in the appropriate cell (B2) on the visible worksheet.
- Click another worksheet tab to deselect the worksheet grouping, and then check that the change has been made in all locations.

Keep in mind that this method only works well on worksheets with identical structures. Furthermore, caution should be used when creating and modifying a workbook in this manner. Although this method is convenient, you could damage your workbook by inadvertently making changes, such as deleting values or formulas, to multiple selected worksheets when you intended to make the changes on only one worksheet.

To create a multidimensional formula to sum cell C8 for each of the four quarters:

- Click the cell in which you want to enter the formula and type =SUM(to begin the formula.
- Click the 1stQtr worksheet tab, and then press and hold the Shift key and click the 4thQtr worksheet tab (assuming the sheets are in contiguous order in the workbook).
- Click cell C8 and then type a close parenthesis) to complete the formula or just press the Enter key to automatically add the close parenthesis. The resulting formula is =SUM('1stQTR: 4thQTR'!C8).

Using this type of formula enables the user to enter additional values into the calculation by inserting additional worksheets within the range. Perhaps management would like a total for the first six quarters instead of only one year. Be aware that if you insert a worksheet within this range of worksheets, then that worksheet will be included in the formula. For example, if you were to insert worksheet Semi-Annual between 1stQtr and 4thQtr, the Semi-Annual! C8 will be included in the total in Summary!C8.

Steps To Success: Level 3

You have learned a tremendous amount about creating the first year's budget for the original option of the new TZEdge shoe. Now, you need to create quarterly budgets and a summary for the textured leather option using $74.07 per shoe as the cost of materials and $5.39 per shoe as the cost of labor.

Unlike with the original option, only two pricing alternatives are being considered for the textured leather option. Table 1.7 shows the two pricing alternatives, as well as the expected sales volume in each quarter for these alternatives. Overhead is calculated at 30% of the direct labor costs, and the selling expense is assumed to be $10 per pair, or $5 per shoe.

Table 1.7: Shoe prices and estimated sales volumes for the textured leather option

		1stQTR	2ndQTR	3rdQTR	4thQTR
Alternative:	$/Pair	#Pairs	#Pairs	#Pairs	#Pairs
Low Priced	229	660	810	1050	1250
High Priced	278	225	269	335	340

Complete the following:

1. Create a new workbook named **Textured Budget.xlsx** and save it in the Chapter 1 folder.

2. Using the finished first quarter budget worksheet for the original option as a model (see Figure 1.24), create a similar first quarter budget worksheet for the textured leather option, as follows:

    a. In cells A1:B2, enter the necessary inputs for number of shoes per pair and overhead.

    b. In cell C1, enter the title **TZEdge 1st Quarter Budget Textured Leather Option** in bold and italic; merge and center this title across cells C1:D1. Apply a gray shaded background to the title cells.

    c. In rows 4 through 6, enter the sales volume and selling price data, with the column headings **Low Priced** and **High Priced** in cells C4 and D4, respectively. Use similar formatting as shown in Figure 1.24.

    d. In cells A7:A18 and B7:D7, enter the same labels as for the original option (see Figure 1.24).

    e. In cells B11, B12, and B16, enter the costs per shoe for Materials, Labor, and Selling Expense, respectively.

    f. In cell B13, enter a formula to calculate the Overhead cost.

    g. In columns C and D, enter the necessary formulas to determine revenue, cost of goods sold, selling expense, and projected earnings for each pricing alternative. (Keep in mind that projected earnings is defined as revenue minus cost of goods sold minus selling expense.) Be sure to use the correct relative, absolute, and mixed cell referencing so that the formulas can be copied wherever it makes sense to do so, and so that the formulas will automatically update if any of the data inputs are later modified. Format the values and calculated results on your worksheet in a similar manner to those in Figure 1.24.

    h. Refer to Figure 1.24 and apply similar borders to the appropriate cells on your worksheet.

    i. Rename the Sheet1 worksheet tab as **1stQTR**.

3. With the 1stQTR worksheet complete, use an appropriate method to create similar worksheets for the other three quarters. Name these worksheets **2ndQTR**, **3rdQTR**, and **4thQTR**. Modify values and labels as necessary on these three worksheets.

4. Create a final comparison sheet named **Summary**, which displays each of the budget components summarized by year for each pricing alternative. For the worksheet title in cells C1:D1, enter **TZEdge Annual Budget Textured Leather Option**.

5. In cell A20, insert text to indicate which pricing alternative you would recommend and why. Highlight this text with a yellow background.

6. Save and close the completed Textured Budget.xlsx workbook.

Chapter Summary

This chapter presented some of the basic tools and concepts you need to understand when working with Excel to solve problems and support decisions. In Level 1, you learned that working with a spreadsheet created by someone else can be a challenging task—especially if the worksheet contains errors in formatting or formulas. You also learned how to locate and correct some of the more common errors to make the worksheet readable and functional. Related concepts, such as order of precedence and precision versus display, were also presented.

Level 2 covered simple functions, such as SUM and AVERAGE, and how to use these functions in formulas. You learned the syntax of these functions and their underlying algorithms, and how the AutoSum tool lets you apply these functions quickly and easily.

In Level 3, you had the opportunity to explore in greater detail the tasks of writing and copying formulas. It is clear that Excel gives you powerful tools for copying formulas using relative, absolute, and mixed cell references. Understanding the impact of these different cell references when copying formulas is critical to building successful worksheets.

Conceptual Review

1. What is the meaning of each of the following error messages?

- ######
- #NAME?
- #N/A
- #REF!
- #VALUE!
- #NUM!
- #DIV/0!

2. If you enter 1,149+25 in a cell exactly as shown (without an equal sign), what value would result?

3. If you enter =2+4*10 in a cell exactly as shown, what value would result?

4. List each of the following operations in order of precedence, from 1 to 4 (first to last):

- Multiplication and division
- Parentheses ( )
- Addition and subtraction
- Exponentiation

5. When writing formulas, why is it preferable to use cell references rather than typing in values?

6. In the worksheet below, cell A3 contains the formula =A1+A2. Explain the most likely reason the value calculated appears incorrect.

	A	B	C
1	1	10%	
2	2		
3	4		
4			
5			

7. Referring to the preceding worksheet, if you wrote the formula =B1*110, what value would result (assuming the displayed value is the precise value)?

8. What formula would you write to do each of the following?

a. Add a range of numbers in cells A2:X2.

b. Find the largest value in cells C2:C8.

c. Find the smallest value in cells B2 through Z12.

d. Find the average value in cells C1 through C10, assuming blank cells will be ignored.

e. Find the total number of values listed in cells C1 through C10, excluding any that contain text.

9. Define the following terms: syntax, arguments, and algorithm.

10. If the formula =$B$4–SUM(C1:C5) is copied from cell A9 to cell C10, what is the resulting formula?

11. Refer to the following worksheet. What formula would you write in cell B2 that can be copied down the column and across the row to complete the multiplication table?

	A	B	C	D	E	F	G
1		1	2	3	4	5	
2	1	1	2	3	4	5	
3	2	2	4	6	8	10	
4	3	3	6	9	12	15	
5	4	4	8	12	16	20	
6	5	5	10	15	20	25	
7							
8							

12. What new formula results for each of the following if the formula is copied from cell C10 to cell E13?

   a.   =A1+A2

   b.   =$A$1+A2

   c.   =$A1+A2

   d.   =A$1+A2

13. What formula could you use to add up cell B1 from Sheet1!, Sheet 2!, and Sheet 3! (assuming the worksheets are contiguous and in the same workbook)?

14. Cell B1 has been given the range name **discount**. How would you write a formula in cell C1 that multiplies discount by cell A1? What new formula results if you copy this formula into cell C2?

Case Problems

Level 1 – Purchasing a Computer for Walsh & Associates

You are currently employed at a medium-sized financial management firm, Walsh & Associates, as a financial analyst. Your boss has recently authorized the purchase of a new laptop computer for your use at home and in the office, and has asked you to obtain three competitive bids before approving the purchase. The minimum requirements of the system you want to buy are as follows:

Operations Management

- Processor with minimum 2 GHz processor speed and 3 GB RAM
- 15" screen
- Camera built in
- Long-life battery
- DVD read/write
- Windows 7 Professional

- Video card
- Broadband, Wi-Fi, and Bluetooth connections
- Carrying case
- Full 3-year warranty
- Minimum 250 GB hard drive

Table 1.8 shows information for three possible computers based on published circulars Web site pricing. The data provided does not exactly match up, so you need to create a worksheet comparing all three systems and their total prices.

Table 1.8: Data for three computers

Please note that these features/prices do not necessarily reflect actual available PCs.

Dell - Laptop	Sony – Laptop	Lenovo - Laptop
Dell Latitude E65: Intel Core 2 Duo processor including (2.53 GHz) 3 GB of RAM, 250 GB hard drive, DVD-R/W, 15" display, long-life battery, video camera and video card, Windows 7 Professional, Wi-Fi/Bluetooth/broadband capable, 3-year warranty, shipping included... $1578	Sony VAIO BZ56 w/Intel Core 2 Duo processor (2.53 GHz) including 2 GB of RAM, 250 GB hard drive, 15.4" display, video card, DVD-R/W, built-in camera, Windows 7 Professional, Wi-Fi/broadband/Bluetooth capable, carry case, standard 1-year warranty... $1459	Lenovo ThinkCentre W5 Intel Core 2 Duo processor (2.53 GHz), 2 GB RAM, 150 GB hard drives, 15.4" display, DVD recordable device, Windows 7 Home Premium and video card, Wi-Fi and broadband capable, 1-year warranty, free shipping... $1349
Additional items:	Additional items:	Additional items:
Carrying case $100	Upgrade to 3 GB RAM $10	Upgrade to 3 GB RAM $30
	Long-life battery upgrade $100	Upgrade to 320 GB hard drive 7200 rpm $100
	3-year warranty $329.99	Upgrade to Windows 7 – Professional $19.99
	Shipping cost $46	Integrated camera $30
		Bluetooth $20
		Long-life battery $70
		3-year warranty $279
		Carrying case $65

Complete the following:

1. Create a new workbook named **Computer Purchase.xlsx** and save it in the Chapter 1 folder.

2. Create a worksheet that compares the cost of each of the listed items for the three computers. Organize the worksheet so that each component is listed separately. If an item is included in the base computer price, enter a zero. Be sure to include the following elements:

   - A title formatted in Cambria, size 14, bold, and italic. Merge and center the title above your worksheet and add a light blue fill.
   - Appropriate column and row headings so that your worksheet is easy to understand. If necessary, wrap the text headings into more than one row in the cell.
   - Numbers in the first row and in any summation rows formatted with the Currency Style. All other dollar values should be formatted with the Comma Style.

3. Calculate the total cost of each system assuming all items listed for that system are purchased. Right align the total cost title and use bold italic formatting.

4. Verify that the totals are accurate even if other values are later substituted for any of the system component costs.

5. Highlight the cell containing the name of the least expensive computer system in yellow.

6. You learn from your boss that the corporation is planning to purchase at least 40 similar systems. Because of this volume, the following price reductions are now available:

- Sony has agreed to give a 17% across-the-board discount on everything but the shipping and handling fee, which remains at $46 per system.
- Lenovo has agreed to a rebate of $250 per machine.
- Dell has declined to give any volume purchase discount.

Skip at least two rows at the bottom of your current data. In a separate area, calculate the total cost of a single machine from each competitor using this new pricing structure. Reference the values you have previously calculated as needed.

7. Just below the calculation for Step 6, calculate the cost of purchasing the 40 machines with this new pricing structure for each option.

8. Highlight the cell containing the lowest final cost for 40 machines in a shade of pale green.

9. Save and close the Computer Purchase.xlsx workbook.

Level 2 – Compiling Relocation Information for Devcon Finn, Inc.

You work in the Human Resources Department of Devcon Finn, Inc., a computer consulting firm. An employee is considering a transfer to one of the company's other locations, and is qualified for several different positions. Your task is to help the employee choose the most appropriate position based on a number of criteria. For example, you need to determine the value of each position in terms of the disposable income the employee can expect. The position with the highest salary is located in the company's New York City office, but a studio apartment there costs about $2,350 per month; however, the employee would not need a car.

**Human
Resources**

You have documented each position in an Excel worksheet. On this sheet, you have recorded the positions, the annual salary, the cost of living multiplier that you obtained from a Web site, and estimates of a monthly car payment, assuming for some of these jobs the employee will need to purchase a car. You have also recorded information regarding the bonus (a one-time payment at the beginning of the year) offered to the employee. Now, you need to finalize the worksheet.

Complete the following:

1. Open the workbook named **Position.xlsx** located in the Chapter 1 folder, and then save it as **Position Analysis.xlsx**.

2. In cells F2:F4, calculate the associated annual adjusted salary. This adjusted salary is the annual salary divided by the cost of living multiplier minus the expected annual car payments. (Note that car payments are given in $/month.)

3. In cell F6, write a formula to calculate the average adjusted salary of the three positions.

4. In cell F7, write a formula to determine the value of the lowest adjusted salary. This formula should automatically update if any of the data inputs are later changed.

5. In cell F8, write a formula to determine the value of the highest adjusted salary. This formula should automatically update if any of the data inputs are later changed.

6. In cell G9, write a formula to determine the number of positions that include a bonus.

7. In cells H2:H4, calculate the value of the adjusted salary package for each position over a two-year period, including bonuses. The bonus does not need to be adjusted for location because the employee plans to use the bonus toward a vacation. Assume that the employee will receive a 3% raise after the first year of employment in the new position.

8. Display dollar values in columns E to H without cents, and include a dollar sign only in the first row of columns with dollars. Format the cost of living multipliers with two decimal places displayed, and align these values on the decimal point.

9. Another position for which the employee is qualified has just become available. This position, a senior consultant position, is also located in New York City, has an annual salary of $66,500, and includes a $1,500 bonus. Because the position is located in New York City, assume that the employee will not be purchasing a car, and that the cost of living multiplier is 1.4. Insert the data for this new position just below the other New York position. Complete the calculations for adjusted salary and total two-year financial package. Verify that all of the other values you've calculated update correctly. Adjust the formatting of the new data, as needed, to match the formatting of the existing data.

10. Highlight in yellow the row of the position with the highest two-year financial package, and bold the text in this row.

11. Save and close the Position Analysis.xlsx workbook.

Level 3 – Analyzing Regional Sales Information for CKG Auto

Sales

As a regional sales manager for CKG Auto, you have just finished summarizing sales data for the first half of this year (January through June) aggregated by car model. You have started to enter data in an Excel worksheet, which lists by model the following:

- Sales Volume, indicating the number of cars sold to dealers.
- Manufacturing (Mfg.) Cost per Vehicle.

- Total Cost of all vehicles sold for the model. You will need to calculate this based on the sales volume and the manufacturing costs per vehicle.
- Markup Percentage, which is the percentage charged above manufacturing cost to dealers.
- Total Sales to dealers. You will need to calculate this as Total Cost plus Markup. (Markup is the markup percentage times the manufacturer cost of the vehicle.)
- % of Total Volume. You will need to calculate this based on volume for the model as compared with the volume of all models sold for the time period.

First, you need to complete the January through June computations based on the data contained in the worksheet and the information given. Then, you have been asked to create a similar worksheet to estimate sales for July through December based on volume supplied by the marketing group. These volumes are based on the historical values adjusted for seasonal demand of specific car types and from market research data on car popularity. After you have completed both the first half actual sales and the second half estimated sales, you need to combine this data to determine expected yearly sales. Management is interested in not only the absolute value of those sales, but also each model's contribution to the total yearly sales in each half of the year and in aggregate.

When completing the workbook, be sure that all data is correctly referenced so that your formulas will work as you copy them down the column or across the row, as necessary.

To complete the workbook, use the following steps:

1. Open the workbook named **Sales.xlsx** located in the Chapter 1 folder, and then save it as **Auto Sales.xlsx**. Rename the Sheet1 worksheet tab as **1st Half**.

2. In the highlighted cells, enter formulas to perform the necessary calculations for January through June and summarize. Be sure to write all formulas so that they can be copied as necessary. Note the following:

   - Display all dollar values in whole dollars and include the dollar sign in the first row and total rows only.
   - When calculating averages, do not include any models that had no sales. Display all average values (other than the percentage) with commas and no decimal places.
   - When calculating summary data (total, average, etc.) keep in mind that additional car models (rows) may eventually be inserted at the bottom of the list.
   - The formulas in column G need to determine the percent of total volume sales that the vehicle represents. (That is, if model A sold 100 cars and a total of 1000 cars were sold for all models, then model A would represent 10% of the total volume.) Format the cells in column G to display values to the nearest tenth of a percent. Be sure to calculate the number of models available for sale.

3. Your next task is to create an estimate of the July through December sales based on marketing data and the first half-year sales values. The marketing group has provided

a list of all car models in identical order to the original data you received, with the expected sales volumes for each car model. This list is found in the workbook named **Market.xlsx**, which is located in the Chapter 1 folder. Manufacturing costs and markups are assumed to be the same for the second half of the year as they were for the first half. With the data and assumptions in mind, create a new worksheet named **2nd Half** in the Auto Sales.xlsx workbook, identical to the 1st Half worksheet. Copy and paste the sales volumes from the Market.xlsx workbook into your new worksheet. Verify that all the calculations in the new worksheet reflect the new data.

TROUBLESHOOTING: In order to complete this task successfully, copy the entire 1st Half worksheet to a new worksheet. Then copy only the values for the sales volume, excluding the heading, from the Market workbook by highlighting the column values and clicking the Copy button. Next, place the insertion point in the column/row of this new worksheet corresponding to the first vehicle's volume and then paste the data. Be sure to check the calculated fields (Total Cost, Total Sales to Dealers, etc.) to be sure vehicles that were not sold during the first half of the year have values calculated and vehicles not sold during the second half do not have values.

4. Create another new worksheet named **Summary**, and include the column headings shown in Table 1.10 on this new worksheet.

Table 1.10: Column headings for Summary worksheet

Model	Annual Volume	Jan–June Sales to Dealers	July–Dec Sales to Dealers	Total Sales to Dealers	%Total Sales to Dealers Jan–June	%Total Sales to Dealers July–Dec	%Total Sales to Dealers Annual

a. Insert the model numbers in the identical format as shown on the 1st Half and 2nd Half worksheets.

b. Insert the annual volume for each model—the combined totals of the January through June and the July through December volumes. Make sure that the values will automatically update if any of the input values are changed at a later time.

c. Insert the Jan–June sales to dealers, again ensuring that these values will automatically update if any of the input data changes.

d. Insert the July–Dec sales to dealers, again ensuring that these values will automatically update if any of the input data changes.

e. Create a combined total of sales to dealers for the entire year.

f. Calculate the total volumes and the total sales to dealers for each time period and annually in a row below the data.

g. Calculate the percentage of sales to dealers that each model represents, as a percentage of the total sales to dealers for all models—first for the Jan–June time frame, then the July–Dec time frame, and finally for the annual values. Use *only one formula for this calculation* and make sure that the formula can be copied down the column to calculate the percentages for the corresponding models, and across the row to calculate the percentages for the corresponding time frames. Display the percentage values with an appropriate format and number of decimal places.

5. Format all three worksheets so that they have a professional appearance.

6. Save and close the Auto Sales.xlsx workbook.

SAM: Skills Assessment Manager

For current SAM information, including versions and content details, visit SAM Central (http://samcentral.course.com). If you have a SAM user profile, you may have access to hands-on instruction, practice, and assessment of the skills covered in this chapter. Since various versions of SAM are supported throughout the life of this text, check with your instructor for the correct instructions and URL/Web site for accessing assignments.

Solving Problems with Statistical Analysis Tools
Manufacturing: Evaluating Quality Control Data to Perform a Cost-Benefit Analysis

"Averages don't always reveal the most telling realities. You know Shaquille O'Neal and I have an average height of six feet."
—Robert Reich
(Mr. Reich is 4'10" tall; whereas the basketball star is 7'1" tall.)

LEARNING OBJECTIVES

Level 1

Understand basic concepts related to statistics
Specify the precision of values using the ROUND function
Copy and paste information in a worksheet using Paste Special options
Calculate basic statistics: arithmetic mean, mode, median, standard deviation
Manage large worksheets by freezing panes and splitting the window

Level 2

Evaluate the rank of each value in a data set
Determine the highest and lowest values in a data set
Determine the number of items that meet specified criteria
Determine a total value for items that meet specified criteria

Level 3

Evaluate a large data set
Apply custom number formats to data
Perform what-if analyses
Perform reverse what-if analyses using Goal Seek
Analyze data by category by combining functions
Simulate data to evaluate different outcomes

FUNCTIONS COVERED IN THIS CHAPTER

AVERAGE	MEDIAN	ROUND
AVERAGEIF	MODE.SNGL	SMALL
COUNTIF	RAND	STDEV.S
LARGE	RANDBETWEEN	SUMIF
	RANK.EQ	

2

Chapter Introduction

In this chapter, you will learn to use several data analysis tools that assist in problem solving. Microsoft Excel provides a variety of predefined functions, including statistical functions that you can use to determine such values as the arithmetic mean, median, mode, and standard deviation of a set of data. These statistical values can then be compared with previously measured historical values, allowing you to determine both the differences and percent differences between the values. In addition to working with statistical functions, you will also explore other functions, such as LARGE, SMALL, and RANK.EQ, that help you to structure and analyze data in meaningful ways. The COUNTIF, SUMIF and AVERAGEIF functions, which enable you to count and total and average data that meets specified criteria, are also covered. Using such functions can give you better insight into the values in a set of data and help you identify any patterns or trends in the data.

The chapter also teaches you how to perform a what-if analysis to examine the effects of changing specific worksheet values and introduces Goal Seek, an Excel tool that allows you to work backward to determine the input required that will ensure a specific outcome. You will generate additional data by simulating possible outcomes with a set of inputs, which vary randomly between a certain set of values. You will also explore the use of custom formatting techniques to make your workbook easier to use and read.

Case Scenario

TheZone manufactures and sells the TZBlazer line of skis, which features an innovative design that makes it one of the most popular on the market. The TZBlazer ski comes in three different styles: one designed for average skiers (A), one designed for expert skiers (E), and one designed for racing (R). Each model is available in different sizes.

Finance

Due to the popularity of this ski line, the company is challenged to keep up with the demand. The manufacturing facility has been forced to add work shifts to meet the increased sales volume. TheZone is committed to maintaining the high standards for which the company is known, but there is increasing concern that these standards will be compromised as a result of the increased production. This concern is partly because one of the bottlenecks in the production process is Quality Control, often referred to as "QC." Here, each ski is thoroughly inspected and tested before being released for sale. Every time a ski is found to have a defect, the part is traced back to the original production line that manufactured and assembled the ski.

The QC team leader, Joanna Cavallo, is responsible for coordinating quality-control efforts for the ski line, including interacting with the purchasing and sales groups regarding any matters pertaining to the quality of the products. Since the increase in production, Joanna has noticed an increase in the number of TZBlazer skis being rejected by the QC group for quality defects. If this trend continues, it will directly affect the company's ability to meet the current ambitious production schedules, as well as add significant costs to the manufacturing process. Joanna needs to evaluate the new data and compare it with historical data to determine if any improvements in the manufacturing process might be required. As part of her analysis, Joanna will work with statistics.

LEVEL 1
Using Statistical Functions to Compare Data Values

Understanding Fundamentals of Statistics

Statistics is a subset of mathematics that is applied to observed data. It is widely used for explaining groups of data, also referred to as **data sets**, and how the data within a group varies. Statistical methods are also used to compare different groups or data sets. The following is a list of some common statistics terms and their definitions:

- **Mean** is the arithmetic average of a set of numbers.
- **Median** is the arithmetic value that occurs in the middle of a data set when organized from lowest to highest, where half the values are less than and half the values are greater than the median value.
- **Mode** is the arithmetic value that occurs most frequently in a data set.
- **Standard deviation** is a measure of how widely the data values are dispersed from the arithmetic mean.

For example, consider the following five values: 1, 1, 6, 7, and 10. The arithmetic mean, or average, of these values is 5, which is determined as follows: $(1+1+6+7+10)/5$. The median value is the middle value when the data is listed in ascending order; in this list of numbers, the middle value is 6, with two lower values and two higher values. The mode is the value that occurs most often; in this case, 1 is the mode value. Finally, the standard deviation is 3.94. A somewhat complex formula is required to determine the standard deviation; the Help system in Excel explains this formula in detail.

Although this simple example illustrates these statistical values, to obtain meaningful statistics, you generally need to work with much larger data sets. Frequently when discussing these large sets of data, a statistician will examine the population distribution—comparing groups of values in ascending order to the frequency in which these groups of values occur. One such distribution is referred to as a **normal distribution**, which is illustrated in Figure 2.1.

A normal distribution exhibits an equal number of occurrences of data values both below and above the arithmetic mean. The mean, median, and mode of a normal distribution are the same value. Figure 2.1 shows a normal distribution with a mean value of 5 and a standard deviation of 2. The shaded portions of the figure represent values included within

Figure 2.1: Normal distribution with a mean of 5 and standard deviation of 2

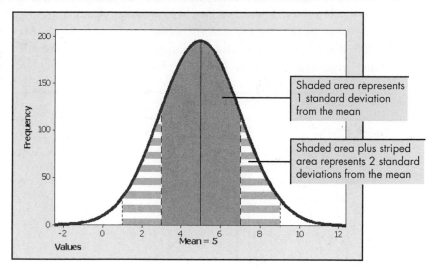

1 standard deviation of the mean (mean 5 +/− standard deviation 2 includes the range 3 to 7). The values in the shaded portion plus the values in the striped portion represent values within 2 standard deviations (mean 5 +/− standard deviation 2*2 represents values within the range 1 to 9). A normal distribution is characterized by the fact that approximately 95% of the values lie within plus or minus 2 standard deviations of the mean.

Figure 2.2 shows another normally distributed set of data with the same mean value of 5. Notice that these values mostly occur much closer to the mean than do the values in the data set shown in Figure 2.1. The standard deviation for the data set in Figure 2.2 is smaller, only 1.

Figure 2.2: Normal distribution with a mean of 5 and standard deviation of 1

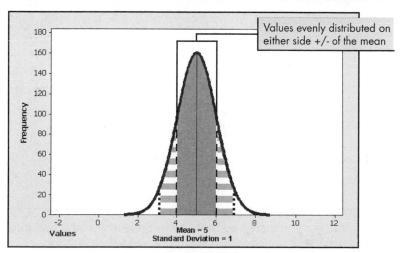

In Figure 2.3, the data set is not normally distributed. Here, the mean value is also 5, but the data has a few very high values and a large number of smaller values. In such a distribution, the arithmetic mean will not be equal to the mode or median values. Also, notice the large "tail" exhibited at one end of the distribution. The tail in this distribution indicates that a few values are at a high extreme above the median.

Figure 2.3: Non-normal distribution with a mean of 5

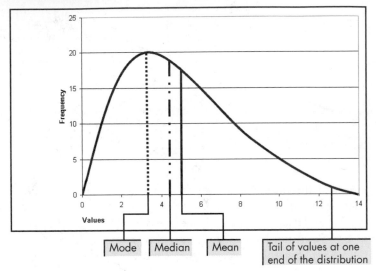

As you can see, the values of each of these statistics provide valuable information about the data set being analyzed. Whereas the mean value gives you an arithmetic average, the standard deviation tells you how closely together the values are distributed. The comparison of mean, mode, and median gives insight into the type of distribution— evenly distributed around the mean or skewed to one end or the other. Two sets of data might have the same mean but different standard deviations, indicating that the data is more or less widely distributed or even exhibits an entirely different distribution profile. Conversely, two data sets might have the same standard deviation, but the mean values in the data sets can be vastly different, indicating two dissimilar sets of data that vary in a similar manner.

In the case of the TZBlazer ski production, Joanna must analyze the recent trend in skis being rejected by the QC group for quality defects. The two most common defects being found in the TZBlazer ski models are as follows:

- High Friction Coefficient, indicating poor surface finishing that can result in poor ski performance. Skis are rejected if they have a Friction Coefficient value of greater than 1.23.
- Low Torsion Strength, indicating that the material strength is insufficient for the rigors of high-performance skiing, usually resulting from problems in the molding process. Skis are rejected if they have a Torsion Strength value of less than 2.

Joanna wants to compare the current Friction Coefficient and Torsion Strength values from the past several days to historical data to see if there has, indeed, been a significant change. She also wants to determine how many skis will be rejected because of these defects and the cost of the rejected skis to the company. This, in turn, can indicate to management the benefits that could be reaped from improving the manufacturing process. Finally, Joanna wants to review the costs of 100% inspection of skis (the current process) and compare them to the possible costs TheZone would incur if skis had to be replaced after they entered the marketplace.

Joanna has already created an Excel workbook named QC Analysis, which contains data about each ski that has been inspected. The Current worksheet, shown in Figure 2.4, includes the following information for each ski:

- Unique manufacturing identification number (Mfg ID#)
- Size
- Style
- Date Manufactured
- Production Line on which the ski was manufactured
- Friction Coefficient value
- Torsion Strength value

Figure 2.4: Current worksheet in the QC Analysis workbook

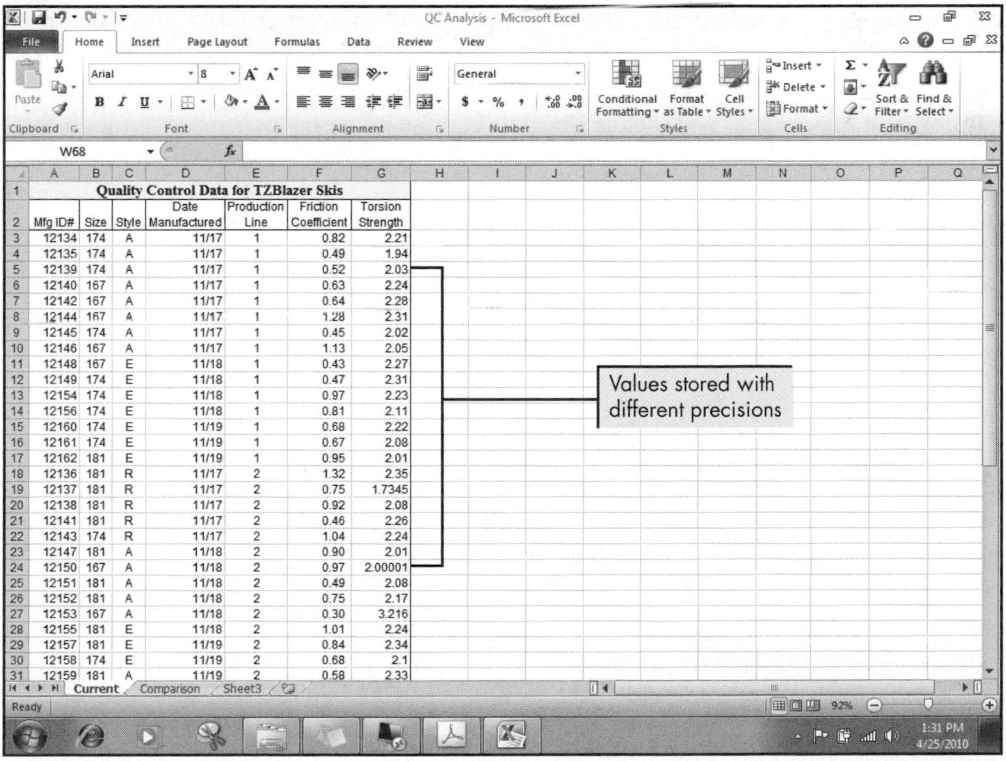

	A	B	C	D	E	F	G
1	Quality Control Data for TZBlazer Skis						
2	Mfg ID#	Size	Style	Date Manufactured	Production Line	Friction Coefficient	Torsion Strength
3	12134	174	A	11/17	1	0.82	2.21
4	12135	174	A	11/17	1	0.49	1.94
5	12139	174	A	11/17	1	0.52	2.03
6	12140	167	A	11/17	1	0.63	2.24
7	12142	167	A	11/17	1	0.64	2.28
8	12144	167	A	11/17	1	1.28	2.31
9	12145	174	A	11/17	1	0.45	2.02
10	12146	167	A	11/17	1	1.13	2.05
11	12148	167	E	11/18	1	0.43	2.27
12	12149	174	E	11/18	1	0.47	2.31
13	12154	174	E	11/18	1	0.97	2.23
14	12156	174	E	11/18	1	0.81	2.11
15	12160	174	E	11/19	1	0.68	2.22
16	12161	174	E	11/19	1	0.67	2.08
17	12162	181	E	11/19	1	0.95	2.01
18	12136	181	R	11/17	2	1.32	2.35
19	12137	181	R	11/17	2	0.75	1.7345
20	12138	181	R	11/17	2	0.92	2.08
21	12141	181	R	11/17	2	0.46	2.26
22	12143	174	R	11/17	2	1.04	2.24
23	12147	181	A	11/18	2	0.90	2.01
24	12150	167	A	11/18	2	0.97	2.00001
25	12151	181	A	11/18	2	0.49	2.08
26	12152	181	A	11/18	2	0.75	2.17
27	12153	167	A	11/18	2	0.30	3.216
28	12155	181	E	11/18	2	1.01	2.24
29	12157	181	E	11/19	2	0.84	2.34
30	12158	174	E	11/19	2	0.68	2.1
31	12159	181	A	11/19	2	0.58	2.33

The Current worksheet includes values for only the skis that Joanna has been analyzing for the past several days. Joanna also has gathered the historical data, which includes the mean Friction Coefficient and Torsion Strength values for skis manufactured last month, as well as the median, mode, and standard deviation values, as shown in Table 2.1.

Table 2.1: Historical values of Friction Coefficient and Torsion Strength

	Friction Coefficient	Torsion Strength
Mean	0.76	2.27
Median	0.73	2.24
Mode	0.53	2.15
Standard Deviation	0.27	0.24

Joanna wants to determine similar statistical data for the skis tested during the past several days, and then compare this information with the historical values to ascertain if there is, indeed, a problem. Therefore, she needs to calculate the values for mean, median, mode, and standard deviation for the skis shown in Figure 2.4. After calculating these values, Joanna will approach the comparison using both of the following techniques:

- Calculate the difference in values: current value – historical value
- Calculate the percent difference: (current value – historical value)/historical value

Joanna will use fairly simple statistical tests to analyze and compare the data. By examining the Friction Coefficient and Torsion Strength values for the current skis as compared with the historical values, Joanna should be able to draw some conclusions regarding whether the number of rejected skis and the distribution of these values have changed significantly. For those with a more sophisticated understanding of statistical concepts, Excel provides a variety of additional tools that allow you to measure the significance of such differences by comparing the means of the current data and historical data sets. Joanna will simply compare the difference and percent difference to draw her conclusions.

Controlling the Precision of Data Using the ROUND Function

In reviewing the Current worksheet (Figure 2.4), Joanna notices that the Torsion Strength values were entered with different formats and precisions. Some were entered to the nearest hundredth, some to the nearest thousandth, and so on. To be consistent in analyzing the data, Joanna first needs to round off the Torsion Strength values to a specified number of decimal places. She decides to round to the nearest hundredth.

Could Joanna use the Decrease Decimal button [icon] in the Number group on the Home tab on the Ribbon to adjust the number of decimal places in column G? No; adjusting the number of decimal places using either the Decrease Decimal button or the Increase Decimal button [icon] simply alters the cell display, but has *no effect on the precision* of the value stored in the cell. Excel 2010 has the capability to store 15 significant digits for each value. To specify that the Torsion Strength values in column G should be precisely stored to the nearest hundredth, Joanna needs to use the **ROUND function**. Rounding, unlike formatting, actually changes the precision of the data values stored. The syntax of the ROUND function is as follows:

```
ROUND(number,num_digits)[END CODE]
```

Notice that the ROUND function is somewhat different from the functions presented in Chapter 1. The ROUND function has two different types of arguments:

- The first argument, *number*, is a single value that can be a constant, a cell reference where the cell contains a numerical value, or another formula that results in a single number value.
- The second argument, *num_digits*, is the specified number of decimal places. A value of 0 for the second argument rounds to the nearest whole number. A value of 1 for the second argument rounds to the nearest tenth (0.1, 0.2, and so on). A value of 2 rounds to the nearest hundredth. Note that a value of –2 for the second argument tells Excel to round to the nearest hundred (100, 200, and so on).

Best Practice

Adhering to Function Syntax When Working with Multiple Arguments

When using a function that contains multiple arguments where each argument represents different information, you must be careful to supply the information in the exact order and format specified by the function's syntax.

Unlike the SUM, AVERAGE, MIN, and MAX functions, whose arguments all take the same type of information (values and/or cell ranges), each of the ROUND function's arguments represents different information. So, for example, to round the two values 6.25 and 3.21 to the nearest whole number, you cannot write =ROUND(6.25,3.21,0). This formula would generate an error message indicating that too many arguments have been given. Excel cannot interpret the intent to round both values, nor can it determine which value to return.

Furthermore, the order of the arguments is critical to correct usage of the ROUND function. Although =SUM(3.21,1) is equivalent to =SUM(1,3.21), the same is not true for functions, such as ROUND, that contain different types of arguments. The formula =ROUND(3.21,1) results in the value 3.2 because it takes the number 3.21 and rounds it to the nearest tenth; by contrast, the formula =ROUND(1,3.21) returns the value 1 because it takes the number 1 and attempts to round it to 3.21 decimal places. In such a case, Excel does not generate an error message indicating incorrect usage of the function; rather, it simply displays an erroneous result if your intent was to round the value 3.21 to the nearest tenth. The first value in the ROUND function is always interpreted as the value you want to round, and anything following the first comma Excel encounters is interpreted as the number of decimal places to be shown.

As with all functions, you must also use caution when entering large values. Typing in commas often causes a formula to be evaluated incorrectly. For example, the formula =ROUND(1,221.34,0) would produce an error message indicating too many arguments have been given because Excel would assume it is rounding the value 1, not the value 1,221.34.

When you work with functions that contain multiple arguments, it's advisable to double-check the function's syntax to be certain you are using the function correctly. The Help system in Excel provides detailed information about each function's syntax, and is a good resource to check for proper function use and syntax.

The ROUND function algorithm rounds down all values of less than half the range, and rounds up values from half the range and above. For example, =ROUND(1.49,0) results in the value 1; whereas the formula =ROUND(1.50,0) results in the value 2. As with all other functions, you can use the ROUND function alone or as part of a larger formula, or even include a ROUND function inside other functions. Table 2.2 provides a few examples of the ROUND function.

Table 2.2: Examples of the ROUND function

Formula	Description	Resulting Value
=ROUND(25.449,0)	Rounds 25.449 to the nearest whole number	25
=ROUND(B2,1)	Where B2 contains the value 23.39, rounds 23.39 to the nearest tenth	23.4
=ROUND(103234, −2)	Rounds 103,234 to the nearest hundred	103,200
=ROUND(23.75%,2)	Rounds 23.75% to the nearest hundredth, which is the same as the nearest percent because the precise value is .2375	24%
=ROUND(SUM(10.33,10.44),0)	First sums 10.33 and 10.44, resulting in 20.77, then rounds this value to the nearest whole number	21

Similar functions are provided in Excel, such as ROUNDUP and ROUNDDOWN, which contain the same arguments but return a value that is always either rounded up or rounded down depending on the function used. For example, the formula =ROUNDUP(3.432,1) rounds the value 3.432 up to the next highest tenth, or 3.5. To round the value 25.83% down to the nearest percent, you could write the formula =ROUNDDOWN(25.83%,2) resulting in the value 25%. Notice that, in this case, the num_digits argument is 2 not 0 because the **precise value** of 25.83% is 0.2583. When using ROUNDUP and ROUNDDOWN functions with negative values, the absolute value is rounded up or down and then the negative sign is reapplied. Table 2.3 summarizes some of the functions you can use to change the precision of a value.

Table 2.3: Examples of functions that modify the precision of a value

Function	Description	Syntax and Example	Resulting Value
ROUND	Rounds a number to a specified number of decimal places	ROUND(number,num_digits) =ROUND(25.33%,2)	25%
ROUNDUP	Rounds a number up to the specified number of decimal places	ROUNDUP(number,num_digits) =ROUNDUP(4.3,0) =ROUNDUP(−4.3,0)	5 −5
ROUNDDOWN	Rounds a number down to the specified number of decimal places	ROUNDDOWN (number,num_digits) =ROUNDDOWN(4.3,0) =ROUNDDOWN(−4.3,0)	4 −4
EVEN	Rounds a number up to the next highest even integer	EVEN(number) =EVEN(2.23)	4
ODD	Rounds a number up to the next highest odd integer	ODD(number) =ODD(1.23)	3
INT	Rounds a number down to the nearest integer	INT(number) =INT(4.3) =INT(−4.3)	4 −5
TRUNC	Truncates a number to the specified number of decimal places by removing digits of lesser precision	TRUNC(number,num_digits) =TRUNC(4.3,0) =TRUNC(−4.3,0)	4 −4

Rounding Values to the Nearest Hundredth

Joanna decides to use the ROUND function to alter the Torsion Strength values in column G of the Current worksheet so that they have a consistent precision. One way she can accomplish this is by calculating the rounded values in a separate column (column H) and then copying the rounded values back into the original Torsion Strength column. Could Joanna simply write the formula with the ROUND function in cell G3 and copy it down the column? No; doing so would result in a circular reference error because the values in the formula would be referencing themselves.

In cell H3, Joanna calculates the corresponding rounded value by writing the formula =ROUND(G3,2). She copies this formula down the column, relatively changing the cell reference G3 as it is copied down. Because the values in column H are formatted according to the general format, only significant digits are displayed. To ensure that values with two decimal places display correctly, Joanna applies the Number format (which specifies two decimal places) to cell H3 and then copies this format into cells H4:H31. To do this, Joanna will use the Format Painter button located in the Clipboard group on the Home tab. This tool can be used to copy a selected format from one cell or cells to another cell or range of cells without affecting the content (text/value). The resulting worksheet values are shown in Figure 2.5.

The ROUND function in cell H3, =ROUND(G3,2), changes the precision of the value listed in cell G3 to two decimal places. For example, if the actual value in cell G3 is 2.214 and is displayed with two decimal places as 2.21, then the formula = G3*1000 results in the value 2214, not 2210. However, the formula =ROUND(G3,2)*1000 results in the value 2210 because the precise value of G3 is changed to 2.21 by the ROUND function.

Figure 2.5: Using the ROUND function to change the precision of the Torsion Strength values

Mfg ID#	Size	Style	Date Manufactured	Production Line	Friction Coefficient	Torsion Strength	H
12134	174	A	11/17	1	0.82	2.21	2.21
12135	174	A	11/17	1	0.49	1.94	1.94
12139	174	A	11/17	1	0.52	2.03	2.03
12140	167	A	11/17	1	0.63	2.24	2.24
12142	167	A	11/17	1	0.64	2.28	2.28
12144	167	A	11/17	1	1.28	2.31	2.31
12145	174	A	11/17	1	0.45	2.02	2.02
12146	167	A	11/17	1	1.13	2.05	2.05
12148	167	E	11/18	1	0.43	2.27	2.27
12149	174	E	11/18	1	0.47	2.31	2.31
12154	174	E	11/18	1	0.97	2.23	2.23
12156	174	E	11/18	1	0.81	2.11	2.11
12160	174	E	11/19	1	0.68	2.22	2.22
12161	174	E	11/19	1	0.67	2.08	2.08
12162	181	E	11/19	1	0.95	2.01	2.01
12136	181	R	11/17	2	1.32	2.35	2.35
12137	181	R	11/17	2	0.75	1.7345	1.73
12138	181	R	11/17	2	0.92	2.08	2.08
12141	181	R	11/17	2	0.46	2.26	2.26
12143	174	R	11/17	2	1.04	2.24	2.24
12147	181	A	11/18	2	0.90	2.01	2.01
12150	167	A	11/18	2	0.97	2.00001	2.00
12151	181	A	11/18	2	0.49	2.08	2.08
12152	181	A	11/18	2	0.75	2.17	2.17
12153	167	A	11/18	2	0.30	3.216	3.22
12155	181	E	11/18	2	1.01	2.24	2.24
12157	181	E	11/19	2	0.84	2.34	2.34
12158	174	E	11/19	2	0.68	2.1	2.10
12159	181	A	11/19	2	0.58	2.33	2.33

Value in cell G3 is rounded to the nearest hundredth

ROUND function changes the precision of the value in cell G24 to two decimal places, so 2.00001 is now 2.00

How To

Use the Format Painter
1. Select the cell(s) containing the format to be copied.
2. Click the Home tab on the Ribbon, and then click the Format Painter button in the Clipboard group. The pointer should now appear as a cross/brush instead of an arrow.
3. To copy this format, do one of the following:

- To copy the format to a single cell, simply click that cell.
- To copy the format to multiple contiguous cells, select the cells while holding down the mouse button and then release.

You can use the Format Painter to copy a format into multiple noncontiguous cells. To accomplish this, select the cell with the format to be copied and then double-click the Format Painter button. Using the Format Painter pointer, click each cell or drag the pointer across multiple ranges of cells to apply the format. This technique also works when copying formats between sheets and even from one workbook to another. When you are finished, click the Format Painter button again, or press the Escape key to turn off this feature.

An alternate way to simultaneously round values and set the display is to use the Set precision as displayed workbook option. Be aware that this feature is applied to the entire workbook. Selecting this option could instantly result in loss of data precision of previously entered or calculated data. To set this option, you use the Excel Options dialog box, which you access from the File tab on the Ribbon. Use the Set precision as displayed workbook option. Once the feature has been enabled, all values in all workbook cells are permanently changed from full precision (for example, 15 digits) to whatever format is displayed in that cell, including the number of decimal places (for example, nine digits and two places to the right of the decimal). Any subsequent use of the Increase Decimal or Decrease Decimal button not only changes the display, but also changes the precision of the values in the selected cells. You should use this feature with extreme caution to avoid unwanted consequences. In general, the use of the ROUND function for specific values is preferable.

How To

Change Workbook Default to Set Precision as Displayed

1. Click the File tab on the Ribbon.
2. Select the Options button on the navigation bar. The Excel Options dialog box opens.
3. Click the Advanced category on the left side of the dialog box.
4. Scroll down the list to display the When calculating this workbook topic, as seen in Figure 2.6.
5. Click the Set precision as displayed check box to enable this option. A warning box appears, alerting you of the possible loss of data accuracy.
6. Click the OK button to acknowledge this warning.
7. Click the OK button to apply this setting and close the dialog box.

Figure 2.6: Excel Options dialog box

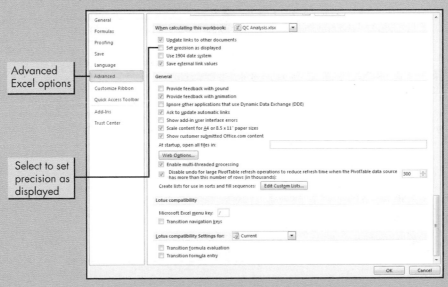

Many other workbook and worksheet options can be modified from the Excel Options dialog box, including calculation options, error checking, file directory defaults, and add-ins.

Now that Joanna has rounded the Torsion Strength values to the nearest hundredth, she can replace the original values in column G with these rounded values. If she tried to simply delete column G, she would receive a #REF! error in column H because the formulas in that column would reference a column that no longer exists. A better way to handle this is to copy and paste just the rounded values, not the formulas that produced the values, into the original column G listing the Torsion Strength values. To do this, Joanna can use the Paste Special feature.

Using Paste Special to Copy and Paste Data

A variety of methods are available to copy information from one part of a worksheet to another, to other worksheets, or even from one workbook to another. The simplest method is to first select the information you want to copy, and then use the Copy button 🗐 and the Paste button in the Clipboard group on the Home tab. When you use this method, Excel pastes the contents of the copied cell or range of cells, including any formatting applied to the original cell(s). You can adjust the way Excel pastes copied data by clicking the Paste button arrow and choosing one of the context-sensitive Paste option buttons or Paste Special on the menu, which are described in Table 2.4.

Table 2.4: Context-sensitive Paste options

Paste Option	Button Name	Description
	Paste	Pastes formulas and formatting
	Formulas	Pastes formulas only
	Formulas & Number Formatting	Pastes formulas with only number formatting
	Keep Source Formatting	Pastes formulas with source formatting
	No Borders	Pastes the formulas and formatting from the original cell(s), but not the format of the cell borders
	Keep Source Column Widths	Pastes formulas and formatting, and matches source column width
	Transpose	Pastes the formulas and formatting from the original range of cells, but reverses the orientation so that the rows of the original cell range become the columns in the pasted range, and the original columns become rows
	Values	Pastes only the values from the original cell(s); the formulas and any formatting are not pasted
	Values & Number Formatting	Pastes values from the original cell(s) and number formats
	Values & Source Formatting	Paste values from the original cell(s) and formatting
	Formatting	Pastes only the cell format of the original cell, not values or formulas
	Paste Link	Pastes a connection, or link, to the original cells, including the applied formatting

Table 2.4: Context-sensitive Paste options (cont.)

Paste Option	Button Name	Description
▣	Picture	Pastes the contents of the copied cell(s) as a picture
▣	Linked Picture	Pastes a linked picture to original content; so if the copied cell's value changes, the linked picture will update to reflect this change
Paste Special		Opens the Paste Special dialog box, which provides all of the preceding options plus additional paste options

Upon completion of pasting content, the Paste Options button arrow 🗐 (Ctrl) ▾ appears next to the pasted values. Clicking on this button again displays context-sensitive pasting options, with the exception of Paste Special.

In this case, Joanna wants to copy only the values with the number formatting in column H without any of the formulas. To do so, Joanna selects the range H3:H31, clicks the Copy button in the Clipboard group on the Home tab, clicks the upper-left cell of the range into which the values will be pasted (in this case, cell G3), clicks the Paste button arrow in the Clipboard group on the Home tab, and then selects Paste Special. In the Paste Special dialog box, Joanna clicks the Values and number formats option button. After moving the values from column H to column G, Joanna deletes column H by highlighting the column and pressing the Delete key. The updated worksheet is shown in Figure 2.7.

Figure 2.7: Updated Torsion Strength values displaying two decimal places

	A	B	C	D	E	F	G	H
2	Mfg ID#	Size	Style	Date Manufactured	Production Line	Friction Coefficient	Torsion Strength	
3	12134	174	A	11/17	1	0.82	2.21	
4	12135	174	A	11/17	1	0.49	1.94	
5	12139	174	A	11/17	1	0.52	2.03	
6	12140	167	A	11/17	1	0.63	2.24	
7	12142	167	A	11/17	1	0.64	2.28	
8	12144	167	A	11/17	1	1.28	2.31	
9	12145	174	A	11/17	1	0.45	2.02	
10	12146	167	A	11/17	1	1.13	2.05	
11	12148	167	E	11/18	1	0.43	2.27	
12	12149	174	E	11/18	1	0.47	2.31	
13	12154	174	E	11/18	1	0.97	2.23	
14	12156	174	E	11/18	1	0.81	2.11	
15	12160	174	E	11/19	1	0.68	2.22	
16	12161	174	E	11/19	1	0.67	2.08	
17	12162	181	E	11/19	1	0.95	2.01	
18	12136	181	R	11/17	2	1.32	2.35	
19	12137	181	R	11/17	2	0.75	1.73	
20	12138	181	R	11/17	2	0.92	2.08	
21	12141	181	R	11/17	2	0.46	2.26	
22	12143	174	R	11/17	2	1.04	2.24	
23	12147	181	A	11/18	2	0.90	2.01	
24	12150	167	A	11/18	2	0.97	2.00	
25	12151	181	A	11/18	2	0.49	2.08	
26	12152	181	A	11/18	2	0.75	2.17	
27	12153	167	A	11/18	2	0.30	3.22	
28	12155	181	E	11/18	2	1.01	2.24	
29	12157	181	E	11/19	2	0.84	2.34	
30	12158	174	E	11/19	2	0.68	2.10	
31	12159	181	A	11/19	2	0.58	2.33	
32								

Values updated with precision to two decimal places and displaying two decimal places

How To

Use Paste Special Options

1. Select the cell or range of cells to be copied, and then click the Copy button 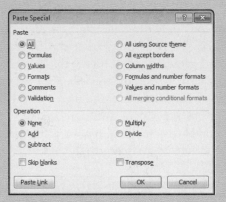 in the Clipboard group on the Home tab on the Ribbon.
2. Select the location to which you want to copy the data by clicking the cell in the upper-left corner of the range. This cell can be on the same worksheet, on another worksheet, or even in a different workbook.
3. Click the Paste button arrow in the Clipboard group on the Home tab, and then click Paste Special to open the Paste Special dialog box. See Figure 2.8.

Figure 2.8: Paste Special dialog box

This dialog box contains all the options provided for pasting copied cells, including several that are not available using the other paste options described earlier (that is, available by clicking the Paste button arrow or the Paste Options button arrow). These additional options include the following:

- **Operation** allows you to paste values using one of four arithmetic operations: Add, Subtract, Multiply, and Divide. For example, assume that cell A2 contains the value 2 and cell B2 contains the value 4. You could copy the value in cell A2 into cell B2 using the Multiply operation to produce the result 8 in cell B2.
- **Skip blanks** enables you to copy and paste a cell range that contains one or more blank cells. The cell range into which the copied cells are pasted retains its original values for any cells that correspond to the blank cells in the copied range; in other words, the blank cells are not pasted over any existing values in the range into which they are pasted. You can select the Skip blanks option in combination with any of the other pasting options.

4. After selecting the options you want in the dialog box, click the OK button.

Calculating the Mean, Median, Mode, and Standard Deviation

Now, Joanna is ready to calculate the arithmetic mean, median, mode, and standard deviation of the Friction Coefficient and Torsion Strength values in the Current worksheet. Table 2.5 lists some of the choices Excel provides to perform these calculations. Joanna will use the AVERAGE function, which was discussed in Chapter 1, and the **MODE.SNGL**, **MEDIAN**, and **STDEV.S** functions. These functions work in a similar way to the AVERAGE function, containing only one type of argument—a list of values. Recall that this list can contain one or more of the following: constants, cell references, a range of cells along a column, a range of cells along a row, or a two-dimensional block of cells.

Table 2.5: Excel statistical functions

Statistic	Function and Syntax	Description
Arithmetic mean	AVERAGE(number1,number2,...)	Returns the average (arithmetic mean) of the arguments
Median	MEDIAN(number1,number2,...)	Returns the median of the given numbers, which is the number in the middle of a set of numbers; that is, half the numbers have values that are greater than the median, and half have values that are less than the median
Mode (singular value)	MODE.SNGL(number1,number2,...)	Returns the most frequently occurring value in a range of data This function is new to Excel 2010 and is not backward compatible.
Standard deviation (sample)	STDEV.S(number1,number2,...)	Estimates standard deviation based on a sample; ignores logical values and text This function is new to Excel 2010 and is not backward compatible.

Table 2.5 contains new Excel 2010 functions for calculating mode and standard deviation that are not available in earlier versions of Excel. If these functions are used in Excel 2010 workbooks and those workbooks are then opened in older versions of Excel, a #NAME? error will result. Excel 2010 does allow for the use of the old functions (MODE, STDEV) in cases where backward compatibility is required.

To calculate these statistics for the Friction Coefficient values in the Current worksheet, Joanna enters the following formulas in the cells indicated:

- Cell F33: =AVERAGE(F3:F31)
- Cell F34: =MEDIAN(F3:F31)
- Cell F35: =MODE.SNGL(F3:F31)
- Cell F36: =STDEV.S(F3:F31)

Joanna then formats these values with the comma style and copies these formulas across the row into column G to calculate the respective values for the Torsion Strength data. Figure 2.9 shows the worksheet with the statistics calculated. Note that Joanna included labels in cells A33:A36 to identify each statistic and applied outside borders.

Figure 2.9: Worksheet with statistics calculated

	A	B	C	D	E	F	G	H
11	12148	167	E	11/18	1	0.43	2.27	
12	12149	174	E	11/18	1	0.47	2.31	
13	12154	174	E	11/18	1	0.97	2.23	
14	12156	174	E	11/18	1	0.81	2.11	
15	12160	174	E	11/19	1	0.68	2.22	
16	12161	174	E	11/19	1	0.67	2.08	
17	12162	181	E	11/19	1	0.95	2.01	
18	12136	181	R	11/17	2	1.32	2.35	
19	12137	181	R	11/17	2	0.75	1.73	
20	12138	181	R	11/17	2	0.92	2.08	
21	12141	181	R	11/17	2	0.46	2.26	
22	12143	174	R	11/17	2	1.04	2.24	
23	12147	181	A	11/18	2	0.90	2.01	
24	12150	167	A	11/18	2	0.97	2.00	
25	12151	181	A	11/18	2	0.49	2.08	
26	12152	181	A	11/18	2	0.75	2.17	
27	12153	167	A	11/18	2	0.30	3.22	
28	12155	181	E	11/18	2	1.01	2.24	
29	12157	181	E	11/19	2	0.84	2.34	
30	12158	174	E	11/19	2	0.68	2.10	
31	12159	181	A	11/19	2	0.58	2.33	
32								
33	Mean					0.76	2.19	
34	Median					0.75	2.21	
35	Mode					0.49	2.24	
36	Standard Deviation					0.26	0.25	
37								

Column titles and the calculations in rows 33–36 cannot be displayed simultaneously at this window height

=AVERAGE(F3:F31)
=MEDIAN(F3:F31)
=MODE.SNGL(F3:F31)
=STDEV.S(F3:F31)

Best Practice

Working with Nested Functions

Statistical values such as mean, median, mode, and standard deviation often are computed with many decimal places. What if you want these values rounded to the nearest hundredth, for example? One way to do this is to write a formula in another cell referencing the value you want to round—for example, =ROUND(F33,2). A more efficient way to do this is to use a technique called **nesting** functions. When you nest a function, you include that function inside another formula or function as one of its arguments. So you could calculate the rounded value by nesting the AVERAGE function directly inside the ROUND function, as follows: =ROUND(AVERAGE(F3:F31),2). In this formula, Excel first evaluates the nested function for the average. The result of this calculation is then used as the first argument of the ROUND function, effectively combining two distinct steps into one calculation.

Almost all the functions you use in Excel allow for functions and formulas to be nested inside each other. For example, the following formula calculates the minimum value in a list: =MIN (2,3+7,AVERAGE(B2:B3)). Assuming that cells B2 and B3 contain the values 10 and 20, respectively, this formula is reduced to =MIN(2,10,15) and, ultimately, results in the value 2. Excel 2010 allows for up to 64 levels of nesting, though more than 3 or 4 can become unwieldy. Previous versions of Excel are incompatible with formulas containing more than 7 levels of nesting.

One important detail to note when nesting functions is the importance of matching parentheses. The formula must have the exact number of opening parentheses as closing parentheses, and they must be placed correctly to ensure that the formula is calculated properly. The topic of nesting functions and formulas is covered in detail in Chapter 4.

As shown in Figure 2.9, Joanna has to scroll the worksheet to view rows 33 through 36. This makes the worksheet difficult to understand because now the column titles are hidden from view. Fortunately, Excel provides several tools to help you view data on different parts of the worksheet simultaneously.

Managing Large Worksheets by Freezing Panes and Splitting the Window

To make larger worksheets more manageable, Excel provides several tools for displaying and scrolling columns and/or rows so that certain areas can be fixed, or frozen, and the remainder of the worksheet can be scrolled easily. The technique used to fix certain rows while you scroll to other rows in a worksheet is called **freezing panes**. An example is shown in Figure 2.10. Freezing rows 1 and 2 keeps the titles displayed in the top pane, allowing the bottom pane to be scrolled so that values farther down the worksheet are displayed along with the titles. Joanna can use this technique so that the identifying titles are always displayed.

Figure 2.10: Freezing panes in the worksheet

Rows 1 and 2 are displayed in the frozen pane, separated by a line, and the bottom portion of the worksheet has been scrolled to begin at row 26

	A	B	C	D	E	F	G	H
1	Quality Control Data for TZBlazer Skis							
2	Mfg ID#	Size	Style	Date Manufactured	Production Line	Friction Coefficient	Torsion Strength	
26	12152	181	A	11/18	2	0.75	2.17	
27	12153	167	A	11/18	2	0.30	3.22	
28	12155	181	E	11/18	2	1.01	2.24	
29	12157	181	E	11/19	2	0.84	2.34	
30	12158	174	E	11/19	2	0.68	2.10	
31	12159	181	A	11/19	2	0.58	2.33	
32								
33	Mean					0.76	2.19	
34	Median					0.75	2.21	
35	Mode					0.49	2.24	
36	Standard Deviation					0.26	0.25	
37								

How To

Freeze Panes

1. Arrange the worksheet showing the column(s) and/or row(s) in the location you want them to appear at all times (usually at the top of the worksheet).

2. Place the pointer in the cell that is one column to the right and/or one row below the columns and/or rows you want to freeze in place.

3. Click the View tab on the Ribbon, and then click the Freeze Panes button located in the Window group. A list of Freeze Pane options appears.

4. Choose the desired option:

- **Freeze Panes** freezes a combination of one or more rows and columns, based on which cell has been selected. All rows above the selected cell and all columns to the left of the selected cell will be frozen. A black line appears below the rows that are frozen, and a black line appears to the right of the columns that are frozen.

- **Freeze Top Row** freezes only the top row of the worksheet regardless of which cell is selected in the worksheet.
- **Freeze First Column** freezes only the first column (A) of your worksheet. Selecting Freeze Top Row and then selecting Freeze First Column in series freezes both the first column and the first row but does not allow for multiple columns or rows to be frozen.

5. To restore normal navigation through a worksheet, click the Freeze Panes button in the Window group, and then select the Unfreeze Panes option.

Another technique you can use to see different parts of the screen at the same time is to **split** the window by dragging either the horizontal split box or the vertical split box to create separate, scrollable panes. You can also split the window by first positioning the pointer below or to the right of where you want the split, and then choosing the Split button in the Window group on the View tab on the Ribbon.

How To

Split the Window
Method 1—Using the Split Boxes:

- To split the window vertically, drag the split box at the lower-right corner of the worksheet to the location where you want to divide the window. The window splits into separate panes, each of which can be scrolled individually.
- To divide the window horizontally, drag the split box at the upper-right corner of the worksheet to the location where you want to divide the window.
- To split the worksheet both vertically and horizontally, complete the first two methods in succession. Figure 2.11 shows a worksheet that has been split both vertically and horizontally.
- To remove the split, simply drag the split line off the window, either to the left side (for a vertical split) or to the top or bottom (for a horizontal split). You can also double-click a split line to remove it. If you have vertical and horizontal split lines, double-click the area where they cross to remove both at the same time. The Split button in the Window group on the View tab on the Ribbon can also be used to set and remove splits.

Method 2—Using the Split Button:

1. Place the pointer in the cell that is one column to the right and/or one row below the columns and/or rows where you want to split the screen.

- To split the screen horizontally so there are five rows in the top section with the remaining rows in the bottom section, click in the first column displayed on the screen in the sixth row.
- To split the screen vertically so there are three columns in the left section with the remaining columns in the right section, click in the fourth column displayed on the screen in the first row.
- To split the screen both vertically and horizontally so there are five rows at the top and three columns on the left, click in the fourth column displayed on the screen in the sixth row of the worksheet.

2. Click the View tab, and then click the Split button located in the Window group.

3. To remove the split, again click the Split button or use one of the alternate techniques listed in Method 1.

Unlike freezing panes, using the Split tool allows you to scroll the top and left areas as well as the bottom and right areas.

Figure 2.11: Splitting the window

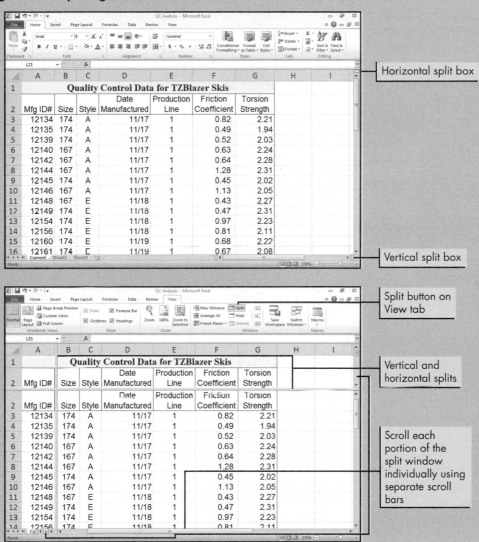

Comparing Current Values with Historical Values

The final step in Joanna's analysis is to compare the current (calculated) values with the historical values provided by QC. One way to do this is to place the current values and the historical values side by side on a separate worksheet in the workbook and then perform the comparisons. Joanna creates a new worksheet named Comparison to accomplish this. Figure 2.12 shows the values in this new Comparison worksheet at the top and the corresponding formulas at the bottom. Note that the formulas relate back to the calculated values on the Current worksheet. Recall from Chapter 1 that references to cells on other worksheets include the worksheet name.

Figure 2.12: Comparison worksheet values and corresponding formulas

The Comparison worksheet in the QC Analysis workbook contains the following elements:

- Cells B4:B7 contain the historical values for the Friction Coefficient that were given to Joanna by the QC group for mean, median, mode, and standard deviation. These values have been entered directly into the cells.
- Cells C4:C7 contain the formulas =Current!F33, =Current!F34, and so on. These formulas simply reference the cells that contain the values previously calculated for mean, median, mode, and standard deviation for Friction Coefficient on the Current worksheet.
- Cells G4:G7 contain the historical values for Torsion Strength that were given to Joanna by the QC group for mean, median, mode, and standard deviation. These values have been entered directly into the cells.
- Cells H4:H7 contain the formulas =Current!G33, =Current!G34, and so on. Again, these formulas simply reference the cells that contain the values previously calculated for mean, median, mode, and standard deviation for Torsion Strength on the Current worksheet.

Now that these values are side by side, Joanna can easily compare them, deriving both the difference between the current values and the historical values, as well as the percent difference between these values.

Calculating the Difference Between Two Sets of Data

To calculate the difference, Joanna needs to subtract the historical values from the current values she just calculated. A positive result indicates that the value has increased; a negative result indicates that the value has decreased. Joanna enters the formula =C4−B4 in cell D4 and copies it down the column (without formatting) to calculate the differences for mean, median, mode, and standard deviation, as shown in Figure 2.13. It appears, for example, that the mean of the Friction Coefficient has decreased by 0.003 (cell D4).

Figure 2.13: Calculating the difference between current and historical values

| | D4 | | | fx | =C4-B4 | | | | | | |

	A	B	C	D	E	F	G	H	I	J	K
1	Analysis of Statistical Values - Current Data vs. Historical Data										
2		Friction Coefficient					Torsion Strength				
3	Value:	Historical	Current	Difference	%Difference		Historical	Current	Difference	%Difference	
4	Mean	0.76	0.76	-0.003			2.27	2.19			
5	Median	0.73	0.75	0.020			2.24	2.21			
6	Mode	0.53	0.49	-0.040			2.15	2.24			
7	Standard Deviation	0.27	0.26	-0.008			0.24	0.25			
8											
9											
10											

=C4-B4 is the difference between the current values and the historical values

A difference of −0.003 for the mean value between the current data and the historical data might or might not be significant, depending on the actual mean values of the data. For example, when comparing mean values such as .01 with .02, a decrease of 0.003 is significant; but when comparing mean values such as 1000.003 with 1000.000, the same decrease is not nearly as significant. So another way to analyze the differences between two sets of data is to look at the *percent difference* of a value in one data set compared with that value in the second data set.

Calculating the Percent Difference Between Two Sets of Data

To calculate a percent difference between two data sets, you subtract the old value from the new value and then divide the difference by the old value. The general format for this formula is as follows:

```
(New Value-Old Value)/Old Value
```

In this case, Joanna needs to write a formula that calculates (Current Value−Historical Value)/Historical Value to compare the values she just calculated from the last few days with the historical values given to her by QC. She begins with the mean values for the Friction Coefficient and enters the following formula in cell E4 on the Comparison worksheet: =(C4–B4)/B4. She then copies this formula down the column to calculate the percent difference for the other statistics.

Joanna also needs to calculate these same values for Torsion Strength. Notice that the headings in columns G, H, I, and J correspond exactly to the Friction Coefficient headings in columns B, C, D, and E. Joanna copies the formulas relative to the columns and rows by selecting cells D4:E7 and using the Copy and Paste buttons to copy the formulas into cells I4:J7. The final comparative analysis is shown in Figure 2.14.

Figure 2.14: Calculating the percent difference between current and historical values

	A	B	C	D	E	F	G	H	I	J	K
1		Analysis of Statistical Values - Current Data vs. Historical Data									
2		Friction Coefficient					Torsion Strength				
3	Value:	Historical	Current	Difference	%Difference		Historical	Current	Difference	%Difference	
4	Mean	0.76	0.76	-0.003	-0.41%		2.27	2.19	-0.082	-3.60%	
5	Median	0.73	0.75	0.020	2.74%		2.24	2.21	-0.030	-1.34%	
6	Mode	0.53	0.49	-0.040	-7.55%		2.15	2.24	0.090	4.19%	
7	Standard Deviation	0.27	0.26	-0.008	-2.95%		0.24	0.25	0.005	2.29%	
8											

=(C4-B4)/B4 calculates the percent difference of current versus historical values

Formulas are copied from cells D4:E7 into cells I4:J7 to determine the difference and percent difference for the Torsion Strength values

What does this data show? Has the quality data changed in the last few days as compared with the historical data and, if so, for better or worse? Joanna first looks at the Friction Coefficient data and notices there is very little change in the mean value (–.41%, as shown in cell E4). The mean is slightly lower, and because a lower Friction Coefficient value is preferred, there is no indication here of any problems. Recall that Friction Coefficient values of greater than 1.23 result in rejection of the ski. The standard deviation has also decreased, as shown in cell E7, indicating the production process is more, rather than less, consistent. The only large difference appears to be for the mode value, which decreased from the historical value of .53 to .49 (cells B6:C6). Again, because a lower Friction Coefficient is better than a higher one, this change does not signal a problem.

When Joanna evaluates the data on Torsion Strength, however, she sees a different trend. The mean seems to have decreased as well, but by a much greater percentage, as shown in cell J4. Higher Torsion Strength values are desirable because the QC process rejects values of less than 2.0; therefore, a 3.6% decrease in the mean value indicates a possible problem. The standard deviation for Torsion Strength has increased, as shown in cell I7. An increase in the standard deviation indicates less consistency in the production process, and this might warrant further investigation. The median value for the current data appears to be close to that of the historical data, as indicated by the result in cell J5; so the problem is not being caused by a large number of tail values at one end of the data set. The mode has increased by .09 (as shown in cell I6), indicating the most common value is now somewhat higher (better) than in the historical data set.

Joanna concludes that if there is a problem, it probably has something to do with the molding of the ski rather than the finishing. Such variations might be the result of machinery problems, modified production line procedures, changes in raw materials, or other factors. Joanna plans to share her results with the molding supervisor to try to isolate the problem quickly, before it has a major impact on production output and costs.

The statistical tools Joanna used are but a few of the most basic ones available. Excel offers a wide variety of more sophisticated statistical tools for data analysis. The Help system in Excel provides detailed information on all the statistical functions and tools available.

Steps To Success: Level 1

A separate processing line assembles the binding mechanisms for the TZBlazer skis. Recently, a new machine was installed on this line to automate the assembly for several components that had previously been done by hand. The new machine was installed about a month ago and seems to be working smoothly. The QC group wants to determine if the binding assemblies made on this new automated machine meet the same high standards as when the bindings were assembled by hand. The QC group tests ski bindings in two ways:

- Minimum pressure at which the binding mechanism will automatically unlock measured in pounds (lbs). Bindings that unlock at less than 10 lbs of pressure are rejected.
- Temperature at which the materials of construction fail, given that the cold temperatures affect the binding performance, measured in degrees Celsius (°C). The lower the failure temperature, the better the ski binding. The maximum allowable failure temperature is −60°C. To avoid any damage to the ski, failure is determined at the point at which the flexibility of the materials falls below a specified level.

The QC group has provided the historical values for these quality attributes, as shown in Table 2.6, and entered the production data for the past four days in an Excel workbook named Binding1.xlsx on a worksheet named BindingData.

Table 2.6: Historical data for bindings

	Pressure in lbs	Temperature in °C
Mean	10.335	−66.887
Median	10.221	−66.91
Mode	10	−66
Standard Deviation	0.701	2.201

In these steps, your task is to compare the mean, median, mode, and standard deviation of the current values with the historical values. Complete the following:

1. Open the workbook named **Binding1.xlsx** located in the Chapter 2 folder, and then save it as **QC Binding Data Analysis 1.xlsx**.

2. Modify the temperature data so that all values are precisely stored to the nearest tenth of a degree and are displayed with one decimal place.

3. In rows below the data in columns D and E, calculate the mean, median, mode, and standard deviation for the pressure and temperature values. Display pressure values in thousandths and temperature values in tenths. Make sure to include labels for all of your calculations.

4. Use the Freeze Panes feature to display the column titles and the values calculated in Step 3 simultaneously.

5. On a separate worksheet named **Compare**, enter the historical values for pressure and temperature (see Table 2.6), using a format similar to that shown in Figure 2.14.

6. On the Compare worksheet, show the values calculated for mean, median, mode, and standard deviation by referencing the values you calculated in Step 3.

7. Calculate the difference between the current values and the historical values for pressure and temperature.

8. Calculate the percent difference between the current values and the historical values for pressure and temperature.

9. In an area below the analysis, list your conclusions about the effect of the new production machine on the quality of the bindings produced, based on current temperature and pressure failure data versus historical data.

10. Format the Compare worksheet so that it is easy to read and includes a title. Use cell shading and/or colors to differentiate the pressure values from the temperature values. Format the values using appropriate numbers of decimal places to display the necessary information. Use percentage formats where indicated.

11. Save and close the QC Binding Data Analysis 1.xlsx workbook.

LEVEL 2

Organizing and Evaluating Different Data Groupings

Determining a Rank for Each Value in a Data Set

So far, Joanna has calculated various statistical values for the QC data and compared them with historical data. This has given her a good understanding of the average values and distributions, but no real insight into the extreme values that were obtained. Joanna now wants to look at the quality data at each of the extremes—the highest values and lowest values. She also wants to determine a rank for each data point relative to the data set. This ranking will serve as a point of reference if one of the skis is returned sometime in the future.

Joanna has slightly modified the Current worksheet, as shown in Figure 2.15, to include the component costs associated with each ski model and size. She plans to use this data later to determine some of the costs associated with rejecting a ski. First, Joanna wants to obtain a ranking for each ski tested, by both Friction Coefficient value and Torsion Strength value, so that if any future problems arise with an individual ski, she can easily see the ski's relative positions for these values compared to the other skis produced. If most of the skis that come back from retailers and consumers are at one end or another of a specific quality value, the manufacturing group will be able to quickly modify its process or quality standards for that specific variable.

Figure 2.15: Worksheet modified to include cost of skis

	A	B	C	D	E	F	G	H	I
1		Quality Control Data for TZBlazer Skis							
2	Mfg ID#	Size	Style	Date Manufactured	Production Line	Friction Coefficient	Torsion Strength	Ski Cost	
3	12134	174	A	11/17	1	0.82	2.21	$54.50	
4	12135	174	A	11/17	1	0.49	1.94	54.50	
5	12139	174	A	11/17	1	0.52	2.03	54.50	
6	12140	167	A	11/17	1	0.63	2.24	45.50	
7	12142	167	A	11/17	1	0.64	2.28	45.50	
8	12144	167	A	11/17	1	1.28	2.31	45.50	
9	12145	174	A	11/17	1	0.45	2.02	54.50	
10	12146	167	A	11/17	1	1.13	2.05	45.50	
11	12148	167	E	11/18	1	0.43	2.27	55.50	
12	12149	174	E	11/18	1	0.47	2.31	64.50	
13	12154	174	E	11/18	1	0.97	2.23	64.50	
14	12156	174	E	11/18	1	0.81	2.11	64.50	
15	12160	174	E	11/19	1	0.68	2.22	64.50	
16	12161	174	E	11/19	1	0.67	2.08	64.50	
17	12162	181	E	11/19	1	0.95	2.01	70.50	

Ski costs added

If you were to manually rank a value from a given list, you would sort the list and then count the number of entries either above or below the value in question. This can be rather tedious as the sample data sets become larger. The **RANK.EQ function** in Excel allows you to quickly and easily complete this same task. The syntax of this function is as follows:

$$\text{RANK.EQ(number,ref,order)}$$

The *number* argument refers to the value to be ranked; the *ref* argument is the range of values the number is being compared with; and the *order* argument specifies the sort order. The function's algorithm defines its behavior as follows: if the order argument is 0 or left blank, Excel ranks the values in descending order; if the order argument is a positive number, Excel ranks the values in ascending order. Duplicate values are all given top rank of that set of values. Note that the RANK.EQ function is also new to Excel 2010 and is not backward compatible.

Joanna wants to rank both the Friction Coefficient and Torsion Strength values so that rank #1 corresponds to the "best" ski. The lower the Friction Coefficient value, the better the ski quality, so Joanna wants the rank of 1 to correspond to the lowest value. This requires the ranking to be done in ascending order. Joanna begins by ranking the first item on the Current worksheet (#12134), as compared with the items in rows 3 through 31, in ascending order by writing the following formula in cell I3:

$$\text{=RANK.EQ(F3,F\$3:F\$31,1)}$$

This formula finds the ranking of the value in cell F3 (0.82) as compared with the values in cells F3 through F31. The last argument, 1, specifies ascending order for the ranking. Also note that Joanna has used absolute row references in the ref argument so that this formula will work when copied down the column into cells I4 through I31. To calculate the ranking for the Torsion Strength, Joanna again wants rank #1 to represent the best ski. In this case, the higher the Torsion Strength value, the better. To represent ranking with the highest value corresponding to rank #1, Joanna needs to specify descending order in the RANK.EQ function for Torsion Strength. Because descending order is the default order type, this argument can be omitted. Joanna writes the following formula in cell J3:

$$\texttt{=RANK.EQ(G3,G\$3:G\$31)}$$

Again, the cell range in the ref argument contains absolute row references so that the formula can be copied down the column into cells J4 through J31. The resulting values are shown in columns I and J of Figure 2.16.

Figure 2.16: Determining rankings for Friction Coefficient and Torsion Strength

=RANK.EQ(F3,F$3:F$31,1) in cell I3 ranks Friction Coefficient values in ascending order

=RANK.EQ(G3,G$3:G$31) in cell J3 ranks Torsion Strength values in descending order

	A	B	C	D	E	F	G	H	I	J	K
		Mfg			Date	Production	Friction	Torsion		Rank Friction	Rank Torsion
2		ID#	Size	Style	Manufactured	Line	Coefficient	Strength	Ski Cost	Coefficient	Strength
3	12134	174	A	11/17	1	0.82	2.21	$54.50	18	15	
4	12135	174	A	11/17	1	0.49	1.94	54.50	6	28	
5	12139	174	A	11/17	1	0.52	2.03	54.50	8	23	
6	12140	167	A	11/17	1	0.63	2.24	45.50	10	10	
7	12142	167	A	11/17	1	0.64	2.28	45.50	11	7	
8	12144	167	A	11/17	1	1.28	2.31	45.50	28	5	
9	12145	174	A	11/17	1	0.45	2.02	54.50	3	24	
10	12146	167	A	11/17	1	1.13	2.05	45.50	27	22	
11	12148	167	E	11/18	1	0.43	2.27	55.50	2	8	
12	12149	174	E	11/18	1	0.47	2.31	64.50	5	5	
13	12154	174	E	11/18	1	0.97	2.23	64.50	23	13	
14	12156	174	E	11/18	1	0.81	2.11	64.50	17	17	
15	12160	174	E	11/19	1	0.68	2.22	64.50	13	14	
16	12161	174	E	11/19	1	0.67	2.08	64.50	12	19	
17	12162	181	E	11/19	1	0.95	2.01	70.50	22	25	
18	12136	181	R	11/17	2	1.32	2.35	82.50	29	2	
19	12137	181	R	11/17	2	0.75	1.73	82.50	15	29	
20	12138	181	R	11/17	2	0.92	2.08	82.50	21	19	
21	12141	181	R	11/17	2	0.46	2.26	82.50	4	9	
22	12143	174	R	11/17	2	1.04	2.24	76.50	26	10	
23	12147	181	A	11/18	2	0.90	2.01	60.50	20	25	
24	12150	167	A	11/18	2	0.97	2.00	45.50	23	27	
25	12151	181	A	11/18	2	0.49	2.08	60.50	6	19	
26	12152	181	A	11/18	2	0.75	2.17	60.50	15	16	
27	12153	167	A	11/18	2	0.30	3.22	45.50	1	1	
28	12155	181	E	11/18	2	1.01	2.24	70.50	25	10	
29	12157	181	E	11/19	2	0.84	2.34	70.50	19	3	
30	12158	174	E	11/19	2	0.68	2.10	64.50	13	18	
31	12159	181	A	11/19	2	0.58	2.33	70.50	9	4	
32											

Skis with the same Friction Coefficient value share the same ranking

Notice that several rows have duplicate ranking values. This function ranks repeated values with an identical ranking. If there are two instances of the Friction Coefficient value 0.97, both are given the same rank—in this case, 23. The next rank given to the next highest Friction Coefficient value is 25. Also notice that, coincidentally, ski number 12153 has both the best Friction Coefficient value and the best Torsion Strength value.

Determining the Highest and Lowest Values in a Data Set

With a long list, ranking the data might not highlight those elements that appear at each extreme, specifically the highest and lowest values. Although the data set Joanna is working with is relatively small, she anticipates using this analysis with larger data sets in the future and, therefore, wants to set up a separate worksheet to examine only the five highest and lowest test values for Friction Coefficient and Torsion Strength. Joanna has created a new worksheet in the QC Analysis workbook named HighLow, as shown in Figure 2.17.

Figure 2.17: HighLow worksheet

	A	B	C	D	E	F
1	Analysis of QC Data Extreme Values					
2		Top 5 (Highest)		Bottom 5 (Lowest)		
3		Friction Coefficient	Torsion Strength	Friction Coefficient	Torsion Strength	
4	1					
5	2					
6	3					
7	4					
8	5					
9						
10						

Determining the Highest Value with the LARGE Function

To obtain the value for the lowest or highest Friction Coefficient values, the MIN and MAX functions would suffice. However, these functions cannot show Joanna the second or third lowest and highest values. One way to create a list of the top five (highest) Friction Coefficient values from the QC data is to manually go through the rankings and select the highest five values—again, a tedious task. The **LARGE function** determines the *n*th largest value in a range. The syntax of this function is as follows:

```
LARGE(array,k)
```

The *array* argument is the range of cells being evaluated. It can be a one-dimensional range along a row or a column, or a two-dimensional range for a block of cells. The second argument, *k*, is the desired ranking, where 1 is the largest value. The *k* argument can be either a constant or a cell reference to a cell containing a positive value. Using a 0 or negative value for *k* results in a #NUM! error. For example, to choose the 13th largest value from a list of values in cells A1:A1000, the formula =LARGE(A1:A1000,13) could be used.

To fill in a list of the top five (highest) Friction Coefficient values and the top five Torsion Strength values, Joanna set up the HighLow worksheet with the numbers 1 through 5 in column A and the headings for Friction Coefficient and Torsion Strength across the rows (see Figure 2.17). Now Joanna can use the LARGE function to find the corresponding top five (highest) values for each. She needs to reference values on the Current worksheet to do so (see Figure 2.16).

What formula should Joanna write in cell HighLow!B4, which she can then copy down and across into cells HighLow!B4 through C8 to give the corresponding *n*th highest value for the given data set? If only considering cell HighLow!B4, she could write the formula =LARGE(Current!F3:F31,A4), where Current!F3:F31 is the array argument (cell range) representing the Friction Coefficient data set, and cell A4 contains the value 1 on the HighLow worksheet, representing the first highest value. But will this formula work when copied down the column to obtain the second highest value or across the row to calculate the first highest value for Torsion Strength? Consider the following:

- When this formula is copied down, the array range will change from Current!F3:F31 to Current!F4:F32. Is this correct? No; Joanna wants the array ranges to remain the same as she copies the formula down. To accomplish this, she can make the rows in the range absolute. Next, consider the second argument, A4. Should this reference change as she copies the formula down? Yes; this should change to determine the second highest value as represented in cell A5, the value 2. Therefore, cell A4 should be copied down the column relatively.
- Now, what happens when the formula is copied across the row? Does the range Current!F3:F31 change to Current!G3:G31 corresponding to the Torsion Strength data set? Yes; this range should change when copied across, so the column address should remain relative. What about cell A4; should it change to cell B4 when copied across? In this case, Joanna still wants to reference the value 1 in cell A4, so she needs to make the column absolute for this reference. The formula needed in this case is as follows:

$$=LARGE(Current!F\$3:F\$31,\$A4)$$

Joanna enters this formula in cell HighLow!B4, and then copies it down the column and across the row, as shown in Figure 2.18.

Figure 2.18: Calculating the top five values

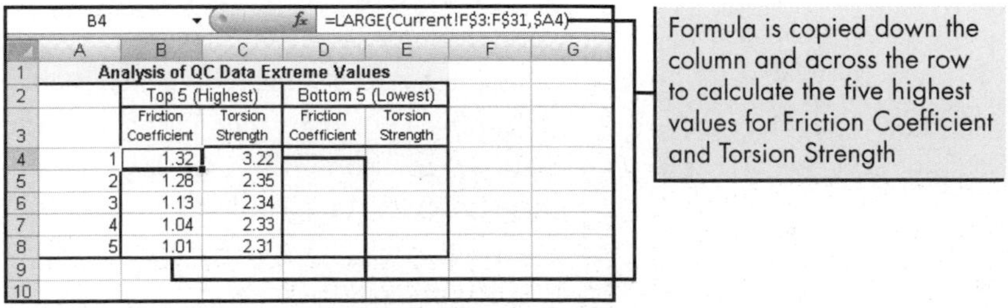

Formula is copied down the column and across the row to calculate the five highest values for Friction Coefficient and Torsion Strength

What do the largest values represent for this data set? For the Friction Coefficient, the larger the value, the worse the ski performance; the largest five values represent the five worst performing skis. For the Torsion Strength, the larger the value, the better the ski performance; the five largest values represent the five best performing skis.

Determining the Lowest Value with the SMALL Function

Using a similar technique, Joanna can also calculate the lowest values for each data set. The **SMALL function** determines the nth smallest value in a range. The syntax of the SMALL function is identical to that of the LARGE function, with the exception of the function name:

$$\text{SMALL(array,k)}$$

The *array* is, again, a range of cells, and k is the desired ranking, where 1 is now the smallest value rather than the largest. These arguments work in the same manner as their counterparts in the LARGE function.

To create a list of the five lowest values for both Friction Coefficient and Torsion Strength, Joanna can use the identical formula that she entered to find the top five values, but substitute the function name SMALL for LARGE. Joanna enters the following formula in cell HighLow!D4:

$$\text{=SMALL(Current!F\$3:F\$31,\$A4)}$$

Note the absolute row references required in the *array* range and the absolute column reference required for the k argument. The finished worksheet is shown in Figure 2.19.

Figure 2.19: Calculating the bottom five values

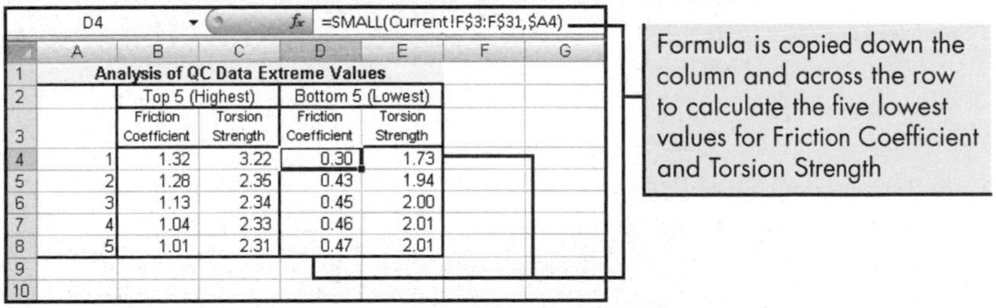

Formula is copied down the column and across the row to calculate the five lowest values for Friction Coefficient and Torsion Strength

What do the smallest values represent for this data set? For Friction Coefficient, the smaller the value, the better the ski performance; so the smallest five values represent the five best performing skis. For Torsion Strength, the smaller the value, the worse the ski performance; therefore, the five smallest values represent the five worst performing skis.

Best Practice

Shortcuts for Working with Large Lists

It can be cumbersome to enter the large number of cell references into a function, such as the formula =LARGE(Current!F$3:F$31,$A4). Excel provides the following two options:

- Determine the beginning and ending of the range to be summed and then type that range directly into the formula. This may require scrolling through the worksheet before beginning the entry.
- Enter the formula name, such as =SUM, and then select the range by highlighting it.

Both techniques might require the repeated use of the scroll bars. There are several useful shortcuts for getting to the top and bottom of a list of numbers using the Ctrl, Shift, and Arrow keys, as listed in Table 2.7. Note that the plus sign (+) is used to indicate that both keys should be pressed, not that the plus sign key is used.

Table 2.7: Shortcut keys for working with large lists

Shortcut Keys	Resulting Action
Ctrl+Home	Moves the cursor to cell A1 and selects cell A1.
Ctrl+End	Moves the cursor to the last rightmost occupied cell in the worksheet. For example, if the last row used for an entry is 999 and the rightmost entry used is in column Z, then the cursor would move to cell Z999.
Ctrl+Arrow Key	Moves the active cell in the direction indicated to the edge of the current data region. To get to the top of a long list, press Ctrl+Up arrow (↑). To get to the bottom, press Ctrl+Down arrow (↓).
Ctrl+Shift+Arrow Key	Selects all cells from the active cell in the direction indicated to the edge of the data region. To highlight a list of numbers, click on the cell at the top of the list and then press Ctrl+Shift+↓. All values will be highlighted in that column until a blank cell is reached.

To quickly enter the formula =LARGE(Current!F$3:F$31,$A4) in cell HighLow!B4, the following steps can be used:

- Select cell HighLow!B4 to make it active and type =LARGE(to begin the formula.
- Click cell Current!F3 on the Current worksheet.
- Press Shift+Ctrl+↓ to highlight the continuous range of cells containing the data, that is, Current!F3:Current!F31.
- Type ,A4 to complete the formula (don't forget the comma before the cell reference) and press the Enter key.

As you learned in Chapter 1, when you need to copy a formula down a long column that is adjacent to a column of equal length, click the cell with the formula to be copied, use the pointer to activate the fill handle, and then double-click. The formula will automatically be copied down to all of the cells in the column without your having to scroll to the last cell in the column.

Determining the Number of Items That Meet Specified Criteria

Joanna wants to continue her analyses to determine exactly how many of the TZBlazer skis were rejected based on each rejection criterion and, ultimately, determine the resulting cost to the company. Recall that skis are rejected based on the following criteria:

- A Friction Coefficient value of greater than 1.23. A high Friction Coefficient value indicates poor surface finishing and results in poor ski performance.
- A Torsion Strength value of less than 2.0. A low Torsion Strength value indicates the material strength is insufficient for the rigors of high-performance skiing; this usually results from problems in the molding process.

To manually calculate the number of skis rejected based on a Friction Coefficient value that is too high, Joanna could look at this value for each ski and make a tally mark for any value greater than 1.23. After reviewing the Friction Coefficient value for all inspected skis, she could count up the number of tally marks to determine the number of skis rejected due to their Friction Coefficient being too high. For a large data set, this manual process would not be practical.

Excel provides a function that mimics this manual process. The **COUNTIF function** counts the number of items in a range that meet specified criteria. The syntax of the COUNTIF function is as follows:

```
COUNTIF(range,criteria)
```

The COUNTIF function has two arguments, the cell *range* and the *criteria*:

- The range argument must be a *contiguous* set of cells down a column (A1:A100) or across a row (A1:Z1), or a block of cells (A1:Z100). If a noncontiguous range is provided with comma separators, the function interprets the second item as the criteria argument, which is not the intended interpretation.
- The criteria argument is essentially a test that the data must meet in order for it to be counted in the grouping. You can use various syntactical formats for this argument depending on the type of criteria test that is specified. To understand the valid methods of specifying this criteria argument, consider the worksheet shown in Figure 2.20, which is a modified version of Joanna's Current worksheet.

Figure 2.20: Examples of the COUNTIF function

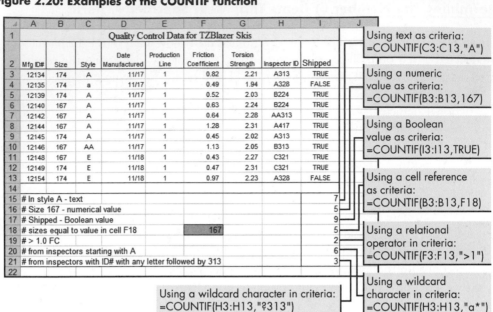

Figure 2.20 shows different types of criteria specified for the COUNTIF function, as described in the following list:

- **Criteria with a specified text value.** The formula =COUNTIF(C3:C13,"A") in cell I15 calculates the number of skis listed that have the style A. The formula finds all instances of the text string "A" in the contiguous range C3 through C13, returning the value 7. This formula does not count cells with "AA" or any other combination of letters containing "A." Note, however, that the function is not case sensitive, so the resulting value includes the lowercase "a" in cell C4 as part of the count.
  What if you wrote the formula as =COUNTIF(C3:C13,A), excluding the quotation marks surrounding the A? The formula would return the value 0 because it would look for the value as defined in a range named A. Even if a range named A actually existed, the formula still would not return the number of values with the text string "A." To correctly specify a text string for the criteria argument, you must enclose the string in quotation marks.
- **Criteria with a specified numeric value.** The formula =COUNTIF(B3:B13,167) in cell I16 calculates the number of skis with the size 167. The formula finds all instances of the numerical value 167 in the range B3 through B13. Notice that the value 167 is not enclosed in quotation marks; specific numerical values do not require quotation marks when used as the criteria argument.
- **Criteria with a specified Boolean value.** The values TRUE and FALSE are referred to as **Boolean values**. They are distinguished from the text values "TRUE" and "FALSE" in the same way that the numerical value 1 is different from the text value "1." The formula =COUNTIF(I3:I13,TRUE) in cell I17 calculates the number of items shipped

by counting the number of items with the Boolean value TRUE in column I. Note that Boolean values should not be enclosed in quotation marks; doing so in this example would result in counting only text strings with "TRUE" rather than counting the Boolean value TRUE. You will learn more about Boolean values in Chapter 4.

- **Criteria with a cell reference containing a specific text, numeric, or Boolean value.** The formula =COUNTIF(B3:B13,F18) in cell I18 calculates the number of skis with the size indicated in cell F18. Because cell F18 contains the value 167, the formula counts the number of instances of the value 167 in the range B3 to B13, returning the value 5. If the value in cell F18 is later changed, the value in cell I18 will be automatically updated. A cell reference works for numerical values, as shown here, and for text or Boolean values. Note that cell reference criteria should *not* be enclosed in quotation marks, or the formula will look for a text string such as "F18" rather than for the contents of cell F18. This method is extremely useful when copying formulas in which the criteria change relative to the row and/or column.

- **Criteria that include relational operators (>, <, >=, <=, <>). Relational operators** are used to compare data, as described in Table 2.8. Each of these operators can be used to establish criteria, such as determining if a value is greater than a specific value, not equal to a specific value, and so on. In Figure 2.20, the formula =COUNTIF (F3:F13,">1") in cell I19 counts the occurrences of all values for the Friction Coefficient that are greater than the value 1. Note that criteria containing a relational operator must be enclosed in quotation marks in a COUNTIF function. Also note that, in its current format, criteria with a relational operator cannot contain a cell reference (for example, " >B2"), only an actual text or numeric value. For more information on using relation operators, use Excel Help .The use of relational operators is explored in much greater detail in Chapter 4.

- **Criteria that include wildcards (*, ?). Wildcards** are symbols that you can use as part of the criteria to search for *text strings* in which the wildcard can be substituted for another character or set of characters. The asterisk wildcard (*) specifies that any number of characters can be substituted. The question mark wildcard (?) specifies that a single character can be substituted. Wildcards can be substituted before, within, or after the text or in combination with other wildcards. Wildcards do not work with values that are numbers or dates, only text. In Figure 2.20, the formula =COUNTIF(H3:H13,"a*") in cell I20 counts the number of values in cells H3 through H13 that begin with the letter "a" followed by any number of characters. Again, because the function is not case sensitive, the formula counts all the Inspector ID values in column H that begin with the letter "A," returning the value 6. Table 2.9 provides additional examples of criteria using wildcards, based on the data in Figure 2.20.

Table 2.8: Relational operators used with the COUNTIF function

Relational Operator	Description	Example in a COUNTIF Function
>	Greater than	=COUNTIF(F3:F13,">1") counts values greater than 1
<	Less than	=COUNTIF(C3:C13,"<E") counts values that appear alphabetically before the letter E
>=	Greater than or equal to	=COUNTIF(F3:F13,">=1") counts values greater than or equal to 1
<=	Less than or equal to	=COUNTIF(G3:G13,"<=2") counts values less than or equal to 2
=	Equal to	=COUNTIF(F3:F13,"=1") counts values equal to 1; this formula is equivalent to =COUNTIF(F3:F13,1)
<>	Not equal to	=COUNTIF(E3:E13,"<>1") counts values not equal to 1

Table 2.9: Wildcards used with the COUNTIF function

Wildcard	Formula	Result	Description
*	=COUNTIF(H2:H13,"*3")	4	Counts all Inspector IDs that end with the text value 3.
*	=COUNTIF(H2:H13,"*1*")	7	Counts all Inspector IDs that contain the text value 1 anywhere in the value (A313, C321, B313, and so on).
?	=COUNTIF(H3:H13,"?313")	3	Counts all Inspector IDs with a single character followed by the characters 313. Notice that cell H7 is not counted because it contains two characters preceding the characters 313. This formula is illustrated in cell I21 in Figure 2.20.
?	=COUNTIF(H3:H13,"*3??")	8	Counts all Inspector IDs that have the value 3 in the third-to-last position in the text value, regardless of the number of preceding characters.

How To

Write a Formula Using the COUNTIF Function

1. Click the cell in which you want to write the formula.
2. Type =COUNTIF(to begin the formula.
3. Locate the range that contains the criteria you want to test. This range must be a contiguous set of columns or rows, or a contiguous block of cells. Type the range (for example, A1:A10) into the function as the first argument, followed by a comma.
4. Determine the selection criteria you want to use, applying the correct syntax for numerical values, text, Boolean values, relational operators, and/or wildcards. Enter the criteria as the second argument of the function.
5. Type the closing parenthesis mark) to end the formula.
6. If you intend to copy the formula, be certain to apply the appropriate relative or absolute cell referencing needed for each argument.

Joanna can now use the COUNTIF function in the Current worksheet to calculate the number of skis rejected because their Friction Coefficient value is too high, and the number of skis rejected because their Torsion Strength value is too low. Joanna enters the necessary formulas in cells F33 and G33, as shown in Figure 2.21. Cell F33 contains the formula =COUNTIF(F3:F31,">1.23"), where the contiguous range F3 through F31 represents the data to be tested and ">1.23" represents the criteria the data must meet in order to be counted—in other words, the function counts all cells in the range F3:F31 containing values greater than 1.23. Similarly, cell G33 contains the formula =COUNTIF (G3:G31,"<2"), which counts all values in the contiguous range G3 through G31 that contain values that are less than 2.

Figure 2.21: Calculating the number of rejected skis using the COUNTIF function

	A	B	C	D	E	F	G	H	I	J	K
1				Quality Control Data for TZBlazer Skis							
2	Mfg ID#	Size	Style	Date Manufactured	Production Line	Friction Coefficient	Torsion Strength	Ski Cost	Rank Friction Coefficient	Rank Torsion Strength	
3	12134	174	A	11/17	1	0.82	2.21	$54.50	18	15	
4	12135	174	A	11/17	1	0.49	1.94	54.50	6	28	
5	12139	174	A	11/17	1	0.52	2.03	54.50	8	23	
6	12140	167	A	11/17	1	0.63	2.24	45.50	10	10	
7	12142	167	A	11/17	1	0.64	2.28	45.50	11	7	
8	12144	167	A	11/17	1	1.28	2.31	45.50	28	5	
9	12145	174	A	11/17	1	0.45	2.02	54.50	3	24	
10	12146	167	A	11/17	1	1.13	2.05	45.50	27	22	
11	12148	167	E	11/18	1	0.43	2.27	55.50	2	8	
12	12149	174	E	11/18	1	0.47	2.31	64.50	5	5	
13	12154	174	E	11/18	1	0.97	2.23	64.50	23	13	
14	12156	174	E	11/18	1	0.81	2.11	64.50	17	17	
15	12160	174	E	11/19	1	0.68	2.22	64.50	13	14	
16	12161	174	E	11/19	1	0.67	2.08	64.50	12	19	
17	12162	181	E	11/19	1	0.95	2.01	70.50	22	25	
18	12136	181	R	11/17	2	1.32	2.35	82.50	29	2	
19	12137	181	R	11/17	2	0.75	1.73	82.50	15	29	
20	12138	181	R	11/17	2	0.92	2.08	82.50	21	19	
21	12141	181	R	11/17	2	0.46	2.26	82.50	4	9	
22	12143	174	R	11/17	2	1.04	2.24	76.50	26	10	
23	12147	181	A	11/18	2	0.90	2.01	60.50	20	25	
24	12150	167	A	11/18	2	0.97	2.00	45.50	23	27	
25	12151	181	A	11/18	2	0.49	2.08	60.50	6	19	
26	12152	181	A	11/18	2	0.75	2.17	60.50	15	16	
27	12153	167	A	11/18	2	0.30	3.22	45.50	1	1	
28	12155	181	E	11/18	2	1.01	2.24	70.50	25	10	
29	12157	181	E	11/19	2	0.84	2.34	70.50	19	3	
30	12158	174	E	11/19	2	0.68	2.10	64.50	13	18	
31	12159	181	A	11/19	2	0.58	2.33	70.50	9	4	
32											
33	# Rejected					2	2				

=COUNTIF(F3:F31,">1.23") in cell F33 calculates the number of skis with a Friction Coefficient value greater than 1.23

=COUNTIF(G3:G31,"<2") in cell G33 calculates the number of skis with a Torsion Strength value less than 2

In reviewing the results of the two COUNTIF functions, would it be accurate to assume that the total number of skis rejected is equal to the sum of the two values resulting from the COUNTIF functions? In this case, two skis were rejected due to their Friction Coefficient values being too high, and two skis were rejected due to their Torsion Strength values being too low, so the sum of these two values is equal to the total number of skis rejected (4). But what if one ski had failed *both* the Friction Coefficient and Torsion Strength criteria? Then this wouldn't be an accurate way to calculate the total number of skis rejected. In later chapters, you will learn about other tools that can help to solve this seemingly simple problem.

Best Practice

Working with Noncontiguous Ranges—Divide and Conquer

One limitation of the COUNTIF function is that it can only accommodate a single contiguous range argument (a one- or two-dimensional range or a block of cells). A list of cell references and/or noncontiguous ranges cannot be interpreted by this function because the first time it encounters the comma delimiter, it assumes that what follows is the criteria—not additional ranges. For example, referring to Figure 2.21, if you wanted to eliminate ski #12137 in row 19 from a count, you could not write the formula =COUNTIF(F3:F18,F20:F31,">0"). This formula has no meaning because Excel would assume that F20:F31 is the criteria argument, which it is unable to evaluate. To solve this type of problem, you can divide the formula into parts, first counting the items that meet the criteria in the first contiguous range and adding that to a count of items that meet the criteria in the second contiguous range, as follows:

$$\texttt{=COUNTIF(F3:F18,">0")+COUNTIF(F20:F31,">0")}$$

This method works well if ranges are in nonadjacent columns or rows, or are even located on other worksheets.

Determining a Total Value for Items That Meet Specified Criteria

Next, Joanna wants to quantify the cost TheZone incurs if a ski is rejected. Significant rejection costs could indicate to management that investing time and money in improving the production process might result in increased profits in the long run. Joanna assumes that after a ski has been rejected, it cannot be reused and, therefore, calculates the rejection cost as the cost to manufacture the ski.

For the purposes of this discussion, assume that no skis can be rejected for having both too high of a Friction Coefficient value and too low of a Torsion Strength value. This might be handled by assuming that after a ski has failed one test, it is immediately rejected and no further tests are performed. If a ski is first tested for Friction Coefficient and fails, it would never be tested for its Torsion Strength, and vice versa. With this technique, a rejected ski cost would never be "double counted." Before calculating the total value of the rejected skis, to avoid any potential problems of double counting, Joanna has modified the data in the Current worksheet. For any ski that failed one test, she deleted the value for the other test for that ski and the corresponding rankings. This modified worksheet is shown in Figure 2.22.

Figure 2.22: Worksheet modified to avoid double counting of failed skis

	A	B	C	D	E	F	G	H	I	J	K
1				Quality Control Data for TZBlazer Skis							
2	Mfg ID#	Size	Style	Date Manufactured	Production Line	Friction Coefficient	Torsion Strength	Ski Cost	Rank Friction Coefficient	Rank Torsion Strength	
3	12134	174	A	11/17	1	0.82	2.21	$54.50	16	13	
4	12135	174	A	11/17	1		1.94	54.50		26	
5	12139	174	A	11/17	1	0.52	2.03	54.50	7	21	
6	12140	167	A	11/17	1	0.63	2.24	45.50	9	8	
7	12142	167	A	11/17	1	0.64	2.28	45.50	10	5	
8	12144	167	A	11/17	1	1.28		45.50	26		
9	12145	174	A	11/17	1	0.45	2.02	54.50	3	22	
10	12146	167	A	11/17	1	1.13	2.05	45.50	25	20	
11	12148	167	E	11/18	1	0.43	2.27	55.50	2	6	
12	12149	174	E	11/18	1	0.47	2.31	64.50	5	4	
13	12154	174	E	11/18	1	0.97	2.23	64.50	21	11	
14	12156	174	E	11/18	1	0.81	2.11	64.50	15	15	
15	12160	174	E	11/19	1	0.68	2.22	64.50	12	12	
16	12161	174	E	11/19	1	0.67	2.08	64.50	11	17	
17	12162	181	E	11/19	1	0.95	2.01	70.50	20	23	
18	12136	181	R	11/17	2	1.32		82.50	27		
19	12137	181	R	11/17	2		1.73	82.50		27	
20	12138	181	R	11/17	2	0.92	2.08	82.50	19	17	
21	12141	181	R	11/17	2	0.46	2.26	82.50	4	7	
22	12143	174	R	11/17	2	1.04	2.24	76.50	24	8	
23	12147	181	A	11/18	2	0.90	2.01	60.50	18	23	
24	12150	167	A	11/18	2	0.97	2.00	45.50	21	25	
25	12151	181	A	11/18	2	0.49	2.08	60.50	6	17	
26	12152	181	A	11/18	2	0.75	2.17	60.50	14	14	
27	12153	167	A	11/18	2	0.30	3.22	45.50	1	1	
28	12155	181	E	11/18	2	1.01	2.24	70.50	23	8	
29	12157	181	E	11/19	2	0.84	2.34	70.50	17	2	
30	12158	174	E	11/19	2	0.68	2.10	64.50	12	16	
31	12159	181	A	11/19	2	0.58	2.33	70.50	8	3	
32											
33	# Rejected					2	2				
34											
35											

Values deleted for second test if ski fails first test

For example, the ski in row 4 does not meet the criteria for the Torsion Strength test (that is, its Torsion Strength value is less than 2), so Joanna manually deleted both its Friction Coefficient value from cell F4 and its Rank Friction Coefficient value from cell I4. (In later chapters, you will learn how to accomplish this automatically.)

Now, Joanna is ready to calculate the cost of all rejected skis. Ideally, she wants to calculate this cost so that if any of the Friction Coefficient or Torsion Strength values are changed later, the worksheet will be automatically updated, making it easy to reuse for future analyses. Simply adding the values for the rejected skis directly would not work. Again, Joanna first considers what manual process she would need to complete the task before implementing a solution in Excel. She could sum the Ski Cost values (column H) for only those skis that meet specified criteria. In this case, because Joanna is considering two different rejection criteria, she needs to do the following:

1. Examine the values for Friction Coefficient (column F) to sum the Ski Cost values (column H) for skis that were rejected because their Friction Coefficient values are too high.

2. Examine the values for Torsion Strength (column G) to sum the Ski Cost values for skis that were rejected because their Torsion Strength values are too low.

3. Add the resulting values from Steps 1 and 2.

Excel provides a function that accomplishes this automatically. The **SUMIF function** adds all the values in a range that meet specified criteria. The syntax of the SUMIF function is as follows:

```
SUMIF(range,criteria,sum_range)
```

The SUMIF function has three arguments:

- The *range* argument identifies the cell range where the criteria are located.
- The *criteria* argument specifies which values should be selected.
- The *sum_range* argument identifies the corresponding cell range to sum if the specified criteria have been met in the range established by the range argument. If the sum_range argument is omitted, the function adds the values in the range indicated by the first argument.

The SUMIF function works almost identically to the COUNTIF function in that its ranges must be contiguous and the criteria can be a value, text, cell reference, or relational expression. The criteria syntax rules are identical to those in the COUNTIF function, as summarized in Table 2.10. It is also important to note that SUMIF, like the COUNTIF function, ignores blank cells, as seen in the examples shown. The examples in Table 2.10 are based on the Current worksheet (see Figure 2.22).

Table 2.10: Examples of the SUMIF function

Criteria Type	Example	Description
Single numeric or Boolean value	=SUMIF(B3:B31,174,H3:H31)	Adds all ski costs (cells H3:H31) where the corresponding ski size is 174.
Text string	=SUMIF(C3:C31,"R",H3:H31)	Adds all ski costs (cells H3:H31) where the corresponding ski style is R.
Cell reference	=SUMIF(C3:C31,C50,H3:H31)	Adds all ski costs (cells H3:H31) where the corresponding ski style is E, assuming that cell C50 contains E.

Table 2.10: Examples of the SUMIF function (cont.)

Criteria Type	Example	Description
Relational operator	=SUMIF(H3:H31,">60")	Adds all ski costs (cells H3:H31) for only those skis that cost more than $60. Note that because the sum_range argument is not specified in this example, the formula uses H3:H31 as both the criteria range and the sum range.
Wildcard	=SUMIF (A3:A31,"12???",H3:H31)	Adds all ski costs (cells H3:H31) where the corresponding Mfg ID# begins with 12 and is followed by three additional characters. This formula only works if cells A3 to A31 are formatted as text values and not as numeric values.

How To

Write a Formula Using the SUMIF Function

1. Click the cell in which you want to write the formula.

2. Type: =SUMIF(to begin the formula.

3. Locate the range that contains the criteria you want to test. This range must be a contiguous set of columns or rows, or a contiguous block of cells. Select or type the range (for example, A1:A10) into the function as the first argument, followed by a comma.

4. Determine the selection criteria you want to use, applying the correct syntax for numerical values, text, Boolean values, relational operators, and/or wildcards. Enter the criteria as the second argument of the function, followed by a comma.

5. Locate the range that contains the values you want to sum if the criterion is met. This range must be a contiguous set of columns or rows, or a contiguous block of cells. Select or type the range into the function as the third argument. If the sum range is the same as the criteria range, this third argument can be omitted.

6. Type the closing parenthesis) to complete the formula.

7. If you intend to copy the formula, be certain to apply the appropriate relative or absolute cell referencing needed for each argument.

To apply the SUMIF function to the problem at hand, Joanna breaks down the problem into its components, as follows:

1. Calculate the Ski Cost values (column H) for skis rejected because their Friction Coefficient values (column F) are too high:

$$SUMIF(F3:F31,">1.23",H3:H31)$$

2. Calculate the Ski Cost values (column H) for skis rejected because their Torsion Strength values (column G) are too low:

$$SUMIF(G3:G31,"<2",H3:H31)$$

3. Add the resulting values from Steps 1 and 2. Joanna could enter each of the preceding formulas in separate cells, or create the entire formula in one cell. She decides to enter the entire formula in cell H33, as follows:

```
=SUMIF(F3:F31,">1.23",H3:H31)+SUMIF(G3:G31,"<2",H3:H31)
```

Figure 2.23 shows the resulting worksheet. Note that the panes are frozen in the worksheet so that the column titles and the result of the SUMIF function can be viewed simultaneously.

Figure 2.23: Calculating the total value of the rejected skis using the SUMIF function

	A	B	C	D	E	F	G	H	I	J	K	L
	H33					f_x	=SUMIF(F3:F31,">1.23",H3:H31)+SUMIF(G3:G31, "<2",H3:H31)				
1			Quality Control Data for TZBlazer Skis									
2	Mfg ID#	Size	Style	Date Manufactured	Production Line	Friction Coefficient	Torsion Strength	Ski Cost	Rank Friction Coefficient	Rank Torsion Strength		
10	12146	167	A	11/17	1	1.13	2.05	45.50	25	20		
11	12148	167	E	11/18	1	0.43	2.27	55.50	2	6		
12	12149	174	E	11/18	1	0.47	2.31	64.50	5	4		
13	12154	174	E	11/18	1	0.97	2.23	64.50	21	11		
14	12156	174	E	11/18	1	0.81	2.11	64.50	15	15		
15	12160	174	E	11/19	1	0.68	2.22	64.50	12	12		
16	12161	174	E	11/19	1	0.67	2.08	64.50	11	17		
17	12162	181	E	11/19	1	0.95	2.01	70.50	20	23		
18	12136	181	R	11/17	2	1.32		82.50	27			
19	12137	181	R	11/17	2		1.73	82.50		27		
20	12138	181	R	11/17	2	0.92	2.08	82.50	19	17		
21	12141	181	R	11/17	2	0.46	2.26	82.50	4	7		
22	12143	174	R	11/17	2	1.04	2.24	76.50	24	8		
23	12147	181	A	11/18	2	0.90	2.01	60.50	18	23		
24	12150	167	A	11/18	2	0.97	2.00	45.50	21	25		
25	12151	181	A	11/18	2	0.49	2.08	60.50	6	17		
26	12152	181	A	11/18	2	0.75	2.17	60.50	14	14		
27	12153	167	A	11/18	2	0.30	3.22	45.50	1	1		
28	12155	181	E	11/18	2	1.01	2.24	70.50	23	8		
29	12157	181	E	11/19	2	0.84	2.34	70.50	17	2		
30	12158	174	E	11/19	2	0.68	2.10	64.50	12	16		
31	12159	181	A	11/19	2	0.58	2.33	70.50	8	3		
32												
33	# Rejected					2	2	$265.00				
34												
35												

Formula first sums the value of all skis rejected due to a Friction Coefficient value that is too high, then sums the value of all skis rejected due to a Torsion Strength value that is too low, and then adds the two resulting values together

As always, it is important to check that any formulas are working properly. With the COUNTIF function, Joanna can manually count the number of skis rejected. With the SUMIF function, she needs to check if the value that is calculated in cell H33 is actually $265.00. To do this manually, Joanna adds $54.50 for ski #12135, which was rejected due to a low Torsion Strength value; $45.50 for ski #12144, which was rejected due to a high Friction Coefficient value; $82.50 for ski #12136, which was rejected due to a high Friction Coefficient value; and finally, $82.50 for ski #12137, which was rejected due to a low Torsion Strength value. The sum of these four values is, indeed, $265.00, so the formula in cell H33 is working correctly.

Best Practice

Watch Those Commas

When you are using more complex functions such as SUMIF, even an extra comma in the wrong place could result in a perfectly plausible but incorrect value. Consider the example shown in Figure 2.24. If Joanna used the formula in cell H33 instead of the correct one, the extra comma in the second SUMIF function in front of the 2 would cause that part of the formula to return a 0, so the resulting value of the SUMIF function would be $128 instead of $265. This type of error is hard to find because no error message is displayed; Excel simply evaluates the incorrect formula and returns a result. In Chapter 10, you will learn about several built-in tools Excel provides to help you troubleshoot formulas to find and correct such errors.

Figure 2.24: Results of using incorrect syntax in a formula

	H33			f_x	=SUMIF(F3:F31,">1.23",H3:H31)+SUMIF(G3:G31, "<,2",H3:H31)						
	A	B	C	D	E	F	G	H	I	J	K	L
1			Quality Control Data for TZBlazer Skis									
2	Mfg ID#	Size	Style	Date Manufactured	Production Line	Friction Coefficient	Torsion Strength	Ski Cost	Rank Friction Coefficient	Rank Torsion Strength		
10	12146	167	A	11/17	1	1.13	2.05	45.50	25	20		
11	12148	167	E	11/18	1	0.43	2.27	55.50	2	6		
12	12149	174	E	11/18	1	0.47	2.31	64.50	5	4		
13	12154	174	C	11/18	1	0.97	2.23	64.50	21	11		
14	12156	174	E	11/18	1	0.81	2.11	64.50	15	15		
15	12160	174	E	11/19	1	0.68	2.22	64.50	12	12		
16	12161	174	E	11/19	1	0.67	2.08	64.50	11	17		
17	12162	181	E	11/19	1	0.95	2.01	70.50	20	23		
18	12136	181	R	11/17	2	1.32		82.50	27			
19	12137	181	R	11/17	2		1.73	82.50		27		
20	12138	181	R	11/17	2	0.92	2.08	82.50	19	17		
21	12141	181	R	11/17	2	0.46	2.26	82.50	4	7		
22	12143	174	R	11/17	2	1.04	2.24	76.50	24	8		
23	12147	181	A	11/18	2	0.90	2.01	60.50	18	23		
24	12150	167	A	11/18	2	0.97	2.00	45.50	21	25		
25	12151	181	A	11/18	2	0.49	2.08	60.50	6	17		
26	12152	181	A	11/18	2	0.75	2.17	60.50	14	14		
27	12153	167	A	11/18	2	0.30	3.22	45.50	1	1		
28	12155	181	E	11/18	2	1.01	2.24	70.50	23	8		
29	12157	181	E	11/19	2	0.84	2.34	70.50	17	2		
30	12158	174	E	11/19	2	0.68	2.10	64.50	12	16		
31	12159	181	A	11/19	2	0.58	2.33	70.50	8	3		
32												
33	# Rejected					2	2	$128.00				
34												
35												

Extra comma in the formula results in the value $128 instead of the correct value $265

Joanna has now taken a more detailed look at the high and low values of the Friction Coefficient and Torsion Strength data, and she has also determined the quantities and ski costs associated with rejected skis—four skis totaling $265. Although this might not seem like a large sum, keep in mind that Joanna started out with a relatively small data set. The real question to consider is what the overall impact will be, such as per day or per year, for this type of rejection quantity. There might be ways to reduce the number of rejected skis, but will the cost of doing so be justified compared with the cost of the rejected skis? In the next level, Joanna will explore the cost of 100% inspection of skis versus the possible costs to the company of retailers and consumers returning these skis because of poor performance.

Steps To Success: Level 2

The QC group wants to extend the ski binding quality control data analysis to determine the rankings, examine the tail ends of the data—both high and low values—and determine the number of bindings that will be rejected. The latest data being analyzed is located in a workbook named Binding2.xlsx. Your task in these steps is to complete this analysis.

The criteria for rejecting bindings are based on two different quality tests, as follows:

- Minimum pressure at which the binding mechanism will automatically unlock, measured in pounds (lbs). The higher the pressure at which the binding unlocks, the better the binding. Bindings that unlock at less than 10 lbs of pressure are rejected.
- Temperature at which the materials of construction fail, given that cold temperatures affect the binding performance, measured in degrees Celsius (°C). The lower the failure temperature, the better the ski binding. The maximum allowable failure temperature is –60°C.

Complete the following:

1. Open the workbook named **Binding2.xlsx** located in the Chapter 2 folder, and then save it as **QC Binding Data Analysis 2.xlsx**.

2. Write a formula in cell G3 that can be copied down the column to calculate the relative rankings of each data element for the pressure test. Set up your rankings so that the best ski is given a ranking of 1 (based on the rejection criteria described in the problem). Include an appropriate column heading in cell G2. In a similar way, set up the rankings for the Temperature test in column H so that the best ski is given a ranking of 1.

3. In cell D49, write a formula to determine the number of ski bindings that failed to meet the minimum pressure requirements for quality testing. Write the formula so that if any of the data inputs change later, this value will be automatically updated. For easier viewing, use the split feature to divide the worksheet into two sections, with the top containing the title and column headings.

4. In cell E49, write a formula to determine the number of ski bindings that failed to meet the minimum temperature requirements for quality testing. Write the formula so that if any of the data inputs change later, this value will be automatically updated.

5. In cell F49, write a formula to determine the total value of the ski bindings that have been rejected. Assume that no binding has failed both tests. Format this cell with the Currency Style. Include the label **Rejection Summary** in cell A49.

6. Set up a separate worksheet named **Tail** in the workbook, and then create a table on the Tail worksheet listing the five highest and lowest values, as shown in Table 2.11. Be certain to include a title on this new worksheet and format the worksheet so that it is easy to read.

Table 2.11: Five highest and lowest values for binding tests

	Top 5 (Highest)		Bottom 5 (Lowest)	
	Pressure	Temperature	Pressure	Temperature
1				
2				
3				
4				
5				

7. Write a formula to calculate the highest pressure value so that it will be automatically updated if the binding data is later revised. Write the formula so that it can be copied down the column to determine the second highest pressure, the third highest pressure, and so on, and across the row to determine the highest temperature.

8. Write a formula to calculate the lowest pressure value so that it will be automatically updated if the binding data is later revised. Write the formula so that it can be copied down the column to determine the second lowest pressure, the third lowest pressure, and so on, and across the row to determine the lowest temperature value.

9. Save and close the QC Binding Data Analysis 2.xlsx workbook.

LEVEL 3

Extending the Analysis with What-If, Goal Seek, and Simulation

Evaluating a Larger Data Set

In the next phase of her cost-benefit analysis, Joanna needs to examine the costs of inspecting each ski and then total these values to determine the total inspection costs. Joanna also wants to calculate these values by ski style to determine if there is a significant variable in the inspection cost per style of ski. Once the QC costs are better understood, Joanna can begin to compare the costs of doing a 100% inspection of the skis versus the cost of just paying the additional charges associated with replacing skis that fail. This, of course, does not take into account factors that can affect sales, such as customer satisfaction or the liability risk involved if ski failure results in personal injury or property damage. However, TheZone's management is responsible for weighing all of the costs, benefits, and risks; Joanna's job is simply to quantify these costs.

The majority of the cost involved in ski quality testing is the cost of labor. The quality inspectors earn approximately $35 per hour, on average. To quantify the time it takes to inspect a ski, the QC group has been asked to keep a record of each test for each ski tested. To make the analysis more meaningful, the QC group has expanded the data set to include 100 different skis. The time data for these 100 skis has been entered in a new worksheet named Time, as shown in Figure 2.25. This worksheet lists the Mfg ID# of the ski, the ski style, and the time it took to perform each of the two quality tests (Friction Coefficient and Torsion Strength) for each individual ski.

Figure 2.25: Time worksheet

	A	B	C	D	E	F
1	Time Data for Quality Control Testing - Per Ski					
2			Actual Time in Minutes			
3	Mfg ID#	Style	Friction Coefficient Testing	Torsion Strength Testing		
4	2345	R	1.0	1.5		
5	2346	R	1.0	1.0		
6	2347	R	1.0	3.0		
7	2348	R	2.0	5.0		
8	2349	R	1.0	1.5		
9	2350	R	1.5	5.0		
10	2351	R				
11	2352	E	2.5	3.5		
12	2353	R	1.0	4.0		
13	2354	E	2.0	1.0		
14	2355	R	1.5	1.5		
15	2356	A	1.0	7.0		
16	2357	R	2.0	3.5		
17	2358	E	1.0	4.5		
18	2359	A	3.0	2.0		
19	2360	A	3.5	3.0		
20	2361	R	2.0	4.5		
21	2362	A	1.0	1.0		
22	2363	A	1.5	6.0		
23	2364	R	1.0	4.5		
24	2365	E	2.0	4.5		
25	2366	R	1.0	1.0		
26	2367	A	1.0	1.5		
27	2368	A	1.0	7.5		
28	2369	A	1.0	3.0		
29	2370	E	1.0	5.0		
30	2371	A	2.0	6.5		
31	2372	E	1.5	6.0		

Joanna needs to use this data to calculate the costs to quality test a ski. To accomplish this task, she can add the number of minutes spent to test a particular ski and then apply those total minutes to the cost per hour of an inspector. In theory, this should be the sum of total minutes to inspect a ski divided by the number of minutes per hour times the dollars per hour ($/hr) of labor for the inspector:

```
SUM(minutes to inspect)/minutes per hour*$ per hour of labor
```

To calculate the cost of testing the first ski, Joanna can write the formula =SUM(C4:D4)/60*35 in cell E4. Notice the use of two constants in this formula, 60 and 35. In general, when designing a worksheet, it is important to separately list inputs, especially inputs that are likely to change or that you might want to explore with "what-if" scenarios. Because 60 (the number of minutes per hour) will not change, it can remain as a constant in the formula. The $35 hourly labor rate, however, is a number that Joanna might want to vary and, therefore, should be listed elsewhere.

If a worksheet contains a large number of data inputs, it is often best to place these inputs on a separate worksheet or in a separate area on the same worksheet. In this case, there is only one data input ($35 hourly labor rate) and it is used in a single calculation. An easy solution might be to simply list the value in a worksheet cell such as cell E2, above the Total Cost to Inspect label. However, the value $35 on its own might not convey what it represents; on the other hand, if Joanna types in the text "$35/hr-labor," the cell value cannot be used as part of the calculation for the cost per hour. One solution is to alter the format of the cell without altering the value by creating a custom number format. This formatting change will allow Joanna to write the formula =SUM(C4:D4)/60*E2 in cell E4 to calculate the Total Cost to Inspect the corresponding ski.

Specifying a Custom Number Format

The Format Cells dialog box, which can be opened from the Number group dialog box launcher on the Home tab, provides many options for changing the display of cell values. The Number tab in this dialog box lists all the available number formats in Excel and also provides an option for creating a custom number format. Here, Joanna wants to enter the more descriptive value "$35.00/hr-labor" in cell E2, but also use just the number 35 from this cell in the formula she needs to write.

Joanna uses the Format Cells dialog box to specify the custom number format $0.00"/hr-labor" for cell E2 and then enters the value 35 in the cell. Now she can write the formula to calculate the costs to quality test a ski. Because Joanna does not want the cost of labor to change when she copies the formula down the column into cells E4 through E103, she needs to make the row reference for the hourly rate an absolute reference. The format of the formula is as follows:

```
=SUM(C4:D4)/60*E$2
```

How To

Apply Custom Number Formats to Cells

1. Select the cell or cells you want to format.

2. Click the Number group dialog box launcher on the Home tab on the Ribbon to open the Format Cells dialog box. The dialog box opens with the Number tab displayed.

3. In the Category list, click Custom.

4. In the Type box, enter the appropriate formatting, using quotation marks to enclose text as in the following example: $0.00"/hr-labor". See Figure 2.26.

Figure 2.26: Format Cells dialog box with Custom formatting selected

5. Click the OK button when you have finished specifying the custom format.

Joanna enters the formula in cell E4, copies it down the column through cell E103, and applies appropriate formatting. Figure 2.27 shows the resulting worksheet.

Understanding Custom Formatting Codes

As shown in Figure 2.27, there are no values in cells C10 and D10. For some reason, this ski was not inspected for either test, even though it appears on the QC list. Notice that a dash (-) appears instead of the value $0 for the cost to inspect in cell E10. The current format of cell E10 uses the Comma Style, which by default represents values of 0 as a dash. Although this has no effect on any subsequent formulas, Joanna prefers to display a 0 in this cell for clarity. To do so, she again needs to specify a custom number format.

Figure 2.27: Worksheet with custom number formatting applied

	A	B	C	D	E	F
E4				f_x =SUM(C4:D4)/60*E$2		
1	Time Data for Quality Control Testing - Per Ski					
2			Actual Time in Minutes		$35.00/hr-labor	
3	Mfg ID#	Style	Friction Coefficient Testing	Torsion Strength Testing	Total Cost to Inspect	
4	2345	R	1.0	1.5	$ 1.46	
5	2346	R	1.0	1.0	1.17	
6	2347	R	1.0	3.0	2.33	
7	2348	R	2.0	5.0	4.08	
8	2349	R	1.0	1.5	1.46	
9	2350	R	1.5	5.0	3.79	
10	2351	R			-	
11	2352	E	2.5	3.5	3.50	
12	2353	R	1.0	4.0	2.92	
13	2354	E	2.0	1.0	1.75	
14	2355	R	1.5	1.5	1.75	
15	2356	A	1.0	7.0	4.67	
16	2357	R	2.0	3.5	3.21	
17	2358	E	1.0	4.5	3.21	
18	2359	A	3.0	2.0	2.92	
19	2360	A	3.5	3.0	3.79	
20	2361	R	2.0	4.5	3.79	
21	2362	A	1.0	1.0	1.17	

Custom formatting in this cell allows the number value to be displayed with text

Formula to calculate the cost of testing skis

Dash is displayed instead of the value $0

To learn more about how custom formats work, Joanna clicks cell E10, opens the Format Cells dialog box, and selects the Custom category. The Type box displays following code:

```
_(* #,##0.00_);_(* (#,##0.00);_(* "-"??_);_(@_)
```

This is the format code currently in place for cell E10; the format is the Comma Style. A format code can include up to four parts, each separated by a semicolon, as follows: Positive number format; Negative number format; Zero value format; Additional text format.

These formats consist of combinations of symbols, such as underscores, question marks, pound signs, asterisks, and so on. Each symbol has a specific meaning that Excel translates into a specific format. Table 2.12 lists some of the common number formatting codes. Some codes display digits that are significant, and others display digits regardless of whether they are significant. Some codes are simply placeholders. An insignificant digit refers to a 0 that does not change the value of the number. For example, in the number 2.030, the 0 at the end of the number is insignificant because 2.03 is the same as 2.030. However, the 0 in the tenths place is significant because eliminating it would change the value.

As stated earlier, up to four different formats can be applied to a cell: one for positive numbers, one for negative numbers, one for zero values, and one for text. Each format must be separated by a semicolon. If you specify only two formats, the first is used for positive numbers and zeros, and the second is used for negative numbers. If you specify only one format, it is used for all numbers. Figure 2.28 illustrates the format code for cell E10 in the Time worksheet.

Table 2.12: Examples of number formatting codes

Symbol	Usage	Typed Digits	Display
#	Acts as a digit placeholder that displays significant digits Example: ####.#	12.87 03.00	12.9 3.
0	Acts as a digit placeholder that displays both significant and insignificant zeros Example: 0.00	.358 245	0.36 245.00
?	Acts as a digit placeholder that does not display insignificant digits but does hold a place so that decimal points will align Example: 0.00?	27.3 5.132	27.30 5.132
%	Inserts a percentage sign and automatically multiplies the value inserted by 100 for display Example: #%	.3	30%
,	Inserts a comma as a thousands separator or as a scaling operator Example as separator: #,### Example as scaling operator: ##,,	12000000 12000000	12,000,000 12
*	Indicates repetition of the following character enough times to fill the column to its complete width Example: $* 00.00 (note that the * is followed by a blank space)	1250	$ 1250.00
_	Indicates to skip the width of the next character; frequently used with ( ) to make sure positive numbers align with negative numbers displayed with ( ) Example used for positive number: _($* #,###_) Example used to align with negative number: ($* #,###)	1250 −1250	$ 1,250 ($ 1,250)
" "	Specifies that text enclosed in quotation marks should be inserted as shown Example: 00.00 "$/hr"	43.333	43.33 $/hr
@	Indicates the location where text should be inserted in cells formatted with a custom format; if the @ is not included in the code, the text will not be displayed Example: $@	None	$None

Figure 2.28: Custom number formatting codes

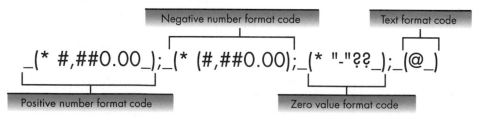

Notice that four sections are defined, so positive, negative, zero, and text values each have their own format. The positive value is defined as _(* #,##0.00_). The first underscore with an opening parenthesis mark indicates a placeholder so that all positive values contain a space on the left side of the cell equal to the width of an opening parenthesis mark. Next is the asterisk (*) followed by a space, indicating to fill the cell with blank spaces in this location after all of the digits have been displayed; this also ensures that values will align on the decimal point. The #,##0.00 placeholders specify that a minimum of the ones, tenths, and hundredths digits be shown and commas be displayed for thousands. At the end, another space is reserved equivalent to the width of a closing parenthesis mark. In a similar manner, the negative value format can be analyzed. Here, parentheses are used to enclose the value. The text format following the last semicolon shows that text will appear if typed into the cell. Again, blank spaces before and after the text in the width of the parentheses characters are indicated.

Joanna wants to change the format of the zero value display. This is the code following the second semicolon. She wants to modify the display from the standard Comma Style so that zero values will display the digit 0 rather than a dash. To edit the format code, Joanna simply replaces the dash with a 0 in the Type box. To align the 0 to the right, she also removes the two question marks that follow and clicks the OK button in the Format Cells dialog box to apply this format. This format can be copied using the Format Painter tool.

Considering Alternatives: What-If Analysis and Goal Seek

With cell E2 properly formatted to display the value 35 with the text "$/hr-labor," Joanna is now ready to do a few simple calculations to determine the total and average minutes for each test and the total and average costs to inspect the skis. She has also decided to calculate the standard deviation of the data to get an idea of its variability. To do this, she enters the following formulas in the cells indicated and copies them into columns D and E:

- C105: =SUM(C4:C103)
- C106: =AVERAGE(C4:C103)
- C107: =STDEV.S(C4:C103)

Figure 2.29 shows the resulting worksheet. Note that the panes are frozen in the worksheet so that the column titles and the statistics calculated can be viewed simultaneously, column widths are adjusted to accommodate text, and appropriate formatting has been applied.

The total cost to inspect the skis is $277.67, as shown in cell E105. The average minutes and standard deviation of minutes to inspect a ski for each test type are calculated in cells C106:D107. The results indicate a significant variance in the time it takes to inspect a ski, both for the Friction Coefficient test and Torsion Strength test. Such results make it hard to predict how long it will take to inspect a given ski. The average total time (cells C106 plus D106) is approximately 4.8 minutes of an inspector's time, who currently makes approximately $35 per hour. The overall costs ($2.78 per ski on average) can now be used as a benchmark of 100% inspection. At a later time, management might choose to look

Figure 2.29: Calculating statistics for quality test times and costs

	A	B	C	D	E	F
1	*Time Data for Quality Control Testing - Per Ski*					
2			Actual Time in Minutes		$35.00/hr-labor	
3	Mfg ID#	Style	Friction Coefficient Testing	Torsion Strength Testing	Total Cost to Inspect	
96	2437	R	1.5	1.0	1.46	
97	2438	R	1.5	1.0	1.46	
98	2439	A	1.0	5.5	3.79	
99	2440	R	1.0	5.0	3.50	
100	2441	R	1.0	2.0	1.75	
101	2442	A	3.5	5.0	4.96	
102	2443	E	1.0	4.0	2.92	
103	2444	A	1.5	1.0	1.46	
104						
105	Total:		154.5	321.5	$ 277.67	
106	Average:		1.6	3.2	2.78	
107	Std. Deviation:		0.7	1.9	1.23	
108						
109						

Calculations done for labor costs of $35/hour

Total cost to inspect skis

=AVERAGE(C4:C103)

=SUM(C4:C103)   =STDEV.S(C4:C103)

into methods of reducing these costs through different testing techniques and/or improved efficiency.

Performing What-If Analysis

So, what if, after all this work, Joanna finds out that the average labor rate for a quality control inspector is $45 per hour rather than $35 per hour? Would she need to recalculate the total cost to inspect each item and then again perform the summary calculations? Or, what if item #2444 was erroneously listed as requiring 1 minute for the Torsion Strength test, but it actually took 10 minutes? Would she need to recalculate all of the totals, averages, and standard deviations?

Because Joanna planned the worksheet well, updating a single cell is all that she would need to do in each of these "what-if" scenarios. Performing a **what-if analysis** means, simply, to determine the outcome of changing one or more input values and evaluate the recalculated results. In the first what-if analysis, Joanna can easily substitute the value $45 for the value $35 in cell E2 to determine the impact of a higher labor rate. All of the other values are calculated from formulas that ultimately refer back to this value, as shown in Figure 2.30. In the second what-if analysis, Joanna can simply change the Torsion Strength test time of item #2444 to 10 in cell D103. Because each of the SUM, AVERAGE, and STDEV.S formulas reference the range containing this value, these calculations will automatically update. You will explore more sophisticated techniques of varying inputs in later chapters.

Figure 2.30: Performing a what-if analysis using $45/hour for labor

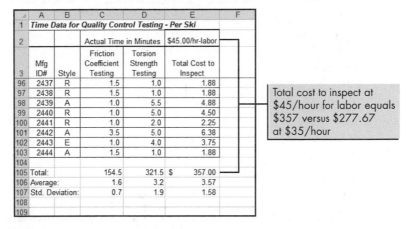

2

Level 3

Using the Goal Seek Tool to Work Backward

What if Joanna wants to change an input value in order to reach a *specified output?* For example, what would the labor rate have to be for the cost of inspection to be $225 instead of the original $277.67? One possible way to solve this is to keep trying various values for labor rate, narrowing it down until the answer is reached. However, Excel provides a tool called **Goal Seek** that enables you to accomplish this automatically. When using Goal Seek, you can specify the outcome you want and which input value you want to vary, and Excel automatically calculates the solution.

To use the Goal Seek tool, Joanna needs to select the What-If Analysis button found in the Data Tools group on the Data tab on the Ribbon. The Goal Seek dialog box is shown in Figure 2.31.

Figure 2.31: Goal Seek dialog box

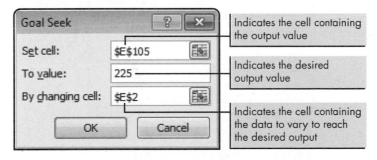

In this dialog box, you use the Set cell box to specify the cell in which the output value will appear. In the To value box, you enter the value you want to achieve as the output value—in other words, the goal you are seeking. In the By changing cell box, you specify the cell containing the dependent data that you want to vary to achieve the desired output, or goal.

How To

Use the Goal Seek Tool

1. Click the Data tab on the Ribbon.

2. Click the What-If Analysis button in the Data Tools group to display the menu. Select Goal Seek to open the Goal Seek dialog box.

3. In the Set cell box, enter the cell reference where the output value will appear.

4. In the To value box, enter the desired outcome value.

5. In the By changing cell box, enter the cell reference of the input you want to vary.

6. Click the OK button to close the Goal Seek dialog box and open the Goal Seek Status dialog box, which displays your target value. If the target value cannot be reached exactly, the closest value found will be listed as the current value.

7. Click the OK button to update the worksheet with these new values, or click the Cancel button to maintain the original values in the worksheet.

For Joanna's analysis, she opens the Goal Seek dialog box and specifies the following (as shown in Figure 2.31):

- Set cell: E105 (the cell containing the total cost to inspect). Note that Excel automatically adds the absolute cell referencing.
- To value: 225 (the total inspection cost that Joanna wants to achieve).
- By changing cell: E2 (the cell containing the hourly labor rate). Note that Excel automatically adds the absolute cell referencing.

When Joanna clicks the OK button in the Goal Seek dialog box, the Goal Seek Status dialog box opens, as shown in Figure 2.32.

Figure 2.32: Goal Seek Status dialog box

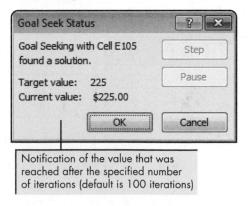

The Goal Seek Status dialog box gives the target value. If the target value cannot be reached exactly, the closest value found is listed as the current value. In this case, the target value of 225 can be reached exactly. Joanna clicks the OK button to update the worksheet, substituting these new values, as shown in Figure 2.33.

Figure 2.33: Worksheet with values updated based on the Goal Seek results

	A	B	C	D	E	F
1	Time Data for Quality Control Testing - Per Ski					
2			Actual Time in Minutes		$28.36/hr-labor	
3	Mfg ID#	Style	Friction Coefficient Testing	Torsion Strength Testing	Total Cost to Inspect	
96	2437	R	1.5	1.0	1.18	
97	2438	R	1.5	1.0	1.18	
98	2439	A	1.0	5.5	3.07	
99	2440	R	1.0	5.0	2.84	
100	2441	R	1.0	2.0	1.42	
101	2442	A	3.5	5.0	4.02	
102	2443	E	1.0	4.0	2.36	
103	2444	A	1.5	1.0	1.18	
104						
105	Total:		154.5	321.5	$ 225.00	
106	Average:		1.6	3.2	2.25	
107	Std. Deviation:		0.7	1.9	0.99	
108						
109						

Goal Seek updated the labor rate to $28.36 from $35 to attain a total labor cost of $225

By using the Goal Seek tool, Excel has calculated that a labor rate of $28.36/hr results in a total cost to inspect of $225.00.

Best Practice

Testing Values with Goal Seek

The Goal Seek Status dialog box gives the target value when you use the Goal Seek tool. At this point in the process, you can click the OK button to update your worksheet with the new values based on the Goal Seek results, or you can click the Cancel button to maintain the original values. Sometimes it's a good idea to keep both the original values and the values resulting from using Goal Seek, so that you can test various values before achieving the solution you want, while keeping your original data intact. This might be especially important if your original data is fairly complex. To do so, simply save your original workbook and then, after completing the Goal Seek, save it again with a different filename.

Goal Seek uses an iterative approach to finding the right input that achieves the desired result, or goal, in the dependent cell. Excel keeps changing values in the changing cell until it reaches the solution or finds the closest value it can. Goal Seek continues to enter values until it reaches a value that is within 0.001 of the goal or 100 iterations. You can change these defaults by modifying the workbook calculation options as follows: click the File tab and then select the Options command in the navigation bar to open the Excel Options dialog box. Select the Formulas category in the listing on the left. Click the Enable iterative calculation check box in the Calculation options section, as shown in Figure 2.34.

In cases where numerous iterations are needed to find a solution, the Goal Seek Status dialog box continually updates as values are tested. To pause this process, click the Pause button. The Step button allows you to step through each iteration one step at a time.

Figure 2.34: Modifying iterations options

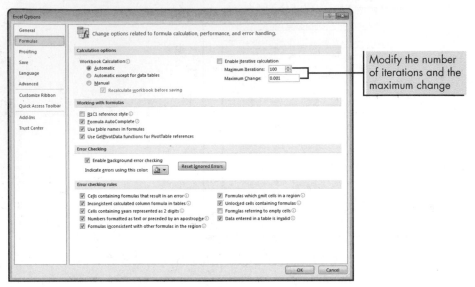

As you can see, the Goal Seek tool enables you to explore this type of "reverse" what-if analysis quickly and easily. Although Goal Seek is simple to use, it does have limitations:

- Goal Seek allows you to vary only a single input. For example, Joanna could vary the labor rate or vary the number of minutes it takes to perform a single test for a single ski, but not both simultaneously.
- The input cannot be a value derived from a formula; it must be a constant value, such as 10, 100, and so on. In Joanna's case, the labor cost is in cell E2. This cell cannot contain a formula such as =30+5; it must contain the value 35. Otherwise, the warning "The cell must contain a value" will be displayed.

Combining COUNTIF and AVERAGEIF to Analyze Data in Specific Categories

In addition to providing the number of minutes it takes to perform each test for each ski, the Time worksheet also includes information about the ski style (column B). Joanna wants to know whether the average times for each test vary based on the ski style. To determine this, Joanna needs to calculate the average times for each test by ski style.

Joanna has set up a new worksheet named SkiType to use in conjunction with the original Time worksheet, which contains the data provided by the QC group. In the SkiType worksheet, Joanna has set up a table with ski type categories listed as individual rows and the following data headings as individual columns: Quantity of Skis Tested, Average Friction Test Time, Average Torsion Test Time, and Average Cost.

In cell SkiType!B3, shown in Figure 2.35, Joanna calculates the total number of items tested by style using the following formula:

=COUNTIF(Time!B$4:B$103,A3)

Figure 2.35: Calculating values by category

	A	B	C	D	E	F
1	Time Data for Quality Control Testing - Per Ski					
2			Actual Time in Minutes		$35.00/hr-labor	
3	Mfg ID#	Style	Friction Coefficient Testing	Torsion Strength Testing	Total Cost to Inspect	
96	2437	R	1.5	1.0	1.46	
97	2438	R	1.5	1.0	1.46	
98	2439	A	1.0	5.5	3.79	
99	2440	R	1.0	5.0	3.50	
100	2441	R	1.0	2.0	1.75	
101	2442	A	3.5	5.0	4.96	
102	2443	E	1.0	4.0	2.92	
103	2444	A	1.5	1.0	1.46	
104						
105	Total:		154.5	321.5	$ 277.67	
106	Average:		1.6	3.2	2.78	
107	Std. Deviation:		0.7	1.9	1.23	
108						

Time worksheet

=COUNTIF(Time!B$4:B$103,A3)

	A	B	C	D	E	F
1		Summary - By Ski Type				
2	Style	Quantity of Skis Tested	Average Friction Test Time	Average Torsion Test Time	Average Cost	
3	A	27	2.04	4.02	$ 3.53	
4	E	21	1.60	3.83	3.17	
5	R	52	1.29	2.60	2.23	
6						
7						

SkiType worksheet

=AVERAGEIF(Time!$B$4:$B$103,$A3,Time!C$4:C$103)

In this COUNTIF function, the criteria range is the cell range B4:B103 on the Time worksheet; this range contains the ski style information. Because this range remains constant regardless of which style is being counted—style A, E, or R—the range rows are absolute. This formula will be copied down the column, but not across rows, so only the row references need to be absolute. The criterion used is the ski style being counted, as specified in cell A3 of the SkiType worksheet. By using the cell reference A3, which contains the value "A" for ski style A, the criteria will vary when the formula is copied down the column into rows 4 and 5. Note that the sheet name is not required in the A3 cell reference because this cell is on the same worksheet as the active cell where the formula is being entered.

Columns C through E on the SkiType worksheet contain the averages for each of the test times and for the cost. To calculate the average test time for ski style A, Excel provides the **AVERAGEIF function**, designed to average a set of values if a specified criterion is met.

This function is very similar to the SUMIF function, requiring the same three arguments: the range where the criteria are evaluated, the selection criteria, and the range of values in this case to average. The AVERAGEIF function ignores cells where either the criteria or the value to be averaged is blank, giving a different result than simply dividing a SUMIF by a COUNTIF. For additional details on the usage and rules of the AVERAGEIF function, use the Excel Help feature. The syntax for AVERAGEIF function is as follows:

```
AVERAGEIF(range,criteria,average_range)
```

Starting in cell C3, Joanna averages all the friction test times for style A using the AVERAGEIF function:

```
=AVERAGEIF(Time!$B$4:$B$103,$A3,Time!C$4:C$103)
```

Notice the relative and absolute cell referencing used in this formula:

- The range containing the criteria for the AVERAGEIF function remains the same whether the formula is copied down the column or across the row. Column B on the Time worksheet is always used to find the criteria and therefore must be referenced absolutely in terms of both rows and columns (Time!$B$4:$B$103).
- The criteria argument of the AVERAGEIF function (the ski style) changes as the formula is copied down the column, but remains the same when copied across the row for each corresponding test and the total cost. So the column of the criteria argument must be referenced absolutely ($A3).
- The average_range argument of the AVERAGEIF function does not change when copied down the column as the styles change, but it does change when copied across the row to calculate each test and then the total cost. If values are being summed for either the friction test or the torsion test, the rows of the range containing the data will remain the same, whereas the columns will vary depending on the values being summed. To indicate this, the rows of the range must be absolute (Time!C$4:C$103).

Note that the AVERAGEIF function is not compatible with some earlier versions of Excel.

Based on the information Joanna has derived from the data, there are indeed significant time and cost differences associated with each of the different ski styles, as shown in the SkiType worksheet. For example, Style A costs roughly 58% more to test than Style R. The reason for this is not immediately obvious to Joanna, but will be an important factor to explore further if management decides to reevaluate the quality tests.

Best Practice

Viewing Multiple Worksheets Simultaneously

When writing formulas that require cell references to values on multiple worksheets, you often may find it helpful to have all of these worksheets displayed simultaneously. You can open multiple worksheets and resize them in the Excel window for easy viewing and referencing as follows:

1. Assuming the current worksheet is maximized in the Excel window, click the Restore Window button. Note that there are two similar icons like this in the upper-right corner of the Excel window. The top button sizes the Excel program window; the one below it sizes the worksheet window. Be sure to click the button that resizes the worksheet window.

2. Once the worksheet is no longer maximized, move the pointer to one of the corners or sides of the window to activate a resizing handle. Resize the worksheet so that there is enough space to view the needed data, keeping in mind additional room in the Excel window is needed to open additional worksheets.

3. As needed, click the top of this window in the gray area above the column headers to drag the window to a desired location—for example, upper left or lower right, depending on the window shape.

4. Open a new worksheet window by clicking New Window button located in the Window group on the View tab on the Ribbon.

5. In this newly opened worksheet window, click the sheet tab for the next sheet you want to display. Once it is visible, repeat Steps 2 and 3 to resize this window and drag it to a convenient location in the Excel window.

6. Open additional windows as needed by repeating Steps 4 and 5. You can close each window by clicking its Close button.

Figure 2.36 shows an example of two windows open simultaneously.

Figure 2.36: Displaying multiple worksheets in the Excel window

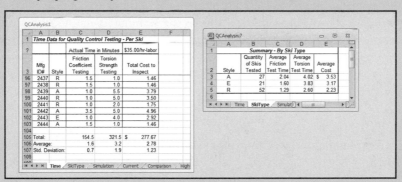

Once the desired worksheets are visible, you can begin typing a formula into the active cell and then click any cell on either the active worksheet or another visible worksheet to include that cell reference in the formula. Cells on worksheets other than the active worksheet will be preceded by their sheet name. As long as you do not click on a worksheet tab, cells on the active worksheet will not be preceded by a worksheet name.

Analyzing Data Through Simulation

Joanna knows the cost of 100% quality testing of skis ($277.67) and now wants to compare this to the option of not doing 100% quality testing. The actual defective ski cost does not change whether the defect is found at QC testing or by a customer, but an additional cost of shipping and handling is incurred if the ski actually goes to a customer and needs to be returned. Again, these costs do not take into account customer satisfaction or liability. Also, remember that the costs of producing 100% defective-free skis might be too prohibitive; it is management's job to balance the risks the company is willing to incur versus the costs.

Joanna needs to determine the costs of not inspecting, specifically the costs of handling and returning the defective ski and getting a new ski to the customer. At this point, Joanna knows that replacement costs vary between $25 and $200, depending on the area of the country, and that the expected failure rates for all ski types is between 3% and 5%. She could just take the average replacement cost and multiply that by the average failure rate times the number of skis. For the number of skis, Joanna will use 100 to match the QC test costs previously calculated when she first started working with the larger data set of 100 skis. The average cost of not testing 100 skis would, therefore, be =(.03+.05)/2*(25+200)/2*100, which results in 450. To calculate the cost by ski type, Joanna can divide this value by 3 because there are three different ski styles. The average cost of not inspecting according to this calculation is about $450, which is more than the total cost of inspecting the skis, $277.67. But, as demonstrated earlier, the average value doesn't necessarily tell the whole story.

Another possible method of determining the costs involved in returning defective skis is to simulate these costs on a worksheet model. **Simulation** is an analytical method that creates artificially generated data to imitate real data. The advantage of a simulation is that it can be easily calculated and recalculated to show some of the different possible outcomes as opposed to the most probable outcome or even the extreme limits. A simulation that is based on randomly generating specific values that have an equal chance of appearing, such as numbers on a set of dice, is often referred to as a "Monte Carlo" simulation. Joanna will use a similar technique to generate the number of defective skis that might be returned and the costs to return them. More sophisticated simulation techniques are covered in a later chapter.

Joanna begins her simulation by setting up a worksheet named Simulation, as shown in Figure 2.37.

First, in column A, Joanna will randomly assign a ski style to each of 100 rows to obtain a sample size similar to the one provided by the QC group, where 1 represents ski style A, 2 represents ski style E, and 3 represents ski style R. In column B, she will calculate a random value for the return costs varying between $25 and $200. In column C, she will calculate the probability that this ski will be defective. Joanna has been directed to use a failure rate

Figure 2.37: Simulation worksheet

	A	B	C	D	E	F	G	H	I
1	Ski Return Cost Simulation					Costs for 100 Skis			
2	Style	Return Costs	Probability of Failure	Probable Cost				Average Cost of Returned Skis	
3								$ 450.00	
4							Style	Simulated Probable Costs	
5							1 A	$ -	
6							2 E	$ -	
7							3 R	$ -	
8								$ -	
9									
10									

Data area for simulation   Summary area

varying randomly from 3% to 5%. The probable cost of a ski being returned can be calculated as this failure rate times the cost of returning the ski (column D). The costs will then be aggregated by type and in total in the area set up in cells F1:H8. Note that the calculation for the average costs of returning defective skis for a group size of 100 has been placed in cell H3.

Randomly Assigning a Number Between Two Values Using the RANDBETWEEN Function

Skis are always of style A, E, or R, as represented by 1, 2, or 3, respectively. To randomly assign one of these values to a cell, you can use a **RANDBETWEEN function**, which randomly assigns a number between two specified values. The syntax of the function is as follows:

RANDBETWEEN(bottom,top)

This function randomly returns an *integer* between the top and bottom values, including the values listed. So the formula =RANDBETWEEN(1,3) randomly returns a 1, 2, or 3. This formula can then be copied down column A of the Simulation worksheet to generate 100 random occurrences of the values 1, 2, and 3.

Note that the RANDBETWEEN function is automatically provided with Excel 2010 and 2007, but not with earlier versions. It can be accessed in Excel 2003 by loading the Analysis ToolPak.

Assigning a Random Value Using the RAND Function

Now, Joanna needs to estimate the cost of a returned ski as a random value between $25 and $200. Because this value does not need to be an integer, she can use another function to create a value. The **RAND function** returns a random value between 0 and 1. The syntax for this function is RAND( ). Notice that it has no arguments, but the syntax requires that the parentheses be included when using the function. To arrive at a value between 25 and 200, Joanna could do the following:

- Start with the minimum value of 25.
- Calculate a random value between 0 and 175 because 175 is the difference between the minimum and maximum value (200–25). If the RAND function gives a random number between 0 and 1, then multiplying RAND() by 175 should give a random number between 0 and 175.
- Add the minimum value of 25 to this random value.
- The resulting formula is =RAND()*175+25.

Joanna writes this formula in cell B3 of the Simulation worksheet and copies it down the column to generate a total of 100 random values between 25 and 200.

In a similar way, Joanna can estimate the probability of failure. To accomplish this, she can again start with the minimum value (3%) and then randomly generate a value from 0 to the difference between the lowest and highest limits, in this case 2% (5%–3%). To randomly calculate a value between 0 and .02, she could simply multiply the random value (a number between 0 and 1) by .02. The resulting formula is =0.03+RAND()*0.02. Joanna enters this formula in cell C3 of the Simulation worksheet and copies it down the column to generate a total of 100 random values between .03 and .05.

Calculating Probable Costs Using a ROUND Function

After each component value has been simulated, Joanna can combine them to arrive at a probable cost. Return cost times the probability of failure results in the expected failure cost for each item. Joanna enters the formula =ROUND(B3*C3,2) in cell D3 and copies it down the column. Including a ROUND function here allows Joanna to arrive at a specified number of dollars and cents. It is best to round off these values after all of the random values have been calculated and combined to minimize the effect of rounding errors. Figure 2.38 illustrates the use of these formulas in Joanna's Simulation worksheet.

The final component of the worksheet is the calculation that totals the simulated probable costs for this 100 ski sample by adding up the values in column D. Joanna has done this by ski style and in total, as shown in cells H5:H7. To total by ski style, she used the formula =SUMIF(A$3:A$102,F5,D$3:D$102) in cell H5 and copied it into cells H6 and H7. Cell H8 contains the formula =SUM(H5:H7).

When working with the RAND and RANDBETWEEN functions, an interesting result occurs. Every time you enter another value or formula in a cell anywhere on the worksheet, the random values automatically change. This is because every time a value or formula is entered in a cell, the entire worksheet is recalculated, including these random value functions, thereby generating new random values. Automatic calculation can be turned off from the Ribbon or from the Excel Options dialog box accessed via the File tab.

2

Level 3

Figure 2.38: Simulated data and summary of ski return costs

	A	B	C	D	E	F	G	H	I
1	*Ski Return Cost Simulation*					*Costs for 100 Skis*			
2	Style	Return Costs	Probability of Failure	Probable Cost				*Average Cost of Returned Skis*	
3	3	90.26344	0.04595703	$ 4.15				$ 450.00	
4	1	105.5341	0.03790161	4.00			Style	*Simulated Probable Costs*	
5	2	53.1886	0.03407964	1.81		1	A	$ 170.90	
6	3	94.45784	0.03396217	3.21		2	E	$ 148.81	
7	3	198.7256	0.04701945	9.34		3	R	$ 113.10	
8	1	34.9016	0.04656778	1.63				$ 432.81	
9	1	185.7113	0.03417853	6.35					
94	3	38.73424	0.03628785	1.41					
95	1	161.3553	0.04723126	7.62					
96	3	90.20179	0.03695332	3.33					
97	2	178.5758	0.04216753	7.53					
98	2	43.55346	0.03250621	1.42					
99	1	111.7173	0.04329966	4.84					
100	2	38.70431	0.04888751	1.89					
101	1	89.06423	0.04217833	3.76					
102	1	151.3678	0.03285205	4.97					
103									

Values resulting from the simulation   Values in summary

	A	B	C	D	E	F	G	H	I
1	*Ski Return Cost Simulation*					Cost			
2	Style	Return Costs	Probability of Failure	Probable Cost				*Average Cost of Returned Skis*	
3	=RANDBETWEEN(1,3)	=RAND()*175 +25	=0.03+RAND()*0.02	=ROUND(B3*C3,2)				=0.04*(25+200)/2*100	
4	=RANDBETWEEN(1,3)	=RAND()*175 +25	=0.03+RAND()*0.02	=ROUND(B4*C4,2)			Style	*Simulated Probable Costs*	
5	=RANDBETWEEN(1,3)	=RAND()*175 +25	=0.03+RAND()*0.02	=ROUND(B5*C5,2)		1	A	=SUMIF(A$3:A$102,F5,D$3:D$102)	
6	=RANDBETWEEN(1,3)	=RAND()*175 +25	=0.03+RAND()*0.02	=ROUND(B6*C6,2)		2	E	=SUMIF(A$3:A$102,F6,D$3:D$102)	
7	=RANDBETWEEN(1,3)	=RAND()*175 +25	=0.03+RAND()*0.02	=ROUND(B7*C7,2)		3	R	=SUMIF(A$3:A$102,F7,D$3:D$102)	
8	=RANDBETWEEN(1,3)	=RAND()*175 +25	=0.03+RAND()*0.02	=ROUND(B8*C8,2)				=SUM(H5:H7)	
9	=RANDBETWEEN(1,3)	=RAND()*175 +25	=0.03+RAND()*0.02	=ROUND(B9*C9,2)					
10	=RANDBETWEEN(1,3)	=RAND()*175 +25	=0.03+RAND()*0.02	=ROUND(B10*C10,2)					
11	=RANDBETWEEN(1,3)	=RAND()*175 +25	=0.03+RAND()*0.02	=ROUND(B11*C11,2)					
12	=RANDBETWEEN(1,3)	=RAND()*175 +25	=0.03+RAND()*0.02	=ROUND(B12*C12,2)					
13	=RANDBETWEEN(1,3)	=RAND()*175 +25	=0.03+RAND()*0.02	=ROUND(B13*C13,2)					
14	=RANDBETWEEN(1,3)	=RAND()*175 +25	=0.03+RAND()*0.02	=ROUND(B14*C14,2)					
15	=RANDBETWEEN(1,3)	=RAND()*175 +25	=0.03+RAND()*0.02	=ROUND(B15*C15,2)					

Formulas used for simulation   Formulas in summary

How To

Turn Off Automatic Calculation

1. Click the Formulas tab on the Ribbon.

2. Select the Calculation Options button in the Calculation group.

3. Click Manual on the menu to change from Automatic (the default) to Manual calculation.

4. To revert back to Automatic calculation, repeat these steps, this time selecting Automatic. See Figure 2.39.

Figure 2.39: Turning off Automatic calculation

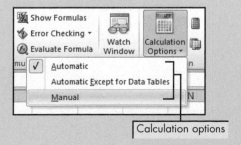

Calculation options

You can recalculate a worksheet at any time by pressing the F9 function key or by selecting the Calculate Now button also found in the Calculation group on the Formulas tab on the Ribbon. Doing so allows you to observe different results obtained by entering different values and then pressing F9. When you press F9, the worksheet is automatically recalculated, altering the values in cells containing the RAND and RANDBETWEEN functions, allowing for the user to simulate new values.

Completing the Cost-Benefit Analysis

Joanna can now complete her cost-benefit analysis comparing the costs of doing 100% quality testing on 100 skis versus allowing the skis to be sold, and having defective skis returned and replaced. The values generated as the cost to return defective skis (skis normally in the $400–$500 range generated by the simulations) are all significantly above the cost of 100% quality testing each ski ($278); so testing each ski is probably not only the right thing to do from the standpoint of customer satisfaction, but also appears to be the most cost-effective process.

After completing her analysis, Joanna now considers the following questions:

- Can the quality testing itself be improved, given the large variance in time between not only ski styles but skis in general?
- Given that the rejection rate is estimated at 3% to 5%, are there cost-effective ways of improving production to reduce this rate?

Joanna plans to raise these questions with management for further study to arrive at the best solution.

Steps To Success: Level 3

Now, you will conduct a cost-benefit analysis to quantify the cost of inspecting the ski bindings versus the additional costs of not inspecting bindings and having skis returned from customers. As with the ski itself, the majority of the inspection cost with bindings is the labor. The average labor rate for the binding inspectors is $38 per hour. Historical data has shown that, on average, 1% to 3% of ski bindings fail. The additional costs incurred if a ski binding fails after purchase are approximately $20 to $75. Based on this information, complete the following:

1. Open the workbook named **Binding3.xlsx** located in the Chapter 2 folder, and then save it as **QC Binding Data Analysis 3.xlsx**. The worksheet named **InspectionCosts** contains two hours of inspection data from the QC inspectors detailing the amount of time spent testing the bindings for each of the two different tests performed: Pressure and Temperature.

2. Calculate the cost to test each ski binding and the total costs for all bindings over this two-hour period. Insert the labor cost per hour above the column heading and display the cell to include "$/hr-labor" following the value, centering it in the cell. If an error message regarding omitting adjacent cells is generated, instruct Excel to ignore this error. (*Hint*: If the error occurs for multiple adjacent cells, highlight all cells and then click on the error message adjacent to the first cell to apply the setting to all cells.) Format the first value using the Accounting Number Format and format the remaining values using the Comma Style. Use similar cell outlining to the adjacent cells.

3. Several rows below the data, calculate the mean, median, and standard deviation of these inspection costs (pressure, temperature) rounded to the nearest cent. Label the rows appropriately. Format these values in Accounting Number Format.

4. On a separate worksheet named **TypeSummary**, summarize these values by binding type (1 to 5), including both a count of the number of bindings inspected of that type and the averages for bindings of that type, as listed in Table 2.13. Be certain to use formulas that will be automatically updated if any of the binding types, values, or cost data is later updated. The formula for average pressure should work when copied down the column to determine pressure for each corresponding binding type, and across the row to determine the average temperature and average costs for each type. Format the table appropriately. Also include a value for the total number of bindings tested and the total cost of all bindings tested.

Table 2.13: Setup for binding cost analysis

Type	#Bindings Tested	Average Pressure	Average Temperature	Average Costs
1				
2				
3				
4				
5				
Total				

5. On a third worksheet named **Simulate**, simulate the cost of not inspecting the bindings for a sample of 100 skis as follows. Use the headings as indicated in Table 2.14 and format the data appropriately.

Table 2.14: Setup for binding simulation

Ski Binding Return Cost Simulation			
Binding Type	Return Costs	Probability of Failure	Probable Cost

- In the first column, simulate a ski binding type assuming bindings are equally likely to be any of the types 1 through 5. (Remember, you want a list of 100 simulated values.)

- In the second column, simulate the return costs based on the historical range given, assuming equal probability of any value within this range.
- In the third column, simulate the probability that this binding will fail, based on the range provided historically. Again, assume equal probability of any value within the range.
- In the fourth column, combine this information to calculate the expected cost of this ski failing, rounded to the nearest cent.

6. In an area adjacent to the simulation calculations, set up a small table summarizing the expected costs by binding type and in total. Recalculate the data five times and record the total cost values obtained in cells below the summary, labeled accordingly. Highlight these values in pink.

7. In a cell below this data, highlighted in yellow, enter text to describe (in a few words) which is the more expensive option for the company—100% inspection of bindings or return of defective bindings—and why.

8. Assume that the labor rates for inspection have decreased to $15 per hour. What is the revised cost to inspect, and will that affect your cost-benefit analysis? Place this value in a cell below your first analysis, and highlight it in light green. Modify the worksheet to contain the original hourly labor rate.

9. Calculate the hourly labor cost that would be needed if total costs of inspection were $100. Record this value in a third cell below the other two analyses, highlighted in light blue. Do not save the worksheet with this value. (*Hint*: To be able to view the new labor rate easily without having to accept the changes, start your analysis from the Inspection Costs worksheet.)

10. Save and close the QC Binding Data Analysis 3.xlsx workbook.

Chapter Summary

In Level 1 of this chapter, you applied problem-solving skills to a variety of data sets, analyzing their statistical values such as mean, mode, median, and standard deviation. Then, using these statistics, you learned how to compare different data sets to assess absolute as well as percentage changes. You also learned how to use the ROUND function to modify the precision of the values in data sets.

Level 2 focused on expanding the analysis to better understand the tail values—the highest and lowest five elements of each data set—and the relative rankings of the values. You learned how to summarize the analyses by counting the number of items that met specific criteria and summing items that met specific criteria. You also learned how to include relational operators and wildcards in functions and formulas.

In Level 3, you learned how to perform a cost-benefit analysis using a larger data set. The level started with an explanation of how to specify a custom number format. Then, you learned about performing what-if analyses and using Goal Seek as ways of considering alternatives for the data set. You saw how to combine the COUNTIF and AVERAGEIF functions to analyze data in categories. Finally, you learned how to analyze data through simulation using the RAND and RANDBETWEEN functions.

Conceptual Review

1. What formula could you write to calculate the mean of the following data set: 2, 5, 4, 3, 1, 2, 7? (Note that a resulting value is not required.)

2. What is the median value of the data set given in Question 1?

3. What is the mode of the data set given in Question 1?

4. The data set given in Question 1 has a standard deviation of 1.58 as compared with another data set that has the same mean but a standard deviation of 2.5. What general differences would you expect to find between the two sets of data?

5. In the chapter, the original labor rate for inspectors was given as $35 per hour. However, due to a contract renegotiation, this value is now $37.50. What algebraic expression could you use to determine the percent increase in labor costs? (Note that a resulting value is not required.)

6. When using the Increase Decimal button on the toolbar, the precise value in the cell is modified. True or False?

7. The formula =ROUND(345.43,0) results in what precise value?

8. Write a formula to round up 63.34% to the nearest percent.

9. What is the symbol for the greater than or equal to relational operator in Excel?

10. What is the symbol for the not equal to relational operator in Excel?

11. Review the following worksheet, and then use the COUNTIF function to write a formula that determines the number of GM cars on this list.

	A	B	C
1	Make	Price	
2	Ford	$ 15,837	
3	GM	$ 12,883	
4	GM	$ 21,210	
5	Ford	$ 27,837	
6	Honda	$ 20,432	
7	Ford	$ 24,552	
8	Toyota	$ 21,553	
9	Lexus	$ 32,412	
10	Nissan	$ 23,134	
11	Total	$ 199,850	
12			
13			

12. Using the worksheet shown in Question 11, write a formula to determine the number of cars that cost less than $20,000.

13. Using the worksheet shown in Question 11, write a formula to determine the total value of all Ford cars.

14. Explain the difference between a "what-if" analysis and Goal Seek by giving an example based on the worksheet shown in Question 11.

15. Using the worksheet shown in Question 11, write a formula to determine the value of the third most expensive car.

16. If each car shown in Question 11 is marked up between $50 and $250 in dollar increments, what function could be used to randomly assign the amount to be added to the car price in this formula?: =B2+ _____

17. The formula =RAND( ) gives what result?

18. What formula could you write to average the values in cells A10 through A20, excluding blank cells, rounded to the nearest 10?

19. Write a formula to determine the average price of only Ford vehicles using the worksheet in Question 11.

20. Write a formula to generate a random integer value between 10 and 20.

Case Problems

Level 1 – Analyzing Sales for Crèmes Ice Cream

Marketing

Judd Hemming is the eastern regional marketing manager for Crèmes Ice Cream. Each quarter, he completes two separate analyses: an analysis comparing ice cream flavor sales volumes from all regional locations with the same quarter sales volumes from the previous year, and an analysis comparing total sales in dollars, including mean, median, mode, and standard deviation, of sales by store.

Sales by Flavor in Gallons

The first analysis, sales by flavor, compares the total quantities sold in gallons. The data collected provides for each flavor the number of pints, gallons, and 10-gallon tubs sold for all stores. Pints and gallons are sold directly to the public, whereas 10-gallon tubs are used for in-store sales of cones, cups, and specialty items such as sundaes and banana splits. To eliminate any impact of pricing changes or special promotions, Judd simply uses the ice cream volumes in gallons to compare sales by flavor. Judd has asked for your help this quarter in completing this analysis. Judd created two workbook files: Creme.xlsx, which contains the current quarter's sales on a worksheet named Flavors, and HCreme.xlsx, which contains the corresponding historical quarterly data for the previous year on a worksheet named HFlavors. For ease of data handling, the flavors in both data sets are in identical order except for two new flavors introduced this year, which appear at the bottom of the current data set. Keep in mind the following conversions when analyzing this data:

- There are 8 pints per gallon.
- Each tub holds 10 gallons.

Also, when calculating values for 10-gallon tubs, Judd has asked you to use the convention of rounding down the values to the nearest whole tub.

Sales by Store in Dollars

The second analysis you need to complete is to summarize sales in dollars by store and compare the result with the previous year's sales. The Stores worksheet in the same workbook contains the individual store sales for the current quarter in dollars rounded to the nearest thousand dollars; this data is for the analysis by store. You need to calculate some basic statistics for store sales. In the same quarter of the previous year, these values were as follows:

- Mean: $8,817
- Median: $8,000
- Mode: $5,500
- Standard Deviation: $6,920

Throughout the steps, when writing formulas, be certain to use the most efficient method, including the use of functions as well as relative and absolute cell referencing.

Complete the following:

1. Open the workbook named **Creme.xlsx** located in the Chapter 2 folder, and then save it as **Creme Current Sales Analysis.xlsx**.

2. On the Flavors worksheet, for the current quarter, calculate for each flavor the total number of gallons sold. Place this calculation in the column adjacent to the data provided. List any conversion values used at the top of the worksheet in a separate area. Remember to round down the tub quantities to the nearest whole tub when completing the calculation.

3. Add another column in which to enter the total number of gallons from last year. Copy the values for the total amount of ice cream sold for the corresponding flavor for last year from the **HCreme.xlsx** workbook, found in the Chapter 2 folder, into a newly added column of the Flavors worksheet.

4. Calculate the overall total and mean number of gallons sold for all flavors for this quarter and for this quarter last year. (Note: Include all flavors in your calculation, whether or not there are sales for them in that given year.)

5. Calculate for each flavor the percent of total gallons this flavor represents compared with total sales for the current quarter of all flavors. Copy this formula to the adjacent column to calculate the percent of total gallons this flavor represents compared with historical total sales.

6. In the two adjacent columns, calculate for each flavor and for the totals the difference and percent difference in sales, assuming a positive value represents an increase in sales. Flavors without sales in the previous year should be left blank (these cells should be completely empty).

TROUBLESHOOTING: In order to complete this step successfully, pay attention to the order of precedence rules when writing the formula. Percent difference is defined as the difference between the new value minus the old value divided by the old value, so specifying the order in which the operations must occur is critical.

7. Switch to the Stores worksheet. Calculate the total sales, mean, median, mode, and standard deviation for this data set. Label the cells so that they can be easily identified.

8. On the same worksheet, set up a table to analyze the change and percent change of each of these statistical values as compared with the historical values given in the problem description. Based on the changes, explain on the worksheet (just below your analysis) whether you feel stores are doing better this year, and if sales in stores are more or less likely to vary from mean sales than they did last year.

9. Based on sales to all stores and total gallons sold for the current quarter, what is the price of a gallon of ice cream on average? Write a formula to determine this value and place it below the statistical analysis on the Stores worksheet.

10. Add appropriate worksheet titles and formatting to make the worksheets easy to read.

11. Save and close the Creme Current Sales Analysis.xlsx workbook.

Level 2 – Analyzing Demographic Data for La Rosa Restaurant

Marketing

You have recently decided to test your entrepreneurial skills by opening a restaurant that you plan to name La Rosa. In your restaurant, you plan to feature specialty desserts, along with fine cuisine. One critical decision you must make is where to locate the restaurant. Right now, you are considering two different locations—one near a large retail area on the fringe of several affluent suburbs (site X), and the other in the downtown district (site Y). Before making the decision, you have hired a local market research firm to provide you with some demographics of the areas and the specific dining habits of the local population that frequent other restaurants in these areas. The raw results of this research have been placed on several worksheets in the LaRosa.xlsx workbook.

Each worksheet (SiteX and SiteY) contains the detailed responses of each of the participants of the study, including questions about their age, their income, and the number of meals and desserts they eat outside of their homes per month.

The market research firm used the following age categories. Respondents were also asked to choose the income level closest to their own from the following list.

Age Categories	Income Levels
18 to 21	$5,000
22 to 25	$10,000
26 to 30	$20,000
31 to 35	$30,000
over 35	$40,000
	$50,000
	$75,000
	$100,000

Complete the following:

1. Open the workbook named **LaRosa.xlsx** located in the Chapter 2 folder, and then save it as **La Rosa Demographic Analysis.xlsx**.

2. On the SiteX and SiteY worksheets, rank each respondent by the number of meals they eat out per month and the number of desserts they eat out per month, respectively— ranking from most meals and desserts out to the least. Freeze the panes of the window on each worksheet to make the category headings at the top visible at all times.

3. On a separate worksheet named **Compare**, display and compare by calculating the difference and percent difference of the mean and standard deviation for the data sets (X and Y) for the number of meals and number of desserts per month obtained. On the same worksheet, set up a table to list the four highest number of desserts per month from each data set (X and Y) and the 10 lowest number of meals eaten out by respondents for each of the data sets (X and Y). Below the data, discuss how these values differ between the data sets and recommend either X or Y for further analysis, highlighted in pink.

4. On a separate worksheet named **Summary**, determine the following for the location you think should be selected:

    • The total number of respondents
    • The total number of respondents with incomes at or above $100,000
    • The total number of respondents who eat fewer than four desserts out each month

- The total number of meals eaten out per month reported by respondents who earn below $50,000
- The total number of desserts per month reported by respondents who are in the 30 to 35 age category or in the 26 to 30 age category

5. Include appropriate titles, labels, and formatting so that the worksheets are easy to read.

6. Save and close the La Rosa Demographic Analysis.xlsx workbook.

Level 3 – Determining Inventory Levels for CKG Auto

Operations Management

Another profitable facet of CKG Auto's business is supplying parts for auto repairs. The most critical component of the parts supply business is having enough of the right parts on hand so that repair shops can receive same-day delivery. The key to profits is minimizing the number of parts that need to be warehoused while also ensuring that sufficient parts are on hand to meet orders. Because each warehouse distribution center serves a different set of customers with different needs, each center must be considered separately. Distribution centers have a five-day lead time for ordering of parts; this must be taken into consideration when determining target inventory levels.

The costs involved in warehousing the parts include the working capital tied up in the inventory itself (the cost of each part) as well as the space to store the part. These costs can be substantial. On the other hand, alternative "generic" parts are often available from rival suppliers, and keeping the auto repair centers supplied and customers satisfied is critical.

One of the most problematic items to supply and store are bearings. This part is both high volume and relatively large, taking up considerable warehousing space. A bearing is also relatively expensive. Analyzing bearing needs is a good place for CKG to start, specifically in one of its largest distribution centers such as Central New Jersey, which serves 10 major customers. You have been asked to analyze the bearing inventory level requirements for this center, including simulating demand levels based on 30-day historical extremes, calculating a target inventory level based on this simulation, and then comparing simulated values to actual values from the past five days from the targeted warehouse.

Complete the following:

1. Open the workbook named **Parts.xlsx** located in the Chapter 2 folder, and then save it as **CKG Parts Analysis.xlsx**.

2. Modify the format of the data on the BearingData worksheet so that zero values are displayed with a 0 instead of the default dash, aligned in the ones column.

3. On the BearingData worksheet, take the existing 30-day data for these bearings for each customer to calculate the high and low limits of the bearing demand by customer.

4. On a new worksheet named **Simulation**, use the high/low limits you just calculated to simulate daily requirements for each customer to obtain a combined daily requirement. Assume that the daily requirements will vary for each customer randomly between the high/low limits you have calculated from the existing 30-day data for that customer. Generate the data for approximately 100 instances, and then copy the results *as values* to another new worksheet in the workbook, keeping the original analysis intact on the Simulation worksheet so that it can be used again later. Name the new worksheet **Simulation Data 1**. Be sure that your worksheets have titles and cell formatting.

5. On the Simulation Data 1 worksheet, in an adjacent column, calculate the total demand by day for all 10 customers. Then use this daily demand total data to calculate the daily mean, mode, median, and standard deviation for the combined requirements of all 10 customers. Use cell shading to clearly identify your calculation area.

6. Extend your analysis (on the same worksheet) to include a ranking of the data (1 to 100) so that the day with the least total demand has a rank of 1. Again use cell shading to clearly identify columns with your calculations.

7. To the right of the data on this same worksheet, create a listing of the top and bottom five daily combined demands from the 100 simulated instances. Clearly identify this listing using borders and shading.

8. Recommend a target inventory level needed for a five-day period based on the following; to be on the cautious side, assume each day's supply will be equal to the average daily demand for all locations combined, plus two standard deviations:

   - Because the mean and standard deviations might not already be integers, round the daily demand up to the nearest whole number.
   - Then, use this calculated daily demand (average plus 2 standard deviations) to calculate demand over a five-day period.

Place this recommendation just below the top/bottom analysis, again clearly identifying it. Add the label **Bearing Recommended** to identify the cell containing the actual value.

9. The warehouse manager has tracked a total of five different parts over the past five days, recording for each shipment the value of the part and the number of days it was in storage. One of these tracked parts is the bearing you have just analyzed. The data has been compiled in a workbook named Demand.xlsx. Each line item represents a single shipment of one item. Copy the data from the **Demand.xlsx** workbook, located in the Chapter 2 folder, to your workbook and place it on a sheet named **Actual Demand**.

10. On the same worksheet, summarize the data to determine the number shipped by part, the total values of those shipments by part, and the average number of days that part was stored, using the format shown in Table 2.15.

Table 2.15: Setup for parts data summary

Item Description	#Items Shipped	Total Dollar Value of Items Shipped	Average #Days Held in Inventory
Bearings			
Timing Belts			
Air Filters			
Fan Belt			
Electronic Board			

In the #Items Shipped column, write the necessary formula to determine the number of bearings shipped. Write the formula so that it can be copied down the column to automatically determine the number of timing belts shipped, the number of air filters shipped, and so on. In the Total Dollar Value of Items Shipped column, write the necessary formula to determine the value of all bearings shipped. Again, write the formula so that it can be copied down the column to automatically determine the value of timing belts, air filters, and so on. In the Average #Days Held in Inventory column, write the necessary formula to determine the average number of days bearings shipped were held in inventory; again, write the formula so that it can be copied down the column. Be certain that these formulas will work even if the data is updated in the future.

11. Based on the recommended inventory level you previously calculated for bearings, would you have had enough bearings in the warehouse to cover these orders? Place your answer in a cell below your analysis on the Actual Demand worksheet. Clearly identify this answer and highlight it in yellow.

12. Double-check all values and formulas for correct implementation. Be certain that you included sufficient formatting and titles to clearly identify the worksheet elements.

13. Save and close the CKG Parts Analysis.xlsx workbook.

SAM: Skills Assessment Manager

For current SAM information, including versions and content details, visit SAM Central (http://samcentral.course.com). If you have a SAM user profile, you may have access to hands-on instruction, practice, and assessment of the skills covered in this chapter. Since various versions of SAM are supported throughout the life of this text, check with your instructor for the correct instructions and URL/Web site for accessing assignments.

2

Chapter Exercises

Determining Effective Data Display with Charts
Marketing: Analyzing Trends in the Sporting Goods Industry

"Information is a source of learning. But unless it is organized, processed, and available to the right people in a format for decision making, it is a burden, not a benefit."
—William Pollard

LEARNING OBJECTIVES

Level 1

Understand the principles of effective data display
Analyze various Excel chart types
Determine appropriate uses for different chart types
Modify the chart type and the chart source data
Specify chart options, including chart and axis titles, legends, and data labels

Level 2

Examine the effectiveness of different chart sub-types
Evaluate the stacked and 100% stacked sub-types
Explore the Pie of Pie and Bar of Pie sub-types
Create various stock charts to display financial data
Clarify data with trendlines and moving averages

Level 3

Understand and evaluate radar, bubble, and dashboard charts
Compare a bubble chart with a 3-D column chart
Explore and customize a dashboard chart
Create and customize a doughnut chart

CHART TYPES COVERED IN THIS CHAPTER

Area	**Pie**
Bubble	**Radar**
Column	**Stock**
Doughnut	**X Y (Scatter)**
Line	

3

Chapter Introduction

This chapter teaches you how to use Microsoft Excel to provide a visual representation of quantitative information, giving the viewer an overall picture of a set of data. In many ways, this view is easier to interpret than large amounts of tabular data. This chapter presents some guiding principles you can follow to create effective graphics of quantitative information. Excel provides many ways to present data visually. The choice of method depends on the data and the goal of the presentation.

The chapter begins with a discussion of data visualization based on the graphic principles laid out by Edward R. Tufte. Sparklines, an innovation created by Tufte, are introduced as an example of these principles. The chapter continues with the basics of creating and modifying line and column charts while discussing how the choice of chart type can influence a viewer's perception of the information presented. Each chart type presents information in different ways that can affect the viewer's interpretation of the data. The chapter covers some basic principles to follow when creating charts and provides examples of how charts can be used in specific situations. Coverage of chart sub-types, including different types of stock charts, is also provided. Radar and bubble charts are then used to illustrate some advanced chart techniques. Finally, the last part of the chapter presents techniques for building a management dashboard by combining different chart types within the same chart.

Case Scenario

Michelle Kim is an analyst in the marketing department at TheZone's corporate headquarters in Colorado. Michelle monitors company performance and assists the president and CEO by gathering the data necessary for managing the company. Michelle works with counterparts in each of the company's three divisions—Equipment, Footwear, and Apparel—to monitor how well the company implements its corporate strategy. Una Baatar, president and CEO of The Zone, has asked Michelle for a report and presentation on the company's performance compared with other industry competitors. The presentation will cover industry trends and the company's overall performance with specific information from each of the divisions. The performance of the company's stock in the market will also be discussed. Una is particularly interested in the Footwear division's work in bringing the new TZEdge athletic shoe line to market. Michelle will use Excel to create the necessary charts for the report and presentation.

Marketing

LEVEL 1
Visualizing Data

If a picture is worth a thousand words, can a chart be worth a thousand data points? Figure 3.1 shows one example from Edward R. Tufte's groundbreaking book, *The Visual Display of Quantitative Information.*

Figure 3.1: Historical chart of New York City weather in 1980

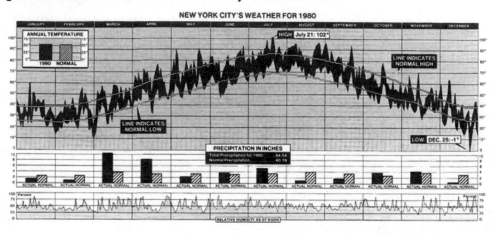

This New York City weather summary for 1980 depicts 2,220 numbers. The daily high and low temperatures are shown in relation to the long-range average. The path of the normal temperatures also provides a forecast of expected change over the year; in the middle of February, for instance, New York City residents can look forward to warming at the rate of about 1.5 degrees per week all the way to July, the yearly peak. This distinguished graphic successfully organizes a large collection of numbers, makes comparisons between different parts of the data, and tells a story.

Let's take a look at a typical Excel chart in Figure 3.2, showing consumer purchase data for TheZone's three divisions—Equipment, Footwear, and Apparel—over an eight-year period beginning in 2006. As you can see, the chart contains the following elements:

- **Chart title**—The descriptive text that identifies the chart's contents
- **Y-axis**—The vertical axis where data values are plotted
- **Y-axis labels**—The labels that identify the data values plotted on the y-axis
- **X-axis**—The horizontal axis where categories are plotted
- **X-axis labels**—The labels that identify the categories plotted on the x-axis
- **Data series**—The related data points that are plotted on the chart; each data series on a chart has a unique color or pattern and is identified in the chart legend
- **Data points**—The points in a data series at which the x-axis and y-axis values intersect
- **Legend**—A box that identifies the patterns or colors assigned to the data series in a chart
- **Data label**—Provides additional information about a data point or value

- **Data table**—Presents a tabular view of the data used to generate the chart
- **Gridlines**—Highlight the horizontal and vertical lines representing values on the chart axes

Figure 3.2: An example of "chart junk"

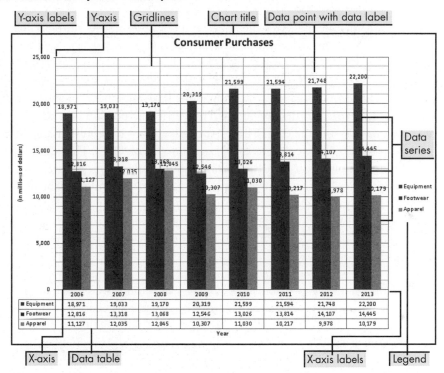

When compared with the weather chart in Figure 3.1, the chart in Figure 3.2 does not communicate its intended message as successfully as the weather chart. The weather chart manages to present a large amount of data very effectively, whereas the consumer purchases chart presents very little data in a very dense and redundant format.

Effective Data Display

Tufte's book is concerned with the design of statistical graphics—the combined use of points, lines, numbers, words, shading, and color to present quantitative information. Tufte believes that graphical excellence depends on clarity, precision, and efficiency. Excellent graphics give the viewer "the greatest number of ideas in the shortest time with the least ink in the smallest space," according to Tufte. The "ink" here refers to everything that prints on paper. In the case of an Excel chart, the ink is the combination of data, labels, and chart effects. Tufte presents five data graphics principles related to "ink" in *The Visual Display of Quantitative Information*:

- Above all else show the data.
- Maximize the data-ink ratio, within reason.
- Erase non-data-ink, within reason.
- Erase redundant data ink, within reason.
- Revise and edit.

The first principle, "Above all else show the data," is a reminder not to clutter a chart by adding unnecessary illustration or decoration. Everything on a chart needs to have a reason for being there. The excessive use of gridlines and data labels in the chart in Figure 3.2 is an example of what Tufte refers to as "chart junk," which can make charts difficult to read, use, and interpret. The second principle, "Maximize the data-ink ratio," refers to the portion of the ink that is devoted to displaying the data versus the portion of a graphic that can be removed without losing the data. The chart uses columns to represent annual sales for each of three products. These columns use a large amount of "ink." The result is a low data-ink ratio—in other words, lots of ink used to display a small amount of data. The third and fourth data principles, "Erase non-data-ink" and "Erase redundant data ink," are somewhat related to maximizing the data-ink ratio. Non-data-ink is a part of the chart that decorates more than informs. Redundant data ink is ink that repeats information. For example, the use of a data table and labels on each point in the chart in Figure 3.2 is redundant.

The fifth and final principle is "Revise and edit." Charts can be improved much in the same way that writing is improved by revision and editing. Feedback on a chart's usefulness and clarity should be sought wherever possible, and the chart should be adjusted accordingly. The intended message of the chart must be considered. A positive feature in one chart type might become negative if it doesn't support what the chart creator is trying to illustrate. Often, the best way to choose a chart is through trial and error. When a chart is found to be useful, it should be saved as a template or working model for future use.

In business, charts are typically used to summarize information so that it can be presented easily to others. The numerous charting options that Excel offers, however, can sometimes lead to chart junk—in this case, the embellishment of charts with a lot of chart effects (ink) that don't tell the viewer anything new. The purpose of formatting is to make a chart easier for the viewer to understand. Too little formatting can leave a chart ambiguous; too much formatting can cause viewers to notice the formatting, not the data. With this in mind, Figure 3.3 shows a much improved chart compared to Figure 3.2. The data-ink ratio has been improved by using lines instead of columns. The lines present the same information as the columns while making trends much easier to notice. The chart junk has been reduced significantly by removing the grid lines, data table, and labels. The addition of data markers makes it easy to align a value with a year, and the legend provides a key to which division a line represents. A **data marker** is a graphical representation of data in a data series of a chart.

Figure 3.3: "Chart junk" removed

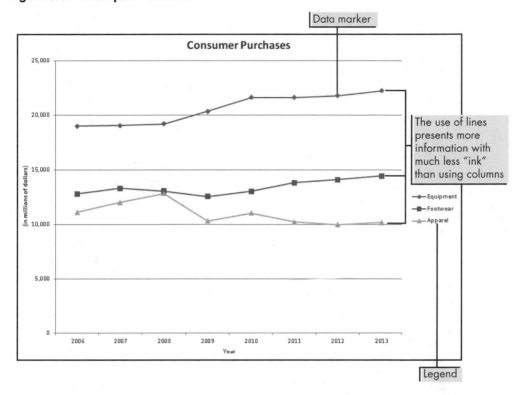

Visualizing Data with Sparklines

Applying Edward Tufte's graphic principles resulted in a much more effective presentation of the consumer purchase data, but the chart is hardly using "the least ink in the smallest space." We can look at more of Tufte's work for another way to improve our chart's effectiveness. In his later book, *Beautiful Evidence*, Tufte introduced the idea of using **sparklines**. These small word-sized charts or graphics are embedded within the words, numbers, and images they represent. The idea is wonderfully simple and represents the ideal of Tufte's five data graphics principles. Placing these word-sized graphics in the context of what they represent makes multiple comparisons of trends and patterns much easier. In previous versions of Excel, data visualization was exclusively handled by inserting stand-alone charts of various types into a worksheet. These older versions of Excel could be used to create sparklines, but the process was fairly time consuming because of scaling problems that required a lot of trial and error manipulation of the chart properties. Excel 2010 makes this process much simpler and effective by adding sparklines to the Insert tab on the Ribbon.

As noted earlier, Michelle Kim is responsible for monitoring how well the company implements its corporate strategy. She has been analyzing industry trends for the company's three divisions, and has just started to put together a spreadsheet showing the sporting goods industry's last eight years of consumer purchase data by equipment, footwear, and apparel.

The information contained in spreadsheets is stored as tabular data arranged in rows, columns, and worksheets. This allows you to organize and analyze a large amount of data effectively, but can you see what the data means? You turn raw data into information by organizing it into something meaningful. You make information useful and give it a purpose by using it to make decisions—decisions that you couldn't have made as well without the knowledge gained from your analysis. Presenting data visually gives a global view that allows you to effectively convey the meaning hidden in a large data set, compare sets of data, and perhaps uncover a critical relationship or trend that would be hard to reveal with tabular data alone.

Michelle is using Excel to organize and analyze the various sets of data shown in Figure 3.4, looking for potential problems that could disrupt the company's strategic plans. The sparklines she added allow for a quick comparison of the sales results for each category over the past eight years. Inserting the sparklines is as simple as highlighting a range of data and indicating which cells should be used to display the sparklines. Sparklines can take the form of lines and columns as well as a special Win/Loss version of columns. You can modify the sparklines to highlight various points in the data using the contextual Sparkline Tools Design tab on the Ribbon, as shown in Figure 3.4.

Figure 3.4: Worksheet of consumer purchase data with sparklines

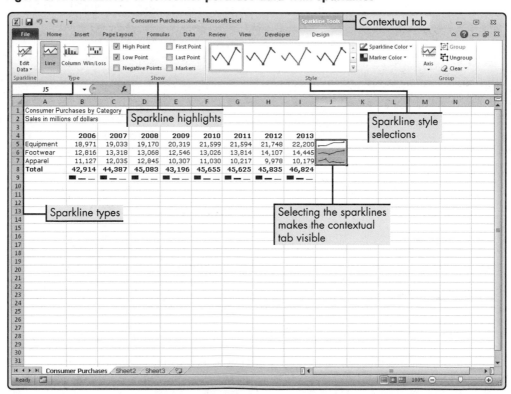

3

How To

Add Sparklines to a Worksheet
1. Click the Insert tab on the Ribbon.
2. In the Sparklines group, click the Line, Column, or Win/Loss button.
3. In the Create Sparklines dialog box, choose the data you want by selecting the Data Range. Choose where you want the sparklines to be placed by selecting the Location Range. Click the OK button.
4. With the sparklines location still selected, click the contextual Sparkline Tools Design tab on the Ribbon. Make any desired formatting changes.

As she examines the sparklines, Michelle realizes that they are better suited to comparing trends within the data illustrated by each sparkline. The lack of a common axis makes it difficult to compare the values represented in multiple sets of data. The lack of a common axis would be useful for quickly visualizing trends for large sets of data or for embedding a chart within the text of a report, but not for Michelle's purpose. She only has three categories to examine and the sparklines are not giving her enough detail. She decides she will need to make extensive use of charts to summarize and present the data visually for further analysis.

Effective Charting in Excel

To create a chart in Excel, you first select the data you want to display in the chart, click the Insert tab, and then click a button in the Charts group or the Dialog Box Launcher in the Charts group if you want to choose from all available chart types and sub-types.

Best Practice

Choosing a Chart Location
A chart can either be embedded as an object on the same worksheet as the source data for the chart or placed on a separate worksheet referred to as a "chart sheet." You can modify the location of a chart at any time using the Move Chart dialog box, which is available in the Location group on the Chart Tools Design tab on the Ribbon. Chart location is a matter of personal preference. Some users find it easier to work with charts that are embedded with the worksheet data because changes to the worksheet are immediately visible in the chart. Other users find that placing the chart on a separate chart sheet makes editing and printing the chart much easier. As a general rule, you should place charts that are developed for presentation and printing on a chart sheet. These charts are typically based on a specific reporting period and the source data usually doesn't change significantly. If the source data is dynamic, seeing the effect of the changes in the chart can be very handy. In this case, the chart should be placed on the worksheet with the data.

Determining the Appropriate Chart Type and Chart Options

Excel provides 11 standard chart types, with 73 sub-types that can be used to present information graphically. In addition, you have the ability to combine these different chart types and sub-types within the same chart. Charts can display a combination of numeric and category data. An Excel chart requires at least one numeric data series and at least one label data series. Excel refers to the label data series as category data. The number of data series and data points that Excel can display in a chart is only limited by available computer memory and capacity.

The chart type you choose depends on what you are trying to illustrate with the data. Table 3.1 identifies and describes the chart types available in Excel.

Table 3.1: Excel chart types

Chart Type	Icon	Description
Column		Compares values across categories in a vertical orientation. Values are indicated by the height of the columns.
Bar		Compares values across categories in a horizontal orientation. Values are indicated by the length of the bars.
Line		Displays trends over time or by category. Values are indicated by the height of the lines.
Area		Displays trends over time or by category. Values are indicated by the filled areas below the lines.
Pie		Compares the contribution each value in a single numeric data series makes to the whole, or 100%. Values are indicated by the size of the pie slices.
Doughnut		Compares the contribution each value in multiple numeric data series makes to the whole, or 100%. Values are indicated by the size of the doughnut segments.
X Y (Scatter)		Compares pairs of numeric values on the x- and y-axes with the data points plotted proportionally to the values on the x-axis; can also be used to display a functional relationship, such as $y=mx+b$. Values are indicated by the position of the data points.
Stock		Displays stock price and volume trends over time. Plotted values can include volume, opening price, highest price, lowest price, and closing price.
Radar		Compares values across categories in a circular orientation. Values are indicated by the distance from a center point.
Bubble		Compares sets of three values. Values are indicated by the size of the bubbles (filled circles).
Surface		Displays value trends in three dimensions. Values are indicated by areas with colors or patterns on the surface of the chart.

Understanding Line and Column Charts

As noted in Table 3.1, a line chart displays trends over time or by category, and a column chart compares values across categories in a vertical orientation. Michelle has already created a line chart based on the consumer purchase data, with markers displayed at each data value (see Figure 3.5). This line chart is useful if the overall trend of the data needs to be emphasized. The vertical y-axis shows the total sales (numeric values) and the horizontal x-axis shows the years (categories). Each line represents the trend in sales of the equipment, footwear, and apparel categories over an eight-year period. In this case, Michelle wants to compare the values in each category more than the overall trend over time, making a column chart the best choice. The two charts shown in Figure 3.5 are based on the same data series; the differences are due to the type of chart chosen. The line chart emphasizes the trend in each category over time, whereas the column chart makes it easier to compare the contribution each category made in a particular year. Note that the column chart in Figure 3.5 is displayed in the default column chart sub-type, the clustered sub-type.

Figure 3.5: Line chart vs. column chart

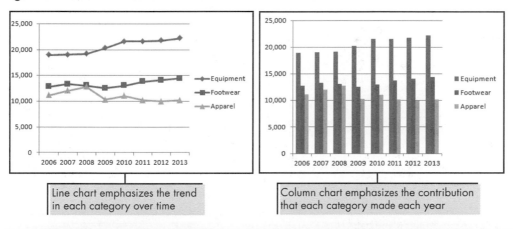

Line chart emphasizes the trend in each category over time

Column chart emphasizes the contribution that each category made each year

How To

Change the Chart Type

1. Select the chart or chart series whose type you want to change. Clicking anywhere in a chart selects the chart. When a chart is selected, three contextual Chart Tools tabs—Design, Layout, and Format—appear on the Ribbon. To change the chart type of a single data series, select that data series either by clicking it in the selected chart, or by selecting it from the Chart Elements box in the Current Selection group on the Layout tab or Format tab.

2. In the Type group on the Design tab, click the Change Chart Type button to open the Change Chart Type dialog box. This dialog box provides the same options available in the Insert Chart dialog box for selecting the chart type.

3. Click the chart type you want to change to, and then click the sub-type (if necessary).

4. Click the OK button.

Comparing Line and X Y (Scatter) Charts

There can be confusion about when to use a line chart and when to use an X Y (Scatter) chart. The data used to plot an X Y (Scatter) chart is different from the data used to create a line chart (or column or bar chart). An X Y (Scatter) chart plots numeric values on both the x- and y-axes based on the value of the data, whereas a line chart plots numeric values on one axis and category labels equidistantly on the other axis. Consider what happens if the order of the consumer purchase data is switched, as shown in Figure 3.6. The years in the worksheet are listed in descending order, from 2013 to 2006, to make the difference between plotting the x-axis as a category and as a numeric value more obvious. The same set of data is used to plot both a line chart and an X Y (Scatter) chart.

Figure 3.6: Line chart vs. X Y (Scatter) chart

	A	B	C	D	E	F	G	H	I	J
1	Consumer Purchases by Category									
2	Sales in millions of dollars									
3										
4		2013	2012	2011	2010	2009	2008	2007	2006	
5	Equipment	22,200	21,748	21,594	21,599	20,319	19,170	19,033	18,971	
6	Footwear	14,445	14,107	13,814	13,026	12,546	13,068	13,318	12,816	
7	Apparel	10,179	9,978	10,217	11,030	10,307	12,845	12,035	11,127	
8	Total	46,824	45,835	45,625	45,655	43,196	45,083	44,387	42,914	
9										

The line chart plots the x-axis based on the position of the categories in the data range

The X Y (Scatter) chart plots the x-axis in numeric order based on the values in the data range

As you can see in the figure, the line chart plots the data points along the y-axis based on the value (sales volume), but the x-axis is based on position because this axis contains categories (years). The line chart's x-axis treats the year data as a category and plots based on position, beginning with 2013. By comparison, the X Y (Scatter) chart plots both the y- and x-axis data as numeric values. So its x-axis treats the year data as numeric values and plots them from lowest to highest, based on the year number. Note that the X Y (Scatter) chart is formatted with lines connecting the points; other formats are available for this chart type as well. Also note that the X Y (Scatter) chart automatically generates an x-axis that applies a buffer at both ends, so the years shown on this axis range from 2004 to 2014. An X Y (Scatter) chart should be used instead of a line chart when comparing sets of numerical data on both the x-axis and the y-axis.

Changing the Chart Source Data

After changing the line chart to a column chart, Michelle decides that the chart is too busy and should show data from only the last five years instead of eight. The Select Data Source dialog box, which is available from the shortcut menu for a selected chart, provides options for modifying the values used to generate a chart. Refer back to Figure 3.4; notice that the categories and numeric data are not in a continuous range of cells. Michelle uses the Ctrl key to select both the categories (Equipment, Footwear, and Apparel) and the data for the years 2009–2013. The data source range changes from A4:I7 to A4:A7, E4:I7.

How To

Change the Source Data

1. Select the chart to display the contextual Chart Tools tabs on the Ribbon.
2. Click the Select Data button in the Data group on the Design tab to open the Select Data Source dialog box. See Figure 3.7. The dialog box can also be reached from the shortcut menu from a selected chart.

Figure 3.7: Select Data Source dialog box

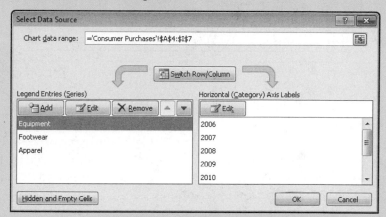

3. In the Chart data range box, modify the current range of values or select a new range as the source of data for the chart. In the case of a chart with multiple data series, you can change individual data series using the options in the Legend Entries (Series) section of the Select Data Source dialog box.
4. Click the OK button after changing the source data.

Notice the Switch Row/Column button in the Select Data Source dialog box (see Figure 3.7). This option provides settings for displaying the data series by rows or by columns. What would the impact be of changing this option in the current chart? Choosing to display the data by either rows or columns can illustrate different trends and force a different comparison of the data. See Figure 3.8. When plotted by columns, the chart compares the amount of each year's sales for each of the three categories (Equipment, Footwear, and Apparel). When plotted by rows, the chart emphasizes the contribution that each category made to each year's performance.

Michelle is more interested in the amount of each year's sales of equipment, footwear, and apparel, so she chooses to plot the data by columns. She doesn't have to open up the Select Data Source dialog box (Figure 3.7). She simply clicks the Switch Row/Column button in the Data group on the Chart Tools Design tab on the Ribbon. Plotting the data by columns makes it easier to see that sales for the Equipment and Footwear categories appear to be increasing from year to year; whereas sales for the Apparel category are leveling off somewhat.

Figure 3.8: Displaying the data series by columns or by rows

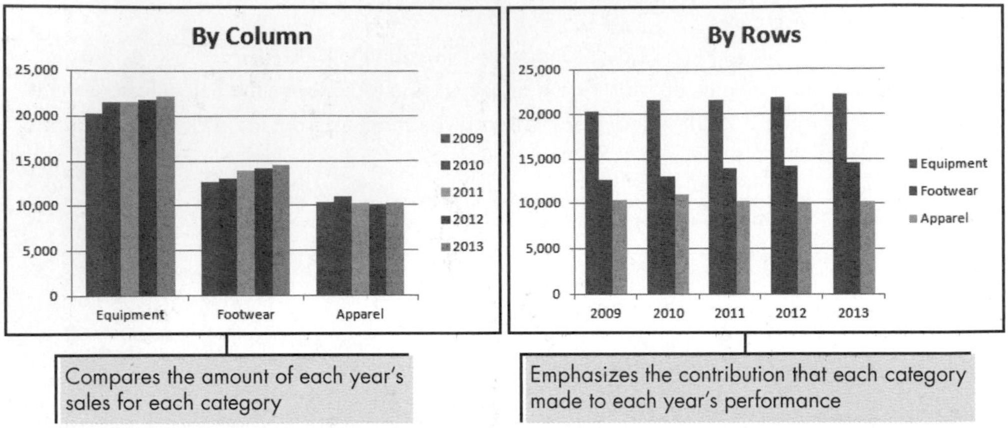

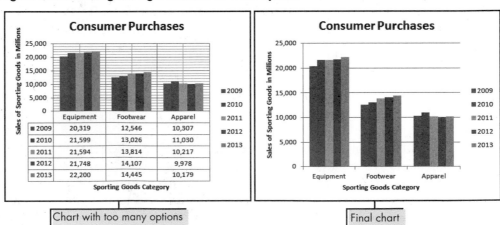

Compares the amount of each year's sales for each category

Emphasizes the contribution that each category made to each year's performance

Specifying Chart Layout Options

Excel offers many formatting and display options for changing the layout of chart elements, including chart and axis titles, legends, data labels, data tables, axes, gridlines, and plot areas. The buttons that lead to options for each of these are found on the Chart Tools Layout tab grouped by Labels, Axes, and Background.

Now that Michelle has selected the chart type and determined how to display the source data, she decides to add axis titles that better describe the data on the chart. Many of the Chart Options settings can cause problems with generating excessive "ink" that obscures the information in the chart. As an illustration of this issue, Figure 3.9 shows the chart that results when too many options are selected, compared with Michelle's final chart, which contains only the elements needed to best describe the data and not overwhelm it.

Figure 3.9: Selecting the right number of chart options

Chart with too many options

Final chart

3

Level 1

How To

Specify Chart Layout Options

1. Click anywhere in the chart to display the contextual Chart Tools tabs on the Ribbon.

2. Click the Layout tab to see available options grouped by Labels, Axes, and Background. See Figure 3.10.

Figure 3.10: Chart Tools Layout tab

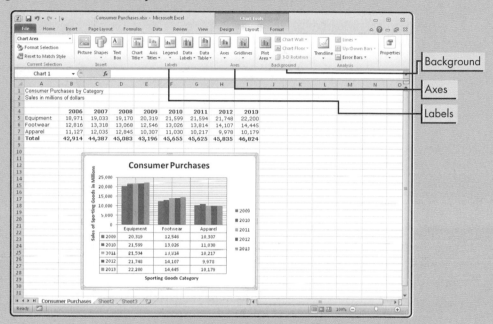

These three groups provide buttons you can use to specify chart layout options:

Labels group

- **Chart Title and Axis Titles**—Use the options under these buttons to modify the layout of the chart title or the axis titles.

- **Legend**—The options under this button control the display and placement of the chart legend. The legend shows the name of each data series along with the appropriate data marker. You can choose to display the legend in a variety of positions around the plot area.

- **Data Labels**—The options under this button allow you to add and control the display of labels for the data points on the chart. Display options include showing the value of each data point as well as the series and category to which each data point belongs. Percentages can also be displayed, if appropriate to the chart type. The selections on this tab display labels for each data point, which can become visually overwhelming. You can control the display of individual labels by selecting them on the plot area or using the Chart Elements box in the Current Selection group.

- **Data Table**—Use the options under this button to display a table of values for each data series in a grid below the chart.

Axes group

- **Axes**—Use the options under this button to specify whether the x- and y-axes are displayed. You can also choose to display the x-axis as a text or a date series axis, instead of automatically choosing a setting based on the chart data. The Date setting shows evenly spaced tick marks across the x-axis, based on the major and minor units of days, months, or years.
- **Gridlines**—Use the options under this button to modify the display of gridlines in the chart plot area. You can also modify the display of major and minor gridlines for each axis.

Background group

- **Plot Area**—Use the options under this button to change the formatting of the plot area, the area bounded by the axes.
- **Chart Wall**—Use the options under this button to change the formatting of the chart wall, the two vertical surfaces created in any of the 3-D chart types.
- **Chart Floor**—Use the options under this button to change the formatting of the chart floor, the horizontal surface created in any of the 3-D chart types.
- **3-D Rotation**—Use the options under this button to change the viewing angle of a 3-D chart.

Understanding Area and Pie Charts

An area chart combines the features of a line chart with a bar or column chart by filling in the area below the line, and displaying the trend of values over time or categories. A pie chart is used to display the percentage contribution that each category makes to the whole, or 100%. The sum of the value of the categories must total 100% to use a pie chart. The highlighted numeric data range used in a pie chart is assumed to identify the individual components of some total. Excel calculates the percentage that each cell in the range contributes to the total.

Percentages are used every day in business to summarize and compare sets of data. For example, comparing the amount of labor used to create products with different overall prices can be made easier if the labor amount is expressed as a percentage of the total cost. Comparisons of salary rates and pay increases across various departments in a company are much clearer if the pay increases are expressed in percentages instead of actual amounts. Use a pie chart when it's most important to show relative percentages rather than values. Graphing these percentages can allow a viewer to make a quick visual comparison.

Earlier, Michelle chose a column chart instead of a line chart to compare the amount of each year's sales for each category rather than emphasize the trend in each category over time. How would an area chart display that same data? Figure 3.11 compares a column chart with an area chart of the consumer purchase data for all eight years (2006–2013). As you can see, the area chart does a better job of illustrating the sales trend in the equipment, footwear, and apparel categories over the longer time period (eight years), while still emphasizing the contribution that each category made to a particular year's performance.

The area chart is somewhat easier to grasp than the column chart because the large number of columns makes the column chart more difficult to interpret.

Figure 3.11: Column chart vs. area chart

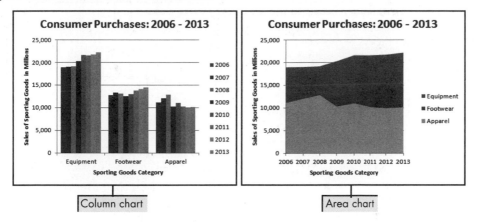

Michelle now wants to examine the contribution that the equipment, footwear, and apparel categories made to 2013 sales as a percentage. She first creates a new worksheet, named "Consumer Purchases – 2013," and places the consumer purchase data on this worksheet. She decides to use a 3-D pie chart type to produce a more appealing visual effect compared with a flat pie chart. Because the category labels in cells A5:A7 are separated from the data in cells I5:I7, Michelle must use the Ctrl key to select the two ranges as the data source. An alternative method is to select cells I5:I7 as the data source, create a pie chart using the Pie button in the Charts group on the Insert tab, and then add the range containing the category labels (A5:A7) using the Edit button in the Horizontal (Category) Axis Labels section of the Select Data Source dialog box, shown in Figure 3.12. Be sure that you don't select the total in cell I8 as part of the source data for the pie chart. Doing so would result in a pie chart that has one slice equal to half the pie, and all the other slices together making up the other half of the pie.

The chart shown on the left in Figure 3.13 is the default 3-D pie chart produced using the Pie button in the Charts group. To improve the appearance of the default chart, Michelle makes the following modifications to produce the final version of the chart, which is shown on the right in Figure 3.13:

- Removes the chart legend and adds a chart title
- Includes category names and percentages as data labels on the pie slices
- Formats the data labels in a larger bold font to make them more visible
- Increases the rotation, or tilt, of the chart around the y-axis from 30 degrees to 40 degrees to provide more space on the pie slices for displaying the data labels and percentages
- Enlarges the chart overall by dragging one of its resizing handles on the plot area

- Explodes the pie slice for the Footwear category, for emphasis, by dragging it away from the other pie slices, because Una is particularly interested in the status of the new TZEdge athletic shoe line

Figure 3.12: Adding category labels to the pie chart source data

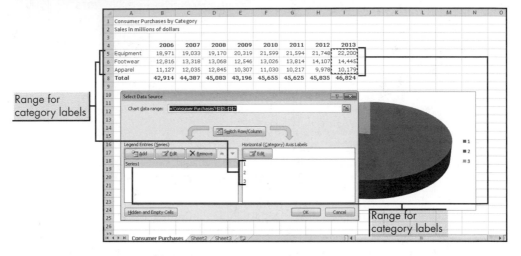

Figure 3.13: Default and modified pie charts

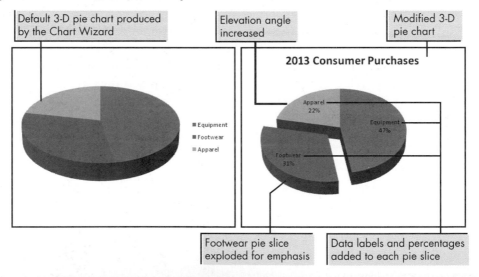

How To

Change a 3-D Pie Chart View
1. Click the chart to display the contextual Chart Tools tabs on the Ribbon.
2. Click the 3-D Rotation button in the Background group on the Layout tab to open the Format Chart Area dialog box. See Figure 3.14.

Figure 3.14: 3-D Rotation in the Format Chart Area dialog box

3. To adjust the rotation of the chart, or spin, around the x-axis, change the value of the degree in X: Rotation box, or click the X: Rotation up or down arrow button. You can also adjust the angle of the x-axis using the Left or Right button.

4. To adjust the rotation, or tilt, of the chart around the y-axis, change the value of the degree in Y: Rotation box, or click the Y: Rotation up or down arrow button. You can also adjust the angle of the y-axis using the Left or Right button.

5. In a 3D chart, adjust the perspective (or thickness) of a pie slice, change the value of the degree in Perspective box, or click the Perspective up or down arrow button. You can also adjust the angle of the z-axis using the Narrow field of view or Widen field of view button.

6. Click the Close button.

How To

Format Data Labels

1. Click any data label on the chart to select the entire series of data labels, or to select a single data label, click the label again after first selecting the entire series. The second click selects only the data label clicked.

2. With either all the labels for a series or a single label selected, click the Data Labels button in the Labels group on the Layout tab.

3. Select the More Data Labels option to open the Format Data Labels dialog box. See Figure 3.15.

Figure 3.15: Format Data Labels dialog box

This dialog box provides a variety of formatting options for data labels, organized into categories:

- **Label Options**—This category provides options for changing the information the label displays as well as the label position.
- **Number**—This category provides options for changing the appearance of numbers in the data labels.
- **Fill, Border Color, Border Styles, Shadow, Glow and Soft Edges, and 3-D Format**—These categories provide options for changing the appearance of the data labels.
- **Alignment**—Use the options in this category to specify the alignment (horizontal or vertical), orientation, position, and direction of the data labels.

4. Click a category in the list on the left of the dialog box to display the available options.
5. After specifying all the necessary formatting options, click the Close button.

Best Practice

Working with 3-D Charts
A 3-D pie chart can be much more visually appealing than a flat pie chart. Most of the chart types have 3-D options, but these should be used with caution. Although the use of 3-D can add visual interest, it might be at the expense of the data being presented. Figure 3.16 compares regular line and column charts with their 3-D equivalents. The 3-D charts are more

attractive and interesting, but they are also more difficult to interpret. In the 3-D line chart, the relationship between the apparel and footwear in any particular year is difficult to determine because the lines are no longer on the same axis. The 3-D column chart does a better job of showing this, but it is still not as clear as the regular 2-D line and column charts. Additional care must be taken to ensure that one series isn't hidden behind the other. The data series order can be changed as necessary to avoid this; but if the data points are very close or cross, often this is not enough to prevent one data series from hiding a portion of another. Because 3-D charts are more visually appealing than 2-D charts in many instances, they are a good choice for presentations and reports, provided that the preceding interpretation issues are taken into consideration.

Figure 3.16: Regular charts vs. 3-D charts

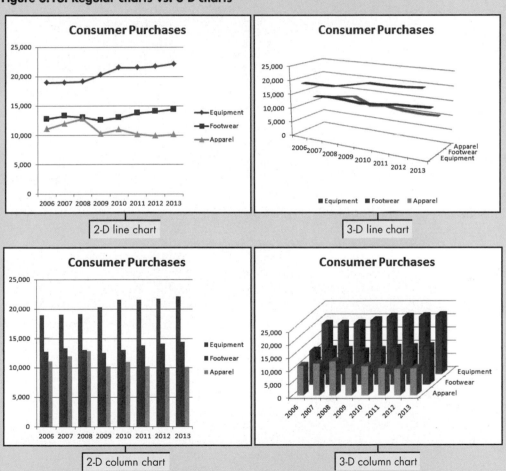

2-D line chart

3-D line chart

2-D column chart

3-D column chart

Steps To Success: Level 1

In these steps, you need to prepare some charts showing trends in the sporting goods industry. A workbook containing a variety of information on industry-wide trends has already been created. You will begin with data showing the number of people who participate in a variety of sports and activities.

Complete the following:

1. Open the workbook named **Trends.xlsx** located in the Chapter 3 folder, and then save it as **Industry Trends.xlsx**. Review the data sets on the four worksheets. You need to determine the most important information in each worksheet and select the best method for displaying that information in a chart. Remember that charts can be used to display single data series, compare multiple data series, show trends, and compare the percentage contribution to the whole.

2. The 2013 Participation worksheet contains participation data for a variety of sports, ranked in descending order by the values in the Total column. Create one column chart, one bar chart, and one line chart from the data. Place each chart on the same worksheet as the source data. In an area below each chart, explain what the chart type emphasizes about the data. Select which chart is the best choice for comparing each sport's participation level. Place this chart on a separate chart sheet named **2013 Participation Chart** as the first worksheet in the Industry Trends workbook, and add appropriate y-axis and chart titles to finalize this chart. Return to the 2013 Participation worksheet, and in an area below the chart you selected to place on the chart sheet, explain the advantages and any disadvantages of this chart.

3. The 10-Year Participation worksheet contains sports participation data over a 10-year period, with values shown for every other year, for a variety of sports. Add sparklines for each sport category in the worksheet. Highlight the high, low, and last data point in each of the sparklines. Create an appropriate chart to illustrate the participation changes in each sport over the 10-year period. Place this chart on the same worksheet as the source data. Add appropriate titles and a legend to finalize the chart. To the right of the chart, compare the information provided by the sparklines with that provided by your chart. Explain the advantages and disadvantages of each in this specific instance.

4. The Female Sports Participation worksheet shows the changes in female sports participation between 2008 and 2013. Create an appropriate chart that shows the changing trends in the percentage of female participation in each sport. Place this chart on the same worksheet as the source data. Add appropriate titles to finalize the chart. In a cell below the chart, explain the advantages and any disadvantages of the chart type you chose.

5. The Purchases by Sport worksheet shows the dollar amount of consumer equipment purchases for 2011, 2012, and 2013. Create an appropriate chart to compare the contribution of each sport and illustrate the changes in consumer purchases from year to year. Place this chart on the same worksheet as the source data. Add appropriate titles and a legend to finalize the chart. To the right of the chart, explain the advantages and any disadvantages of the chart type you chose.

6. Save and close the Industry Trends.xlsx workbook.

LEVEL 2
Evaluating Chart Sub-Types

Examining Sub-Types for Various Chart Types

As discussed earlier, the chart type you choose depends on what you are trying to illustrate. Charts can compare values across categories (bar and column), display trends over time or category (line and area), and compare the contribution each value in a single data series makes to the whole, or 100% (pie). Some of the chart sub-types available for the basic chart types enable you to sum or stack the values in each category, giving a slightly different perspective on the contribution that each category makes to the sum or the whole. Another option is to create a 100% stacked chart, in which the plotted values are converted into percentages of the total amount within each category. A 100% stacked chart is similar to a pie except that the pieces are in a column instead of a circle.

After reviewing the sample charts in the Consumer Purchases workbook she prepared for the company, Michelle is pleased with how the visual display of data makes it easier to compare the data across categories. Now she wants to modify the consumer purchases chart, which is currently an area chart, to show the total sales in each year and how much each category contributes to that total. The current chart shows the sales amount for each category, but does not show the total sales amount for each year.

Adding Things Up: Stacked Chart Options

Stacked charts do a good job of illustrating the cumulative effects of data in categories. Line, bar, column, and area charts all have a stacked chart sub-type. Figure 3.17 shows the current consumer purchases area chart compared with three stacked charts of the same data.

Michelle decides that the stacked column chart is the one that most clearly shows the totals for each category (in this case, each year). The stacked area and stacked line charts don't clearly show that the lines represent the cumulative total of each year. These charts can give the impression that each line represents the actual values in the data series, and not the cumulative amounts for each category. This could lead to some misinterpretation and require too much explanation of the chart to make the meaning clear.

Figure 3.17: Area chart compared with stacked charts

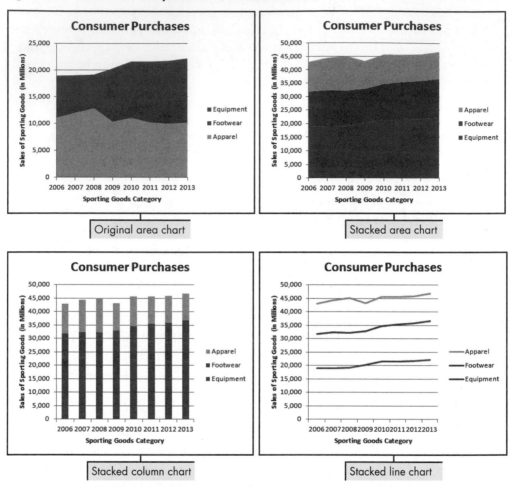

How To

Change the Chart Sub-Type

1. Click the chart to display the contextual Chart Tools tabs on the Ribbon.

2. Click the Change Chart Type button in the Type group on the Design tab to open the Change Chart Type dialog box. The chart type for the current chart is already selected. An alternative method of opening this dialog box is to right-click on the chart and then select Change Chart Type.

3. Click the icon for the chart sub-type you want in the Chart sub-type section.

4. Click the OK button.

Summing to 100%: Alternatives to Pie Charts

Another option for illustrating the cumulative contribution for each category is to express this contribution as a percentage. As was the case with the stacked sub-type, line, bar, column, and area charts offer a 100% stacked sub-type as well. Showing the cumulative contribution for each category as a percentage can reduce confusion over whether the line on the chart represents the *individual* or *cumulative* contribution to the whole. These charts combine the features of a pie chart with the features of line, column, or area charts. Figure 3.18 compares the original area chart of consumer purchase data with 100% stacked versions of the same data. Although each of these charts clearly shows the cumulative contribution each of the three divisions—Apparel, Footwear, and Equipment—makes to the whole, or 100%, for each year, Michelle chooses to use the 100% stacked column chart. She feels that displaying each year in a column makes the percentage contribution that each of the three divisions made in each year more obvious. In a way, this 100% stacked column chart is the equivalent of eight pie charts—one for each year. Each column presents the same information that would exist in a pie chart for that year; the only difference is the shape.

Figure 3.18: Comparison of 100% stacked charts

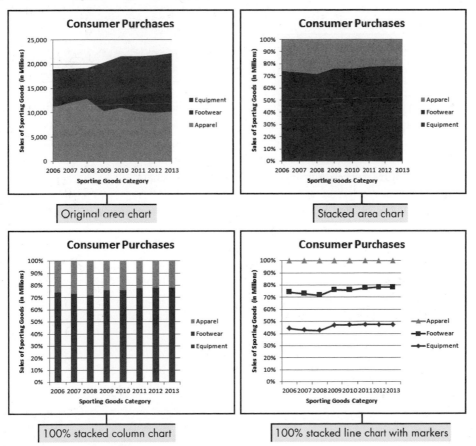

Slicing the Pie Too Thin: Summarizing Too Much Detail in Pie Charts

Having too many categories can be a problem with pie charts. If you have an excessive number of pie slices, the chart can become very cluttered and confusing. For example, the data in Figure 3.19 shows consumer equipment purchases by sport in both worksheet format and a corresponding pie chart, which Michelle created based on some industry trend data. She wants to analyze which sports generate the most equipment purchases every year by displaying the data in a pie chart format to show the percent contribution of each sport for 2013.

Figure 3.19: Consumer equipment purchases

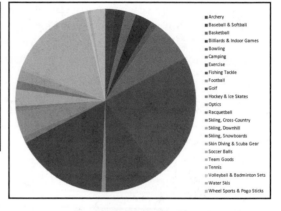

Consumer Equipment Purchases by Sport (in millions)	2013	2012	2011
Archery	$382.77	$372.66	$356.74
Baseball & Softball	$415.17	$404.41	$400.70
Basketball	$427.05	$422.67	$363.64
Billiards & Indoor Games	$678.69	$660.70	$629.12
Bowling	$267.21	$260.45	$240.10
Camping	$1,649.61	$1,602.35	$1,539.67
Exercise	$4,992.21	$4,757.14	$4,269.54
Fishing Tackle	$2,266.21	$2,259.53	$2,281.95
Football	$167.95	$171.24	$155.43
Golf	$3,716.73	$3,680.05	$4,240.32
Hockey & Ice Skates	$258.57	$252.67	$222.07
Optics	$992.97	$965.91	$904.52
Racquetball	$105.21	$104.93	$89.98
Skiing, Cross-Country	$116.01	$114.33	$99.27
Skiing, Downhill	$657.09	$644.71	$614.76
Skiing, Snowboards	$347.13	$338.53	$322.83
Skin Diving & Scuba Gear	$439.93	$431.41	$435.26
Soccer Balls	$146.25	$141.54	$132.86
Team Goods	$2,836.45	$2,807.09	$2,795.04
Tennis	$508.05	$502.37	$459.78
Volleyball & Badminton Sets	$110.61	$108.93	$93.87
Water Skis	$139.77	$137.22	$122.92
Wheel Sports & Pogo Sticks	$581.49	$607.13	$843.61
Total	$22,200.00	$21,748.00	$21,594.00

As illustrated in Figure 3.19, the number of categories makes the pie chart confusing and difficult to interpret. The data is currently sorted alphabetically by category. As a result, the chart is arranged by category. The first category (Archery) starts at the 12 o'clock position, and the remaining categories are placed in an alphabetical clockwise rotation. The sort order contributes to the disarray and confusion in the chart.

Michelle decides to sort the data by the size of the equipment purchases in descending order, so that the data goes from highest to lowest. She creates a new chart, shown in Figure 3.20, using the data sorted in this order. The new chart appears more orderly and less confusing when compared with the original pie chart (see Figure 3.19). Michelle still isn't satisfied with the results, however, because the chart continues to have an excessive number of segments. There are 23 categories shown in the pie chart—which, of course, is too great a number—resulting in many small, indistinguishable pie segments.

Figure 3.20: Re-sorted pie chart

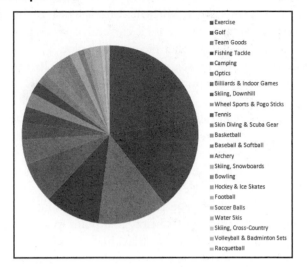

Exploring the Pie of Pie and Bar of Pie Chart Sub-Types

How can Michelle modify the pie chart to address the problem of too many segments? One way would be to choose a different sub-type for the chart. Excel offers two interesting pie chart sub- types that can be used to combine many smaller segments of a pie chart into an "Other" category, which can then be shown as a smaller pie chart or as a single vertical bar chart next to the original pie chart. The two chart sub-types, Pie of Pie and Bar of Pie, are similar, with the exception of the chart type of the second plot in the chart. Michelle wants to emphasize the categories with the largest purchases. Either chart sub-type would do this well, but she chooses the Pie of Pie sub-type because she feels that the Bar of Pie sub-type could cause confusion over whether the bar represents percentages or values. The resulting chart, shown in Figure 3.21, does decrease the number of pie segments to improve the visual display of data, but it still needs formatting enhancements to meet Michelle's needs.

Figure 3.21: Pie of Pie sub-type applied to the chart

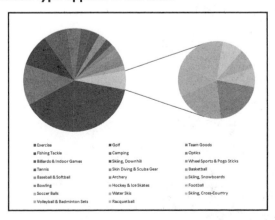

After adding the chart title "Consumer Purchases by Sport" and removing the legend from the chart to make the pie segments larger, Michelle considers how to format the data series to make the chart easier to interpret. The series is currently split by position, with the last eight values displayed in the second, smaller pie chart, or plot. The total of the values in the second plot is represented by the pie segment on the main pie chart to which the smaller plot is connected. There are four options for splitting the data series:

- **Position**—This option automatically assigns a specific number of values to the second plot. In the current chart, the last eight values in the data range are assigned to the second plot.
- **Value**—This option allows you to select a cutoff point that assigns all the values below that point to the second plot.
- **Percent Value**—This option allows you to select a cutoff point by percentage, rather than value, and assign all the percentages below that point to the second plot.
- **Custom**—This option allows you to drag individual pie segments between the two charts so you can include exactly the segments you want in the main pie chart and the second plot.

When the data series is selected, the Format Data Series dialog box is available by clicking the Format Selection button in the Current Selection group on the Chart Tools Format tab on the Ribbon. The dialog box, which is also available by right-clicking on the data set to open the shortcut menu, provides an option for changing how the series is split, as well as other options affecting the data series display. Michelle decides to make the following changes to the current chart to improve its appearance:

- Split the series by position, with the last 10 values assigned to the second plot.
- Emphasize the information in the main pie chart by reducing the overall size of the second plot and increasing the gap width between the two pie charts.

Figure 3.22 shows the Format Data Series dialog box settings that will implement these formatting changes.

Figure 3.22: Changing the format of the Pie of Pie chart

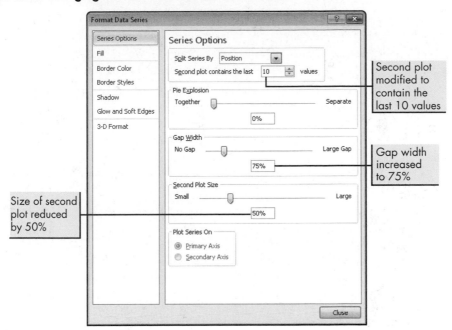

To further enhance the chart, Michelle adds category name data labels. The resulting chart is shown in Figure 3.23. Notice the label "Other," which identifies the pie slice that represents the total of all the slices in the smaller pie plot. You will make some further formatting changes to this chart, which is still too "busy," in the Steps To Success exercise at the end of Level 2.

Figure 3.23: Pie of Pie chart with formatting changes

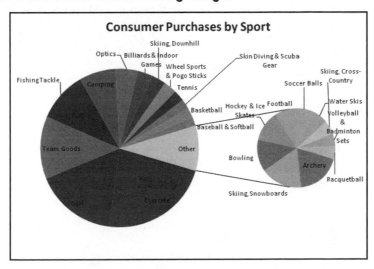

How To

Format Data Series in a Pie of Pie Chart

1. Right-click on either of the pie charts to open the shortcut menu, and then click Format Data Series on the shortcut menu to open the Format Data Series dialog box (see Figure 3.22).

2. Under Series Options, you can select which data points are included in the second pie chart, or plot. The split between the first and second pie chart can be made by the position, value, or percentage of the individual data points on the worksheet. A custom setting allows pie slices to be dragged between the two pie charts. You can also modify the size of the second plot as well as the distance between the main pie chart and the second plot.

3. Use the Fill, Border Color, and Border Styles selections to specify the settings you want for the border and area of the entire data series. Changes to the border style affect all of the pie slice borders. Any changes to the area color or fill effects settings result in the same appearance for all of the pie slices.

4. After making the necessary formatting changes, click the Close button.

Note: Any changes to the data label content must be made using the Data Labels button in the Labels group on the Layout tab. You can choose to display the series name, category name, value, and/or percentage. The Layout tab also provides options for the legend display.

From Pies to Doughnuts: Showing Individual Percentages with Multiple Series
Although doughnut charts are not a chart sub-type, they are related to 100% stacked charts and pie charts because of the type of data displayed. One of the limitations—or advantages, depending on your perspective—of 100% stacked charts is that they show cumulative rather than individual percentages. That is, the value for the second data point is the sum of the first and second values. Pie charts can show individual percentages, but only for one data series. Doughnut charts show the information contained in a pie chart for more than one series.

Michelle wants to show how the percentages of consumer purchases for the three divisions (Apparel, Equipment, and Footwear) have changed from year to year. She has prepared two sample doughnut charts, shown in Figure 3.24, from the same consumer purchase data she has been working with. One of the problems with doughnut charts is that they can easily become confusing if too many data series are charted at once. Michelle decides that even if she charted only two numeric data series, the doughnut charts would be difficult to understand. She thinks that multiple pie charts—one for each year, for example—would be much easier for decision makers to interpret.

Figure 3.24: Two doughnut charts

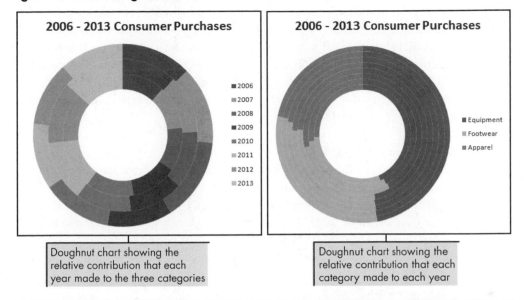

| Doughnut chart showing the relative contribution that each year made to the three categories | Doughnut chart showing the relative contribution that each category made to each year |

Monitoring a Business with Stock Charts

On a regular basis, Michelle compares TheZone's performance in the stock market with that of other competitors in the sporting goods industry. Probably the most important investor data in business can be found in the financial sections of newspapers around the world. The international stock market is the lifeblood of business. Information about the daily variations in a company's value is tracked by everyone from day traders, to investment bankers, to individual investors, and to the companies themselves. Commonly reported stock information includes the opening and closing prices, the highest and lowest prices achieved, and the volume of stock sales in a particular period.

Excel line charts can be used to track changes in the prices of stocks at the end of each period, but they are not ideal because each of the values mentioned previously requires a single line representing one data series on the chart. A single line representing the closing prices for the time period would be the easiest to understand, but the range of values that a stock has during the reported period can be as significant as the ending price to many investors. Each of the commonly reported items of stock information can be of importance to investors. Excel can be used to create a form of "candlestick" plot, which is commonly used in financial stock reporting, to show all of this information in a compact chart. A candlestick plot can be thought of as a combination of a column chart and a line chart, where the column represents the range of values over a period of time. In this case, the values would be the opening price and then the closing price for a stock. The lines represent the range of values achieved between opening and closing. The candlestick plot is a modification of the "box-and-whisker" plot, which is common in statistics. All of the stock reporting charts available in Excel are somewhat based on the candlestick plot format, taking pieces of it as appropriate to report specific data.

Michelle needs to create a chart that summarizes the company's stock prices for the last year. She has a separate workbook named TheZone Financial Data, containing the daily stock price and volume information for the last several years, and now she must choose one of the four available stock chart sub-types to display the data. The different sub-types display varying combinations of the high and low stock prices that are achieved for a day, as well as the day's opening and closing stock prices. Some sub-types add the volume or number of shares traded in a day to the chart. All of these chart sub-types require that the data in the worksheet be arranged in a specific order.

Creating a Chart with the High-Low-Close Sub-Type

First, Michelle uses a subset of the company's stock prices from April that have been copied and pasted into a new worksheet so she can examine the High-Low-Close chart sub-type. With this sub-type, the data to be plotted must be placed by column in this order: high stock value for the day, low stock value, and, finally, closing stock value, as shown in Figure 3.25. The range of lowest to highest stock prices for each time period is shown by a vertical line. The tip of the arrowhead represents the closing price for the time period.

Figure 3.25: High-Low-Close chart

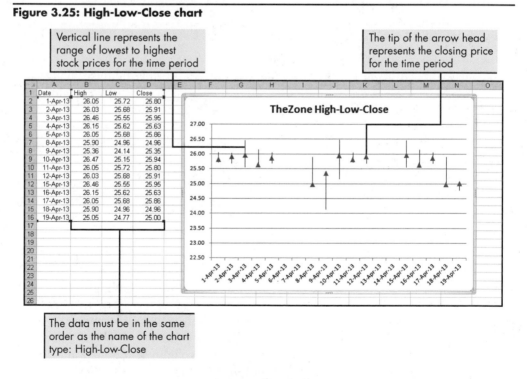

Creating a Chart with the Open-High-Low-Close Sub-Type

The Open-High-Low-Close chart sub-type adds information on the opening price of the stock for the time period. This chart sub-type also requires the data to be in a specific order in the worksheet. The order matches the name of the chart sub-type; in this case, the data must be listed in Open-High-Low-Close order to plot the chart properly. After adding the opening stock price to the data series, Michelle creates a chart with the Open-High-Low-Close sub-type, shown in Figure 3.26. The range of lowest to highest stock prices is still represented by a vertical line for each time period. A box is included to show the opening and closing prices. The bottom of the box represents the lower of the opening or closing values, while the top of the box represents the higher. Color is used to show if the stock closed at a higher or lower price than its opening price. If the box is white, the stock increased in value for the time period. The white box is referred to as the "up bar." If the box is black, the stock decreased in value for the time period. The black box is referred to as the "down bar."

Figure 3.26: Open-High-Low-Close chart

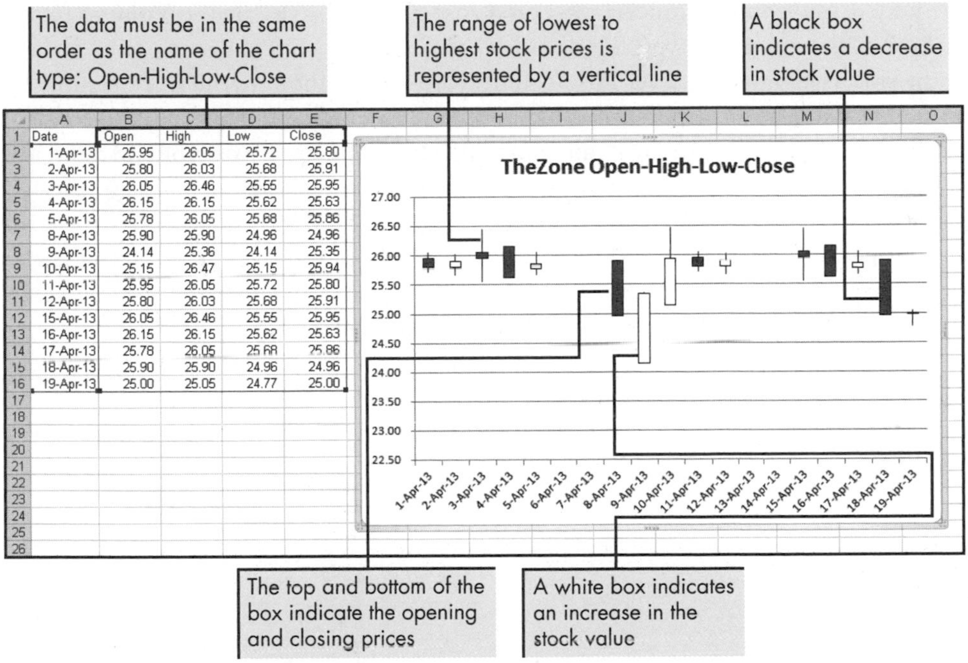

The data must be in the same order as the name of the chart type: Open-High-Low-Close

The range of lowest to highest stock prices is represented by a vertical line

A black box indicates a decrease in stock value

The top and bottom of the box indicate the opening and closing prices

A white box indicates an increase in the stock value

Best Practice

Changing the Default Colors for Excel Stock Charts

Many analysts dislike the default colors that Excel uses to indicate if a stock closed lower or higher than its opening price. Most businesspeople consider "in the black" to be positive for a company, but the default Excel stock charts in candlestick format use a black bar to indicate that the stock closed down. One option is to change the color of the "up" bars to green and the "down" bars to red, so that the colors better reflect the positive or negative aspect of the bars.

Format Up and Down Bars in Stock Charts

1. Right-click either an up bar or a down bar in the stock chart to display the shortcut menu.

2. Click either the Format Up Bars option or the Format Down Bars option on the shortcut menu, depending on which type of bar you right-clicked, to display the appropriate dialog box.

3. Select the Fill category, and then specify the color and/or pattern you want to apply to the bars.

4. Click the Close button.

Adding Volume to Stock Charts

Volume information showing how many shares of stocks were traded in the time period can be added using the Volume-High-Low-Close chart sub-type or the Volume-Open-High-Low-Close chart sub-type. These two chart sub-types shift the stock price scale to the right-side axis, or secondary y-axis. Columns are used to indicate the stock volume for each time period. The primary y-axis shows the stock volume on the left, and the columns representing the share volume are compared to it. The secondary y-axis is on the right, and the stock prices shown by the lines/bars/boxes are measured against it. Using the secondary axis in a chart is a common way to include widely differing sets of data from the same time period. These types of stock charts also require the data to be arranged in a specific order in the worksheet. After moving the column containing the volume to the correct location, Michelle creates the chart shown in Figure 3.27.

Figure 3.27: Volume-High-Low-Close chart

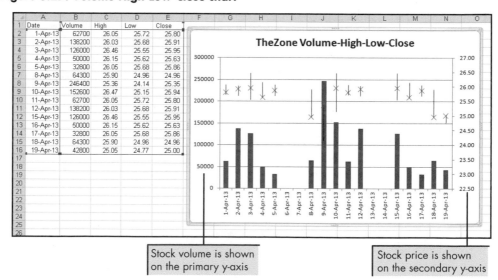

Stock volume is shown on the primary y-axis

Stock price is shown on the secondary y-axis

The default color setting on the column portion of the chart can obscure the High-Low line for time periods with exceptional volume. One option is to format the column data series with a different color that allows the High-Low lines to be displayed, as illustrated in Figure 3.28. Notice that the first volume column is in the same space as the stock price data for that time period. A dark column color would make the stock price information very difficult to interpret. Michelle modifies the column color to make the stock price data easier to see.

Figure 3.28: Modified Volume-High-Low-Close chart

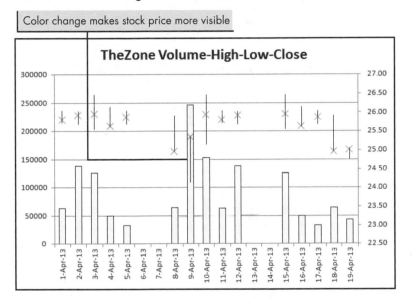

What would the impact be if the chart showed all the price and stock information for the previous year, as opposed to showing the information for only April 2013 as it does now? The Volume-Open-High-Low-Close chart sub-type combines all of the available information into one chart: lines for the high-low price range, boxes showing the opening and closing prices, and columns indicating the time period volumes. This information looks great with a small data set, but when all the daily stock information for an entire year is charted, as shown in Figure 3.29, the chart becomes almost illegible. This chart is, essentially, a cluttered line chart superimposed over a column chart. This format won't work at all for the analysis of annual stock information.

Figure 3.29: Volume-Open-High-Low-Close chart showing data for one year

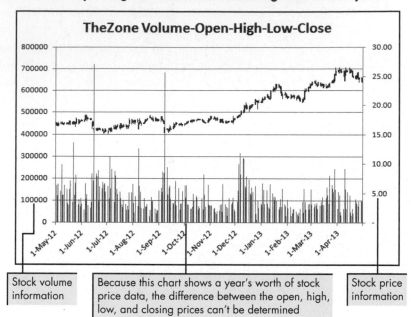

Adding Trendlines and Moving Averages

Michelle can use a line chart to show the overall trend in the closing price of the stock for the past year, combined with a column chart indicating the stock volume. Or, she could summarize the daily stock prices by month, retaining all the information in the chart. Michelle chooses the first alternative and decides to do the following:

- Create a line chart from the closing prices for each day and place it directly above the original chart.
- Add a linear trendline and a 30-day moving average to smooth out the day-to-day variations in the data.
- Change the source data in the original chart to the stock volume only.
- Change the chart type of the original chart to column.
- Remove the title from the new volume chart and make the plot area shorter.

The resulting chart is shown in Figure 3.30.

Figure 3.30: Alternative line and column chart combination

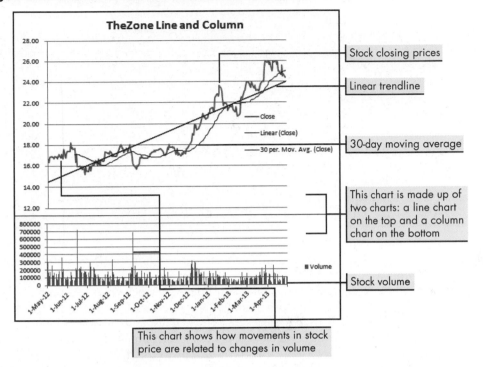

This chart shows how movements in stock price are related to changes in volume

This chart is similar to those used by many financial publications to illustrate trends in a company's stock prices and the volume of stock sold in a given period. The purpose of a chart like the one in Figure 3.30 is to show overall trends, not to show the price or volume of a stock for a particular day. Notice that the chart shows that some spikes in the volume of stock sold have occurred at the same time that the stock price has reduced dramatically. This usually indicates that investors have sold off the stock in response to particularly bad news about the company's financial strength or future prospects. The linear trendline shows a definite upward trend in the stock price. **Trendlines** graphically illustrate trends in the data using a statistical technique known as regression. More advanced uses of trendlines include forecasting forward or backward by a set number of periods in the data set, but these topics are best left to those with a strong background in regression to avoid misapplying the tool. The 30-day **moving average** trendline is used to smooth out the data, making it easier to spot trends. Each point on the 30-day moving average line represents an average of the stock closing prices for the last 30 days. The term moving average is used because the average is calculated each day for the last 30 days—moving the average along the chart. Varying degrees of smoothing are achieved by changing the length of the moving average. The longer the time period, the less sensitive the line is to day-to- day variability in the price. Generally when a stock price moves above the moving average trendline, it is a good indicator of an upward trend.

How To

Add Trendlines and Moving Averages to a Chart

1. Click the data series to which you want to add a trendline or moving average.

2. On the Layout tab, in the Analysis group, click the Trendline button to open the Trendline options.

3. Select the Trendline type you want to apply to the data series. The choices include linear, exponential, and linear forecast logarithmic. A two-period moving average selection is also available in this list of options.

4. If you want to change the number of periods in the moving average, click More Trendline Options. This opens the Format Trendline dialog box, where you can specify the number of periods over which you want to calculate the average. This dialog box allows you to modify the setting for the various trendlines available in Excel.

5. In the Format Trendline dialog box, set the number of periods and the forecast parameters for the trendline, as necessary.

6. Click the Close button.

Michelle is pleased with the results, but still wants to explore how to show annual stock data using a Volume-Open-High-Low-Close stock chart. She copies the worksheet and begins to consider how to summarize the data. Displaying the stock volume is simple; she needs to add up the stock traded during the month and can use a SUM function to do so. MAX and MIN functions can be used to take care of the highest and lowest stock price for each month. Displaying the opening and closing prices for each time period presents more of a problem. How do you select a value that corresponds to the first and last day of the month from a range of values? Michelle decides that the quickest way to do this is to simply select these cells in the worksheet. She uses the WEEKDAY and MONTH functions to calculate the day of the week and month from the date in column A. She creates a summary table of the monthly stock prices and volumes, shown in Figure 3.31.

Figure 3.31: Worksheet with summary table

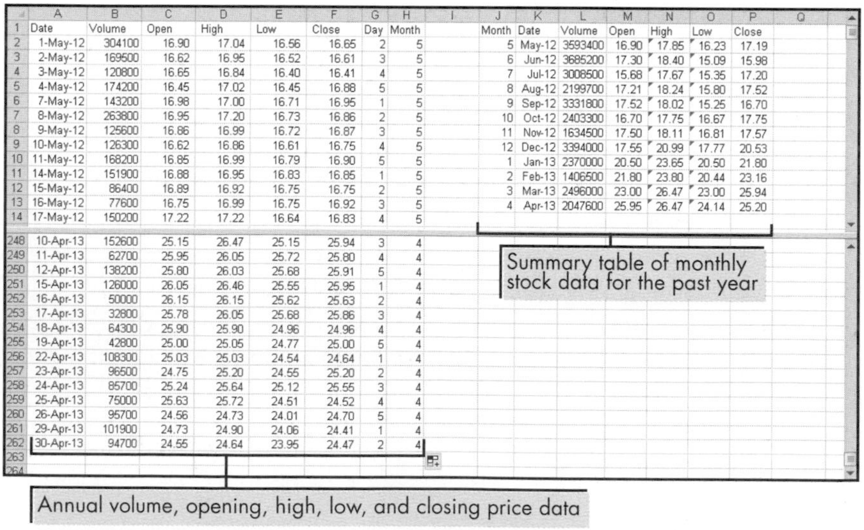

Summary table of monthly stock data for the past year

Annual volume, opening, high, low, and closing price data

The resulting Volume-Open-High-Low-Close stock chart is shown in Figure 3.32. Notice that the primary y-axis scale showing stock volumes has been increased to keep the stock volume columns from interfering with the stock price information.

Figure 3.32: Annual Volume-Open-High-Low-Close stock chart

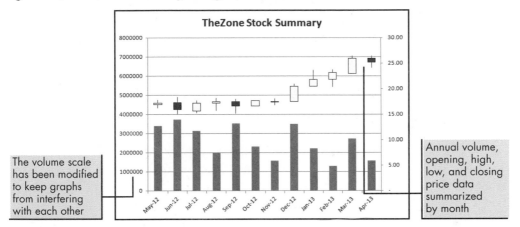

Steps To Success: Level 2

In these steps, you will work with the same consumer equipment purchasing data used to complete the Pie of Pie chart that Michelle worked on earlier. This data and the Pie of Pie chart are contained in the Excel workbook named Purchase.xlsx. You'll use this data to create a Bar of Pie chart. This same workbook contains detailed purchasing data broken out by age and gender for the following: footwear, camping, fitness, and golf. You'll use this data to create charts that illustrate the relationship between age and gender. The goal is to apply Tufte's principles to effectively present this quantitative information.

Complete the following:

1. Open the workbook named **Purchases.xlsx** in the Chapter 3 folder, and then save it as **Consumer Purchases.xlsx**. Review the data sets on the six worksheets. You need to determine how the chart sub-types covered in Level 2 can be used to illustrate the most important information in each worksheet.

2. The Pie of Pie worksheet contains the consumer purchase data organized by sport that Michelle used to create the Pie of Pie chart earlier. Use this data to create a Pie of Pie chart for the 2012 data. Place this chart on the same worksheet as the source data. Format the chart to look like the chart shown in Figure 3.23. Include the chart title **2012 Consumer Purchases by Sport** on your chart.

3. Use the data found on the Purchases by Sport worksheet to create a Bar of Pie chart that illustrates the percentage contribution by each sport to the total purchase amount. Create one Bar of Pie chart for each year. Place the three charts on the same worksheet

as the source data. Include a chart title for each chart that is similar to the chart title you included in the Pie of Pie chart in Step 2.

4. The Footwear Purchases worksheet contains percentage data for footwear purchases organized by age groups and gender. The data also includes a breakout of the age and gender of the U.S. population by percentage. Create a clustered column chart, a stacked column chart, and a 100% stacked column chart to compare the purchases by different age groups each year with the U.S. population. Place the three charts on the same worksheet as the source data. Include appropriate titles and a legend in each chart. In a cell below each chart, explain what you think the chart illustrates.

5. The Camping Purchases worksheet contains percentage data for camping purchases organized by age groups and gender. The data also includes a breakout of the age and gender of the U.S. population by percentage. Create an area chart, a stacked area chart, and a 100% stacked area chart to compare the purchases by different age groups each year with the U.S. population. Place the three charts on the same worksheet as the source data. Include appropriate titles and a legend in each chart. In a cell below each chart, explain what you think the chart illustrates.

6. The Fitness Purchases worksheet contains percentage data for fitness purchases organized by age groups and gender. The data also includes a breakout of the age and gender of the U.S. population by percentage. Create a line chart, a stacked line chart, and a 100% stacked line chart to compare the purchases by different age groups each year with the U.S. population. Place the three charts on the same worksheet as the source data. Include appropriate titles and a legend in each chart. In a cell below each chart, explain what you think the chart illustrates.

7. The Golf Purchases worksheet contains percentage data for golf purchases organized by age groups and gender. The data also includes a breakout of the age and gender of the U.S. population by percentage. Create a doughnut chart and one other chart of your choice to compare the purchases by gender each year with the U.S. population. Place the two charts on the same worksheet as the source data. Include appropriate titles and a legend in each chart. In a cell below each chart, explain what you think the chart illustrates.

8. Save and close the Consumer Purchases.xlsx workbook.

LEVEL 3
Exploring More Advanced Chart Types

Evaluating the Effectiveness of Radar, Bubble, and Dashboard Charts

Michelle is very pleased with the progress that she has made using Excel to chart and visually analyze data. However, after further reviewing both the Pie of Pie and Bar of Pie charts showing consumer purchase data, she doesn't feel that these charts adequately convey the information. She decides to look into radar charts as an alternative way to chart the consumer purchase data. Another data set she is working with has three data points for each category. Charting on three axes can be very challenging. Some options for handling this type of data include a 3-D column chart and a bubble chart. In addition, Michelle wants to set up a "management dashboard" that shows a visual summary of various performance data she uses on a regular basis.

Understanding Radar Charts

Excel has many advanced chart features and types that can be used to present data in a variety of ways. One of the more advanced chart types is the radar chart. Radar charts are named for their resemblance to the plots on radar screens as they scan a 360-degree circle. Values radiate from the center of the chart in a way that can be compared to radar screen plots, showing the distance of an object from the radar in the center. The categories are represented by lines that radiate out from the center. Although radar charts somewhat resemble pie charts, each segment in a radar chart is always the same size as the other segments. The number of categories determines the number of segments in the chart. The radar chart is also similar in structure to a spiderweb, with each "web strand" that roughly forms a circle representing the data values. The area under the curves in a radar chart can be shaded, similar to an area chart. Radar charts are like area charts in that they both allow you to compare the contributions of different categories. Whereas area charts emphasize the amount of the contribution, radar charts emphasize the relative comparison of the categories. Radar charts combine the comparison features across categories that area charts provide, with the comparison of the relative contribution to the whole that pie charts provide.

As she continues to analyze the data set of consumer equipment purchases by sport, Michelle wants to show which sports generate the most equipment purchases every year. The Pie of Pie chart created earlier shows the percentage contribution of each sport to the industry. Now Michelle decides to try using a filled radar chart to show the numerical value that each sport contributed to the industry. The worksheet data is sorted alphabetically by category with data for the three-year period 2011–2013. Michelle selects the 2013 data and produces the chart shown in Figure 3.33. The bold values next to each web strand represent the values of the data.

Figure 3.33: Consumer equipment purchase data plotted as a radar chart

	A	B	C	D
1	Consumer Equipment Purchases by Sport (in millions)			
2				
3				
4		2013	2012	2011
5	Archery	$382.77	$372.66	$356.74
6	Baseball & Softball	$415.17	$404.41	$400.70
7	Basketball	$427.05	$422.67	$383.64
8	Billiards & Indoor Games	$678.69	$660.70	$629.12
9	Bowling	$267.21	$260.45	$240.10
10	Camping	$1,649.61	$1,602.35	$1,539.67
11	Exercise	$4,992.21	$4,757.14	$4,259.54
12	Fishing Tackle	$2,265.21	$2,259.53	$2,281.95
13	Football	$167.85	$171.24	$155.43
14	Golf	$3,716.73	$3,680.05	$4,240.32
15	Hockey & Ice Skates	$258.57	$252.67	$222.07
16	Optics	$992.97	$965.91	$904.52
17	Racquetball	$105.21	$104.93	$89.98
18	Skiing, Cross-Country	$116.01	$114.33	$99.27
19	Skiing, Downhill	$657.09	$644.71	$614.76
20	Skiing, Snowboards	$347.13	$338.53	$322.83
21	Skin Diving & Scuba Gear	$438.93	$431.41	$435.26
22	Soccer Balls	$146.25	$141.54	$132.86
23	Team Goods	$2,835.45	$2,807.09	$2,765.04
24	Tennis	$508.05	$502.37	$459.78
25	Volleyball & Badminton Sets	$110.61	$108.93	$93.87
26	Water Skis	$139.77	$137.22	$122.92
27	Wheel Sports & Pogo Sticks	$581.49	$607.13	$843.61
28				
29	Total equipment	$22,200.00	$21,748.00	$21,594.00
30				
31				

The circular lines that radiate out from the center represent the axis values for this chart—in this case, the $4,000 value

The straight lines that radiate out from the center represent categories—in this case, the Archery category

This chart isn't very informative. The large range of values in the data set results in large jumps in the chart, as evidenced by the wide variances in the shaded areas representing the data values. Viewing the chart, you can pick out only the largest contributors to industry purchases, such as Exercise and Fishing Tackle, with little idea of the values contributed by the rest. Sorting the data in descending order by purchases in 2013 would reorganize the information presented in the radar chart. However, the resulting chart would only do a slightly better job of showing the dollar amount contributed by each sport category and allowing you to see the relative contribution from each sport category.

One problem is the range of values present in the data. There are too many insignificant data points that add more clutter than information to the chart. One option is to reduce the range of data charted to those categories that are more significant. Michelle decides that she is most interested in categories that have over $300 million in consumer purchases in 2013. There are 15 equipment categories that meet the criteria, as shown in the radar chart in Figure 3.34. Note that the shaded area moves in a circular fashion around the chart, going up and down as necessary to indicate the data values. For example, the Exercise category data value is $4,992.21, so the shaded area for this category appears very close to the circular line representing $5,000. By contrast, the Fishing Tackle category data value is $2,265.21, so the shaded area moves down for this category and appears close to the circular line representing $2,000. How could you show the categories with the smaller values? If needed, a second chart could be created with the smaller values. Care would have to be taken that the difference in values for the two charts is obvious or a problem with interpreting the data could result. A note describing this would have to be added to the second chart.

Figure 3.34: Revised radar chart limited to purchases over $300 million

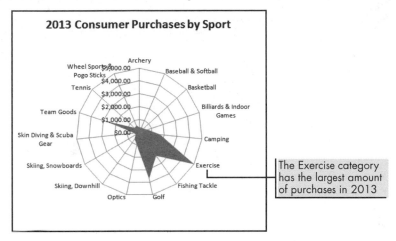

Radar charts can display more than one series, but displaying too much information on the chart can cause problems. For example, Figure 3.35 shows the consumer purchases above $300 million by sport for the last three years in the chart on the left, which is labeled as a filled radar chart. The series overlap in many values, making it very difficult to determine the values represented by the chart. Changing the chart type from a filled radar to a non-filled (standard) radar chart, shown on the right in Figure 3.35, doesn't help much because the values are so close.

Figure 3.35: Radar charts with multiple data series

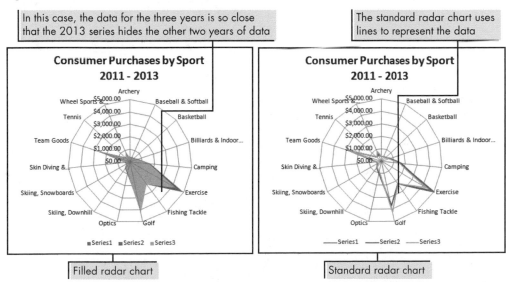

Radar charts offer a powerful method of displaying and comparing data across categories. As with all of the charts in Excel, the intended message of the chart must be considered. A positive feature in one chart type might become negative if it doesn't support what the chart creator is trying to illustrate. Often, the best way to choose a chart is through trial and error.

Understanding Bubble Charts

Bubble charts allow three-dimensional data to be plotted in 2-D on two axes. A bubble chart is similar to an X Y (Scatter) chart. Both the x- and y-axes are numeric rather than having one axis containing categories, as in bar and column charts. The third dimension is also numeric and is represented by varying the size of the data point that intersects with the x- and y-axis—the larger the bubble, the larger the value. The varying sized data points, or bubbles, give this chart its name.

Plotting 3-D Data in Two Axes: Bubble Charts vs. 3-D Column Charts

Michelle has been working with some market share data for the Footwear division and wants to display the relationship between the number of styles offered, sales, and market share. A 3-D column chart has three axes and should, therefore, work for this data. Figure 3.36 shows the 3-D column chart; in this chart, the plot area was rotated to better show each data series. The great difference in scale for the number of styles, sales, and market share make this chart less than useful.

Figure 3.36: 3-D column chart of Footwear division market share

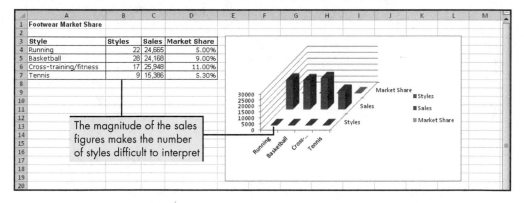

Michelle decides to try a bubble chart to display this set of data. She also removes the legend from the right side of the chart and adds a title. The resulting chart is shown in Figure 3.37.

Figure 3.37: Bubble chart of Footwear division market share

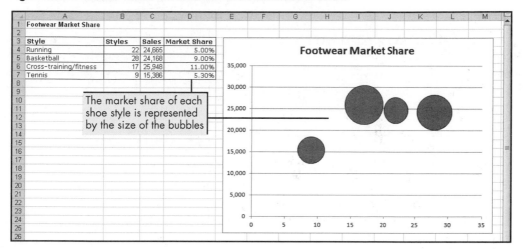

The bubble chart displays the number of styles on the x-axis and the sales on the y-axis; the market share is represented by the size of each bubble on the chart. Now the chart needs some descriptions to clarify the data on the chart. Michelle runs into a slight problem when attempting to add the shoe style categories to the chart. Adding the series name as a data label to the chart results in the problem shown in Figure 3.38. The series name has no meaning because all the data is in one series.

Figure 3.38: Adding a series name to the bubble chart

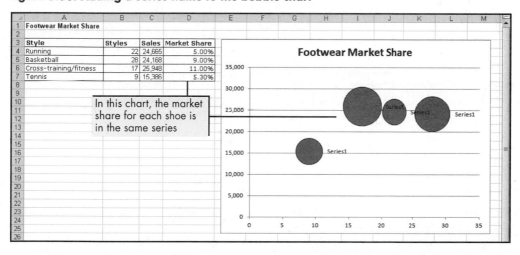

The shoe category names can be assigned to the bubble chart by adding each shoe type as an individual series in the Legend Entries (Series) section of the Select Data Source dialog box. Adding the series requires the individual entry of the name, x-value, y-value, and bubble size. Michelle adds the x- and y-axis titles and selects the series name as a data label to create the final chart shown in Figure 3.39.

Figure 3.39: Final bubble chart showing Footwear division market share vs. sales vs. number of styles

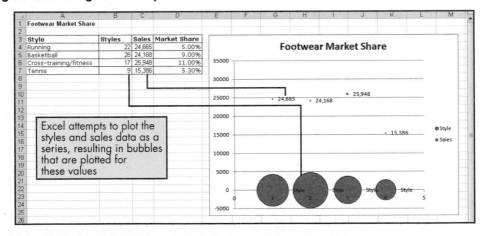

Solving Bubble Chart Problems

Bubble charts can be problematic. The source data must be selected without including labels. Figure 3.40 shows what happens if the row and column labels are selected along with the source data. Excel is "confused" by the addition of what appears to be category data and attempts to assign numerical values to it, thereby rendering the chart useless.

Figure 3.40: Range selection problems with bubble charts

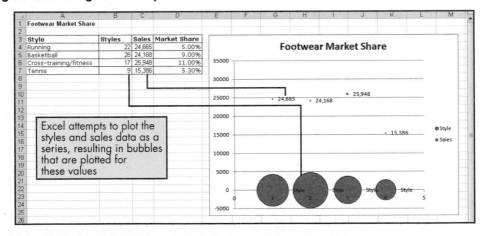

Best Practice

Adding Category Labels to Bubble Charts Without Using Multiple Series

There is a way to "trick" Excel into displaying category labels without having to go to the trouble of entering individual name, x-value, y-value, and bubble size values for each item: use custom formatting to hide the displayed value for the range of cells associated with the bubble size—in this case, market share. The value data label displays the cell contents for the range of cells identified as the data source for the bubble size, as shown in Figure 3.41. The chart data range for this figure is (B4:C7, E4:E7).

Figure 3.41: Bubble chart "tricks"

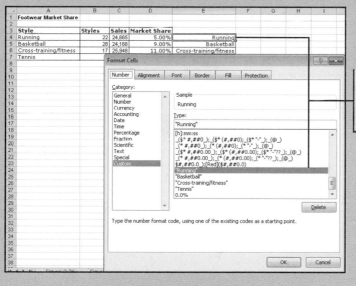

To create a custom cell format that accomplishes this trick, display the Number tab of the Format Cells dialog box; then enter the category text within quotation marks, as shown in Figure 3.42. The category name becomes the displayed contents of the cell. The actual cell contents are hidden behind the text string and are used for any calculations.

Figure 3.42: Custom cell formats

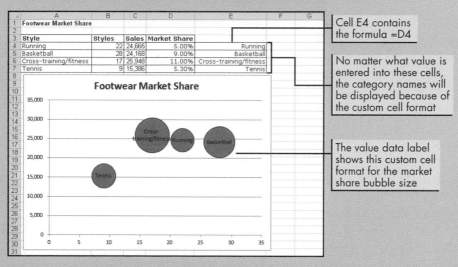

Creating a Management Dashboard

Michelle has been reviewing several business intelligence software packages featuring **dashboards** that display performance indicators in a fashion similar to the instrument panel in a car's dashboard. These dashboards usually feature a set of charts that summarize several sets of data graphically. The most intriguing ones feature charts that resemble actual dashboards. Michelle prefers the flexibility that using Excel gives her, but would like to add a dashboard worksheet to provide a quick, visual summary of performance indicators such as customer satisfaction, customer returns, on-time deliveries, monthly sales, and other accounting measures. She decides the first step is to create a chart that duplicates the gauges found on many of the software packages she has been reviewing. The chart will illustrate the average customer purchases per year for TheZone's top customers.

Building a Dashboard Chart

Michelle builds the dashboard chart shown in Figure 3.43. This chart is a doughnut chart with some of the data segments hidden to create the 180-degree circular band. Doughnut charts assign the relative size of each segment according to the segment's contribution to the total. For example, in a two-segment doughnut chart, each with the same value, each segment takes up one-half of the doughnut. Three equal segments each take up one-third, four segments each take up one-fourth, and so on. Because a doughnut chart is really a circle, Michelle can use the properties of a circle to fit the values into her dashboard chart.

Figure 3.43: Final dashboard chart

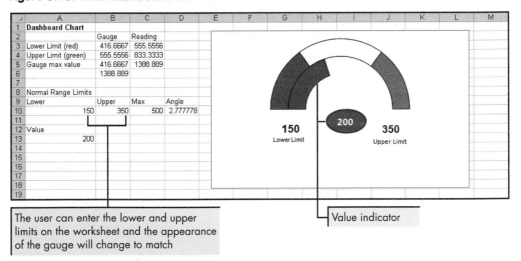

The user can enter the lower and upper limits on the worksheet and the appearance of the gauge will change to match

Value indicator

Defining the Normal Operating Range

The chart shows three segments in the top arch: the far-left section for values below the normal operating range limit, the normal operating range section, and the far-right section for values above the upper limit. A fourth segment of the doughnut chart takes up one-half of the chart and is hidden at the lower part of the chart. Because there are 360 degrees in a circle, the easiest thing to do is to convert all values into degrees. The dashboard chart needs to display only one-half of the circle, so the lower hidden segment will always have a value of 180 degrees. Michelle wants to be able to dynamically adjust the normal operating range limits on the chart by typing values into the worksheet that define the lower and upper limits. She will use the worksheet in Figure 3.44 to accomplish this.

Figure 3.44: Dashboard chart setup

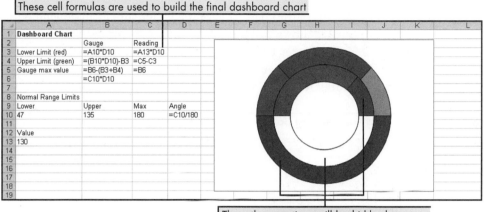

These cell formulas are used to build the final dashboard chart

	A	B	C	D	E	F	G	H	I	J	K	L
1	Dashboard Chart											
2		Gauge	Reading									
3	Lower Limit (red)	=A10*D10	=A13*D10									
4	Upper Limit (green)	=(B10*D10)-B3	=C5-C3									
5	Gauge max value	=B6-(B3+B4)	=B6									
6		=C10*D10										
7												
8	Normal Range Limits											
9	Lower	Upper	Max	Angle								
10	47	135	180	=C10/180								
11												
12	Value											
13	130											
14												
15												
16												
17												
18												
19												

These three sections will be hidden by changing the color to match the background

Michelle enters the lower limit, upper limit, and maximum (max) value of the gauge into the cells in row 10 of the worksheet. The max value will always occur at the 180-degree position of this chart, so it is divided by 180 degrees, in cell D10, to get a conversion value to use for the other values. The chart source data for the first gauge segment is created in cell B3 by multiplying the lower limit value in cell A10 by cell D10, converting the lower limit into degrees. The second chart segment is calculated in cell B4 by multiplying the upper limit value in cell B10 by the conversion factor in cell D10 and then subtracting the value for the first segment in cell B3. The third segment is whatever remains in the 180-degree arc; this is calculated in cell B5 by subtracting the value for the first two segments from the value of the lower hidden segment in cell B6.

Creating the Value Indicator

The value indicator is the portion of the doughnut chart that is below the main arch of the dashboard chart (see Figure 3.43). The value indicator only requires three segments for its doughnut chart instead of the four needed for the gauge. The first segment is calculated in cell C3 by multiplying the value entered into cell A13 by the angular conversion factor in cell D10. The value of the second segment is calculated in cell C4 by subtracting the value of the third and final segment in cell C5 from the first segment in cell C3. The third segment is the portion of the doughnut that will be hidden at the bottom of the chart and is equal in value to the normal operating range fourth segment that is to be hidden in the same way.

Creating the Doughnut Chart

Michelle uses the Insert tab to create the doughnut chart shown in Figure 3.44. She uses the Ctrl key to select the range C3:B5, B3:B6. The default doughnut chart starts the angle of the first slice at the 12 o'clock position, or 0 degrees. Michelle right-clicks the data series and opens the Format Data Series dialog box. The angle of the first segment setting is located on the Series Options tab. Michelle sets the angle to 270 degrees to have the chart start the gauge at the 9 o'clock position. This hides the bottom half of the doughnut chart.

Michelle hides the lower segments of the chart by selecting each segment and opening the Format Data Point dialog box, as shown in Figure 3.45. In the Fill category she sets the Fill option to No fill, and in the Border Color category she sets the Border Color to No line, making these segments seem to disappear. The second segment of the value doughnut can also be hidden in this manner.

Figure 3.45: Format Data Point dialog box

Adding Digital Values to the Chart

The lower and upper normal operating range limits and the plotted value can be added to the chart to improve the information that the chart provides. The Shapes button in the Insert group on the Layout tab contains a variety of shapes that can be added to the chart. The plotted value digital display is an oval object found in the Shapes gallery. Michelle selects the chart, clicks the Oval button in the Shapes gallery, and then draws the oval in the middle of the chart (see Figure 3.43). To display the value in the oval, she clicks the oval on the chart, enters an equal sign (=) in the Formula Bar, and then selects the cell containing the value she wants to link to this shape. For the plotted value, this is cell A13. Michelle then formats the text with bold and a larger font size to improve clarity. She creates text boxes, again using the Shapes gallery, to display the upper and lower limits in the dashboard chart. These can be linked to cell values in the same way that the oval shape was.

With the dashboard chart complete, Michelle tests it by entering different numbers for the normal operating range lower and upper limits, the max gauge value, and the value to be plotted. She ensures that the chart responds properly to these changes.

Michelle is pleased with her work on this dashboard style chart. She will use this chart as a template for the other dashboard style charts she is planning to use to monitor performance indicators or metrics for the company.

Steps To Success: Level 3

In these steps, you will create charts to illustrate and analyze consumer purchase data for the Footwear division of TheZone.

Complete the following:

1. Open the workbook named **Footwear.xlsx** in the Chapter 3 folder, and then save it as **Footwear Analysis.xlsx**.

2. Use the Footwear Purchases by Price worksheet in the workbook to produce charts that compare the average price for each category of footwear. Create a radar chart and an appropriate version of a bar chart to see which one best illustrates the information. Place the two charts on the same worksheet as the source data. Include appropriate titles and a legend in each chart. Determine which chart does the best job of illustrating the relative contribution of each category to the purchase amount, and which one is best for emphasizing the year-to-year trend for each category. In a cell below each chart, explain what you think the chart illustrates.

3. Michelle has been working on sport participation data by gender and equipment sales. She built a worksheet by combining data from the 2013 overall and 2013 women's participation in sports data with the equipment purchases by sport data. Use the data in the Participants and Equipment worksheet to create a bubble chart that shows the number of women and the number of men participating in sports, as well as the amount of equipment sales that each sport generates. Place the chart on the same worksheet as the source data. Include appropriate titles and category labels in the chart.

   TROUBLESHOOTING: To help you complete this task quickly and more efficiently, remember that you can use a custom cell format. This allows you to add category labels to the bubbles without having to enter items individually. Refer to the bubble chart Best Practice in the chapter.

4. Save and close the Footwear Analysis.xlsx workbook.

Chapter Summary

This chapter presented many ways that Excel can be used to illustrate quantitative information. Sparklines were introduced as a quick way to visualize changes in trends and patterns in data sets. Both sparklines and charts offer the opportunity to add visual analysis to problem solving. Tufte's guiding principles on the creation of graphics can be applied in Excel to create excellent charts that present quantitative information clearly, precisely, and efficiently.

In Level 1, you learned how the choice of chart type can influence a viewer's perception of the information presented. Differences between the main chart types—line, column, bar, area, pie, and X Y (Scatter)—were examined, as these charts were used to summarize and present a variety of data. Many of the chart types can be used with the same types of data, resulting in different interpretations of that data.

Level 2 covered chart sub-types, such as stacked and 100% stacked, for line, column, and area charts. These sub-types further summarize the data being presented, allowing a comparison of the contribution of a particular data series to a greater whole. The Pie of Pie and Bar of Pie chart sub-types were introduced to show how particular elements of pie charts can be summarized in another format. The different sub-types of stock charts were covered in some detail, showing the strengths and weaknesses of the various ways that Excel presents stock price and volume information. You also learned how trendlines and moving averages can help to clarify the data in stock charts.

In Level 3, the discussion was expanded to include more advanced chart types, such as radar and bubble charts. You also saw how to combine chart types within the same chart to build a management dashboard. This management dashboard consists of "speedometer-like" gauges that can be used to monitor various business metrics at a glance, allowing the viewer to see if any particular areas of a business require more investigation.

Table 3.2 summarizes the chart types and sub-types presented in this chapter.

Table 3.2: Summary of Excel chart types and sub-types

Chart Type	Description
Column	
Clustered Column	Compares values across categories
Stacked Column	Compares the contribution of each value to a total across categories
100% Stacked Column	Compares the percentage each value contributes to a total across categories
3-D Column	Compares values across categories and across series
Bar	
Clustered Bar	Compares values across categories

Table 3.2: Summary of Excel chart types and sub-types (cont.)

Chart Type	Description
Stacked Bar	Compares the contribution of each value to a total across categories
100% Stacked Bar	Compares the percentage each value contributes to a total across categories
Line	
Line	Displays a trend over time or categories
Stacked Line	Displays the trend of the contribution of each value over time or categories
100% Stacked Line	Displays the trend of the percentage each value contributes over time or categories
3-D Line	Displays a line with a 3-D visual effect
Pie	
Pie	Displays the contribution of each value to a total
3-D Pie	Displays the contribution of each value to a total with a 3-D visual effect
Pie of Pie	Displays a main pie chart with user-defined values extracted and combined into a second pie plot
Exploded Pie	Displays the contribution of each value to a total value while emphasizing individual values
Bar of Pie	Displays a main pie chart with user-defined values extracted and combined into a stacked bar as the second plot
X Y (Scatter)	Compares pairs of values; display options include Scatter with data points connected by lines, Scatter with data points connected by smoothed lines without markers, and Scatter with data points connected by lines without markers
Area	
Area	Displays the trend of values over time or categories
Stacked Area	Displays the trend of the contribution of each value over time or categories
100% Stacked Area	Displays the trend of the percentage each value contributes over time or categories
Doughnut	
Doughnut	Displays the contribution of each value to a total (similar to a pie chart), but can contain multiple series
Exploded Doughnut	Displays the contribution of each value to a total value while emphasizing individual values (similar to an exploded pie chart), but can contain multiple series
Radar	Displays changes in values relative to a center point
Bubble	Compares sets of three values; similar to a scatter chart with the third value displayed as the size of a bubble marker
Stock	
High-Low-Close	Requires three series of values in this order
Open-High-Low-Close	Requires four series of values in this order
Volume-High-Low-Close	Requires four series of values in this order
Volume-Open-High-Low-Close	Requires five series of values in this order

Conceptual Review

1. List and describe the significance of each of Tufte's five data graphics principles.

2. How do sparklines differ from charts?

3. What are the three steps involved in using the Insert tab to create a chart?

4. Give an example of a low data-ink ratio in a chart.

5. How do you change the chart type of an existing chart?

6. What charting limits does Excel have in terms of data points and series?

7. How many standard chart types and sub-types are available in Excel?

8. What are the differences and similarities between a line chart and an X Y (Scatter) chart? When should you use each one?

9. Explain the difference between the data points in a line chart and an X Y (Scatter) chart.

10. What are the differences between a bar chart and a column chart? Give an example of when you would use each one.

11. What are the differences between a column chart and an area chart? Give an example of when you would use each one.

12. How do pie charts differ from doughnut charts?

13. When should you use a stacked line, column, or area chart? How do the stacked charts differ from regular charts?

14. When should you use a 100% stacked line, column, or area chart? How do the 100% stacked charts differ from stacked charts?

15. What chart sub-types are available for the stock chart in Excel? Explain how you interpret the data markers on each of the sub-types.

16. How does a radar chart differ from other charts? Give an example of when you would consider using a radar chart.

17. Define a bubble chart and explain what type of data is suitable for plotting on a bubble chart.

18. When should you use a dashboard chart?

Case Problems

Level 1 – Illustrating Travel Data for the Indiana Department of Tourism

As a travel industry consultant, you have been working for the state of Indiana Department of Tourism. The department manager has asked you to present a report on where Indiana residents travel to and where Indiana visitors come from. The modes of transportation must also be presented. You will also include some information from a survey that your firm has recently completed. The travel survey is located in the workbook named Indiana.xlsx.

Complete the following:

1. Open the workbook named **Indiana.xlsx** in the Chapter 3 folder, and then save it as **Indiana Travel.xlsx**.

2. Create a bar chart to illustrate the differences in Trips per Traveler and Miles per Traveler of the average Indiana resident, the average U.S. resident, and the average Indiana visitor.

3. Create a bar chart to illustrate a state-by-state comparison of the number of residents from the rest of the nation who visit Indiana, and the number of Indiana residents who visit other states. Rank the information in this chart by the states with the most visitors to Indiana.

4. The Indiana Department of Tourism is very interested in learning more about how people travel in Indiana. They want to use this information to better target advertising to specific demographic groups and methods of travel. Use the appropriate chart or series of charts to illustrate how people travel; the purpose of their travel; and their income levels, age, and gender. This information should be presented for people who live within the state and those visiting the state with a comparison between the two groups.

5. Save and close the Indiana Travel.xlsx workbook.

Level 2 – Analyzing Stock Performance for Universal Investments

As an analyst at the Universal Investments financial company, you regularly monitor the performance of your clients' investments. You are preparing for a meeting with one of your investors to discuss how their stocks have performed over the last year and changes they should make to their portfolio. Your client has asked for information on four companies: Intel, AMD, Time Warner, and Wal-Mart. You will find daily stock price and volume information contained in the Invest.xlsx workbook.

Finance

Complete the following:

1. Open the workbook named **Invest.xlsx** located in the Chapter 3 folder, and then save it as **Investment Performance.xlsx**.

2. Create a chart for each company using the appropriate stock chart sub-type. Be certain to use each chart sub-type only once.

3. Summarize the data to clearly show some of the data markers in the charts.

4. Place each chart on a new sheet in the workbook.

5. Use the appropriate chart to compare the change in stock price for each company over the last year.

6. Using the information on the Portfolio worksheet, prepare the appropriate chart to display the relative contribution of each stock to the value of the portfolio.

7. Save and close the Investment Performance.xlsx workbook.

Level 3 – Illustrating Patterns in Gas Prices for CKG Auto

Sales

You have been assigned to CKG Auto's sales department as an analyst. The marketing team for the new Safari Wildebeest Sport Utility Vehicle has become concerned that the rising cost of gas will negatively affect vehicle sales. They are considering introducing limited rebates at times when gas prices are especially high. The company might also increase its marketing of the Safari Meer Cat, the new compact, sporty SUV the company introduced late last year. Your supervisor has asked you to put together a report and presentation showing the price per gallon of gas by region and large metropolitan areas. The company is interested to see if there are any patterns in the data that can be used to better time the rebate promotions. The Safari.xlsx file contains data on gas prices for various regions and metropolitan areas around the country.

Complete the following:

1. Open the workbook named **Safari.xlsx** located in the Chapter 3 folder, and then save it as **Safari Analysis.xlsx**.

2. Create a series of charts that compare gas prices by time of the year and by location. The time can be in quarters, months, or week of the month, as you deem appropriate. The location should be charted separately by region, by state, and by city.

3. For each location—region, state, and city—determine if a particular location has higher gas prices than the others. Add a comment near each chart to explain your findings.

4. Determine if a particular time of year has higher gas prices than the other times of the year. Add a comment near each chart to explain your findings.

5. Create a bubble chart to illustrate the number of weeks that each city's gas price is above the gas price for the entire United States; the number of weeks that it is below the gas price for the entire United States; and the average gas price in dollars per gallon for the year. Add appropriate titles, labels, and a legend to the chart.

6. Save and close the Safari Analysis.xlsx workbook.

SAM: Skills Assessment Manager

For current SAM information, including versions and content details, visit SAM Central (http://samcentral.course.com). If you have a SAM user profile, you may have access to hands-on instruction, practice, and assessment of the skills covered in this chapter. Since various versions of SAM are supported throughout the life of this text, check with your instructor for the correct instructions and URL/Web site for accessing assignments.

Applying Logic in Decision Making
Accounting: Establishing a Credit Approval Process for Accounts Receivable

"No, no, you're not thinking; you're just being logical."
—Niels Bohr

LEARNING OBJECTIVES

Level 1

Understand the Boolean logical values TRUE and FALSE
Build formulas with relational operators
Evaluate criteria using the Boolean logical functions AND, OR, and NOT
Apply conditional formatting to highlight key information in a worksheet

Level 2

Understand how to build formulas with nested functions
Write IF functions to evaluate TRUE/FALSE values and perform calculations
Nest functions within an IF statement
Construct a simple nested IF function

Level 3

Combine sets of criteria in an IF function
Create a *none of* construct to perform a logical test
Create an *only* construct to perform a logical test
Solve more complex problems using nested IFs and Boolean logical functions

FUNCTIONS COVERED IN THIS CHAPTER

AND
IF
NOT
OR

Chapter Introduction

So far in this text, you have used arithmetic operators and functions to produce a numeric result. But what if you want to evaluate the following statement: "The company sold more skis last year than this year"? The result of this statement is not a numeric value, but rather the response *true* or *false*. **TRUE** and **FALSE** are referred to as Boolean logical values.

In this chapter, you will take data analysis to the next level, exploring tools that allow you to compare data as well as analyze sets of data using multiple criteria. Analyzing data in this way enables you to determine if the data meets *all* of the criteria, or *at least one* of the criteria, or even *none* of the criteria—resulting in a TRUE or FALSE Boolean value. You will accomplish these tasks using relational operators and the Boolean logical functions AND, OR, and NOT. You will also learn how to specify different cell formats based on whether a set of criteria is met. In later sections of the chapter, you will take the results of logical tests and apply different outcomes to those that are TRUE versus those that are FALSE. Finally, you will learn to combine these tools together, further enhancing your ability to analyze more complex data and make decisions based on the results.

Case Scenario

Accounting

As an international sporting goods company, TheZone maintains some of its own retail outlets. However, the most significant part of the company's sales is derived from selling large amounts of sporting goods equipment and apparel to other retailers and to large organizations, such as school systems and athletic teams. Most companies like TheZone have processes in place to determine the creditworthiness of potential customers before entering into business relationships with them, thereby ensuring that the company's accounts receivable group is able to collect payments from customers in a timely manner. The accounts receivable group at TheZone performs many vital tasks that affect the success of the company. The data provided by this group during the credit approval process has a direct impact on the cash flow and financial stability of the company. This process includes both obtaining financial data for new and existing customers, and determining the current credit status of each customer's account. These tasks are ongoing and can be challenging due to customers' changing status and the variability of economic conditions.

Eric Carter is an accountant working in the accounts receivable group at TheZone. He has recently been asked to develop a formal system to streamline and automate the credit approval process. Eventually, the information compiled will be handed off to the finance group for final analysis and approval. The finance group is responsible for making the ultimate decisions, factoring in the effects that these decisions will have on corporate profitability, customer relations, adherence to government regulations, and so on.

LEVEL 1

Analyzing Data Using Relational Operators and Boolean Logical Functions

Reviewing Financial Criteria Related to Credit

Before Eric can evaluate a customer's account for credit availability, he must first assemble the financial information required to make the credit decisions. The internal data, such as a customer's purchasing and payment history with TheZone, is available from TheZone's corporate accounting system. Eric also plans to utilize information on each customer as compiled by Dun & Bradstreet. **Dun & Bradstreet® (D&B)** is one of the most widely used financial reporting services that provides, among other products, financial information about corporations and institutions, and extensive analyses on each company's credit-worthiness and payment history. The values supplied by D&B on the companies that TheZone does business with will be updated on a quarterly basis by a clerical employee in TheZone's accounts receivable group. Specifically, Eric plans to use D&B's services to obtain values on the net worth of companies requesting credit, a company's credit rating, and a company's payment record, as follows:

- The net worth of a company is based on the assets and liabilities listed on its balance sheet.
- The credit rating consists of two parts, as listed in Table 4.1. The first is a classification ranging from 5A to HH indicating the net worth category of the company. The second is a value from 1 to 4 indicating a composite credit appraisal score, where 1 is the best and 4 is the worst. The score represents D&B's determination of the company's risk factors that affect its ability to pay its bills.

Table 4.1: D&B credit rating system*

Rating Classification		Composite Credit Appraisal			
Based on Worth from Interim or Fiscal Balance Sheet		High	Good	Fair	Limited
5A	50,000,000 and over	1	2	3	4
4A	10,000,000 to 49,999,999	1	2	3	4
3A	1,000,000 to 9,999,999	1	2	3	4
2A	750,000 to 999,999	1	2	3	4
1A	500,000 to 749,999	1	2	3	4
BA	300,000 to 499,999	1	2	3	4
BB	200,000 to 299,999	1	2	3	4
CB	125,000 to 199,999	1	2	3	4
CC	75,000 to 124,999	1	2	3	4
DC	50,000 to 74,999	1	2	3	4

Table 4.1: D&B credit rating system* (cont.)

Rating Classification		Composite Credit Appraisal			
DD	35,000 to 49,999	1	2	3	4
EE	20,000 to 34,999	1	2	3	4
FF	10,000 to 19,999	1	2	3	4
GG	5,000 to 9,999	1	2	3	4
HH	Up to 4,999	1	2	3	4
*Based on information available at www.dnb.com/					

4

Level 1

- The PAYDEX® index is an indicator of the payment habits of the company, as listed in Table 4.2. The index provides a score from 1 to 100, with 1 representing the worst payment record and 100 representing the best.

Table 4.2: D&B PAYDEX score*

Score	Payment
100	Payments received prior to date of invoice (Anticipate)
90	Payments received within trade discount period (Discount)
80	Payments received within terms granted (Prompt)
70	15 days beyond terms
60	22 days beyond terms
50	30 days beyond terms
40	60 days beyond terms
30	90 days beyond terms
20	120 days beyond terms
UN	Unavailable
*Based on information available at www.dnb.com/	

- The financial stress risk class is a rating from 1 to 5 indicating the risk of a company ending up in financial distress, where 1 represents businesses with the lowest probability of risk, as detailed in Table 4.3.

Table 4.3: D&B financial stress risk class*

Class	% of Businesses Within This Class	Financial Stress Percentile	Financial Stress Score
1	80%	21–100	1377–1875
2	10%	11–20	1353–1376
3	6%	5–10	1303–1352
4	3%	2–4	1225–1302
5	1%	1	1001–1224
*Based on information available at www.dnb.com/			

Eric's first task is to develop a worksheet that will list these data elements for each of The-Zone's customers. He will start with a small, selected customer list and develop the necessary formulas. Later he will expand the list to include all credit customers. He begins by entering data for each customer into a worksheet named CreditData in a workbook named Customer Credit and Payment History.xlsx, as shown in Figure 4.1. This worksheet includes the following information:

- Customer name (column A)
- Current credit limit (column B)
- Total sales to the customer from the previous fiscal year (column C)
- Current fiscal year's total sales to date (column D)
- Value of the customer's past due balance, which is for any unpaid invoices over 30 days (column E)
- Net worth of the company according to its D&B report in thousands of dollars (column F)
- D&B credit rating classification value (column G)
- D&B composite credit appraisal value (column H)
- D&B PAYDEX score (column I)
- D&B financial stress risk class (column J)

Eric needs to develop the formulas that will allow him and other accounts receivable staff members to automatically reauthorize and approve new credit applications based on a set of criteria. The first step in this process is to apply several credit approval indicator rules to each customer's data. Each of these rules presents criteria that suggest credit approval might be warranted. Later, Eric will take the results of these indicator rules and combine them to make final credit recommendations. First, he needs to create the required formulas, which must be based on TheZone's credit determination rules, as follows:

Rule #1: Accept a customer that has a past due balance that is less than 10% of this year's total sales. This is not calculated for new customers. A customer that has a past due balance of 10% or more of this year's sales, regardless of its financial stability, has failed to consistently pay its previous bills with TheZone and, therefore, has not demonstrated a satisfactory business relationship. A customer without such a past due balance demonstrates creditworthiness.

Rule #2: Accept a customer that has either a composite credit appraisal value of 1 or a PAYDEX score over 90. These values indicate a strong, financially stable enterprise with an outstanding reputation for paying its bills on time.

Rule #3: Accept a customer that has all of the following: a net worth of at least $500,000; a composite credit appraisal value of 2 or lower; a PAYDEX score over 70; and a stress risk class of 1. These values indicate that the customer has a good overall financial position, a reasonable level of risk, and a reputation for paying its creditors.

Figure 4.1: CreditData worksheet in the Customer Credit and Payment History workbook*

TheZone's accounts receivable data   D&B data

Customer Name	Current Credit Limit	Previous Year's Sales	Current Year's Sales	Past Due Balance	Net Worth in (000)	D&B Credit Rating Class	D&B Composite Credit Appraisal (1 Best)	D&B PAYDEX (100 Best)	D&B Stress Risk Class (1 Best)
Athletic Gear Corp.	$ 9,000	$ 15,382	$ 11,952	$ 0	$ 450	BA	4	15	3
Baltimore O's	39,000	10,033	7,789	0	1,950	3A	1	51	1
Baseball & More	75,000	60,009	55,342	13,892	37,500	4A	2	70	1
Canadian Ski Club	33,000	35,039	50,921	495	1,650	BA	2	43	1
Concord Pro Shop					10,000	4A	1	91	1
Everything Golf	25,000	15,221	9,483	2,899	1,250	3A	3	76	1
Lake Pro Shops	42,000	80,498	81,126	0	2,100	3A	2	87	1
Mars Dept. Store	27,000	35,354	20,666	0	213	BB	3	94	1
RG Bradley	46,000	90,970	18,343	0	2,300	3A	1	21	1
RX for Sports	15,000	5,663	3,014	0	750	2A	1	59	1
School Sports Supply	45,000	50,278	32,338	0	2,250	3A	3	91	1
Ski World	26,000	25,864	28,154	0	300	BA	2	82	1
Sneaker Kingdom	45,000	40,157	25,379	0	2,250	3A	2	71	1
Sports & Stuff	15,000	15,898	14,732	14,383	450	BA	1	67	1
Toy Kingdom	22,000	10,073	1,047	0	1,100	3A	3	14	1
Under the Sea	45,000	95,411	64,418	0	150	CB	4	79	2
US Olympic Team	20,000	5,621	6,171	0	1,000	3A	1	07	1
WWW Sports Inc.	100,000	60,009	60,354	0	500,000	5A	2	97	1
Zip & Sons	10,000	15,490	22,760	0	620	1A	2	96	1

Accounts Receivable Department - Customer Credit Analysis

New customer with no previous account history

*Please note that companies used in this example are fictitious, but the text uses the investment ratings of the Dun & Bradstreet® credit rating system.

What does it mean if a customer does *not* meet the criteria for a specific rule? Does this mean that credit should be rejected? Not necessarily. Consider the example of a college that might automatically accept an applicant if that applicant's SAT scores are above 2250. It cannot be assumed that if the applicant's scores are below this threshold, the school will automatically reject the applicant for admission—only that further evaluation is required. Similarly, in the case of TheZone, the three rules suggest a customer's creditworthiness, but failure to meet the criteria for any single rule does not translate to automatic denial of credit.

Evaluation of these rules is the first step in making Eric's worksheet operational. Additional information will be forthcoming from management to determine what combinations of results for these rules will cause a customer to be accepted automatically to a specific credit level or rejected outright. Automating this process in Excel will leave a greater amount of time for the accounts receivable staff to further analyze the more problematic accounts, such as customers with very large orders and less than perfect credit or smaller companies with limited assets.

Using Relational Operators to Compare Two Values

Eric needs to determine if a company listed on the CreditData worksheet meets the specific conditions set forth in each of the three rules noted previously. Consider the first rule: "Accept a customer that has a past due balance that is less than 10% of this year's total sales. This is not calculated for new customers." A customer that meets the criteria has, for the most part, paid its bills. To manually determine if this condition is TRUE, Eric would need to calculate the past due percentage and determine if it is lower than 10%.

In Excel, you can use relational operators to compare two values to determine if the relational expression is TRUE or FALSE. Relational operators were first introduced in Chapter 2, when the problem in that chapter required creating criteria for the COUNTIF and SUMIF functions. Here, relational operators are used to compare two values, as shown in Table 4.4.

Table 4.4: Relational operators used when comparing two values

Description	Operator	Example	Resulting Value
Equal to	=	=3+5=8	TRUE
Not equal to	<>	=SUM(3,7)<>10	FALSE
Greater than	>	=100>MAX(5,10,20)	TRUE
Less than	<	=B3<C3 where cell B3=5 and cell C3=4	FALSE
Greater than or equal to	>=	=B3>=C3 where cell B3 contains the date 1/1/2014 and cell C3 contains the date 12/31/2013	TRUE
Less than or equal to	<=	=C1<=D1 where cell C1 contains the label "AA" and cell D1 contains the label "BB"	TRUE

For example, if you want to compare the value 3 to the value 5 to see if 3 is greater than 5, you would enter the following formula: =3>5. The resulting value displayed in the cell would be FALSE. It is important to note the order of precedence in which these relational expressions are evaluated. Relational operators are evaluated after arithmetic operators, exponents, and parentheses. The formula =(1+2)/3<>10 is evaluated as follows:

- First, Excel evaluates 1+2 in the parentheses to produce the value 3.
- Next, Excel evaluates 3 divided by 3, resulting in the value 1.
- After completing all of the arithmetic operations, Excel evaluates the <> not equal relational operator, 1<>10, resulting in a TRUE value.

Notice that like all other formulas, relational expressions begin with an equal sign. In the formula =B2=C2, Excel evaluates this expression to see if the value in cell B2 equals the value in cell C2. The first equal sign (=) indicates the beginning of a formula; the second equal sign is interpreted as a relational operator.

You can use relational operators to evaluate text labels. For example, you can test to see if a cell contains a specific label, such as =C2="Hello". If C2 contains the label Hello, then the value TRUE is returned. The >, >=, <, and <= operators also work with text, where a greater value is one that appears later in the alphabet. For example, ="Goodbye">"Hello" returns the value FALSE because Goodbye comes alphabetically before Hello.

Best Practice

#NAME! Error
Question: What is the result of the formula =Goodbye>Hello?

This formula is written without the quotation marks around each of the labels—that is Goodbye and Hello. Excel looks for a range named Goodbye and a range named Hello in the worksheet. If these had not been previously set up as valid range names corresponding to cell addresses, Excel would return the error message #NAME?. On the other hand, if the range named Goodbye contained the value 5 and the range named Hello contained the value 3, the value TRUE would be returned representing the formula =5>3. Note that relational expressions are not case sensitive, so any combination of lowercase and uppercase letters does not affect the outcome.

You can also use relational operators to evaluate dates. Recall that dates are stored as sequential numbers, but can be formatted in the month/day/year format or even written out, such as January 1, 2014. You can use dates in both relational and arithmetic expressions; however, you cannot enter a date, such as 1/1/2014, directly into a formula because Excel interprets the entry as a numerical expression. For example, assuming that cell D4 contains the date 12/31/2013 and cell D1 contains the date 1/1/2014, you could write the formula =D4>=D1. The result would be FALSE because 12/31/2013 comes before 1/1/2014.

Using relational operators, Eric can easily set up a formula to test if the condition specified in Rule #1 is TRUE: "A customer has a past due balance that is less than 10% of this year's total sales." If the resulting value is TRUE, the customer's request for credit will be recommended for approval. If the resulting value is FALSE, the customer might be rejected for credit for failing to meet the credit approval criteria specified in this rule.

Eric begins by setting up a new column in the CreditData worksheet, column K, with the heading Rule #1 in cell K2. To obtain the percentage of past due balance versus this year's total sales for the first company listed in the CreditData worksheet, Athletic Gear Corp., Eric divides the past due balance in cell E3 ($0) by the current year's sales value in cell D3 ($11,952). The result is 0, which is less than the benchmark of 10% specified in Rule #1—so the value TRUE should be displayed in cell K3. To implement this, Eric writes the following formula in cell K3:

```
=E3/D3<0.1
```

Because all of the operands copy relatively, no absolute references are required. The resulting values are displayed in cells K3:K21 on the worksheet, as shown in Figure 4.2. Notice the value TRUE in cell K3, which indicates that the customer Athletic Gear Corp. could be granted credit approval because it meets the criteria established in Rule #1.

Figure 4.2: Applying Rule #1 using a relational operator

`=E3/D3<0.1`

	A	B	C	D	E	F	G	H	I	J	K	L
1	Accounts Receivable Department - Customer Credit Analysis											
2	Customer Name	Current Credit Limit	Previous Year's Sales	Current Year's Sales	Past Due Balance	Net Worth in (000)	D&B Credit Rating Class	D&B Composite Credit Appraisal (1 Best)	D&B PAYDEX (100 Best)	D&B Stress Risk Class (1 Best)	Rule #1	
3	Athletic Gear Corp.	$ 9,000	$ 15,382	$11,952	$ 0	$ 450	BA	4	15	3	TRUE	
4	Baltimore O's	39,000	10,033	7,789	0	1,950	3A	1	51	1	TRUE	
5	Baseball & More	75,000	60,009	55,342	13,892	37,500	4A	2	70	1	FALSE	
6	Canadian Ski Club	33,000	35,039	50,921	495	1,650	BA	2	43	1	TRUE	
7	Concord Pro Shop					10,000	4A	1	91	1		
8	Everything Golf	25,000	15,221	9,483	2,899	1,250	3A	3	76	1	FALSE	
9	Lake Pro Shops	42,000	80,498	81,126	0	2,100	3A	2	87	1	TRUE	
10	Mars Dept. Store	27,000	35,354	20,666	0	213	BB	3	94	1	TRUE	
11	RG Bradley	46,000	90,970	18,343	0	2,300	3A	1	21	1	TRUE	
12	RX for Sports	15,000	5,663	3,014	0	750	2A	1	59	1	TRUE	
13	School Sports Supply	45,000	50,278	32,338	0	2,250	3A	3	91	1	TRUE	
14	Ski World	26,000	25,864	28,154	0	300	BA	2	82	1	TRUE	
15	Sneaker Kingdom	45,000	40,157	25,379	0	2,250	3A	2	71	1	TRUE	
16	Sports & Stuff	15,000	15,898	14,732	14,383	450	BA	1	67	1	FALSE	
17	Toy Kingdom	22,000	10,073	1,047	0	1,100	3A	3	14	1	TRUE	
18	Under the Sea	45,000	95,411	64,418	0	150	CB	4	79	2	TRUE	
19	US Olympic Team	20,000	5,621	6,171	0	1,000	3A	1	87	1	TRUE	
20	WWW Sports Inc.	100,000	60,009	60,354	0	500,000	5A	2	97	1	TRUE	
21	Zip & Sons	10,000	15,490	22,760	0	620	1A	2	96	1	TRUE	
22												
23												

A FALSE value indicates that the customer does not meet the criteria for credit approval for Rule #1

Notice that row 7 contains the data for Concord Pro Shop. There are no values for past due balance or this year's total sales for this customer, so Eric deletes the formula in cell K7 to eliminate a #DIV/0! error message in the cell. A better method of dealing with this type of situation is explored later in this chapter. Based on the results displayed in column K, it appears that three customers—Baseball & More, Everything Golf, and Sports & Stuff—might be rejected due to poor payment history with TheZone.

Using Boolean Logical Functions to Evaluate a List of Values and Determine a Single True or False Value

So far, Eric has compared two different values using relational operators in an expression to determine if that expression is TRUE or FALSE. To evaluate Rule #2, "Accept a customer that has either a composite credit appraisal value of 1 or a PAYDEX score over 90," he can individually test to see if a customer's composite credit appraisal value equals 1, and then test to see if the customer's PAYDEX score is over 90. Doing so would result in two separate TRUE/FALSE values. However, Eric wants to display only a single TRUE or FALSE value in column L of the worksheet to evaluate this rule.

How can Eric determine if *at least* one item meets the specified criteria? At some point, he might also need to consider if *all* the items in a group meet specified criteria, or if an item does *not* meet specified criteria. To evaluate a list of Boolean values, you can use the AND and OR functions. Another function, the NOT function, switches a single Boolean value to the opposite value. These functions are described in the following list:

- The **AND function** evaluates a list of logical arguments to determine if *all* arguments are TRUE. The AND function returns a value of TRUE if all arguments in the function are TRUE.
- The **OR function** evaluates a list of logical arguments to determine if *at least one* argument is TRUE. The OR function returns a value of FALSE only if all of the arguments in the function are FALSE.
- The **NOT function** evaluates only one logical argument to determine if it is FALSE. The NOT function essentially changes the value TRUE to FALSE or the value FALSE to TRUE.

Figure 4.3 lists the outcomes for the AND function using two inputs, Condition #1 and Condition #2, in a format commonly referred to as a **truth table**.

Figure 4.3: AND truth table

	If Condition #1 is	
AND Condition #2 is	**TRUE**	**FALSE**
TRUE	TRUE	FALSE
FALSE	FALSE	FALSE

An AND function only results in a TRUE value if both Condition #1 and Condition #2 are TRUE. An AND function results in a FALSE value if either Condition #1 or Condition #2 is FALSE.

Figure 4.4 lists the outcomes for the OR function using two inputs, Condition #1 and Condition #2.

Figure 4.4: OR truth table

	If Condition #1 is	
OR Condition #2 is	**TRUE**	**FALSE**
TRUE	TRUE	TRUE
FALSE	TRUE	FALSE

An OR function results in a TRUE value if either Condition #1 or Condition #2 is TRUE. An OR function only results in a FALSE value if both Condition #1 and Condition #2 are FALSE.

Level 1

4

Figure 4.5 lists the outcomes of the NOT function, which, unlike the AND and OR functions, evaluates only a single input: Condition.

Figure 4.5: NOT truth table

	If Condition is	
	TRUE	**FALSE**
Resulting value is	FALSE	TRUE

A NOT function results in a TRUE value if the Condition is FALSE.
A NOT function results in a FALSE value if the Condition is TRUE.

Using the OR Function to Evaluate Criteria

Which Boolean operator does Eric need to evaluate the second rule for determining creditworthiness? The rule states: "Accept a customer that has either a composite credit appraisal value of 1 (column H) or a PAYDEX score over 90 (column I)." The key words in this case are *either* and *or*. If either condition is met, then credit should be approved, which indicates the need for an OR function.

The OR function evaluates a list of logical arguments to determine if at least one argument is TRUE. The arguments can consist of any combination of cell references, values, or ranges that each individually reduce to a TRUE or FALSE value. The syntax of the OR function is as follows:

```
OR(logical1,logical2,...)
```

An OR function is FALSE only if all arguments are FALSE. Consider the following Excel formulas that use the OR function:

- =OR(I3>90,I4>90,I5>90,I6>90) returns a FALSE value if the values in cells I3, I4, I5, and I6 all contain values of 90 or less.
- =OR(K3:K21) returns a TRUE value if any of the values in K3 through K21 contain the value TRUE. When using a range in a Boolean function, the range must contain only TRUE and FALSE values.
- =OR(25<24,MIN(1,10)<2,3<=2+1) returns a TRUE value. This formula begins by evaluating the expression 25<24, which is FALSE; then evaluates the expression MIN(1,10)<2, or 1<2, which is TRUE; and finally evaluates the expression 3<=2+1, which is also TRUE. So, the formula reduces to =OR(FALSE,TRUE,TRUE), resulting in the final value of TRUE because at least one of the arguments is TRUE.

Eric can use the OR function to determine if the first customer listed in the CreditData worksheet, Athletic Gear Corp., should be granted credit approval based on Rule #2. To do this, he first needs to evaluate each individual criterion and then combine them with the OR Boolean function to calculate a single TRUE or FALSE result to be placed in column L, as follows:

- Determine if the composite credit appraisal value in column H equals 1 using the relational expression H3=1.
- Determine if the PAYDEX score given in column I is greater than 90 using the relational expression I3>90.
- Determine if either of the preceding statements is TRUE using the OR function, and then display the resulting TRUE or FALSE value.

Eric enters the following formula in cell L3 and then copies the formula down the column to determine the results for each of the other customers:

$$=OR(H3=1,I3>90)$$

Because both cell H3 and cell I3 need to copy relatively, no absolute references are required. The resulting TRUE and FALSE values are displayed in column L, as shown in Figure 4.6.

Figure 4.6: Applying Rule #2 using an OR function

=OR(H3=1,I3>90)

	A	B	C	D	E	F	G	H	I	J	K	L	M
1	Accounts Receivable Department - Customer Credit Analysis												
2	Customer Name	Current Credit Limit	Previous Year's Sales	Current Year's Sales	Past Due Balance	Net Worth in (000)	D&B Credit Rating Class	D&B Composite Credit Appraisal (1 Best)	D&B PAYDEX (100 Best)	D&B Stress Risk Class (1 Best)	Rule #1	Rule #2	
3	Athletic Gear Corp.	$ 9,000	$15,382	$11,952	$ 0	$ 450	BA	4	15	3	TRUE	FALSE	
4	Baltimore O's	39,000	10,033	7,709	0	1,950	3A	1	51	1	TRUE	TRUE	
5	Baseball & More	75,000	60,009	55,342	13,892	37,500	4A	2	70	1	FALSE	FALSE	
6	Canadian Ski Club	33,000	35,039	50,921	495	1,650	BA	2	43	1	TRUE	FALSE	
7	Concord Pro Shop					10,000	4A	1	91	1		TRUE	
8	Everything Golf	25,000	15,221	9,483	2,899	1,250	3A	3	76	1	FALSE	FALSE	
9	Lake Pro Shops	42,000	80,498	81,126	0	2,100	3A	2	87	1	TRUE	FALSE	
10	Mars Dept. Store	27,000	35,354	20,666	0	213	BB	3	94	1	TRUE	TRUE	
11	RG Bradley	46,000	90,970	18,343	0	2,300	3A	1	21	1	TRUE	TRUE	
12	RX for Sports	15,000	5,663	3,014	0	750	2A	1	59	1	TRUE	TRUE	
13	School Sports Supply	45,000	50,278	32,338	0	2,250	3A	3	91	1	TRUE	TRUE	
14	Ski World	26,000	25,864	28,154	0	300	BA	2	82	1	TRUE	FALSE	
15	Sneaker Kingdom	45,000	40,157	25,379	0	2,250	3A	2	71	1	TRUE	FALSE	
16	Sports & Stuff	15,000	15,898	14,732	14,383	450	BA	1	67	1	FALSE	TRUE	
17	Toy Kingdom	22,000	10,073	1,047	0	1,100	3A	3	14	1	TRUE	FALSE	
18	Under the Sea	45,000	95,411	64,418	0	150	CB	4	79	2	TRUE	FALSE	
19	US Olympic Team	20,000	5,621	6,171	0	1,000	3A	1	87	1	TRUE	TRUE	
20	WWW Sports Inc.	100,000	60,009	60,354	0	500,000	5A	2	97	1	TRUE	TRUE	
21	Zip & Sons	10,000	15,490	22,760	0	620	1A	2	96	1	TRUE	TRUE	
22													
23													

Substituting the values in the cells corresponding to the first customer listed in the worksheet, Athletic Gear Corp., the formula can be interpreted as follows:

- Substitute the values corresponding to the cell references, =OR(4=1,15>90).
- Analyze the first logical argument. Because 4 does not equal 1, this argument evaluates to the value FALSE.
- Analyze the second logical argument. Because 15 is not greater than 90, this argument also evaluates to the value FALSE.
- The resulting expression is =OR(FALSE,FALSE). For an OR function to be TRUE, at least one of its arguments must be TRUE, which is not the case here. So, the value resulting from this formula for Athletic Gear Corp. is the value FALSE, which is displayed in cell L3. This customer does not meet the criteria established in Rule #2 and, therefore, is not recommended for credit approval based on this measurement.

Best Practice

Comparing a Long List of Elements to the Same Value

Referring to the worksheet in Figure 4.6, consider the following question: "Do any customers have a PAYDEX score over 90?" To find the answer to this question, you could write an expression such as =OR(I3>90,I4>90,I5>90,I6>90...I21>90), listing every cell in column I from cell I3 all the way to cell I21. However, this is a cumbersome way to evaluate a list of elements, especially given that the relational expression is essentially the same in each case. Could you write the formula as =OR(I3:I21>90)? No; this is not a legitimate syntactical use of the function. Indeed, a FALSE value will be returned and not an error message, even though cell I7 contains a PAYDEX score of 91. This formula would perform the relational operation with cell I3 only.

In situations where you have a long list and want each element to be compared to the same value, an effective, two-step approach is to first create a separate column. For example, in Figure 4.7, the formula in column M calculates the relationship for each individual element. You can copy the formula =I3>90 in cell M3 down the column, resulting in a TRUE or FALSE value for each element. Then, in a separate cell (cell M23 in Figure 4.7), you can write the formula =OR(M3:M21) to determine if any of the elements are TRUE. Because column M contains only TRUE or FALSE values, you can use a range in the formula for this OR function. In Figure 4.7, the final result is TRUE (cell M23), indicating that at least one customer has a PAYDEX score greater than 90.

Figure 4.7: Two-step approach to calculate a PAYDEX score greater than 90

The formula =I3>90 has been entered in cell M3 and copied down the column

	A	B	C	D	E	F	G	H	I	J	K	L	M	N
1	**Accounts Receivable Department - Customer Credit Analysis**													
2	Customer Name	Current Credit Limit	Previous Year's Sales	Current Year's Sales	Past Due Balance	Net Worth in (000)	D&B Credit Rating Class	D&B Composite Credit Appraisal (1 Best)	D&B PAYDEX (100 Best)	D&B Stress Risk Class (1 Best)	Rule #1	Rule #2	PAYDEX > 90	
3	Athletic Gear Corp.	$ 9,000	$15,382	$11,952	$ 0	$ 450	BA	4	15	3	TRUE	FALSE	FALSE	
4	Baltimore O's	39,000	10,033	7,789	0	1,950	3A	1	51	1	TRUE	TRUE	FALSE	
5	Baseball & More	75,000	60,009	55,342	13,892	37,500	4A	2	70	1	FALSE	FALSE	FALSE	
6	Canadian Ski Club	33,000	35,039	50,921	495	1,650	BA	2	43	1	TRUE	FALSE	FALSE	
7	Concord Pro Shop					10,000	4A	1	91	1		TRUE	TRUE	
8	Everything Golf	25,000	15,221	9,483	2,899	1,250	3A	3	76	1	FALSE	FALSE	FALSE	
9	Lake Pro Shops	42,000	80,498	81,126	0	2,100	3A	2	87	1	TRUE	FALSE	FALSE	
10	Mars Dept. Store	27,000	35,354	20,666	0	213	BB	3	94	1	TRUE	TRUE	TRUE	
11	RG Bradley	46,000	90,970	18,343	0	2,300	3A	1	21	1	TRUE	TRUE	FALSE	
12	RX for Sports	15,000	5,663	3,014	0	750	2A	1	59	1	TRUE	TRUE	FALSE	
13	School Sports Supply	45,000	50,278	32,338	0	2,250	3A	3	91	1	TRUE	TRUE	TRUE	
14	Ski World	26,000	25,864	28,154	0	300	BA	2	82	1	TRUE	FALSE	FALSE	
15	Sneaker Kingdom	45,000	40,157	25,379	0	2,250	3A	2	71	1	TRUE	FALSE	FALSE	
16	Sports & Stuff	15,000	15,898	14,732	14,383	450	BA	1	67	1	FALSE	TRUE	FALSE	
17	Toy Kingdom	22,000	10,073	1,047	0	1,100	3A	3	14	1	TRUE	FALSE	FALSE	
18	Under the Sea	45,000	95,411	64,418	0	150	CB	4	79	2	TRUE	FALSE	FALSE	
19	US Olympic Team	20,000	5,621	6,171	0	1,000	3A	1	87	1	TRUE	TRUE	FALSE	
20	WWW Sports Inc.	100,000	60,009	60,354	0	500,000	5A	2	97	1	TRUE	TRUE	TRUE	
21	Zip & Sons	10,000	15,490	22,760	0	620	1A	2	96	1	TRUE	TRUE	TRUE	
22														
23												At least 1 PAYDEX score >90	TRUE	

The formula =OR(M3:M21) determines if *any* PAYDEX score is greater than 90

Using the AND Function to Evaluate Criteria

Next, Eric needs to consider Rule #3: "Accept a customer that has all of the following: a net worth of at least $500,000; a composite credit appraisal value of 2 or lower; a PAYDEX score over 70; and a stress risk class of 1." The key word in this case is *all*. Because each one of the four criteria must be met for the rule to be TRUE, an AND function is required.

The AND function is used to evaluate a list of logical arguments to determine if *all* of the arguments are TRUE. As with the OR function, each argument can consist of any of the following: cell references or a range of cells containing Boolean logical values, relational expressions, and functions that reduce to a single TRUE or FALSE value. The syntax of the AND function is as follows:

```
AND(logical1,logical2,...)
```

An AND function is TRUE only if all its arguments are TRUE.

Eric can use the AND function to evaluate the data in the CreditData worksheet to determine which customers of TheZone meet *all* the criteria in Rule #3. He can first evaluate each individual criterion and then combine them with the AND function to calculate a single TRUE or FALSE result, as follows:

Figure 4.8: Applying Rule #3 using an AND function

=AND(F3*1000>=500000,H3<=2,I3>70,J3=1)

	A	B	C	D	E	F	G	H	I	J	K	L	M	N
1	**Accounts Receivable Department - Customer Credit Analysis**													
2	**Customer Name**	**Current Credit Limit**	**Previous Year's Sales**	**Current Year's Sales**	**Past Due Balance**	**Net Worth in (000)**	**D&B Credit Rating Class**	**D&B Composite Credit Appraisal (1 Best)**	**D&B PAYDEX (100 Best)**	**D&B Stress Risk Class (1 Best)**	**Rule #1**	**Rule #2**	**Rule #3**	
3	Athletic Gear Corp.	$ 9,000	$15,382	$11,952	$ 0	$ 450	BA	4	15	3	TRUE	FALSE	FALSE	
4	Baltimore O's	39,000	10,033	7,789	0	1,950	3A	1	51	1	TRUE	TRUE	FALSE	
5	Baseball & More	75,000	60,009	55,342	13,892	37,500	4A	2	70	1	FALSE	FALSE	FALSE	
6	Canadian Ski Club	33,000	35,039	50,921	495	1,650	BA	2	43	1	TRUE	FALSE	FALSE	
7	Concord Pro Shop					10,000	4A	1	91	1		TRUE	TRUE	
8	Everything Golf	25,000	15,221	9,483	2,899	1,250	3A	3	76	1	FALSE	FALSE	FALSE	
9	Lake Pro Shops	42,000	80,498	81,126	0	2,100	3A	2	87	1	TRUE	FALSE	TRUE	
10	Mars Dept. Store	27,000	35,354	20,666	0	213	BB	3	94	1	TRUE	TRUE	FALSE	
11	RG Bradley	46,000	90,970	18,343	0	2,300	3A	1	21	1	TRUE	TRUE	FALSE	
12	RX for Sports	15,000	5,663	3,014	0	750	2A	1	59	1	TRUE	TRUE	FALSE	
13	School Sports Supply	45,000	50,278	32,338	0	2,250	3A	3	91	1	TRUE	TRUE	FALSE	
14	Ski World	26,000	25,864	28,154	0	300	BA	2	82	1	TRUE	FALSE	FALSE	
15	Sneaker Kingdom	45,000	40,157	25,379	0	2,250	3A	2	71	1	TRUE	FALSE	TRUE	
16	Sports & Stuff	15,000	15,898	14,732	14,383	450	BA	1	67	1	FALSE	TRUE	FALSE	
17	Toy Kingdom	22,000	10,073	1,047	0	1,100	3A	3	14	1	TRUE	FALSE	FALSE	
18	Under the Sea	45,000	95,411	64,418	0	150	CB	4	79	2	TRUE	FALSE	FALSE	
19	US Olympic Team	20,000	5,621	6,171	0	1,000	3A	1	87	1	TRUE	TRUE	TRUE	
20	WWW Sports Inc.	100,000	60,009	60,354	0	500,000	5A	2	97	1	TRUE	TRUE	TRUE	
21	Zip & Sons	10,000	15,490	22,760	0	620	1A	2	96	1	TRUE	TRUE	TRUE	

- Determine if the net worth of the customer given in column F is at least $500,000 using the relational expression F3*1000>=500000 (for the first customer listed, Athletic Gear Corp.). Note that the net worth is listed in column F of the worksheet in thousands of dollars, not by the actual value; therefore, the expression must multiply the net worth by 1000 so that the resulting value can be compared with 500,000. Other algebraic equivalents of this expression that could also be used are F3>=500000/1000 or F3>=500.
- Determine if the composite credit appraisal value given in column H is 2 or lower using the relational expression H3<=2.
- Determine if the PAYDEX score given in column I is over 70 using the relational expression I3>70.
- Determine if the stress risk class given in column J is equal to 1 using the relational expression J3=1.
- Determine if all of the preceding statements are TRUE using the AND function, and then display the resulting TRUE or FALSE value.

Eric enters this formula in cell M3 and copies it down column M. The resulting TRUE and FALSE values are displayed, as shown in Figure 4.8.

```
=AND(F3*1000>=500000,H3<=2,I3>70,J3=1)
```

Substituting the values in the cells corresponding to the first customer listed in the work-sheet, Athletic Gear Corp., the formula can be interpreted as follows:

- Substitute the values corresponding to the cell references in the formula =AND(450*1000>=500000,4<=2,15>70,3=1).
- Analyze the first logical argument. Because 450*1000 is not greater than or equal to 500000, this argument evaluates to the value FALSE.
- Analyze the second logical argument. Because 4 is not less than or equal to 2, this argument also evaluates to the value FALSE.
- Analyze the third logical argument. Because 15 is not greater than 70, this argument also evaluates to the value FALSE.
- Analyze the fourth logical argument. Because 3 does not equal 1, this argument also evaluates to the value FALSE.
- The resulting expression is =AND(FALSE,FALSE,FALSE,FALSE). For an AND function to be TRUE, all of its arguments must be TRUE, which is not the case here. So, the value resulting from this formula for Athletic Gear Corp. is the value FALSE, which is displayed in cell M3. This customer does not meet the criteria established in Rule #3 and therefore is not recommended for credit approval based on this measurement.

Figure 4.9 illustrates this analysis.

Figure 4.9: Analyzing the resulting value in cell M3

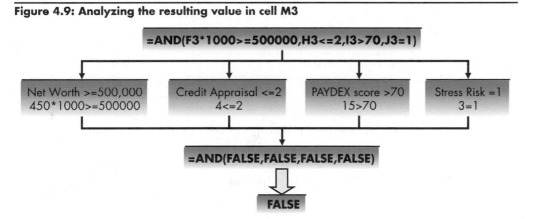

With the formulas for the three rules in place, Eric now wants to determine if the following statement is TRUE: "At least one company is recommended for credit approval based on a TRUE value for Rule #1 (K3:K21)." In reviewing the worksheet at this point (Figure 4.8), notice that there are many TRUE values in column K, so the statement is TRUE. But what if the list of customers was significantly longer with few, if any, TRUE values, and scanning the list was not practical? Eric could write a formula using an OR function to determine if the statement is TRUE. In the example shown in Figure 4.10, Eric writes the formula =OR(K3:K21) in cell K23 and copies it across the row into cells L23 and M23 to determine if at least one customer meets Rule #2 and Rule #3, respectively. Because all of the cell references change relatively, no absolute references are required in the formula.

Figure 4.10: Determining if at least one customer meets each rule

	A	B	C	D	E	F	G	H	I	J	K	L	M	N
1	Accounts Receivable Department - Customer Credit Analysis													
2	Customer Name	Current Credit Limit	Previous Year's Sales	Current Year's Sales	Past Due Balance	Net Worth in (000)	D&B Credit Rating Class	D&B Composite Credit Appraisal (1 Best)	D&B PAYDEX (100 Best)	D&B Stress Risk Class (1 Best)	Rule #1	Rule #2	Rule #3	
3	Athletic Gear Corp.	$ 9,000	$ 15,382	$ 11,952	$ 0	$ 450	BA	4	15	3	TRUE	FALSE	FALSE	
4	Baltimore O's	39,000	10,033	7,789	0	1,950	3A	1	51	1	TRUE	TRUE	FALSE	
5	Baseball & More	75,000	60,009	55,342	13,892	37,500	4A	2	70	1	FALSE	FALSE	FALSE	
6	Canadian Ski Club	33,000	35,039	50,921	495	1,650	BA	2	43	1	TRUE	FALSE	FALSE	
7	Concord Pro Shop					10,000	4A	1	91	1		TRUE	TRUE	
8	Everything Golf	25,000	15,221	9,483	2,899	1,250	3A	3	76	1	FALSE	FALSE	FALSE	
9	Lake Pro Shops	42,000	80,498	81,126	0	2,100	3A	2	87	1	TRUE	FALSE	TRUE	
10	Mars Dept. Store	27,000	35,354	20,666	0	213	BB	3	94	1	TRUE	TRUE	FALSE	
11	RG Bradley	46,000	90,970	18,343	0	2,300	3A	1	21	1	TRUE	TRUE	FALSE	
12	RX for Sports	15,000	5,663	3,014	0	750	2A	1	59	1	TRUE	TRUE	FALSE	
13	School Sports Supply	45,000	50,278	32,338	0	2,250	3A	3	91	1	TRUE	TRUE	FALSE	
14	Ski World	26,000	25,864	28,154	0	300	BA	2	82	1	TRUE	FALSE	FALSE	
15	Sneaker Kingdom	45,000	40,157	25,379	0	2,250	3A	2	71	1	TRUE	FALSE	TRUE	
16	Sports & Stuff	15,000	15,898	14,732	14,383	450	BA	1	67	1	FALSE	TRUE	FALSE	
17	Toy Kingdom	22,000	10,073	1,047	0	1,100	3A	3	14	1	TRUE	FALSE	FALSE	
18	Under the Sea	45,000	95,411	64,418	0	150	CB	4	79	2	TRUE	FALSE	FALSE	
19	US Olympic Team	20,000	5,621	6,171	0	1,000	3A	1	87	1	TRUE	TRUE	TRUE	
20	WWW Sports Inc.	100,000	60,009	60,354	0	500,000	5A	2	97	1	TRUE	TRUE	TRUE	
21	Zip & Sons	10,000	15,490	22,760	0	620	1A	2	96	1	TRUE	TRUE	TRUE	
22														
23								Do any meet the rule?			TRUE	TRUE	TRUE	

`=OR(K3:K21)`

As noted earlier, a range can be used in a Boolean logical AND or OR function if the range refers to cells containing only TRUE or FALSE values. Excel ignores empty cells, such as cell K7 in Figure 4.10, although it might display a warning message in such a case.

Using the NOT Function to Evaluate Criteria

How could Eric determine if none of the customers meet the criteria for Rule #1? In this case, Eric simply wants the opposite value that was calculated in cell K23:

- Because at least one customer meets the criteria for Rule #1, cell K23 contains the value TRUE, and the statement "None of the customers meet Rule #1" is FALSE.
- If no customers met the criteria for Rule #1, the resulting value in cell K23 would be FALSE, and the statement "None of the customers meet Rule #1" would be TRUE.

How do you change a TRUE value to FALSE or a FALSE value to TRUE? Eric accomplishes this using the NOT function with the formula =NOT(K23). He enters this formula in cell K24 and copies it to cells L24:M24, as shown in Figure 4.11.

Could Eric also have written this formula as =NOT(K3:K21)? No; unlike the AND and OR functions, the NOT function takes only one argument and essentially changes a single TRUE value to FALSE or a single FALSE value to TRUE. The logical argument can consist of a single cell reference that contains a Boolean value or an expression that will reduce to a TRUE or FALSE value. The syntax of the NOT function is as follows:

```
NOT(logical1)[END CODE]
```

Figure 4.11: Determining if no customers meet each rule

Customer Name	Current Credit Limit	Previous Year's Sales	Current Year's Sales	Past Due Balance	Net Worth in (000)	D&B Credit Rating Class	D&B Composite Credit Appraisal (1 Best)	D&B PAYDEX (100 Best)	D&B Stress Risk Class (1 Best)	Rule #1	Rule #2	Rule #3	
Athletic Gear Corp.	$ 9,000	$15,382	$11,952	$ 0	$ 450	BA	4	15	3	TRUE	FALSE	FALSE	
Baltimore O's	39,000	10,033	7,789	0	1,950	3A	1	51	1	TRUE	TRUE	FALSE	
Baseball & More	75,000	60,009	55,342	13,892	37,500	4A	2	70	1	FALSE	FALSE	FALSE	
Canadian Ski Club	33,000	35,039	50,921	495	1,650	BA	2	43	1	TRUE	FALSE	FALSE	
Concord Pro Shop					10,000	4A	1	91	1		TRUE	TRUE	
Everything Golf	25,000	15,221	9,483	2,899	1,250	3A	3	76	1	FALSE	FALSE	FALSE	
Lake Pro Shops	42,000	80,498	81,126	0	2,100	3A	2	87	1	TRUE	FALSE	TRUE	
Mars Dept. Store	27,000	35,354	20,666	0	213	BB	3	94	1	TRUE	TRUE	FALSE	
RG Bradley	46,000	90,970	18,343	0	2,300	3A	1	21	1	TRUE	TRUE	FALSE	
RX for Sports	15,000	5,663	3,014	0	750	2A	1	59	1	TRUE	TRUE	FALSE	
School Sports Supply	45,000	50,278	32,338	0	2,250	3A	3	91	1	TRUE	TRUE	FALSE	
Ski World	26,000	25,864	28,154	0	300	BA	2	82	1	TRUE	FALSE	FALSE	
Sneaker Kingdom	45,000	40,157	25,379	0	2,250	3A	2	71	1	TRUE	FALSE	TRUE	
Sports & Stuff	15,000	15,898	14,732	14,383	450	BA	1	67	1	FALSE	TRUE	FALSE	
Toy Kingdom	22,000	10,073	1,047	0	1,100	3A	3	14	1	TRUE	FALSE	FALSE	
Under the Sea	45,000	95,411	64,418	0	150	CB	4	79	2	TRUE	FALSE	FALSE	
US Olympic Team	20,000	5,621	6,171	0	1,000	3A	1	87	1	TRUE	TRUE	TRUE	
WWW Sports Inc.	100,000	60,009	60,354	0	500,000	5A	2	97	1	TRUE	TRUE	TRUE	
Zip & Sons	10,000	15,490	22,760	0	620	1A	2	96	1	TRUE	TRUE	TRUE	
						Do any meet the rule?				TRUE	TRUE	TRUE	
						Do none meet the rule?				FALSE	FALSE	FALSE	

Accounts Receivable Department - Customer Credit Analysis

=NOT(K23)

The following are some examples of the NOT function used in formulas:

- NOT(TRUE) returns the value FALSE
- NOT(FALSE) returns the value TRUE
- NOT(7<10) returns the value FALSE because 7 is less than 10
- NOT(H2=2) returns the value TRUE assuming that cell H2 contains any value other than 2

More information and analysis are required before decisions can be made regarding whether the accounts receivable staff should recommend credit for a specific customer. For some customers, the rules clearly indicate whether to recommend accepting or rejecting a credit application; whereas for other customers, such as Sports & Stuff, the rules have returned contradictory results—to both reject credit (cells K16 and M16) and to accept credit (cell L16). Eric will revisit this worksheet later with further input from management to resolve these types of issues and make a final recommendation.

Applying Conditional Formatting to a Worksheet

Before completing the worksheet, Eric wants to include formatting to highlight the results that were obtained. When a worksheet contains a large set of data, highlighting specific values in a format different from the rest of the worksheet data can make those values stand out or help the reader recognize trends in data. As you learned in Chapter 1, you can change the formatting of a cell quite easily using the formatting buttons in several of the groups, such as Font, Alignment, and Number, on the Home tab. However, the disadvantage of formatting in this way is that if a value changes, you might need to manually reformat the cells affected.

Excel provides **Conditional Formatting** tools, which are tools you can use to identify a set of conditions and specify the formatting if those conditions are met. If a cell value changes, the formatting will be updated automatically according to the specified criteria. The Excel Conditional Formatting tools allow you to insert colored bars (called data bars), multicolor gradients (called color scales), and small graphics (called icons) in addition to standard formatting such as bold, italic, and font size, and user-specified formatting combinations. You can apply conditional formatting to cells based on either the value in that cell or the results of a specified formula that returns a Boolean value. When applying a conditional format, you can specify multiple conditions and modify the format based on whether these conditions are met. If the conditions are not *mutually exclusive* (that is, where one data element cannot fall into more than one category, resulting in more than one specified condition being TRUE), then the formatting of the last specified rule overrides those of earlier rules.

Applying Preset Conditional Formatting Features

One of the easiest ways to use conditional formatting is to apply preset formats such as Data Bars, Color Scales, and Icon Sets. Eric has applied two different formats to his worksheet, as seen in columns B and H of Figure 4.12. In column B, Eric has applied Gradient Fill Blue Data Bars to highlight the values for each company's current credit limit. In column H, Eric has applied the 3 Arrows Colored Icon Set and modified the criteria rules such that the up arrow appears for appraisal scores equal to 1, the horizontal arrow appears for appraisal scores of 2 and 3, and a down arrow appears for appraisal scores equal to 4.

Figure 4.12: Applying conditional formatting presets

	A	B	C	D	E	F	G	H
1	*Accounts Receivable Department - Customer Credit Analysis*							
2	Customer Name	Current Credit Limit	Previous Year's Sales	Current Year's Sales	Past Due Balance	Net Worth in (000)	D&B Credit Rating Class	D&B Composite Credit Appraisal (1 Best)
3	Athletic Gear Corp.	$ 9,000	$ 15,382	$ 11,952	$ 0	$ 450	BA	⬇ 4
4	Baltimore O's	39,000	10,033	7,789	0	1,950	3A	⬆ 1
5	Baseball & More	75,000	60,009	55,342	13,892	37,500	4A	➡ 2
6	Canadian Ski Club	33,000	35,039	50,921	495	1,650	BA	➡ 2
7	Concord Pro Shop					10,000	4A	⬆ 1
8	Everything Golf	25,000	15,221	9,483	2,899	1,250	3A	➡ 3
9	Lake Pro Shops	42,000	80,498	81,126	0	2,100	3A	➡ 2
10	Mars Dept. Store	27,000	35,354	20,666	0	213	BB	➡ 3
11	RG Bradley	46,000	90,970	18,343	0	2,300	3A	⬆ 1

Data Bars preset   Icon Set preset

How To

Apply Conditional Formatting Presets

1. Highlight the cell or cells to be formatted.
2. Click the Conditional Formatting button arrow in the Styles group on the Home tab to open the menu.
3. Select Data Bars, Color Scales, or Icon Sets from the menu to open a gallery of options.
4. Point to a format to preview it in the selected cells, and click the desired format to apply it.

Figure 4.13 shows the Conditional Formatting menu and Data Bars gallery.

Figure 4.13: Applying Data Bars to selected cells

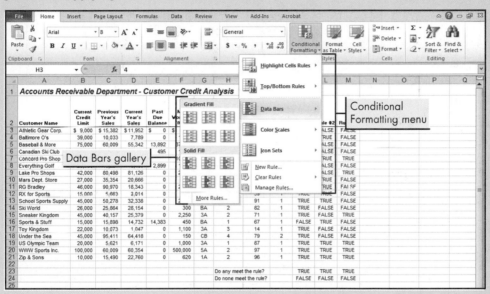

You can also modify the criteria for a conditional formatting preset by clicking the More Rules command in the gallery. The arrows used in column H of the spreadsheet are created by selecting the arrow icon and modifying the values associated with each arrow direction.

How To

Modify a Conditional Formatting Preset

1. Highlight the cell or cells to be formatted and then click the Conditional Formatting button to display the Conditional Formatting menu.
2. Select Icon Sets on the menu to open the Icon Sets gallery, as shown in Figure 4.14. To customize the formatting or criteria for this format, continue to Step 3.

Figure 4.14: Applying Icon Sets to selected cells

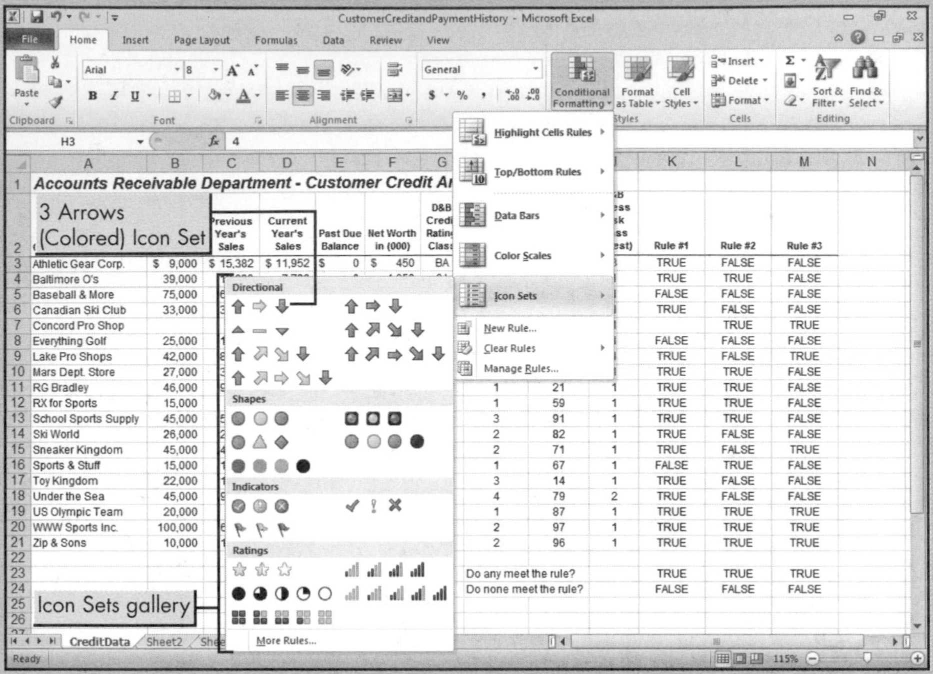

3. Select the More Rules option at the bottom of the gallery. The New Formatting Rule dialog box opens. This dialog box varies for each conditional formatting preset, but the basic options are the same; you can further customize the look of the preset and/or modify the criteria to use in applying this formatting.

4. Click the Icon Style arrow in the Edit the Rule Description section (lower half of the dialog box), and then select the desired style; in this case, three colored arrows (scroll to the top of the list as needed). Icon Style options include Data Bars, Icon Sets, and 2- or 3-Color Scale gradients.

5. To change the order in which the icons will appear, click the Reverse Icon Order button. In this case, you want an up arrow to represents the value 1, the best credit appraisal score, so you also need to specify the values associated with each icon.

6. Once you have selected the Format Style and/or Icon Style, modify the icon rules for the new icons; in this case, the down and horizontal arrows:

   - For the down arrow, first set the Type box to Number (the default is Percent) and then set the Value box at >=4.
   - For the horizontal arrow, set the Type box to Number then set the Value box at >=2.
   - Press the Tab key. This automatically sets the value of the up arrow to <2; you cannot modify the rules for this icon manually.

Figure 4.15 illustrates the New Formatting Rule dialog box after these options have been set.

Figure 4.15: Modifying rules for Icon Sets using the New Formatting Rule dialog box

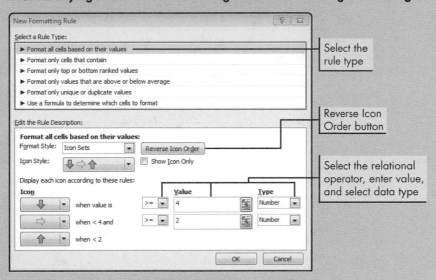

4

Level 1

7. Click the OK button to apply these formatting rules.

Note that you can modify the criteria for other conditional formatting presets by clicking the More Rules option in the appropriate gallery; your choices for modifying the formatting and criteria vary depending on the type of conditional formatting you are applying. The Excel Help tool provides a more complete description of all the options available with the Conditional Formatting tool.

Although these formats are colorful, Eric has decided to use some other techniques to emphasize different data from his analysis. To remove all of the conditional formatting on the worksheet, Eric selects the Conditional Formatting button arrow, points to Clear Rules on the menu, and then clicks Clear Rules from Entire Sheet. To clear conditional formatting from only certain cells in a worksheet, highlight the desired cells, click the Conditional Formatting button, point to Clear Rules, and then click Clear Rules from Selected Cells.

Applying Conditional Formatting Based on Cell Value

Instead of using preset formats, Eric wants to apply specific formats only if a cell value meets a specified criterion. He can accomplish this using the Highlight Cells Rules submenu of the Conditional Formatting menu. Table 4.5 lists the Highlight Cells Rules options. Also available from the Conditional Formatting menu is the Top/Bottom Rules submenu, with options for applying formats based on values in the top 10 or bottom 10 (or other specified number), top or bottom 10% (or other specified percentage), or above or below average values in a selected range.

Table 4.5: Highlight Cells Rules submenu options

Option	Use To
Greater Than	Identify values greater than the specified value
Less Than	Identify values less than the specified value
Between	Set lower and upper limits inclusive
Equal To	Identify values equal to the specified value
Text that Contains	Identify text strings matching a specific string
A Date Occurring	Identify dates such as Today, Tomorrow, Last Week, Last Month, etc.
Duplicate Values	Identify either duplicate values with a specific format or unique values
More Rules	Open the New Formatting Rule dialog box, which contains additional relational operators, including not equal to, not between, greater than or equal to, less than or equal to; also available are options to highlight blank or nonblank cells and cells with or without errors

After the relational comparison is selected, criteria can be set based on any of the following types of data:

- Arithmetic values (1, 2, 3, and so on): >=1000.
- Boolean values (TRUE, FALSE): =TRUE.
- Text values (Accept, Reject, and so on): Note that quotation marks are not required because the Conditional Formatting tool adds them automatically: =BA.
- References or named ranges to other cells containing arithmetic, Boolean, or text values: Note that when using either a cell reference or a named range to specify a rule, be sure to enter an equal sign (=) *before* the cell reference or name; otherwise it will be interpreted at text.

After establishing both the relational operator and the condition, you need to specify the formatting to be applied if the condition is met. This can include the font style and color, borders, and/or cell patterns. Note that you cannot change the font type (such as Times New Roman) or the font size.

How To

Apply *Cell Value Is* Conditional Formatting
1. Select the cell or cells to which you want to apply conditional formatting.
2. Click the Conditional Formatting button in the Styles group on the Home tab, and then point to Highlight Cells Rules to display its gallery of options, as shown in Figure 4.16.
3. Set up the desired relational operation using either of these methods:

- Select one of the listed relational operations (Equal To, Less Than, etc.) from the submenu. This launches the appropriate dialog box such as the Greater Than dialog box, as shown in Figure 4.17. Enter the comparison value or values as required. From the with list, select a preset format or select Custom Format to launch the Format Cells Dialog box.

Figure 4.16: Highlight Cells Rules options

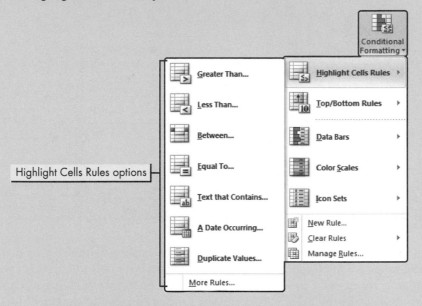

Highlight Cells Rules options

Figure 4.17 Greater Than dialog box

Comparison value box

Formatting options

- Alternatively, select the More Rules option at the bottom of the list to launch the New Formatting Rule dialog box, as shown in Figure 4.18. The Format only cells that contain rule type is highlighted in the top section of the dialog box and will be selected. In the bottom half of the dialog box, fill in the Edit the Rule Description section as follows:

  - In the far-left box, specify the rule type (Cell Value, Specific Text, Blanks, Errors, etc.).
  - In the center box, select a relational operation (equal to, not equal to, etc.).
  - In the right box (or boxes depending on the relational operation), enter the comparison value or values. To use a value in another cell, click on that cell or type the reference using correct syntax (start with = and then use $ as default).
  - Click the Format button to launch the Format Cells Dialog box.

4. To set a custom format, use the Format Cells dialog box. This dialog box is similar to the Font tab of the Format Cells dialog box, which is available when applying regular formatting to cells. In this dialog box, you can select the desired font style (italicized bold) and text color, or you can use the tabs to select options for borders, fill (patterns), or even number types. To close the dialog box, click the OK button.
5. Click the OK button to apply the conditional formatting rule to the selected cells.

Figure 4.18: Creating cell value rules in the New Formatting Rule dialog box

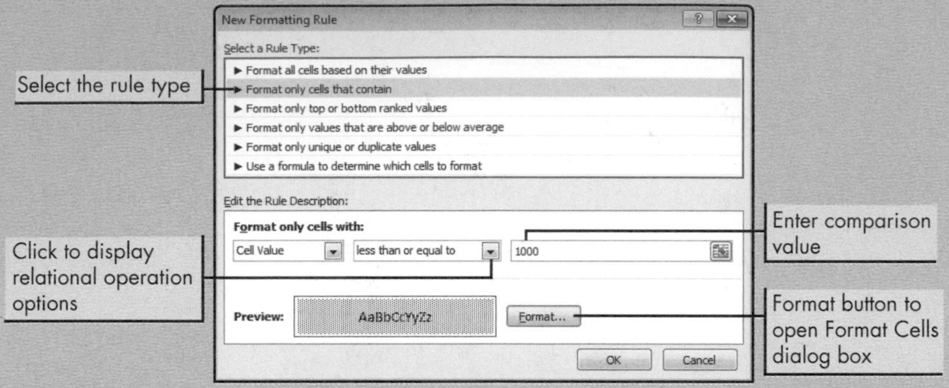

Select the rule type

Click to display relational operation options

Enter comparison value

Format button to open Format Cells dialog box

Eric wants to apply conditional formatting in the CreditData worksheet so that all TRUE values in the range K3:M21 appear in a bold, italicized format. This will make it easier for him and other accounts receivable staff members to see which customers might be granted credit approval because the value TRUE appears for one or more of the three rules. Eric has chosen this formatting because he needs to make black-and-white copies and wants to avoid color schemes that might not show up. To do this, he points to the Highlight Cells Rules option and then selects Equal To. Eric sets the Format cells that are EQUAL TO condition to TRUE, and opens the Format Cells dialog box by clicking the *with* arrow and then selecting Custom Format. He then specifies the Bold Italic font style on the Font tab. Figure 4.19 shows the resulting worksheet.

Figure 4.19: Worksheet with TRUE values highlighted in bold italic font style

TRUE values in cells K3:M21 are displayed in bold and italic

	A	B	C	D	E	F	G	H	I	J	K	L	M	N
1	*Accounts Receivable Department - Customer Credit Analysis*													
2	Customer Name	Current Credit Limit	Previous Year's Sales	Current Year's Sales	Past Due Balance	Net Worth in (000)	D&B Credit Rating Class	D&B Composite Credit Appraisal (1 Best)	D&B PAYDEX (100 Best)	D&B Stress Risk Class (1 Best)	Rule #1	Rule #2	Rule #3	
3	Athletic Gear Corp.	$ 9,000	$ 15,382	$ 11,952	$ 0	$ 450	BA	4	15	3	*TRUE*	FALSE	FALSE	
4	Baltimore O's	39,000	10,033	7,789	0	1,950	3A	1	51	1	*TRUE*	*TRUE*	FALSE	
5	Baseball & More	75,000	60,009	55,342	13,892	37,500	4A	2	70	1	FALSE	FALSE	FALSE	
6	Canadian Ski Club	33,000	35,039	50,921	495	1,650	BA	2	43	1	*TRUE*	FALSE	FALSE	
7	Concord Pro Shop					10,000	4A	1	91	1		*TRUE*	*TRUE*	
8	Everything Golf	25,000	15,221	9,483	2,899	1,250	3A	3	76	1	FALSE	FALSE	FALSE	
9	Lake Pro Shops	42,000	80,498	81,126	0	2,100	3A	2	87	1	*TRUE*	FALSE	*TRUE*	
10	Mars Dept. Store	27,000	35,354	20,666	0	213	BB	3	94	1	*TRUE*	*TRUE*	FALSE	
11	RG Bradley	46,000	90,970	18,343	0	2,300	3A	1	21	1	*TRUE*	*TRUE*	FALSE	
12	RX for Sports	15,000	5,663	3,014	0	750	2A	1	59	1	*TRUE*	*TRUE*	FALSE	
13	School Sports Supply	45,000	50,278	32,338	0	2,250	3A	3	91	1	*TRUE*	*TRUE*	FALSE	
14	Ski World	26,000	25,864	28,154	0	300	BA	2	82	1	*TRUE*	FALSE	FALSE	
15	Sneaker Kingdom	45,000	40,157	25,379	0	2,250	3A	2	71	1	*TRUE*	FALSE	*TRUE*	
16	Sports & Stuff	15,000	15,898	14,732	14,383	450	BA	1	67	1	FALSE	*TRUE*	FALSE	
17	Toy Kingdom	22,000	10,073	1,047	0	1,100	3A	3	14	1	*TRUE*	FALSE	FALSE	
18	Under the Sea	45,000	95,411	64,418	0	150	CB	4	79	2	*TRUE*	FALSE	FALSE	
19	US Olympic Team	20,000	5,621	6,171	0	1,000	3A	1	87	1	*TRUE*	*TRUE*	*TRUE*	
20	WWW Sports Inc.	100,000	60,009	60,354	0	500,000	5A	2	97	1	*TRUE*	*TRUE*	*TRUE*	
21	Zip & Sons	10,000	15,490	22,760	0	620	1A	2	96	1	*TRUE*	*TRUE*	*TRUE*	
22														
23								Do any meet the rule?			TRUE	TRUE	TRUE	
24								Do none meet the rule?			FALSE	FALSE	FALSE	
25														

Applying Conditional Formatting Based on the Results of a Formula

What if Eric wants to apply conditional formatting by shading an entire row if a customer's net worth is less than $1 million and shading an entire row with a polka-dot pattern if a company's net worth is above $10 million? He can again use conditional formatting, this time based on the results of a formula.

Eric will need to highlight a single row as the range (in this case, row 3), and then apply the appropriate conditional formatting option. Because Eric wants to apply multiple rules, he can enter and manage these rules from the Conditional Formatting Rules Manager dialog box, which he opens from the Conditional Formatting menu. See Figure 4.20. First, Eric clicks the Delete Rule button to delete the existing rule, and then he selects the New Rule button to define the new conditional format.

Figure 4.20: Conditional Formatting Rules Manager dialog box

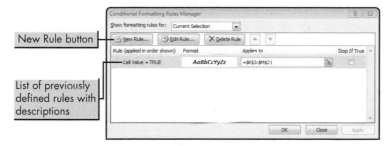

After clicking the New Rule button to launch the New Formatting Rule dialog box, Eric then adds each formula, one at a time. Eric has used this feature before, but this time he needs to choose the rule type, which is Use a formula to determine which cells to format, in the top half of the dialog box, as shown in Figure 4.21.

Figure 4.21: Applying a *Formula Is* condition

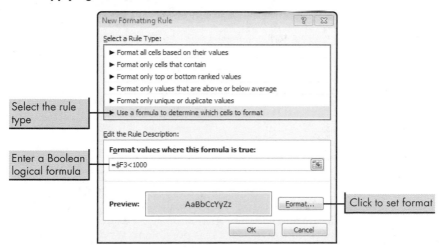

The first condition, a company's net worth is less than $1 million, can be expressed using the formula =$F3<1000. Because Eric needs to copy this conditional formatting down the column, he needs to ensure that the cell reference in the formula has a relative row reference. Unlike cell referencing within the worksheet, the default for conditional formatting is an absolute cell reference. He then sets the format to a gray fill and a gray fill with a polka dot pattern.

To apply the second condition, a company's net worth is above $10 million, Eric must repeat this process but substitute the formula =$F3>10000, which again has an absolute reference to the column and a relative reference to the row. Eric must specify the desired formatting if this formula is evaluated as TRUE, which is a pattern of 25% gray polka dots. Could Eric simply use one expression, such as =OR($F3<1000,$F3>10000)? Yes; this is a valid conditional formatting formula. However, this approach allows only one format to be applied (either gray fill or a polka dot pattern) as opposed to the two different formats Eric wants (gray fill with a polka dot pattern).

After establishing the conditional formatting in one row, Eric uses the Format Painter tool to copy the formatting down the column to the remaining rows. The resulting worksheet is shown in Figure 4.22.

Figure 4.22: Worksheet with conditional formatting based on formulas

Because F3<1000 (Condition 1), gray shading is applied to this row

Because F5>10000 (Condition 2), gray shading with polka dots is applied to this row

	A	B	C	D	E	F	G	H	I	J	K	L	M	N
1	Accounts Receivable Department - Customer Credit Analysis													
2	Customer Name	Current Credit Limit	Previous Year's Sales	Current Year's Sales	Past Due Balance	Net Worth in (000)	D&B Credit Rating Class	D&B Composite Credit Appraisal (1 Best)	D&B PAYDEX (100 Best)	D&B Stress Risk Class (1 Best)	Rule #1	Rule #2	Rule #3	
3	Athletic Gear Corp.	$ 9,000	$ 15,382	$11,952	$ 0	$ 450	BA	4	15	3	TRUE	FALSE	FALSE	
4	Baltimore O's	$ 39,000	$ 10,033	$ 7,789	$ 0	$ 1,950	3A	1	51	1	TRUE	TRUE	FALSE	
5	Baseball & More	$ 75,000	$ 60,009	$55,342	$13,892	$ 37,500	4A	2	70	1	FALSE	FALSE	FALSE	
6	Canadian Ski Club	$ 33,000	$ 35,039	$50,921	$ 495	$ 1,650	BA	2	43	1	TRUE	FALSE	FALSE	
7	Concord Pro Shop					$ 10,000	4A	1	91	1		TRUE	TRUE	
8	Everything Golf	$ 25,000	$ 15,221	$ 9,483	$ 2,899	$ 1,250	3A	3	76	1	FALSE	FALSE	FALSE	
9	Lake Pro Shops	$ 42,000	$ 80,498	$81,126	$ 0	$ 2,100	3A	2	87	1	TRUE	FALSE	TRUE	
10	Mars Dept. Store	$ 27,000	$ 35,354	$20,666	$ 0	$ 213	BB	3	94	1	TRUE	TRUE	FALSE	
11	RG Bradley	$ 46,000	$ 90,970	$18,343	$ 0	$ 2,300	3A	1	21	1	TRUE	TRUE	FALSE	
12	RX for Sports	$ 15,000	$ 5,663	$ 3,014	$ 0	$ 750	2A	1	59	1	TRUE	TRUE	FALSE	
13	School Sports Supply	$ 45,000	$ 50,278	$32,338	$ 0	$ 2,250	3A	3	91	1	TRUE	TRUE	FALSE	
14	Ski World	$ 26,000	$ 25,864	$26,154	$ 0	$ 300	BA	2	82	1	TRUE	FALSE	FALSE	
15	Sneaker Kingdom	$ 45,000	$ 40,157	$25,379	$ 0	$ 2,250	3A	2	71	1	TRUE	FALSE	TRUE	
16	Sports & Stuff	$ 15,000	$ 15,898	$14,732	$14,383	$ 450	BA	1	67	1	FALSE	TRUE	FALSE	
17	Toy Kingdom	$ 22,000	$ 10,073	$ 1,047	$ 0	$ 1,100	3A	3	14	1	TRUE	FALSE	FALSE	
18	Under the Sea	$ 45,000	$ 95,411	$64,418	$ 0	$ 150	CB	4	79	2	TRUE	FALSE	FALSE	
19	US Olympic Team	$ 20,000	$ 5,621	$ 6,171	$ 0	$ 1,000	3A	1	87	1	TRUE	TRUE	TRUE	
20	WWW Sports Inc.	$100,000	$ 60,009	$60,354	$ 0	$500,000	5A	2	97	1	TRUE	TRUE	TRUE	
21	Zip & Sons	$ 10,000	$ 15,490	$22,760	$ 0	$ 620	1A	2	96	1	TRUE	TRUE	TRUE	
22														
23								Do any meet the rule?			TRUE	TRUE	TRUE	
24								Do none meet the rule?			FALSE	FALSE	FALSE	
25														

Because F19 meets neither condition, the formatting remains unchanged for this row

Eric's formulas will return mutually exclusive results because a company's net worth cannot be both greater than $10 million and less than $1 million at the same time. Thus, no more than one format will be applied to a given cell. It is possible to set up criteria that are *not* mutually exclusive where multiple sets of criteria can be TRUE. For example, you could have one rule that formats cells in italic if a specific criterion is TRUE and another rule that formats those same cells with a blue background if another criterion is TRUE. In such cases, if both criteria are TRUE, the cell would be formatted with italic text and a blue background. However, if both types of formatting cannot be applied to the cell simultaneously—for example, the text color blue for the first condition versus the text color red for the second condition—the rule that appears first in the rules list overrides other rules for that specific cell. Note also that the *last* rule created will appear *first* in the list, unless you change the order of the rules. You can use the Conditional Formatting Rules Manager dialog box to create new rules, edit or delete existing rules, or change the order of these rules.

How To

Apply *Formula Is* Conditional Formatting

1. Select the cell or cells to which you want to apply conditional formatting, click the Conditional Formatting button in the Styles group on the Home tab, and then click Manage Rules on the menu. The Conditional Formatting Rules Manager dialog box opens.
2. Click the New Rule button in the Conditional Formatting Rules Manager dialog box to open the New Formatting Rule dialog box.
3. In the Select a Rule Type box (upper half of the dialog box), select the Use a formula to determine which cells to format option.
4. Specify criteria for this new rule by entering a formula (beginning with an equal sign) in the box in the Edit the Rule Description section (lower half of the dialog box). The formula must result in a TRUE or FALSE value using any of the relational operators or Boolean functions.
5. Click the Format button to open the Font tab of the Format Cells dialog box, and then specify the formatting to be applied if the condition is met.
6. Click the OK button to return to the New Formatting Rule dialog box, and then click the OK button again to return to the Conditional Formatting Rules Manager dialog box.
7. To specify one or more additional conditions (up to 64), repeat this procedure. Figure 4.23 shows the Conditional Formatting Rules Manager dialog box with two rules displayed.

Figure 4.23: Conditional Formatting Rules Manager dialog box with two rules

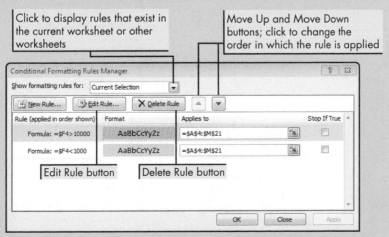

8. To modify any of the rules or to reprioritize how these rules are applied, use the option buttons within the Conditional Formatting Rules Manager dialog box. When two or more conditional formatting rules apply to a range of cells, these rules are evaluated in order of precedence by how they are listed in this dialog box.

A rule higher in the list has greater precedence than a rule lower in the list. By default, new rules are always added to the top of the list. The rule order can be modified using the Move Up and Move Down arrows in the dialog box.

9. Click the Apply button to apply the rules listed, and then click the OK button to close the Conditional Formatting Rules Manager dialog box.

Eric will determine which, if any, conditional formatting he will maintain in the CreditData worksheet based on the data he wants to emphasize. In the next section, he will continue to work with payment data for TheZone's customers to streamline some of the accounts receivable tasks.

Steps to Success: Level 1

The accounting group routinely collects and analyzes credit data on the suppliers with which TheZone does business. Management is always concerned about entering into business relationships with suppliers that are financially unstable and might not be able to meet their commitments. So before any major new contract is awarded, the accounting group collects both D&B data and previous experience data on each bidder (supplier) and makes recommendations to the Purchasing Department regarding the financial stability of each bidder.

Currently, the Purchasing Department is bidding out a contract (PO #527) for supplying a new computer-based warehousing system to all warehousing facilities. The contract includes computer equipment, software, installation, and ongoing maintenance and technical support. The contract is expected to be in the $1 to $2 million range. A list of companies bidding on this contract, together with their financial data, has been compiled in the Bidder worksheet (see Figure 4.24) in a workbook named PO527.xlsx.

Figure 4.24: Bidder credit analysis worksheet

	A	B	C	D	E	F	G
1	PO 527 Bidder List Financial Evaluation						
2	Bidder List	Previous Experience Grade	Net Worth (Dollars)	D&B Composite Credit Appraisal (1 Best)	D&B PAYDEX (100 Best)	D&B Stress Risk Class (1 Best)	
3	Riva Technology	Unsatisfactory	$ 70,000	2	39	2	
4	RDT Corporation	Satisfactory	250,000,000	1	90	1	
5	ComputerX Assoc.	Satisfactory	1,723,000	1	55	2	
6	Exceed WR	None	2,500,000	2	74	1	
7	Roberts Inc.	Satisfactory	580,000	3	68	1	
8							
9							

In these steps, you will help complete the credit analysis by applying the following set of rules:

Rule #1: Consider a bidder if its D&B stress risk class is equal to 1.

Rule #2: Consider a bidder if *all* of the following criteria are met:

- The company's D&B PAYDEX score is greater than 65.
- The company's D&B composite credit appraisal is less than or equal to 2.
- The company's net worth is greater than $900,000. (Net worth values are listed in dollars on the worksheet.)

Rule #3: Consider a bidder if *any* of the following criteria are met:

- The company's D&B PAYDEX score is greater than or equal to 90.
- The company's previous experience grade is Satisfactory.

Complete the following:

1. Open the workbook named **PO527.xlsx** located in the Chapter 4 folder, and then save it as **PO527 Credit Analysis.xlsx**.

2. In a column adjacent to the data, calculate whether or not (TRUE/FALSE) the first company listed meets the criteria for Rule #1. Place an appropriate heading at the top of the column. Copy this formula down the column to analyze this rule for each of the other bidders.

3. In the next column, calculate whether or not (TRUE/FALSE) the first company listed meets the criteria for Rule #2. Place an appropriate heading at the top of the column. Copy this formula down the column to analyze this rule for each of the other bidders.

4. In the next column, calculate whether or not (TRUE/FALSE) the first company listed meets the criteria for Rule #3. Place an appropriate heading at the top of the column. Copy this formula down the column to analyze this rule for each of the other bidders.

5. In cell G9, write a formula to determine if any of the bidders has a TRUE value for Rule #1. Copy the formula across the row to determine if any of the bidders has a TRUE value for Rule #2 and then do the same for Rule #3. In cell A9, enter an appropriate label for this row.

6. In cell G10, write a formula to determine if none of the bidders has a TRUE value for Rule #1. Copy this formula across the row to determine this for Rules #2 and #3. In cell A10, enter an appropriate label for this row.

7. Use conditional formatting to place three-way arrows highlighting composite credit appraisal scores. The up arrow should represent a score of 1, the horizontal arrow should represent a score of 2, and the down arrow should represent a score of 3 and higher.

8. Using conditional formatting, highlight the cells in the range G3:I7 that contain a value of FALSE with pink shading, and highlight all the cells that contain a value of TRUE with light green shading.

9. Using conditional formatting, format in bold italic the name of any bidder (column A) whose previous experience grade is None.

10. Save and close the PO527 Credit Analysis.xlsx workbook.

LEVEL 2
Analyzing Data Using IF Functions and Nested Functions

Introduction to IF Functions and Nested Functions

As you learned in Level 1, you can use relational operators and Boolean functions to evaluate sets of conditions resulting in TRUE or FALSE values. Often, the goal is not just to determine if a value is TRUE or FALSE, however, but to use that information to perform another action. In Level 1, Eric used conditional formatting to change the display of worksheet data if a specified condition is met. But so far, he has not used this information to make changes to cell values, either by displaying any information other than TRUE or FALSE, or by performing a calculation based on the outcome of the logical expression. Both of these tasks can be accomplished using an IF function. An **IF function** is a Boolean logical function that returns one value if a specified condition evaluates to TRUE and another value if the specified condition evaluates to FALSE.

In this level, the logical operations presented in Level 1 are combined with IF functions to specify different tasks depending on whether the value is TRUE or FALSE. For example, if an account is past due, Eric might want to calculate finance charges and add them to the previous balance; whereas accounts that are not past due would not incur finance charges.

Like other Excel functions, the IF function allows you to nest additional formulas and functions within each of its arguments. The term **nested** means that a function contains additional formulas and/or functions as one or more of its arguments. For example, if you want to calculate the average of cells B1 through B10 rounded to the nearest whole number, you could write the formula =ROUND(AVERAGE(B1:B10),0). Here, the AVERAGE function is "nested" inside the ROUND function. Excel first calculates the average and then uses that value as the first argument of the ROUND function. This level explores some simple examples of nesting functions inside the IF function arguments, including nesting of additional IF statements. This technique gives you the flexibility of choosing between three or more sets of criteria.

Writing Simple IF Functions

Recall that part of Eric's task is to develop a way to track a customer's credit and payment status with TheZone—information such as when a customer's credit was last evaluated, if the customer has been approved or denied credit, and the customer's current balance. In the Customer Credit and Payment History workbook, Eric has created a second worksheet named Status, which is shown in Figure 4.25. This worksheet is similar to a standard accounts receivable aging schedule, except that Eric will be using the data for his analysis.

Figure 4.25: Status worksheet

	A	B	C	D	E	F	G	H	I
1	TheZone Customer Accounts - Credit & Payment Status								
2	Customer Name	Customer Type	Current Balance Due	30-Days Past Due	60-Days Past Due	90-Days Past Due	Total Past Due Balance	Current Credit Status	
3	Athletic Gear Corp.	A	$8,612	$ 0	$ 0	$ 0	$ 0	TRUE	
4	Baltimore O's	B	0	0	0	0	0	TRUE	
5	Baseball & More	A	2,345	3,473	5,557	4,862	13,892	TRUE	
6	Canadian Ski Club	C	0	345	0	150	495	TRUE	
7	Everything Golf	A	0	0	2,000	899	2,899	FALSE	
8	Sports & Stuff	A	0	14,000	383	0	14,383	FALSE	
9									
10									

The Status worksheet contains the following information:

* Customer name (column A)
* Customer type, which is a designation of the type of business in which the customer is engaged (column B)
* Current balance due, which is the value of unpaid purchases made within the past 30 days (column C)
* 30-days past due balance, which is the value of unpaid purchases made more than 30 days ago but within the last 60 days (column D)
* 60-days past due balance, which is the value of unpaid purchases made more than 60 days ago but within the last 90 days (column E)
* 90-days past due balance, which is the value of unpaid purchases made more than 90 days ago (column F)
* Total past due balance, which is the value of all 30-, 60-, and 90-days past due balances (column G)
* Current credit status as indicated by the Boolean value TRUE if the accounting group has previously approved or renewed credit for the customer, or by the Boolean value FALSE if credit has been denied (column H). In some cases, a customer might still have a past due balance with a credit status of FALSE, indicating that the customer was recently denied credit but has not yet paid its outstanding balance. These values are the results of the previous manual credit approval process that Eric is endeavoring to automate.

One critical element of this worksheet is the current credit status (column H). The value TRUE could be confusing to staff members trying to interpret the data; does the value TRUE indicate that credit was approved or denied? The status of each customer's credit would be clearer if another column was added that explicitly states whether credit has been approved or denied. If the value in cell H3 is TRUE, Eric wants to display the text "credit approved" in cell I3; otherwise, he wants to display the text "credit denied" in cell I3. To accomplish this, Eric can use an IF function, which evaluates a logical test and then applies one solution if the value is TRUE and another solution if the value is FALSE. The syntax of the IF function is as follows:

```
IF(logical_test,value_if_true,value_if_false)
```

The first argument of the IF function is the *logical_test*. This is the hypothesis to be tested, which results in a TRUE or FALSE value. This argument can consist of any of the following:

- The value TRUE or FALSE
- A reference to a cell containing a TRUE or FALSE value
- A relational expression resulting in a single TRUE or FALSE value
- A Boolean logical function (AND, OR, NOT) resulting in a single TRUE or FALSE value
- Any other formula that results in a TRUE or FALSE value

The second argument of the IF function is the *value_if_true*. This value is applied only if the condition in the first argument is evaluated as TRUE. This argument can simply be a text string to display a label, which is what Eric wants to do, or it can contain a cell reference or even formulas containing operators and/or nested functions. If you want the argument to display a text label, you must enclose the text within quotation marks; otherwise, Excel interprets the string as a named range.

The third argument of the IF function is the *value_if_false*. This value is applied only if the condition in the first argument is evaluated as FALSE. Again, this argument can simply be a text label to be displayed or it can contain cell references, formulas, operators, and/or nested functions. This third argument is considered to be optional. If it is omitted from the function, a FALSE value is displayed if the IF statement is evaluated to be FALSE; however, this is not the recommended way to structure an IF function. To return a blank cell in an IF function, you can include an empty text string " ".

How To

Write a Simple IF Function

1. Select the cell in which you want to write the IF function.
2. Type =IF(to begin the function.
3. Enter the first argument for the function, the logical test, followed by a comma.

4. Enter the second argument for the function, the value if the logical test results in a TRUE value, followed by a comma.

5. Enter the third argument for the function, the value if the logical test results in a FALSE value.

6. Type a closing parenthesis) to end the function.

Writing an IF Function with a Logical Test That Evaluates TRUE/FALSE Values

To perform the task of displaying "credit approved" or "credit denied" based on the corresponding Boolean value in column H, Eric can write a formula in cell I3 containing an IF function, as follows:

```
=IF(H3,"credit approved","credit denied")
```

The first argument, the logical test, simply references a cell that contains a Boolean value. So this first argument tests whether cell H3 contains the value TRUE or the value FALSE. The value_if_true and value_if_false arguments are the text strings that will be displayed if the logical test is TRUE or FALSE, respectively. If cell H3 contains the value TRUE, then the text string "credit approved" will be displayed in cell I3; otherwise, the text string "credit denied" will be displayed in cell I3. Eric copies this formula down the column relatively, to determine if each customer was approved or denied credit, as shown in Figure 4.26.

Figure 4.26: Using the IF function to identify the credit decision

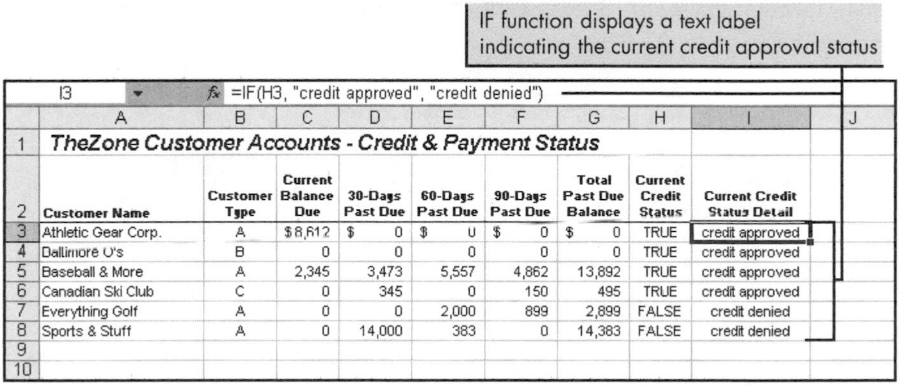

IF function displays a text label indicating the current credit approval status

I3   fx =IF(H3, "credit approved", "credit denied")

	A	B	C	D	E	F	G	H	I	J
1	**TheZone Customer Accounts - Credit & Payment Status**									
2	**Customer Name**	**Customer Type**	**Current Balance Due**	**30-Days Past Due**	**60-Days Past Due**	**90-Days Past Due**	**Total Past Due Balance**	**Current Credit Status**	**Current Credit Status Detail**	
3	Athletic Gear Corp.	A	$8,612	$ 0	$ 0	$ 0	$ 0	TRUE	credit approved	
4	Dallimore O's	B	0	0	0	0	0	TRUE	credit approved	
5	Baseball & More	A	2,345	3,473	5,557	4,862	13,892	TRUE	credit approved	
6	Canadian Ski Club	C	0	345	0	150	495	TRUE	credit approved	
7	Everything Golf	A	0	0	2,000	899	2,899	FALSE	credit denied	
8	Sports & Stuff	A	0	14,000	383	0	14,383	FALSE	credit denied	
9										
10										

Writing an IF Function That Performs a Simple Calculation

Next, Eric wants to look at several schemes of applying penalties to those accounts with past due balances. TheZone is considering several alternatives in an effort to discourage late payments and cut down on interest expenses. At the same time, the alternative must be chosen carefully, taking into consideration how it could affect sales and customer relations.

The first alternative being considered is a flat fee of $25 charged against all past due accounts. Columns C through G of the Status worksheet (Figure 4.26) list the balances due on each customer's account and how many days past due each amount is. To evaluate the effect of the first alternative, a flat fee of $25 as a finance charge, Eric needs to calculate a total balance including this finance charge using the following criteria:

- For customers that have no total past due balance (column G), the total balance including the finance charge will be equal to the customer's current balance (column C).
- For customers that have a total past due balance greater than 0 (column G), the total balance including the finance charge will be equal to the customer's current balance (column C), plus the customer's total past due balance (column G), plus the $25 finance charge.

How can Eric apply this logic in the worksheet? In this situation, he wants to determine if the total past due balance is equal to 0 and, if it is, he wants to simply display the current balance. If the total past due balance is not equal to 0, then he wants Excel to complete the following calculation: current balance plus total past due balance plus 25. Instead of simply displaying a TRUE or FALSE value, Eric wants Excel to complete one action if the formula evaluates to TRUE and another if it evaluates to FALSE. Consequently, Eric needs to use an IF function that performs a calculation.

Figure 4.27 shows a decision tree Eric created to help illustrate this logic. In a decision tree, a logical test is represented by a diamond shape. Stemming from the logical test is one action to take if the test is TRUE and another action to take if it is FALSE; these actions are presented in rectangles.

Figure 4.27: Decision tree to evaluate new total balance

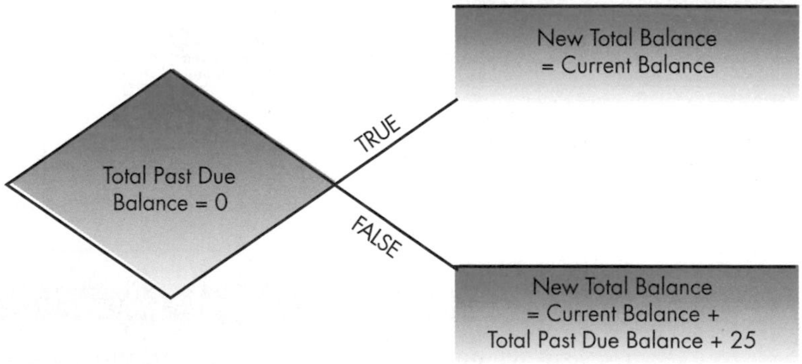

What will the first argument of the IF function be for this problem? The logical test is whether the past due balance is 0, which can be expressed as the relational expression G3=0 (for the first customer in the worksheet). The second argument is the result to be displayed if the test is TRUE; in this case, the current balance, which is in cell C3, should be displayed. The third argument is the result to be displayed if the test is FALSE, which is represented by the numerical expression C3+G3+25 (current balance + past due balance + 25). In Excel syntax, the formula is constructed as follows:

$$=\texttt{IF(G3=0,C3,C3+G3+25)}$$

This formula will work quite well as is; however, Eric knows that the finance charge value (currently $25) is subject to change. He decides to insert several rows at the top of the Status worksheet to explicitly list this input value, as shown in Figure 4.28. He also updates the formula, which is now located in cell J6, to the following:

$$=\texttt{IF(G6=0,C6,C6+G6+B\$2)}$$

Figure 4.28: Using an IF function to calculate the total balance including finance charge

IF function determines if the total past due balance = 0; if true, the current balance due is displayed; if false, the result of the calculation is displayed

	A	B	C	D	E	F	G	H	I	J	K
					f_x	=IF(G6=0, C6, C6+G6+B$2)					
1	Data Inputs:										
2	Base Penalty Fee	$ 25									
3											
4	**TheZone Customer Accounts - Credit & Payment Status**										
5	Customer Name	Customer Type	Current Balance Due	30-Days Past Due	60-Days Past Due	90-Days Past Due	Total Past Due Balance	Current Credit Status	Current Credit Status Detail	Total Balance Including Finance Charge	
6	Athletic Gear Corp.	A	$8,612	$ 0	$ 0	$ 0	$ 0	TRUE	credit approved	$ 8,612	
7	Baltimore O's	B	0	0	0	0	0	TRUE	credit approved	0	
8	Baseball & More	A	2,345	3,473	5,557	4,862	13,892	TRUE	credit approved	16,262	
9	Canadian Ski Club	C	0	345	0	150	495	TRUE	credit approved	520	
10	Everything Golf	A	0	0	2,000	899	2,899	FALSE	credit denied	2,924	
11	Sports & Stuff	A	0	14,000	383	0	14,383	FALSE	credit denied	14,408	
12											

Because each cell reference for a balance changes relatively when the formula is copied down the column, no absolute referencing is required for them. However, the value in cell B2 (penalty fee representing the finance charge) should not change when copied down column J. Therefore, the row in this cell reference must be absolute because the formula is copied only down the column and not across rows.

Could Eric have written the expression =IF(G6<>0,C6+G6+B$2,C6) instead? This formula is logically equivalent to the formula shown in Figure 4.28. The only difference is that this alternative formula uses a logical test to determine if the total past due balance is *not equal to 0* instead of testing to determine if it is *equal to 0*. Consequently, the value_if_true and value_if_false arguments are switched. What if a total past due value was negative? If this was a possibility, the logical test would need to be written as G6>0 instead of G6<>0. As you can see, there are often several ways of implementing a set of criteria with an IF function.

Best Practice

Using the IF Function Appropriately

Sometimes users are tempted to include an IF function in a formula even when it is not required. When you are only comparing two values and require only a TRUE or FALSE result, an IF function is not needed. For example, if you simply want to determine if the total past due balance is greater than 0, you only need to write the formula =G6>0 to produce a TRUE or FALSE result. The formula =IF(G6>0,TRUE,FALSE) produces the same result, but is a more complicated expression and, therefore, is not recommended.

Writing IF Functions with Nested Functions

As Eric continues to develop the Status worksheet to assess and apply penalties, the managers in the accounts receivable group have determined that a simple finance charge of $25 might not be sufficient to deter customers from not paying their bills, especially those bills that are over 90 days past due. Furthermore, this charge might not always be sufficient to cover the interest expense TheZone incurs from not having collected funds. An additional penalty surcharge has been suggested under certain circumstances, as follows:

- If the 90-days past due amount is greater than $200, then an additional surcharge will be imposed of either $100 or 10% of the 90-days past due balance, whichever is higher.
- If the 90-days past due amount is not greater than $200, then no additional surcharge will be imposed, and a value of $0 should be displayed.

Eric needs to calculate this additional penalty as a separate value on the worksheet. Because the criteria might need to be modified depending on the outcomes, he again inserts additional rows at the top of the worksheet to list these input values, as shown in Figure 4.29.

Figure 4.29: Additional rows with new data inputs

New input values added

	A	B	C	D	E	F	G	H	I	J	K
1	Data Inputs:										
2	Base Penalty Fee	$ 25									
3	Minimum 90-Days Balance for Surcharge	$ 200									
4	Minimum Surcharge	$ 100									
5	Surcharge Percentage	10%									
6											
7	**TheZone Customer Accounts - Credit & Payment Status**										
8	**Customer Name**	Customer Type	Current Balance Due	30-Days Past Due	60-Days Past Due	90-Days Past Due	Total Past Due Balance	Current Credit Status	Current Credit Status Detail	Total Balance Including Finance Charge	
9	Athletic Gear Corp.	A	$8,612	$ 0	$ 0	$ 0	$ 0	TRUE	credit approved	$ 8,612	
10	Baltimore O's	B	0	0	0	0	0	TRUE	credit approved	0	
11	Baseball & More	A	2,345	3,473	5,557	4,862	13,892	TRUE	credit approved	16,262	
12	Canadian Ski Club	C	0	345	0	150	495	TRUE	credit approved	520	
13	Everything Golf	A	0	0	2,000	899	2,899	FALSE	credit denied	2,924	
14	Sports & Stuff	A	0	14,000	383		14,383	FALSE	credit denied	14,408	
15											

The new inputs are as follows:

- Minimum 90-days past due balance before applying the surcharge—$200 (cell B3)
- Minimum surcharge value—$100 (cell B4)
- Surcharge percentage—10% (cell B5)

Again, Eric uses an IF function because the problem requires him to make a decision and then generate different values depending on whether the logical test results in a TRUE or FALSE value. So far, Eric has used an IF function where the resulting values are generated by displaying either a simple text message or the results of a simple arithmetic formula. In this case, the problem requires him to use a nested function to calculate the necessary values. One method of solving the problem is to use the MAX function to select the higher value of $100 or 10% of the 90-days past due amount. Consider each of the three arguments of this IF function:

- *Logical_test*—This test must determine if the 90-days past due amount is greater than $200. In this case, the logical test requires the following relational expression: 90-days past due amount > 200.
- *Value_if_true*—If the logical test results in a TRUE value, the worksheet needs to display either the value $100 or 10% of the 90-days past due amount, whichever is larger. Recall that the MAX function can select the highest value from a list of values; in this case, MAX(100,10%*90-Days Past Due Amount). This MAX function must be nested inside the IF function as the value_if_true argument. If the logical test evaluates to a TRUE value, then Excel will calculate the value of this nested expression.
- *Value_if_false*—If the logical test results in a FALSE value, the worksheet needs to display the value $0.

Translating these elements into Excel syntax results in the following formula, which Eric will enter in cell K9 of the Status worksheet:

```
=IF(F9>B3,MAX(B4,B5*F9),0)
```

Before he can copy this formula down the column, Eric needs to consider which of the cell references copy relatively and which copy absolutely. Each input value (cells B3, B4, and B5) must remain the same as the formula is copied down the column, so each must contain an absolute row reference. Figure 4.30 illustrates the formula and describes its arguments.

Eric enters the formula in cell K9 and copies it down the column. See Figure 4.31 for the resulting values.

Figure 4.30: IF function with nested function for *value_if_true*

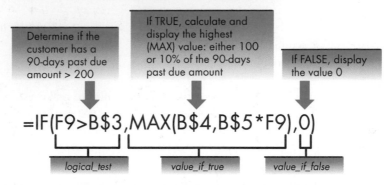

Determine if the customer has a 90-days past due amount > 200

If TRUE, calculate and display the highest (MAX) value: either 100 or 10% of the 90-days past due amount

If FALSE, display the value 0

$$=IF(F9>B\$3,MAX(B\$4,B\$5*F9),0)$$

logical_test   value_if_true   value_if_false

Figure 4.31: Results of the 90-days past due surcharge calculation

IF function determines if the 90-days past due amount > 200; if true, the MAX of 100 or 10% of 90-days past due amount is displayed; if false, 0 is displayed

K9 f_x =IF(F9>B\$3, MAX(B\$4, B\$5*F9),0)

	A	B	C	D	E	F	G	H	I	J	K	L
1	Data Inputs:											
2	Base Penalty Fee	$ 25										
3	Minimum 90-Days Balance for Surcharge	$ 200										
4	Minimum Surcharge	$ 100										
5	Surcharge Percentage	10%										
6												
7	**TheZone Customer Accounts - Credit & Payment Status**											
8	Customer Name	Customer Type	Current Balance Due	30-Days Past Due	60-Days Past Due	90-Days Past Due	Total Past Due Balance	Current Credit Status	Current Credit Status Detail	Total Balance Including Finance Charge	90-Days Past Due Surcharge	
9	Athletic Gear Corp.	A	$8,612	$ 0	$ 0	$ 0	$ 0	TRUE	credit approved	$ 8,612	$ 0	
10	Baltimore O's	B	0	0	0	0	0	TRUE	credit approved	0	0	
11	Baseball & More	A	2,345	3,473	5,557	4,862	13,892	TRUE	credit approved	16,262	486	
12	Canadian Ski Club	C	0	345	0	150	495	TRUE	credit approved	520	0	
13	Everything Golf	A	0	0	2,000	899	2,899	FALSE	credit denied	2,924	100	
14	Sports & Stuff	A	0	14,000	383	0	14,383	FALSE	credit denied	14,408	0	
15												

Constructing a Simple Nested IF Function

Another alternative penalty scheme under consideration to discourage customers from being delinquent in paying their bills is to charge a different monthly penalty depending on how late the payments are. This could be used instead of the across-the-board $25 penalty or the previously calculated surcharge. This alternative penalty would work as follows:

- Customers that have balances of 90-days past due would be charged a $100 flat fee.
- Customers that have no 90-days past due balance but have a 60-days past due balance would be charged a $50 flat fee.
- Customers that have only a 30-days past due balance would be charged a $25 flat fee.
- Customers that have no past due balance would not be charged a penalty fee.

As you have seen, an IF function can be used to evaluate a logical test, such as determining if the 90-days past due balance is greater than 0, with only two resulting values: a value_if_true and a value_if_false. In this case, however, if the logical test results in a FALSE value, another calculation is needed to determine if the value of the 60-days past due balance is greater than 0—and, if that results in a FALSE value, perform yet another calculation.

How can Eric write a formula to ask a question, then another question depending on the outcome of the first question, and so on? In the previous formula, Eric nested the MAX function so that its resulting value was one component of the IF function. He can use a similar technique of nesting IF functions, one inside the other.

Before trying to solve this directly, it might be easier to first understand the logic by constructing a decision tree to illustrate the process, as shown in Figure 4.32.

Figure 4.32: Decision tree with nested IF

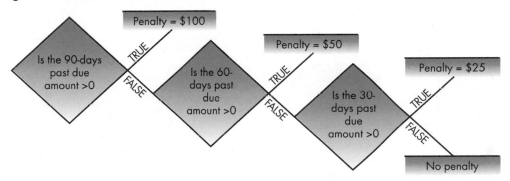

Again, each diamond represents a question leading to a different action depending on whether the answer is TRUE or FALSE. First, test to see if a company has a 90-days past due balance. If this is TRUE, apply a $100 penalty and the calculation is complete. If the company does not have a 90-days past due balance, then the next step is to test to see if it has a 60-days past due balance; if it does, apply a $50 penalty. If the company has neither a 90-days nor a 60-days past due balance, then the last step would be to check for a 30-days past due balance. If this is TRUE, apply a $25 penalty; if it's FALSE, then there are no past due balances and a value of $0 should be returned.

Using this logic, Eric can establish what his formula will look like for the first customer listed, Athletic Gear Corp., using a **pseudocode**, which is a kind of shorthand formula showing the structure of the formula without the syntactical details. After doing so, Eric can easily substitute the appropriate cell references. The following is the pseudocode for Eric's formula:

```
IF (Athletic Gear Corp.'s 90-days past due amount is >0, then
   the penalty is $100, otherwise
      IF(Athletic Gear Corp.'s 60-days past due amount is >0,
         then the penalty is $50, otherwise
            IF(Athletic Gear Corp.'s 30-days past due balance
               is >0, then the penalty is $25, otherwise no
                  penalty $0)))
```

Eric sets up an additional input area on the Status worksheet in cells D1:G4 and plans to use column L to calculate this alternative penalty scheme, converting his pseudocode into a formula in Excel syntax. The values in the cells containing the penalty amounts (cells G2:G4) should not change when the formula is copied down the column, so these cell references must have an absolute row reference. The resulting formula is as follows:

$$=IF(F9>0,G\$2,IF(E9>0,G\$3,IF(D9>0,G\$4,0)))$$

This formula is described in detail in Figure 4.33.

Figure 4.33: Nested IF function for the alternative penalty scheme

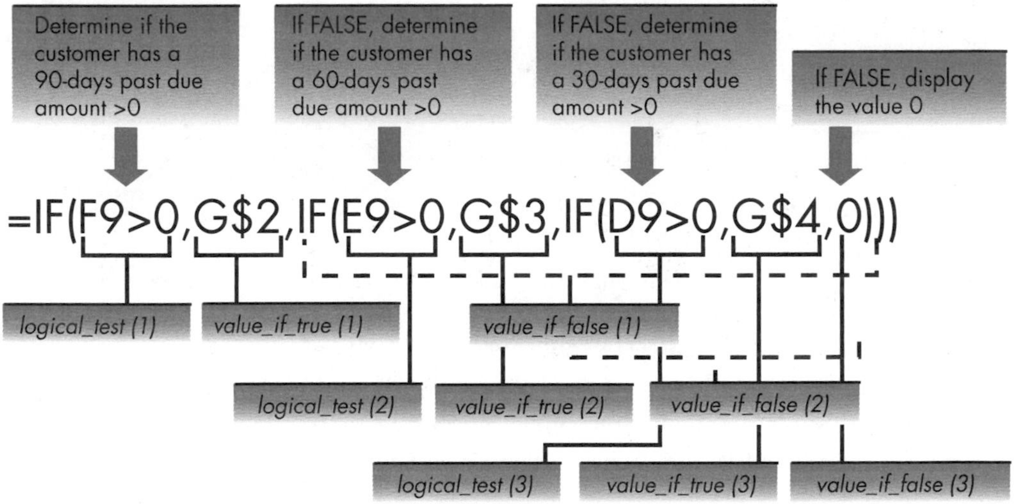

Eric enters the formula in cell L9 and copies it down the column. The resulting worksheet is shown in Figure 4.34.

How are the formula arguments evaluated? Excel begins by evaluating the first IF function. If *logical_test* results in a TRUE value, Excel evaluates the *value_if_true* argument; otherwise, it evaluates the *value_if_false* argument. In a nested IF function, the second argument (value_if_true) and/or the third argument (value_if_false) can contain another IF function. In Eric's formula, both the first and second IF functions have nested IFs for the third argument (value_if_false).

Figure 4.34: Results of the nested IF for the alternative penalty scheme

Nested IF function determines the penalty based on the past due amount

| L9 | | fx | =IF(F9>0,G$2,IF(E9>0,G$3,IF(D9>0,G$4,0))) |

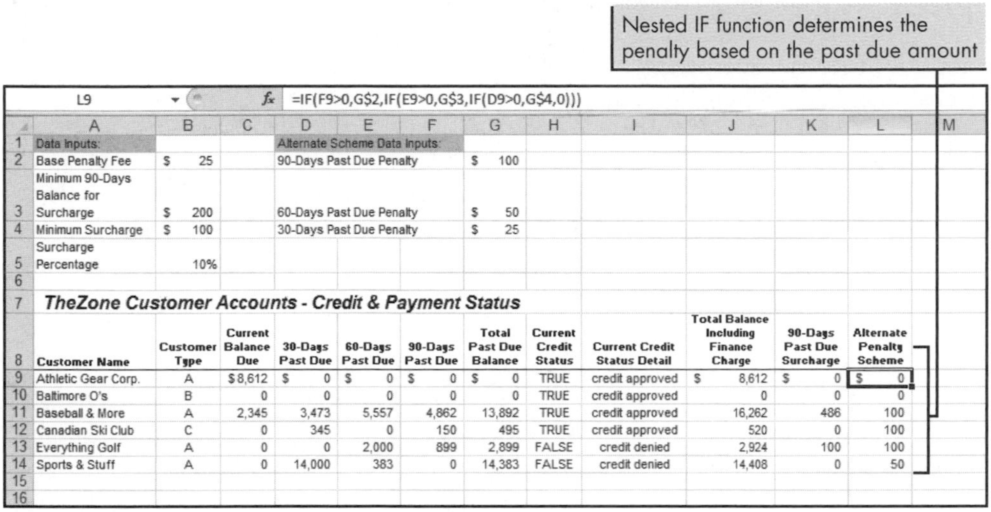

	A	B	C	D	E	F	G	H	I	J	K	L	M
1	Data Inputs:			Alternate Scheme Data Inputs:									
2	Base Penalty Fee	$ 25		90-Days Past Due Penalty			$ 100						
3	Minimum 90-Days Balance for Surcharge	$ 200		60-Days Past Due Penalty			$ 50						
4	Minimum Surcharge	$ 100		30-Days Past Due Penalty			$ 25						
5	Surcharge Percentage	10%											
6													
7	**TheZone Customer Accounts - Credit & Payment Status**												
8	Customer Name	Customer Type	Current Balance Due	30-Days Past Due	60-Days Past Due	90-Days Past Due	Total Past Due Balance	Current Credit Status	Current Credit Status Detail	Total Balance Including Finance Charge	90-Days Past Due Surcharge	Alternate Penalty Scheme	
9	Athletic Gear Corp.	A	$8,612	$ 0	$ 0	$ 0	$ 0	TRUE	credit approved	$ 8,612	$ 0	$ 0	
10	Baltimore O's	B	0	0	0	0	0	TRUE	credit approved	0	0	0	
11	Baseball & More	A	2,345	3,473	5,557	4,862	13,892	TRUE	credit approved	16,262	486	100	
12	Canadian Ski Club	C	0	345	0	150	495	TRUE	credit approved	520	0	100	
13	Everything Golf	A	0	0	2,000	899	2,899	FALSE	credit denied	2,924	100	100	
14	Sports & Stuff	A	0	14,000	383	0	14,383	FALSE	credit denied	14,408	0	50	

In this case, if the customer has a 90-days past due amount greater than 0, logical_test (1), Excel returns the value_if_true (1) result of $100 and the evaluation ends. None of the other arguments are evaluated once the formula encounters a condition that is met. Because Athletic Gear Corp. does not have a 90-days past due amount greater than 0 (its amount is equal to 0), Excel evaluates the value_if_false (1) argument, which, in turn, is another IF function.

Now, Excel evaluates the second IF function, or logical_test (2), which determines if the customer has a 60-days past due amount greater than 0. If this test results in a TRUE value, Excel returns the value_if_true (2) result of $50 and the evaluation ends. In Figure 4.34, note that the customer Sports & Stuff meets this condition—a 60-days past due amount greater than 0 (cell E14), so the result of the nested IF function for this customer is $50 (cell L14). However, the customer Athletic Gear Corp. again does not meet the condition. In this case, Excel next evaluates the value_if_false (2) argument—which, in turn, is yet another IF function. The customer Athletic Gear Corp. does not meet this condition either (a 30-days past due amount greater than 0); in fact, this customer has no past due amount at all. So the amount $0 is returned and displayed in cell L9, which is the result of the value_if_false (3) argument of the last nested IF function.

In Figure 4.34, note that cells L11, L12, and L13 each display the amount $100. Each of these customers met the condition of a 90-days past due amount greater than 0 (cells F11, F12, and F13, respectively), so these customers would be assessed the highest penalty under this alternative penalty scheme.

The Order of Logical Tests for Nonmutually Exclusive Criteria

Eric's formula first determines if an amount is past due in the 90-days category before testing for 60-days or 30-days past due amounts. Does it matter which condition is tested for first? If each customer falls into only one category (90-days, 60-days, or 30-days), it does not matter which condition is tested for first. This is not the case here, however, because a given customer can have a 30-days past due amount greater than 0 and also have a 90-days past due amount greater than 0. If the formula first tested for the 30-days past due amount, then the $25 penalty would be applied before the formula ever determined if the customer had a 90-days past due amount.

Consider, for example, the customer Baseball & More, which has past due amounts in all three categories. The formula as written first tests the 90-days past due amount, resulting in the value $100 in cell L11 (see Figure 4.34). What would happen if the formula was written with the order of logical arguments switched, testing the 30-days past due amount first, as follows:

$$=IF(D9>0,G\$4,IF(E9>0,G\$3,IF(F9>0,G\$2,0)))$$

This formula would result in an incorrect alternative penalty value of $25 for the customer Baseball & More. This formula first tests to see if the 30-days past due amount is greater than 0 (D9>0). Because this results in a TRUE value, the value_if_true argument (G$4) is returned. In this formula, as soon as the function evaluates an argument to be TRUE, the evaluation ends; consequently, this formula would never test to determine if the customer has a 90-days past due amount greater than 0. So when writing a formula with nested IF functions to determine nonmutually exclusive criteria, the order in which the logical tests are placed must match the established criteria.

The Order of Logical Tests for Mutually Exclusive Criteria

In other situations, the criteria are mutually exclusive, where one data element cannot fall into more than one category. The following is an example of mutually exclusive criteria:

- If the customer is a Customer Type A, apply a $50 penalty.
- If the customer is a Customer Type B, apply a $100 penalty.
- For all other customer types, apply a $150 penalty.

Because each customer is assigned to a single type category, as listed in column B on the Status worksheet, the criteria are mutually exclusive and only one TRUE value can result. Consider the following formula:

$$=IF(B9="A",50,IF(B9="B",100,150))$$

With this formula, the customer Athletic Gear Corp. would be charged a $50 penalty because it is identified as a Customer Type A. No matter what order the logical tests are in, the penalty applied will be $50 for this customer because it is a Customer Type A (cell B9). The formula =IF(B9="B",100,IF(B9="A",50,150)) would produce the same results because the criteria are mutually exclusive. Therefore, when writing a formula with nested IF functions to determine mutually exclusive criteria, you can place the logical tests in any order.

The Order of Logical Tests for Criteria Between a Range of Values

In cases where you want to test criteria between a range of values, placing the logical tests in a specific order—either from highest to lowest or lowest to highest—can save a considerable amount of work. Consider the following criteria for applying a penalty based on the total past due balance:

- If the total past due balance is less than $1,000, then the penalty is $25.
- If the total past due balance is at least $1,000 but less than $5,000, then the penalty is $50.
- If the total past due balance is $5,000 or greater, then the penalty is $100.

In this case, could you test to see if the total past due amount is at least $1,000 but less than $5,000 first, and then test to see if the amount is less than $1,000? The logical test would have to first determine that the amount is both greater than or equal to $1,000 *and* less than $5,000, as follows:

```
=IF(AND(G9>=1000,G9<5000),50,IF(G9<1000,25,100))
```

This formula requires nesting an AND function in the logical test argument of the IF function. On the other hand, if the formula first tested either the lowest value and went up in order, or first tested the highest value and went down in order, the logical tests could be simplified. Using ascending order, you could write the following formula:

```
=IF(G9<1000,25,IF(G9<5000,50,100))
```

Using descending order, you could write the following formula:

```
=IF(G9>=5000,100,IF(G9>=1000,50,25))
```

With the ascending order formula, if a customer has a total past due balance of $2,899, Excel first determines if $2,899 is less than $1,000. This results in a FALSE value, so Excel next evaluates the value_if_false argument—which is the logical test of the second IF function. This test determines if $2,899 is less than $5,000; it does not also have to determine if the value is at least $1,000 because the first logical test (G9<1000) takes care of this. If the value was less than $1,000 (in other words, it was not at least $1,000), Excel executes the value_if_true argument and returns a value of $25. Therefore, the second logical test would never be executed.

By evaluating the conditions in a specific order, you can simplify the task. This technique works well when evaluating problems with three or four range categories. Up to the maximum of 64 levels of nesting can be used in a formula. In a later chapter, you'll learn a technique that is much more effective when a large number of ranges must be considered.

As you have seen, formulas that contain IF functions and nested functions can be powerful tools for data analysis. In the next level, Eric will revisit the customer credit evaluation developed in Level 1, expanding and combining these tools to further automate the decision-making process.

Steps To Success: Level 2

TheZone accounts payable group can sometimes be delinquent in paying TheZone's vendors in a timely manner. In some cases, this is a deliberate effort to hold off payment as long as possible; in others, it is simply an oversight. The accounts payable group has developed a worksheet listing some of the vendors to which TheZone owes past due balances, organized by past due categories of 30-days past due, 60-days past due, and 90-days past due. Figure 4.35 shows this worksheet.

Figure 4.35: TheZone's accounts payable analysis

	A	B	C	D	E	F	G	H	I	J	K	L
1	Fixed Fee & Penalties			Graduated Penalties - Range				Penalty		Category Penalties		
2	Fixed Penalty	$ 50		Graduated penalty <=			$ 500	$ 0		Utilities	8%	
3	90-days min amt for penalty	$ 100		Graduated penalty >500 but <			5,000	250		Labor	12%	
4	90-days penalty percentage	15%		Graduated penalty >=			5,000	450		Other	5%	
5												
6												
7	TheZone Accounts Payable - Outstanding Balance Report											
8	Vendor Name	Category	Applies Fixed Penalty	30-Days Past Due	60-Days Past Due	90-Days Past Due	Total Past Due Balance	Fixed Penalty	90-Days Penalty	Graduated Penalty	Category Penalty	
9	RTF Electric	Utilities	FALSE	$ 18,100	$ 0	$ 0	$ 18,100					
10	Ross County Water & Sewer	Utilities	FALSE	500	0	0	500					
11	YNC Trucking	Transportation	TRUE	0	0	3,100	3,100					
12	Italian Leather Group Ltd.	Raw Materials	TRUE	0	850	5,674	6,524					
13	Union Plastics	Raw Materials	TRUE	7,250	436	0	7,686					
14	Freight to Go	Transportation	FALSE	0	0	8,730	8,730					
15	Temps R'Us	Labor	FALSE	2,700	0	0	2,700					
16	Notworth Telephone	Telephone	TRUE	0	100	0	100					
17												

Recently, some vendors have started to apply different penalty and discount schemes to overdue accounts, similar to those being proposed by TheZone's accounts receivable group. As a preemptive measure, you have been asked to help calculate some of these possible penalty scenarios that TheZone might incur based on its current outstanding balances. A list of these past due balances is provided in the workbook named Unpaid.xlsx. This file also contains the data input values that you need to calculate the penalties in the top portion of the worksheet (similar to the spreadsheet in Figure 4.34). Keep in mind that you should use cell references in your formulas wherever possible.

Complete the following:

1. Open the workbook named **Unpaid.xlsx** located in the Chapter 4 folder, and then save it as **Unpaid Invoice Penalties.xlsx**.

2. Some vendors have agreed on an industry standard penalty of $50 on all past due accounts regardless of the past due amount or number of days past due. These vendors

are identified by the value TRUE in the corresponding row of column C. Write a formula in column H, which can be copied down the column, listing the penalty for the corresponding account: $50 for vendors that are participating in this standard penalty and $0 for all other vendors. Only vendors that are owed past due balances are listed on this sheet.

3. Calculate another possible penalty whereby only those accounts with 90-days past due balances are owed a fee. In column I, write a formula that can be copied down the column to calculate the penalty based on the following criteria:

- For accounts with a 90-days past due balance of $100 or more, apply a fee of 15% of the 90-days past due balance.
- For all other accounts, no penalty is applied.

4. Another penalty scheme being used by vendors is a graduated method based on the total past due balances (column G). In column J, write a formula that can be copied down the column to calculate the penalty based on the following criteria:

- For accounts with a total past due balance of less than or equal to $500, do not apply a penalty.
- For accounts with a past due balance of greater than $500 but less than $5,000, apply a penalty of $250.
- For accounts with a past due balance of $5,000 or more, apply a penalty of $450.

5. Penalties can sometimes be specific to vendor category. In column K, write a formula that can be copied down the column to calculate the penalty based on the following criteria:

- For vendors in the Utilities category, apply a fee of 8% of the total past due balance (column G).
- For vendors in the Labor category, apply a fee of 12% of the total past due balance.
- For vendors in all other categories, apply a fee of 5% of the total past due balance.

6. Format columns H through K to match column G.

7. Save and close the Unpaid Invoice Penalties.xlsx workbook.

LEVEL 3
Creating Complex Logical Constructs for Solving Problems

Evaluating More Complex Criteria

The previous level explored relational expressions in formulas and nested functions. This level presents similar techniques to create more complex logical constructs—combinations of multiple logical operations—to determine if *none of* the criteria are TRUE for a list of items, and even if *only certain* criteria are TRUE for a list of items.

In addition to working with logical constructs that require nesting AND, OR, and NOT functions, this level also covers, in more depth, the techniques of nesting IF functions to solve more complex problems.

Eric is now ready to go back to the CreditData worksheet in the Customer Credit and Payment History workbook to come up with a single recommendation regarding credit approval, which he can then provide to the accounts receivable manager and the finance group for final analysis and approval. He will use the information already generated based on customer accounts plus additional guidelines from management to determine the recommendation.

Recall that in Level 1, Eric created formulas using relational operators and Boolean logical functions (AND, OR, and NOT) to evaluate TheZone's credit approval rules, as follows:

Rule #1: Accept a customer that has a past due balance that is less than 10% of this year's total sales. This is not calculated for new customers.

Rule #2: Accept a customer that has either a composite credit appraisal value of 1 or a PAYDEX score over 90.

Rule #3: Accept a customer that has all of the following: a net worth of at least $500,000; a composite credit appraisal value of 2 or lower; a PAYDEX score over 70; and a stress risk class of 1.

Figure 4.36 shows the current CreditData worksheet. Notice that Eric chose to apply the conditional formatting so that all TRUE values in the range K3:M21 appear in a bold, italic font.

Reviewing the worksheet, it is not always clear how to proceed in finalizing the credit approval for a particular customer. The determination is fairly straightforward for those customers that have a TRUE value for all three rules and for those that have a FALSE value for all three rules. What about those customers with combinations of TRUE and FALSE values? Management has provided Eric with the following directions regarding credit approval decisions:

Figure 4.36: Customer credit analysis revisited

	A	B	C	D	E	F	G	H	I	J	K	L	M	N
1	Accounts Receivable Department - Customer Credit Analysis													
2	Customer Name	Current Credit Limit	Previous Year's Sales	Current Year's Sales	Past Due Balance	Net Worth in (000)	D&B Credit Rating Class	D&B Composite Credit Appraisal (1 Best)	D&B PAYDEX (100 Best)	D&B Stress Risk Class (1 Best)	Rule #1	Rule #2	Rule #3	
3	Athletic Gear Corp.	$ 9,000	$ 15,382	$11,952	$ 0	$ 450	BA	4	15	3	TRUE	FALSE	FALSE	
4	Baltimore O's	39,000	10,033	7,789	0	1,950	3A	1	51	1	TRUE	TRUE	FALSE	
5	Baseball & More	75,000	60,009	55,342	13,892	37,500	4A	2	70	1	FALSE	FALSE	FALSE	
6	Canadian Ski Club	33,000	35,039	50,921	495	1,650	BA	2	43	1	TRUE	FALSE	FALSE	
7	Concord Pro Shop					10,000	4A	1	91	1		TRUE	TRUE	
8	Everything Golf	25,000	15,221	9,483	2,899	1,250	3A	3	76	1	FALSE	FALSE	FALSE	
9	Lake Pro Shops	42,000	80,498	81,126	0	2,100	3A	2	87	1	TRUE	FALSE	TRUE	
10	Mars Dept. Store	27,000	35,354	20,666	0	213	BB	3	94	1	TRUE	TRUE	FALSE	
11	RG Bradley	46,000	90,970	18,343	0	2,300	3A	1	21	1	TRUE	TRUE	FALSE	
12	RX for Sports	15,000	5,663	3,014	0	750	2A	1	59	1	TRUE	TRUE	FALSE	
13	School Sports Supply	45,000	50,278	32,338	0	2,250	3A	3	91	1	TRUE	TRUE	FALSE	
14	Ski World	26,000	25,864	28,154	0	300	BA	2	82	1	TRUE	FALSE	FALSE	
15	Sneaker Kingdom	45,000	40,157	25,379	0	2,250	3A	2	71	1	TRUE	FALSE	TRUE	
16	Sports & Stuff	15,000	15,898	14,732	14,383	450	BA	1	67	1	FALSE	TRUE	FALSE	
17	Toy Kingdom	22,000	10,073	1,047	0	1,100	3A	3	14	1	TRUE	FALSE	FALSE	
18	Under the Sea	45,000	95,411	64,418	0	150	CB	4	79	2	TRUE	FALSE	FALSE	
19	US Olympic Team	20,000	5,621	8,171	0	1,000	3A	1	87	1	TRUE	TRUE	TRUE	
20	WWW Sports Inc.	100,000	60,009	60,354	0	500,000	5A	2	97	1	TRUE	TRUE	TRUE	
21	Zip & Sons	10,000	15,490	22,760	0	620	1A	2	96	1	TRUE	TRUE	TRUE	
22														
23							Do any meet the rule?				TRUE	TRUE	TRUE	
24							Do none meet the rule?				FALSE	FALSE	FALSE	
25														

- Automatically *reject* credit if a customer meets none of the approval rules. Such customers have demonstrated none of the desired attributes—either financially through their D&B credit information or through their past dealings with TheZone.
- Recommend *further evaluation* if a customer meets either of the following sets of criteria:

  – The customer has a TRUE value for *only* Rule #1 (that is, has less than a 10% past due balance). Although such a customer has a satisfactory payment history with TheZone, its D&B financial data indicates possible problems in its future ability to pay.
  – The customer has a TRUE value for *only* Rule #2 and/or Rule #3 and has a FALSE value for Rule #1. Although such a customer has satisfactory D&B financial indicators, its previous payment history with TheZone is less than satisfactory.

Customer accounts identified for further evaluation will be handled manually by an experienced accountant, requiring additional financial information and consideration of this customer's current business relationship with TheZone.

- Automatically *accept* for credit those customers that have a TRUE value for Rule #1 and a TRUE value for Rule #2 and/or Rule #3. These customers have demonstrated both financial stability and a satisfactory payment history with TheZone.

Eric now needs to assess the customer data against this final set of criteria and return one of the following results for each customer: "Reject," "Further Evaluate," or "Accept." How can he analyze criteria and return a value other than TRUE or FALSE? Recall that the IF function can evaluate a set of criteria and return one value if it is TRUE and another value if it is FALSE. By nesting levels of IF functions, multiple sets of criteria can be sequentially analyzed until a final value is returned.

Using an IF Function to Combine Sets of Criteria

Before Eric can formulate a specific implementation of the rules, he must explore several aspects of the problem. For example, are the different criteria mutually exclusive, or can a customer fall into more than one category? In fact, the different criteria are mutually exclusive; a customer can fall into only one of the three categories (Accept, Further Evaluate, Reject). So the order in which the different criteria are analyzed should not matter, except perhaps to make the analysis easier to interpret. In this case, Eric decides to follow the guidelines in the order presented earlier. First, he will determine if a company meets none of the rules (Reject); then if only Rule #1 is met or if only Rules #2 or #3 are met (Further Evaluate); and finally, if the customer meets the approval criteria (Accept).

Another question to be answered before proposing an implementation is the following: Can it be assumed if a customer is neither rejected nor identified for further evaluation that the customer, by default, will fall into the Accept category? Consider the truth table shown in Figure 4.37.

Figure 4.37: Truth table showing all possible combinations of values for Rules #1 through #3

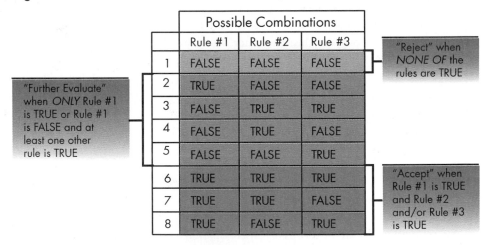

This table lists all possible combinations of values for Rules #1 through #3. There are two possible results for each rule (TRUE or FALSE), resulting in 2^3 (2*2*2) or eight possible outcomes. Outcome 1 at the top of the truth table in Figure 4.37 results in a customer's credit being rejected. Outcomes 2 through 5 represent the results for customers who require further evaluation. This leaves outcomes 6 through 8. Do these three remaining outcomes all meet the criteria of a TRUE value for Rule #1 and a TRUE value for Rule #2 and/or Rule #3, indicating that the customer should be accepted for credit? Yes; each of these three possible combinations contains a TRUE value for Rule #1 and a TRUE value for Rule #2 or Rule #3, or both. So a third IF statement is not required. After the criteria for Reject and Further Evaluate are complete, the only other possible outcome is Accept.

The best way to proceed is to take the information and represent this process schematically in a decision tree, as illustrated in Figure 4.38. First, the rejection criteria will be analyzed, then the further evaluation criteria. And, finally, if a customer is neither rejected nor identified for further evaluation, the customer will automatically be accepted for credit.

Figure 4.38: Decision tree to determine the category: Reject, Further Evaluate, or Accept

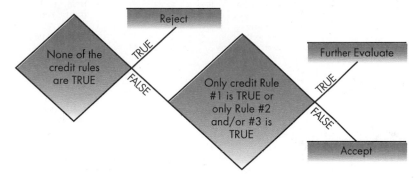

This process can also be represented in pseudocode, as follows:

```
IF (none of the rules are TRUE, "Reject",
   IF(OR(only Rule #1 is TRUE, only Rule #2 and/or Rule #3
      is TRUE), "Further Evaluate", otherwise "Accept"))
```

To implement this formula, Eric will consider each component separately and then combine them in cell N3. After building the formula in cell N3, he will copy it down the column. As shown in the pseudocode, this formula requires nested levels of IF statements and Boolean logical constructs within the arguments of the IF statements.

Using the None Of Construct

The first step Eric takes is to evaluate if *none of* the credit rules are met. Eric has not yet tested for a *none of* criterion directly. However, recall that he entered the formula =OR(K3:K21) in cell K23 (see Figure 4.39), which determines whether any customer meets the criteria for Rule #1. Then the question "Do none meet the rule?" is asked, with the answer value placed in cell K24. Eric simply flipped the "any" to "none of" by turning the TRUE value to FALSE. He implemented this by writing the formula =NOT(K23) in cell K24. Note that Eric froze the first column in the worksheet so that he could focus more easily on the customers and the three credit rules.

Figure 4.39: Previous rule summary using OR and NOT functions in two steps to obtain a *none of* construct

Pane frozen

Formulas in cell K23 =OR(K3:K21) and cell K24 =NOT(K23) can be combined using the formula =NOT(OR(K3:K21)) to determine if *none* of the values for Rule #1 are TRUE

	A	H	I	J	K	L	M
1	**Accounts Recalysis**						
2	Customer Name	D&B Composite Credit Appraisal (1 Best)	D&B PAYDEX (100 Best)	D&B Stress Risk Class (1 Best)	Rule#1	Rule#2	Rule#3
3	Athletic Gear Corp.	4	15	3	TRUE	FALSE	FALSE
4	Baltimore O's	1	51	1	TRUE	TRUE	FALSE
5	Baseball & More	2	70	1	FALSE	FALSE	FALSE
6	Canadian Ski Club	2	43	1	TRUE	FALSE	FALSE
7	Concord Pro Shop	1	91	1		TRUE	TRUE
8	Everything Golf	3	76	1	FALSE	FALSE	FALSE
9	Lake Pro Shops	2	87	1	TRUE	FALSE	TRUE
10	Mars Dept. Store	3	94	1	TRUE	TRUE	FALSE
11	RG Bradley	1	21	1	TRUE	TRUE	FALSE
12	RX for Sports	1	59	1	TRUE	TRUE	FALSE
13	School Sports Supply	3	91	1	TRUE	TRUE	FALSE
14	Ski World	2	82	1	TRUE	FALSE	FALSE
15	Sneaker Kingdom	2	71	1	TRUE	FALSE	TRUE
16	Sports & Stuff	1	67	1	FALSE	TRUE	FALSE
17	Toy Kingdom	3	14	1	TRUE	FALSE	FALSE
18	Under the Sea	4	79	2	TRUE	FALSE	FALSE
19	US Olympic Team	1	87	1	TRUE	TRUE	TRUE
20	WWW Sports Inc.	2	97	1	TRUE	TRUE	TRUE
21	Zip & Sons	2	96	1	TRUE	TRUE	TRUE
22							
23		Do any meet the rule?			TRUE	TRUE	TRUE
24		Do none meet the rule?			FALSE	FALSE	FALSE

The two steps Eric took can be combined into one by nesting the formula as follows: =NOT(OR(K3:K21)). This formula directly determines (TRUE or FALSE) if none of the customers meet the criteria for Rule #1. The formula essentially finds that, if even one customer meets the criteria, then the statement "none of the customers meet the criteria" is FALSE.

Now, Eric considers how to determine if a customer meets the criteria for *none of* the rules—neither Rule #1, Rule #2, nor Rule #3—as listed in columns K through M of the worksheet. He can use a similar technique by first testing to see if *any* of the rules are TRUE for a specific customer, and then flip the result with a NOT function. The following is the logical test he uses in his formula for the first customer listed, Athletic Gear Corp.:

$$NOT(OR(K3:M3))$$

Eric substitutes this as the logical_test of the first IF statement in the pseudocode, as follows:

```
IF (NOT(OR(K3:M3)), "Reject",
    IF(OR(only Rule #1 is TRUE, only Rule #2 and/or Rule #3
     is TRUE), "Further Evaluate", otherwise "Accept"))
```

To better illustrate which customers will be affected by the Reject criteria, they have been highlighted on the worksheet in Figure 4.40. As you can see, two customers, Baseball & More and Everything Golf, have all FALSE values for Rules #1 through #3.

Figure 4.40: Customers that will be automatically rejected

	A	K	L	M	N
1	Accounts Rec				
2	Customer Name	Rule #1	Rule #2	Rule #3	
3	Athletic Gear Corp.	TRUE	FALSE	FALSE	
4	Baltimore O's	TRUE	TRUE	FALSE	
5	Baseball & More	FALSE	FALSE	FALSE	
6	Canadian Ski Club	TRUE	FALSE	FALSE	
7	Concord Pro Shop		TRUE	TRUE	
8	Everything Golf	FALSE	FALSE	FALSE	
9	Lake Pro Shops	TRUE	FALSE	TRUE	
10	Mars Dept. Store	TRUE	TRUE	FALSE	
11	RG Bradley	TRUE	TRUE	FALSE	
12	RX for Sports	TRUE	TRUE	FALSE	
13	School Sports Supply	TRUE	TRUE	FALSE	
14	Ski World	TRUE	FALSE	FALSE	
15	Sneaker Kingdom	TRUE	FALSE	TRUE	
16	Sports & Stuff	FALSE	TRUE	FALSE	
17	Toy Kingdom	TRUE	FALSE	FALSE	
18	Under the Sea	TRUE	FALSE	FALSE	
19	US Olympic Team	TRUE	TRUE	TRUE	
20	WWW Sports Inc.	TRUE	TRUE	TRUE	
21	Zip & Sons	TRUE	TRUE	TRUE	
22					
23		TRUE	TRUE	TRUE	
24		FALSE	FALSE	FALSE	
25					

Customers shaded in gray will be automatically rejected based on the criteria used in the IF function

Best Practice

Implementing the *None Of* Construct Most Efficiently

The most efficient way to execute a *none of* construct is to nest the OR function within a NOT function. A less efficient but logically equivalent approach to determining if none of the rules are TRUE for a specific customer is to figure out if each rule results in a FALSE value. So if Rule #1, Rule #2, and Rule #3 all result in the value FALSE for a customer, then the statement "None of the rules are true" is TRUE. You can accomplish this by "flipping" the value of each rule with a NOT function to obtain a TRUE value if the rule had a FALSE value, and then combine all values with an AND function to test whether all of the rules are FALSE. The following logical construct is used in this case:

AND(NOT(K3),NOT(L3),NOT(M3))

No matter how long the list of values to be checked is, each cell in the range needs to be listed separately using this type of construct. Clearly this method, although usable, is much more cumbersome to execute than the NOT(OR(K3:M3)) construct and, consequently, is not recommended, especially with large lists.

Could you simply write the expression NOT(K3:M3)? No; recall that the syntax of the NOT function evaluates only a single TRUE or FALSE value, not a range of values. This expression is not valid, and cannot be interpreted as either "all the items are FALSE" or as "at least one item is FALSE."

Using the Only Construct

The next step in constructing the formula is to determine if *only* Rule #1 evaluates to TRUE and, if so, to recommend further evaluation; *OR* if *only* Rule #2 and/or Rule #3 evaluate to TRUE and not Rule #1, as represented by the following pseudocode:

```
OR(only Rule #1 is TRUE, only Rule #2 and/or Rule #3 is TRUE)
```

How can Eric determine if a customer has *only* a TRUE value for Rule #1 but for neither of the other two rules? Breaking down this part of the problem into smaller logical tasks makes the process clearer. To prove this *only* construct, Eric must prove that *both* of the following statements are TRUE:

- Rule #1 has a TRUE value.

AND

- None of the other rules have a TRUE value (in this instance, both Rule #2 and Rule #3 are FALSE).

Note that an *only* construct always has a positive condition to be evaluated AND a negative condition to be evaluated. An OR function is required for either the positive condition or the negative condition if more than one item being evaluated falls in that category.

To evaluate if either Rule #2 or Rule #3 is TRUE or if both are TRUE, and that Rule #1 is not TRUE, Eric can similarly explain this as follows:

- Rule #2 OR Rule #3 has a TRUE value.

AND

- Rule #1 does not have a TRUE value (it is FALSE).

The diagram in Figure 4.41 illustrates this logic.

The pseudocode for the Further Evaluate criteria can now be detailed as follows:

```
OR(AND(Rule #1 is TRUE, neither Rule #2 nor Rule #3 is
   TRUE),AND(OR(Rule #2 and/or Rule #3 is TRUE), Rule #1
     is FALSE))
```

Now Eric needs to translate the statement "This customer *only* has a TRUE value for Rule #1" into Excel syntax. To test if K3 is TRUE, Eric only needs to list the cell reference inside the AND statement. To test if neither L3 nor M3 is TRUE (both are FALSE), Eric can use the *none of* construct he used earlier. Substituting the appropriate cell references results in the following expression:

```
AND(K3,NOT(OR(L3:M3)))
```

Figure 4.41: Defining the Further Evaluate criteria using *only* constructs

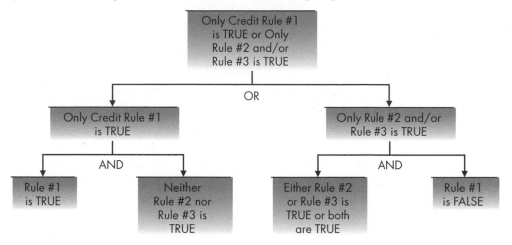

This expression tests that both K3 is TRUE (Rule #1) and that *none of* the other values are TRUE by using an AND function and nesting a *none of* construct inside it as the second argument.

How To

Build an *Only* Construct with Multiple Positive and Negative Items

Consider the example shown in Figure 4.42 to determine if only companies with a current credit limit of more than $50,000 have a TRUE value for Rule #1.

Figure 4.42: Example of an *only* construct containing multiple items in each category

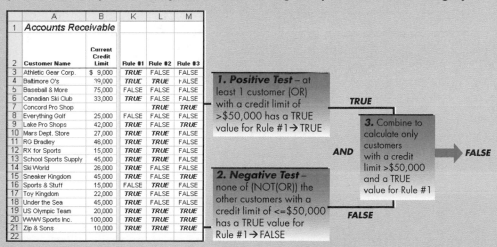

Do we need to prove all companies with over a $50,000 credit limit have a TRUE value, or that at least one of these companies has a TRUE value for Rule #1? Do we need to prove that all companies with a $50,000 or less credit limit have a FALSE value for Rule #1 or only some? Logically, the statement requires at least one company with over a $50,000 credit limit to have a TRUE value for Rule #1, and that all of the companies with $50,000 or less have a FALSE value. This logic can be applied using the following approach:

1. Complete the *Positive Test*: Evaluate if any of the customers with a credit limit of more than $50,000 have a TRUE value for Rule #1. In this case, Baseball & More (cell B5) and WWW Sports Inc. (cell B20) both have credit limits exceeding $50,000. To consider if either of these companies has a TRUE value for Rule #1, you can write the following:

OR(K5,K20)

2. Complete the *Negative Test*: Evaluate if none of the other customers have a TRUE value for Rule #1. To evaluate all customers except Baseball & More and WWW Sports Inc., you can write the following *none of* construct:

NOT(OR(K3:K4,K6:K19,K21))

3. Combine the Positive Test and the Negative Test to determine if both sets of criteria are met:

=AND(OR(K5,K20),NOT(OR(K3:K4,K6:K19,K21)))

Note that this formula does not automatically determine which customers have a credit limit of over $50,000, but instead these cells are directly referenced manually in the formula. Much more sophisticated techniques would be required to do this automatically.

Nesting Boolean Logical Operators to Analyze Criteria

Eric now evaluates the second part of the Further Evaluate criteria. Here, he needs to prove that both of the following statements are TRUE:

• Either Rule #2 or Rule #3 is TRUE or both are TRUE.
• Rule #1 is FALSE.

Logically, this can be expressed as AND(OR(Rule #2 is TRUE, Rule #3 is TRUE), Rule #1 is FALSE). Substituting the appropriate cell references results in the following expression:

AND(OR(L3,M3),NOT(K3))

Eric has now evaluated both parts of the Further Evaluate criteria using the following two expressions:

AND(K3,NOT(OR(L3:M3)))

$$AND(OR(L3,M3),NOT(K3))$$

The guidelines that management provided Eric require that only one of these statements be TRUE for a customer to be identified for further evaluation. The statements must be combined using an OR operation, as follows:

$$OR(AND(K3,NOT(OR(L3:M3))),AND(OR(L3,M3),NOT(K3)))$$

Eric can substitute this expression as the second logical test of the pseudocode, as follows:

```
IF (NOT(OR(K3:M3)), "Reject",
   IF(OR(AND(K3,NOT(OR(L3:M3))),AND(OR(L3,M3),NOT(K3))),
      "Further Evaluate", otherwise "Accept"))
```

Again, to better illustrate which customers will be affected by the Further Evaluate criteria, these rows have been highlighted in Figure 4.43.

Figure 4.43: Customers that will be recommended for further evaluation

	A	K	L	M	N
1	*Accounts Rec*				
2	**Customer Name**	**Rule #1**	**Rule #2**	**Rule #3**	
3	Athletic Gear Corp.	TRUE	FALSE	FALSE	
4	Baltimore O's	TRUE	TRUE	FALSE	
5	Baseball & More	FALSE	FALSE	FALSE	
6	Canadian Ski Club	TRUE	FALSE	FALSE	
7	Concord Pro Shop		TRUE	TRUE	
8	Everything Golf	FALSE	FALSE	FALSE	
9	Lake Pro Shops	TRUE	FALSE	TRUE	
10	Mars Dept. Store	TRUE	TRUE	FALSE	
11	RG Bradley	TRUE	TRUE	FALSE	
12	RX for Sports	TRUE	TRUE	FALSE	
13	School Sports Supply	TRUE	TRUE	FALSE	
14	Ski World	TRUE	FALSE	FALSE	
15	Sneaker Kingdom	TRUE	FALSE	TRUE	
16	Sports & Stuff	FALSE	TRUE	FALSE	
17	Toy Kingdom	TRUE	FALSE	FALSE	
18	Under the Sea	TRUE	FALSE	FALSE	
19	US Olympic Team	TRUE	TRUE	TRUE	
20	WWW Sports Inc.	TRUE	TRUE	TRUE	
21	Zip & Sons	TRUE	TRUE	TRUE	
22					
23		TRUE	TRUE	TRUE	
24		FALSE	FALSE	FALSE	
25					
26					

Customers shaded in gray will be placed in the "Further Evaluate" category based on the criteria used in the IF function

As shown in Figure 4.43, it appears that seven customers will require further evaluation. For example, Athletic Gear Corp. meets the criterion that only Rule #1 is TRUE, while Sports & Stuff meets the criteria that either Rule #2 or Rule #3 is TRUE and Rule #1 is FALSE.

Completing the Complex Nested IF Formula

The last step is to determine the Accept criteria. However, as previously demonstrated, this requires no analysis because if a customer is neither rejected nor identified for further evaluation, there is no other choice but to accept that customer for credit. Modifying the remainder of the pseudocode results in the following formula:

```
IF(NOT(OR(K3:M3)),"Reject",
   IF(OR(AND(K3,NOT(OR(L3:M3))),AND(OR(L3:M3),NOT(K3))),
      "Further Evaluate", otherwise "Accept"))
```

To better illustrate which customers will result in a TRUE value for the Accept criteria, their rows have been highlighted in Figure 4.44.

Figure 4.44: Customers that will be accepted automatically

	A	K	L	M	N
1	Accounts Rec				
2	Customer Name	Rule #1	Rule #2	Rule #3	
3	Athletic Gear Corp.	TRUE	FALSE	FALSE	
4	Baltimore O's	TRUE	TRUE	FALSE	
5	Baseball & More	FALSE	FALSE	FALSE	
6	Canadian Ski Club	TRUE	FALSE	FALSE	
7	Concord Pro Shop		TRUE	TRUE	
8	Everything Golf	FALSE	FALSE	FALSE	
9	Lake Pro Shops	TRUE	FALSE	TRUE	
10	Mars Dept. Store	TRUE	TRUE	FALSE	
11	RG Bradley	TRUE	TRUE	FALSE	
12	RX for Sports	TRUE	TRUE	FALSE	
13	School Sports Supply	TRUE	TRUE	FALSE	
14	Ski World	TRUE	FALSE	FALSE	
15	Sneaker Kingdom	TRUE	FALSE	TRUE	
16	Sports & Stuff	FALSE	TRUE	FALSE	
17	Toy Kingdom	TRUE	FALSE	FALSE	
18	Under the Sea	TRUE	FALSE	FALSE	
19	US Olympic Team	TRUE	TRUE	TRUE	
20	WWW Sports Inc.	TRUE	TRUE	TRUE	
21	Zip & Sons	TRUE	TRUE	TRUE	
22					
23		TRUE	TRUE	TRUE	
24		FALSE	FALSE	FALSE	
25					
26					

Customers shaded in gray will be accepted for credit based on the criteria used in the IF function

It appears that 11 customers will be accepted for credit. Note that the Concord Pro Shop, which has no prior sales history with TheZone, is highlighted for both the Further Evaluate criteria (see Figure 4.43) and for the Accept criteria, as shown in Figure 4.44. This happens because cell K7 is blank, and blank cells are ignored. However, because the Further Evaluate criteria are evaluated in the formula before the Accept criteria are evaluated, the result for Concord Pro Shop will be "Further Evaluate," which is appropriate for most new customers.

All that is left for Eric to do is build this carefully constructed IF formula in cell N3 and copy it down the column. Because each cell reference changes relative to the row being evaluated, no absolute references are required. The final formula is listed below and detailed in Figure 4.45:

```
=IF(NOT(OR(K3:M3)), "Reject",
   IF(OR(AND(K3,NOT(OR(L3:M3))),AND(OR(L3:M3),NOT(K3))),
      "Further Evaluate", "Accept"))
```

Figure 4.45: Final complex nested IF formula to determine credit status

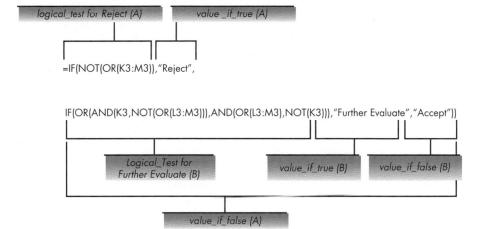

Eric copies this formula into cells N3:N21. The resulting worksheet is shown in Figure 4.46.

Eric now has a clear, easy-to-read set of final recommendations to pass along to management in the accounts receivable group and to the finance group. Of course, further evaluation will be needed for some of the customers listed, and many of the decisions ultimately made for those customers will depend on risk assessment versus the profit potential from a specific customer. TheZone might be willing to take a risk to foster a relationship with a customer believed to have the potential for large sales, but might be less willing to take the same risk for a customer that has little potential.

Figure 4.46: CreditData worksheet with final recommendations

Final complex nested IF formula

N3   fx =IF(NOT(OR(K3:M3)), "Reject",IF(OR(AND(K3,NOT(OR(L3:M3))),AND(OR(L3:M3),NOT(K3))),"Further Evaluate","Accept"))

Customer Name	Current Credit Limit	Previous Year's Sales	Current Year's Sales	Past Due Balance	Net Worth in (000)	D&B Credit Rating Class	D&B Composite Credit Appraisal (1 Best)	D&B PAYDEX (100 Best)	D&B Stress Risk Class (1 Best)	Rule #1	Rule #2	Rule #3	Final Recommendation
Athletic Gear Corp.	$ 9,000	$ 15,382	$11,952	$ 0	$ 450	BA	4	15	3	TRUE	FALSE	FALSE	Further Evaluate
Baltimore O's	39,000	10,033	7,789	0	1,950	3A	1	51	1	TRUE	TRUE	FALSE	Accept
Baseball & More	75,000	60,009	55,342	13,892	37,500	4A	2	70	1	FALSE	FALSE	FALSE	Reject
Canadian Ski Club	33,000	35,039	50,921	495	1,650	BA	2	43	1	TRUE	FALSE	FALSE	Further Evaluate
Concord Pro Shop					10,000	4A	1	91	1		TRUE	TRUE	Further Evaluate
Everything Golf	25,000	15,221	9,483	2,899	1,250	3A	3	76	1	FALSE	FALSE	FALSE	Reject
Lake Pro Shops	42,000	80,498	81,126	0	2,100	3A	2	87	1	TRUE	FALSE	TRUE	Accept
Mars Dept. Store	27,000	35,354	20,666	0	213	BB	3	94	1	TRUE	TRUE	FALSE	Accept
RG Bradley	46,000	90,970	18,343	0	2,300	3A	1	21	1	TRUE	TRUE	FALSE	Accept
RX for Sports	15,000	5,663	3,014	0	750	2A	1	59	1	TRUE	TRUE	FALSE	Accept
School Sports Supply	45,000	50,278	32,338	0	2,250	3A	3	91	1	TRUE	TRUE	FALSE	Accept
Ski World	26,000	25,864	28,154	0	300	BA	2	82	1	TRUE	FALSE	FALSE	Further Evaluate
Sneaker Kingdom	45,000	40,157	25,379	0	2,250	3A	2	71	1	TRUE	FALSE	TRUE	Accept
Sports & Stuff	15,000	15,898	14,732	14,383	450	BA	1	67	1	FALSE	TRUE	FALSE	Further Evaluate
Toy Kingdom	22,000	10,073	1,047	0	1,100	3A	3	14	1	TRUE	FALSE	FALSE	Further Evaluate
Under the Sea	45,000	95,411	64,418	0	150	CB	4	79	2	TRUE	FALSE	FALSE	Further Evaluate
US Olympic Team	20,000	5,621	6,171	0	1,000	3A	1	87	1	TRUE	TRUE	TRUE	Accept
WWW Sports Inc.	100,000	60,009	60,354	0	500,000	5A	2	97	1	TRUE	TRUE	TRUE	Accept
Zip & Sons	10,000	15,490	22,760	0	620	1A	2	96	1	TRUE	TRUE	TRUE	Accept
						Do any meet the rule?				TRUE	TRUE	TRUE	
						Do none meet the rule?				FALSE	FALSE	FALSE	

Accounts Receivable Department - Customer Credit Analysis

Best Practice

Matching Parentheses and Including Correct Commas

The final formula to determine the recommendations for credit evaluation is long and complex consisting of eleven parentheses pairs and seven commas.

```
=IF(NOT(OR(K3:M3)), "Reject",
    IF(OR(AND(K3,NOT(OR(L3:M3))),AND(OR(L3:M3),NOT(K3))),
        "Further Evaluate", "Accept"))
```

Needless to say, it is very easy to misplace, fail to include, or include extra commas and parentheses when entering this type of complex formula. Unfortunately, such errors can greatly affect the resulting value. In the best case scenario, Excel alerts you to an error and suggests a correction, such as a closing parenthesis. Sometimes an error message (#VALUE! or #NAME!) will result, giving the user a clue as to what type of problem has occurred. In the worst case scenario, Excel just evaluates what's written without the user being aware that the formula did not reach its intended results.

Once a formula such as this is entered, it is always a good idea for the user to go through and match the parenthesis pairs and be sure each argument is separated by a comma. Excel color coordinates the parenthesis pairs, making it easier to spot errors. A good idea is to manually follow the logic for several examples to see if the desired result is reached. In Chapter 10, a more formal methodology using the Formula Auditing tools is introduced.

Steps To Success: Level 3

TheZone is considering different bids for the supply of plastic resins used to manufacture skis and needs to determine which bidder should be awarded the contract (PO #611). TheZone's accounts payable group has asked you to make some determinations regarding whether specific bidders should be rejected based on their lack of financial stability. Part of the analysis has already been completed, as shown in Figure 4.47.

Figure 4.47: Bidder List Financial Evaluation worksheet

	A	B	C	D	E	F	G	H	I	J
1	PO 611 Bidder List Financial Evaluation									
2	Customer Name	Net Worth (Dollars)	D&B CCAR (1 Best)	D&B PAYDEX (100 Best)	D&B Stress Risk Class (1 Best)	Rule #1	Rule #2	Rule #3	Final Recommendation	
3	BFF Industries	$ 158,000	1	90	1	FALSE	TRUE	FALSE		
4	NE Plastic	64,830,000	2	85	1	TRUE	FALSE	FALSE		
5	Pergo Molding	780,000	2	98	1	TRUE	FALSE	TRUE		
6	Allma	17,043,000	3	55	2	TRUE	FALSE	FALSE		
7	JF & Sons	35,500,000	1	32	1	TRUE	TRUE	FALSE		
8	Argree Inc.	613,800,000	3	0	1	TRUE	FALSE	FALSE		
9	RGM Plastics	452,000	4	83	3	FALSE	FALSE	FALSE		
10	Soto Services	182,680,000	1	73	1	TRUE	TRUE	FALSE		
11	NRKK	239,227,000	2	79	2	TRUE	FALSE	FALSE		
12	SPDM	487,000	2	87	1	FALSE	FALSE	FALSE		
13										

This worksheet contains the names of the bidders, their D&B ratings, and the results of the following analysis:

- Column F contains the results of applying Rule #1: Allow to bid if the bidder's net worth is greater than $500,000.
- Column G contains the results of applying Rule #2: Allow to bid if the bidder has a CCAR of 1 and a stress risk class of 1.
- Column H contains the results of applying Rule #3: Allow to bid if the bidder's PAYDEX score is over 90.

Complete the following:

1. Open the workbook named **PO611.xlsx** in the Chapter 4 folder, and then save it as **PO611 Credit Analysis.xlsx**.

2. Write a formula in column I that can be copied down the column to make a final determination of "Allow to bid," "Do not include," or "Get more data" based on the following criteria:

   - Recommend to "Do not include" if none of the rules are TRUE.
   - Recommend to "Get more data" if only Rule #1 is TRUE or only Rule #2 is TRUE.
   - Recommend to "Allow to bid" if the bidder is recommended neither to "Do not include" nor to "Get more data."

TROUBLESHOOTING: To complete this exercise, be sure to use parentheses in pairs and commas to separate arguments. It is very easy to misplace, fail to include, or include extra parentheses and commas when entering this type of complex formula resulting in error messages or incorrect values. Excel color coordinates the pairs of parentheses pairs, making it easier to spot errors.

3. To make the worksheet easier to view, split the window to show the titles in rows 1 and 2 and the row heading in column A.

4. Save and close the PO611 Credit Analysis.xlsx workbook.

Chapter Summary

Level 1 of this chapter explored several tools that allow you to evaluate and compare both text and numeric data. These tools include relational operators (>, <, >=, <=, =, <>) and the Boolean logical functions AND, OR, and NOT. Both relational operators and Boolean functions return a Boolean logical value, TRUE or FALSE. Using these tools, you were able to determine if a specific data element or set of data elements met the required criteria. You also applied relational operators and Boolean logic using conditional formatting tools.

In Level 2, you gained additional flexibility by applying Boolean logic within an IF statement. The IF function allows you to not only determine if an expression is TRUE or FALSE, but to also return a value other than TRUE or FALSE, such as text or numeric values depending on the outcome of a logical test. Both additional IF statements and other Excel functions can be nested within an IF function to complete more complicated tasks.

In Level 3, you learned about more complex logical constructs, specifically the *none of* construct and the *only* construct. You also combined the concepts presented in Levels 1 and 2 to solve more complex logical tasks, nesting IF functions, relational operators, and Boolean functions within the same formula. Table 4.6 provides a summary of commonly used logical constructs.

Table 4.6: Common logical constructs

Logical Construct	Description
Assuming cells A1:A4 contain TRUE/FALSE values	*Use this logical construct:*
AND(A1:A4)	When all items must be TRUE to return a TRUE value
OR(A1:A4)	When only one item must be TRUE to return a TRUE value
NOT(A1)	To change a single TRUE to FALSE or a single FALSE to TRUE
NOT(OR(A1:A4))	To return a TRUE if none of the items are TRUE (equivalent to all of the items are FALSE)
AND(NOT(A1),NOT(A2),NOT(A3),NOT(A4))	To return a TRUE if all of the items are FALSE (equivalent to none of the items are TRUE)
NOT(AND(A1:A4))	To return a FALSE if all of the items are TRUE (equivalent to returning a TRUE if even one item is FALSE)
OR(NOT(A1),NOT(A2),NOT(A3),NOT(A4))	To return a TRUE if even one item is FALSE (equivalent to returning a FALSE if all items are TRUE)
AND(A1,NOT(OR(A1:A4)))	To return a TRUE if only A1 is TRUE and none of the other values are TRUE
AND(OR(A1,A2),NOT(OR(A3:A4)))	To return a TRUE if only A1 or A2 is TRUE and none of the other values are TRUE
IF(OR(A1:A4),"This is true","This is false") IF(A1,25,IF(A2,50,0))	To return any value, text or numeric, depending on if the logical test is evaluated as TRUE or FALSE; a logical test can be any expression that reduces to a TRUE or FALSE value; additional logical tests can be performed within the same expression by nesting IFs up to seven levels

Conceptual Review

1. Evaluate the following expressions:

   a. =AND(FALSE,TRUE,TRUE)

   b. =OR(3>5,TRUE)

   c. =NOT(OR(FALSE,FALSE,FALSE))

   d. =AND(A2>6,NOT(FALSE)) where A2 contains the value 25

2. Describe how you would format a cell so that if the value is greater than 50 it would be automatically bolded.

   Answer Questions 3–15 using the following worksheet shown. Assume that all of your answers will be placed in cells on the same worksheet.

	A	B	C	D	E	F
1		Sales Meeting in NY				
2	Item	Optional/ Required	Budget	Actual	Within Budget	
3	Food	R	$ 250	$ 185	TRUE	
4	Hotel	R	500	525	FALSE	
5	Transportation	R	100	40	TRUE	
6	Theater Tickets	O	100	125	FALSE	
7	Airfare	R	225	199	TRUE	
8	Tour Package	O	50	40	TRUE	
9	Total		$1,225	$1,114		
10						

3. What formula is used in cell E3, which can be copied down the column to determine (TRUE or FALSE) if this item is within budget?

4. Write a formula to determine if all of the items are within budget.

5. Write a formula to determine if at least one item is within budget.

6. Write a formula in cell F3 that can be copied down the column to determine if this food item is not within budget.

7. What formula would you use if you wanted to set a conditional format of cell A3 using the Formula Is method—such that the item name would be shaded in yellow if this item has an Actual cost of at least $400?

8. Write a formula to determine if none of the items are within budget.

9. Write a formula to determine if (TRUE or FALSE) only the required items (R) are within budget. Note that this formula does not have to work if the optional/required categories are later modified.

10. Are the following two Boolean expressions equivalent? Why or why not?
=NOT(OR(E3:E8))
=AND(NOT(E3),NOT(E4),NOT(E5),NOT(E6),NOT(E7),NOT(E8))

11. Is the following formula valid? Why or why not?
=NOT(E3:E8)

12. What value would the following formula return?
=IF(D4<=C4,"within budget","over budget")

13. What value would the following formula return?
=IF(SUM(D6,D8)<200,"go to both",IF(SUM(D6,D8)>450,"go to neither",
"choose one"))

14. Write a formula in cell G3 that can be copied down the column to return the following:

- If this item has an actual cost of less than $100, then return the text "Minor Component Cost".
- If this item has an actual cost of $100 or more, then return the text "Major Component Cost".

15. Write an Excel formula in cell H3 that can be copied down the column to calculate the cost of this component for a larger sales meeting based on the following:

- If this item is optional as indicated in column B, then the cost will be equal to the original budgeted amount.
- If this item is required as indicated in column B, then the cost will be three times the original budgeted amount.

Case Problems

Level 1 – Evaluating Job Applicants for Winston, Winston & Coombs

You work in the Human Resources Department for the accounting firm Winston, Winston & Coombs. The firm has recently increased its client base and decided to hire several university graduates for entry-level positions. The human resources manager has established a formal process for evaluating job applicants. This process takes into account not only the applicant's academic performance, but also his or her work experience and impression made during the personal interview. In addition, all applicants are given a separate skills-based exam to determine their proficiency in spreadsheet and database applications. Because some of the applicants are not business majors but might be otherwise qualified for a position, the exam also covers some basic business concepts in accounting, finance, and marketing. You have been asked to evaluate the information on the candidates being considered.

Human Resources

Each job application provides the following information:

- College GPA (valid scores range from 1.5 to 4.0)
- Standardized universal Major Code indicating the applicant's undergraduate major; for example, Engineering=1, Business=2, Economics=3, Physical Science=4, and so on (valid codes for majors are 1 through 200)
- The total number of references submitted by the applicant
- A personal interview rating
- If the applicant has previous work experience (TRUE or FALSE)
- The Employment Exam score (valid scores are between 200 and 800)
- The undergraduate school ranking (compared with all colleges across the country)

The human resources manager has established criteria to determine if an applicant will be automatically disqualified or automatically hired, or if no decision is made. The criteria, which are applied in order, are described in the following list.

An applicant is *automatically disqualified* if any of the following criteria are TRUE:

- The applicant has submitted an invalid GPA score, Employment Exam score, or Major Code.
- The applicant has a GPA less than 2.8.
- The applicant provided fewer than two references.
- The applicant has an Employment Exam score below 650.
- The applicant has a personal interview rating of less than 3.

An applicant is *automatically hired* if all of the following criteria are TRUE:

- The applicant has not been automatically disqualified.
- The applicant has a GPA score over 3.7.
- The applicant has a Major Code between 1 and 20 (inclusive).
- The applicant graduated from one of the top 20 schools (ranking of 20 or less).
- The applicant has an Employment Exam score above 700.
- The applicant has a personal interview rating of 4 or higher.
- The applicant has prior work experience.

If an applicant is neither automatically disqualified nor automatically hired, that applicant's status is *undecided*.

Complete the following:

1. Open the workbook named **Hiring.xlsx** located in the Chapter 4 folder, and then save it as **WWC Hiring Analysis.xlsx**.

2. Write a formula in cell I4 that can be copied down the column to determine if (TRUE or FALSE) *any* of the following scores/codes listed for this applicant are invalid: GPA, Major Code, Employment Exam. (*Hint*: Use the information provided in the problem description to determine the appropriate criteria.)

3. Write a formula in cell J4 that can be copied down the column to determine if (TRUE or FALSE) the applicant should be automatically disqualified based on the criteria given.

4. Write a formula in cell K4 that can be copied down the column to determine if this candidate is *not* automatically disqualified. (*Hint:* Use the results determined in Step 3.)

5. In cell L4, write a formula that can be copied down the column to determine if (TRUE or FALSE) the candidate should be automatically hired based on the criteria given. (*Hint:* For criteria between two values, test that the value is both >= the lower limit and <= the higher limit.)

6. Write a formula in cell M4 that can be copied down the column to determine if this candidate is *not* automatically hired. (*Hint:* Use the results determined in Step 5.)

7. Write a formula in cell N4 that can be copied down the column to determine if no decision is made on this applicant. Recall that no decision is made if the applicant is *both* not automatically disqualified (K) and not automatically hired (M).

8. Write a formula in cell I14 that can be copied across the row (through column N) to determine if all of the applicants have invalid scores.

9. Write a formula in cell I15 that can be copied across the row (through column N) to determine if any of the applicants have invalid scores.

10. To summarize the results, write a formula in cell I16 that displays the total number of applicants who have invalid scores. Copy this formula across the row (through column N). This formula should automatically update if any of the scores or criteria are later modified.

11. Apply conditional formatting to highlight the important points, as follows:

a. Highlight all of the TRUE values obtained for the Automatically Disqualified column (J4:J12) in a red, bold text format.

b. Use gradient fill blue data bars to highlight the Personal Interview Rating scores of the applicants.

c. Highlight the name of any applicant with an Employment Exam Score of more than 700 using a light green background.

12. Save and close the WWC Hiring Analysis.xlsx workbook.

Level 2 – Estimating Painting Job Costs for RJ Construction

Finance

For the past year, you have been working with a medium-sized painting contractor, RJ Construction, doing everything from running errands to cutting the weekly paychecks and filing the appropriate quarterly employment withholding forms with the IRS. Given your knowledge of spreadsheets, your boss has asked you to create an Excel worksheet for estimating painting jobs that are done by a subgroup of the construction firm, either as part of larger jobs or as stand-alone projects. Your boss wants the worksheet to contain some basic input information and automatically calculate an estimated price so that a customer can quickly know the cost of the work. The variables to be considered are as follows:

- The dimensions of each room—length, width, and height
- The condition of the wall surfaces, where 1 represents excellent, 2 represents reasonable but has some peeling and/or old paint, and 3 represents poor condition with major holes, peeling, and/or very old paint
- Whether or not the requested new color is lighter than the existing wall color (TRUE or FALSE)
- Grade of paint being requested—premium, superior, or economy

Complete the following:

1. Create a new workbook and save it as **Painting Estimator.xlsx** in the Chapter 4 folder. Create a worksheet with the columns and data shown in Table 4.7. Also include a meaningful title at the top of your worksheet. Ultimately, this worksheet will be used as a template and filled out on site by the painter.

Table 4.7: Worksheet data for painting estimator

Room	Length in Feet	Width in Feet	Height in Feet	Square Feet (sf) of Wall/Ceiling	Wall Condition	New Color Lighter	Paint Quality
Family Room	25	15	12		1	FALSE	Premium
Bedroom1	16	11	8		2	FALSE	Economy
Bedroom2	12	12	8		1	FALSE	Superior
Bath	8	6	8		3	TRUE	Superior

To complete Steps 2–10, you need to calculate the individual component costs by room, writing all formulas so that they can be copied down the column. List all other inputs that are needed for your calculations on a separate worksheet in the workbook—named appropriately. Assume all wall surfaces, including the ceiling area, are to be included when calculating repair and painting costs. Remember, your formulas will need to work when new quantities are substituted into the data-entry area.

2. In the column you've already listed, calculate the total square footage (sf) of walls and ceiling. If a room is 10' by 12' with an 8' ceiling height, it would have two walls that are 10' × 8' (total of 160 sf) and two walls that are 12' × 8' (total of 192 sf), and a ceiling of 10' × 12' (120 sf) for a total of 472 sf. Do not subtract any area for windows, doors, and so on.

3. To the right of the Paint Quality column, calculate the cost of wall repairs and primer. Only walls with a wall condition of poor (3) will require wall repair and primer. This cost is estimated as $0.75 per sf. If no primer is required, a value of 0 should be entered. Remember to list any additional inputs on a separate worksheet as described above.

4. In an adjacent column, calculate the cost of the first coat of paint. If the condition of the wall is 1, the cost of paint is $0.55 per sf; if the condition of the wall is 2, the cost of paint is $0.60 per sf; otherwise, the cost is $0.70 per sf.

5. In an adjacent column, calculate the cost of the second coat of paint based on the following criteria:

   • If the condition of the wall is 3, a second coat of paint will be required at $0.45 per sf.
   • If the condition of the walls is not poor (3), but new wall color is lighter than the existing color, a second coat of paint will be required at $0.40 per sf.
   • Otherwise, no second coat will be required, and a value of $0 should be entered.

6. In an adjacent column, calculate the cost adjustment for paint quality based on the following criteria:

- If premium paint is used, add $0.15 per sf.
- If economy paint is used, deduct $0.10 per sf.

7. In an adjacent column, calculate the total cost to paint this room (primer, first coat, second coat, and adjustments for paint quality).

8. In an adjacent column, determine if (TRUE or FALSE) this is a high-priced room. A high-priced room is one that is estimated to cost more than $450.

9. Create a row below the data that totals the costs of each item (primer, first coat, and so on) and then a grand total of all items for all rooms.

10. Because larger jobs have certain economies of scale in setup and cleanup, a discount is given based on these estimated values to jobs based on their total size. Just below the grand total, determine the total discounted price of the job based on the following:

   - If the total cost of the painting job is less than $800, then there is no discount.
   - If the total cost of the painting job is at least $800 but less than $2,000, then an 8% discount will be given (discount is calculated based on the grand total cost for all items and all rooms).
   - If the total cost of the painting job is at least $2,000 but less than $5,000, then a 12% discount will be given.
   - If the total cost of the painting job is $5,000 or more, then a 15% discount will be given.

11. Format your worksheets so that they are easy to read and information is clearly identifiable. Highlight the result of Step 10 in yellow.

12. Save and close the Painting Estimator.xlsx workbook.

Level 3 – Analyzing Dealership Promotions for CKG Auto

Marketing

CKG Auto runs several promotions each year to reward dealerships for their sales efforts, sometimes on specific car models and other times for overall sales. CKG Auto is running three different promotions for large dealerships, based on performance over this past calendar year. Small and medium-sized dealerships have similar promotions but based on different expected volumes and rebate percentages. The promotions are as follows:

- A rebate on shipping expenses based on exceeding expected quarterly volumes: These are savings CKG Auto realizes from its trucking carriers and has decided to pass along as a reward to dealerships that have exceeded expectations. Rebates for each quarter were set by management as follows: 1st quarter, $65 per car sold (actual volume); 2nd quarter, $80 per car sold; 3rd quarter, $65 per car sold; and 4th quarter, $122 per car sold. Dealerships are awarded the rebate on a quarter-by-quarter basis, only for quarters

4

where their actual sales exceeded expected volumes for that quarter. Expected sales volumes for large dealerships for each quarter are as follows:

- 1st Quarter: 325
- 2nd Quarter: 425
- 3rd Quarter: 440
- 4th Quarter: 350

- An overall sales volume bonus based on exceeding expected annual volumes: Dealerships that exceeded the expected annual sales volume by more than 7% are awarded a $10,000 bonus. Dealerships that exceeded the expected annual sales volume by 7% or less are awarded a $5,000 bonus. Otherwise, no bonus is awarded ($0).
- A "Best in Class" bonus of $6,000 awarded to the one dealership with the highest overall sales volume in its class

You have been asked to set up a worksheet to record the dealer information for the past year and apply the appropriate promotions to each dealership. The actual dealership quarterly sales volumes have already been entered in a worksheet. Now, you will finalize the analysis.

Complete the following:

1. Open the workbook named **CKGPromo.xlsx** located in the Chapter 4 folder, and then save it as **Promo Large Dealerships.xlsx**. This past year's quarterly sales volumes and expected sales volumes for large dealerships have already been entered into this workbook. Complete the analysis using any additional columns and/or rows as you deem necessary. All formulas should work when copied either across or down, as needed. Include titles in each column and/or row to identify the corresponding data. Add any appropriate formatting to make the worksheet easy to read.

2. Insert rows at the top of the worksheet to create an input area where you can list the inputs such as bonus amounts, shipping rebates, and so on. List the inputs explicitly and use only one worksheet for this task, so that any inputs can be easily displayed for management and then later copied and modified to calculate the promotions for both the medium and small dealership classes. Insert rows as needed, and be sure to clearly label each input so that the data can be interpreted and modified easily next year. Wrap text and format the data as needed.

3. In a column adjacent to the quarterly sales data, calculate the corresponding annual sales volume for each dealership.

4. Calculate the value of the shipping rebate for each dealer for each quarter (use four new columns). This should require only one formula that can be copied down the column and across the row. Be sure your inputs are set up so that this can be easily accomplished. Remember, dealers will only receive rebates in quarters where their actual quarterly sales volumes exceeded expected sales volumes. In an adjacent column, determine the total value of the shipping rebate for all four quarters by dealership.

5. Analyze the quality of these volume estimates by categorizing the quality of the annual volume estimate versus the actual annual volumes for each dealership into the following categories:

   - Display "Excellent" if the estimate is within 5% (higher or lower) of the actual sales volume. (*Hint:* For example, if you wanted to determine if the value 26 is within +/− 25% of 40, you would need to test this value to make sure that *both* 26>=40−.25*40 and 26<=40+.25*40.)
   - Display "Good" if the estimate is greater than 5% higher or lower, but within 10% higher or lower of the actual volume.
   - Display "Poor" if the estimate is greater than 10% higher or lower.

6. In an adjacent column or columns, calculate the value of the annual sales volume bonus for each dealership.

7. In an adjacent column, calculate the value of the "Best in Class" bonus for each dealership. (Only the dealership with the highest annual sales volume will receive this; all others will receive $0.)

8. In a row below the data, calculate the total values for all dealers for sales volume, shipping rebates, sales, and best in class bonuses.

9. In an adjacent column, determine if (TRUE or FALSE) this dealership received money during this year for both a shipping rebate and a sales volume bonus. Copy the formula down the column to obtain the corresponding value for each dealership.

10. Skipping one row below the totals, in the column just used in Step 9, determine (TRUE or FALSE) if none of the dealerships received both shipping rebates and a volume bonus. Label the row accordingly.

11. Just below the result of Step 10, determine if only dealerships with Excellent estimate qualities (determined in Step 5) received both shipping rebates and a sales volume bonus. This formula need not work if any of the input data or formulas are later updated. Label the row accordingly.

12. Again, skip a row below the data. Then, in the following rows, determine for each rebate/bonus the number of dealerships receiving this rebate/bonus and the average value of the bonus (include dealerships that did not earn a bonus in the average calculation).

13. Save and close the Promo Large Dealerships.xlsx workbook.

SAM: Skills Assessment Manager

For current SAM information, including versions and content details, visit SAM Central (http://samcentral.course.com). If you have a SAM user profile, you may have access to hands-on instruction, practice, and assessment of the skills covered in this chapter. Since various versions of SAM are supported throughout the life of this text, check with your instructor for the correct instructions and URL/Web site for accessing assignments.

4

Chapter Exercises

Retrieving Data for Computation, Analysis, and Reference
Sales: Creating Product Order Forms for Equipment Purchases

LEARNING OBJECTIVES

Level 1

Organize and evaluate data in vertical and horizontal lookup tables
Examine the VLOOKUP and HLOOKUP function rules
Retrieve data from a vertical lookup table
Retrieve data from a horizontal lookup table

Level 2

Analyze and retrieve data from multiple worksheets
Look up data in a one-row or one-column range
Use named range references in formulas
Retrieve data from multidimensional tables

Level 3

Prevent errors in data retrieval
Nest lookup and reference functions to perform more complex calculations
Choose a value or a range of values for analysis
Retrieve data by matching the relative position of an item in a list

FUNCTIONS COVERED IN THIS CHAPTER

CHOOSE
HLOOKUP
IFERROR
INDEX
ISBLANK
LOOKUP
MATCH
VLOOKUP

Chapter Introduction

In previous chapters, you learned how to create formulas with IF and nested IF functions to make decisions based on specified criteria. However, these formulas are not well suited in some circumstances, such as selecting a particular value from a long list of values. Instead of using nested IF statements, you can use a group of Excel functions known as the **Reference and Lookup functions**. These functions expand your ability to vary values based on criteria and find an input value that produces a specific result. In this chapter, you will use Reference and Lookup functions to retrieve data stored in the same or a different worksheet, and then use that data in formulas or reference it in another location.

Data is often stored in a list format on a worksheet. A data list that categorizes values you want to retrieve is called a **lookup table**. You can use the data in a lookup table to create worksheets that list items, such as products ordered and their corresponding prices, and then perform calculations. The Reference and Lookup functions enable you to retrieve the appropriate data from a lookup table for use in such calculations.

In this chapter, you will learn how to create an automated order form that uses the Reference and Lookup functions to provide prices, shipping, and other order information. Level 1 begins with VLOOKUP and HLOOKUP, the most common of these functions, which lookup data based on its location in a table, and then retrieve a corresponding value that matches specified criteria. In Level 2, the LOOKUP function is used to retrieve a value in a column or a row, and the INDEX function is used to look up a value in a two- dimensional range. Level 3 shows how to nest various Reference and Lookup functions, including CHOOSE and MATCH, to perform more complex calculations.

Case Scenario

Vijay Patel is a sales representative in TheZone's Equipment division, and calls on large and small sporting goods stores to promote TheZone's products and assist customers with their orders. Although he can provide the full line of TheZone's sporting goods to his customers, Vijay concentrates on racket sports and golf equipment. One important part of Vijay's job is maintaining up-to-date product specifications and pricing information that he can quickly retrieve to answer customer questions. Vijay and the other sales representatives can access information about their product line from anywhere as long as they have Web access. Unfortunately, Web access is not always reliable or fast, and in such cases, Vijay is unable to answer questions such as "What would a case of golf balls cost?" or "What volume discounts are available for tennis rackets?" The corporate database system also requires that Vijay enter an actual order to obtain this information, making it difficult to look at different what-if scenarios.

Marketing

To solve this problem, Vijay now wants to create an application that will work on a laptop computer using Excel, not necessarily connected to the Web. Vijay would like to simulate an order form that will look up item prices, customer discounts, and any other information required to complete an order. These forms will serve as templates that Vijay and the other sales representatives can use to more efficiently explore customer options. Once he has a working application, he can then ask the corporate technology group to create an interface to upload any real orders that may be generated.

LEVEL 1
Performing Basic Lookups to Calculate and Evaluate Data

Working with Lookup Tables

When working with customers, Vijay looks up item numbers, descriptions, discount amounts, and shipping amounts, and then calculates unit and total prices. Now he wants to automate this process by creating a form (template) in Excel. He begins by creating a workbook named Tennis Orders in which he wants to develop a Tennis Balls worksheet that contains a unit pricing lookup table. TheZone sells tennis balls in bulk, priced per canister, so Vijay uses a canister as the unit to calculate prices. Unit prices are based on the total quantity being ordered, as listed in Table 5.1.

Table 5.1: Unit prices for tennis balls

Quantity (in units)	$/each
Under 60	$2.45
60–119	$2.27
120–239	$2.12
240 or more	$2.00

Vijay also wants to add a shipping costs lookup table to the worksheet. When calculating order amounts, he has to account for shipping charges, which depend on the transportation method. Table 5.2 shows the shipping charges.

Table 5.2: Shipping charges for tennis balls

Shipping Method	Charge per Unit
Truck	$0.25
Rail	$0.20
Ship	$0.15
Customer arranges for shipping	$0.00

Vijay can then include an area of the worksheet for an order form that lists the order information and calculates the total price. Vijay creates the Tennis Balls worksheet, shown in

Figure 5.1, and begins to add data from recent orders. Vijay entered the order number, customer ID, shipping method, and quantity ordered. He wants to insert the unit price based on the values stored in the Unit Pricing table (cells A7:B10), and the unit shipping charge based on the values stored in the Shipping Costs table (cells D7:E10). Then he can calculate the totals for price and shipping, and sum those to calculate the grand total.

Figure 5.1: Tennis Balls worksheet

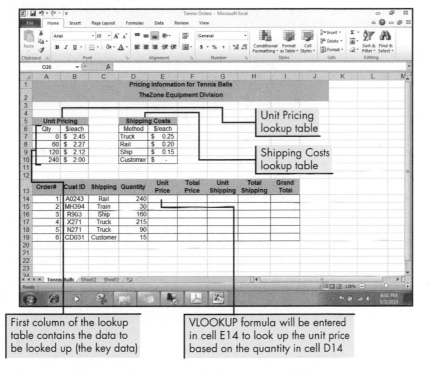

First column of the lookup table contains the data to be looked up (the key data)

VLOOKUP formula will be entered in cell E14 to look up the unit price based on the quantity in cell D14

Vijay briefly considers using an IF function to insert the unit prices and unit shipping charges. He could use nested IF logic that evaluates if the quantity ordered is less than 60, charge $2.45 per unit; if the quantity ordered is greater than or equal to 60 but less than 120, charge $2.27 per unit; if the quantity ordered is greater than or equal to 120 but less than 240, charge $2.12 per unit; and if the quantity ordered is greater than or equal to 240, charge $2.00 per unit. He could construct a similar nested IF formula to calculate the unit shipping charges. However, that would require two long nested IF formulas. Furthermore, Vijay thinks that the unit prices and shipping methods will be expanded to include more prices and methods, so using the IF function is not practical for this worksheet.

Instead, he can use the **VLOOKUP function** to look up a unit price based on quantity, and look up a shipping charge based on method.

Retrieving Data from a Vertical Lookup Table

When you organize data in a **vertical lookup table**, a lookup table in which the data to be searched is organized in columns, the most effective and flexible way to retrieve data is to use the VLOOKUP function. (The *V* in VLOOKUP stands for *vertical*.) This function searches a specified part of a worksheet for data. It starts by searching for data in the first column. When it finds the required data, it retrieves the value in a specified column that is in the same row as the data found by the lookup. You use VLOOKUP when the first column of the lookup table contains the data you are looking up, also called the **key data**, and the corresponding information you want to find is in one of the columns to the right of the key data column, as shown in Figure 5.1.

The VLOOKUP function is appropriate for finding the correct unit price in Vijay's Unit Pricing table and inserting it in cell E14, and for finding the correct unit shipping charge in the Shipping Costs table and inserting it in cell G14. As shown in Figure 5.1, the first column of the Unit Pricing table contains the quantities, which is what Vijay will look up. The information he wants to find—the unit price—is included in the column to the right of the Qty column. Similarly, the first column of the Shipping Costs table contains the shipping methods, which Vijay will look up, and the second column lists the corresponding unit charges, which is the information he wants to find.

When you write a VLOOKUP formula, you indicate the value you want to look up in a table. VLOOKUP searches for a matching value in the leftmost column of the table, and then retrieves the value in the same row but in another column that you specify. Vijay plans to enter a VLOOKUP formula in cell E14 to look up the unit price based on the quantity entered in cell D14.

The syntax of the VLOOKUP function is as follows and its arguments are described in Table 5.3:

VLOOKUP(lookup_value,table_array,col_index_num,range_lookup)

Table 5.3: VLOOKUP function arguments

Argument	Description
lookup_value	The data you want to look up. This value can be a number, text, a logical value, or a name or cell reference that refers to a value.
table_array	The range containing the data that you want to search to find the lookup value. This range must start in the column with the lookup values and extend at least as far as the column containing the data to be returned.
col_index_num	The number of the column containing the data you want to retrieve. The number 1 indicates the first column of the lookup table, 2 indicates the second column, and so on.
range_lookup	The type of lookup you want to perform—TRUE or FALSE. With a TRUE type (the default), the VLOOKUP function finds the greatest value that does not exceed the lookup_value. When the lookup type is TRUE, the values in the first column of the lookup table must be sorted in ascending sort order; otherwise, VLOOKUP might not retrieve the correct value. With a FALSE type, the VLOOKUP function looks only for an exact match of the lookup_value. If it does not find an exact match, the text #N/A is displayed in the cell.

How To

Write a VLOOKUP Formula

1. Type =VLOOKUP(to begin the formula.

2. Enter the value you want to match or look up, such as a cell reference, text, or a number.

3. Enter the range or table_array that contains the data you want to look up, where the first column of the range lists the matching values, or key data.

4. Enter the number of the column that contains the data you want to find, where 1 is the first column of the array.

5. Enter the type of lookup you want to perform: TRUE to search sorted data for the greatest value that does not exceed your criteria or FALSE to find an exact match.

6. Type a closing parenthesis mark) to complete the formula, and then press Enter.

5

Level 1

Looking Up Unit Prices Using a VLOOKUP

Vijay will need to look up the quantity ordered to find the unit price, so the lookup_value is cell D14. Cells A7:B10 contain the unit pricing data; these are the cells the function will search (table_array). In the Unit Pricing lookup table, column 2 lists the unit prices, so the col_index_num argument is 2. The range_lookup argument requires the TRUE type because the function must look for the greatest value in the first column of the Unit Pricing table that is not greater than 240, the value specified in cell D14. With a FALSE type, the function would look only for the exact value 240 in the first column of the Unit Pricing table. Because customers might order amounts of cans of tennis balls that do not match exactly the amounts in the Unit Pricing table, the TRUE type is needed in this case. To insert the correct unit price in cell E14, Vijay enters the following formula:

$$\texttt{=VLOOKUP(D14,A7:B10,2,TRUE)}$$

This formula considers the value in cell D14 (240), and tries to match it in the first column of the range A7:B10. When it finds 240 (cell A10), it looks in column 2 for the data to retrieve, which is $2.00, and places this result in cell E14.

Vijay's next step is to copy the VLOOKUP formula from cell E14 to cells E15:E19 to include the unit prices for the other orders in the order table. He considers each argument of the VLOOKUP function in cell E14. If he copies the formula from cell E14 to E15, should the lookup_value change from D14 to D15? Yes, the second order in row 15 should calculate unit price according to the quantity stored in D15. Therefore, the cell reference in the first argument should be relative. Should the table_array A7:B10 become A8:B11? No, the formula should reference the Unit Pricing table and, therefore, requires absolute row references. (The column references will stay the same when the formula is copied; only absolute row references are needed.) The col_index_num and range_lookup are constants and will remain the same. Therefore, Vijay changes the formula in cell E14 to use absolute row references in the second argument, as follows:

$$\texttt{=VLOOKUP(D14,A\$7:B\$10,2,TRUE)}$$

He copies the formula from cell E14 to E15:E19. Next, Vijay wants to calculate the total order value by multiplying quantity by price. In cell F14, he enters the formula =D14*E14, and then he copies this formula to cells F15:F19, as shown in Figure 5.2.

Figure 5.2: Calculating the unit price and total price

	A	B	C	D	E	F	G	H	I	J
1				Pricing Information for Tennis Balls						
2				TheZone Equipment Division						
3										
4										
5	Unit Pricing			Shipping Costs						
6	Qty	$/each		Method	$/each					
7	0	$ 2.45		Truck	$ 0.25					
8	60	$ 2.27		Rail	$ 0.20					
9	120	$ 2.12		Ship	$ 0.15					
10	240	$ 2.00		Customer	$ -		=VLOOKUP(D14,A$7:B$10,2,TRUE)			
11							formula copied to cells E15:E19			
12										
13	Order#	Cust ID	Shipping	Quantity	Unit Price	Total Price	Unit Shipping	Total Shipping	Grand Total	
14	1	A0243	Rail	240	$ 2.00	$480.00				
15	2	MH394	Train	30	$ 2.45	$ 73.50				
16	3	R903	Ship	160	$ 2.12	$339.20				
17	4	X271	Truck	215	$ 2.12	$455.80				
18	5	N271	Truck	90	$ 2.27	$204.30				
19	6	CD031	Customer	15	$ 2.45	$ 36.75				
20										
21										

VLOOKUP formula searches this column for a value that matches the one in cell D14

Formula for calculating total price: =D14*E14

Examining the VLOOKUP Rules

It is easy to imagine the steps Excel might perform to match the specified value of 240 in the Unit Pricing lookup table as the lookup value is explicitly listed in leftmost column of the lookup table. Order #2, however, has a quantity of 30, which is not a listed key value in the Unit Pricing table. In cell E15, shown in Figure 5.2, Excel retrieves a value of $2.45 from the Unit Pricing lookup table. How does Excel match the lookup_value of 30 to the quantities listed in cells A7:A10 to return the correct price?

To best answer this question, you would need to trace each step of the VLOOKUP algorithm. Unfortunately, Excel does not include an explanation of the algorithmic steps used by VLOOKUP, but it does provide the function syntax and a set of rules. When these rules are followed, the function is guaranteed to return the correct matching value: for a type TRUE, the greatest value that does not exceed the lookup value; and for a type FALSE, an exact match. These rules are defined in Excel Help. The most important stipulations are as follows:

- If a lookup_value is smaller than the smallest value in the first column of table_array, VLOOKUP returns the #N/A error value.
- If a type TRUE is specified, an exact or approximate match is returned. If an exact match is not found, the next largest value that is less than lookup_value is returned. When creating a range for use with a type TRUE VLOOKUP table, make sure to sort the values in the first column of table_array in ascending order; otherwise, VLOOKUP might not return the correct value.
- If a type FALSE is specified, VLOOKUP returns only an exact match if one is found. In this case, the values in the first column of table_array do not need to be sorted. If there are two or more values in the first column of table_array that match the lookup_value, the first value found (not necessarily the first value listed) is used. If an exact match is not found, the error value #N/A is returned.

To see an example of how results can differ, consider the three worksheets shown in Figure 5.3. In each worksheet, a lookup table has been placed in cells A2:B5. Worksheet (A) follows the rule requiring that the first column of the lookup table for a type TRUE lookup be sorted in ascending order (0, 60, 120, 240). Worksheet (B) and Worksheet (C) contain alternate configurations of the lookup table that do not follow this required rule. In each worksheet, cells B7:B9 contain formulas that look up the corresponding cost for quantities of 30, 160, and 215, respectively. These formulas are as follows:

```
Cell B7:  =VLOOKUP(30,A2:B5,2,TRUE)
Cell B8:  =VLOOKUP(160,A2:B5,2,TRUE)
Cell B9:  =VLOOKUP(215,A2:B5,2,TRUE)
```

Figure 5.3: Results of VLOOKUP function based on different lookup tables

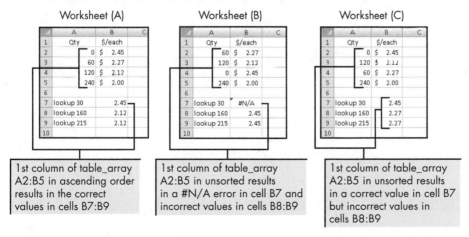

Worksheet (A) correctly returns the greatest value that does not exceed the lookup value for all three examples. A quantity of 30 is less than 60 and, thus, should correspond to a unit cost of $2.45 associated with the minimum quantity of 0. The quantities 160 and 215

are both more than 120 but less than 240, and correspond to the pricing for the minimum volume of 120, which is $2.12.

In Worksheet (B), where the first column of the lookup table is not sorted in ascending order, the VLOOKUP formula returns an error message #N/A for the quantity 30, indicating that no match was found. This is consistent with the rule requiring that the lookup value for a type TRUE lookup be greater than or equal to the first value in the leftmost column of the lookup table. The lookup values returned for the quantities 160 and 215 are also incorrect.

Worksheet (C)'s lookup value table is also not sorted in ascending order; the values are in a random order: 0, 120, 60, 240. Notice that the value returned for a quantity of 30 is correct ($2.45), but that the values returned for the lookups of the 160 and 215 quantities are incorrect.

Because there are so many variables involved when using a VLOOKUP function, and it's not always obvious when a returned value is incorrect, it's important to closely follow the specified rules; otherwise, the possibility exists that the value returned will be incorrect.

Best Practice

Unexpected VLOOKUP Results

It's not uncommon to find that your VLOOKUP formula results in an error message or even a value from the list that was not your intended result. These errors can occur for the following reasons:

- If the col_index_num argument is less than 1, VLOOKUP returns the #VALUE! error value. If the col_index_num argument is greater than the number of columns in the table_array, VLOOKUP returns the #REF! error.
- If using a type TRUE lookup and the first column of the table_array is not sorted in ascending order, a #N/A error may occur or an incorrect value may be returned. This error will also occur if the lookup_value is smaller than the first value in the first column of the table_array.
- If using a type FALSE lookup and the lookup value does not appear in the first column of the lookup_range, a #N/A error will be returned. When dealing with text, this can occur because either the lookup_value or the table_array text may contain leading spaces, trailing spaces, inconsistent use of straight (' or ") and curly (' or ") quotation marks, or nonprinting characters.

Retrieving an Exact Match

Vijay also wants to use a VLOOKUP formula to retrieve the appropriate unit shipping charges from the Shipping Costs table. At first, Vijay decides to use the same type of formula to calculate the unit shipping value in cell G14. He uses the formula =VLOOKUP(C14,D$7:E$10,2,TRUE) to calculate the unit shipping charges, and then copies the formula to cells G15:G19. However, the results as shown in Figure 5.4 are correct only for orders 1 and 3. Vijay checks the cell references and the syntax of the formula, and realizes he should use FALSE instead of TRUE as the lookup type.

Figure 5.4: Incorrect shipping values obtained using a type TRUE VLOOKUP

	A	B	C	D	E	F	G	H	I	J
1				Pricing Information for Tennis Balls						
2				TheZone Equipment Division						
3										
4										
5	Unit Pricing			Shipping Costs						
6	Qty	$/each		Method	$/each					
7	0	$ 2.45		Truck	$ 0.25		Except for Order# 1 and Order# 3, incorrect			
8	60	$ 2.27		Rail	$ 0.20		shipping values are obtained using the			
9	120	$ 2.12		Ship	$ 0.15		formula: =VLOOKUP(C14,D$7:E$10,2,TRUE)			
10	240	$ 2.00		Customer	$ -					
11										
12										
13	Order#	Cust ID	Shipping	Quantity	Unit Price	Total Price	Unit Shipping	Total Shipping	Grand Total	
14	1	A0243	Rail	240	$ 2.00	$480.00	$ 0.20			
15	2	MH394	Train	30	$ 2.45	$ 73.50	$ -			
16	3	R903	Ship	160	$ 2.12	$339.20	$ 0.15			
17	4	X271	Truck	215	$ 2.12	$455.80	$ -			
18	5	N271	Truck	90	$ 2.27	$204.30	$ -			
19	6	CD031	Customer	15	$ 2.45	$ 36.75	#N/A			
20										
21										

When you use a lookup type of FALSE, the VLOOKUP function looks only for an exact match of the lookup value. In this case, the values in the lookup table do not need to be sorted in ascending order, as they do with the TRUE type. As you have learned, if the function does not find an exact match, it displays *#N/A* in the cell, so you don't have to arrange the values in a way to return correct approximate matches.

When Vijay uses a lookup type of TRUE to calculate unit shipping charges, it causes a number of problems. First, the table is not sorted in ascending order. More important, he wants an exact match—for example, he wants to find *Rail* and not the closest value. The lookup type for this formula should, therefore, be FALSE. Vijay changes the formula in cell G14 so that it uses a lookup type of FALSE, as follows:

=VLOOKUP(C14,D$7:E$10,2,FALSE)

To solve this formula, the function considers the value in cell C14 (Rail). Because the lookup type is FALSE, the function looks only for an exact match to *Rail* in the first column of the D7:E10 range, which is the Shipping Costs table. When it finds an exact match, it retrieves the corresponding value—$0.20—from the second column in the specified range.

Vijay copies the formula from cell G14 to cells G15:G19. Figure 5.5 shows the resulting worksheet.

Figure 5.5: VLOOKUP function with a FALSE lookup type

	A	B	C	D	E	F	G	H	I	J
1				Pricing Information for Tennis Balls						
2				TheZone Equipment Division						
3										
4										
5	Unit Pricing			Shipping Costs						
6	Qty	$/each		Method	$/each					
7	0	$ 2.45		Truck	$ 0.25					
8	60	$ 2.27		Rail	$ 0.20					
9	120	$ 2.12		Ship	$ 0.15					
10	240	$ 2.00		Customer	$ -					
11										
12										
13	Order#	Cust ID	Shipping	Quantity	Unit Price	Total Price	Unit Shipping	Total Shipping	Grand Total	
14	1	A0243	Rail	240	$ 2.00	$480.00	$ 0.20			
15	2	MH394	Train	30	$ 2.45	$ 73.50	#N/A			
16	3	R903	Ship	160	$ 2.12	$339.20	$ 0.15			
17	4	X271	Truck	215	$ 2.12	$455.80	$ 0.25			
18	5	N271	Truck	90	$ 2.27	$204.30	$ 0.25			
19	6	CD031	Customer	15	$ 2.45	$ 36.75	$ -			
20										
21										

=VLOOKUP(C14,D$7:E$10,2,FALSE)
formula with the FALSE lookup type retrieves the correct values for the Unit Shipping cells except for Order# 2

With the FALSE lookup type, the VLOOKUP function retrieves the correct values for all of the Unit Shipping cells except cell G15. It retrieves the correct values for cell G14 and cells G16:G19 because it looks for an exact match of the lookup value, which is the Shipping value in cells C14:C19. The function retrieves the values even though the list is unsorted. The text #N/A is displayed in cell G15 because the function cannot find an exact match to the value in cell C15, which is *Train*. This is a data entry error that Vijay can correct by changing *Train* in cell C15 to *Rail*, as shown in Figure 5.6.

Figure 5.6: Completing the unit shipping information

	Order#	Cust ID	Shipping	Quantity	Unit Price	Total Price	Unit Shipping	Total Shipping	Grand Total
13									
14	1	A0243	Rail	240	$ 2.00	$480.00	$ 0.20		
15	2	MH394	Rail	30	$ 2.45	$ 73.50	$ 0.20		
16	3	R903	Ship	160	$ 2.12	$339.20	$ 0.15		
17	4	X271	Truck	215	$ 2.12	$455.80	$ 0.25		
18	5	N271	Truck	90	$ 2.27	$204.30	$ 0.25		
19	6	CD031	Customer	15	$ 2.45	$ 36.75	$ -		
20									
21									

When Train is changed to Rail in cell C15, the function retrieves the correct shipping cost and displays it in cell G15

Now that Vijay has set up the VLOOKUP formulas in cells E14:E19 and G14:G19, he calculates the total shipping cost by multiplying the unit shipping charge by the quantity ordered, as shown in Figure 5.7.

Figure 5.7: Calculating the total shipping charge

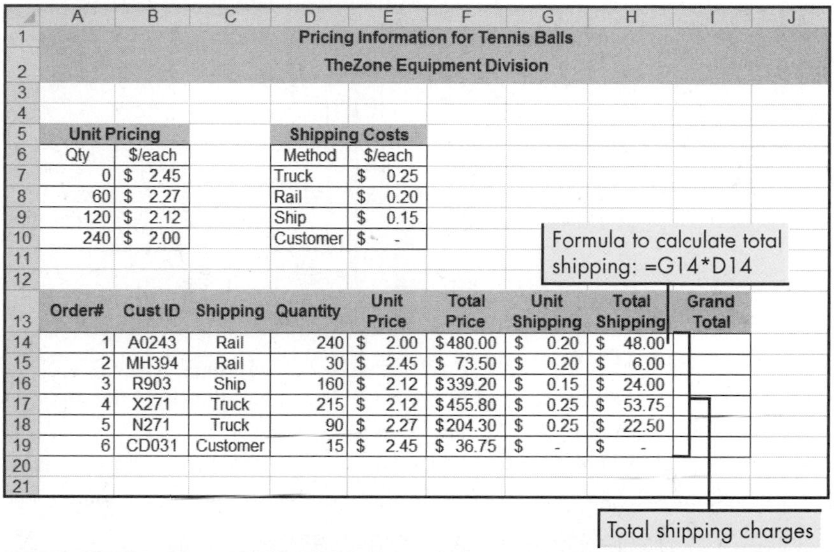

Formula to calculate total shipping: =G14*D14

Total shipping charges

Best Practice

Creating an Effective Vertical Lookup Table

To find and retrieve data from a vertical lookup table in the most efficient way, create a simple worksheet that contains related data, and organize this data in columns to form the vertical lookup table. Include a heading at the top of each column to easily identify the information, though these titles should not be included as part of the lookup_range in the VLOOKUP formula. List the key values in the first column. If a type TRUE lookup is needed, sort the key column data in ascending order. Key values are those pieces of data that you know, such as customer names, quantities, or product descriptions. The remaining columns should contain values that you want to look up, such as customer numbers or product codes or pricing. You can use Excel lookup functions to find data when it's organized in a different way, but vertical lookup tables reflect the way you find information manually—by scanning the left column until you find the value for which you need information, and then looking to the right for the column containing the detail you need.

A lookup table can have only one key value in each cell of its first column. For example, you can list 0, 60, 120, and 240 in the first column, but not 0–59, 60–119, and 120–239, as seen in Worksheet (A) in Figure 5.8. When creating a vertical lookup table with the TRUE type, be certain to start with the lowest possible value, such as 0, so that the table covers all the possible data. For example, you might be tempted to start the Unit Pricing table with 60, as shown in Worksheet (B) of Figure 5.8, because it's the first quantity associated with a unit price. However, if you need to look up a quantity such as 30, the function will display the text #N/A because 30 is less than the first key value in the lookup table—instead of correctly displaying the unit price of $2.45.

Figure 5.8: Incorrect VLOOKUP table configurations

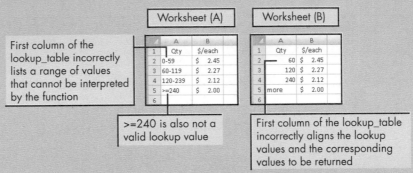

If you have a valid range that is not in ascending order, you can sort it using the Sort commands in the Editing group on the Home tab on the Ribbon or in the Sort & Filter group on the Data tab on the Ribbon. Select the range you plan to use as the lookup table and then click the Sort A to Z button to sort the selection in ascending order, in alphabetical order from A to Z, or from lowest to highest (1, 2, 3...) if the selection contains numbers. Click the Sort Z to A button to sort the selection in descending order.

Retrieving Data from a Horizontal Lookup Table

TheZone is considering offering customers a discount on shipping, depending on the total price of the customer's tennis ball order. Table 5.4 shows the two possible shipping discounts under consideration.

Table 5.4: Shipping discounts

Shipping Discount			
Total Price:	$0	$300	$1,000
Shipping Discount 1	0%	15%	25%
Shipping Discount 2	0%	10%	15%

For example, with Shipping Discount 1, a customer with an order totaling $350 would receive a 15% discount on the shipping costs. With Shipping Discount 2, this same order would receive a 10% discount.

Vijay now needs to evaluate the effect of this potential shipping discount on the overall total order. He begins by inserting the Shipping Discount lookup table as well as a new column labeled Shipping Discount in the Tennis Balls worksheet, as shown in Figure 5.9.

Figure 5.9: Worksheet with shipping discount data entered

Shipping Discount lookup table with values displayed in rows

	A	B	C	D	E	F	G	H	I	J	K	L
1					Pricing Information for Tennis Balls							
2					TheZone Equipment Division							
3												
4												
5	Unit Pricing			Shipping Costs					Shipping Discount			
6	Qty	$/each		Method	$/each							
7	0	$ 2.45		Truck	$ 0.25		Total Price:		$ 0	$ 300	$ 1,000	
8	60	$ 2.27		Rail	$ 0.20		Shipping Discount 1		0%	15%	25%	
9	120	$ 2.12		Ship	$ 0.15		Shipping Discount 2		0%	10%	15%	
10	240	$ 2.00		Customer	$ -							
11												
12												
13	Order#	Cust ID	Shipping	Quantity	Unit Price	Total Price	Unit Shipping	Total Shipping	Shipping Discount	Grand Total		
14	1	A0243	Rail	240	$ 2.00	$480.00	$ 0.20	$ 48.00				
15	2	MH394	Rail	30	$ 2.45	$ 73.50	$ 0.20	$ 6.00				
16	3	R903	Ship	160	$ 2.12	$339.20	$ 0.15	$ 24.00				
17	4	X271	Truck	215	$ 2.12	$455.80	$ 0.25	$ 53.75				
18	5	N271	Truck	90	$ 2.27	$204.30	$ 0.25	$ 22.50				
19	6	CD031	Customer	15	$ 2.45	$ 36.75	$ -	$ -				
20												
21												

Shipping Discount column inserted to be included in the grand total calculation

Notice that the shipping discounts are presented in a horizontal format, so Vijay cannot use the VLOOKUP function to retrieve the correct discount amount and display it in the Shipping Discount column. Instead, he can use a similar function, called HLOOKUP. (The *H* in HLOOKUP stands for *horizontal*.) When solving an **HLOOKUP formula**, Excel looks up a value by testing for a criterion across a row, instead of down a column. The syntax of the HLOOKUP function is as follows:

```
HLOOKUP(lookup_value,table_array,row_index_num,range_lookup)
```

The HLOOKUP function is similar to the VLOOKUP function except that it searches a **horizontal lookup table**, in which data is stored in rows instead of in columns. When you use the HLOOKUP function, you specify the row_index_num instead of col_index_num. Excel then searches for the *lookup_value* in the first row of the *table_array*, or lookup table, and returns the value in the specified row. The *row_index_num* is counted from the first row in the lookup table, not the worksheet, so the first row in the lookup table is row 1 and the second is row 2, even if the lookup table occupies other rows in the worksheet. Table 5.5 describes the four arguments in the HLOOKUP function.

Table 5.5: HLOOKUP function arguments

Argument	Description
lookup_value	The data you want to look up. This value can be a number, text, a logical value, or a name or cell reference that refers to a value.
table_array	The range containing the data that you want to search to find the lookup value. This range must start in the row with the lookup values and extend at least as far as the row containing the data to be returned.

Table 5.5: HLOOKUP function arguments (cont.)

Argument	Description
row_index_num	The number of the row containing the data you want to retrieve. The number 1 indicates the first row of the lookup table, 2 indicates the second row, and so on.
range_lookup	The type of lookup you want to perform—TRUE or FALSE. With a TRUE type (the default), the HLOOKUP function finds the greatest value that does not exceed the lookup_value. When the lookup type is TRUE, the values in the first row of the lookup table must be sorted in ascending sort order; otherwise, HLOOKUP might not retrieve the correct value. With a FALSE type, the HLOOKUP function looks only for an exact match of the lookup_value. If it does not find an exact match, the text #N/A is displayed in the cell.

How To

Write an HLOOKUP Formula
1. Type =HLOOKUP(to begin the formula.
2. Enter the value you want to match, such as a cell reference, number, or text.
3. Enter the range that contains the data you want to look up, where the first row includes the matching values, or key data.
4. Enter the number of the row that contains the data you want to find.
5. Enter the type of lookup you want to perform: TRUE to search sorted data for the greatest value that does not exceed your criteria or FALSE to find an exact match.
6. Type a closing parenthesis mark) and then press the Enter key.

Vijay believes the company is more likely to choose Shipping Discount 2, which offers smaller discounts, so he decides to examine this discount first. The formula he needs to enter in cell I14 must look up the total price given in cell F14 and find the corresponding discount. The lookup range (table_array argument) is the Shipping Discount lookup table in cells I7:K9. This range must start in the row with the lookup values and extend at least as far down as the row containing the data to be returned. Because Vijay wants to evaluate Shipping Discount 2, the function must retrieve data from row 3 of the lookup table (row_index_num argument). Finally, the function must use the TRUE type so that it will look for the greatest value in the first row of the lookup table that is not greater than the value in cell F14 ($480). The FALSE type, which would look for an exact match only, is not appropriate in this case.

Note that the rules for an HLOOKUP function with a TRUE lookup type work in the same way as for a VLOOKUP function, except that values are tested *across the first row* instead of *down the first column*. Therefore, the first row (key values) of the lookup table must be sorted in ascending order to use an HLOOKUP function with a TRUE lookup type.

Vijay is now ready to use the HLOOKUP function to calculate the shipping discount value. The discount will be the shipping discount percentage multiplied by the shipping costs. He enters the following formula in cell I14:

```
=-HLOOKUP(F14,I$7:K$9,3,TRUE)*H14
```

The formula is preceded by a negative sign so that the resulting value will be negative, because the discount reduces the order cost. Also note that the table_array argument must contain absolute row references so that the row values will not change when the formula is copied down the column.

Vijay's final calculation is to determine the grand total (column J). To do so, he sums the following: total price (column F) plus total shipping (column H) plus shipping discount (column I). Because the shipping discount values are negative, the formula he enters will actually subtract this discount amount from the total. Vijay enters the formula =F14+H14+I14 in cell J14. The final Tennis Balls worksheet is shown in Figure 5.10.

Figure 5.10: Calculating the shipping discount and grand total

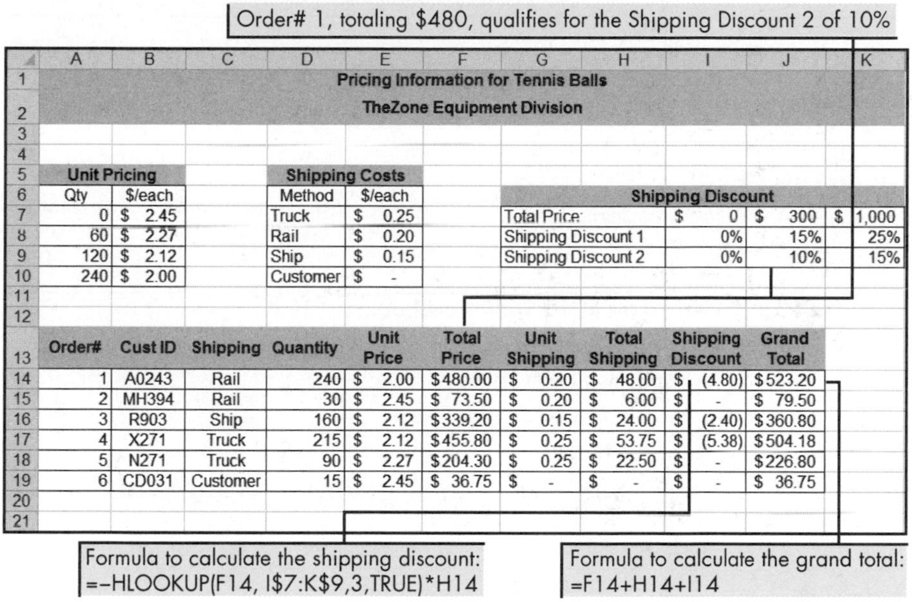

Order# 1, totaling $480, qualifies for the Shipping Discount 2 of 10%

	A	B	C	D	E	F	G	H	I	J	K
1					Pricing Information for Tennis Balls						
2					TheZone Equipment Division						
3											
4											
5	Unit Pricing			Shipping Costs							
6	Qty	$/each		Method	$/each				Shipping Discount		
7	0	$ 2.45		Truck	$ 0.25		Total Price:		$ 0	$ 300	$ 1,000
8	60	$ 2.27		Rail	$ 0.20		Shipping Discount 1		0%	15%	25%
9	120	$ 2.12		Ship	$ 0.15		Shipping Discount 2		0%	10%	15%
10	240	$ 2.00		Customer	$ -						
11											
12											
13	Order#	Cust ID	Shipping	Quantity	Unit Price	Total Price	Unit Shipping	Total Shipping	Shipping Discount	Grand Total	
14	1	A0243	Rail	240	$ 2.00	$480.00	$ 0.20	$ 48.00	$ (4.80)	$523.20	
15	2	MH394	Rail	30	$ 2.45	$ 73.50	$ 0.20	$ 6.00	$ -	$ 79.50	
16	3	R903	Ship	160	$ 2.12	$339.20	$ 0.15	$ 24.00	$ (2.40)	$360.80	
17	4	X271	Truck	215	$ 2.12	$455.80	$ 0.25	$ 53.75	$ (5.38)	$504.18	
18	5	N271	Truck	90	$ 2.27	$204.30	$ 0.25	$ 22.50	$ -	$226.80	
19	6	CD031	Customer	15	$ 2.45	$ 36.75	$ -	$ -	$ -	$ 36.75	
20											
21											

Formula to calculate the shipping discount:
=-HLOOKUP(F14, I$7:K$9,3,TRUE)*H14

Formula to calculate the grand total:
=F14+H14+I14

Consider Order #1, which totals $480. The HLOOKUP function searched the Shipping Discount 2 row in the lookup table and retrieved the corresponding discount of 10%. This discount was then multiplied by the total shipping charge (cell H14) to produce the correct shipping discount of $4.80 (cell I14).

Now that Vijay has completed the pricing calculations for tennis balls, he can create the order form for all tennis products, which he will do in the next section.

Steps To Success: Level 1

In addition to creating an order form for tennis balls, Vijay also needs to create an order form for golf balls. TheZone sells golf balls in various packages, such as a box of a dozen balls, but prices them per unit. The shipping charges for golf balls are slightly different from those for tennis balls. Table 5.6 shows the unit prices and shipping charges for golf balls.

Table 5.6: Unit prices and shipping charges for golf balls

Quantity (in units)	$/each	Shipping Method	$/each
Under 36	$2.85	Rail	$0.19
36–95	2.63	Truck	0.22
96–179	2.27	Ship	0.14
180 or more	2.00	Customer arranges shipping	0.00

Vijay has already created a Golf workbook containing lookup tables and an order form in a worksheet named Golf Balls. See Figure 5.11.

In these steps, you need to complete this worksheet using the appropriate lookup functions to calculate the total prices, total shipping charges, and grand totals. Complete the following:

Figure 5.11: Golf Balls worksheet in the Golf workbook

1. Open the workbook named **Golf.xlsx** located in the Chapter 5 folder, and then save it as **Golf Orders1.xlsx**.

2. In the Golf Balls worksheet, complete the Unit Pricing lookup table to include the units and corresponding prices that TheZone charges for golf balls.

3. Complete the Shipping Costs table to list the appropriate unit shipping charges.

4. In cell E14, use the appropriate lookup function to calculate the unit price for this order based on the quantity ordered. Write the formula so that it can be copied down the column, and then copy the formula into cells E15:E19.

5. In cell F14, calculate the total price of this order (excluding shipping). Write the formula so that it can be copied down the column, and then copy the formula into cells F15:F19.

6. In cell G14, calculate the unit shipping charge based on the shipping method. Write the formula so that it can be copied down the column, and then copy the formula into cells G15:G19. Correct data entry errors, as necessary.

7. In cell H14, calculate the total shipping cost. Write the formula so that it can be copied down the column, and then copy the formula into cells H15:H19. Ignore any inconsistent formula errors.

8. In cell I14, calculate the shipping discount, using Shipping Discount 2, based on the total price (column F). The discounted value will be the corresponding percentage times the total shipping cost previously calculated. Write the formula so that it can be copied down the column, and then copy the formula into cells I15:I19.

9. In cell J14, calculate the grand total for this item. Write the formula so that it can be copied down the column, and then copy the formula into cells J15:J19.

10. Save and close the Golf Orders1.xlsx workbook.

LEVEL 2

Performing More Complex Lookups Involving Multiple Worksheets and Multidimensional Tables

Retrieving Data from Multiple Worksheets

As you learned in Level 1, you can use a VLOOKUP formula and an HLOOKUP formula to retrieve data stored in lookup tables on the same worksheet. You can also use VLOOKUP and HLOOKUP to retrieve data stored in lookup tables on other worksheets. This is especially useful when lookup tables are long, such as those that contain products and prices, or when you need to retrieve data from more than one lookup table.

Now that Vijay has completed the Tennis Balls worksheet and order form, which calculates the cost of an item based on the quantity ordered, he is ready to develop a worksheet for other types of tennis equipment, such as rackets and bags, which are based on a fixed price per unit. This worksheet must accommodate orders for products that have fixed prices per unit, and include many products in a single order. Vijay decides to develop this worksheet for now without including bulk tennis balls, which are priced based on quantity ordered. Later, he will explore creating an order form that can handle both fixed and variable prices per unit.

Vijay begins by adding a worksheet named Costs to the Tennis Orders workbook. This worksheet is a partial list of the tennis equipment TheZone sells for a fixed price. The list includes a product description and its associated unit cost.

Vijay also adds a worksheet named Orders to the Tennis Orders workbook, which will serve as an order form, or template. This worksheet will include the data for a single customer's order, which can contain one or more items. Vijay's idea is that salespeople will enter an item number and quantity, and formulas will retrieve or calculate the item description and item total price. Formulas will also calculate the subtotal of all items, discounts, shipping charges, and a grand total. Figure 5.12 shows how the Costs and Orders worksheets will be used together to achieve the desired results.

The first product ordered is item# 12 (Touring Bag - One Size) and has a quantity of 10. To create the formula that multiplies the quantity ordered by the product's unit price, Vijay considers writing the following formula in cell D3 of the Orders worksheet:

```
=Costs!C13*B3
```

This formula multiplies the value in cell C13 of the Costs worksheet by the value in cell B3 of the current worksheet. (Cell Costs!C13 contains the unit price of item# 12.) This formula would calculate the correct result, $599.90, for the first item.

However, Vijay cannot copy this formula to cells D4:D7 to calculate the total price for other items. For example, if the formula =Costs!C13*B3 is copied to cell D4, it becomes =Costs!C14*B4. The reference to cell B4 is correct because that cell will contain the quantity ordered for the second item. The reference to cell C14 in the Costs worksheet, however, might or might not contain the correct unit price—it depends on the item ordered. An absolute cell reference, as in =Costs!C$13*B4, does not solve the problem either—that only references the touring bag, not any of the other 14 products. You can usually solve this type of problem by using a lookup function. Because the data is organized on the Costs sheet in a vertical format, the VLOOKUP function will work in this case.

Figure 5.12: Orders worksheet with calculations to be based on the Costs worksheet

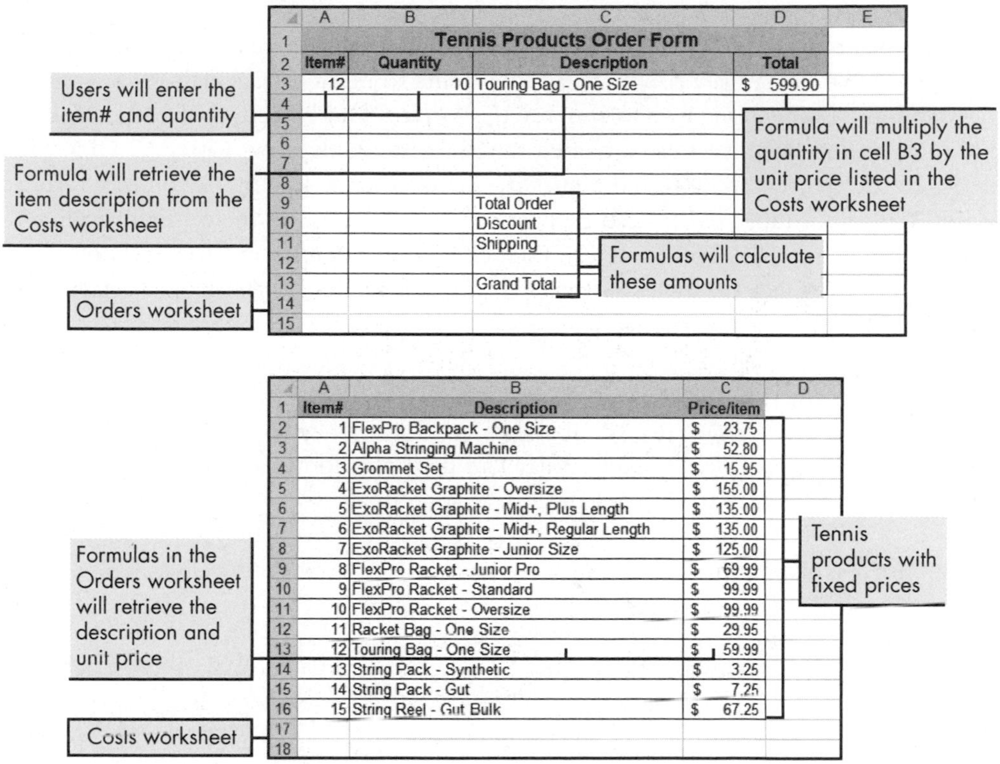

	A	B	C	D	E
1	Tennis Products Order Form				
2	Item#	Quantity	Description	Total	
3	12	10	Touring Bag - One Size	$ 599.90	
4					
5					
6					
7					
8					
9			Total Order		
10			Discount		
11			Shipping		
12					
13			Grand Total		
14					
15					

	A	B	C	D
1	Item#	Description	Price/item	
2	1	FlexPro Backpack - One Size	$ 23.75	
3	2	Alpha Stringing Machine	$ 52.80	
4	3	Grommet Set	$ 15.95	
5	4	ExoRacket Graphite - Oversize	$ 155.00	
6	5	ExoRacket Graphite - Mid+, Plus Length	$ 135.00	
7	6	ExoRacket Graphite - Mid+, Regular Length	$ 135.00	
8	7	ExoRacket Graphite - Junior Size	$ 125.00	
9	8	FlexPro Racket - Junior Pro	$ 69.99	
10	9	FlexPro Racket - Standard	$ 99.99	
11	10	FlexPro Racket - Oversize	$ 99.99	
12	11	Racket Bag - One Size	$ 29.95	
13	12	Touring Bag - One Size	$ 59.99	
14	13	String Pack - Synthetic	$ 3.25	
15	14	String Pack - Gut	$ 7.25	
16	15	String Reel - Gut Bulk	$ 67.25	
17				
18				

Using VLOOKUP with Multiple Worksheets

Vijay will use the VLOOKUP function in cell D3 to retrieve the unit price that corresponds to the item number in cell A3, as in the following formula:

```
=VLOOKUP(A3,Costs!A2:C16,3,FALSE)*B3
```

To solve this formula, the function looks for the item number value in cell A3 (12, in this case) in the first column of the range A2:C16 in the Costs worksheet. When it finds an exact match to that value, it retrieves the data in column 3 of the lookup table, which lists the unit prices. Note that the formula uses a lookup type of FALSE because Vijay wants to find an exact match to the data entered in cell A3. What will happen when he copies this formula to the other cells in the column? Although cells A3 and B3 will vary relatively, the lookup range (A2:C16) needs to be absolute because it will not vary when the formula is copied. Therefore, Vijay modifies the formula as follows:

```
=VLOOKUP(A3,Costs!A$2:C$16,3,FALSE)*B3
```

Vijay plans to provide the Tennis Orders workbook to other sales representatives so they can adapt it for their primary products, and he wants to make his calculations as easy to understand as possible. One way to simplify the formula and be certain that the lookup range remains the same is to use a named range for the table_array Costs!A2:C16. He switches to the Costs worksheet and names the A2:C16 range Pricing. If you recall from Chapter 2, a cell or range of cells can be given a name by selecting the cells and typing a name into the Name Box. This name can then be used in formulas and copies absolutely. Then he changes the VLOOKUP formula in cell D3 of the Orders worksheet to the following:

```
=VLOOKUP(A3,Pricing,3,FALSE)*B3
```

Because range names copy absolutely, Vijay can copy this formula to cells D4:D7 and change only the references to cells A3 and B3, as appropriate.

Vijay can use a similar formula to insert the correct item description in cells C3:C7 of the Orders worksheet:

```
=VLOOKUP(A3,Pricing,2,FALSE)
```

To solve this formula, the function looks for the item number value in cell A3 (12, in this case) in the first column of the Pricing range in the Costs worksheet. When it finds an exact match to that value, it retrieves the data in column 2 of the table, which lists the item descriptions. Vijay enters the item number (12) and quantity (10) for the first product ordered in the Orders worksheet. He also enters both VLOOKUP formulas in the appropriate cells, as shown in Figure 5.13.

Vijay enters additional items for this order by entering item numbers in cells A4:A7 and the quantities ordered in cells B4:B7. These are as follows: item# 4 – 50, item# 8 – 25, item# 10 – 25, item# 13 – 100. Then he copies the VLOOKUP formula in cell C3 to cells C4:C7 to insert the appropriate item descriptions. He also copies the VLOOKUP formula in cell D3 to cells D4:D7 to calculate the correct order totals. He calculates the total order amount by summing the prices in cells D3:D7. (Note a blank row was included in the SUM to facilitate easy insertion of additional rows.) Figure 5.14 shows the Orders worksheet with both values and formulas displayed.

Figure 5.13: VLOOKUP formulas in the Orders worksheet

VLOOKUP formula calculates the total cost of item# 12 from the Costs worksheet

	A	B	C	D	E
1			**Tennis Products Order Form**		
2	**Item#**	**Quantity**	**Description**	**Total**	
3	12	10	Touring Bag - One Size	$ 599.90	
4					
5					
6					
7					
8					
9			Total Order		
10			Discount		
11			Shipping		
12					
13			Grand Total		
14					
15					

VLOOKUP formula retrieves the description for item# 12 from the Costs worksheet

Figure 5.14: Complete Orders worksheet values and formulas

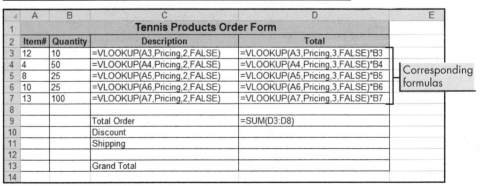

	A	B	C	D	E
1			**Tennis Products Order Form**		
2	**Item#**	**Quantity**	**Description**	**Total**	
3	12	10	Touring Bag - One Size	$ 599.90	
4	4	50	ExoRacket Graphite - Oversize	$ 7,750.00	
5	8	25	FlexPro Racket - Junior Pro	$ 1,749.75	
6	10	25	FlexPro Racket - Oversize	$ 2,499.75	
7	13	100	String Pack - Synthetic	$ 325.00	
8					
9			Total Order	$ 12,924.40	
10			Discount		
11			Shipping		
12					
13			Grand Total		
14					

Values resulting from calculations

	A	B	C	D	E
1			**Tennis Products Order Form**		
2	**Item#**	**Quantity**	**Description**	**Total**	
3	12	10	=VLOOKUP(A3,Pricing,2,FALSE)	=VLOOKUP(A3,Pricing,3,FALSE)*B3	
4	4	50	=VLOOKUP(A4,Pricing,2,FALSE)	=VLOOKUP(A4,Pricing,3,FALSE)*B4	
5	8	25	=VLOOKUP(A5,Pricing,2,FALSE)	=VLOOKUP(A5,Pricing,3,FALSE)*B5	
6	10	25	=VLOOKUP(A6,Pricing,2,FALSE)	=VLOOKUP(A6,Pricing,3,FALSE)*B6	
7	13	100	=VLOOKUP(A7,Pricing,2,FALSE)	=VLOOKUP(A7,Pricing,3,FALSE)*B7	
8					
9			Total Order	=SUM(D3:D8)	
10			Discount		
11			Shipping		
12					
13			Grand Total		
14					

Corresponding formulas

Looking Up Data in a One-Row or One-Column Range

Vijay's next task is to calculate the value of the discount being offered to large-volume customers. TheZone offers a $150 discount on all tennis equipment orders of $5,000 or more, a $400 discount on orders of $10,000 or more, and a $1,000 discount on orders of $25,000 or more. Vijay's sales manager has already created a workbook containing this discount information on a worksheet named Discount. Vijay copies this worksheet into his Tennis Orders workbook, as shown in Figure 5.15.

Figure 5.15: Discount worksheet

	A	B	C	D
1	Discount	Total Order Value	Description	
2	$ 0	$ 0	Less than $5000, no discount	
3	$ 150	$ 5,000	At least $5000 but less than $10,000, $150 discount	
4	$ 400	$ 10,000	At least $10,000 but less than $25,000, $400 discount	
5	$ 1,000	$ 25,000	$25,000 or more, $1000 discount	
6				

The total order values in this worksheet are based on the order subtotal before shipping. Vijay examines the Discount worksheet to see if he can use a VLOOKUP function to retrieve the appropriate discounts. The values he wants to look up are in column B and the values to retrieve are in column A, which means he cannot use the VLOOKUP function. One possible solution is to reconfigure the table. However, the Discount worksheet will be updated periodically by Vijay's sales manager. This means Vijay would have to reconfigure the worksheet every time he receives an updated one. Another possibility is to use the LOOKUP function. Unlike VLOOKUP, the LOOKUP function looks up the greatest value that does not exceed a specified value *anywhere* in a table or range. It can retrieve data from a lookup table with a vertical or horizontal orientation. LOOKUP also uses only a TRUE lookup type, so the column or row containing the lookup values must be in ascending order. The syntax of the LOOKUP function is as follows:

LOOKUP(lookup_value,lookup_vector,result_vector)

Table 5.7 describes the three arguments of the LOOKUP function.

Table 5.7: LOOKUP function arguments

Argument	Description
lookup_value	The data you want to look up. This value can be a number, text, a logical value, or a cell reference or a name that refers to a value.
lookup_vector	The location of the data you want to look up. This location is a range of only one row or column that contains the value you want to look up.
result_vector	The location of the data you want to retrieve. This location is a range of only one row or column that contains the data you want to retrieve. This range must be the same size as the lookup_vector; for example, if there are 10 values in the lookup_vector, there must be 10 corresponding values in the result_vector.

How To

Write a LOOKUP Formula

1. Type =LOOKUP(to begin the formula.

2. Enter the value you want to look up, such as a cell reference, text, or a number.

3. Enter the range that contains the data you want to look up.

4. Enter the range that contains the data you want to retrieve.

5. Type a closing parenthesis mark) and then the press Enter key.

You can often use a LOOKUP function instead of a VLOOKUP or an HLOOKUP function with a TRUE lookup type. You can only use a LOOKUP function when you want to retrieve a value that is stored to the left of a key data column in a vertical lookup table or above a key data row in a horizontal lookup table. Figure 5.16 illustrates this fact using data for some of TheZone's customers.

Figure 5.16: Vertical and horizontal lookup tables that work only with LOOKUP

Customer names are stored to the left of the customer numbers

	A	B	C	D	E	F	G
1	**Customer Name**	**Number**	**Street**	**City**	**State**	**Zip**	
2	A-line Athletic Goods	100-2	1366 W. Treeline Rd.	Denver	CO	80202	
3	AllBest Sporting Goods	100-3	72 S. Boyd St.	Denver	CO	80214	
4	BBK Athletics	100-4	8232 W. Rockies	Aurora	CO	80013	
5	CC Sports Supply	100-5	5378 Airport Blvd.	Denver	CO	80224	
6	First Western Sports	100-6	55 N. Cougar Way	Boulder	CO	80306	
7	Full Spectrum Sporting Goods	100-7	11285 National Rd.	Boulder	CO	80329	
8	Milton Athletic Supply	100-8	313 N. Dowler St.	Aurora	CO	80013	
9	Northern Sporting Goods	100-9	2574 Churchill Rd.	Denver	CO	80221	
10	Stedco Athletic Gear	100-10	2215 W. Jefferson	Fort Collins	CO	80525	
11							
12							

This is a vertical lookup table, but if you want to look up a customer number to find the correct name, you can't use VLOOKUP—you must use LOOKUP

Customer names are stored in the row above the customer numbers

	A	B	C	D	E
1	**Customer name**	A-line Athletic Goods	AllBest Sporting Goods	BBK Athletics	
2	**Number**	100-2	100-3	100-4	
3	**Zip**	80202	80214	80013	
4					
5					

This is a horizontal lookup table, but if you want to look up a customer number to find the correct name, you can't use HLOOKUP—you must use LOOKUP

Note that when you use the LOOKUP function, the data in the lookup table must be sorted in ascending order. As with the VLOOKUP and HLOOKUP functions with the TRUE lookup type, the LOOKUP function looks for a value that matches the criterion by comparing values based on their position in the lookup table. It can only make these comparisons correctly if the values are sorted in ascending order. Also, if the lookup_value is less than the smallest value in the lookup_vector, LOOKUP displays the text #N/A, just as VLOOKUP and HLOOKUP do. The horizontal lookup table in Figure 5.16 could cause problems when you are looking for an exact match. For example, if you are looking up customer number 100-3, but it does not appear in the list, LOOKUP would return the value for customer number 100-2. Because LOOKUP does not have a FALSE lookup type, it might not be the best choice in such a situation.

In this case, because Vijay wants to look up the total order amount to insert the discount amount in the Orders worksheet, he must use a lookup_value of D9, which is the cell in the Orders worksheet that stores the total order amount. In the Discount worksheet (Figure 5.15), cells B2:B5 contain the total order value amounts, so this cell range will constitute the lookup_vector. Also in the Discount worksheet, cells A2:A5 contain the discount amounts, so this cell range will constitute the result_vector.

To simplify the LOOKUP formula, Vijay names the range B2:B5 in the Discount worksheet Totals. Then he can use Totals as the second argument, the lookup_vector, in the LOOKUP formula. He also names the range A2:A5 in the Discount worksheet Discounts so he can use Discounts as the third argument, the result_vector. In the Orders worksheet, Vijay enters the following formula in cell D10:

$$=-\texttt{LOOKUP(D9,Totals,Discounts)}$$

Figure 5.17: Using a LOOKUP function to calculate the discount

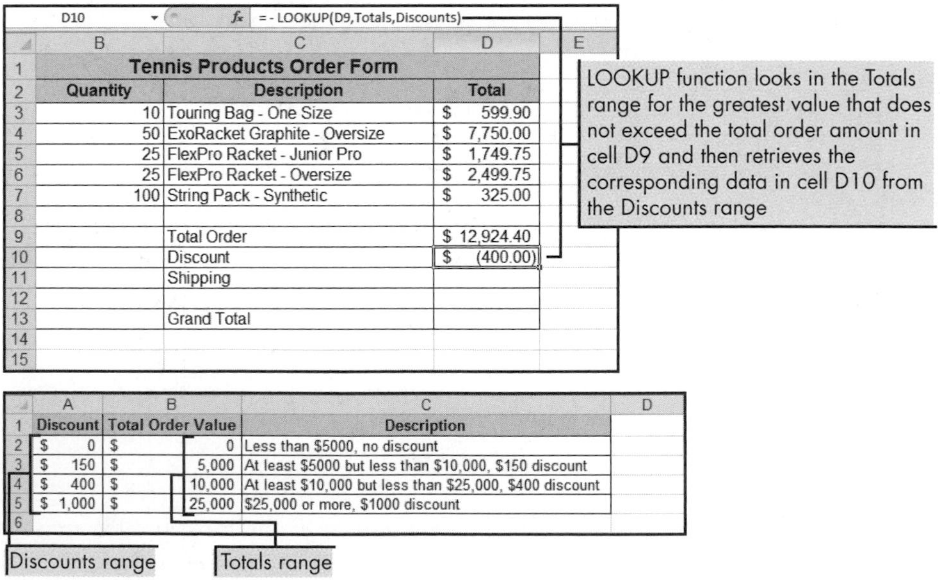

The negative sign at the beginning of the formula indicates that Excel should display the results as a negative value, as the discount will be deducted from the total. To solve the rest of the formula, Excel looks for the total order amount in cell D9 ($12,924.40) in the range named Totals (cells B2:B5 in the Discount worksheet). When it finds the greatest value that does not exceed $12,924.40, it retrieves the corresponding data from the range named Discounts (cells A2:A5 in the Discount worksheet), as shown in Figure 5.17.

Vijay learns that TheZone's shipping procedures are changing. Before he can complete the Orders worksheet, he needs to determine the appropriate shipping charges, based on the new information.

Retrieving Data from Multidimensional Tables

TheZone has contracted with an outside company to handle all of its shipping. This means Vijay must change his method of calculating shipping charges. Instead of basing the charge only on the shipping method or order value, he must now determine the charge according to the weight of the order in pounds. The price per pound is based on two variables: the shipping method and the shipping destination. The shipping company has segmented the United States into five shipping regions: 1 (Northeast), 2 (Southeast), 3 (Midwest), 4 (Southwest), and 5 (West). Shipments outside the United States must be priced separately. The shipping company also prices according to four shipping methods: 1 (Truck), 2 (Rail), 3 (Air), and 4 (Boat). The actual shipments originate from TheZone's warehouse located in the Northeast.

So far, Vijay has used different lookup functions to find only one value, such as quantity, to determine a result, such as price. Vijay now needs to vary both the shipping region and the shipment method to calculate the shipping price in dollars per pound. To make this calculation, Vijay can use the INDEX function, which allows you to retrieve data from multidimensional tables.

Vijay adds a new worksheet named Shipping, which lists prices per pound, to the Tennis Orders workbook. Figure 5.18 shows this worksheet. If a shipping method is not available to a specific region, the worksheet displays the value *NA*. Prices for Air (3) and Boat (4) include local hauling to and from the freight terminal.

Figure 5.18: Shipping worksheet

	A	B	C	D	E	F
1		Shipping Method - Standard				
2	Region	1	2	3	4	
3	1	$ 0.10	$ 0.11	$ 1.50	NA	
4	2	$ 0.18	$ 0.12	$ 2.00	NA	
5	3	$ 0.24	$ 0.14	$ 2.10	$ 0.20	
6	4	$ 0.28	$ 0.16	$ 2.25	$ 0.20	
7	5	$ 0.45	$ 0.40	$ 3.50	$ 0.35	
8						

Price per pound depends on two variables—region and shipping method

This lookup table is a **two-dimensional table**. In a one-dimensional table, Excel can search a row or column to find key data, and then use that data to locate the correct value. To find a value in a two-dimensional table, Excel searches one dimension, such as the rows, and then searches another dimension, such as the columns, to find the value at the inter-section of a single row and column.

The order in the Orders worksheet has a total shipping weight of 100 pounds, and it is being shipped to Region 3 via truck (Shipping Method 1). Vijay modifies the Orders worksheet to include this shipping information at the top, as shown in Figure 5.19. Because this order form will be used as a template, these data inputs must be included so that they can be changed, as needed, based on the specific order.

Figure 5.19: Modified Orders worksheet

Shipping information added to the Orders worksheet

	A	B	C	D	E
1			Tennis Products Order Form		
2		Shipping weight	100		
3		Region number	3		
4		Shipping method	1		
5					
6	Item#	Quantity	Description	Total	
7	12	10	Touring Bag - One Size	$ 599.90	
8	4	50	ExoRacket Graphite - Oversize	$ 7,750.00	
9	8	25	FlexPro Racket - Junior Pro	$ 1,749.75	
10	10	25	FlexPro Racket - Oversize	$ 2,499.75	
11	13	100	String Pack - Synthetic	$ 325.00	
12					
13			Total Order	$ 12,924.40	
14			Discount	$ (400.00)	
15			Shipping		
16					
17			Grand Total		
18					

So, what is the total shipping charge for this order? To determine this, Vijay needs to find the correct price per pound for the associated region and shipping method. He could do this manually by searching column A in the Shipping worksheet to find Region 3, which is stored in cell A5. Then he could search row 5 for Shipping Method 1, which appears in column B. He finds that the price per pound to ship to Region 3 via Shipping Method 1 is $0.24 per pound, shown in cell B5. The total cost of shipping the 100-pound shipment is 100*$0.24, or $24. However, Vijay wants to automate this process using the **INDEX function**.

Using the INDEX Function with a Two-Dimensional Table

To calculate the shipping charge in cell D15 of the Orders worksheet, Vijay must now account for three variables: shipping weight, region number, and shipping method. He wants to look up the region number and shipping method in the two-dimensional table stored in the Shipping worksheet (Figure 5.18). He cannot use the VLOOKUP, HLOOKUP, or LOOKUP functions with a two-dimensional table. Instead, he must use the INDEX function, which returns the value in a table based on the row and column numbers that you specify. Excel provides several forms of the INDEX function. The one that Vijay will use has the following syntax and is described in Table 5.8:

`INDEX(reference,row_num,column_num,area_num)`

Table 5.8: INDEX function arguments

Argument	Description
reference	The range containing the data you want to find. The range can be a contiguous range or a set of nonadjacent ranges.
row_num	The number of the row in the range referenced in the first argument. You number the rows within the range, not the worksheet, so the first row of the range is row 1, even if it is stored in a different row in the worksheet.
column_num	The number of the column in the range referenced in the first argument. You number the columns within the range, not the worksheet, so the first column of the range is column 1, even if it is stored in a different column in the worksheet.
area_num	The part of a nonadjacent range referenced in the first argument. You use this argument only if you specified a nonadjacent range in the first argument. Use an area_num of 1 to indicate the first part of a nonadjacent range, 2 to indicate the second part, and so on.

How To

Write an INDEX Formula

1. Type =INDEX(to begin the formula.
2. Enter the range containing the data you want to retrieve.
3. Enter the number of the row in which the data is stored.
4. Enter the number of the column in which the data is stored.
5. If the cells containing the data include nonadjacent ranges, enter the number of the area in which the data is stored.
6. Type a closing parenthesis mark) and then press Enter.

To facilitate creating the necessary formula, Vijay first names the cell range B3:E7 in the Shipping worksheet Shipping1.

Vijay wants to find values stored in the Shipping1 range, which contains the per pound charges for shipments according to region number and shipping method. The Shipping1 range will be the reference argument in the formula. In the Shipping1 range, rows 1 through 5 contain the region numbers. The region number for the order is stored in cell C3 of the Orders worksheet, so Vijay can use C3 as the second argument (row_num) when he creates the INDEX formula. In the Shipping1 range, columns 1 through 4 contain the Shipping Methods. The shipping method for the order is stored in cell C4 of the Orders worksheet, so Vijay can use C4 as the third argument (column_num) in the INDEX formula. Finally, because Shipping1 is a contiguous range, Vijay does not need to specify the area_num argument.

Vijay wants to insert the INDEX function in cell D15 of the Orders worksheet to calculate the shipping charge according to TheZone's new policy. He enters the following formula in cell D15:

```
=INDEX(Shipping1,C3,C4)
```

To solve this formula, the function refers to the data stored in the Shipping1 range. It retrieves the value at the intersection of the row specified in cell C3 (row 3) and the column specified in cell C4 (column 1).

The formula only returns the shipping charge per pound. Vijay also must multiply the results of the INDEX formula by the shipping weight, which is stored in cell C2. He modifies the formula as follows:

```
=INDEX(Shipping1,C3,C4)*C2
```

Figure 5.20 shows the resulting worksheet.

Figure 5.20: Using an INDEX function to calculate the shipping charge

	A	B	C	D	E
1			Tennis Products Order Form		
2		Shipping weight		100	
3		Region number		3	
4		Shipping method		1	
5					
6	Item#	Quantity	Description	Total	
7	12	10	Touring Bag - One Size	$ 599.90	
8	4	50	ExoRacket Graphite - Oversize	$ 7,750.00	
9	8	25	FlexPro Racket - Junior Pro	$ 1,749.75	
10	10	25	FlexPro Racket - Oversize	$ 2,499.75	
11	13	100	String Pack - Synthetic	$ 325.00	
12					
13			Total Order	$ 12,924.40	
14			Discount	$ (400.00)	
15			Shipping	$ 24.00	
16					
17			Grand Total		
18					

=INDEX(Shipping1,C3,C4)*C2 finds the value in the Shipping1 range corresponding to the row specified in cell C3 (3) and the column specified in cell C4 (1) and then multiplies that value by the weight in cell C2 (100)

	A	B	C	D	E	F
1			Shipping Method - Standard			
2	Region	1	2	3	4	
3	1	$ 0.10	$ 0.11	$ 1.50	NA	
4	2	$ 0.18	$ 0.12	$ 2.00	NA	
5	3	$ 0.24	$ 0.14	$ 2.10	$ 0.20	
6	4	$ 0.28	$ 0.16	$ 2.25	$ 0.20	
7	5	$ 0.45	$ 0.40	$ 3.50	$ 0.35	
8						

Shipping1 range

Value at the intersection of row 3, column 1 in the Shipping1 range is $0.24

Best Practice

Nesting Functions to Set a Minimum or Maximum Value

The formula =INDEX(Shipping1,C3,C4)*C2 results in a value of $24 for the order shown in Figure 5.20. What if there were a minimum charge for shipping and handling set at $25 per order? How could this minimum charge be incorporated into the calculation?

To set a minimum price, you need the formula to take the higher of two prices—in this case, $25 or the result of the formula =INDEX(Shipping1,C3,C4)*C2. One simple way to do this is to nest the INDEX function inside a MAX function, as follows:

```
=MAX(25,INDEX(Shipping1,C3,C4)*C2)
```

If this formula were substituted in cell D15, the resulting value would be $25 instead of $24.

Using a similar technique, a maximum value for the cost of shipping could be set at $1,000. The formula =MIN(1000,INDEX(Shipping1,C3,C4)*C2) would return the smaller of the two values. In this case, the value $24 would be returned because 24 (which results from the nested INDEX function) is less than $1,000.

Consider using such nested functions when you want to both retrieve data and compare it to a minimum or maximum value to determine the appropriate value to use in a calculation.

Using the INDEX Function with a Three-Dimensional Table

Vijay learns from his sales manager that because TheZone does substantial business with certain customers on some shipping routes, the company has negotiated more favorable freight rates with its new shipping company. TheZone wants to pass along these preferential shipping rates to its large customers. So TheZone will now calculate shipping charges for three types of customers: standard, preferred, and most preferred. Vijay modifies the Shipping worksheet to reflect this additional information, as shown in Figure 5.21.

To retrieve the shipping charges in dollars per pound for an order, Vijay must now work with three different variables: shipping region, shipping method, and customer type (as given by the three different shipping schedules). The INDEX function allows you to specify a list of nonadjacent ranges as the reference argument, and then specify which of these ranges to use in the area_num argument. This means the INDEX function can solve for two or more variables. Vijay can use the INDEX function to find the shipping charge per pound, but must now include the ranges for the three schedules in the first argument. The following statement shows the logic Vijay can use in the INDEX formula:

Figure 5.21: Modified Shipping worksheet

	A	B	C	D	E	F
1		Shipping Method - Standard				
2	Region	1	2	3	4	
3	1	$ 0.10	$ 0.11	$ 1.50	NA	
4	2	$ 0.18	$ 0.12	$ 2.00	NA	
5	3	$ 0.24	$ 0.14	$ 2.10	$ 0.20	
6	4	$ 0.28	$ 0.16	$ 2.25	$ 0.20	
7	5	$ 0.45	$ 0.40	$ 3.50	$ 0.35	
8						
9		Shipping Method - Preferred				
10	Region	1	2	3	4	
11	1	$ 0.09	$ 0.10	$ 1.35	NA	
12	2	$ 0.16	$ 0.11	$ 1.80	NA	
13	3	$ 0.22	$ 0.13	$ 1.89	$ 0.18	
14	4	$ 0.25	$ 0.14	$ 2.03	$ 0.18	
15	5	$ 0.41	$ 0.36	$ 3.15	$ 0.32	
16						
17		Shipping Method - Most Preferred				
18	Region	1	2	3	4	
19	1	$ 0.08	$ 0.09	$ 1.22	NA	
20	2	$ 0.15	$ 0.10	$ 1.62	NA	
21	3	$ 0.19	$ 0.11	$ 1.70	$ 0.16	
22	4	$ 0.23	$ 0.13	$ 1.82	$ 0.16	
23	5	$ 0.36	$ 0.32	$ 2.84	$ 0.28	
24						

Shipping costs for "standard" customer type (1)

Shipping costs for "preferred" customer type (2)

Shipping costs for "most preferred" customer type (3)

```
INDEX((range for standard customers, range for preferred
customers, range for most preferred customers), row number of
the shipping region, column number of the shipping method,
area number of the selected customer type)
```

Before entering the formula, Vijay names each range in the Shipping worksheet, using the names Shipping1 (previously set up), Shipping2 (Shipping!B11:E15), and Shipping3 (Shipping!B19:E23). He also adds a new item to the Orders worksheet for entering the appropriate shipping schedule according to customer type, as shown in Figure 5.22.

Figure 5.22: Customer type data added to the Orders worksheet

Order form now includes the customer type to determine from which shipping range on the Shipping worksheet to retrieve the shipping cost

	A	B	C	D
1		Tennis Products Order Form		
2		Shipping weight	100	
3		Region number	3	
4		Shipping method	1	
5		Customer type	2	
6	Item#	Quantity	Description	Total
7	12	10	Touring Bag - One Size	$ 599.90
8	4	50	ExoRacket Graphite - Oversize	$ 7,750.00
9	8	25	FlexPro Racket - Junior Pro	$ 1,749.75
10	10	25	FlexPro Racket - Oversize	$ 2,499.75

In the Orders worksheet, Vijay enters the following formula in cell D15 to calculate the shipping charge:

=INDEX((Shipping1,Shipping2,Shipping3),C3,C4,C5)*C2

To solve this formula, the function refers to three named ranges: Shipping1, which contains the shipping charges for standard customers; Shipping2, which contains the shipping charges for preferred customers; and Shipping3, which contains the shipping charges for most preferred customers. The function retrieves the value at the intersection of the row specified in cell C3 (row 3 in a shipping range) and the column number specified in cell C4 (column 1 in a shipping range) in the area specified in cell C5 (2 for range Shipping2). Then it multiplies the result by the weight (lbs) in cell C2 (100). Figure 5.23 shows the resulting worksheet.

Figure 5.23: Calculating the shipping charge by shipping region, shipping method, and customer type

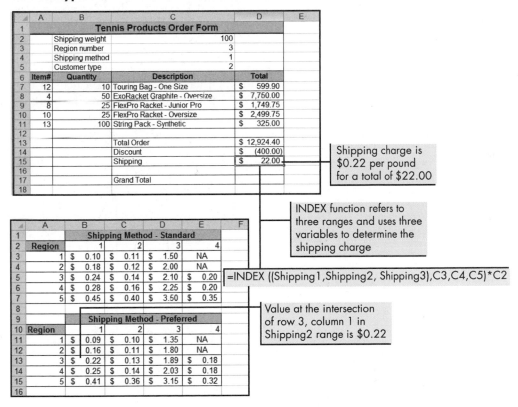

When you use the INDEX function, keep in mind the following guidelines:

- If you are using a noncontiguous range, you must enclose the entire reference in parentheses, as in (A1:B3,A7:B9,A15:B17). In this range reference, A1:B3 is area 1, A7:B9 is area 2, and A15:B17 is area 3.
- If you specify only one contiguous range, you can omit the area_num argument.
- You can use the INDEX function to look up data stored in a single row, such as B3:E3, or a single column, such as B3:B7. In this case, you enter the range as the first argument, and then enter only the row_num or the column_num, as appropriate.
- If you enter a row_num, column_num, or area_num outside of the range you referenced in the first argument, Excel displays the #REF! error.
- You can use a row_num of 0 to retrieve all the values in a specified column. Similarly, you can use a column_num of 0 to retrieve all the values in a specified row.
- If you want to use the INDEX function to retrieve data stored in more than one range, be certain to store all the lookup ranges on the same worksheet. The INDEX function can refer to ranges that are stored on a worksheet different from the one containing the formula, but it expects to find the ranges on the same worksheet, even if you use named ranges. If you do use an INDEX formula that refers to ranges on separate worksheets, Excel displays the #VALUE error.

Vijay's final step to complete the order form in the Orders worksheet is to calculate the grand total in cell D17 with the formula =SUM(D13:D15). Figure 5.24 shows the finished order form.

Figure 5.24: Final tennis products order form

	A	B	C	D	E
1	Tennis Products Order Form				
2		Shipping weight	100		
3		Region number	3		
4		Shipping method	1		
5		Customer type	2		
6	Item#	Quantity	Description	Total	
7	12	10	Touring Bag - One Size	$ 599.90	
8	4	50	ExoRacket Graphite - Oversize	$ 7,750.00	
9	8	25	FlexPro Racket - Junior Pro	$ 1,749.75	
10	10	25	FlexPro Racket - Oversize	$ 2,499.75	
11	13	100	String Pack - Synthetic	$ 325.00	
12					
13			Total Order	$ 12,924.40	
14			Discount	$ (400.00)	
15			Shipping	$ 22.00	
16					
17			Grand Total	$ 12,546.40	
18					

Formula to calculate the grand total: =SUM(D13:D15)

Vijay takes some time to review his work on the Tennis Orders workbook, concentrating on the Orders worksheet. He would like this order form to be more flexible and streamlined. For example, this form cannot accommodate items with variable unit pricing, such as tennis balls. He also wants to list the price per unit directly on the order form. Entering codes such as 1 or 3 for shipping method and region is awkward—Vijay usually thinks of a region by its state abbreviation, such as CO, and a shipping method by its name, such as Rail. He will continue to refine the order form in the next section.

Steps To Success: Level 2

Now that Vijay has completed the order form for tennis products, he needs to work on the order form for golf equipment. As with tennis products, Vijay must include shipping charges and a discount for orders according to their total amount. In addition, he must add a handling charge because most golf equipment must be packed by hand. TheZone calculates handling costs for golf equipment as shown in Table 5.9.

Table 5.9: Handling charges for golf equipment

Order Amount	Handling Charge
Under $2,500	7% of the total order amount
$2,500–$5,000	6% of the total order amount
$5,000–$7,500	5% of the total order amount
$7,500–$10,000	4% of the total order amount
$10,500–$12,500	3% of the total order amount
$12,500 and over	2% of the total order amount
All orders	A minimum handling charge of $20 is applied to all orders

Vijay has updated the Golf workbook and renamed it Golf2. He consolidated the order information on a worksheet named Orders, and added worksheets for pricing information, handling charges (including a minimum fee), discounts, and shipping charges. Figure 5.25 shows the Orders worksheet with some order-related data already entered.

Figure 5.25: Orders worksheet in the Golf2 workbook

	A	B	C	D	E
1			Golf Products Order Form		
2		Shipping weight	200		
3		Region number	3		
4		Shipping method	2		
5		Customer type	2		
6					
7	Item#	Quantity	Description	Total	
8	16	5			
9	3	6			
10	2	5			
11	8	10			
12	13	6			
13					
14					
15			Total Order		
16			Shipping		
17			Handling		
18			Discount		
19					
20			Grand Total		
21					

In these steps, you need to complete the Orders worksheet using lookup functions to display the product description, and to calculate the order total and shipping, handling, and discount charges. Complete the following:

1. Open the workbook named **Golf2.xlsx** located in the Chapter 5 folder, and then save it as **Golf Orders2.xlsx**.

2. Examine the contents of each worksheet, and name the ranges as indicated in Table 5.10. Use these range names as appropriate in Questions 3 through 9.

Table 5.10: Naming ranges in the Golf Orders2 workbook

Range Name	Worksheet	Cells
ItemPrice	Costs	A5:C20
HandlingFee	Handling	B2:G3
Disc	Discounts	A2:A5
TotalOrderValue	Discounts	B2:B5
Shipping1	Shipping	B3:E7
Shipping2	Shipping	B11:E15
Shipping3	Shipping	B19:E23

3. In cell C8 of the Orders worksheet, write a formula that displays the product description for the first item in the order. Copy the formula into cells C9:C12.

4. In cell D8 of the Orders worksheet, calculate the total value of the item (price multiplied by quantity). Copy the formula into cells D9:D12.

5. In cell D15 of the Orders worksheet, calculate the total cost of the order.

6. In cell D16 of the Orders worksheet, calculate the total shipping charge for this order based on four variables: the ship to region, the customer type (standard, preferred, or most preferred), the total weight, and the method of shipping.

7. In cell D17 of the Orders worksheet, calculate the handling cost. Be certain to account for the minimum handling charge. Handling fees are based on the total order value excluding shipping and discounts.

8. In cell D18 of the Orders worksheet, calculate the discount. Be certain to write the formula so that the discount is deducted from the total amount when all values are added. Discounts are again based on the total order value excluding shipping and handling fees.

9. In cell D20 of the Orders worksheet, calculate the grand total for the order.

10. Save and close the Golf Orders2.xlsx workbook.

LEVEL 3

Nesting Lookup and Reference Functions to Retrieve and Calculate Data

---

Refining the Order Form

Vijay reviews the current order form for tennis products and decides that the form should be more professional looking and flexible so that other sales representatives can use it easily. He plans to reformat the Orders worksheet to make it easier for users to enter the necessary data. He also wants to modify the worksheet to include products with both variable and fixed unit pricing, and to list the price per unit on the order form.

To achieve these goals, Vijay will change the Tennis Orders workbook as follows:

- Redesign the order form to incorporate the new state and shipping method entries, and to list shipping weight and unit prices.
- Accommodate fixed and variable unit pricing by assigning a price schedule code to each item: 1 for fixed unit priced items and 2 for tennis balls. Based on the price schedule code, Vijay can look up the unit price.
- Add two worksheets, one for each price schedule. The Pricing Schedule 1 worksheet, to be used with items with a price schedule code of 1, will list fixed unit prices for tennis equipment. The Pricing Schedule 2 worksheet, to be used with items with a price schedule code of 2, will list variable prices for tennis balls. If TheZone adds other products with variable prices, Vijay can create other pricing schedule worksheets and related price schedule codes. These worksheets will replace the Costs and the original Tennis Balls worksheets.
- Support the redesigned state entry by adding a worksheet that lists each U.S. state abbreviation and its corresponding region number. Users can then enter a state directly and Excel will calculate shipping based on the region.

Vijay begins by revising the Orders worksheets. Next, he switches to the Costs worksheet and renames it as Products. Next, he names the range in the Products worksheet in which he will be looking up data as Products, and then he adds a Price Schedule column and a Ship Weight column to the Products worksheet. He revises the Discount worksheet with a simplified horizontal format. Figure 5.26 shows these three worksheets.

Figure 5.26: Updated Orders, Products, and Discount worksheets

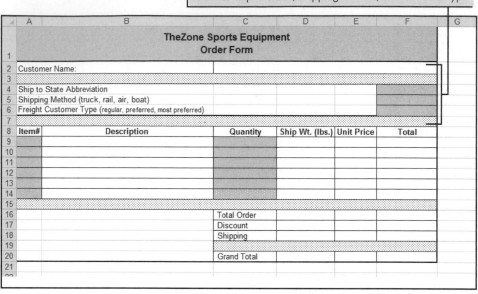

Redesigned Orders worksheet includes simplified user-entry fields for ship to states, shipping method, and customer type

TheZone Sports Equipment Order Form

	A	B	C	D	E	F	G
2	Customer Name:						
3							
4	Ship to State Abbreviation						
5	Shipping Method (truck, rail, air, boat)						
6	Freight Customer Type (regular, preferred, most preferred)						
7							
8	Item#	Description	Quantity	Ship Wt. (lbs.)	Unit Price	Total	
9							
10							
11							
12							
13							
14							
15							
16			Total Order				
17			Discount				
18			Shipping				
19							
20			Grand Total				
21							

Product Information for Tennis Equipment
TheZone Equipment Division

Products worksheet (formerly the Costs worksheet) now includes Price Schedule and Ship Weight columns (but no prices) with range A5:D20 named Products

	A	B	C	D	E
4	Item#	Description	Price Schedule	Ship Weight	
5	1	FlexPro Backpack - One Size	1	2.1	
6	2	Alpha Stringing Machine	1	2.5	
7	3	Grommet Set	1	1.2	
8	4	ExoRacket Graphite - Oversize	1	16.0	
9	5	ExoRacket Graphite - Mid+, Plus Length	1	16.0	
10	6	ExoRacket Graphite - Mid+, Regular Length	1	15.0	
11	7	ExoRacket Graphite - Junior Size	1	16.0	
12	8	FlexPro Racket - Junior Pro	1	14.0	
13	9	FlexPro Racket - Standard	1	18.0	
14	10	FlexPro Racket - Oversize	1	19.0	
15	11	Racket Bag - One Size	1	6.0	
16	12	Touring Bag - One Size	1	12.0	
17	13	String Pack - Synthetic	1	1.2	
18	14	String Pack - Gut	1	1.2	
19	15	String Reel - Gut Bulk	1	2.0	
20	100	Tennis Balls - Bulk	2	0.1	
21					

	A	B	C	D	E	F
1	Total Order Value	$ 0	$ 5,000	$ 10,000	$ 25,000	
2	Discount	$ 0	$ 150	$ 400	$ 1,000	
3						

Discount worksheet redesigned in a horizontal format

Vijay also adds the Pricing Schedule 1, Pricing Schedule 2, and States worksheets, and modifies the Shipping worksheet. Figure 5.27 shows these four worksheets.

Figure 5.27: Pricing Schedule 1, Pricing Schedule 2, Shipping, and States worksheets

Pricing Schedule 1 worksheet with Item# and prices for fixed-price products

	A	B	C
1	Price List for Tennis Products Fixed-Price Items		
2			
3	Item#	$/each	
4	1	$ 23.75	
5	2	$ 52.80	
6	3	$ 15.95	
7	4	$ 135.00	
8	5	$ 135.00	
9	6	$ 139.99	
10	7	$ 142.50	
11	8	$ 69.99	
12	9	$ 99.99	
13	10	$ 99.99	
14	11	$ 29.95	
15	12	$ 59.99	
16	13	$ 3.25	
17	14	$ 7.25	
18			

Pricing Schedule 2 worksheet with quantities and unit prices for tennis balls

	A	B	C
1	Price List for Tennis Balls Variable-Priced Items		
2			
3	Qty	$/each	
4	0	$ 2.45	
5	60	$ 2.27	
6	120	$ 2.12	
7	240	$ 2.00	
8			

Pricing Schedule 2 worksheet

States worksheet with state name, abbreviation, region name, and region number

	A	B	C	D
1	Name	Abbreviation	Region	Region#
2	Alabama	AL	SE	2
3	Alaska	AK	W	5
4	Arizona	AZ	SW	4
5	Arkansas	AR	SE	2
6	California	CA	W	5
7	Colorado	CO	W	5
8	Connecticut	CT	NE	1
9	Delaware	DE	NE	1
10	District of Columbia	DC	NE	1
11	Florida	FL	SE	2
12	Georgia	GA	SE	2
13	Hawaii	HI	W	5

Shipping worksheet with three shipping tables based on customer type

	A	B	C	D	E	F
1	Shipping Charges by Customer Type, Region, and Method					
2						
3		Shipping Method - Standard				
4	Region	Truck	Rail	Air	Boat	
5	1	$ 0.10	$ 0.11	$ 1.50	NA	
6	2	$ 0.18	$ 0.12	$ 2.00	NA	
7	3	$ 0.24	$ 0.14	$ 2.10	$ 0.20	
8	4	$ 0.28	$ 0.16	$ 2.25	$ 0.20	
9	5	$ 0.45	$ 0.40	$ 3.50	$ 0.35	
10						
11		Shipping Method - Preferred				
12	Region	Truck	Rail	Air	Boat	
13	1	$ 0.09	$ 0.10	$ 1.35	NA	
14	2	$ 0.16	$ 0.11	$ 1.80	NA	
15	3	$ 0.22	$ 0.13	$ 1.89	$ 0.18	
16	4	$ 0.25	$ 0.14	$ 2.03	$ 0.18	
17	5	$ 0.41	$ 0.36	$ 3.15	$ 0.32	
18						
19		Shipping Method - Most Preferred				
20	Region	Truck	Rail	Air	Boat	
21	1	$ 0.08	$ 0.09	$ 1.22	NA	
22	2	$ 0.15	$ 0.10	$ 1.62	NA	
23	3	$ 0.19	$ 0.11	$ 1.70	$ 0.16	
24	4	$ 0.23	$ 0.13	$ 1.82	$ 0.16	
25	5	$ 0.36	$ 0.32	$ 2.84	$ 0.28	
26						

To complete the order form on the Orders worksheet, Vijay needs to set up the following calculations:

- Look up the item description in the Products range.
- Look up the shipping weight for each item in the Products range.
- Look up the unit price for each item by referring to the tables in the Pricing Schedule 1 or Pricing Schedule 2 worksheet, which also requires first looking up the Price Schedule number from the Product table.
- Calculate the total for each item by multiplying price by quantity.

- Calculate the total order amount by summing the item totals.
- Calculate the total shipping weight by summing the weight for each item.
- Look up the appropriate discount in the Discounts range.
- Look up the associated shipping charge per pound in the Shipping worksheet, which also requires looking up the region number associated with the state entered.
- Calculate the shipping charge by multiplying the shipping weight by the charge per pound.
- Calculate the grand total, including discounts and shipping.

Figure 5.28 shows the lookup calculations required to complete all of these tasks.

Figure 5.28: Lookup calculations to be made in the Orders worksheet

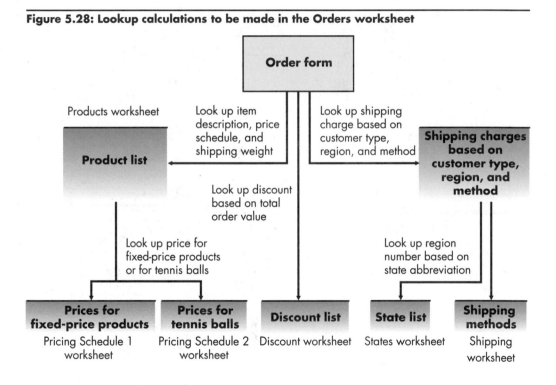

Vijay has already performed some of these calculations in the original order form, such as looking up the item description, so he only needs to repeat those formulas in the modified order form. Retrieving the unit price for each item and finding the correct shipping charge, however, require more complex formulas that nest one or more functions.

To test the order form as he enters the formulas, Vijay plans to use the sample order information shown in Table 5.11.

Table 5.11: Sample order information

Item#	Product	Quantity
5	ExoRacket Graphite - Mid+, Plus Length	60
6	ExoRacket Graphite - Mid+, Regular Length	15
12	Touring Bag - One Size	100
100	Tennis Balls - Bulk	300

Now, Vijay is ready to create the complex lookup formulas he needs to complete the order form. He'll nest Reference functions within the IF functions and use IS functions to develop a powerful, automated order form.

Preventing Errors in Data Retrieval

Vijay starts developing the new order form by entering a VLOOKUP formula in cell B9 of the Orders worksheet to retrieve the product description for the first item. He enters the following formula:

```
=VLOOKUP(A9,Products,2,FALSE)
```

To solve this formula, the VLOOKUP function scans the lookup range named Products for an exact match to the value specified in cell A9, which is 5. When it finds that value, it retrieves the corresponding data in column 2 of the lookup range, which contains the description for item# 5. Vijay copies this VLOOKUP formula from cell B9 to cells B10:B14. Figure 5.29 shows the resulting worksheet.

Cells B13 and B14 display the error #N/A because Vijay has provided item numbers for four products, but the form has room for six. The formula in cell B13 refers to the empty cell A13, and the formula in cell B14 refers to the empty cell A14. Vijay could respond to the #N/A error by deleting the VLOOKUP formulas in cells B13 and B14, but if he receives an order of more than four items, he would have to enter the formulas again. Instead, he can use the **ISBLANK function** to prevent the #N/A error.

Figure 5.29: Retrieving the item description using a VLOOKUP formula

Orders worksheet

	A	B	C	D	E	F
1		TheZone Sports Equipment Order Form				
2	Customer Name:					
3						
4	Ship to State Abbreviation					
5	Shipping Method (truck, rail, air, boat)					
6	Freight Customer Type (regular, preferred, most preferred)					
7						
8	Item#	Description	Quantity	Ship Wt. (lbs.)	Unit Price	Total
9	5	ExoRacket Graphite - Mid+, Plus Length	60			
10	6	ExoRacket Graphite - Mid+, Regular Length	15			
11	12	Touring Bag - One Size	100			
12	100	Tennis Balls - Bulk	300			
13		#N/A				
14		#N/A				
15						

=VLOOKUP(A9,Products,2,FALSE) copied to cells B10:B14, resulting in #N/A error messages if the Item# is blank

	A	B	C	D
1		Product Information for Tennis Equipment		
2		TheZone Equipment Division		
3				
4	Item#	Description	Price Schedule	Ship Weight
5	1	FlexPro Backpack - One Size	1	2.1
6	2	Alpha Stringing Machine	1	2.5
7	3	Grommet Set	1	1.2
8	4	ExoRacket Graphite - Oversize	1	16.0
9	5	ExoRacket Graphite - Mid+, Plus Length	1	16.0
10	6	ExoRacket Graphite - Mid+, Regular Length	1	15.0
11	7	ExoRacket Graphite - Junior Size	1	16.0
12	8	FlexPro Racket - Junior Pro	1	14.0
13	9	FlexPro Racket - Standard	1	18.0
14	10	FlexPro Racket - Oversize	1	19.0
15	11	Racket Bag - One Size	1	6.0
16	12	Touring Bag - One Size	1	12.0
17	13	String Pack - Synthetic	1	1.2
18	14	String Pack - Gut	1	1.2
19	15	String Reel - Gut Bulk	1	2.0
20	100	Tennis Balls - Bulk	2	0.1

Products worksheet

VLOOKUP function in cell Orders!B9 looks for the lookup value in cell Orders!A9 (5) in the Products range that matches and then retrieves the corresponding data

Using the ISBLANK Function

Excel provides nine functions, called the IS functions, that test a value or cell reference, and then return a TRUE or FALSE value depending on the results. For example, you can use the ISBLANK function to test a cell reference. If the cell is blank, or empty, the function returns the value TRUE. You can specify what Excel should do in this case, such as display a dash (-) or N/A in the cell.

The **IS functions** are often used in formulas to test the outcome of a calculation. If you combine them with the IF function, they help you locate data-entry errors. For example, you could write a formula using the ISTEXT function to check whether cell A5 contains text, such as a customer name. If a user committed a data-entry error by entering a number in cell A5 instead of text, you could display a message such as "Cell A5 must contain text." Table 5.12 lists and describes the nine IS functions, which all check for a condition and then return a TRUE or FALSE value.

Table 5.12: IS functions

IS Function	Description
ISBLANK	Value refers to an empty cell
ISERR	Value refers to any error value except #N/A
ISERROR	Value refers to any error value (#N/A, #VALUE!, #REF!, #DIV/0!, #NUM!, #NAME?, or #NULL!)
ISLOGICAL	Value refers to a logical value
ISNA	Value refers to the #N/A (value not available) error value
ISNONTEXT	Value refers to any item that is not text (this function returns TRUE if the value refers to a blank cell)
ISNUMBER	Value refers to a number
ISREF	Value refers to a reference
ISTEXT	Value refers to text

The **ISBLANK function** checks whether a specified value refers to an empty cell. The syntax of this function is as follows:

```
ISBLANK(value)
```

In the Orders worksheet, the formula =ISBLANK(A13) would return the value TRUE because cell A13 is empty. Vijay can combine this ISBLANK formula with an IF function to determine if cell A13 is blank, and if it is, modify the contents of cell B13. Vijay revises the formula in cell B9 as follows:

```
=IF(ISBLANK(A9)," ",VLOOKUP(A9,Products,2,FALSE))
```

To solve this formula, Excel first checks to see if cell A9 is blank. If it is, Excel displays a string of empty characters, the " " in the formula. If cell A9 contains a value, VLOOKUP returns the corresponding item description, as it did originally.

Vijay copies this formula from cell B9 to cells B10:B14. In a similar manner, Vijay can nest the IF, ISBLANK, and VLOOKUP functions to calculate the shipping weight in cell D9, as in the following formula:

```
=IF(ISBLANK(A9)," ",VLOOKUP(A9,Products,4,FALSE)*C9)
```

To solve this formula, Excel checks to see if cell A9 is blank. If it is, Excel displays a string of empty characters. If cell A9 contains a value, Excel performs the VLOOKUP part of the formula. In the Products range, it looks for an exact match to the value in cell A9, which is 5, the item number. When it finds an exact match, it retrieves the value in column 4, which is the shipping weight of 16 pounds. It then multiplies 16 by the value in C9, which is the quantity of 60, and displays the results of 960. Vijay copies this formula from cell D9 to cells D10:D14. Figure 5.30 shows the resulting worksheet.

Figure 5.30: Using IF, ISBLANK, and VLOOKUP to calculate the shipping weight

Formula in cell D9:
=IF(ISBLANK(A9)," ",VLOOKUP(A9, Products,4,FALSE)*C9)

	A	B	C	D	E	F	G
1			TheZone Sports Equipment Order Form				
2	Customer Name:						
3							
4	Ship to State Abbreviation						
5	Shipping Method (truck, rail, air, boat)						
6	Freight Customer Type (regular, preferred, most preferred)						
7							
8	Item#	Description	Quantity	Ship Wt. (lbs.)	Unit Price	Total	
9	5	ExoRacket Graphite - Mid+, Plus Length	60	960			
10	6	ExoRacket Graphite - Mid+, Regular Length	15	225			
11	12	Touring Bag - One Size	100	1200			
12	100	Tennis Balls - Bulk	300	30			
13							
14							
15							
16			Total Order				
17			Discount				
18			Shipping				
19							
20			Grand Total				
21							

Because cells A13 and A14 are blank, cells D13 and D14 contain a string of empty characters appearing blank

How To

Write an ISBLANK Formula

1. Type =ISBLANK(to begin the formula.

2. Enter the reference of the cell you want to check to determine if it is blank.

3. Type a closing parenthesis mark) and then press the Enter key.

Another function named IFERROR could also be used here in combination with the VLOOKUP function to simplify error-checking. It combines aspects of the IF function and the ISERROR function. It's less specific than the ISBLANK function, which only tests for a blank cell as opposed to an error message resulting from the use of a blank cell in your formula (#N/A, #REF!, #DIV/0!, etc.). With IFERROR, you can specify your own text (or even a blank cell) when an error is encountered rather than the standard Excel message.

The syntax of this function is IFERROR(value, value_if_error). For example, applying the formula =IFERROR(VLOOKUP(A9,Products,4,FALSE)*C9," ") would essentially return a blank if *any* error were to result for the VLOOKUP formula. Vijay has decided to use the original method of nesting an ISBLANK function within an IF function because he does not want other types of errors such as #REF! to go unnoticed.

Now, Vijay can turn to a complicated part of the worksheet—calculating the unit prices.

Nesting LOOKUP and IF Functions to Calculate the Price per Unit

In the first version of the order form that Vijay created, the price per unit was based on the quantity ordered. Because he was only considering tennis balls, Vijay could use a basic VLOOKUP type TRUE formula to find the appropriate unit price. In the next version of his order form, the price per unit was based on the item ordered, and he used a VLOOKUP type FALSE formula to retrieve the fixed price of a tennis product based on its item number. Now, he wants to combine these two capabilities.

As TheZone expands its tennis line, Vijay might also need to accommodate other fixed- and variable-priced items. Vijay has, therefore, substituted the unit price in the Products worksheet for a Price Schedule column, which contains price schedule codes. Price schedule code 1 refers to fixed-price products, and price schedule code 2 refers to tennis balls, which are based on prices that vary by quantity. For each price schedule code there is a separate corresponding pricing schedule worksheet, which contains the unit costs for the items. This process is diagramed in Figure 5.31. If TheZone expands its tennis products to include other fixed-price items, Vijay can include the items in the Pricing Schedule 1 worksheet and assign price schedule code 1 to these products. If TheZone adds other types of variable-priced products, he can create additional worksheets, such as Pricing Schedule 3 and Pricing Schedule 4, and assign price schedule codes 3 and 4 to these items in the Products worksheet.

Figure 5.31 Schematic for obtaining unit prices for products

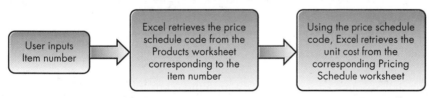

Because each price schedule lookup table on the pricing schedule worksheets is in a vertical format, one way to look up the correct unit price is to create a VLOOKUP function and vary the arguments of the function depending on the price schedule code of the item. The difficult part of the formula is that some arguments of the VLOOKUP will require Excel to, in turn, look up the price schedule code before it can be determined what value is needed for that argument. Figure 5.32 diagrams the logic of the formula that Vijay needs to create.

Figure 5.32: Logic for retrieving product prices using a VLOOKUP

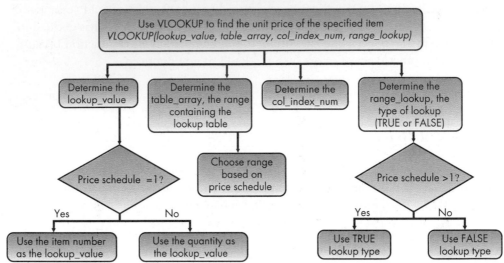

According to Figure 5.32, Vijay needs to specify the four arguments for the VLOOKUP function as follows:

- First argument: *lookup_value*—Choose the lookup_value, the value he wants Excel to match in the lookup table. If that value is associated with price schedule code 1, use the item number as the lookup_value. If the price schedule code is not 1, use the quantity as the lookup_value.
- Second argument: *table_array*—Choose the table_array, the range containing the lookup table, according to the price schedule code. If the price schedule code is 1, use the lookup table in the Pricing Schedule 1 worksheet. If the price schedule code is 2, use the lookup table in the Pricing Schedule 2 worksheet.
- Third argument: *col_index_num*—Choose the col_index_num depending on which column contains the prices. For both lookup tables, this is column 2.
- Fourth argument: *range_lookup*—Choose a TRUE or FALSE lookup type according to the price schedule code. If the price schedule code is greater than 1, use TRUE; if the price schedule code is 1, use FALSE.

For example, if a customer orders item# 5, a graphite tennis racket, the VLOOKUP function can look up the item on the Products worksheet and retrieve its price schedule code, which is 1. For a product with this price schedule code, a second VLOOKUP function uses the *item number* to look up the unit cost in the Pricing Schedule 1 worksheet. Because item# 5 uses price schedule code 1, the second VLOOKUP function uses 5 as its first argument. Excel looks up item# 5 in the Pricing Schedule 1 worksheet and retrieves the unit price of $135.00.

If a customer orders 50 canisters of item 100, bulk tennis balls, the VLOOKUP function can look up item 100 and retrieve its price schedule code, which is 2. For a product with this price schedule code, the second VLOOKUP function uses the quantity ordered to look up the unit cost in the Pricing Schedule 2 worksheet. Because item 100 uses price schedule code 2, the second VLOOKUP function will use 50—the *quantity ordered*—as its first argument. Excel looks up a quantity of 50 in the Pricing Schedule 2 worksheet, and retrieves the unit cost of $2.45.

The following sections discuss how to translate these steps into the arguments of the VLOOKUP function.

Choosing the Lookup_Value Using an IF Function with a Nested VLOOKUP

The first argument Vijay will write in his VLOOKUP formula to determine unit price is the lookup_value. The lookup_value is either the item number entered in cell A9 for fixed-priced items or the quantity entered in cell C9 for variable priced items. Vijay wants Excel to first test whether this item has a fixed price per unit using an IF function. The logical test of the IF function requires Excel to retrieve the price schedule code for this item on the Products table using a VLOOKUP. If the price schedule code value equals 1, then the item number (A9) will be the lookup_value of the original VLOOKUP; otherwise, the quantity (C9) will be the lookup_value. To determine the unit price for an ordered item, Vijay will enter the following expression as the first argument of the longer VLOOKUP formula in cell E9 of the Orders worksheet:

```
IF(VLOOKUP(A9,Products,3,FALSE)=1,A9,C9)
```

To solve this expression for the first item (item# 5), Excel looks up the price schedule code in the Products range (Products!A5:D20) for item# 5, retrieving only an exact match (type FALSE). The price schedule code for item# 5 is 1; thus the IF function will select the value in cell A9 (5) as the lookup_value. Figure 5.33 details the progress Vijay has made in writing the formula to determine the unit price.

Figure 5.33: First argument of the VLOOKUP formula to determine unit price

=VLOOKUP(IF(VLOOKUP(A9, Products, 3, FALSE) = 1, A9, C9),

2nd argument – table_array,

3rd argument – col_index_num,

4th argument – range_lookup type)

Choosing the Table_Array Using the CHOOSE Function

Next, Vijay must specify the second argument of the VLOOKUP, the table_array that contains the appropriate lookup table, which is determined by the price schedule code. He uses Price1 as the name of the range A4:B17 in the Pricing Schedule 1 worksheet, the range containing the item numbers and unit prices for fixed-price products. He uses Price2 as the name of the range A4:B7 in the Pricing Schedule 2 worksheet, the range containing the quantity and unit prices for tennis balls.

If the price schedule code is 1, Excel uses the Price1 range. If the price schedule code is 2, Excel uses the Price2 range. In short, Vijay wants to look up the value 1 or 2 and return the range Price1 or Price2. But how can he look up a value and return a range?

None of the Reference and Lookup functions he has used so far can solve the problem of returning a range and not a single value. One way to accomplish this might be to use another VLOOKUP function nested within an IF function. However, TheZone might add more pricing schedules, which would require an unnecessarily complex formula with many levels of nesting. Instead, Vijay considers using the **CHOOSE function**, another Reference and Lookup function that can return a value or a range for up to 254 different values. The syntax of the CHOOSE function is as follows:

$$\texttt{CHOOSE(index\_num,value1,value2,...)}$$

The index_num argument specifies which value to select from the list that follows. Index_num must be a number between 1 and 254, a formula, or a reference to a cell containing a number between 1 and 254. The list of values (value1, value2, and so on) can be numbers, text, cell references, or even ranges. For example, in the formula =CHOOSE(2,A2:A7,B2:B7,C2:C7), the first argument (2) means that Excel should choose the second value—in this case, the range B2:B7—from the list of four values.

Keep the following conditions in mind when specifying the index_num argument:

- If the index_num is 1, the function returns the first value from the list. If the index_num is 2, the function returns the second value from the list, and so on.
- If the index_num is less than 1 or greater than the last value in the list, the function displays the error #VALUE!
- If the index_num is a fraction, it is truncated to an integer before being used.

How To

Write a CHOOSE Formula
1. Type =CHOOSE(to begin the formula.
2. Enter a number that specifies which value to select from the list that follows. The number can be the result of a formula or a cell reference.
3. Enter the list of values, which can be numbers, text, cell references, or ranges.
4. Type a closing parenthesis mark) and then press the Enter key.

Vijay can use the CHOOSE function to determine the table_array. He can write this part of the VLOOKUP formula so that the CHOOSE function returns the Price1 range or the Price2 range, depending on the price schedule code used for the specified item number.

To create the CHOOSE function, he first considers what to use for the index_num argument. He wants to choose the appropriate price schedule code: 1 or 2. The price schedule code, however, is listed on the Products table by item number. For example, item# 5 uses price schedule code 1. To retrieve the appropriate price schedule code to use as the index_num argument of the CHOOSE function, Vijay can write the same VLOOKUP function used in the first argument to retrieve the price schedule code. The resulting value determines which range to choose: Price1 or Price2. The value1 and value2 arguments are the ranges associated with price schedule code 1 (Price1) and price schedule code 2 (Price2). To select the appropriate price schedule code (table_array argument) for the first item on the order form, Vijay can use the following expression in the VLOOKUP formula in cell E9 of the Orders worksheet:

```
CHOOSE(VLOOKUP(A9,Products,3,FALSE),Price1,Price2)...
```

To solve this expression, Excel chooses the price schedule as determined by the VLOOKUP function. In the Products range, it looks for the item number referenced in cell A9 (5), and retrieves an exact match to the value in column 3, which is 1. Then the CHOOSE function uses that value as the index_num, selecting the first value in the list, which is the Price1 range.

Figure 5.34 shows the second argument (table_array) of the formula in cell E9 for calculating the unit price.

Figure 5.34: Second argument of the VLOOKUP formula to determine unit price

VLOOKUP(IF(VLOOKUP(A9, Products, 3, FALSE) = 1, A9, C9),

CHOOSE(VLOOKUP(A9, Products, 3, FALSE), Price1,Price2)

3rd argument – col_index_num,

4th argument – range_lookup type)

Excel begins to solve the VLOOKUP function by determining whether it should match the item number or the quantity in a lookup table. It chooses which lookup table to use by looking in the Products range for the item number referenced in cell A9 (5), and then retrieving an exact match to the value in column 3, which is the price schedule code 1. Then it chooses the Price1 range (value 1) as the lookup table.

Choosing the Col_Index_Num Using a Constant Value

The next step is to select the col_index_num of the VLOOKUP function. Vijay designed all of the pricing schedules to list the lookup values in column 1 and the prices in column 2. He can, therefore, use the value 2 as the col_index_num because both lookup tables list prices in column 2.

Combining the col_index_num argument with the other two parts of the formula, the partial formula in cell E9 now looks like the one shown in Figure 5.35.

Figure 5.35: Third argument of the VLOOKUP to determine unit price

VLOOKUP(IF(VLOOKUP(A9, Products, 3, FALSE) = 1, A9, C9),

CHOOSE(VLOOKUP(A9, Products, 3, FALSE), Price1,Price2),

2

4th argument – range_lookup type)

Choosing the Range_Lookup Using a VLOOKUP Function

The fourth and final argument of the VLOOKUP function is the range_lookup type, which can be TRUE or FALSE. Like the lookup_value, this argument varies depending on the associated pricing schedule. If Excel uses pricing schedule 1, the Price1 range, it looks up the item number exactly, meaning Vijay should use a FALSE lookup type. If Excel uses any other variable pricing schedule, such as 2 for the tennis balls, it looks up the quantity, which might not exactly match the values in the lookup table, and therefore requires a TRUE lookup type.

To determine the correct range_lookup, Vijay again needs to determine which price schedule code is associated with the specified item number. Similar to how he found the price schedule code in the first and second arguments, he can use another VLOOKUP function. If the price schedule code is equal to 1, this argument should be FALSE; otherwise, it should be TRUE.

To select the appropriate lookup type, Vijay can use the following relational expression that compares the results of the VLOOKUP function to see if it is greater than 1. He adds this argument to the formula he has already begun to enter in cell E9 of the Orders worksheet:

VLOOKUP(A9,Products,3,FALSE)>1...

To solve this expression, Excel looks for an exact match to the value stored in cell A9 (5), and then retrieves the corresponding value from the third column of the Products table, which lists the price schedule code associated with this item. If that price schedule code is greater than 1, Excel returns a TRUE value; otherwise, it returns a FALSE value. Because the price schedule code for item# 5 is 1, the formula will return FALSE.

After combining the range_lookup argument with the other parts of the formula, the complete VLOOKUP function to be entered in cell E9 now looks like the one shown in Figure 5.36.

Figure 5.36: Fourth argument of the VLOOKUP formula to determine unit price

VLOOKUP(IF(VLOOKUP(A9, Products, 3, FALSE) = 1, A9, C9),

CHOOSE(VLOOKUP(A9, Products, 3, FALSE), Price1,Price2),

2

VLOOKUP(A9,Products,3,FALSE)>1)

Creating the Final Formula for Determining Unit Price

Vijay has now determined each of the four arguments of the VLOOKUP formula that will find the unit price. He also wants to avoid displaying the error #N/A, so he will use the IF and ISBLANK functions as he did before to display a blank cell in cell E9 if no item number is entered in cell A9. He enters the formula as shown in Figure 5.37 in cell E9. (Note that each part of the formula is shown on a separate line for readability here; Vijay enters the entire formula on one line in Excel.)

Figure 5.37: Final formula used to determine unit price

=IF(ISBLANK(A9)," ",

VLOOKUP(IF(VLOOKUP(A9,Products,3,FALSE)=1,A9,C9),

CHOOSE(VLOOKUP(A9,Products,3,FALSE),Price1,Price2),

2,

VLOOKUP(A9,Products,3,FALSE)>1))

Vijay copies this formula from cell E9 to cells E10:E14 to provide the unit prices for the other items in the order. Figure 5.38 shows the revised Orders worksheet.

Figure 5.38: Completed unit price formula on Orders worksheet

	A	B	C	D	E	F	G
1		TheZone Sports Equipment Order Form					
2	Customer Name:						
3							
4	Ship to State Abbreviation						
5	Shipping Method (truck, rail, air, boat)						
6	Freight Customer Type (regular, preferred, most preferred)						
7							
8	Item#	Description	Quantity	Ship Wt. (lbs.)	Unit Price	Total	
9	5	ExoRacket Graphite - Mid+, Plus Length	60	960	$ 135.00		
10	6	ExoRacket Graphite - Mid+, Regular Length	15	225	$ 139.99		
11	12	Touring Bag - One Size	100	1200	$ 59.99		
12	100	Tennis Balls - Bulk	300	30	$ 2.00		
13							
14							
15							
16			Total Order				
17			Discount				
18			Shipping				
19							
20			Grand Total				
21							

Planning for Future Changes: The Limitations of Using Nested IF Functions

Can you solve Vijay's problem using a different type of formula? Yes; many people would use a series of nested IF functions according to the following logic:

- If the price schedule code is 1, look up the price based on the item number in Pricing Schedule 1.
- If the price schedule code is 2, look up the price based on the quantity in Pricing Schedule 2.

Although this technique would work equally well to solve Vijay's problem, it may prove cumbersome with three or more pricing schedules. The solution that Vijay used works for up to 254 pricing structures with modifications as required to the CHOOSE function argument list. The nested IF method is limited to 65 pricing structures, and it would require a very long list of complex arguments. If a product or company has more than three or four pricing structures, a relational database, such as Microsoft Access, might be a better choice than using a spreadsheet program. When designing a workbook, designers need to consider how the workbook will be used and what types of modifications are likely in the future.

Calculating Totals

Now that Vijay has solved the complex problem of unit pricing, he can turn to an easier task: calculating the total cost of each item and the total cost of the order. In cell F9, he can calculate the total price by multiplying the unit price by the quantity. Again taking into account blank rows, he enters the following formula in cell F9:

```
=IF(ISBLANK(A9)," ",C9*E9)
```

He copies it to cells F10:F14, and then Vijay can calculate the total order amount in cell F16 by using the following formula:

```
=SUM(F9:F14)
```

Finally, in cell D16, he enters the following formula to calculate the total weight of the order:

```
=SUM(D9:D14)
```

Figure 5.39 shows the Orders worksheet with totals calculated.

Figure 5.39: Totals calculated on the Orders worksheet

Formula in cell F9 calculates the total price of the item

	A	B	C	D	E	F	G
1			TheZone Sports Equipment Order Form				
2	Customer Name:						
3							
4	Ship to State Abbreviation						
5	Shipping Method (truck, rail, air, boat)						
6	Freight Customer Type (regular, preferred, most preferred)						
7							
8	Item#	Description	Quantity	Ship Wt. (lbs.)	Unit Price	Total	
9	5	ExoRacket Graphite - Mid+, Plus Length	60	960	$ 135.00	$ 8,100.00	
10	6	ExoRacket Graphite - Mid+, Regular Length	15	225	$ 139.99	$ 2,099.85	
11	12	Touring Bag - One Size	100	1200	$ 59.99	$ 5,999.00	
12	100	Tennis Balls - Bulk	300	30	$ 2.00	$ 600.00	
13							
14							
15							
16			Total Order	2,415		$ 16,798.85	
17			Discount				
18			Shipping				
19							
20			Grand Total				
21							

SUM functions calculate total weight and order amount

Calculating the Discount Amount

Vijay decides to simplify the Discount worksheet so that it contains a basic horizontal lookup table. He names the range of values Discounts, as shown in Figure 5.40. According to this table, all orders of $5,000 or more qualify for a discount based on a sliding scale.

Figure 5.40: Horizontal lookup table in the modified Discount worksheet

	A	B	C	D	E	F
1	Total Order Value	$ 0	$ 5,000	$ 10,000	$ 25,000	
2	Discount	$ 0	$ 150	$ 400	$ 1,000	
3						

Range B1:E2 named Discounts

Vijay can use a basic HLOOKUP formula in cell F17 in the Orders worksheet to calculate the discount:

```
=-HLOOKUP(F16,Discounts,2,TRUE)
```

Excel solves this formula by looking up the value stored in cell F16 (the order total, $16,798.85) in the Discounts table, and retrieving the value in the second row. The formula uses the TRUE lookup type because it does not need to exactly match the specified value, and includes a negative sign at the beginning so that Excel returns a negative value. Figure 5.41 shows the Orders worksheet with this formula entered.

5

Level 3

Figure 5.41: HLOOKUP formula added to the Orders worksheet

Formula in cell F17 calculates the order discount:
=–HLOOKUP(F16,Discounts,2,TRUE)

	A	B	C	D	E	F	G
1		TheZone Sports Equipment Order Form					
2	Customer Name:						
3							
4	Ship to State Abbreviation						
5	Shipping Method (truck, rail, air, boat)						
6	Freight Customer Type (regular, preferred, most preferred)						
7							
8	Item#	Description	Quantity	Ship Wt. (lbs.)	Unit Price	Total	
9	5	ExoRacket Graphite - Mid+, Plus Length	60	960	$ 135.00	$ 8,100.00	
10	6	ExoRacket Graphite - Mid+, Regular Length	15	225	$ 139.99	$ 2,099.85	
11	12	Touring Bag - One Size	100	1200	$ 59.99	$ 5,999.00	
12	100	Tennis Balls - Bulk	300	30	$ 2.00	$ 600.00	
13							
14							
15							
16			Total Order	2,415		$ 16,798.85	
17			Discount			$ (400.00)	
18			Shipping				
19							
20			Grand Total				
21							
22							

Calculating the Shipping Costs Using MATCH and INDEX Functions

Although Vijay is using the same format for the shipping schedules as he did originally, he needs to change the formula for calculating shipping costs to let users enter the destination state, shipping method, and customer type as text. These text entries will replace the numeric codes used for region, shipping method, and customer type. In addition, Vijay will retrieve the shipping cost in $/lb and then multiply it by the total shipping weight that was previously determined.

Vijay is now basing shipping charges on the following input variables, which are also shown in Figure 5.42:

- **Ship to State Abbreviation**—The destination location is determined from the two-character state abbreviation that users enter in cell F4. Excel will look up the region number based on the state abbreviation.
- **Shipping Method**—Users enter truck, rail, air, or boat as the shipping method. Excel will look up the shipping method number based on this entry.
- **Freight Customer Type**—Users enter regular, preferred, or most preferred as the customer type. Excel will look up the customer type number based on this entry.

Figure 5.42: Shipping charge based on three variables

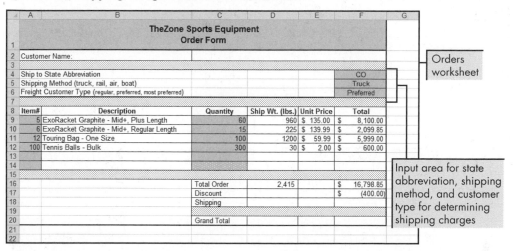

One possible way to perform these tasks is to use the INDEX function, as Vijay did in an earlier version of the order form. However, for this formula, each argument in the INDEX function might require an additional nested lookup function. Recall that the syntax of the INDEX function is as follows:

```
INDEX(reference,row_num,column_num,area_num)
```

Figure 5.43 illustrates this complex logic for determining the shipping charges using this technique.

Figure 5.43: Logic for determining the shipping charges

=INDEX(reference, row_num,column_num, area_num)

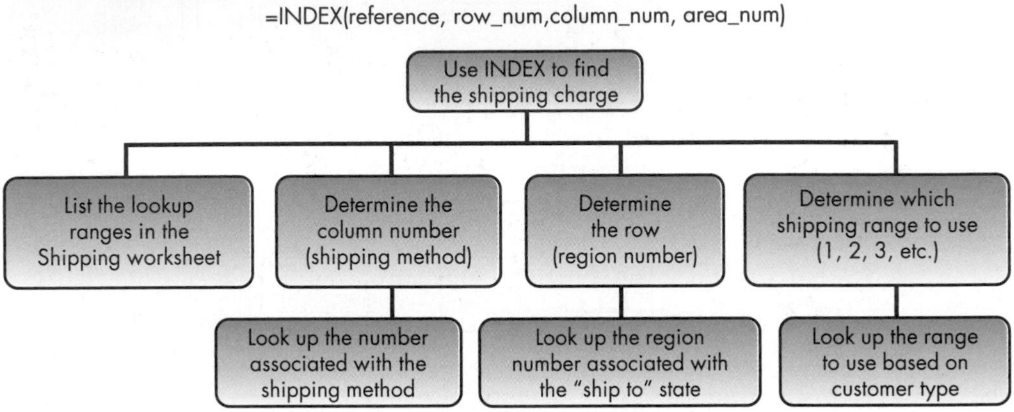

Vijay prepares the Order worksheet for the INDEX function by entering the values for state, shipping method, and freight customer type in cells Orders!F4:F6. He enters CO for state, Truck for shipping method, and Preferred for customer type. Now Vijay can begin to enter his INDEX function. This function, however, needs a row number, column number, and area number, which do not correspond directly to Vijay's inputs of CO, Truck, and Preferred. Each required argument must be retrieved from another table:

- First argument: *reference*—This argument is the listing of possible ranges for the lookup. On the Shipping worksheet, Vijay has named the three noncontiguous ranges Shipping1 (B5:E9), Shipping2 (B13:E17), and Shipping3 (B21:E25).
- Second argument: *row_num*—To retrieve the shipping charge per pound, Vijay will need the row number corresponding to the ship to region. The row_num is determined by the region number, which must be determined by the ship to state entered in cell F4 of the Orders worksheet. To obtain the region from the state abbreviation entered, the user will need to look up the appropriate region number listed in the range B2:D52 on the States worksheet. He names this range States to make it easier to reference in the Orders worksheet.
- Third argument: *column_num*—Also needed to retrieve the shipping charge per pound is the column number. The column number is determined by the shipping method. Vijay needs to find the shipping method column (1, 2, 3, or 4) that corresponds to the shipping method description, which is entered in cell F5 of the Orders worksheet. To obtain this from the user input, a number will need to be assigned to each corresponding description (Truck, Rail, Air, Boat).

- Fourth argument: *area_num*—The last argument, the area_num, determines which noncontiguous range (Shipping1, Shipping2, Shipping3) is used for this lookup. Because this must be a number, Vijay must look up the corresponding number for the selected freight customer type.

When he finds the shipping charge per pound using the INDEX function, he will multiply that value by the total order weight in cell D16. Each step in creating this INDEX function is described in the following sections.

Determining the Reference Argument of the INDEX Function

The first argument in the INDEX function is a list of the three ranges that contain the values Vijay wants to look up. These range names should be enclosed in parentheses. Vijay can use the INDEX function, which is similar to the INDEX function he used earlier:

```
INDEX((Shipping1,Shipping2,Shipping3)
```

After nesting this first argument within the formula, Vijay's next step is to determine the values for each of the remaining arguments.

```
INDEX((Shipping1,Shipping2,Shipping3),row_num,column_num,
              area_num)*total weight)
```

Determining the Row_Num of the INDEX Function Using a VLOOKUP Function

The second argument of the INDEX function is to choose the table row. Vijay organized the shipping tables in the Shipping worksheet with rows listing the regions. Before he can look up the region number in the shipping tables, he must find the region number corresponding to the state abbreviation that users enter. The States range is a vertical lookup table, with the region number listed in the third column. Instead of using a cell reference or a value as he did earlier, Vijay can use a VLOOKUP function to determine the row num of the INDEX function:

```
VLOOKUP(F4,States,3,FALSE)
```

To solve this expression, Excel looks in the States range for the value that exactly matches the one in cell F4 (the state abbreviation), and then retrieves the region number from the third column of that table.

Nesting this argument within the formula before proceeding, Vijay has the following:

```
=INDEX((Shipping1,Shipping2,Shipping3),VLOOKUP(F4,States,
          3,FALSE),column_num,area_num)*total weight
```

Determining the Column_Num of the INDEX Function Using the MATCH Function

The third argument of the INDEX function requires the table column value. In the shipping tables, the columns represent the different shipping methods. To determine the column number to use, Vijay must match the shipping method description entered in cell F5 of the Orders worksheet to the column number in the appropriate shipping table.

One way to do this is to set up a separate lookup table, as Vijay did for the States range, which lists states and region numbers. However, because each shipping description is listed in one column, creating a one-to-one correspondence of shipping descriptions and numbers, a simpler technique is to use a **MATCH function**.

The MATCH function is designed to return the relative position (such as 1, 2, or 3) of an item in a list. Although the LOOKUP function returns a corresponding value in a list, the MATCH function returns the relative position number of the lookup_value in a list. The syntax of the MATCH function is as follows and is described in Table 5.13:

```
MATCH(lookup_value,lookup_array,match_type)
```

Table 5.13: MATCH function arguments

Argument	Description
lookup_value	The value you want to match in the list, which can be a constant value such as 4, a text value such as "Tony", the value FALSE, or a formula that returns a numerical, textual, or Boolean value
lookup_array	A one-dimensional horizontal or vertical list, which can be a range or a list of values enclosed in braces { } (also called curly brackets)
match_type	One of three match types, with 1 as the default: • Type 0 requires the function to find an exact match or display the error #N/A. • Type 1 finds a match that returns the greatest value that is less than or equal to the lookup value. • Type −1 finds a match that returns the smallest value that is greater than or equal to the lookup_value.

Keep the following guidelines in mind when you use the MATCH function:

- The MATCH function returns the relative position of an item in a list, and can be used instead of LOOKUP, VLOOKUP, or HLOOKUP when you need the position of an item in a range instead of the item itself. For example, the formula =MATCH("jones",A1:A5,0) returns a 3 if "jones" is stored in cell A3. The formula =MATCH("b",{"a","b","c"},0) returns 2, the relative position of "b" within the {"a","b","c"} list.
- The MATCH function does not distinguish between uppercase and lowercase letters when matching text values.
- If you use a match_type of 0 (exact match), you can use the asterisk (*) and question mark (?) wildcards in the lookup_value. An asterisk matches any sequence of characters, and a question mark matches any single character.

- If you use a match_type of 1, the function finds the largest value that is less than or equal to the lookup_value. With a 1 match type, the lookup_array must be sorted in ascending order.
- If you use a match_type of –1, the function finds the smallest value that is greater than or equal to the lookup_value. With a –1 match type, the lookup_array must be sorted in descending order.

In this case, Vijay wants to match the value entered in cell F5 in the Orders worksheet, the shipping method text, so this value will be the lookup_value. In the Shipping worksheet, cells B4:E4 list the shipping method text as column headings; this range constitutes the lookup_array. Vijay wants to find an exact match to the shipping method text entered in cell F5, so he will use a match_type of 0. So, Vijay can use the following expression as the column_num argument in the INDEX function:

```
MATCH(F5,Shipping!B4:E4,0)
```

For the MATCH function to work correctly, the shipping methods must be listed using the same text and in the same order in all three of the shipping tables.

Nesting this argument within the formula before proceeding, Vijay has the following:

```
=INDEX((Shipping1,Shipping2,Shipping3),VLOOKUP(F4,States,
3,FALSE),MATCH(F5,Shipping!B4:E4,0),area_num)*total weight
```

Best Practice

Using the MATCH Function
Suppose you are working with the simple table of values shown in Figure 5.44.

Figure 5.44: Sample values for the MATCH function

	A	B	C	D	E
1	0	25	50	100	1000

The following formulas show how you can use the MATCH function:

- =MATCH(32,A1:E1,1) returns the value 2 because the greatest value that does not exceed 32 is 25, which is in the second position. The values in cells A1:E1 must be in ascending order to use this match type.
- =MATCH(32,A1:E1,–1) returns the #N/A error because the lookup array is in ascending, not descending, order. If the order of the values were reversed (1000,100,50,25,0), the value 3 would be returned because the smallest value that is greater than 32 is 50, which is in the third position. The values in cells A1:E1 must be in descending order to use this match type.

- =MATCH("HELP",A1:E1,0) returns the #N/A error because the function cannot find an exact match to HELP in the list.

When using the MATCH function, carefully consider how items should be ordered in the list so that the correct values will be returned.

Determining the Area_Num of the INDEX Function Using the MATCH Function with a Nested List

To complete the INDEX function, Vijay needs to specify the area_num value, which represents the range that contains the value he wants to retrieve—area 1, 2, or 3. He has already listed the reference ranges as Shipping1, Shipping2, and Shipping3. To determine which range to use, Vijay compares the range name to the freight customer type, where Shipping1 is for regular customers, Shipping2 is for preferred customers, and Shipping3 is for most preferred customers.

In cell F6 of the Orders worksheet, users will enter regular, preferred, or most preferred as text. Because there is a one-to-one correspondence between freight customer type descriptions and freight customer type ranges, Vijay can use a MATCH function to determine the area_num, just as he used a MATCH function to determine the column_num. This time Vijay needs to list these descriptions in the appropriate order within the function, as follows:

```
MATCH(F6,{"regular","preferred","most preferred"},0)
```

To solve this expression, Excel exactly matches the value entered in cell F6 to a description in the list nested within the lookup_array argument, and then returns the position of that description in the list. When using the MATCH function with a nested list, the lookup_array must be enclosed in curly braces.

Placing this argument within the formula before proceeding, Vijay has the following:

```
=INDEX((Shipping1,Shipping2,Shipping3),VLOOKUP(F4,States,
3,FALSE),MATCH(F5,Shipping!B4:E4,0),MATCH(F6,{"regular","
preferred","most preferred"},0))*total weight
```

Creating the Complex INDEX Formula and Completing the Worksheet

Vijay has defined each argument in the INDEX function to retrieve the appropriate shipping rate. Now, he can multiply that value by the total number of pounds to create the complete formula, as follows:

```
=INDEX((Shipping1,Shipping2,Shipping3),VLOOKUP(F4,States,
3,FALSE),MATCH(F5,Shipping!B4:E4,0),MATCH(F6,{"regular","
preferred","most preferred"},0))*D16
```

The formula is described in detail in Figure 5.45.

Figure 5.45: Calculating shipping charges with a complex nested INDEX function

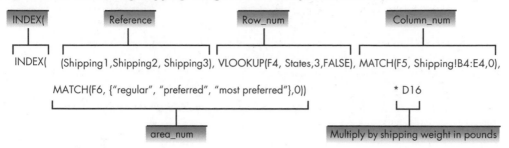

Finally, Vijay can calculate the grand total of the order by summing the discount, order amount, and shipping charge. He enters the following formula in cell F20:

```
=SUM(F16:F18)
```

Figure 5.46 shows the completed order form with sample data.

Figure 5.46: Completed order form

	A	B	C	D	E	F	G
1			TheZone Sports Equipment Order Form				
2	Customer Name:						
3							
4	Ship to State Abbreviation					CO	
5	Shipping Method (truck, rail, air, boat)					Truck	
6	Freight Customer Type (regular, preferred, most preferred)					Preferred	
7							
8	Item#	Description	Quantity	Ship Wt. (lbs.)	Unit Price	Total	
9	5	ExoRacket Graphite - Mid+, Plus Length	60	960	$ 135.00	$ 8,100.00	
10	6	ExoRacket Graphite - Mid+, Regular Length	15	225	$ 139.99	$ 2,099.85	
11	12	Touring Bag - One Size	100	1200	$ 59.99	$ 5,999.00	
12	100	Tennis Balls - Bulk	300	30	$ 2.00	$ 600.00	
13							
14							
15							
16			Total Order	2,415		$ 16,798.85	
17			Discount			$ (400.00)	
18			Shipping			$ 990.15	
19							
20			Grand Total			$ 17,389.00	
21							
22							

Completed order form with user inputs for shipping information, shipping charges calculated, and grand total

Best Practice

Creating a Testing Plan to Verify Accuracy

After you enter the final formula in a worksheet, especially one as complex as the Orders worksheet presented in this level, you should take the time to verify that the formulas result in correct values. One effective way to do so is to create an order with one set of entries, and then systematically vary each entry to test each formula and cell that contains a value.

This includes checking that the formulas you copied from one cell to a range are also displaying correct values.

You could use the following testing plan to verify the accuracy of the Orders worksheet:

1. Verify that the values retrieved for each line item—description, weight, and unit cost—have been correctly calculated for items from pricing schedules 1 and 2.
2. Verify that the total order amount in cell F16 is correct.
3. Test several total values in cell F16 to see if the discount in cell F17 is correctly updated.
4. Enter several state abbreviations in cell F4 in at least two regions to see if the shipping cost is correctly updated.
5. Enter each type of shipping method using the same freight customer type and shipping region to see if the costs are correctly updated.
6. Enter each freight customer type with the same shipping region and shipping mode.

When testing a worksheet, it's best to use round numbers for testing. For example, it's easier to verify 100 items multiplied by 16 pounds per item than 123 items multiplied by 16 pounds. It is also advisable to check values that represent category divisions, such as discounts at $5,000 and $10,000.

Steps To Success: Level 3

Vijay has been asked to develop an order form for fishing equipment. He has already created a workbook named Fishing.xlsx, which contains the worksheets described in Table 5.14.

Table 5.14: Worksheets in the Fishing workbook

Worksheet	Description
Orders	Contains an order form for fishing products.
Item List	Lists items sold by the Fishing division, including the item number, description, shipping volume in cubic feet (cf), and corresponding price schedule.
Sched1	Lists fixed unit prices ($/unit) based on item number.
Sched2	Lists variable unit prices ($/unit) for soft bait in 4 oz. packages.
Discount	Lists discounts based on the total value of an order. For example, orders under $3,000 receive no discount, and orders of at least $3,000 but less than $5,000 receive a 2% discount, as detailed on the worksheet.
Ship	Contains shipping data. Shipping costs are based on the shipping method (Truck, Rail, or Air), the shipping region, and the volume of the order. The prices given are dollars per cubic foot ($/CF). Regions vary by state. Regular customers are charged at the rates listed in the first shipping table, and rates for preferred customers are in the second shipping table.
States	Lists all the U.S. states and their corresponding region abbreviations (NE, SE, SW, etc.), and a list of corresponding region numbers.

In these steps, you will complete the order form, creating the formulas so that new items can be added easily to the item list. You'll need to design the order form on the Orders worksheet so that it works as follows:

- Prices for fixed-price items are listed in the Sched1 worksheet. Prices for variable-priced soft bait packages are listed in the Sched2 worksheet. A price schedule code (1 for fixed priced, 2 for soft bait variable priced) is included in the Item List worksheet.
- Shipping costs are based on the freight customer type, destination region, shipping method, and total shipping volume. Users enter the freight customer type text and state abbreviation. You need to use this information to retrieve the freight customer type number and region number. Calculate the shipping volume based on the volumes listed by item number in the Item List worksheet.
- Discounts are calculated as a percentage of the total order value as listed in the Discounts worksheet. For example, orders of less than $3,000 receive no discount, and orders of at least $3,000 but less than $5,000 receive a 2% discount, as detailed on the worksheet table. Orders of $25,000 or more receive a 6% discount.

As you complete the Orders worksheet, select functions that are flexible enough to allow for additional items or up to 23 pricing schedules. Use range names to make the form easy to use and troubleshoot. If the item number field is blank, be certain your form displays a blank cell for the resulting unit price and total. Test that your workbook calculates the correct values. Where appropriate, formulas should work when copied down the column or across the row. Format your values appropriately.

Complete the following:

1. Open the workbook named **Fishing.xlsx** located in the Chapter 5 folder, and then save it as **Fishing Orders.xlsx**.

2. In the Orders worksheet, use the following test data:

   - Orders: Item #213 (250 items), Item #218 (400 items), Item #201 (25 items)
   - Shipped by rail to Massachusetts to a regular customer

3. In cell B9 of the Orders worksheet, write a formula that enters the item description. Copy the formula to cells B10:B14.

4. In cell D9 of the Orders worksheet, write a formula that calculates the total volume of the first line item (quantity multiplied by volume per item). Copy the formula to cells D10:D14.

5. In cell E9 of the Orders worksheet, write a formula that calculates the unit price. Copy the formula to cells E10:E14.

6. In cell F9 of the Orders worksheet, write a formula that calculates the total value of this line item. Copy the formula to cells F10:F14.

7. In cell F16 of the Orders worksheet, write a formula that calculates the total for all items, excluding discounts and shipping.

8. In cell D16 of the Orders worksheet, write a formula that calculates the total shipping volume of this order.

9. In cell F17 of the Orders worksheet, write a formula that calculates the discount, if any, on this order.

10. In cell F18 of the Orders worksheet, write a formula that calculates the shipping costs directly from the state and ship method (Truck, Rail, or Air).

   TROUBLESHOOTING: In order to complete this step so that the cost of shipping automatically updates correctly based on the shipping parameters, you should calculate the value manually for several different options and compare it against the resulting values on your worksheet. Using range names will help simplify the formulas. If incorrect values result, break down the formula, argument by argument to determine where the discrepancies can be found.

11. In cell F20 of the Orders worksheet, write a formula that calculates the grand total of this order.

12. Double-check your formulas to be certain that different test data produces valid results.

13. Save and close the Fishing Orders.xlsx workbook.

Chapter Summary

In this chapter, you learned how using the Excel Reference and Lookup functions VLOOKUP, HLOOKUP, LOOKUP, INDEX, CHOOSE, and MATCH can transform a multistep task that required users to enter many values more than once into a well-designed worksheet in which users enter only a few items to perform sophisticated calculations.

When you organize data in a vertical lookup table, the most effective and flexible way to retrieve the data is to use the VLOOKUP function. Use VLOOKUP when the first column of the lookup table contains the key data, and the information you want to retrieve is in one of the columns to the right of the key data column. HLOOKUP works in a similar way, except that it retrieves data stored in horizontal lookup tables. Use HLOOKUP when the first row of the lookup table contains the key data, and the information you want to retrieve is in a row below the key data row. Unlike VLOOKUP and HLOOKUP, the LOOKUP function looks up the greatest value that does not exceed a specified value anywhere in a table or range. It can retrieve data from a lookup table with a vertical or horizontal orientation.

To solve more complex problems, such as those involving multiple worksheets, you can nest the Reference and Lookup functions using the IF, IS, INDEX, CHOOSE, and

MATCH functions. The ISBLANK function is one of the nine IS functions, which all check for a condition and then return a TRUE or FALSE value. ISBLANK checks whether a specified value refers to an empty cell. Use the INDEX function to return the value in a table based on the row and column numbers that you specify. Use the CHOOSE function to return a value or a range for up to 254 corresponding values. The MATCH function returns the relative position (such as 1, 2, or 3) of an item in a list.

Completing complex tasks that require several levels of lookups, as demonstrated in Level 3, might indicate that you should use a tool other than Excel. Relational databases such as Microsoft Access are designed to handle large quantities of information, especially those that involve multiple sets of related data. However, Excel does provide the capability to complete such tasks through the use of more complex formulas containing multiple nested functions.

Conceptual Review

Answer Questions 1–10 as True or False.

1. _____ The lookup_value of a VLOOKUP function can be a contiguous cell range.

2. _____ In a VLOOKUP formula with a TRUE lookup type, the first column of the lookup table referenced must be in ascending order to retrieve the correct value.

3. _____ The result_vector of a LOOKUP function must be sorted in ascending order.

4. _____ Reference and Lookup functions may not contain nested functions as arguments.

5. _____ The default range_lookup type for the VLOOKUP and HLOOKUP functions is FALSE.

6. _____ Excel matches the lookup_value "tom" with the entry "TOM" in a lookup table.

7. _____ The row and column arguments in the INDEX function can be numeric values, Boolean values, or text.

8. _____ The formula =INDEX((B2:D7,B12:D17,B22:D17),2,3,2) returns the value in cell D13.

9. _____ The formula =AVERAGE(CHOOSE(1,B12:D17,B22:D17)) averages the value 1 with the values in cells B12 to D17 and B22 to D17.

10. _____ The formula =MATCH(40,{10,40,50,90},0) returns the value 2.

Answer the following questions.

11. What happens when Excel is solving a VLOOKUP formula with a FALSE range_lookup type and does not find an exact match in the lookup table?

12. What is the difference between the LOOKUP function and the VLOOKUP or HLOOKUP function?

13. Which Excel function should you use when you want to look up a value from a two-dimensional table, where both the columns and rows can be varied?

14. Write a formula to choose the name of the fifth day of the week from the list starting with Sunday, Monday, Tuesday...Saturday.

15. What is the difference between the LOOKUP function and the MATCH function?

Base your answers for Questions 16–18 on the Pricing and Delivery worksheets shown here. Cells Pricing!A1:B7 list the costs per copy based on the total number of copies being made. The price for less than 10 copies corresponds to $0.07 per copy, the price for at least 10 copies but less than 100 copies corresponds to $0.06 per copy, etc.

	A	B	C	D
1	Number of copies	Price per copy		
2	1	0.07		
3	10	0.06		
4	100	0.05		
5	200	0.04		
6	500	0.03		
7	1000	0.02		
8				
9				
10				
11	Copies made:	Total cost:	Delivery cost	
12				
13	3			
14	10			
15	200			
16	1001			
17				

Pricing worksheet

	A	B	C	D	E
1			Delivery charges		
2					
3					
4					
5					
6					
7					
8					
9					
10					
11					
12					
13					
14					
15					
16					
17					

Delivery worksheet

16. Write a formula in cell B13 in the Pricing worksheet to determine the total cost of making copies for this order (3 copies). Write the formula so that it works when copied into cells B14:B16.

17. The delivery charges used in the Delivery worksheet are as follows:

- For orders under $20, there is a $5 delivery fee.
- For orders at least $20 but less than $50, there is an $8 delivery fee.
- For orders over $50, delivery is free of charge.

Create a lookup table for the Delivery worksheet so that you can use a lookup function to calculate the delivery cost for each order. Organize the table in a horizontal format, as shown here:

	A	B	C	D
1		Delivery charges		
2				
3				
4				

18. Write a formula in cell C13 in the Pricing worksheet to look up the correct delivery cost using the lookup table you created in Question 17. Write the formula so that it can be copied down the column.

Base your answers for Questions 19–20 on the Scores and Grades worksheets shown here.

	A	B	C	D
1	Name	Score	Final Grade	
2	Mary	930		
3	Davide	450		
4	Tang	880		
5	Bindu	750		
6	Thomas	320		
7	Rebecca	850		
8	Mallory	970		
9				
10				

Scores worksheet

	A	B	C	D	E	F
1	900	800	700	600	0	
2	A	B	C	D	F	
3						
4						
5	0	600	700	800	900	
6	F	D	C	B	A	
7						
8						
9						
10						

Grades worksheet

19. As shown in the Grades worksheet, final grades are determined using the following grading scheme:

- Students earning over 900 points receive an A.
- Students earning less than 900 points but at least 800 points receive a B.
- Students earning less than 800 points but at least 700 points receive a C.
- Students earning less than 700 points but at least 600 points receive a D.
- Students earning less than 600 points receive an F.

Write a formula in cell C2 in the Scores worksheet that determines the final grade for the first student based on the grading scheme. Use the appropriate Reference and Lookup function and write the formula so that it can be copied down the column.

20. Explain the difference between the lookup table in cells A1:E2 of the Grades worksheet and the lookup table in cells A5:E6 in the same worksheet.

Case Problems

Level 1 – Evaluating Tax Rates for the Takoma Group

Note: The information in this Case Problem does not reflect any actual tax rates, tax rate calculation methodologies, or IRS policies, and should not be constituted as tax advice.

Accounting

The Takoma Group is a "think tank" in Washington, D.C., that provides research data to lobbyists and members of the federal government. As a tax analyst for the Takoma Group, your job is to report how tax policies affect federal, state, and local revenues. A lobbyist asks you to study how alternate flat tax rate proposals could affect the total taxes owed and residual amount of taxes owed on April 15, based on a list of sample individual tax return information. A flat tax rate is a rate applied to the total income earned. For example, a flat tax rate of 10% on $20,000 in income is $2,000. The current graduated system applies different percentages to ranges of income for each taxpayer. For example, a graduated tax on a $20,000 income might be as follows: 0% of the first $5,000, 10% of the amounts between $5,001 and $10,000, and 15% of the amounts over $10,000.

A worksheet in an Excel workbook named Takoma.xlsx has been set up listing sample tax return data and the actual amount of taxes owed based on the current tax rates (column F). The worksheet also includes schedules for the proposed flat tax rates, penalties, and state allowances.

To complete this study, your task is to analyze the total taxes owed based on two new flat-rate tax alternatives. In addition, you will compare the residual amount owed and penalties applied to that residual amount for each alternative. The residual amount owed on April 15 is calculated as follows: total tax owed minus the sum of the actual withholding taxes paid and the estimated taxes paid.

Withholding taxes are those amounts withheld from an employee's paycheck each pay period and remitted to the IRS by the employer. Estimated taxes are direct tax payments made by taxpayers to the IRS each quarter. Depending on the amount owed, penalties might be applied to the residual amount owed. Complete the following:

1. Open the workbook named **Takoma.xlsx** located in the Chapter 5 folder, and then save it as **Takoma Tax Analysis.xlsx**.

2. In cell G12, write a formula that uses the Alternate 1 flat tax rate to determine the total dollar value of the tax for the income in cell B12. As detailed in the Flat Tax Rate table (cells A1:F4), this tax scheme calculates taxes by multiplying the total income by the corresponding rate. For example, incomes below $25,000 pay no tax; incomes of at least $25,000 but less than $42,000 pay 4.5% of the income in taxes; incomes of at least $42,000 but less than $72,000 pay 12.5% of the income in taxes;

and incomes of $129,500 or more pay a 28% tax rate. Write the formula so that it can be copied down the column, and then copy it to cells G13:G21.

3. In cell H12, write a formula that uses the Alternative 2 flat tax rate to determine the total dollar value of the tax for the income in cell B12. As detailed in the Flat Tax Rate table (cells A1:F4), this tax scheme also calculates taxes by multiplying the total income by the corresponding rate. For example, incomes below $25,000 pay no tax; incomes of at least $25,000 but less than $42,000 pay 5% of the income in taxes; incomes of at least $42,000 but less than $72,000 pay 9% of the income in taxes; and incomes of $129,500 or more pay a 25% tax rate. Write the formula so that it can be copied down the column, and then copy it to cells H13:H21.

4. In cell I12, write a formula that calculates the amount of unpaid taxes the first taxpayer still owes on April 15. The unpaid taxes are based on the actual amount of taxes owed, the actual withholding taxes paid, and estimated taxes paid. Write the formula so that it can be copied down the column to calculate this amount for each taxpayer. Also, write the formula so that it can be copied across the row to determine the unpaid amount based on the taxes owed for the Alternative 1 and Alternative 2 flat tax calculations. (*Hint:* Assume the same withholding and estimated taxes paid.) Copy the formula to cells I13:I21 and to cells J12:K21.

5. In cell L12, write a formula that determines the actual penalty owed based on the penalty schedule. For example, unpaid tax balances of less than $100 owe no penalty, and unpaid tax balances of at least $100 but less than $1,000 are charged a penalty of 5% of the unpaid tax amount. The range H3:I8 is named Penalty. (*Hint:* Use an IF function to determine if the unpaid tax amount is negative, indicating that the IRS owes the taxpayer a refund and, therefore, no penalties apply.) Copy this formula both down the column to calculate the penalty for the corresponding ID# and across the row to determine the penalties based on each alternative tax scheme.

6. In row 23, calculate the total values for each category (F23:N23) for all 10 tax returns.

7. As part of the flat-rate tax, one possible scheme would include a state allowance to balance the high and low cost of living. The amount of the allowance is listed by state in cells A7:B9. If the list does not contain the appropriate state, the error message #N/A should be displayed. In cell O12, write a formula that determines the state allowance for this taxpayer. Write the formula so that it can be copied down the column, and then copy it to cells O13:O21.

8. Highlight in pink the column of the tax scheme that is most favorable to very high-income taxpayers (Actual, Alternative 1, or Alternative 2).

9. Format the worksheet to make it easy to read and understand.

10. Save and close the Takoma Tax Analysis.xlsx workbook.

Level 2 – Calculating Travel Costs at America Travels

Sales

As a new sales associate at America Travels travel agency, you assist travel agents in finding the best fares for corporate customers. As a high-volume travel agency, America Travels has negotiated several premium discounts with airlines, which you pass along to your customers who do a large amount of business with you. Compared to standard business fares, these discounts can amount to a substantial savings and do not have minimum stay requirements.

Texto, Inc. is a significant customer with a travel department that prices its own fares online, and then contacts America Travels to see if it can provide a better rate. Texto e-mails an Excel workbook containing a list of proposed trips to America Travels each day by 10 a.m., and requests price quotes for these trips by noon. Texto has corporate offices in New York, San Francisco, and London, which is where most of its travel originates. When the Texto workbook arrives, America Travels sales associates must work hard to enter the information that Texto requests and return the workbook to the company on time.

For several months, America Travels has been working on a more automated method of replying to these inquiries. Another sales associate compiled fare data by flight number and researched airport fees. This information has been set up on separate worksheets in an Excel workbook. Your task is to complete the last piece of the project, which is to use the information on the customer's fare request sheet and automatically calculate the best fares. For this project, assume that all flight numbers are included on the flights list.

The following worksheets have already been created in an Excel workbook named Texto.xlsx:

- **Requests**—This worksheet contains a sample request form from Texto, including the date, traveler's name, flight number, and corporate-rate fare.
- **Flights**—This worksheet contains a list of flights sorted by flight number and the associated departure city, arrival city, and base fare.
- **Fees**—This worksheet contains a table listing fare categories and airport fees associated with specific ticket price categories. These airport fees will be added to the price of each ticket. For example, fares of less than $200.00 fall into fare category 1 and have a $15 airport fee, and fares from $200.00 to $299.99 also fall into fare category 1 but have a $25 airport fee.
- **Discounts**—This worksheet contains a two-dimensional table of discount categories based on the fare category and the weekday of the ticket.

Your task is to include formulas in the Requests worksheet to provide fare information. All formulas must work when copied down the column to determine the requested information for each travel request. Complete the following:

1. Open the workbook named **Texto.xlsx** located in the Chapter 5 folder, and then save it as **Texto Travel Quotes.xlsx**.

2. In cell E3 of the Requests worksheet, write a formula that retrieves the name of the departure city for this flight. Copy the formula to cells E4:E6.

3. In cell F3, write a formula that retrieves the name of the arrival city for this flight. Copy the formula to cells F4:F6.

4. In cell G3, write a formula that retrieves the base fare for this flight based on the data given on the Flights worksheet. Copy the formula to cells G4:G6.

5. In cell H3, write a formula that determines the day of the week (1 through 7) of this flight using the WEEKDAY(*date*) function. The WEEKDAY function returns 1 for Sunday, 2 for Monday, and so on. (Refer to the Microsoft Excel Help feature for more details on using the WEEKDAY function.) Copy this formula to cells H4:H6.

6. Airline tickets are assigned a fare category based on the base fare ticket price (column G) and the categories listed on the Fees worksheet. In cell I3, write a formula that determines the fare category for this ticket. Copy the formula to cells I4:I6.

7. The Discounts worksheet contains a two-dimensional table that has been set up to find the discount category of a ticket based on the weekday of travel and the fare category. In cell J3, write a formula that determines the discount category for this ticket. Copy the formula to cells J4:J6.

8. In a separate area of the Discounts worksheet, create a horizontal lookup table based on the following discount information:

- Fare discount category AA: 0% discount of the published base fare
- Fare discount category X: 25% discount of the published base fare
- Fare discount category Y: 50% discount of the published base fare
- Fare discount category Z: 65% discount of the published base fare

9. In cell K3 of the Requests worksheet, write a formula that determines the discounted fare price (base fare minus discount) of this flight using the table you created in the Discounts worksheet. Fares should be rounded to the nearest dollar. (*Hint*: Do not use an IF function.) Copy this formula to cells K4:K6.

10. In cell L3, calculate the airport fee based on the fee schedule in the Fees worksheet. Note that the airport fee is based on the discounted fare. Copy this formula to cells L4:L6.

11. In cell M3, calculate the total ticket price that America Travels can obtain (discounted fare plus airport fees). Copy this formula to cells M4:M6.

12. In cell N3, compare the America Travels total ticket price to the corporate fare that Texto found. Return a TRUE value if the America Travels price is less than the corporate fare Texto was offered. Copy this formula to cells N4:N6.

13. Format your worksheet so that it is easy to read and understand.

14. Save and close the Texto Travel Quotes.xlsx workbook.

Level 3 – Creating a Cost Estimate Form for CKG Auto

Sales

As part of its product line, CKG Auto has nine basic models, each with different options and features. Although many car buyers are concerned about the initial cost of a car, customers are also becoming increasingly concerned about the yearly operating expenses they can expect. They frequently want to compare two or more purchase options to see how much a car costs to run each year. Although they might be willing to spend an extra $5,000 to purchase a sports utility vehicle or luxury car with many options, customers might reconsider when they calculate the annual cost of gas and insurance.

Fuel economy information posted on each car's window is usually stated within a range of 5 to 10 miles per gallon. For example, CKG Auto's compact car, the Pony, lists 29–34 miles per gallon in the city and 33–39 miles per gallon on the highway. This and other car sticker information is difficult to translate into annual costs for gasoline, maintenance, insurance, and other operating costs. Many CKG Auto dealerships have asked for an easy way to provide operating cost information to their customers, much the same way they can give them base car costs and option prices.

To this end, CKG Auto has decided to develop an Excel workbook that can calculate costs associated with the first three years of operating a new car, including gas expenses, maintenance, and insurance premiums. Although these costs are estimates, they will give customers a good understanding of what to expect.

Your task is to work with the **Costs.xlsx** workbook, which is located in the Chapter 5 folder, saving the workbook as **CKG Operating Costs.xlsx**, and developing a worksheet named **Estimate Form** that salespeople can complete to help their customers calculate annual operating costs for a selected vehicle. CKG Auto completed a preliminary analysis summarizing the data required from the salespeople, the information needed for the calculations, and the desired data outputs. The estimate form should compare the operating costs of the selected vehicles. When this form is complete, it should display the data inputs and outputs, and provide space to compare up to five vehicles. If less than five vehicles are listed, blank cells should be displayed in lieu of error messages.

Customer Information – Input on Estimate Form

Users should enter the following data about the customer and use the test customer profile for purposes of calculations:

- Expected number of driving miles per year
- Type of driving: Highway (speeds of 55 mph and over), Mixed (balance of highway and city driving), or City (speeds of 45 mph and below)
- State of residence
- Residential status: City, Suburban, or Rural
- Driving safety record: Excellent, Average, or Poor
- Gas price adjustment percentage, which is a multiplier that accounts for major changes in gas prices; to calculate this multiplier, take the gas price at your local gas station for regular grade gas and divide by 3

Test Customer Profile

- Expected number of driving miles per year: 25,000
- Type of driving: Mixed
- Purchaser's state: IL
- Purchaser's residential status: Suburban
- Purchaser's driving safety record: Average
- Gas price adjustment percentage: Calculate this by dividing the current gas price in your neighborhood by 3.0

Vehicle Inputs – Input on Estimate Form

In the Estimate Form worksheet, users should enter the following data about each vehicle (design the worksheet for up to five vehicles):

- Vehicle model number
- Engine: number of cylinders (4, 6, 8, or turbo)

Test Vehicles Profile

- Model 1: 4 cylinders
- Model 4: 6 cylinders
- Model 5: 8 cylinders
- Model 7: turbo

Data Tables Provided in Costs.xlsx Workbook

Data for car models, mileage, regions, gas pricing, and insurance that will be required to obtain the necessary output is available in the Costs.xlsx workbook on the following worksheets. Use this data to create appropriate named ranges that can be used on your form:

5

Chapter Exercises

- **Models**—This worksheet lists available car models including description, available engines, weight class, and expected maintenance base costs for the first three years (excluding oil changes). For some models these maintenance costs are zero, reflecting dealer incentives to buyers that include free maintenance over a specified period. Also included is the number of recommended miles per oil change and the cost per oil change.
- **Mileage**—This worksheet includes the gas mileage schedules for each driving usage type. Each schedule lists the gas mileage in miles per gallon based on the weight class and engine.
- **States**—This worksheet lists states and their associated regions.
- **Gas Prices**—This worksheet includes regional average gas prices based on $3 per gallon in the Northeast. This value should be adjusted based on the multiplier supplied as part of the user inputs (current gas price/$3). This assumes prices change proportionally throughout the country. A multiplier of greater than 1 increases the price, and a multiplier of less than 1 reduces the price. The estimated $/gallon is equal to the $/gallon from the Gas Prices table (which varies by region) times this multiplier.
- **Insurance**—This worksheet lists regional insurance rate estimates for new cars. These base prices can then be adjusted based on driver safety records and residential status.

Estimate Form Outputs

The Estimate Form worksheet should include the following outputs (for each car model) for up to five selected cars:

- Car make and description based on model number input
- Estimated annual cost of gas based on the selected type of driving, weight class, annual miles traveled, gas price, and engine type
- Estimated annual insurance premium based on the owner's region of residence, driving record, and residential status (*Hint*: Include an intermediate calculation in the form that looks up the region number associated with the state of residence, and then refer to the cell that contains this result in the insurance formula.)
- Estimated average annual maintenance cost for the first three years of operation, based on the selected car model and annual miles traveled (total 3-year maintenance costs divided by 3 plus the cost of 1 year of oil changes); to the base maintenance cost, add $29 per oil change for each 5,000 miles driven
- Estimated total cost of operation per year

Make sure the formulas you enter can be copied to other cells in the same column as needed for each model selected. Your formulas should also be flexible enough to easily accommodate anticipated changes to this data. The form should work without displaying error messages where there are no models. For example, if the model number is blank, the formulas should leave the description field blank. Use named ranges to simplify your formulas.

You can create intermediate calculations and/or additional worksheets, as needed, to develop this form. Be certain your Estimate Form is easy to read and use. Highlight the data inputs so the user can easily recognize what is needed to complete the form. Be sure to test your data to verify that the Estimate Form works for different combinations of buyer profiles and cars.

(*Hint*: Some of the formulas may require several levels of nesting and/or complex function arguments. It is strongly recommended that you create additional intermediate calculations for values you might use over and over again, or to obtain values that might help simplify longer calculations.)

Save and close the CKG Operating Costs.xlsx workbook.

SAM: Skills Assessment Manager

For current SAM information, including versions and content details, visit SAM Central (http://samcentral.course.com). If you have a SAM user profile, you may have access to hands-on instruction, practice, and assessment of the skills covered in this chapter. Since various versions of SAM are supported throughout the life of this text, check with your instructor for the correct instructions and URL/Web site for accessing assignments.

Evaluating the Financial Impact of Loans and Investments
Finance: Forecasting Cash Flows for a Capital Project Analysis

"To succeed in business, to reach the top, an individual must know all it is possible to know about that business."
—J. Paul Getty

LEARNING OBJECTIVES

Level 1

Understand how simple interest and compound interest are calculated
Determine the value of a loan payment
Analyze positive and negative cash flows
Determine the future value and the present value of a financial transaction
Determine the interest rate and the number of periods of a financial transaction

Level 2

Set up an amortization table to evaluate a loan
Calculate principal and interest payments
Calculate cumulative principal and interest payments
Set up named ranges for a list
Calculate depreciation and taxes

Level 3

Set up a worksheet to analyze profitability
Calculate the net present value
Calculate the internal rate of return
Calculate the return on investment
Determine the payback period

FUNCTIONS COVERED IN THIS CHAPTER

CUMIPMT	IRR	PMT	SLN
CUMPRINC	ISNUMBER	PPMT	
FV	NPER	PV	
IPMT	NPV	RATE	

Chapter Introduction

Business decisions are often greatly influenced by financial considerations, such as how much something will cost and how funding will be obtained. Money is usually not the only component in a business decision; companies must also consider long-term market ramifications, jobs, environmental and social issues, or even technical feasibility. However, ultimately, when financing a corporate project or determining where to best invest funds, the issues of money, return on investment, rate of return, and so on are central to the decision-making process.

As you will see in this chapter, keeping track of loans and investments requires more than simply multiplying the payments made or interest earned over a period of time. Level 1 explores some fundamental financial calculations to evaluate different financing options. In Level 2, these basic concepts are expanded upon to develop an amortization table—a listing by period of the cash inflows and outflows. You also will learn about Excel tools for calculating depreciation, a technique used to allocate the costs of an asset over its useful life. Finally, in Level 3, you will explore the ramifications of these cash flows, using a variety of tools to analyze the financial viability of a project.

6

Case Scenario

As you recall, TheZone is planning to bring to market a new athletic shoe called TZEdge. Previously, the project team's financial analyst compiled a list of labor and material costs to manufacture these shoes, and formulated an initial budget, including overhead and selling expenses. One critical element that remains to be analyzed is the capital investment required to manufacture the TZEdge shoe. This capital investment is the money needed to purchase and install the manufacturing equipment necessary to produce the shoe.

Finance

Because the cost of this equipment will ultimately affect the profitability of the venture, TheZone needs to quantify the costs and determine how funds will be obtained before making a final decision to proceed with this project. Approximately $1 million will be needed to purchase and install the equipment to manufacture TZEdge shoes. These funds include modifications to an existing manufacturing facility, the required electrical upgrades, and the costs to purchase and install new state-of-the-art automated cutting and sewing machines.

Ryan Whittier, an analyst in the finance group, must use this information to explore a variety of funding options and to generate cash flow projections. Ultimately, he will use this data to compile the financial information needed by management—information that will be a critical piece in the decision-making process of whether to fund this project.

LEVEL 1
Calculating Values for Simple Financial Transactions

Understanding How Interest Is Calculated

When you borrow money from a bank to make a purchase, for example, to buy a car, you must pay back the amount borrowed plus an additional amount known as **interest**. This interest is like a user fee, because you are paying to "use" the bank's money. The amount of interest charged by the lender depends on many variables, including the following:

- **How long do you want to borrow the money?** In general, having $1 in hand today is preferable to having $1 in hand three years from now. When borrowing money, you need to consider the cost to you for borrowing it. How much would you be willing to pay back in the future in order to have $10,000 today, for example? This concept is often referred to as the "time value of money."
- **What level of risk is the lender assuming in lending the money?** Although a bank might be quite willing to lend a home buyer with an excellent credit rating the necessary amount to purchase a house, the same bank would probably be much less willing to lend a large sum of money to a new business owner for investing in an unproven product or service.
- **What are the current monetary policies and levels of supply and demand to borrow versus lend money?** An investment might be of short duration and very sound, but few lending institutions might be willing to lend money while many are seeking to borrow. Often, the fiscal policy of the Federal Reserve Bank or other monetary policies set by governmental agencies directly affect the supply and demand for funds and, ultimately, the interest rate.

These are just some of the factors that can affect the interest to be paid on an investment or charged to borrow funds. Interest is usually calculated as a percentage of the principal for a specified period of time. The **principal** is the value of the loan or investment. Interest can be accounted for in two ways: simple interest or compound interest.

Calculating Simple Interest

Interest that is paid solely on the amount of the original principal value is called **simple interest**. The computation of simple interest is based on the following formula:

```
Simple interest = Principal * Interest rate per time period *
                  Number of time periods
```

Consider the following example: You have deposited $10,000 in a two-year certificate of deposit (CD) that pays simple interest of 4% per year for a period of two years. At the end of the two years, your $10,000 plus the interest owed to you will be returned. How much interest will be owed to you at the end of two years?

```
Year 1: $10,000 [principal] * .04 [interest rate] = $400
Year 2: $10,000 [principal] * .04 [interest rate] = $400
          Total interest at the end of two years = $800
```

In this example, the principal is $10,000 and the interest is applied yearly at the rate of 4% for a total of two years. This can be represented mathematically as the formula =$10,000*.04*2. Notice that the principal never changes, and the additional $400 of interest earned in year 1 plays no role in the calculation of interest in year 2.

Calculating Compound Interest

Most often in financial transactions, you want to take into account the interest paid in the previous period. In the example of the CD, the value of the CD increases each year by the amount of the previous interest paid. How would this affect the total interest paid if the CD earned interest on this additional amount each period?

Adding interest earned each period to the principal for purposes of computing interest for the next period is known as **compound interest**. As you will see from the examples that follow, the total value of interest payments using compound interest is greater than those using simple interest at the same percentage. Most financial instruments use compound interest; these include bank accounts, CDs, loans, and so on. Using the previous example, consider how much money you will have at the end of the two years, but this time assume that the interest (4%) will be earned on the interest accrued in the previous periods.

```
Year 1: $10,000 [principal] * .04 [interest rate] = $400
Year 2: $10,400 [principal of $10,000 + accrued
           interest of $400] * .04 [interest rate] = $416
             Total interest at the end of two years = $816
```

Notice that the principal changes in the second year to include the interest paid in the previous year. After two years, an additional $16 will be earned with compound interest as compared to simple interest.

Consider another example: Assume you have deposited $10,000 in a credit union, which pays interest at 4% per year *compounded quarterly*. Here, interest is added to the principal each quarter. To determine the amount of money you will have at the end of one year (four quarters), you would calculate the interest as follows:

```
1st Qtr: $10,000 [principal] * .04/4 [interest rate] = $100.00
  2nd Qtr: $10,100 [principal of $10,000 + accrued
           interest of $100] * .04/4 [interest rate] = $101.00
```

```
    3rd Qtr: $10,201 [principal of $10,100 + accrued
         interest of $101) * .04/4 [interest rate] = $102.01
4th Qtr: $10,303.01 [principal of $10,201 + accrued
      interest of $102.01) * .04/4 [interest rate] = $103.03
                Total interest at the end of one year = $406.04
```

Notice that if the annual interest is 4%, the quarterly interest is 4% divided by 4 quarters per year, or 1% per quarter. The total interest paid at the end of one year is $406.04. This amount results in $6.04 more interest paid than if this same interest rate was applied only once in the year.

Financial institutions often use the term **annual percentage yield** (**APY**). This is the equivalent of a yearly simple interest rate, taking into account compounding. In the previous example, the interest rate was 4% per year compounded quarterly. The APY would be 4.0604% because, at the end of the first four quarters, a total of $406.04 would have been paid out on the initial deposit of $10,000. Often, financial institutions advertise their loan interest rates in what is referred to as an **annual percentage rate** (**APR**). This rate reflects the interest being paid on the actual amount borrowed. Because loans often have fees associated with them, the actual amount borrowed is the face value of the loan minus any fees charged. For example, if a $100,000 mortgage requires a $1,000 application fee, the amount borrowed would actually be $99,000 because the borrower had to pay $1,000 to obtain the mortgage. However, the borrower still must pay back the entire mortgage amount of $100,000. This effectively makes the interest rate higher than the stated interest rate. APRs can often be problematic because different banks calculate the APR in various ways, including or excluding certain fees. You can use the Excel tools presented in this chapter to better understand and compare these types of financial transactions.

Although the method presented in this section for calculating compound interest is effective, it is certainly not efficient, requiring multiple steps of multiplying and adding values. Consider that for a 30-year mortgage compounded monthly, you would need to perform this calculation 360 times (30 *12 periods)! Fortunately, Excel provides a wide variety of financial functions that perform these steps automatically.

Reviewing Alternative Financing Options

The first task Ryan faces is to analyze several possible financing options for the TZEdge shoe project. The options being considered by TheZone to raise funds for this project are as follows:

(1) Funding the entire project using a line of credit from CtrBank. CtrBank currently charges a fixed rate of 8% annual interest compounded quarterly. For this type of project, payments are scheduled quarterly over a five-year period.

(2) Funding the project by cashing in a money market account that was set up as an emergency fund. The fund started with an initial deposit of $900,000 and paid 3.5% annual interest compounded monthly. The account was originally set up two years ago.

(3) Funding the project from an initial investment and current profits. This option requires the project to be delayed by one and a half years, investing a portion of TheZone's expected profits ($50,000 per month each month), plus an initial cash outlay to be determined. A money market account will be used to hold these funds. The current money market rates pay 4% annual interest compounded monthly.

(4) Funding the entire project through NWN Bank, an institution that has not previously done business with TheZone. In an effort to win TheZone's business, NWN Bank is offering several different options for funding, as follows:

(a) A loan to be paid back over the next four years, with equal semiannual payments (compounded semiannually) of $150,000

(b) A loan with a fixed interest rate of 6.5% per year compounded quarterly, and fixed quarterly payments of $95,000

Each of the options being considered involves applying compound interest over a specific time period and a constant rate of interest. However, not all of the variables have been identified. Ryan needs to examine each financing method and calculate any of the missing pieces of data. In some cases, this will require determining the periodic payments; in others, the specified loan duration; and in still others, the value of an existing financial asset. Using the manual, step-by-step method of calculating compound interest over multiple periods would be a long and tedious process. Consequently, Ryan will use some of the financial functions that are built into Excel.

Using the PMT Function to Determine a Loan Payment

Recall that the first financing option under consideration is to fund the entire project using a line of credit from CtrBank.

What is known about this financial transaction? Ryan knows that $1 million will be given to TheZone when the loan is initiated. In exchange, for each quarter for the next five years, TheZone will pay back an unspecified amount of money—paying back both the accrued interest and a portion of the principal each period. Because the loan is compounded quarterly, interest will be calculated each quarter based on the remaining principal. The rate per period (quarter) is the annual rate (8% currently being charged by CtrBank) divided by the number of periods per year (4); in this case, 2% per quarter. At the end of the loan duration (five years), the original loan amount and all of the accrued interest will be completely paid off. A timeline of this transaction is shown in Figure 6.1.

Figure 6.1: Timeline of the financial transaction for a $1 million loan

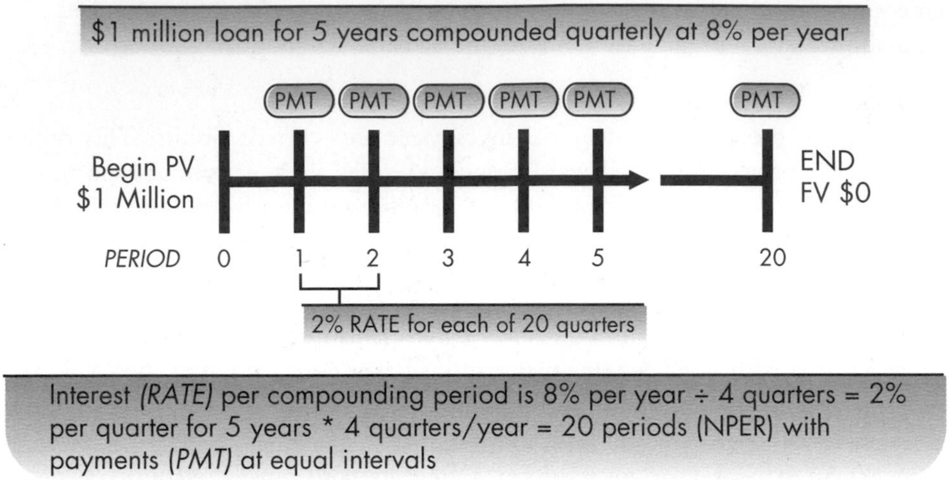

$1 million loan for 5 years compounded quarterly at 8% per year

Interest (RATE) per compounding period is 8% per year ÷ 4 quarters = 2% per quarter for 5 years * 4 quarters/year = 20 periods (NPER) with payments (PMT) at equal intervals

A critical element of this transaction is the unknown quarterly payment. This cannot be calculated by simply dividing $1,000,000 by 20 total quarters because interest will be charged in each quarter based on the remaining principal. Furthermore, in each quarter, the remaining principal will be reduced based on the value of this payment less the accrued interest. To determine the quarterly payment, Ryan will use the **PMT function**. The PMT function finds the value of the payment per period, assuming that there are constant payments and a constant interest rate for the duration of the loan. The syntax of the PMT function is as follows:

$$\texttt{PMT(rate,nper,pv,fv,type)}$$

As with any Excel function, to use the PMT function, you need to supply the correct values for each argument and adhere to any specified rules. The five arguments of the PMT function are defined as follows:

- The *rate* argument is the interest rate per compounding period.
- The *nper* argument is the number of compounding periods.
- The *pv* argument is the present value, also referred to as the original principal value at the beginning of the financial transaction.
- The *fv* argument is the future value (compounded amount), also referred to as the value at the end of the financial transaction.
- The *type* argument designates when payments are made. Type 0, the default type, indicates that payments are made at the end of the period. Type 1 indicates that payments are made at the beginning of the period.

The Help system in Excel provides more detail on how the PMT function and its arguments work.

Understanding Cash Flow (Inputs and Outputs)

The fv and pv arguments, as well as the result of the PMT function, are all cash amounts that are either received or paid out during the course of the financial transaction. These inputs and outputs are often referred to as **cash flow**. For the PMT function to work properly, it must recognize which amounts are flowing to the borrower and which amounts the borrower is paying out. The convention used here is that when cash is *received* it is considered **positive cash flow**, and when cash is *paid out* it is considered **negative cash flow**. These concepts of cash received and cash paid out do not necessarily correspond to who owns the money, but rather reflect where the money is physically going, as illustrated in Figure 6.2.

Figure 6.2: Positive and negative cash flows

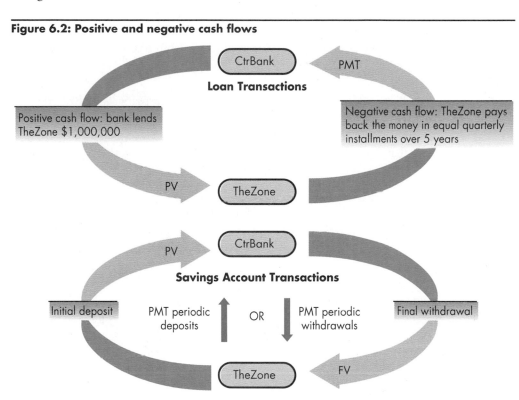

In the loan diagram in the top section of Figure 6.2, the present value (pv) is a positive cash flow from the bank to TheZone. The company can subsequently take this loan to buy the new equipment needed to make shoes. Because the bank has given the money to the company, it is a positive cash flow for TheZone. Each of TheZone's payments back to the bank is a negative cash flow from the company to the bank.

The savings account transaction diagram in the bottom section of Figure 6.2 shows an initial deposit, which is a negative present value (pv) reflecting a transfer of funds to the bank from the company. This deposit is, therefore, a negative cash flow. This diagram also shows a final withdrawal, which is a positive future value (fv) reflecting a transfer of funds back to the company from the bank. Periodic deposits can be made into the account (negative cash flow), or withdrawals can be taken from the account (positive cash flow) as determined by the PMT function.

Specifying Consistent Units of Time

It is also necessary when using Excel financial functions to pay close attention to the compounding period being used. The financial functions apply the *interest rate per period* and the *payment per period* to the principal value over a *specified number of periods*. It does not matter if the compounding period is months, days, quarters, and so on; the function simply applies the appropriate rate and payments the specified number of times. If the rate and nper arguments, and the results of the PMT function, are not all consistent or do not reflect the compounding period, the wrong values will be calculated. As noted previously, $10,000 compounded one time at 4% per period is different from $10,000 compounded four times at 1% per period; the latter resulted in a higher value.

In the original loan being offered by CtrBank, the interest rate per year is 8% over a period of five years. Because the compounding period is quarterly, a rate of 2% per quarter (8% per year / 4 quarters per year) is applied over 20 separate periods (5 years * 4 quarters per year). The value that Ryan is calculating with the PMT function is the payment per quarter.

Determining the Value of the Loan Payment

To calculate the payment per quarter, Ryan can substitute the appropriate values for each of the arguments of the PMT function in an Excel worksheet. This formula is detailed in Figure 6.3.

Figure 6.3: Applying the PMT function

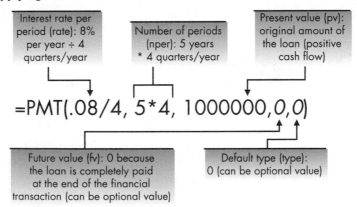

When writing formulas using financial functions, consider the following:

- Commas cannot be used when typing in the value for one million. A comma is interpreted as the beginning of a new argument: =PMT(.08/4,5*4,1,000,000) is interpreted as having a pv of 1.
- To make things simple and clear, the argument values can be nested formulas. For example, the rate per period in this transaction is 2%, but this value is not explicitly stated. Instead of calculating this value elsewhere, nest the calculation within the function argument; divide the annual interest rate by the number of periods per year (8%/4).
- Because the fv and type arguments are both 0 and occur at the end of the function argument list, they can be omitted and the formula written as follows:

$$=PMT(.08/4,5*4,1000000)$$

The resulting calculated value is –$61,156.72. This value is negative because it represents the payment that will be made to the bank (cash flow out of TheZone) each quarter.

Each payment goes partly to pay off the interest accrued each quarter and partly to reduce the principal (Beginning Principal + Interest – Payment). At the beginning of the transaction, when the interest expenses are high, most of the payment is used to pay off the interest. As the principal amount is slowly lowered, more and more of the payment amount is applied to reducing the principal debt.

Using a Financial Function with Cell Referencing

The calculations done so far can be easily performed using most calculators equipped with business functions. However, the power of using a spreadsheet lies in explicitly listing inputs so that values can be easily updated to perform what-if analyses, Goal Seeks, and so on. Ryan creates a new workbook named Financing.xlsx and lists these inputs and outputs on a worksheet named Options. The format that he uses provides an easy way to compare these values as each of the different financing options is analyzed, as shown in Figure 6.4.

Figure 6.4: Options worksheet with financial function data inputs and outputs

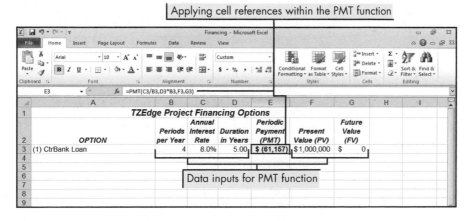

The columns list each of the relevant variables. Row 3 contains the inputs for the first financing option (CtrBank). In cell E3, Ryan entered the formula substituting the cell references for the rate, nper, pv, and fv arguments of the PMT function:

$$=\text{PMT(C3/B3,D3*B3,F3,G3)}$$

Ryan omitted the type argument because he is assuming that the default payment type is being applied for all options. Recall that the default payment type (type 0) specifies that payments are made at the end of the period. The result of the PMT function (cell E3) is displayed in parentheses to indicate it is a negative number.

Using the RATE, NPER, PV, and FV Functions

In the same way Ryan just solved the problem to determine the value of the periodic payment on the loan, he could have solved for any one of the other variables. In fact, each argument of the PMT function (rate, nper, pv, and fv) is also an Excel function in itself. Each of these functions, in turn, is dependent on the other four, as described in Table 6.1.

Table 6.1: Basic financial functions

Function Syntax	Description
RATE(nper,pmt,pv,fv,type)	Solves for the interest rate per period
NPER(rate,pmt,pv,fv,type)	Solves for the number of periods
PMT(rate,nper,pv,fv,type)	Solves for the value of the payment per period
PV(rate,nper,pmt,fv,type)	Solves for the initial value, the amount in or out at the beginning of the financial transaction
FV(rate,nper,pmt,pv,type)	Solves for the final value, the amount in or out at the end of the financial transaction

How To

Write a Basic Financial Function
1. Determine which element of the financial transaction you need to calculate.
2. Type = to begin the formula, followed by the function name: RATE, NPER, PMT, PV, or FV.
3. Fill in each of the remaining variables, excluding the one you are solving for:

- Specify the rate per period (rate). If necessary, divide the annual rate by the number of compounding periods per year to arrive at the rate per period.
- Specify the number of periods (nper). If necessary, multiply the number of years by the number of periods per year.
- Specify the payment per period (pmt). Payments that are inflows should be positive, and payments that are outflows should be negative.
- Specify the present value of the transaction (pv). This value is the amount in or out at the beginning of the transaction.

- Specify the future value of the transaction (fv). This value is the amount in or out at the end of the transaction. A loan that is completely paid off would have an fv of 0; a bank account would have an fv equal to the pv plus any accrued interest, plus or minus any payments into or out of the account.
- Specify the transaction type, if necessary. The default type (0) indicates payments are made at the end of each period (this can be omitted). Use type 1 if payments are made at the beginning of each period.

4. Press the Enter key to complete the formula.

Determining the Future Value of a Financial Transaction

The second financing option being considered is to fund the TZEdge project using some current liquid assets of the company; in this case, a money market account that was set up by TheZone to handle any liquidity cash flow problems that might arise. Fortunately, the funds were never needed, so now this is a possible source being considered to fund the project. The original investment placed in the money market account two years ago was $900,000. The terms of the account include a fixed annual interest rate of 3.5% compounded monthly. What is not known is the current value of this account and whether this value will be sufficient to cover the capital investment required for the project. Note that the current value in this case is actually the end of the financial transaction because the transaction was initiated two years ago. The end of the transaction is referred to as the future value.

Because Ryan requires future value, he needs to use the **FV function**. The syntax of the FV function is:

$$FV(rate,nper,pmt,pv,type)$$

Ryan substitutes the appropriate arguments into the FV function, as follows:

- The *rate* is 3.5% per year. Because the investment is compounded each month, and there are 12 months per year, the rate per period is 3.5% divided by 12 (.035/12). It is not necessary to separately perform this calculation; it can be nested inside the function argument. Note that with this option, the interest rate is how much interest TheZone will earn on its investment; in the first option, the loan from CtrBank, the interest rate shown is the rate TheZone would have to pay on the loan.
- The *nper* is the duration the principal has been accruing interest, which is two years. So, the number of periods equals 2 years * 12 months per year, or 24 periods.
- No periodic payments into or out of the account have been mentioned, so the *pmt* argument can be assumed to be $0. Can this argument be left out of the FV function? Because this 0 does not appear at the end of the function argument list, it cannot be left out; otherwise, Excel would interpret the next value after the nper argument as the

payment, even if it should be the pv argument. This FV function must include a 0 for the pmt argument followed by a comma or just a comma (without the 0) to hold the place of the pmt argument.

- The *pv* (the initial value of the investment) is $900,000. Because this money was taken out of TheZone and placed into the money market account, it is considered a negative cash flow, so the $900,000 will be negative.
- The *type* argument is assumed to be the default 0. Because this is the last argument and the value is 0, it can be omitted.

The resulting formula is:

$$=FV(.035/12,2*12,0,-900000)$$

Ryan enters the inputs for the second financing option in the Options worksheet, as shown in Figure 6.5. The formula Ryan enters in cell G4, using the appropriate cell references, is as follows:

$$=FV(C4/B4,D4*B4,E4,F4)$$

Figure 6.5: Calculating the future value of the money market account

	A	B	C	D	E	F	G	H
G4			f_x =FV(C4/B4,D4*B4,E4,F4)					
	A	B	C	D	E	F	G	H
1		*TZEdge Project Financing Options*						
2	*OPTION*	*Periods per Year*	*Annual Interest Rate*	*Duration in Years*	*Periodic Payment (PMT)*	*Present Value (PV)*	*Future Value (FV)*	
3	(1) CtrBank Loan	4	8.0%	5.00	$ (61,157)	$1,000,000	$ 0	
4	(2) Emergency Fund	12	3.5%	2.00	$ 0	$ (900,000)	$ 965,159	
5								
6								

Using FV to calculate the ending value of a financial transaction

At the end of the two years, the final value of the fund is $965,159. Is this amount sufficient to fund the project, which requires $1 million? By simply looking at the value in the worksheet, it is apparent that the amount is not sufficient. On a more complex worksheet, you could also create a relational expression, such as G4>=1000000. In fact, the entire financial function could be used as part of a relational expression similar to the following:

$$=FV(C4/B4,D4*B4,E4,F4)>=1000000$$

Based on the results of the FV function, there are insufficient funds in the money market account to completely fund the TZEdge project. Either another funding method will be required entirely, or this method could perhaps be used in conjunction with some other transaction.

Best Practice

Working with Positive and Negative Cash Flows

When writing formulas with financial functions, you need to be certain that the functions have the appropriate positive and negative cash flows. The present value (pv), payment (pmt), and future value (fv) are all cash flows of a financial transaction.

- If you are calculating payments to a bank (a negative cash flow), your formula requires at least one positive cash flow—either a positive present value (pv) or a positive future value (fv), or both.
- If you are calculating a positive future value (money being withdrawn from a bank, which is a positive cash flow), your formula requires at least one negative cash flow—either a negative present value (pv) or a negative payment (pmt), or both.
- If you are calculating an interest rate (using the RATE function) or a loan duration (using the NPER function), the transaction, such as a loan, requires both cash into and out of the transaction —combinations of positive and negative pv, pmt, and fv values. A typical loan has a positive cash flow at the beginning of the transaction and a negative cash flow for periodic payments.

Before constructing a formula with a financial function, it's a good idea to determine the timeline of the financial transaction, similar to the timeline shown in Figure 6.1. Doing so helps you to figure out which cash flows are positive and which are negative, and helps to ensure that the formula you create works properly.

Determining the Present Value of a Financial Transaction

The third financing option under consideration is to fund the TZEdge project from an initial investment and current profits. This option requires the project to be delayed by one and a half years, investing a portion of TheZone's expected profits ($50,000 per month each month), plus an initial cash outlay to be determined. A money market account will be used to hold these funds. The current money market rates pay 4% annual interest compounded monthly.

What is still unknown for this option is the amount of money that must be invested now, so that at the end of a year and a half, at least $1 million will be available. The elements that are already known are the interest rate, loan duration, periodic payments, and ending value. So, Ryan needs to calculate the initial outlay, or the present value, which is the amount at the beginning of the transaction. The syntax of the **PV function** is as follows:

```
PV(rate,nper,pmt,fv,type)
```

Ryan substitutes the appropriate arguments into the PV function, as follows:

- The *rate* per year is 4%. Because the account is compounded monthly, the corresponding rate per month is .04/12. As with the second option, this interest rate is the amount of interest TheZone would earn on this investment.

- The *nper* is the duration of the time delay, which is 1.5 years. Because the units of time must be consistent in the function, the nper must be expressed as months: 1.5*12 (months), or 18 periods.
- The *pmt* each month is –$50,000. This is a negative cash flow from TheZone into the account.
- The *fv* is the ending value desired of $1,000,000. Because these funds will be taken out of the account and given to TheZone, this is a positive cash flow for the company, so the fv will be positive.
- The *type* is assumed to be the default 0. Because this is the last argument and the value is 0, it can be omitted.

Substituting these values into the function results in the formula:

$$=PV(.04/12,1.5*12,-50000,1000000)$$

Using the appropriate cell references, Ryan enters the following formula in cell F5:

$$=PV(C5/B5,D5*B5,E5,G5)$$

Figure 6.6 shows the results in the worksheet.

Figure 6.6: Calculating the present value of an investment

F5	▼	*fx* =PV(C5/B5,D5*B5,E5,G5)						
	A	B	C	D	E	F	G	H
1			TZEdge Project Financing Options					
2	OPTION	Periods per Year	Annual Interest Rate	Duration in Years	Periodic Payment (PMT)	Present Value (PV)	Future Value (FV)	
3	(1) CtrBank Loan	4	8.0%	5.00	$ (61,157)	$1,000,000	$ 0	
4	(2) Emergency Fund	12	3.5%	2.00	$ 0	$ (900,000)	$ 965,159	
5	(3) Delay Project & Use Profits	12	4.0%	1.50	$ (50,000)	$ (69,736)	$1,000,000	
6								
7								

Using PV to calculate the beginning value of a financial transaction

The resulting present value is –69,736.10 (in Figure 6.6, the value is displayed to nearest dollar); this is the amount that TheZone would need to invest in a money market account now in order to have $1 million at the end of one-and-a-half years, assuming periodic payments of $50,000 as well. The major issues that management must evaluate in this case are whether the company has this amount of money to set aside now and the long-term effects of delaying the project, in terms of both lost revenues and changes in the marketplace.

Determining the Interest Rate of a Financial Transaction

In an effort to secure TheZone's business, NWN Bank is offering two options for funding the TZEdge project, the first of which is the following:

A loan for the entire $1,000,000 to be paid back over the next four years with equal semiannual payments of $150,000 (compounded semiannually)

Although the value of the loan and the payments are known, the interest rate being charged is unknown. Knowing the rate will give Ryan a good comparison point when he tries to determine which funding option is most favorable. To calculate the rate, Ryan can use the **RATE function**. The RATE function syntax is as follows:

$$\text{RATE(nper,pmt,pv,fv,type)}$$

Ryan substitutes the appropriate arguments into the RATE function, as follows:

- The *nper* is the duration of the loan, four years. Because the loan is compounded semi-annually (twice a year), the number of periods is 8 (4*2).
- The *pmt* per period is –$150,000. This is a negative cash flow for TheZone.
- The *pv* is $1,000,000 (the amount of the initial transaction). This is a positive cash flow for TheZone.
- The *fv* is assumed to be $0 because no mention is made of any residual amounts owed at the end of the loan.
- The *type* is assumed to be the default 0. Because this is the last argument and its value is 0, it can be omitted.

The resulting formula is =RATE(4*2,–150000,1000000). However, is this the information Ryan is seeking? This formula determines the rate per period—in this case, a semian-nual rate. The comparative value Ryan wants to calculate is the annual rate. So, the formula must be multiplied by the number of periods per year (2), as follows:

$$\text{=RATE(4*2,-150000,1000000)*2}$$

Ryan enters this formula in cell C6 using the appropriate cell references. The resulting value is as shown in Figure 6.7. The interest rate calculated is 8.5%, which is higher than the 8.0% interest rate on the loan offered by CtrBank.

Figure 6.7: Calculating the annual interest rate of a loan

Using RATE to calculate the annual interest rate of a financial transaction

Determining the Number of Periods of a Financial Transaction

The final financing option being considered by TheZone is NWN Bank's option b, which is the following:

A loan for the entire $1,000,000 with a fixed interest rate of 6.5% per year compounded quarterly and fixed quarterly payments of $95,000

Although the interest rate on this loan seems favorable, the payments are quite high as compared with some of the other options. Exactly how many years will it take to pay off this loan is not specifically stated. To calculate the duration of the loan, Ryan needs to use the **NPER function**. The syntax of the NPER function is as follows:

```
NPER(rate,pmt,pv,fv,type)
```

Ryan substitutes the appropriate arguments into the NPER function, as follows:

- The *rate* per year is 6.5% compounded quarterly. So, the rate per period is 6.5%/4.
- The *pmt* is –$95,000 per quarter. This is a negative cash flow for TheZone.
- The *pv* is $1,000,000, because the bank has offered to fund all of the capital required for the project. This value is a positive cash flow for TheZone.
- The *fv* is assumed to be $0 because no mention is made of any residual amounts owed at the end of the loan.
- The *type* is assumed to be the default 0. Because this is the last argument and the value is 0, it can be omitted.

Remember that Ryan needs to calculate NPER in terms of the number of compounding periods; in this case, the number of quarters. To calculate the loan duration in years, he must divide the number of periods (NPER) by the number of quarters per year, which produces the following formula:

```
=NPER(6.5%/4,-95000,1000000)/4
```

Ryan enters the following formula in cell D7, as shown in Figure 6.8:

```
=NPER(C7/B7,E7,F7,G7)/B7
```

Figure 6.8: Calculating the number of periods for a loan

D7 fx =NPER(C7/B7,E7,F7,G7)/B7

	A	B	C	D	E	F	G	H
1	*TZEdge Project Financing Options*							
2	*OPTION*	*Periods per Year*	*Annual Interest Rate*	*Duration in Years*	*Periodic Payment (PMT)*	*Present Value (PV)*	*Future Value (FV)*	
3	(1) CtrBank Loan	4	8.0%	5.00	**$ (61,157)**	$1,000,000	$ 0	
4	(2) Emergency Fund	12	3.5%	2.00	$ 0	$ (900,000)	**$ 965,159**	
5	(3) Delay Project & Use Profits	12	4.0%	1.50	$ (50,000)	**$ (69,736)**	$1,000,000	
6	(4a) NWN Bank w/$150,000 Payments	2	**8.5%**	4.00	$(150,000)	$1,000,000	$ 0	
7	(4b) NWN Bank Loan at 6.5% Rate	4	6.5%	**2.91**	$ (95,000)	$1,000,000	$ 0	
8								
9								

Using NPER to calculate the number of periods of a financial transaction

As shown by the results of the NPER function, the number of years it will take to pay off this loan is 2.91 years. This is a considerably shorter time than the duration for the other two loan options being considered, but requires a much higher annual cash outlay.

Best Practice

Accounting for Loan Options

In addition to the loan elements previously discussed—principal, interest rate, payment periods, and so on—some loans include additional options that must be taken into account. The following are some tips for writing formulas to account for these other loan options:

- To account for a financial transaction that includes a **down payment,** which is money required from the borrower toward the purchase of an asset, you must adjust the present value (pv) to reflect the exact value of the loan. For example, a house that costs $200,000 and requires a 10% down payment would have an original loan value (pv) of $180,000 (200,000–.1*200,000).
- To account for a **balloon payment,** which is additional money owed at the end of a loan, you must specify a negative future value (fv). For example, a three-year car loan totaling $15,000 at 3% annual interest can be paid off in equal monthly installments of $436.22. This can be calculated using the formula =PMT(.03/12,12*3,15000). Instead of completely paying off the loan, if a balloon payment of $2000 is built into the loan terms, the monthly payment would be reduced to $383.06 using the formula =PMT(0.03/12,12*3,15000,–2000).
- To account for mortgage fees such as points, loan origination fees, or any other fee that the borrower must pay up front, do the following:

  - Adjust the present value (pv) of the loan by subtracting these fees from the loan amount. Unlike a down payment, these fees do not change the actual face value (amount to be paid back) of the loan.
  - To determine the actual percentage rate being paid, recalculate the interest rate using the same payments and loan periods, but with the new pv amount. Banks in the United States are required to inform borrowers of this "adjusted" percentage rate; however, which fees are charged can vary from bank to bank.

  For example, a bank lending a borrower $200,000 for 15 years with monthly payments of $1,580.59 has a nominal interest rate of 5%. However, if this loan required a 2-point fee, 2% of the loan paid in advance, the actual amount being borrowed would only be $196,000. To calculate the actual interest rate being charged, use the formula =RATE(15*12,–1580.59,196000). The resulting interest rate is 5.31%.

Selecting a Financing Option

With the Options worksheet complete, Ryan must now select the most favorable financing option to recommend to management. Which option should he recommend? The answer is, "that depends." Options 2 and 3 use existing funds that will certainly avoid any additional debt to be incurred by the company. Usually, a lower amount of debt is a desirable attribute on a company's balance sheet, yet this must be weighed against the tax advantages of writing off the interest on a loan. Choosing option 2 also means using emergency liquid assets; and depending on fluctuations in the market, this might have certain risk consequences. Option 3 requires delaying the project while funds are secured from current profits. Again, this has consequences beyond the scope of this analysis because delays will also affect potential profits.

If a loan is selected as the vehicle to raise capital, a lower interest rate is generally preferable to a higher rate, all else being equal. However, not only do the rates vary for the three loans, but the durations and payments vary as well. To better compare these options, Ryan modifies the worksheet to include, in column H, the total annual payment for the three loan options—the periodic payment (values in column E) times the number of periods per year (values in column B). Figure 6.9 shows the modified worksheet.

Figure 6.9: Comparing annual payments for each of the loan options

H3		f_x =E3*B3						
A	B	C	D	E	F	G	H	I
1			TZEdge Project Financing Options					
2 OPTION	Periods per Year	Annual Interest Rate	Duration in Years	Periodic Payment (PMT)	Present Value (PV)	Future Value (FV)	Annual Loan Payments	
3 (1) CtrBank Loan	4	8.0%	5.00	$ (61,157)	$1,000,000	$ 0	$ (244,627)	
4 (2) Emergency Fund	12	3.5%	2.00	$ 0	$ (900,000)	$ 965,159		
5 (3) Delay Project & Use Profits	12	4.0%	1.50	$ (50,000)	$ (69,736)	$1,000,000		
6 (4a) NWN Bank w/$150,000 Payments	2	8.5%	4.00	$(150,000)	$1,000,000	$ 0	$ (300,000)	
7 (4b) NWN Bank Loan at 6.5% Rate	4	6.5%	2.91	$ (95,000)	$1,000,000	$ 0	$ (380,000)	
8								
9								

Total value of the annual loan payment (payment per period * number of periods) for the three loan options

The lowest interest rate is for NWN Bank's option 4b at 6.5%, but this option requires annual loan payments of $380,000. CtrBank's loan with an 8% interest rate requires annual payments of only $244,627, and NWN Bank's first option at 8.5% interest requires annual payments of $300,000. If the cash flow generated in the early years of the project is minimal, it might be difficult to meet the annual loan payments—especially for NWN Bank's 6.5% loan. Depending on the circumstances, option 1 with a higher interest rate but a longer duration and lower annual payments might be a better choice.

Which option should Ryan recommend? Before he can select one of the financing options, Ryan needs to evaluate a few more factors. For example, he needs to understand the projected cash flows from this venture and the possible tax implications. He will explore these factors in Level 2.

Steps To Success: Level 1

To promote the new TZEdge line of athletic shoes, the marketing group has decided to purchase advertising in selected print media, including leading health and fitness magazines and brochures to upscale sport outlets. Although the cost of this advertising has been worked into the selling expense, this money will actually be needed now, in year 0, rather than in years 1 and 2, so that the advertising agencies can begin designing a promotion and arranging for publication. The finance group at TheZone will discuss financing options directly with the advertising agencies, which are willing to accept a variety of different payment terms. Your task in these steps is to set up a worksheet to analyze each of the advertising agency options.

Complete the following:

1. Open a new workbook and save it as **Advertising.xlsx** in the Chapter 6 folder.

2. Create a worksheet with the following column headings:

   - Option#
   - Company Name
   - Number of Compounding Periods per Year
   - Annual Interest Rate
   - Loan Duration in Years
   - Payment per Period
   - Present Value
   - Future Value

3. Include the title **TZEdge Advertising Options** on your worksheet, merged and centered over the data.

4. Fill in the appropriate data inputs and calculations for each option (across the row) so that all information is listed. For all options, assume that the payment period duration will be used as the compounding period and that payments are made at the end of each period.

   - **Option 1**—AD Executives Inc. has proposed a campaign costing $45,000. This agency will accept full payment over the next two years in equal monthly installments of $2,100. For this option, you need to calculate the annual interest rate.
   - **Option 2**—Bradshaw & Hicks has designed a campaign for $45,000 and indicated that it will charge a 6.25% annual rate of interest on this amount, with fixed quarterly payments paid out over the next 18 months. For this option, you need to calculate periodic payments.
   - **Option 3**—AdWest Inc. has proposed the most modestly priced campaign, costing $30,000. This agency is willing to accept monthly payments of $1,400 until the

campaign is completely paid off. AdWest Inc. will charge a 6.5% annual interest rate. For this option, you need to calculate the duration in years that will be required to pay off this debt.

- **Option 4**—Johnson, Bellview & Associates has shown the Marketing team an excellent campaign that will cost $1,500 a month for the next two years. This agency's payment terms are based on an annual interest rate of 5%. For this option, you need to calculate the initial value of this advertising campaign.

5. In an adjacent column, calculate the total yearly payments required for each option.

6. Format your worksheet so that it is easy to read. Be certain that dollars and percentages are included where appropriate and that columns display consistent numbers of decimal places. Wrap text, as necessary, to format the column headings within reasonable column widths. Highlight cells with the data outputs.

7. In a row below your data, select an option to recommend if you were trying to minimize the yearly outlay for this campaign. Highlight your recommendation in pink.

8. Save and close the Advertising.xlsx workbook.

LEVEL 2

Creating a Projected Cash Flow Estimate and Amortization Table

Designing the Cash Flow Estimate Worksheet

The finance group is specifically interested in how the TZEdge project will affect the cash flow of the company—the amount of money coming into or out of the company each year. This information is important so that TheZone can ensure it has the funds needed for day-to-day operations. To estimate the cash flow generated from the TZEdge project, the finance group needs to combine the revenues and expenses associated with the shoe manufacturing with the effects of the required capital investment and financing. If the project is financed using a loan, this estimate must reflect the periodic payments that will be made to service the loan. In addition, corporate taxes allow companies to both allocate portions of the capital investment as an expense and deduct interest associated with a loan, thereby reducing the amount of taxes owed. These are also factors that need to be taken into consideration.

The next task for Ryan is to develop a projected five-year cash flow estimate and a detailed schedule of payments for the selected financing option. Ryan has been directed to assume that TheZone will fund the project using the loan from CtrBank (option 1), requiring quarterly payments of $61,157 over a five-year period. Ryan will also use the revenues and expenses developed previously by the marketing group when evaluating the TZEdge shoe project, and the group's five-year sales projections for the shoe.

Ryan begins by creating a new workbook named TZEdge Cash Flow Estimate. In this workbook, he renames a worksheet as CashFlow and then lists each of the different cash flow elements down the first column and each year across the row. He enters the data provided by the marketing group for the first five years of operation, as shown in cells B4:G12 of Figure 6.10.

Figure 6.10: Worksheet for projected 5-year cash flow estimate

	A	B	C	D	E	F	G	H
1			TZEdge Projected 5-Year Cash Flow Estimate					
2								
3		Year:		1	2	3	4	5
4	Sales Volume			4450	25000	50000	65000	70000
5	Selling Price Per Pair of Shoes		$ 225	$ 225	$ 225	$ 225	$ 225	
6								
7	Revenue		$ 1,001,250	$ 5,625,000	$ 11,250,000	$ 14,625,000	$ 15,750,000	
8		$/shoe						
9	Cost of Goods Sold	$(177.90)	$ (791,655)	$ (4,447,500)	$ (8,895,000)	$ (11,563,500)	$ (12,453,000)	
10	Selling Expense	$ (10.00)	$ (44,500)	$ (250,000)	$ (500,000)	$ (650,000)	$ (700,000)	
11								
12	Operating Income		$ 165,095	$ 927,500	$ 1,855,000	$ 2,411,500	$ 2,597,000	
13								
14								
15								
16								
17								
18								
19								
20								
21								
22								
23								
24	Cash Flow							
25								
26								

Calculations for revenue, cost of goods sold, and selling expense based on projected yearly sales volumes

Ryan has decided to express all revenues as positive values and all costs as negative values. So far, the CashFlow worksheet includes the following information:

- Projected annual sales volume (pairs sold)
- Selling price per pair of shoes
- A calculation for sales revenue—sales volume multiplied by selling price using the formula =C4*C5 in cell C7
- A calculation for cost of goods sold based on a cost of $177.90 per pair, using the formula =C$4*$B9 in cell C9, assuming a constant cost per pair for all five years
- A calculation for the selling expense per pair based on a cost of $10 per pair—the number of pairs sold multiplied by the selling expense per pair—using the formula =C$4*$B10 in cell C10
- A calculation for operating income—summing all positive and negative cash flows using the formula =SUM(C7,C9:C10) in cell C12

These formulas have been copied into the corresponding cells for each year.

Identifying the Missing Data Elements

Ryan now needs to account for the missing data elements of his projected cash flow estimate—those items associated with the loan payments and taxes. Doing so can be somewhat tricky because taxes are calculated based on *taxable income*, which excludes certain elements that are cash flows and includes other non–cash flow items.

When calculating taxes in the United States, a company can expense (subtract from income) only the *interest portion* of a loan payment, and not the portion that goes toward paying off the principal. The principal payment of a loan is not directly tax deductible. So, Ryan needs to determine the interest portion of the loan payments for the corresponding year to estimate taxable income and taxes for that year. After taxes have been calculated, the principal portion of each payment then needs to be subtracted from the cash flow.

What about the $1 million that TheZone will spend on capital equipment; is that considered a taxable expense? Corporations cannot deduct the cost of capital equipment in the same way they can the cost of materials (such as shoe leather) or labor. Corporations must allocate a portion of this expense over the useful life of the equipment using a method known as depreciation.

Depreciation is the process by which a company spreads the expense of an asset over its useful life. In other words, each year only a portion of the money spent initially on capital equipment can be used to reduce income. Depreciation needs to be subtracted from the cash flow in each year to calculate taxes for that year, but then must be added back in because it is not actually a cash flow in that year. There are several methods a company can consider for calculating depreciation, as defined in the tax codes. Ryan will estimate depreciation using a straight line method over a period of five years (this method is discussed in detail later in this section). Although this method will not produce the amount of depreciation allowed by the Internal Revenue Service (IRS), it will serve Ryan's purposes for the cash flow estimate.

After the interest expense and depreciation have been deducted, taxes can be calculated. The taxes owed will then be subtracted from the cash flow. To complete the cash flow calculation, Ryan must add back in the depreciation (which is not a cash flow) and subtract the value of the principal payments on the loan. The process Ryan will use is illustrated in Figure 6.11.

Figure 6.11: Process for calculating cash flow

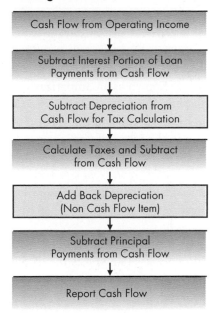

To implement this process, Ryan has expanded his worksheet to include the appropriate labels, as shown in Figure 6.12.

Figure 6.12: Additional cash flow elements included in the worksheet

	A	B	C	D	E	F	G	H
1			TZEdge Projected 5-Year Cash Flow Estimate					
2								
3	Year:		1	2	3	4	5	
4	Sales Volume		4450	25000	50000	65000	70000	
5	Selling Price Per Pair of Shoes	$ 225	$ 225	$ 225	$ 225	$ 225		
6								
7	Revenue		$ 1,001,250	$ 5,625,000	$11,250,000	$ 14,625,000	$ 15,750,000	
8		$/shoe						
9	Cost of Goods Sold	$(177.90)	$ (791,655)	$ (4,447,500)	$ (8,895,000)	$(11,563,500)	$(12,453,000)	
10	Selling Expense	$ (10.00)	$ (44,500)	$ (250,000)	$ (500,000)	$ (650,000)	$ (700,000)	
11								
12	Operating Income		$ 165,095	$ 927,500	$ 1,855,000	$ 2,411,500	$ 2,597,000	
13								
14	Interest Expense							
15	Depreciation							
16	Taxable Income							
17								
18	Taxes							
19	Income After Taxes							
20								
21	Add Back Depreciation							
22	Subtract Principal Payments							
23								
24	**Cash Flow**							
25								
26								

Additional elements required to estimate cash flow

Setting Up an Amortization Table

Now Ryan needs to enter the necessary calculations in the worksheet. The first value that he requires is the interest portion of the loan for each year. This amount will change from year to year as the principal value of the loan is paid off. A standard method of detailing a loan transaction is to set up what is known as an **amortization table** (or schedule). This table lists, for each specific loan period, the remaining principal and the value of the payments being apportioned to interest expense and to principal pay down. Ryan will set up this amortization table according to the terms of CtrBank's option 1 loan, as follows:

Funding the entire project using a line of credit from CtrBank. CtrBank currently charges a fixed rate of 8% annual interest compounded quarterly. For this type of project, payments are scheduled quarterly over a five-year period.

To set up the amortization table, Ryan creates a separate worksheet named Loan in the TZEdge Cash Flow Estimate workbook. He first lists the data inputs (loan value, interest rate, compounding periods, and so on), and then details for each period the corresponding interest and principal payment values, as shown in Figure 6.13.

Figure 6.13: Setting up a loan amortization table

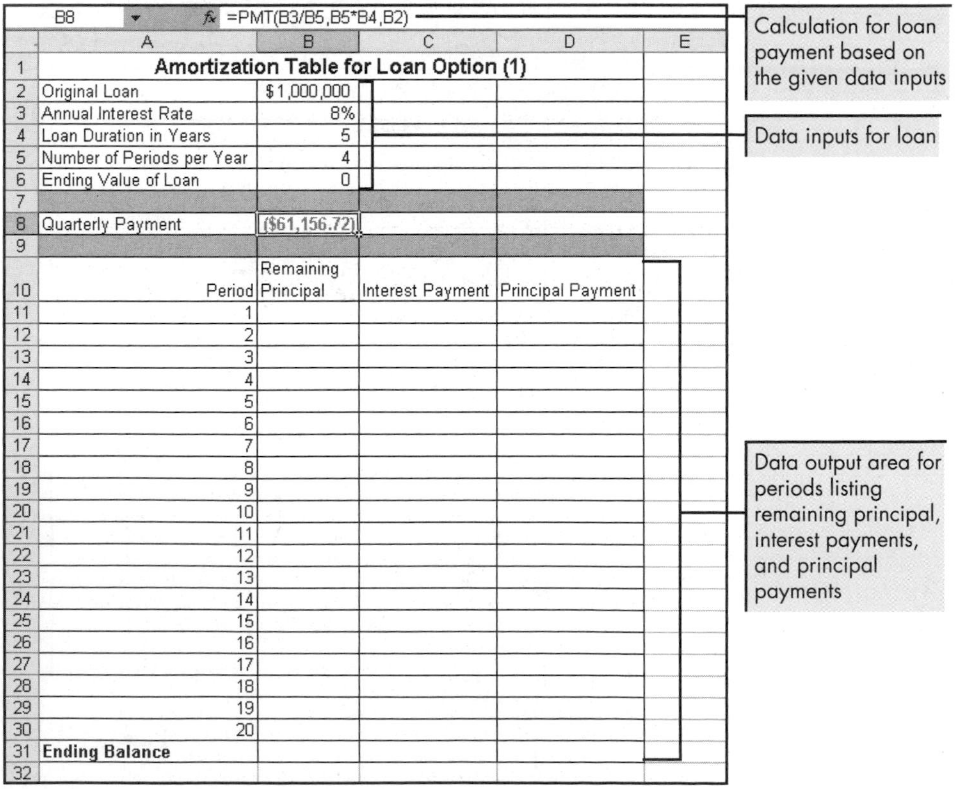

Previously, Ryan used the formula =PMT(.08/4,5*4,1000000,0) to calculate the payments. Here, he has substituted the appropriate cell references for these values as follows:

```
=PMT(B3/B5,B5*B4,B2)
```

He enters this formula in cell B8; the resulting payment value is –$61,156.72. (Note that this value is formatted to display two decimal places on this worksheet.) But how much of the $61,156.72 goes toward paying off the accrued interest for the period, and how much toward paying down the principal? Ryan could go through the calculation for each quarter, calculating the interest per quarter by multiplying the remaining principal by the interest rate and then subtracting this interest from the payment to obtain the principal payment, and, finally, subtracting the principal payment from the remaining principal. Although this is possible, it would be very time consuming and tedious. Excel provides a more efficient method to accomplish this task.

Calculating Principal and Interest Payments

One method of calculating principal and interest payments is to use the PPMT and IPMT functions. The IPMT function calculates the value of the interest payment for a specified period, and the PPMT function calculates the value of the principal payment for a specified period. The syntax for each of these functions is as follows:

```
IPMT(rate,per,nper,pv,fv,type)
```

```
PPMT(rate,per,nper,pv,fv,type)
```

In both of the functions, the arguments are defined as follows:

- The *rate* represents the interest rate per period.
- The *per* is the period for which the interest or principal amount will be calculated. Valid periods begin at 1 and end at the last payment period, which equals nper.
- The *nper* is the total number of periods in the financial transaction.
- The *pv* is the value at the beginning of the financial transaction.
- The *fv* is the value at the end of the financial transaction.
- The type is the payment type of 0 or 1, where 0 represents payments made at the end of each period, and 1 represents payments made at the beginning of each period.

If Ryan wants to calculate the interest expense for period 15 of this $1 million loan compounded quarterly over a five-year period at an 8% annual rate, the formula would be =IPMT(.08/4,15,5*4,1000000,0,0). The resulting value is an interest payment of –$6,851.30. Because this is a quarterly loan, period 15 corresponds to the third quarter of year 4.

To fill in the values on his amortization table, first Ryan enters the original principal value for period 1 in cell B11 by using the formula =B2. He then applies the IPMT function in cell C11 to write a formula that calculates the interest payment for period 1. Substituting the appropriate cell references, Ryan writes the following formula:

$$\texttt{=IPMT(B\$3/B\$5,A11,B\$4*B\$5,B\$2,B\$6,0)}$$

Because Ryan needs to copy this formula down the column, absolute row references must be applied to values that do not change. The values B2, B3, B4, B5, and B6 will all remain constant regardless of the period for which interest is being calculated. The period number (per) is the only argument that will vary. The results of the formula are shown in Figure 6.14.

Figure 6.14: Calculating the interest portion of each payment for the corresponding period

	C11		f_x =IPMT(B$3/B$5,A11,B$4*B$5,B$2,B$6,0)				Calculation for the interest portion of the loan payment for period 1, based on rate, nper, pv, and fv
	A	B	C	D	E		
1	Amortization Table for Loan Option (1)						
2	Original Loan	$1,000,000					
3	Annual Interest Rate	8%					
4	Loan Duration in Years	5					
5	Number of Periods per Year	4					
6	Ending Value of Loan	0					
7							
8	Quarterly Payment	($61,156.72)					
9							
10		Period	Remaining Principal	Interest Payment	Principal Payment		
11		1	$1,000,000	($20,000.00)			Period 1's remaining principal is equal to the original amount of the loan
12		2		(19,176.87)			
13		3		(18,337.27)			
14		4		(17,480.88)			
15		5		(16,607.36)			
16		6		(15,716.38)			
17		7		(14,807.57)			
18		8		(13,880.59)			
19		9		(12,935.06)			
20		10		(11,970.63)			
21		11		(10,986.91)			
22		12		(9,983.51)			
23		13		(8,960.05)			
24		14		(7,916.11)			
25		15		(6,851.30)			
26		16		(5,765.19)			
27		17		(4,657.36)			
28		18		(3,527.38)			
29		19		(2,374.79)			
30		20		(1,199.15)			
31	Ending Balance						
32							

The following is a description of the function arguments used in this formula:

- The *rate* is 8% per year divided by 4 quarters per year (B$3/B$5).
- The *per* is the period number the interest payment is being calculated for; in this case, period 1 (A11). Note that this value changes relatively as each subsequent interest amount is calculated for periods 2 through 20.
- The *nper* is the total number of pay periods, in this case 5 years times 4 quarters per year (B$4*B$5).

- The pv is the present value of the loan: $1,000,000 (B$2).
- The fv is the future value of the loan, which is assumed to be 0 (B$6).
- The $type$ argument is the default 0 because no information is given regarding payments.

The resulting value for the interest portion of this payment in period 1 is –$20,000, which is equal to $1,000,000*.08/4.

In a similar manner, Ryan calculates the value of each of the principal payments by quarter by placing the following formula in cell D11:

$$=PPMT(B\$3/B\$5,A11,B\$4*B\$5,B\$2,B\$6,0)$$

Ryan copies this formula down the column into cells D12:D30. To complete the amortization table, Ryan wants to have a running total of the remaining principal value of the loan in column B. Because the payment is expressed as a negative number, this can be accomplished by taking the previous period's principal value and adding it to the previous period's principal payment. Ryan writes the formula =B11+D11 in cell B12 and copies this formula down the column. The completed amortization table is shown in Figure 6.15.

Figure 6.15: Completed amortization table

	A	B	C	D	E
1	Amortization Table for Loan Option (1)				
2	Original Loan	$1,000,000			
3	Annual Interest Rate	8%			
4	Loan Duration in Years	5			
5	Number of Periods per Year	4			
6	Ending Value of Loan	0			
7					
8	Quarterly Payment	($61,156.72)			
9					
10		Period	Remaining Principal	Interest Payment	Principal Payment	
11		1	$1,000,000	($20,000.00)	($41,156.72)	
12		2	958,843.28	(19,176.87)	(41,979.85)	
13		3	916,863.43	(18,337.27)	(42,819.45)	
14		4	874,043.98	(17,480.88)	(43,675.84)	
15		5	830,368.14	(16,607.36)	(44,549.36)	
16		6	785,818.79	(15,716.38)	(45,440.34)	
17		7	740,378.44	(14,807.57)	(46,349.15)	
18		8	694,029.29	(13,880.59)	(47,276.13)	
19		9	646,753.16	(12,935.06)	(48,221.65)	
20		10	598,531.51	(11,970.63)	(49,186.09)	
21		11	549,345.42	(10,986.91)	(50,169.81)	
22		12	499,175.61	(9,983.51)	(51,173.21)	
23		13	448,002.40	(8,960.05)	(52,196.67)	
24		14	395,805.73	(7,916.11)	(53,240.60)	
25		15	342,565.13	(6,851.30)	(54,305.42)	
26		16	288,259.71	(5,765.19)	(55,391.52)	
27		17	232,868.19	(4,657.36)	(56,499.35)	
28		18	176,368.84	(3,527.38)	(57,629.34)	
29		19	118,739.50	(2,374.79)	(58,781.93)	
30		20	59,957.57	(1,199.15)	(59,957.57)	
31	Ending Balance	$ 0.00			
32					

Calculation for the principal portion of the loan payment for period 1, based on rate, nper, pv, and fv

Remaining principal calculated for each period

Calculating Principal and Interest Payments Between Two Periods

The amortization table includes the interest and principal payments by period; in this case, quarters. However, the projected cash flow estimate that is being prepared requires *yearly* payments. Because each year consists of four periods, Ryan needs to summarize these values in groups of four. If Ryan assumes that the fiscal year coincides with the beginning of the loan, then year 1 consists of periods 1 through 4. He can use several different methods to aggregate the interest and principal values in yearly increments.

One method is to use the **CUMIPMT** and **CUMPRINC functions**. These functions automatically calculate the interest values between two periods and the principal values between two periods, respectively. CUMIPMT returns the cumulative interest paid on a loan between start_period and end_period. CUMPRINC returns the cumulative principal paid on a loan between start_period and end_period. The syntax of each function is as follows:

```
CUMIPMT(rate,nper,pv,start_period,end_period,type)
```

```
CUMPRINC(rate,nper,pv,start_period,end_period,type)
```

Ryan can enter these functions on his CashFlow worksheet, referencing the appropriate input data on the Loan worksheet. Again, consider the projected 5-year cash flow estimate shown in Figure 6.16. Ryan needs to write a formula to calculate the interest portion of the payments for year 1 in cell C14, and the principal portion of the payments in cell C22.

Figure 6.16: CashFlow worksheet with areas for cumulative interest and principal payments

	A	B	C	D	E	F	G	H
1			TZEdge Projected 5-Year Cash Flow Estimate					
2								
3	Year:		1	2	3	4	5	
4	Sales Volume		4450	25000	50000	65000	70000	
5	Selling Price Per Pair of Shoes	$	225	$ 225	$ 225	$ 225	$ 225	
6								
7	Revenue		$ 1,001,250	$ 5,625,000	$11,250,000	$ 14,625,000	$ 15,750,000	
8		$/shoe						
9	Cost of Goods Sold	$(177.90)	$ (791,655)	$(4,447,500)	$ (8,895,000)	$(11,563,500)	$(12,453,000)	
10	Selling Expense	$ (10.00)	$ (44,500)	$ (250,000)	$ (500,000)	$ (650,000)	$ (700,000)	
11								
12	Operating Income		$ 165,095	$ 927,500	$ 1,855,000	$ 2,411,500	$ 2,597,000	
13								
14	Interest Expense							
15	Depreciation		Cumulative interest payments for the corresponding year will be calculated in this row					
16	Taxable Income							
17								
18	Taxes							
19	Income After Taxes							
20								
21	Add Back Depreciation							
22	Subtract Principal Payments		Cumulative principal payments for the corresponding year will be calculated in this row					
23								
24	**Cash Flow**							
25								
26								

Ryan begins to enter the cumulative interest formula by inputting the arguments for rate, nper, pv (located on the Loan worksheet), and starting and ending periods, as follows:

```
=CUMIPMT(Loan!B3/Loan!B5,Loan!B4*Loan!B5,Loan!B2,1,4,0)
```

This formula works fine in cell C14, but can it be copied across the row to calculate the cumulative interest payments for years 2 through 5? The cell references for rate, nper, and pv can be modified to make the column absolute so that these values remain constant. But what will happen to the start_period and end_period arguments when copied across? Here, Ryan uses constants, the values 1 and 4, which will not change when the formula is copied. Ryan either needs to write four additional formulas, instead of copying the formula in cell C14, or needs to nest an expression inside the CUMIPMT function to automatically calculate the starting period and ending period values from the information he has in the workbook.

If Ryan directly references the year (cell CashFlow!C3) as the start_period, this would also not work when the formula is copied across because the cell reference C3 would become D3 for the year 2 calculation. However, year 2 begins with quarter 5, not quarter 2. Instead, Ryan decides to write the algebraic expression C3*4–3 for the starting period—multiplying the number of years by 4 and then subtracting 3. For year 1, this approach results in 1*4–3, or 1; for year 2, this results in 2*4–3, or 5; for year 3, this results in 3*4–3, or 9. This approach will work when copied across the row to determine the starting period for each of the five years.

In a similar way, Ryan can construct an algebraic formula to calculate the ending period; this is simply C3*4 (the year number multiplied by 4 quarters). Ryan substitutes these expressions as the start_period and end_period arguments. His formula now looks like the one shown in Figure 6.17.

Figure 6.17: Formula to determine the cumulative interest payment for year 1

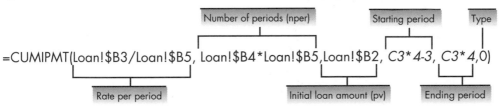

Ryan enters this formula in cell C14 and copies it across the row into cells D14 through G14. Using the same technique, Ryan can also calculate the principal payments that must be accounted for in the projected 5-year cash flow estimate, after taxes. He enters the following formula in cell C22 and copies it across the column:

```
=CUMPRINC(Loan!$B3/Loan!$B5,Loan!$B4*Loan!$B5,Loan!
                  $B2,C3*4-3,C3*4,0)
```

Keep in mind that the principal payments represent negative cash flows—money that the company pays out. Ryan displays these as negative values, as shown in Figure 6.18.

Figure 6.18: Entering the cumulative interest and principal payments

Cumulative interest payments for year 1:
=CUMIPMT(Loan!$B3/Loan!$B5,Loan!$B4*Loan!$B5,Loan!$B2,C3*4-3,C3*4,0)

	A	B	C	D	E	F	G	H
1			TZEdge Projected 5-Year Cash Flow Estimate					
2								
3		Year:	1	2	3	4	5	
4	Sales Volume		4450	25000	50000	65000	70000	
5	Selling Price Per Pair of Shoes		$ 225	$ 225	$ 225	$ 225	$ 225	
6								
7	Revenue		$ 1,001,250	$ 5,625,000	$11,250,000	$ 14,625,000	$ 15,750,000	
8		$/shoe						
9	Cost of Goods Sold	$(177.90)	$ (791,655)	$(4,447,500)	$ (8,895,000)	$(11,563,500)	$(12,453,000)	
10	Selling Expense	$ (10.00)	$ (44,500)	$ (250,000)	$ (500,000)	$ (650,000)	$ (700,000)	
11								
12	Operating Income		$ 165,095	$ 927,500	$ 1,855,000	$ 2,411,500	$ 2,597,000	
13								
14	Interest Expense		$ (74,995)	$ (61,012)	$ (45,876)	$ (29,493)	$ (11,759)	
15	Depreciation							
16	Taxable Income							
17								
18	Taxes							
19	Income After Taxes							
20								
21	Add Back Depreciation							
22	Subtract Principal Payments		$ (169,632)	$ (183,615)	$ (198,751)	$ (215,134)	$ (232,868)	
23								
24	**Cash Flow**							
25								
26								

Cumulative principal payments for year 1:
=CUMPRINC(Loan!$B3/Loan!$B5,Loan!$B4*Loan!$B5,Loan!$B2,C3*4-3,C3*4,0)

Calculating Depreciation Using the SLN Function

The next item to be determined is the depreciation amount for each of the five years related to the $1 million TheZone will spend on equipment to manufacture the TZEdge shoe. Recall that depreciation is the process by which a company spreads the expense of an asset over its useful life. Each year, a portion of the $1,000,000 capital investment will be deducted from income for the purposes of calculating taxes. Ryan will use the straight line depreciation method, which is only an approximation of the actual depreciation allowed by the tax code. The actual depreciation is far too complex to calculate here, and will be left to the corporate accountants if the project goes forward.

Straight line depreciation basically allocates the value of an asset evenly throughout the life of the asset. So, a $12,000 piece of equipment depreciated over 10 years with a salvage value at the end of those 10 years of $2,000 has an annual depreciation value of $1,000. Algebraically, this can be expressed as follows:

```
(Cost of the asset - Salvage value)/Life of the asset
```

Excel provides the SLN function to automatically calculate straight line depreciation. The syntax of this function is as follows:

```
SLN(cost,salvage,life)
```

- The cost argument is the initial cost of the asset.
- The salvage argument is the value at the end of the depreciation, often referred to as the salvage value.
- The life argument is the number of periods over which the asset is depreciated.

The cost of the asset has already been determined as $1 million. Both the salvage value and life of the asset are unknown. The accounting group has recommended that, for planning purposes, a 10-year life is appropriate for the useful life with a salvage value of $25,000. Note that the asset life is different from the period being considered for the cash flow of the TZEdge shoe (five years). If, at the end of the five years, this product line is discontinued, the reuse or tax write-off of the equipment will be dealt with outside of this analysis. Ryan can now calculate yearly depreciation as follows:

```
=-SLN(1000000,25000,10)
```

Notice that Ryan includes a minus sign preceding the function so that the resulting value will be negative, reducing cash flow for the purposes of calculating taxable income. The resulting yearly depreciation is –$97,500. Best practices dictate that these input values be explicitly listed elsewhere in the workbook. Therefore, Ryan sets up a separate worksheet named Depreciation, as shown in Figure 6.19.

Figure 6.19: Depreciation worksheet

	A	B	C
1	Depreciation Values		
2			
3	Capital	$1,000,000	
4	Salvage	$ 25,000	
5	Life	10	
6			

A technique Ryan can use to simplify his formula is to take this list of depreciation values and apply a range name to each, naming cell B3 Capital, cell B4 Salvage, and cell B5 Life. This can be accomplished using the Create Names from Selection dialog box.

How To

Create a List of Named Ranges That Correspond to Descriptions

1. Select the cells containing both the descriptions (labels) and their corresponding values to be named.
2. Click the Create from Selection button in the Defined Names group on the Formulas tab. The Create Names from Selection dialog box opens, as shown in Figure 6.20.

Figure 6.20: Naming ranges from a list

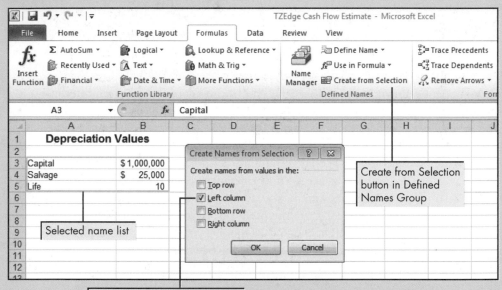

3. Designate the location that contains the labels by selecting the Top row, Left column, Bottom row, or Right column check box. As shown in Figure 6.20, the Left column option is selected because the labels to be used as the range names appear to the left of their corresponding values.
4. Click the OK button.

The cells containing values can now be referenced using these assigned names. Note that symbols such as $ and # are not included in the named ranges.

Ryan creates the three named ranges for the depreciation value and uses them to write the following formula in cell C15 on the CashFlow worksheet:

```
=-SLN(Capital,Salvage,Life)
```

He copies the formula across the row without any further modifications because range names copy absolutely.

Next, Ryan calculates taxable income in cell C16 as the sum of the values for operating income, interest expense, and depreciation, and copies this formula across the row. Figure 6.21 shows the resulting worksheet. Note that Ryan can sum these three values because the interest expense and depreciation values are expressed as negative values; therefore, the sum calculation actually subtracts these two values from the operating income to determine the taxable income.

Figure 6.21: Calculating straight line depreciation and taxable income

Straight line depreciation calculation includes named ranges in formula: =-SLN(Capital,Salvage,Life)

	A	B	C	D	E	F	G	H
1			TZEdge Projected 5-Year Cash Flow Estimate					
2								
3		Year:	1	2	3	4	5	
4	Sales Volume		4450	25000	50000	65000	70000	
5	Selling Price Per Pair of Shoes	$ 225	$ 225	$ 225	$ 225	$ 225		
6								
7	Revenue		$ 1,001,250	$ 5,625,000	$11,250,000	$ 14,625,000	$ 15,750,000	
8		$/shoe						
9	Cost of Goods Sold	$ (177.90)	$ (791,655)	$ (4,447,500)	$ (8,895,000)	$ (11,563,500)	$ (12,453,000)	
10	Selling Expense	$ (10.00)	$ (44,500)	$ (250,000)	$ (500,000)	$ (650,000)	$ (700,000)	
11								
12	Operating Income		$ 165,095	$ 927,500	$ 1,855,000	$ 2,411,500	$ 2,597,000	
13								
14	Interest Expense		$ (74,995)	$ (61,012)	$ (45,876)	$ (29,493)	$ (11,759)	
15	Depreciation		$ (97,500)	$ (97,500)	$ (97,500)	$ (97,500)	$ (97,500)	
16	Taxable Income		$ (7,400)	$ 768,988	$ 1,711,624	$ 2,284,507	$ 2,487,741	
17								
18	Taxes							
19	Income After Taxes							
20								
21	Add Back Depreciation							
22	Subtract Principal Payments		$ (169,632)	$ (183,615)	$ (198,751)	$ (215,134)	$ (232,868)	
23								
24	**Cash Flow**							
25								
26								

Calculating taxable income based on operating income, interest expense, and depreciation for year 1: =C12+C14+C15

Best Practice

Using Named Ranges Globally and Locally

There are several ways to name a range within Excel 2010, including the following:

- Use the Name Box, located to the left of the formula bar, to type a name for the selected cell or range (this can include a selection of nonadjacent cells).
- Use the New Name dialog box, accessed by clicking the Define Name button in the Defined Names group on the Formulas tab, to name a single cell or range of contiguous cells.
- Use the Create from Selection dialog box, accessed by clicking the Create from Selection button in the Defined Names group, to create a list of single cell ranges with names corresponding to the labels listed in adjacent cells.

6

Level 2

The first and second options seem to perform the same task; however, in Excel 2010, using the Define Name button and then selecting the Define Name option allows you to specify a *named range scope*. You can name a *range* and then specify its *scope* as either a workbook (global) or a specific worksheet (local). If you name a range globally for the entire workbook, the range name will be recognized anywhere within the workbook, and you cannot use that range again within the workbook. If you name a range locally for a specific worksheet, the range name will only be recognized within that worksheet, so you can use that range name within other worksheet scopes in the same workbook.

Why use one versus the other? In some cases, a value is needed in multiple worksheets within a workbook; in this case, a global range name is best. However, there might be applications where a worksheet is copied identically and used over and over again within the same workbook. If that worksheet has values that are conveniently named but vary from worksheet to worksheet—for example, a sales volume—then the name Sales_Volume could be used locally on each worksheet, making the formulas easy to work with yet still specific to the local values.

There are specific rules outlining valid range names. Range names must start with a letter, an underscore, or a backslash. Uppercase or lowercase single letters *C* or *R* cannot be used as a range name. Names are also not case sensitive, so the name *Data* is equivalent to *data*. Names cannot be cell references such as *Z200*, cannot contain any blank spaces, and are limited to 255 characters.

Name ranges can also be managed—edited, deleted, and added—from the Name Manager dialog box, which you access by clicking the Name Manager button found in the Defined Names group. This topic is discussed in detail in Chapter 8 – Level 2.

Alternative Depreciation Options Provided in Excel

In addition to straight line depreciation, Excel provides a variety of other functions that calculate depreciation (check Excel online Help for details). These alternative approaches do not correspond exactly to the tax codes, which are complex and ever changing. However, they are frequently used to estimate depreciation for income reporting. Three of the available functions and their methods are described as follows:

- **Double-declining balance**—The double-declining balance method computes depreciation at an accelerated rate. Depreciation is highest in the first period and decreases in successive periods. The syntax for the DDB function is:

```
DDB(cost,salvage,life,period,factor)
```

The DDB function uses the following formula to calculate depreciation for a period:

```
((cost – salvage) – total depreciation from prior periods) *
                    (factor/life)
```

- **Sum of the years digits**—In this method, depreciation is apportioned based on a declining fractional amount of the asset's life. The syntax for the SYD function is:

```
SYD(cost,salvage,life,per)
```

The fraction is calculated as follows:

1. The denominator is determined by taking each digit of the number of years of the asset's life and adding them together. For example, an asset with three years of depreciable life takes the sum of the digits from 1 to 3: (1+2+3), which equals 6.

2. The numerator of the fraction starts with the number of years in the life of an asset for year 1 and descends by 1 for each succeeding year. For an asset with a useful life of three years, the fraction is 3/6 for year 1, 2/6 for year 2, and 1/6 for year 3.

- **Fixed-declining balance**—This method returns the depreciation of an asset for a specified period using the fixed-declining balance method. The syntax for the DB function is:

```
DB(cost,salvage,life,period,month)
```

The DB function uses the following formula to calculate depreciation for a period:

```
(cost - total depreciation from prior periods) * rate
```

- **Variable-declining balance**—This method returns the depreciation of an asset for any period you specify, including partial periods, using the double-declining balance method or some other method you specify. The syntax for the VDB function is:

```
VDB(cost,salvage,life,start_period,end_period,factor,no_switch)
```

Calculating Taxes

Ryan's next step in completing the projected 5-year cash flow estimate is to calculate the estimated value of taxes for each year. Keep in mind that these are taxes against income derived from the projected sales of the TZEdge shoe. For purposes of this analysis, TheZone's corporate taxes will be calculated based on the marginal rate paid last year; in addition, corporate tax rates are assumed to be based on a graduated income scale varying from approximately 15% to 35% of taxable income. TheZone is a large corporation with sales domestically and internationally far exceeding the maximum tax rate range of $18 million in income. So, any additional income sources should be assumed to be taxed at this highest rate of 35%.

Ryan enters the tax rate of 35% in the workbook as a range named Taxrate without first entering the value itself in the workbook. In Excel, you can give a value a range name without actually entering the value in a specific cell. To do so, you use the New Name dialog box.

How To

Define a Range Name for a Value Not Listed in the Worksheet

1. Click the Define Name button arrow in the Defined Names group on the Formulas tab, and then click Define Name. The New Name dialog box opens, as shown in Figure 6.22.

Figure 6.22: New Name dialog box

Enter range name

Delete any cell reference and type value

2. In the Name box, enter the name you want to assign to the value.

3. In the Refers to box, enter the value for which you are defining a range name. If necessary, delete any cell reference that might appear by default before entering the value.

4. To apply the range name globally, make sure that Workbook is selected as the Scope box.

5. Enter a comment if needed for future reference.

6. Click the OK button.

This value can now be referenced anywhere in the workbook using its range name. Note that when you use this method to assign a named range to a value, the range name does not appear in the Name Box.

Ryan also assumes that the actual taxes owed will be rounded to the nearest dollar. Using this information, he enters the following formula in cell C18 to calculate the taxes:

```
=-ROUND(Taxrate*C16,0)
```

Note that the formula is preceded by a negative sign because this value needs to be deducted from the cash flow. Ryan also calculates the projected income after taxes in cell C19 using the following formula. Figure 6.23 shows the resulting worksheet.

$$=C18+C16$$

Figure 6.23: Calculating taxes and income after taxes

Calculating taxes rounded to the nearest dollar
using the named range: =−ROUND(Taxrate*C16,0)

	A	B	C	D	E	F	G	H
1			TZEdge Projected 5-Year Cash Flow Estimate					
2								
3		Year:	1	2	3	4	5	
4	Sales Volume		4450	25000	50000	65000	70000	
5	Selling Price Per Pair of Shoes	$	225	$ 225	$ 225	$ 225	$ 225	
6								
7	Revenue		$ 1,001,250	$ 5,625,000	$11,250,000	$ 14,625,000	$ 15,750,000	
8		$/shoe						
9	Cost of Goods Sold	$(177.90)	$ (791,655)	$(4,447,500)	$ (8,895,000)	$(11,563,500)	$(12,453,000)	
10	Selling Expense	$ (10.00)	$ (44,500)	$ (250,000)	$ (500,000)	$ (650,000)	$ (700,000)	
11								
12	Operating Income		$ 165,095	$ 927,500	$ 1,855,000	$ 2,411,500	$ 2,597,000	
13								
14	Interest Expense		$ (74,995)	$ (61,012)	$ (45,876)	$ (29,493)	$ (11,759)	
15	Depreciation		$ (97,500)	$ (97,500)	$ (97,500)	$ (97,500)	$ (97,500)	
16	Taxable Income		$ (7,400)	$ 768,988	$ 1,711,624	$ 2,284,507	$ 2,487,741	
17								
18	Taxes		$ 2,590	$ (269,146)	$ (599,068)	$ (799,578)	$ (870,709)	
19	Income After Taxes		$ (4,810)	$ 499,842	$ 1,112,556	$ 1,484,929	$ 1,617,032	
20								
21	Add Back Depreciation							
22	Subtract Principal Payments		$ (169,632)	$ (183,615)	$ (198,751)	$ (215,134)	$ (232,868)	
23								
24	Cash Flow							
25								
26								

Calculating income after taxes: =C18+C16

Completing the Analysis

The last two steps required for Ryan to complete the projected 5-year cash flow estimate are as follows:

- Add back the depreciation because this is not actually a cash flow. In this case, Ryan enters the following formula in cell C21 and copies it across the row. Remember that cell C15 contains the depreciable amount represented as a negative value; because the value must be added back in, and the value is already a negative, the formula must change the sign for this value to a positive.

$$=-C15$$

- Total the values of taxable income, depreciation added back to the cash flow, and principal payments deducted from the cash flow (already a negative value) to determine the projected cash flow. Ryan enters the following formula in cell C24 and copies it across the row:

$$=SUM(C19,C21,C22)$$

Ryan's finished worksheet to calculate the projected cash flow estimate is shown in Figure 6.24.

Figure 6.24: Final worksheet for the projected 5-year cash flow estimate

Adding back depreciation: =-C15

	A	B	C	D	E	F	G	H
1			TZEdge Projected 5-Year Cash Flow Estimate					
2								
3		Year:	1	2	3	4	5	
4	Sales Volume		4450	25000	50000	65000	70000	
5	Selling Price Per Pair of Shoes		$ 225	$ 225	$ 225	$ 225	$ 225	
6								
7	Revenue		$ 1,001,250	$ 5,625,000	$11,250,000	$ 14,625,000	$ 15,750,000	
8		$/shoe						
9	Cost of Goods Sold	$(177.90)	$ (791,655)	$ (4,447,500)	$ (8,895,000)	$ (11,563,500)	$ (12,453,000)	
10	Selling Expense	$ (10.00)	$ (44,500)	$ (250,000)	$ (500,000)	$ (650,000)	$ (700,000)	
11								
12	Operating Income		$ 165,095	$ 927,500	$ 1,855,000	$ 2,411,500	$ 2,597,000	
13								
14	Interest Expense		$ (74,995)	$ (61,012)	$ (45,876)	$ (29,493)	$ (11,759)	
15	Depreciation		$ (97,500)	$ (97,500)	$ (97,500)	$ (97,500)	$ (97,500)	
16	Taxable Income		$ (7,400)	$ 768,988	$ 1,711,624	$ 2,284,507	$ 2,487,741	
17								
18	Taxes		$ 2,590	$ (269,146)	$ (599,068)	$ (799,578)	$ (870,709)	
19	Income After Taxes		$ (4,810)	$ 499,842	$ 1,112,556	$ 1,484,929	$ 1,617,032	
20								
21	Add Back Depreciation		$ 97,500	$ 97,500	$ 97,500	$ 97,500	$ 97,500	
22	Subtract Principal Payments		$ (169,632)	$ (183,615)	$ (198,751)	$ (215,134)	$ (232,868)	
23								
24	Cash Flow		$ (76,942)	$ 413,727	$ 1,011,305	$ 1,367,295	$ 1,481,664	
25								
26								

Calculating the projected cash flow estimate for year 1: =SUM(C19,C21,C22)

The projected cash flow estimate shows a moderate negative cash flow in year 1. In all subsequent years, the sales projections predict a positive cash flow, so that by year 5 the TZEdge project is generating $1.48 million in cash. The results of this analysis raise several questions. Will the original CtrBank loan be feasible for financing this project? Certainly over the course of the first five years there is enough cash generated to pay off the loan. However, if TheZone relies solely on cash flows to pay back the loan, then insufficient funds will be generated in year 1 to service the debt. Approximately $245,000 (payment of $61,000*4) is needed each year to make the loan payments. In fact, because there is no positive cash flow generated in year 1, some other type of financial arrangement might be needed, unless TheZone is willing to cover the debt by using funds generated from other corporate enterprises.

But even before the financing issues are resolved, the main question is: Should TheZone go ahead with this project? Or, as an alternative, would the company reap more profits through another means, such as buying treasury bills? If the company wants to continue with the project, can it be modified so that less capital is required, even if additional labor will be needed? These questions will be explored further in Level 3.

Best Practice

Nesting Basic Financial Functions to Calculate Variable Periodic Payments

Excel provides other, more complex financial functions that allow for variable payments, interest rates, and so on. However, using only the basic functions, you can often easily solve this type of financial transaction by nesting functions within each other. Consider the example of CtrBank modifying its loan so that it would lend TheZone $1 million at 8.5% interest compounded quarterly over the next six years, but no payments would be expected for the first year. How would you calculate the payments for such a loan? One way would be to calculate the money owed after year 1, $1 million plus the accrued interest (future value), and then use that amount as the present value of a five-year payment stream. The formula to accomplish this is shown in Figure 6.25.

Figure 6.25: Calculating a loan payment where payments begin after one year of accruing interest

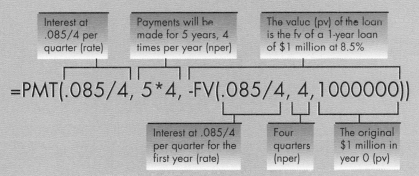

By nesting one financial function inside another—in this case, nesting the FV function inside the PMT function—you can obtain the same results provided by more complex functions. This might be a preferred method, depending on your knowledge of and experience with building formulas with more complicated financial functions.

Steps To Success: Level 2

The Equipment division at TheZone is looking into a new piece of equipment that was developed in Europe to mold skis more precisely and less expensively than the current technology being used at TheZone. The cost of the machine plus installation is estimated to be $1,665,000. The projected cost savings are expected to be $8.50 per pair of skis. You have been asked to estimate a projected cash flow savings (if any) that will be generated by this proposed project over the next four years.

Complete the following:

1. Open the workbook named **Ski.xlsx** in the Chapter 6 folder, and then save it as **Ski Molder Cash Flow Estimate.xlsx**. The structure for the projected cash flow estimate is provided on Sheet1, as shown in Figure 6.26.

Figure 6.26: Worksheet for ski molder projected cash flow estimate

	A	B	C	D	E	F	G
1	Year		1	2	3	4	
2	Sales Volume						
3	Cost Savings per Pair						
4							
5	Cost Savings						
6							
7	Interest Expense						
8	Depreciation						
9	Net Cost Savings						
10							
11	Additional Tax Owed						
12	Savings After Taxes						
13							
14	Add Back Depreciation						
15	Subtract Principal Payments						
16							
17	Projected Cash Flow Estimate						
18							
19							

---

2. Rename the Sheet1 worksheet as **cashflow**. Insert the following title at the top of the worksheet, merged and centered: **Ski Molding Project – Projected 4-Year Cash Flow Estimate**.

3. Enter the sales volume for each year, assuming sales in year 1 of 150,000 pairs. The sales volume for each successive year is assumed to be 6% more than the previous year. Round these values to the nearest whole number.

4. Enter the cost savings as **$8.55** per pair. This will not change in subsequent years.

5. Calculate the cost savings as the number of pairs of skis sold times the cost savings per ski.

6. On a separate worksheet named **loan** (similar to the Loan worksheet shown in Figure 6.15), create an amortization table listing the principal and interest payments and remaining principal in each monthly period, assuming TheZone will borrow the money under the following terms:

   Funding will be arranged for the entire cost of this investment (the cost of the machine plus installation) at 5% interest compounded monthly, paid out in full in equal monthly installments over this same four-year period.

7. On the cashflow worksheet, calculate the cumulative interest expense for year 1 (the interest portion of the loan payments for the corresponding year). You can reference

cells on the loan worksheet as needed. Assume the loan will start at the beginning of year 1, and all payments will be made at the end of each period. Write your formula so that it can be copied across the row to automatically calculate these values for years 2 through 4.

8. Calculate the depreciation for this equipment using the straight line depreciation method. The equipment is assumed to have a 10-year life with a salvage value of $70,000 at the end of that period. For cost, use the cost of the machine plus installation. Set up a separate worksheet named **depreciation** to store these values, and use named ranges in your formula.

9. Calculate the net cost savings—the cost savings less the interest expense and depreciation.

10. Calculate the additional tax that would be owed (based on the net cost savings) assuming that TheZone is taxed at a 35% rate. Use a named range to store this value.

11. Calculate the savings after taxes.

12. Complete the worksheet, adding back in the depreciation that was deducted and adding in the cumulative principal payments for the corresponding year, to arrive at a final projected cash flow estimate for each of the four years. Use the correct absolute and relative cell referencing so that your formulas will work for each of the cash flow years.

13. Format your worksheet as appropriate to make it easy to read and understand.

14. Save and close the Ski Molder Cash Flow Estimate.xlsx workbook.

LEVEL 3
Evaluating the Financial Viability of Alternative Project Options

Setting Up a Worksheet to Analyze Profitability

Ryan has now estimated the cash flow for the manufacture of the TZEdge shoe according to the terms of option 1, which requires $1,000,000 in capital funded through a loan from CtrBank at 8% interest compounded quarterly. The engineering group has also proposed a less capital-intensive solution that requires additional labor instead of the $1 million in upfront capital equipment. This option would be less automated, replacing what a machine can do with manual labor, requiring a $250,000 capital investment and additional labor costs of $20 per pair of shoes. Ryan has calculated the income after taxes for this low capital alternative, assuming that it will be entirely funded from existing cash assets; therefore, no loan will be required. He has also assumed for this alternative that the equipment is depreciated using straight line depreciation over a 10-year period with a salvage value of $5,000.

Ryan's next task is to analyze the profitability of each of these options. To facilitate this analysis, Ryan copies his earlier projected cash flow worksheet to a new workbook named Profitability, and then modifies the worksheet to include all of the relevant data inputs for loan values and depreciation. For financial purposes, he has been directed by management to use the Income After Taxes values in his analysis. Specifically, he makes the following modifications:

- Names the new worksheet High for the high capital option
- Inputs data for the loan, depreciation, and taxes at the top of the worksheet
- Inputs data for the interest rate (or hurdle rate, as defined later) and tax rate
- Deletes the rows below the Income After Taxes row from his original worksheet
- Modifies the formulas to reflect these changes, referencing the corresponding new data input locations

The resulting worksheet is shown in Figure 6.27.

The formulas for the High worksheet are shown in Figure 6.28.

Figure 6.27: High worksheet

Data inputs for loan, depreciation, and hurdle rates

	A	B	C	D	E	F	G
1	OPTION	Annual Rate	Duration in Years	Compounding Periods/Year	PV	FV	PMT
2	(1) CtrBank loan	8.0%	5	4	$ 1,000,000	$ 0	$ (61,157)
3							
4	Depreciation Method		Asset Value	Salvage Value	Life		
5	SLN		$ 1,000,000	$ 25,000	10		
6							
7	Hurdle Rate:	25.0%		Tax Rate	35.0%		
8							
9	Projected 5-Year Income after Taxes - High Capital Option (Original)						
10	Year	0	1	2	3	4	5
11	Sales Volume:		4,450	25,000	50,000	65,000	70,000
12	Selling Price - per pair		$ 225	$ 225	$ 225	$ 225	$ 225
13	Cost of Goods Sold - per pair		$ 177.90	$ 177.90	$ 177.90	$ 177.90	$ 177.90
14	Selling Expenses - per pair		$ 10	$ 10	$ 10	$ 10	$ 10
15							
16	Revenue		$ 1,001,250	$ 5,625,000	$ 11,250,000	$ 14,625,000	$ 15,750,000
17	Cost of Goods Sold:		$ (791,655)	$ (4,447,500)	$ (8,895,000)	$ (11,563,500)	$ (12,453,000)
18	Selling Expense		$ (44,500)	$ (250,000)	$ (500,000)	$ (650,000)	$ (700,000)
19							
20	Operating Income		$ 165,095	$ 927,500	$ 1,855,000	$ 2,411,500	$ 2,597,000
21							
22	Interest Expense		$ (74,995)	$ (61,012)	$ (45,876)	$ (29,493)	$ (11,759)
23	Depreciation		$ (97,500)	$ (97,500)	$ (97,500)	$ (97,500)	$ (97,500)
24	Taxable Income		$ (7,400)	$ 768,988	$ 1,711,624	$ 2,284,507	$ 2,487,741
25							
26	Income Taxes		2,590	(269,146)	(599,068)	(799,578)	(870,709)
27	Income After Taxes	(1,000,000)	(4,810)	499,842	1,112,556	1,484,930	1,617,032

Cashflow worksheet copied from Sales Volume through Income After Taxes

Now Ryan is ready to analyze the data. Companies can use numerous methods to analyze whether to proceed with a project, or to choose among alternatives based on their profitability. Ryan will look at several common methods such as *net present value* and *internal rate of return* in conjunction with calculations for *return on investment* and *payback period*. Ryan will proceed with his analysis using the projected income after taxes to measure these values. Here, TheZone is not focusing on the cash in and out of the company, but rather on income earned, or profits.

Figure 6.28: High worksheet with formulas displayed

Cumulative interest referencing rate, pv, and nper from row 2

9			Projected 5-Year Income
10 Year	0	1	
11 Sales Volume:		4450	
12 Selling Price - per pair		225	
13 Cost of Goods Sold - per pair		177.9	
14 Selling Expenses - per pair		10	
15			
16 Revenue		=C11*C12	
17 Cost of Goods Sold:		=-C13*C11	
18 Selling Expense		=-C11*C14	
19			
20 Operating Income		=SUM(C16:C18)	
21			
22 Interest Expense		=CUMIPMT($B2/$D2,$C2*$D2,$E2,C10*4-3,C10*4,0)	
23 Depreciation		=-SLN($C5,$D5,$E5)	
24 Taxable Income		=SUM(C20,C22:C23)	
25			
26 Income Taxes		=-$E7*C24	
27 Income After Taxes	=-E2	=C26+C24	

Straight line depreciation referencing inputs from row 5

Ultimately, the decision of whether to proceed will depend not only on these specific values for the TZEdge project, but also on other projects the company is considering for different uses of capital, such as expanding the tennis racket line, for example, or building a new corporate office. The decision must also factor in TheZone's ability to fund the project, the level of risk the company is willing to assume, and the company's overall corporate strategies for growth.

Calculating Net Present Value

The High worksheet includes all the necessary elements to analyze the profitability of the high capital option assuming it's funded by the CtrBank loan. The formulas correctly calculate the yearly net income after taxes for the given inputs. Ryan can now begin to complete the financial analysis. The first method he will use is **net present value** (**NPV**). NPV is preferred by most financial theorists because it uses the expected cash flows—in this case, income after taxes—and applies a minimum rate of return to discount these cash flows into current (present) value dollars, essentially finding the present value for each year's income. In other words, NPV enables you to see what the current worth is of the projected cash flows, which helps you to determine the profitability of the venture.

The **rate of return**, often referred to as the **hurdle rate** or **discount rate**, is an interest rate chosen to reflect not only the time value of money, but the desired returns the company expects for the level of risk being taken. Projects with positive NPVs at a given hurdle rate are considered to be ones that will add wealth to the corporation—the more positive the value, the greater the expected returns. Selecting a hurdle rate can be quite controversial because different analysts or managers might not all agree on the hurdle rate to choose. The NPV is often calculated at several alternative hurdle rates to determine the sensitivity of the project to the various rates of return.

Ryan has been instructed to use a hurdle rate of 25% for the high capital option. So, if the NPV is greater than 0 for this minimum rate of return, TheZone should go ahead with the TZEdge project. Projects with positive cash flows indicate that the project will be profitable; the higher the NPV, the more profitable the project.

Entering the NPV Function

To analyze the net present value manually, Ryan would have to systematically calculate the present value based on each year's income after taxes and compound the hurdle rate over a one-year period for year 1's cash flow and then compound the hurdle rate over a two-year period for year 2's cash flow, and so on. The NPV function performs these calculations automatically. This function takes the hurdle rate and the series of cash flow values and automatically calculates the discounted value. The syntax of the NPV function is as follows:

$$\text{NPV(rate,value1,value2,...)}$$

The NPV function has the following requirements:

- The hurdle (discount) *rate* must match the period duration, so that a yearly cash flow would apply to a yearly (annual) discount rate, for example.
- *Value1, value2, value3*, and so on must be equally spaced in time and occur at the end of each period.
- Because NPV uses the order of value1, value2, value3, and so on to determine the number of periods to discount each value, cash flows must be entered in the correct sequence from earliest to latest (year 1, year 2,…year *n*).
- Text values and error messages are ignored.

Best Practice

Avoiding Problems of Year 0 Cash Flows When Using the NPV Function
The NPV function in Excel takes the cash flow from year 0, which is referred to as value1, and discounts the value by one year. Essentially, the first cash flow in or out of the financial transaction is assumed to be one year from now. The function then takes value2 and discounts it back two years at the given discount rate. So, if the actual first cash flow is now (year 0), and you include this in the NPV function, the result would be that the entire cash flow would be discounted an extra year—which is not the intended result.

This problem can be easily corrected. Consider the example of cash flows from years 0 to 4, as follows: –1000, +400, +400, +400, +400. Assuming a 20% hurdle rate, the formula you would write is: =NPV(20%,–1000,400,400,400,400). This formula results in the value 29.58; but, as noted earlier, this formula does not take into account the fact that the first cash flow is now (year 0)—not one year from now. To work around this problem and accurately calculate the cash flow using the NPV function, again assuming a 20% hurdle rate, you could calculate the NPV by adding the value in year 0 to the discounted cash flows in years 1 to *n*, as follows: value1+NPV(discount rate, value2, value3,...value*n*). In this example, the resulting formula is =–1000+NPV(20%,400,400,400,400). The result of this formula is 35.49, which accurately reflects when the cash flows actually occur.

Setting Up a Table of Hurdle Rates

Using the NPV function, Ryan can write the formula to determine the net present value of the income flows for this project, including the initial investment, as follows:

```
–Initial investment + NPV(25%, income year 1, income year
                    2...income year 5)
```

However, Ryan decides to create a small table that calculates the NPV for several values above and below the 25% hurdle rate to give him a better idea of the sensitivity of this project to hurdle rates both above and below the target rate provided by management. For a hurdle rate of 25%, Ryan wants to calculate the NPV starting with a rate of 21% and going up to 29%, as follows:

- Target hurdle rate –4%
- Target hurdle rate –3%
- Target hurdle rate –2%
- Target hurdle rate –1%
- Target hurdle rate
- Target hurdle rate +1%
- Target hurdle rate +2%
- Target hurdle rate +3%
- Target hurdle rate +4%

To create a table that automatically updates if the hurdle rate is modified, Ryan needs to relate this range of values to the hurdle rate input value, as shown in Figure 6.29. Note that Ryan has applied the Freeze Panes tool to easily view the data inputs and outputs simultaneously.

Figure 6.29: Setting up an NPV table for +/- 4% of a given hurdle rate

	A	B	C	D	E	F	G
1	OPTION	Annual Rate	Duration in Years	Compounding Periods/Year	PV	FV	PMT
2	(1) CtrBank loan	8.0%	5	4	$ 1,000,000	$ 0	$ (61,157)
3							
4	Depreciation Method		Asset Value	Salvage Value	Life		
5	SLN		$ 1,000,000	$ 25,000	10		
6							
7	Hurdle Rate:	25.0%		Tax Rate	35.0%		
8							
28							
29		Hurdle rates	NPV				
30		21%		Formula =B34-0.01			
31		22%		in cell B33 is copied			
32		23%		up to cells B32:B30			
33		24%					
34		25%			Formula =B7 in cell B34		
35		26%			points to the hurdle rate		
36		27%					
37		28%		Formula =B34+0.01			
38		29%		in cell B35 is copied down to cells B36:B38			

Cell B7 contains the initial hurdle rate

The process Ryan followed is as follows:

- Start in the center of the hurdle rate column of the table (cell B34) and directly reference the hurdle rate from the inputs at the top of the worksheet by writing the formula =B7.
- Calculate the values below the hurdle rate by writing the formula =B34–0.01 in cell B33, and then copy this formula into the top half of the table (cells B30:B32).
- Calculate the values above the hurdle rate by writing the formula =B34+0.01 in cell B35, and then copy this formula into the bottom half of the table (cells B36:B38).

With the hurdle rates established, Ryan can now write the NPV formula in cell C30 and copy it down the column to cell C38, as follows:

=B$27+NPV(B30,C$27:G$27)

Cell B$27 contains the initial capital investment of –$1,000,000 made in year 0; cell B30 contains the corresponding hurdle rate; and the range C$27:G$27 contains the cash flows from years 1 through 5. Only the hurdle rate will copy relatively; the values for the initial investment and cash flow range will remain fixed. Figure 6.30 shows the resulting worksheet. All the resulting values are positive, indicating that this project, if completed, would benefit the company.

Figure 6.30: Results for NPV at different hurdle rates

	A	B	C	D	E	F	G
1	OPTION	Annual Rate	Duration in Years	Compounding Periods/Year	PV	FV	PMT
2	(1) CtrBank loan	8.0%	5	4	$ 1,000,000	$ 0	$ (61,157)
3							
4	Depreciation Method		Asset Value	Salvage Value	Life		
5	SLN		$ 1,000,000	$ 25,000	10		
6							
7	Hurdle Rate:	25.0%		Tax Rate	35.0%		
8							
26	Income Taxes		2,590	(269,146)	(599,068)	(799,578)	(870,709)
27	Income After Taxes	(1,000,000)	(4,810)	499,842	1,112,556	1,484,930	1,617,032
28							
29			Hurdle rates	NPV			
30			21%	$ 1,281,599			
31			22%	$ 1,213,171			
32			23%	$ 1,147,480			
33			24%	$ 1,084,390			
34			25%	$ 1,023,776			
35			26%	$ 965,518			
36			27%	$ 909,504			
37			28%	$ 855,627			
38			29%	$ 803,788			
39							

Formula to calculate NPV
for a given cash flow:
= B$27+NPV (B30,C$27:G$27)

Calculating the Internal Rate of Return

The second analysis Ryan will undertake is to calculate the internal rate of return (IRR) for the TZEdge project. The **internal rate of return (IRR)** method of evaluating profitability takes a similar approach to that of NPV in that it considers the cash flows and discounts them back to the present value. The difference is that the IRR method calculates the *rate* at which these discounted cash flows in and out are equal, essentially where the NPV is $0. The company can then determine if the IRR is sufficient to make it worthwhile to go ahead with a project. Usually, projects with higher IRRs are preferable to projects with lower IRRs, given that all discount rates below the IRR result in positive cash flows to the company.

In traditional projects with large capital expenditures in the early years followed by positive cash flows in later years, the two analytical methods of NPV and IRR usually (but not always) lead to similar decisions. In projects where cash flows are negative at both the beginning and end of the project life, the results are often contradictory.

To calculate the IRR manually, you would need to guess an IRR value and substitute it as the discount rate in the NPV formula. Depending on the value returned, this process would be repeated with a second guess, and then a third guess, and so on, refining the estimate until a value of 0 is reached. Like all other trial-and-error manual tasks, this would be a laborious process. Fortunately, Excel can do this work automatically with the IRR function.

The syntax of the IRR function is as follows:

```
IRR(values,guess)
```

6

Level 3

The *values* argument is a list of positive and negative cash flows. For this function to work, a minimum of one positive and one negative cash flow must be listed. Cash flows are taken in the order listed, assuming each successive one is one period later. As with the NPV function, the cash flows must occur at regular, equal intervals. The *guess* argument is optional and should not be needed, but can be used if the 20 iterations that are automatically performed by Excel do not result in an accurate value (within .00001%). If this happens, a #NUM! error is returned.

Applying this function to the worksheet in cell B39, Ryan writes the following formula:

```
=IRR(B27:G27)
```

As shown in Figure 6.31, Ryan placed the formula at the bottom of the table containing the hurdle rate and NPV values. He entered the value $0 in the NPV column (C39) applying appropriate cell formats. This facilitates the formulation of a chart, which Ryan plans to create next.

Figure 6.31: Calculating the IRR

	A	B	C	D	E	F	G
		Annual	Duration in	Compounding			
1	OPTION	Rate	Years	Periods/Year	PV	FV	PMT
2	(1) CtrBank loan	8.0%	5	4	$ 1,000,000	$ 0	$ (61,157)
3							
4	Depreciation Method		Asset Value	Salvage Value	Life		
5	SLN		$ 1,000,000	$ 25,000	10		
6							
7	Hurdle Rate:	25.0%		Tax Rate	35.0%		
8							
26	Income Taxes		2,590	(269,146)	(599,068)	(799,578)	(870,709)
27	Income After Taxes	(1,000,000)	(4,810)	499,842	1,112,556	1,484,930	1,617,032
28							
29		Hurdle rates	NPV				
30		21%	$ 1,281,599				
31		22%	$ 1,213,171				
32		23%	$ 1,147,480				
33		24%	$ 1,084,390				
34		25%	$ 1,023,776				
35		26%	$ 965,518				
36		27%	$ 909,504				
37		28%	$ 855,627				
38		29%	$ 803,788				
39	IRR	52%	$ 0				
40							

Formula to calculate IRR: =IRR(B27:G27)

The calculation results in an IRR of 52%. At a discount rate of 52%, the NPV of these cash flows is $0. Using this method alone, TheZone management would accept this project only if they considered a 52% rate of return a sufficient profit for the risks involved.

Creating a Chart Showing the Hurdle Rate vs. NPV

Ryan wants to graphically depict the sensitivity of the NPV to the hurdle rates, as well as the IRR. Because he wants to show a functional relationship—in this case, hurdle rate versus NPV— the best type of chart to use is an X Y Scatter chart, with scattered data points and smooth lines. Ryan creates this chart easily by highlighting the data range $B$30:$C$39 and selecting the Scatter button in the Charts group on the Insert tab. He then selects the Scatter chart type with straight lines and markers. Next, Ryan moves the resulting chart to the desired area of the worksheet and resizes it so that it fits next to the hurdle rate table. Finally, Ryan inserts the appropriate chart and axes titles, plot area, and shading and formatting options, as shown in Figure 6.32.

Figure 6.32: X Y Scatter chart of NPV vs. hurdle rates

The lower the hurdle rate, the higher the NPV

	A	B	C	D	E	F	G	H
		Annual	Duration in	Compounding				
1	OPTION	Rate	Years	Periods/Year	PV	FV	PMT	
2	(1) CtrBank loan	8.0%	5	4	$ 1,000,000	$ 0	$ (61,157)	
3								
4	Depreciation Method		Asset Value	Salvage Value	Life			
5	SLN		$ 1,000,000	$ 25,000	10			
6								
7	Hurdle Rate:	25.0%		Tax Rate	35.0%			
8								
26	Income Taxes		2,590	(269,146)	(599,068)	(799,578)	(870,709)	
27	Income After Taxes	(1,000,000)	(4,810)	499,842	1,112,556	1,484,930	1,617,032	
28								
29		Hurdle rates	NPV					
30		21%	$ 1,281,599					
31		22%	$ 1,213,171					
32		23%	$ 1,147,480					
33		24%	$ 1,084,390					
34		25%	$ 1,023,776					
35		26%	$ 965,518					
36		27%	$ 909,504					
37		28%	$ 855,627					
38		29%	$ 803,788					
39	IRR	52%	$ 0					
40								
41								
42								

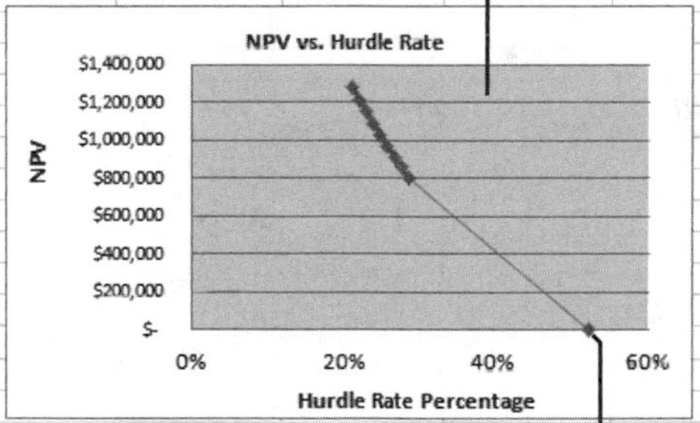

NPV vs. Hurdle Rate

The point where the line crosses the x-axis, at 52%, is the IRR

The chart clearly illustrates that all hurdle rates below 52% (IRR) result in a positive NPV—the lower the hurdle rate, the higher the NPV.

Calculating the Return on Investment

The third value to be calculated in Ryan's analysis is the **return on investment** (**ROI**). The ROI is the sum of the cash flows, excluding the initial investment, divided by the investment value. Stockholders often look at the ROI as a quick measure of how attractive a company's stock is versus other stocks within the industry. Because ROI is easy to calculate, it is often used in addition to more sophisticated measures.

For the high capital case, the ROI is the sum of the income values in years 1 through 5 divided by $1,000,000. In Excel syntax, the formula is:

```
=SUM(C27:G27)/C5
```

Ryan enters this formula in cell B41 of the worksheet. The resulting value for the high capital option is 471%, as shown in Figure 6.33.

Figure 6.33: Calculating ROI

	A	B	C	D	E	F	G	H
1	*OPTION*	*Annual Rate*	*Duration in Years*	*Compounding Periods/Year*	*PV*	*FV*	*PMT*	
2	(1) CtrBank loan	8.0%	5	4	$ 1,000,000	$ 0	$ (61,157)	
3								
4	*Depreciation Method*		*Asset Value*	*Salvage Value*	*Life*			
5	SLN		$ 1,000,000	$ 25,000	10			
6								
7	*Hurdle Rate:*	25.0%		*Tax Rate*	35.0%			
8								
26	Income Taxes		2,590	(269,146)	(599,068)	(799,578)	(870,709)	
27	Income After Taxes	(1,000,000)	(4,810)	499,842	1,112,556	1,484,930	1,617,032	
28								
29		*Hurdle rates*	*NPV*					
30		21%	$ 1,281,599					
31		22%	$ 1,213,171					
32		23%	$ 1,147,480					
33		24%	$ 1,084,390					
34		25%	$ 1,023,776					
35		26%	$ 965,518					
36		27%	$ 909,504					
37		28%	$ 855,627					
38		29%	$ 803,788					
39	IRR	52%	$ 0					
40								
41	*Return on Investment*	471%						
42								

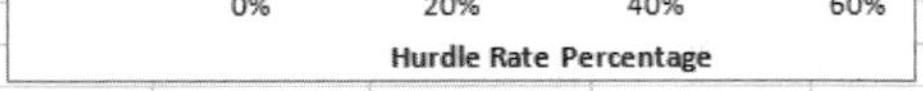

Formula to calculate ROI: =SUM(C27:G27)/C5

Keep in mind that the ROI does not take into account the time value of money. In aggregate, over the entire five-year period, this project would yield $4.71 per dollar of investment. The timing of the money is not taken into account. This 471% would be the same if all of the money was earned in the first period or all in the last. However, despite the lack of accounting for timing, the value clearly shows that over this period, the company would recoup its investment more than fourfold. Over a five-year period, depending on the risk, this might be a reasonable investment.

Determining the Payback Period

The final piece of data Ryan needs to determine is the **payback period**, which is the time it will take to earn sufficient profits so that the loan can be paid back. Projects that are paid back early are preferred. Over the long term, calculating the payback period does not always give the most realistic view of the most profitable venture. Again, this factor is only one of many to consider when making the final decision.

The payback year is the year in which the *cumulative* total cash flow is greater than or equal to $0. To determine this manually, you would need to add the cash flows together using the values in cells B27:G27, starting with year 0 (negative value for the initial investment) and continuing with each successive year until the value reaches $0 or greater as follows:

- Years 0 to 1: –1,000,000 + –4,810 results in the value –1,004,810
- Years 0 to 2: –1,000,000 + –4,810 + 499,842 results in the value –504,968
- Years 0 to 3: –1,000,000 + –4,810 + 499,842 + 1,112,556 results in the value 607,588

It is some time during the third year of operation that the original investment would be recouped. Ryan directly enters the value 3 in cell B42 to indicate year 3 for the payback period, as shown in Figure 6.34.

Figure 6.34: Determining the payback period

	A	B	C	D	E	F	G	H
		Annual	Duration in	Compounding				
1	OPTION	Rate	Years	Periods/Year	PV	FV	PMT	
2	(1) CtrBank loan	8.0%	5	4	$ 1,000,000	$ 0	$ (61,157)	
3								
4	Depreciation Method		Asset Value	Salvage Value	Life			
5	SLN		$ 1,000,000	$ 25,000	10			
6								
7	Hurdle Rate:	25.0%		Tax Rate	35.0%			
8								
26	Income Taxes		2,590	(269,146)	(599,068)	(799,578)	(870,709)	
27	Income After Taxes	(1,000,000)	(4,810)	499,842	1,112,556	1,484,930	1,617,032	
28								
29		Hurdle rates	NPV					
30		21%	$ 1,281,599					
31		22%	$ 1,213,171					
32		23%	$ 1,147,480					
33		24%	$ 1,084,390					
34		25%	$ 1,023,776					
35		26%	$ 965,518					
36		27%	$ 909,504					
37		28%	$ 855,627					
38		29%	$ 803,788					
39		IRR	52%	$ 0				
40								
41	Return on Investment	471%						
42	Payback (years)	3						

Payback period is the earliest year in which the cumulative cash flows are greater than $0

Ryan has calculated a payback of three years. It will take TheZone three years to earn enough money to cover its initial investment costs. Again, this method does not discount cash flows; the same value would be returned if the cash flows for years 1 and 2 were $0, and in year 3 the cash flow was any amount over $1 million. Nor does this method take into account the profitability of the venture versus the risk. In this case, if the TZEdge shoes are expected to sell for only a five-year period, almost half the life cycle of the project would be over before any profits would be realized.

Excel provides a method to automatically calculate the payback period, but it is a somewhat complex process that involves using the MATCH function and calculating a cumulative total.

How To

Automate the Payback Calculation

1. In a row below the data being analyzed (refer to Figure 6.34 for the purposes of this discussion), write a formula in cell B44 to determine if the cumulative cash flow for the corresponding year is greater than $0, as follows:

$$=SUM(\$B27:B27)>0$$

2. Copy this formula across the row to produce a row of TRUE and FALSE values. Note that by adding an absolute cell reference to only the beginning cell column reference of the sum range, copying this formula across will change only the end range reference, thereby creating a row of cumulative totals.

3. Determine the relative position (1, 2, 3) of the first TRUE value and subtract 1 to find the corresponding year using the following formula:

$$=MATCH(TRUE,B44:G44,0)-1$$

Recall that the MATCH function syntax requires a lookup_value, lookup_array, and match type as inputs. In the example, the lookup_value is TRUE to be found in the lookup_array B44:G44, and because an exact match is required, the match type is 0. Because these flows correspond to years 0, 1, 2, and so on, instead of 1, 2, 3, it is necessary to subtract 1 to get the correct number of years in which the amount is paid back.

An implementation of this technique is shown in Figure 6.35. Again, the results show that year 3 is the year in which the loan is paid back, as indicated by the value TRUE in cell E44.

Figure 6.35: Automating the payback calculation

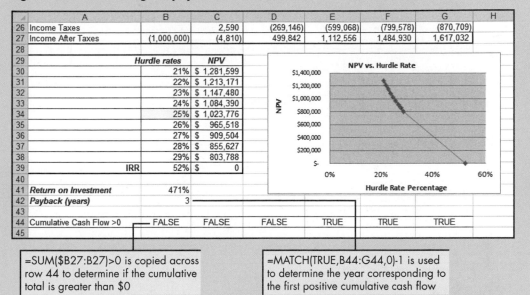

	A	B	C	D	E	F	G	H
26	Income Taxes		2,590	(269,146)	(599,068)	(799,578)	(870,709)	
27	Income After Taxes	(1,000,000)	(4,810)	499,842	1,112,556	1,484,930	1,617,032	
28								
29		Hurdle rates	NPV					
30		21%	$ 1,281,599					
31		22%	$ 1,213,171					
32		23%	$ 1,147,480					
33		24%	$ 1,084,390					
34		25%	$ 1,023,776					
35		26%	$ 965,518					
36		27%	$ 909,504					
37		28%	$ 855,627					
38		29%	$ 803,788					
39	IRR	52%	$ 0					
40								
41	Return on Investment	471%						
42	Payback (years)	3						
43								
44	Cumulative Cash Flow >0	FALSE	FALSE	FALSE	TRUE	TRUE	TRUE	
45								

=SUM($B27:B27)>0 is copied across row 44 to determine if the cumulative total is greater than $0

=MATCH(TRUE,B44:G44,0)-1 is used to determine the year corresponding to the first positive cumulative cash flow

Setting Up the Worksheet for the Low Capital Option

Recall that another option is being considered to fund the TZEdge project, one with lower capital investment requirements and higher labor costs. To set up the worksheet for this option, Ryan copies the High worksheet to create a new worksheet named Low and enters the new input values and headings. Figure 6.36 shows the Low worksheet.

To create the Low worksheet, Ryan did the following:

- Modified the title
- Removed the loan values from row 2, because this option does not involve a loan, leaving only the PV of $250,000, which is the cost of the lower capital investment
- Modified the cost of goods sold per pair of shoes from $177.90 to $197.90 (+$20/ pair) and copied this value across the row (cells C13:G13)
- Modified the depreciation input values in row 5 to account for the new asset value of $250,000 and the new salvage value of $5,000
- Deleted the values in row 22 for Interest Expense

The only element that did not copy relatively to the new Low worksheet is the chart. Chart ranges include both sheet names and absolute cell references. This happens automatically when you highlight a range. This means that when Ryan copied the High worksheet to create the Low worksheet, the chart did not automatically update. Ryan had to manually edit the data range to match that of the new sheet's chart input area, essentially just chang-

Figure 6.36: Calculating the profitability of the low capital option

Updated cost of goods sold

Depreciation values updated

Removed loan values

	A	B	C	D	E	F	G	H
1	OPTION	Annual Rate	Duration in Years	Compounding Periods/Year	PV	FV	PMT	
2					$ 250,000			
3								
4	Depreciation Method		Asset Value	Salvage Value	Life			
5	SLN		$ 250,000	$ 5,000	10			
6								
7	Hurdle Rate:	25.0%		Tax Rate	35.0%			
8								
9			Projected 5-Year Income after Taxes - Low Capital Option					
10	Year		0	1	2	3	4	5
11	Sales Volume:		4,450	25,000	50,000	65,000	70,000	
12	Selling Price – per pair		$ 225	$ 225	$ 225	$ 225	$ 225	
13	Cost of Goods Sold – per pair		$ 197.90	$ 197.90	$ 197.90	$ 197.90	$ 197.90	
14	Selling Expenses – per pair		$ 10	$ 10	$ 10	$ 10	$ 10	
15								
16	Revenue		$ 1,001,250	$ 5,625,000	$ 11,250,000	$ 14,625,000	$ 15,750,000	
17	Cost of Goods Sold:		$ (880,655)	$ (4,947,500)	$ (9,895,000)	$ (12,863,500)	$ (13,853,000)	
18	Selling Expense		$ (44,500)	$ (250,000)	$ (500,000)	$ (650,000)	$ (700,000)	
19								
20	Operating Income		$ 76,095	$ 427,500	$ 855,000	$ 1,111,500	$ 1,197,000	
21								
22	Interest Expense							
23	Depreciation		$ (24,500)	$ (24,500)	$ (24,500)	$ (24,500)	$ (24,500)	
24	Taxable Income		$ 51,595	$ 403,000	$ 830,500	$ 1,087,000	$ 1,172,500	
25								
26	Income Taxes		(18,058)	(141,050)	(290,675)	(380,450)	(410,375)	
27	Income After Taxes	(250,000)	33,537	261,950	539,825	706,550	762,125	
28								
29			Hurdle rates	NPV				
30			21%	$ 884,792				
31			22%	$ 851,691				
32			23%	$ 819,901				
33			24%	$ 789,359				
34			25%	$ 760,004				
35			26%	$ 731,779				
36			27%	$ 704,631				
37			28%	$ 678,509				
38			29%	$ 653,364				
39			IRR	91%	$ 0			
40								
41	Return on Investment	922%						
42	Payback (years)	2						
43								

NPV vs. Hurdle Rate chart (NPV on y-axis $-$ to $1,000,000; Hurdle Rate Percentage on x-axis 0% to 100%)

Chart with updated data range

ing the sheet name of the range. To accomplish this, he selected the chart, clicked the Select Data button in the Data group on the Design tab, and then in the Select Data Source window, he renames the High worksheet as Low.

The values obtained for the low capital option case show positive NPVs for all hurdle rates below 91% (IRR). The return on investment is 922%, and this project would be paid for within the first two years of operation.

Best Practice

Using an ISNUMBER Function to Avoid Displaying an Error Message
In the Low worksheet (see Figure 6.36), notice that the yearly interest payments are blank in cells C22:G22. These cells were manually adjusted to remove the formula

=CUMIPMT($B2/$D2,$C2*$D2,$E2,C10*4-3,C10*4,0), which automatically calculated the cumulative interest paid between the corresponding payment periods. In the low capital option, because there is no loan involved and, therefore, no values in row 2, if this formula had not been removed manually, the error message #DIV/0! would have been displayed. This would happen because the function would try to divide by D2, which contains the value 0.

If this type of worksheet were to be used again and again by the company as a template for these types of capital project analyses, it would be more efficient if this payment value could be automatically "corrected" without manually having to remove the formulas—especially if the worksheet was used for further what-if analyses that did include some type of loan funding. This can be accomplished using the ISNUMBER function (described in Chapter 5) nested inside an IF function. Recall that the ISNUMBER function tests to see if the result of the formula is a number.

In the Low worksheet, the following expression could be written in cell C22 to test to see if the cumulative value of the interest payments results in a number; if so, the results of the cumulative interest function would be displayed; otherwise, the value 0 would be displayed.

```
=IF(ISNUMBER(CUMIPMT($B2/$D2,$C2*$D2,$E2,C10*4-3,C10*4,0)),
     CUMIPMT($B2/$D2,$C2*$D2,$E2,C10*4-3,C10*4,0),0)
```

Again, using this technique is a good idea if you plan to use the worksheet as a template to perform further analyses, both with and without the values associated with a loan.

Evaluating the Results of the Analysis

Which of the two options—the high capital option or the low capital option—should Ryan recommend? Or is neither option worthwhile to pursue? Table 6.2 lists a summary of the key values.

Table 6.2: Comparison of investment values

	High Capital Option	Low Capital Option
NPV	$1,023,776	$760,004
IRR	52%	91%
ROI	471%	922%
Payback period	3	2

If Ryan considers only the NPV measure, both options are over $0, but clearly the high capital option returns a higher value, indicating greater profits. On the other hand, the IRR is higher for the low capital option. Neither of these methods has taken into account the difference in risks, such as a possible increased risk due to labor uncertainties. Perhaps the hurdle rates themselves for the low capital option should be revisited. Consider the

ROI and payback period indicators; these clearly also favor the low capital option, even though the subsequent cash flows are lower. What is the correct answer? There is no clear-cut correct answer in this case; the analyses that Ryan has performed will help TheZone management choose the most viable option, taking into consideration many other factors not included in these analyses. The results of these analyses provide useful tools to guide the decision-making process toward an ultimate solution.

Steps To Success: Level 3

The Tennis Equipment division is considering starting its own line of specialty tennis shops in selected areas of the country. The endeavor would require significant upfront capital, but according to the marketing group, it could reap substantial rewards. Two options are under consideration, as follows:

- **Option 1**—Build three new shops on empty lots in three different locations, all of which are close to tennis facilities.
- **Option 2**—Establish three shops located in existing tennis club facilities.

Table 6.3 summarizes the projected income after taxes for the two options over a six-year period.

Table 6.3: Options for tennis shops

	Option 1	Option 2
Year	Income After Taxes	Income After Taxes
0	$ (10,000,000)	$ (4,500,000)
1	920,743	693,091
2	2,608,380	1,910,509
3	3,920,929	2,552,864
4	5,495,889	2,895,157
5	5,958,256	2,962,386
6	5,958,256	2,962,386

The investment for the first option is the most significant, requiring the construction of new buildings, but has the lowest operating costs because it involves no significant rent or royalty-sharing agreements, as does the second option. Your task in these steps is to complete the financial analysis for each option. Complete the following:

1. Open the workbook named **Tennis.xlsx** located in the Chapter 6 folder, and then save it as **Tennis Option Analysis.xlsx**.

2. Create a hurdle rate sensitivity table in cells A15:C25 that calculates the NPV for each option between +/– 5% of the hurdle rate. Be certain that if the hurdle rate in cell

B13 is modified, the sensitivity table will automatically update to reflect the changed rate.

3. In cells B26:C26, calculate the corresponding internal rate of return for each option. Format the cells as percentages.

4. Calculate the return on investment for each option in cells B28:C28. Format the cells as percentages.

5. In cells D3:D9, calculate the cumulative income (including the initial investment) for each year in option 1 (for example: year 1 would include –10,000,000 + 920,743 for option 1). Write the formula so that it can be copied both down the column and across the row to calculate the cumulative income for option 2. Provide appropriate labels in cells D2:E2.

6. In cells B29:C29, enter the payback period (year number) for each option. (*Optional challenge*: Write the necessary formulas to automatically calculate the year number in which the cumulative total income exceeds $0.)

7. Highlight in yellow the income data for the option you would recommend.

8. Create an X Y Scatter chart for your selected option that displays the functional relationship of the hurdle rates to the NPV values. Size the chart and place it next to the hurdle rate analysis. Give the chart an appropriate title and name the axes accordingly.

   TROUBLESHOOTING: In order to modify the X Y Scatter chart to include chart titles and axis titles, use the contextual Chart Tools Format tab, which appears when the chart is selected. Then select the appropriate property you want to modify.

9. Format your worksheet as needed to convey the information clearly and neatly.

10. Save and close the Tennis Option Analysis.xlsx workbook.

Chapter Summary

Although business decisions are not made solely on the basis of money, financial considerations play a significant role in the decision-making process and, therefore, must be analyzed carefully. As you learned in this chapter, Excel provides a host of tools to help in this process. In Level 1, you learned about some of the basic functions used to calculate the elements of a loan, including PMT, RATE, NPER, PV, and FV, and how they affect the positive and negative cash flows of the financial transaction.

In Level 2, a projected cash flow estimate was presented, including an amortization table, to evaluate how a proposed financial endeavor would affect the cash flow of a company. This analysis involved calculating the principal and interest payments with PPMT and

IPMT; calculating the cumulative principal and interest payments with CUMPRINC and CUMIPMT; calculating depreciation using the straight line method; and calculating taxes. Level 3 extended the analysis to explore the profitability of a financial venture by calculating the NPV and IRR, and determining the ROI and payback period.

The financial functions explored in this chapter are only a small subset of the many available in Excel. Some examples are the financial functions that allow you to calculate values based on variable interest rates or uneven compounding periods. You can use the Help system in Excel to explore the different types of financial functions available.

Conceptual Review

Match the following lettered items with Questions 1–14.

A. Compound Interest	E. IRR	I. PMT	M. ROI
B. CUMPRINC	F. NPER	J. PPMT	N. Simple Interest
C. FV	G. NPV	K. PV	O. SLN
D. IPMT	H. Payback Period	L. RATE	P. Type

1. _____Function to calculate the interest percentage per period of a financial transaction

2. _____Function to calculate the value at the beginning of a financial transaction

3. _____Function to calculate the value at the end of a financial transaction

4. _____Function to calculate periodic payments into or out of a financial transaction

5. _____Function to calculate the number of compounding periods in a financial transaction

6. _____Use a 1 for this argument to indicate that interest will be paid at the beginning of each compounding period

7. _____This type of interest is calculated based on original principal regardless of the previous interest earned

8. _____This type of interest is calculated based on principal and previous interest earned

9. _____Function to calculate straight line depreciation based on the initial capital investment, number of years to be depreciated, and salvage value

10. _____Function to calculate the amount of a specific periodic payment that is principal in a given period

11. _____Function to calculate the amount of a periodic payment that is interest in a given period

12. _____Function to calculate the cumulative principal paid between two periods

13. _____Function to determine the value of a variable set of cash flows discounted to its present value

14. _____Function to determine the rate of return, where the net present value of the cash flows is 0

15. Assume that you are investing $6,000 in a savings plan today and will make additional contributions of $200 per quarter. The plan pays 5% interest per year compounded quarterly. Write an Excel formula to determine how much your savings will be worth in five years.

16. Write an Excel formula to determine the yearly interest rate being charged by the bank on a $375,000, 30-year mortgage. You make a monthly mortgage payment of $3,000 and the value of the loan at the end of 30 years is 0. Interest is compounded monthly.

17. Assume that you are buying a car for $23,500 with a $3,000 down payment, and you are borrowing the rest from a bank at 6.0% annual interest compounded monthly. Your monthly payments are $370.Write an Excel formula to determine the number of years it will take you to pay off this loan.

18. Consider a $100,000 mortgage at 5% annual interest compounded monthly, to be paid back over the next 15 years. The loan will have a $5,000 balloon payment due at the end of the loan. Write an Excel formula to determine the payment that must be made each month on this loan.

19. Assume that you have been left an inheritance and want to save part of it toward the purchase of a car upon graduation, which is three years from now. Write an Excel formula to determine the amount of money you need to invest now to have $15,000 at the end of the three-year period. Assume that you will place this money in a CD that pays 3% interest compounded quarterly and that you will be making no additional deposits into this account.

20. Write an Excel formula to determine the amount of money that can be depreciated each year, using straight line depreciation, for a new packaging machine purchased by your company. The machine originally cost $250,000 and has a useful life of 10 years and an estimated salvage value of $10,000.

CASE PROBLEMS

Level 1 – Evaluating Loan Options for Flowers By Diana

Finance

Diana Bullard currently rents space for her small florist business. As her business continues to grow, Diana has decided to purchase her own building. She has selected a site and now requires financing. After meeting with several banks to discuss financing options for a mortgage, Diana has the data she needs to analyze her options. She lists the purchase price of the building and the different values for each of the loan variables together with the other data inputs in an Excel workbook named Loan.xlsx. Her analysis must also take into account the following:

- **Down payment**—The amount of money Diana will pay at the time she purchases the building. Provided is the percent of the building purchase price that will be required for a down payment on each corresponding loan. The difference between the sale price and the down payment is the loan value—the face value of the loan.
- **Points**—The additional charges banks sometimes require when lending a mortgage. Banks usually offer mortgage loans in a variety of interest rate and point combinations. Frequently, loans with higher points have lower interest rates. One point equals 1% of the loan value, so one point on a $7,500 loan is $75.
- **Fees**—The additional amounts banks sometimes charge when lending a mortgage. These amounts vary by bank and loan type. Typical charges include application fees, appraisal fees, credit report fees, and so on.

Your task is to complete the Loan worksheet for Diana, using cell references whenever possible. The formulas in cells G8 through K8 should be written so that they can be copied down the column to calculate values for each of the options listed. These formulas should also automatically update if the mortgage value is updated. Loan options 1–7 are all compounded monthly.

Complete the following:

1. Open the workbook named **Loan.xlsx** in the Chapter 6 folder, and then save it as **Loan Analysis.xlsx**.

2. In the Loan Value column, calculate the face value of this mortgage. The purchase price of the building is given in cell E3.

3. In the Monthly Payment column, calculate the monthly mortgage payment for this loan amount based on the loan value you just calculated. Use the corresponding loan duration, and nominal interest rate indicated. Assume that the loan is completely paid off at the end of this duration. The number of compounding periods per year is given in cell E4.

4. In the Actual Amount Borrowed column, calculate the actual amount Diana will borrow, subtracting the points and fees from the loan value.

5. To take these fees into account, the lender is required by law to disclose the APR of the loan— the *annual percentage rate of interest* being charged. However, different banks calculate APR in different ways, including or excluding different fees. So, you will calculate the APR based on the actual amount borrowed, which you just calculated. Use this amount as the present value of the loan, the monthly payment you calculated in Step 3, and the corresponding loan duration to calculate an actual annual interest rate being charged on this loan (APR).

6. In the Payment with Balloon column, use the nominal interest rate and loan value (column G) to determine the monthly loan payment if you altered the loan to include a $10,000 balloon payment at the end of the loan.

7. The building seller has also offered Diana a private loan for 80% of the value of the building. In return, Diana must pay $14,000 per quarter for the next 10 years. Determine the annual interest rate being charged (cell E17). Inputs do not have to be explicitly listed elsewhere.

8. Diana is negotiating with the seller and is willing to pay $9,000 per quarter at 7½% interest per year compounded quarterly. She will borrow everything but a 10% down payment. Determine how many years it will take to pay off the loan (cell E18). Inputs do not have to be explicitly listed elsewhere.

9. Eight years ago, Diana invested in a bank CD worth $35,000. The CD has earned 4.25% annual interest compounded yearly. Determine (TRUE/FALSE) if Diana has sufficient funds from this CD for Option #1's down payment (E19).

10. Diana has decided that she prefers a bank loan and, given cash flow issues, wants the loan with the smallest payment. Highlight in light blue the cell in column H containing the payment of the loan Diana should select.

    Optional Challenge: Automatically highlight the cell containing the minimum payment value using Conditional Formatting such that if any of the values on any of the bank loans are later modified, the correct value would be automatically highlighted.

11. Save and close the Loan Analysis.xlsx workbook.

Level 2 – Creating a Mortgage Calculator for TriState Savings & Loan

You have been working as a loan officer at TriState Savings & Loan for just over six months. Most of the work you do involves dealing with mortgages for home buyers and small business owners. Frequently, prospective buyers come in seeking information about payments for a particular size mortgage and/or the maximum size mortgage they can obtain

Finance

for a particular payment. They also frequently require information on the tax implications of their selected mortgages, including cumulative yearly interest and depreciation. The answers to these questions vary based on the interest rates currently being offered and the terms the potential buyer is seeking, such as loan duration, balloon payments, and so on.

Although you have found some excellent Web sites that perform the necessary calculations, relying on the Web is sometimes problematic. You can just as easily construct this type of mortgage calculator in Excel, which is what you will do in these steps.

Complete the following:

1. Create a new workbook and save it as **Mortgage Calculator.xlsx** in the Chapter 6 folder. Rename Sheet1 as **Calculator** and include the following elements:

   • First, construct a small mortgage calculator in which you can fill in the data inputs for the value of the mortgage, the loan duration in years, the number of payment periods per year, and the annual interest rate. Then, using this data, calculate the payment for the mortgage. Assume the payment is rounded to the nearest cent. Format the worksheet so the calculator is easy to read and use with data inputs and outputs clearly defined (labeled).
   • Below the mortgage calculator on the same worksheet, create an amortization table for the loan, organized as follows:

Period Number	Remaining Principal	Interest Payment	Principal Payment

   Make sure the table can accommodate a maximum mortgage duration of 30 years, assuming monthly payments. The remaining principal should start out by referencing the calculator's principal value, and thereafter reflect the previous remaining principal value and principal payment. Write the interest and principal payment formulas so that if any of the calculator elements change, these amounts will be automatically updated. Write them so they can be copied down the column for each corresponding period.

   Optional Challenge: To avoid #NUM! errors in periods past the end of the loan, nest your principal and interest payment formulas inside an IF statement to return a 0 if no further interest or principal payments are required.

2. To test the calculator, use the following customer inputs: determine the monthly payment for Zach Jones, who wants a 20-year $270,000 mortgage. The current annual interest rate is 5.75% compounded monthly. The loan is completely paid off at the end of 20 years. Assume no additional points or fees.

3. On a separate worksheet named **Tax**, create a table listing years 1–30 and calculate the following:

- Cumulative interest payments for each year. Write a formula that automatically calculates this value for the corresponding periods so that it can be copied down for each year. Assume that the loans all begin in January so that no "partial" years need to be calculated. Note that to accommodate variable periods (months, quarters, and so on), the beginning and ending periods must be formulas that reference the number of periods per year on your mortgage calculator. (*Hint*: To automatically determine the starting period, take the year number multiplied by the number of periods per year, and then subtract one less than the number of periods per year.)
- In three adjacent columns, calculate the value of the expected tax deduction for tax rates of 15%, 28%, and 33% for the corresponding year (interest payments * tax rate). Your formula should copy both down the column and across the row. Enter the tax rate in a row above the corresponding column.
- For sample data, use the values from the loan for Zach Jones.
- *Optional Challenge*: Automatically substitute zeros instead of #NUM! errors in periods past the end of the loan.

4. In some cases, small business owners who want to buy the properties for their business endeavors are applying for mortgages. For these customers, it would also be helpful to provide them with depreciation estimates. Create a separate worksheet named **Depreciation** to calculate the depreciation. Include the following:

- At the top of the table, list the inputs that will be required: asset value (which will differ from mortgage to mortgage, so it needs to be entered directly), salvage value, and asset life (which will differ from the loan duration).
- Just below the input area, calculate the yearly depreciable value using straight line depreciation.
- Next, create a table below the straight line depreciation to calculate the depreciation for each year (1–20) based on the double-declining balance (DDB) method. For more details on how to use the DDB function, refer to the Excel Help system. Assume the default factor will be used and, therefore, can be omitted. Your table should include the year and the depreciable amount, using **Year** and **DDB** as headings to identify the values.
- Enter the following test data: asset value of $190,000 with a 17-year life and a salvage value of $8,000.

5. Format the workbook so it is easy to read. Save the changes to your Mortgage Calculator.xlsx workbook.

6. Use the Save As option to create a copy of the entire workbook named **Mortgage Calculator2.xlsx**. Then complete the following:

- Modify your inputs and formulas on the Calculator worksheet so that you can enter a known monthly payment, duration, and interest rate to calculate the associated mortgage value as output. Double check that all of your other formulas work: amortization table, taxes, and depreciation.

- Use the following example for your test data: Kelly Hamilton wants to buy a building she plans to use as rental property. If she can make monthly payments of $1,050 per month for the next 30 years, how large a mortgage can she take, assuming that the current interest rate on a 30-year mortgage is 6% per year compounded monthly? For depreciation, assume an asset value of 105% of the loan value, a salvage value of $25,000, and a depreciable life of 30 years.

7. Save and close both the Mortgage Calculator.xlsx workbook and the Mortgage Calculator2.xlsx workbook.

Level 3 – Analyzing Purchasing vs. Leasing Options for CKG Auto

Operations Management

CKG Auto compact car manufacturing assembly plants rely on parts from multiple outside vendors and internal subassembly plants. Currently, these parts are all transported via independent trucking firms for negotiated fees based on actual tons shipped and miles. The operations management group has been dissatisfied lately with the service levels provided by these outside trucking companies, as well as with the rising costs of roughly 7.5% per year for the last two years. These costs are expected to rise in the foreseeable future at similar rates, according to industry analysts. The operations management group is beginning a study to determine if purchasing or leasing a fleet of trucks would be a more cost-effective solution over the next seven years. To do so, the group has compiled some of the costs for each transport option, as follows:

(1) Trucking by others—Using several different trucking carriers, the CKG Auto compact car manufacturing group currently pays $8,000,000 annually in trucking fees. Again, these costs are expected to rise at an annual rate of 7.5%. All costs are considered expenses, which can be used to reduce income for purposes of calculating taxes.

(2) Buying trucks—If CKG Auto purchased a fleet of 20 trucks, the cost of such a purchase would be based on the following:

- The model of truck being considered with trailers is estimated to cost $135,000 per truck. This amount will be spent in year 0 (now).
- This purchase would be funded using a bank loan. The bank is willing to lend the money at a 5% annual interest rate compounded quarterly over the next four years. A 5% down payment will be required, which can be funded from current assets.
- The operations management group has been directed to assume that if CKG Auto purchases this fleet, it would be depreciated using straight line depreciation over the full seven-year period, assuming a salvage value of 10% of the original purchase price.
- Operating costs for year 1 are estimated at $2.80 per mile; this includes driver wages,

gas, insurance, maintenance, fees, and licenses. It is also assumed that each truck will average 150,000 miles per year. For year 2 and all subsequent years, assume a cost increase of 4% per year above the previous year.

- For the calculation of taxes, CKG Auto can deduct from each year's income the following: operating costs, the interest portion of the loan payments, and depreciation.

(3) Leasing trucks—If CKG Auto leases a fleet of 20 trucks, the cost of such a lease would be based on the following:

- There will be an upfront signing fee of $9,500 per truck due at signing (year 0). These fees will be paid directly out of cash assets and no additional financing will be required. These fees can be used to reduce income in year 0 for tax purposes.
- Each year, the lease cost will be a flat fee of $25,000 per truck for each of the next seven years. This fee is fixed for the duration of the lease based on a 150,000-per-mile limit per year per truck.
- Operating costs for year 1 are estimated at $2.80 per mile; this includes driver wages, gas, insurance, maintenance, fees, and licenses. It is assumed that each truck will average 150,000 miles per year. For year 2 and all subsequent years, assume a cost increase of 4% per year above the previous year.
- Because this is an operating lease, there is no depreciation. The entire cost of the lease is considered an expense and can be used to reduce income for purposes of calculating taxes.

Your task is to analyze the various options for CKG Auto to determine which is the most viable. Complete the following:

1. Create a new workbook and save it as **Lease vs Buy.xlsx** in the Chapter 6 folder. Begin by setting up three separate worksheets, one for each option, with appropriate sheet names and titles.

2. For each option, calculate the net costs after taxes for each year, starting with year 0 through year 7, as follows:

- For year 0, list any capital expenditures (purchase option) and/or upfront fees (lease option).
- For years 1–7, list the costs including any operating expenses, leasing or trucking fees paid in that year, any associated depreciation, and interest (purchase option). Remember that the $8 million for trucking costs will go up by 7.5% in year 1 for the first option, and operating expenses for the purchase and lease options will increase by 4% each year with year 1 costs at $2.80 per mile and 150,000 miles per year.
- Multiply all costs (except capital expenditures) by the marginal tax rate of 25%.

- Then subtract this tax savings from the costs to arrive at the net costs after taxes. For year 0, only consider monies paid toward leases and/or purchases—not the current costs of trucking—and keep in mind that only fees and depreciation, not purchases, will result in tax savings.

3. Insert a fourth worksheet named **Comparison** and include the following on this worksheet:

- List the net cost after taxes for each year for each option in three sequential rows, referencing the original worksheets so that any subsequent changes will be automatically reflected on this sheet.
- Calculate the cost savings between using the current trucking method (by others) and purchasing a fleet; and then in the next row, the cost savings between the current trucking method and leasing. Your Comparison worksheet should have a format similar to the one in Table 6.4.

Table 6.4: Comparison worksheet

Net Costs after Taxes:	Year 0	Year 1	Year 2	Year 3	Year 4	Year 5	Year 6	Year 7
Trucking by others								
Purchasing								
Leasing								
Cost Savings Comparisons	Year 0	Year 1	Year 2	Year 3	Year 4	Year 5	Year 6	Year 7
Trucking by others vs. Purchasing								
Trucking by others vs. Leasing								

- Regardless of which signs you've used in your analysis so far, express cost savings as a positive number. (For example, if the costs for shipping by others for year 1 are $10,000 after taxes, and the costs for shipping with purchased trucks in year 1 are $6,000 after taxes, express the cost savings as a positive $4,000.)

4. Determine the net present value of the *cost savings* cash flows (if any) between trucking by others versus purchasing trucks for years 0 through 7, for hurdle rates between 10% and 20% (at 1% intervals). In a similar way, determine the net present value of the cost savings cash flows between trucking by others versus leasing trucks.

5. Calculate the internal rate of return for the cost savings cash flows (trucking by others versus purchasing, and trucking by others versus leasing).

6. Calculate the return on investment and payback period on the investment vs. the cost savings of the purchasing option.

7. Make a recommendation of which method to use for trucking (by others, purchasing, or leasing). Highlight in yellow the row containing the net cost savings of the option you recommend. In a separate area on the worksheet, highlighted in yellow, explain the reason for your choice.

8. Save and close the Lease vs Buy.xlsx workbook.

SAM: Skills Assessment Manager

For current SAM information, including versions and content details, visit SAM Central (http://samcentral.course.com). If you have a SAM user profile, you may have access to hands-on instruction, practice, and assessment of the skills covered in this chapter. Since various versions of SAM are supported throughout the life of this text, check with your instructor for the correct instructions and URL/Web site for accessing assignments.

Organizing Data for Effective Analysis
Marketing: Transforming Raw Data into Various Formats

"There is no such thing as too much planning and tracking."
—Indra Nooyi

LEARNING OBJECTIVES

Level 1

Import text data into a worksheet
Concatenate values and extract characters from a text string
Converting text into columns of data
Analyze data by creating subtotals
Create, sort, and filter an Excel table

Level 2

Import data stored in a database into Excel
Use dates and times in calculations
Analyze data using a PivotTable report
Create a PivotChart report
Import information from the Web into Excel using a Web query

Level 3

Understand markup languages and XML
Import XML data into Excel as an XML table
Add an XML map to a workbook
Analyzing XML Data with Excel
Export XML data from Excel into an XML document

FUNCTIONS COVERED IN THIS CHAPTER

CONCATENATE
FIND
LEFT
RIGHT
SEARCH
TODAY
TRIM
YEARFRAC

Chapter Introduction

In this book, you have used Excel to analyze data in a variety of ways. You can enter data into a worksheet in several ways—you might type data into cells, import data into a worksheet, or link data to another document or file. The data contained in most spreadsheets is numeric, but a significant amount of text is often used to describe that numeric data. Excel has many functions and tools that you can use to manage and analyze nonnumeric data, such as text, dates, and times. You can also use another tool, called a PivotTable report, to analyze data from a variety of perspectives.

This chapter's main focus is on working with data, especially large amounts of it. You can import data stored in a text file, a database, and an XML document into a worksheet. XML, which stands for Extensible Markup Language, was developed as a method to share data and a description of that data in an open, nonproprietary format for a variety of purposes and for use by different programs. Imported data, especially nonnumeric data, is rarely in the desired format, so it is important for you to know how to manipulate imported data into the format you need for analysis. In this chapter, you will look at ways to manage large amounts of data by using Tables, a PivotTable report, and XML.

Case Scenario

TheZone just received some contact information from a distributor that recently went out of business. TheZone needs to contact the retailers serviced by this distributor to ensure that they will still carry TheZone products. The data is for the Pacific sales region, which includes the states of Alaska, California, Hawaii, Oregon, and Washington. Barbara Jones has been assigned the task of importing data about the retailers that ordered sporting goods and sports apparel from TheZone into a format that will make it easy to sort and arrange the data in ways to help the Marketing Department contact these retailers. Barbara wants to import this data into Excel so she can analyze it. She plans to organize this data so she can determine how long each retailer has been a customer of TheZone products and identify the top retailers in each state and city. Barbara will use the tools in Excel to manage, organize, and analyze the data she obtained from the distributor.

Marketing

LEVEL 1

Importing and Structuring Text Data in Excel Worksheets

Working with Text Data

One term that is commonly encountered when working with text data in a computer application is **string**, which refers to a meaningful sequence of characters. The term has its origins in the computer science field and describes the formal theory behind representing characters, words, and symbols as numbers. This is important because computers store data in memory as numbers. There are many different standard character representation computer codes, such as ASCII (American Standard Code for Information Interchange) and UTF-8 (8-bit UCS/Unicode Transformation Format). A complete description of these codes is beyond the scope of this book; but it's important to note that without them, you wouldn't have the ability to work with text in Excel.

Strings allow you to sort and search for specific character combinations in data. A common way of storing data so that it is usable in other programs is to save it in a **comma-delimited file**. Because this format separates the values in each record with commas, data stored in this way is also called **comma-separated values**, or **CSV**. Excel can convert data stored in a comma-delimited file so that each value in a record appears in a separate cell of the worksheet into which you import it. A paragraph mark identifies the end of each record in a comma-delimited file.

The data that Barbara received from the distributor is not stored in a comma-delimited file, so her job is a challenging one. In the data for the retailers in Alaska, shown in Figure 7.1, each company's name, address, city, state, ZIP code, and phone number appear on separate lines in the text file.

The first goal when working with unstructured data is to determine the format you need so you can find the best way to change the unstructured data into structured data. Because the data for the sporting goods retailers in Alaska is not stored in a comma-delimited file, Barbara cannot import the data into Excel in the format she needs. She decides to copy the data from the text file and paste it into a new workbook. After completing this task, each line in the text file appears in a separate row in the worksheet. Barbara's goal for the unstructured data she received is to be able to change its format so that she can list the retailers by city, state, and ZIP code. To help the Marketing Department plan for its staff to contact these retailers, Barbara also needs to count the number of retailers by city. She needs to change the data into a format so that the company name, street address, city, state, ZIP code, and phone number appear in different cells, and so that the complete information for each company appears in a separate row. After she changes the data into comma-separated values, she can use the sorting tools in Excel to generate the list of retailers in various ways, as requested by the Marketing Department.

Figure 7.1: Text file listing sporting goods retailers in Alaska

Barbara's new workbook, Alaska Retailers.xlsx, contains all of the data from the text file. Notice that the data for each company appears in six rows in the worksheet, as shown in Figure 7.2.

Figure 7.2: Data pasted into an Excel worksheet from a text file

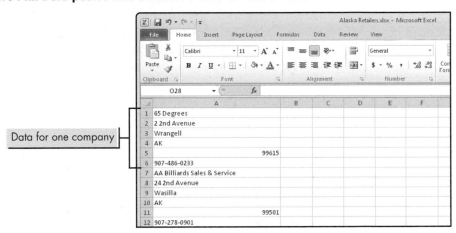

Barbara could move each cell containing a particular company's data into one row, but this work would be very labor intensive and might result in errors. Barbara instead decides to use a text function to link together, or **concatenate**, the information from multiple cells into one cell. To change the data into comma-separated values so it is in a format that makes the data easy to use in the future, she decides to insert commas between each value in a record at the same time.

Combining Text Using the CONCATENATE Function

By concatenating the data in the six cells that make up one company's information, Barbara can change the data into the desired format in which the name, address, city, state, ZIP code, and phone number for each company appear in one row in the worksheet. The **CONCATENATE function** combines the values in a range of cells into one text item in a new cell. The values can be text strings, numbers, or references to single cells.

The syntax for the CONCATENATE function is as follows:

```
CONCATENATE(text1,text2,...)
```

In the CONCATENATE function, text1 and text2 are the text, number, or cell references that contain the characters you want to join into a single text item in a new cell. Another method of concatenating text is to use the concatenation operator (&) instead of the CONCATENATE function. In this case, the formula syntax is =text1 & text2... Barbara enters the following CONCATENATE function into cell B1 to make this change and also to insert commas between the values in each row:

```
=CONCATENATE(A1,",",A2,",",A3,",",A4,",",A5,",",A6)
```

This CONCATENATE function combines the information in cells A1 through A6 as a new value in cell B1. Notice the different uses of the commas in the function. The first comma in the function, which follows the reference to cell A1, separates the first argument in the function from the second one. The second comma in the function, which appears inside the quotation marks, encloses the comma that will appear between the first and second arguments in the displayed results of the formula. The commas in quotation marks in the rest of the formula separate the company data into individual fields, as shown in cell B1 in Figure 7.3. Notice that the original data remains in cells A1:A6. If you deleted the data in cells A1:A6, the displayed results of the formula in cell B1 would contain only the commas that appear within the quotation marks because the function refers to these cells.

Barbara copies the formula in cell B1 to all the cells in column B that have an entry in column A by double-clicking the fill handle in cell B1. The way that Excel copies cells with relative cell references creates a problem with the information in column B. The formula in cell B2 concatenates cells A2, A3, A4, A5, A6, and A7 together, resulting in an entry that incorrectly combines the data from two companies. The structure of the data in groups of six rows in column A means that the information in column B is correct in every sixth row. Barbara could delete all the incorrectly concatenated rows, but there are 606 rows in this worksheet. Manually deleting the incorrect rows would take a lot of time and might

Figure 7.3: Combining text using the CONCATENATE function

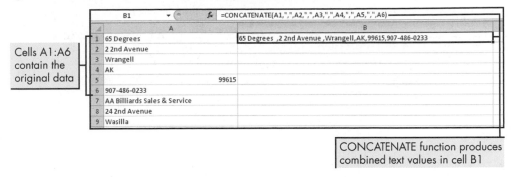

Cells A1:A6 contain the original data

CONCATENATE function produces combined text values in cell B1

result in some unintentional errors. She needs a more consistent way to remove the incorrect entries.

One method is to look for a unique feature that separates the rows of data she wants (the correct rows) from the incorrect rows. Barbara notices that each cell in column B that contains the information in the order she needs ends with a phone number. She can use the phone number to select the correct rows (containing the information for one company and in the proper order) from the incorrect rows. Each correct row in column B ends with a phone number that is displayed as -#### (a dash followed by four numbers). She decides to use this format to extract the correct rows of data.

Extracting Characters from a Text String

Barbara decides to use the **RIGHT function** to extract the last five characters of the text strings in column B. The RIGHT function returns the last character or characters in a text string, based on the number of characters specified. The syntax for the RIGHT function is as follows:

$$RIGHT(text, num\_chars)$$

In this function, *text* is the text string or cell reference that contains the characters you want to extract, and *num_chars* specifies the number of characters to be extracted.

The RIGHT function lets Barbara determine that the dash character, which indicates that the cell contains a correct row of data, is located in the correct position in the text string. The RIGHT function extracts the specified number of characters from the end or *right side* of a text string. The counterpart to this function is the **LEFT** function, which extracts characters from the beginning or *left side* of a text string. The dash character is located five positions from the end of the text string when it appears in a correct row. Barbara enters the following function into cell C1:

$$=RIGHT(B1,5)$$

The RIGHT function appears in Figure 7.4. Notice that the function returns a value of 233 in cell C1.

Figure 7.4: Using the RIGHT function

	A	B	C	D	E	F
C1		=RIGHT(B1,5)				
1	65 Degrees	65 Degrees ,2 2nd Avenue ,Wrangell,AK,99615,907-486-0233	233			
2	2 2nd Avenue	2 2nd Avenue ,Wrangell,AK,99615,907-486-0233 ,AA Billiards Sales & Service				
3	Wrangell	Wrangell,AK,99615,907-486-0233 ,AA Billiards Sales & Service ,24 2nd Avenue				
4	AK	AK,99615,907-486-0233 ,AA Billiards Sales & Service ,24 2nd Avenue ,Wasilla				
5	99615	99615,907-486-0233 ,AA Billiards Sales & Service ,24 2nd Avenue ,Wasilla,AK				
6	907-486-0233	907-486-0233 ,AA Billiards Sales & Service ,24 2nd Avenue ,Wasilla,AK,99501				
7	AA Billiards Sales & Service	AA Billiards Sales & Service ,24 2nd Avenue ,Wasilla,AK,99501,907-278-0901				
8	24 2nd Avenue	24 2nd Avenue ,Wasilla,AK,99501,907-278-0901 ,Alaska Fly Outfitter				
9	Wasilla	Wasilla,AK,99501,907-278-0901 ,Alaska Fly Outfitter ,99 3rd Avenue				
10	AK	AK,99501,907-278-0901 ,Alaska Fly Outfitter ,99 3rd Avenue ,Wasilla				
11	99501	99501,907-278-0901 ,Alaska Fly Outfitter ,99 3rd Avenue ,Wasilla,AK				
12	907-278-0901	907-278-0901 ,Alaska Fly Outfitter ,99 3rd Avenue ,Wasilla,AK,99709				
13	Alaska Fly Outfitter	Alaska Fly Outfitter ,99 3rd Avenue ,Wasilla,AK,99709,907-455-1006				

RIGHT function in cell C1 produces an incorrect value because the fourth and fifth characters are spaces

Removing Spaces from a Text String

The RIGHT function returns the value 233 in cell C1 instead of extracting a dash followed by four numbers as Barbara anticipated. Barbara examines the data in cell B1 and confirms that a correct row includes the company's name, address, city, state, ZIP code, and phone number. Often, data that you copy and paste from another source contains space characters at the end of the values. Because these spaces can cause errors in Excel formulas, Barbara decides to examine the data more carefully to determine if extra spaces are causing the error. Barbara selects cell A6, which is the source of the phone number in cell B1, and then clicks in the Formula Bar. She notices that there are two blank spaces at the end of the phone number. (The blank spaces can be "seen" by using the right arrow key to move to the far-right position of the cell contents in the Formula Bar.) Barbara could use the LEN function to determine the number of characters in the text string. However, because she already knows that there are blank spaces at the end of the phone number, she decides to use another text function to remove the extra spaces. The **TRIM** function removes all spaces in a text string except for the single spaces between words. This function can be very useful when importing data from another data source in which the data might contain spaces at the end of values. The syntax for the TRIM function is as follows:

```
TRIM(text)
```

In the TRIM function, *text* is the text string or cell reference that contains the space(s) that you want to remove. Barbara changes the formula in cell B1 by nesting it within a TRIM function. In this formula, the CONCATENATE function produces the text to be trimmed. The new formula in cell B1 is as follows:

```
=TRIM(CONCATENATE(A1,",",A2,",",A3,",",A4,",",A5,",",A6))
```

Barbara's TRIM function removes the spaces at the end of the phone number and the value –0233 now appears in cell C1, as shown in Figure 7.5. The value –0233 is the last five characters of the phone number, indicating a correct row.

Figure 7.5: Results of the TRIM function

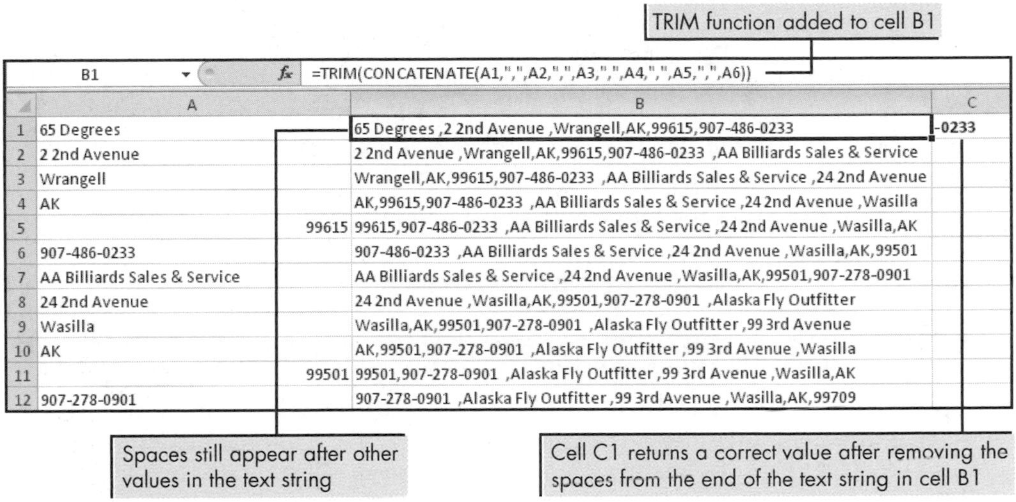

TRIM function added to cell B1

| B1 | fx | =TRIM(CONCATENATE(A1,",",A2,",",A3,",",A4,",",A5,",",A6)) |

	A	B	C
1	65 Degrees	65 Degrees ,2 2nd Avenue ,Wrangell,AK,99615,907-486-0233	-0233
2	2 2nd Avenue	2 2nd Avenue ,Wrangell,AK,99615,907-486-0233 ,AA Billiards Sales & Service	
3	Wrangell	Wrangell,AK,99615,907-486-0233 ,AA Billiards Sales & Service ,24 2nd Avenue	
4	AK	AK,99615,907-486-0233 ,AA Billiards Sales & Service ,24 2nd Avenue ,Wasilla	
5		99615 99615,907-486-0233 ,AA Billiards Sales & Service ,24 2nd Avenue ,Wasilla,AK	
6	907-486-0233	907-486-0233 ,AA Billiards Sales & Service ,24 2nd Avenue ,Wasilla,AK,99501	
7	AA Billiards Sales & Service	AA Billiards Sales & Service ,24 2nd Avenue ,Wasilla,AK,99501,907-278-0901	
8	24 2nd Avenue	24 2nd Avenue ,Wasilla,AK,99501,907-278-0901 ,Alaska Fly Outfitter	
9	Wasilla	Wasilla,AK,99501,907-278-0901 ,Alaska Fly Outfitter ,99 3rd Avenue	
10	AK	AK,99501,907-278-0901 ,Alaska Fly Outfitter ,99 3rd Avenue ,Wasilla	
11		99501 99501,907-278-0901 ,Alaska Fly Outfitter ,99 3rd Avenue ,Wasilla,AK	
12	907-278-0901	907-278-0901 ,Alaska Fly Outfitter ,99 3rd Avenue ,Wasilla,AK,99709	

Spaces still appear after other values in the text string

Cell C1 returns a correct value after removing the spaces from the end of the text string in cell B1

Barbara notices that the TRIM function removed the spaces only at the end of the concatenated value displayed in cell B1. She can see that there are also spaces at the end of the value in A1 and at the end of other values as well by examining the spaces between the values separated by commas in cell B1 and in other cells in column B. She changes the formula in cell B1 to trim each value, which removes all extra spaces in the concatenated text string, to the following:

```
=CONCATENATE(TRIM(A1),",",TRIM(A2),",",TRIM(A3),",",
       TRIM(A4),",",TRIM(A5),",",TRIM(A6))
```

Barbara's new formula correctly returns the value –0233 in cell C1 and also trims the values in cells A1:A6 so that the concatenated value in cell B1 does not contain any spaces, other than the ones between words. Barbara copies the new formula to other cells in column B, and then copies the formula in cell C1 to other cells in column C.

Determining the Position of a Character Within a Text String

Because every correct row in column B includes a phone number as the last text string, valid rows of data in column B have cells in column C that begin with a dash character in the first position, followed by four digits. Incorrect rows of data will display something other than a dash character followed by four digits in column C. Barbara could look for the dash character manually, but decides instead to use another text function to locate the position of the dash character in row C. The **FIND function** returns the starting position of one text value within another text value. The FIND function is case sensitive, so searching for *d* returns a different result than searching for *D*. The **SEARCH function** does the same thing as the FIND function, but the SEARCH function is not case sensitive. The syntax for the FIND function is as follows:

```
FIND(find_text,within_text,start_num)
```

In the FIND function, *find_text* is the text that you want to find, *within_text* is the text or cell reference containing the text that you want to find, and *start_num* is the character position in which to start the search. If you omit *start_num*, Excel assumes a start number of 1. Barbara enters the following formula into cell D1 to search for a dash character in cell C1, and then she copies the formula down column D:

```
=FIND("-",C1)
```

Sorting and Removing Invalid Data

Barbara used the RIGHT function in column C to extract the last five characters of the data in column B. Any cell in column C that has a dash character in the first position is a correct row, in which case the FIND function in column D returns a value of 1 to indicate that the dash character appears as the first character in the string. A dash located in any other position (second, third, fourth, or fifth) returns another value (2, 3, 4, or 5). If a value in column C does not contain a dash, a #VALUE! message is returned, as shown in Figure 7.6.

Figure 7.6: Results of the FIND function

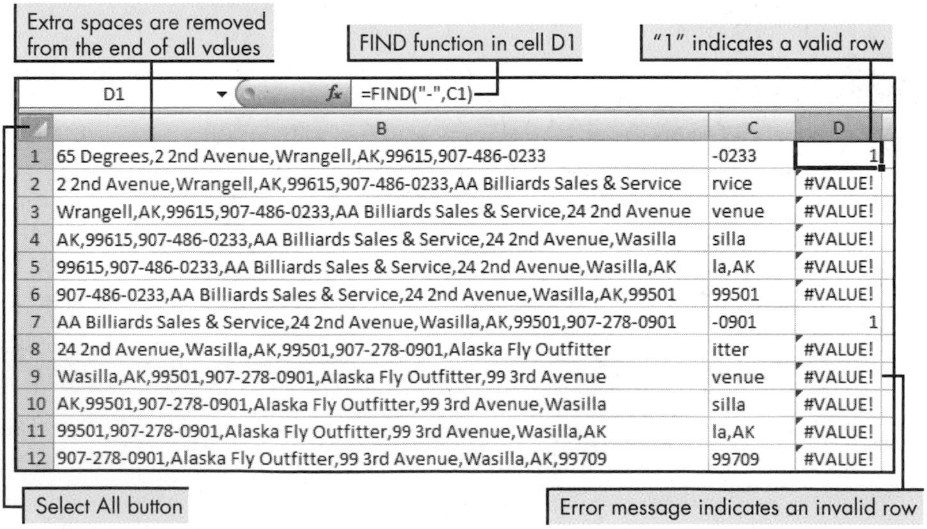

Now that Barbara has created a method to determine which rows contain valid information, she needs to remove the rows that contain invalid data. To preserve her imported data and the work she has done, she renames this worksheet Imported Data. She clicks the Select All button in the upper-left corner of the worksheet to select every cell in the worksheet. She then clicks the Home tab on the Ribbon and uses the Copy button in the Clipboard group to copy the selected cells to the Clipboard. She clicks cell A1 in a new worksheet that she renames as CSV. Next, she clicks the Paste button arrow in the Clipboard group, and then she clicks the Values (V) button on the Paste Options menu. Using the Paste Values option replaces the formula in each cell with its value. This action preserves the original data and eliminates the potential problem of automatically updating formulas as she modifies the data.

Barbara needs to sort the data in the CSV worksheet to separate the valid rows from the invalid rows. She selects the entire CSV worksheet to select all the data it contains, and then she uses the Sort button in the Sort & Filter group on the Data tab on the Ribbon to open the Sort dialog box. Because the data doesn't contain headers, Barbara deselects the My data has headers check box. This changes the Sort by selection from the values in the first cell in each column to column letters. She selects column D as the Sort by field, as shown in Figure 7.7.

Figure 7.7: Sort dialog box

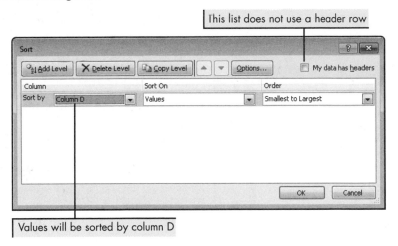

The data is sorted in ascending order on column D, which places the rows with valid entries (those with a 1 in column D) at the top of the document, as shown in Figure 7.8.

Barbara then deletes the rows with a #VALUE! message in column D and deletes everything except the data in column B. Now, the data remaining in column A is in a comma-delimited form—a single cell of data with commas separating the company name, street address, city, state, ZIP code, and phone number for each retailer, as shown in Figure 7.9.

Figure 7.8: Data sorted on column D

	A	B	C	D	E
1	65 Degrees	65 Degrees,2 2nd Avenue,Wrangell,AK,99615,907-486-0233	-0233	1	
2	AA Billiards Sales & Service	AA Billiards Sales & Service,24 2nd Avenue,Wasilla,AK,99501,907-278-0901	-0901	1	
3	Alaska Fly Outfitter	Alaska Fly Outfitter,99 3rd Avenue,Wasilla,AK,99709,907-455-1006	-1006	1	
4	Alaska Hiking	Alaska Hiking,101 Airport Way,Wasilla,AK,99503,907-272-1466	-1466	1	
5	Alaska Mountaineering Supply	Alaska Mountaineering Supply,104 Arctic Boulevard,Valdez,AK,99507,907-770-	-1542	1	
6	Alaska Outfitting Rentals	Alaska Outfitting Rentals,117 Arctic Boulevard,Valdez,AK,99901,907-225-1600	-1600	1	
7	Alaska SportMart	Alaska SportMart,101 6th Avenue,Wasilla,AK,99507,907-346-1244	-1244	1	
8	Alaskan Experience Inc	Alaskan Experience Inc,139 Arena Avenue,Valdez,AK,99901,907-225-1750	-1750	1	
9	Alaskan Outfitters	Alaskan Outfitters,171 Avenue Mall,Valdez,AK,99701,907-452-1811	-1811	1	
10	Anglerman's Inc	Anglerman's Inc,239 Business Boulevard,Soldotna,AK,99929,907-874-2229	-2229	1	
11	Anvil Outfitters	Anvil Outfitters,250 College Road,Soldotna,AK,99559,907-543-2290	-2290	1	
12	Apoc Design Inc	Apoc Design Inc,261 College Road,Soldotna,AK,99701,907-451-2300	-2300	1	
13	Arctic Outfitters	Arctic Outfitters,301 Curlew Way,Sitka,AK,99501,907-279-2401	-2401	1	

Valid rows contain a 1 and appear first in the sort

Figure 7.9: Comma-delimited data

	A	B	C
1	65 Degrees,2 2nd Avenue,Wrangell,AK,99615,907-486-0233		
2	AA Billiards Sales & Service,24 2nd Avenue,Wasilla,AK,99501,907-278-0901		
3	Alaska Fly Outfitter,99 3rd Avenue,Wasilla,AK,99709,907-455-1006		
4	Alaska Hiking,101 Airport Way,Wasilla,AK,99503,907-272-1466		
5	Alaska Mountaineering Supply,104 Arctic Boulevard,Valdez,AK,99507,907-770-1542		
6	Alaska Outfitting Rentals,117 Arctic Boulevard,Valdez,AK,99901,907-225-1600		
7	Alaska SportMart,101 6th Avenue,Wasilla,AK,99507,907-346-1244		
8	Alaskan Experience Inc,139 Arena Avenue,Valdez,AK,99901,907-225-1750		
9	Alaskan Outfitters,171 Avenue Mall,Valdez,AK,99701,907-452-1811		
10	Anglerman's Inc,239 Business Boulevard,Soldotna,AK,99929,907-874-2229		
11	Anvil Outfitters,250 College Road,Soldotna,AK,99559,907-543-2290		

Table 7.1 shows some of the functions that you can use to manipulate data in Excel.

Table 7.1: Common functions that manipulate data

Function (Arguments)	Description
CLEAN(text)	Removes all nonprintable characters from a text string; useful when importing data from an external data source
CONCATENATE(text1,text2,...)	Joins two or more text strings into a single text string
DOLLAR(number,decimals)	Converts a number to text in currency format with a dollar sign and the specified number of decimal places
EXACT(text1,text2)	Compares two text strings to determine if they are identical (case sensitive)
FIND(find_text,within_text,start_num)	Finds one text string within another text string (case sensitive) using the start_num character as a starting point
FIXED(number,decimals,no_commas)	Rounds a number to a specified number of decimals and returns the number as text with commas and a period
LEFT(text,num_chars)	Returns the far-left characters in a text string using num_chars as the starting point
LEN(text)	Returns the number of characters in a text string
LOWER(text)	Converts uppercase letters in a text string to lowercase
MID(text,start_num,num_chars)	Returns a specific number of characters in a text string using start_num as the starting point

Table 7.1: Common functions that manipulate data (cont.)

Function (Arguments)	Description
PROPER(text)	Capitalizes the first letter in each word in a text string and converts all other letters to lowercase; very useful when data has been improperly stored as uppercase characters
REPLACE(old_text,start_num,num_chars,new_text)	Replaces part of a text string with a new text string based on the number of characters specified in num_chars
REPT(text,number_times)	Repeats a text string a specified number of times
RIGHT(text,num_chars)	Returns the far-right characters in a text string using num_chars as the starting point
SEARCH(find_text,within_text,start_num)	Finds one text string within another text string (not case sensitive)
SUBSTITUTE(text,old_text,new_text,instance_num)	Substitutes new text for old text in a text string
TEXT(value,format_text)	Converts a value to text in the specified number format
TRIM(text)	Removes spaces from a text string, except for spaces between words; useful when importing data from an external data source
UPPER(text)	Converts lowercase letters in a text string to uppercase
VALUE(text)	Converts a text string that represents a number (a number, date, or time) to a number

Converting Text into Columns of Data

Now that Barbara has formatted the unstructured data into a list of comma-separated values, she can turn her attention to sorting the data for the Marketing Department. Each row in the worksheet contains the name, address, and phone number for each company that the Marketing Department needs to contact. Each cell containing data is a field. To sort the data in various ways, Barbara needs to separate the data so that each field appears in a separate column in the worksheet. She uses the Convert Text to Columns Wizard to separate the data into columns. As the name suggests, this wizard separates the values in a text string into columns or fields. You can determine how to divide (or parse) the text into columns in two ways. The first way is to identify the character that delimits (separates) the data. In Barbara's comma-delimited file, commas separate the data, so a comma is the delimiter. Another common delimiter is the tab character. The second way to parse data is to set field widths to identify the breaks between data that appears in columns. You use the fixed-width method when the data to parse does not include a consistent character to separate the field values. For example, you might have a line of data in which the first field occupies characters 1 through 10, the next field occupies characters 11 through 15, and so on. In this case, you could create a column break between characters 10 and 11, and then another column break between characters 15 and 16 to parse the data into columns.

How To

Use the Convert Text to Columns Wizard to Parse Data

1. Select the column that contains the data to be converted from text to columns.

2. In the Data Tools group on the Data tab on the Ribbon, click the Text to Columns button.

3. In Step 1 of the Wizard, select the Delimited option button, and then click the Next button.

4. In Step 2, click the check box for the delimiter used in the data. See Figure 7.10.

Figure 7.10: Convert Text to Columns Wizard

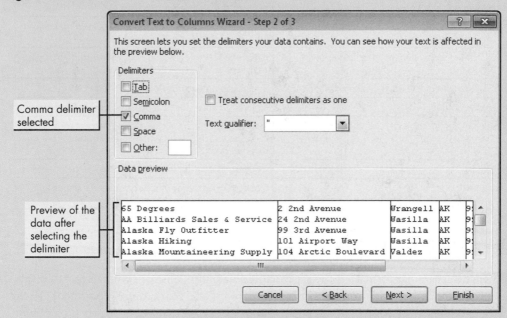

5. Click the Next button.

6. In Step 3, select the column data format for each column.

7. Click the Finish button.

Barbara uses the Convert Text to Columns Wizard to convert the comma-separated values to columns, as shown in Figure 7.11. Now, the data for each field appears in a separate column in the worksheet.

Labeling and Sorting Data

Now that the data is organized correctly, Barbara adds a row at the top of the worksheet (called a **header row**) and types labels that identify the data contained in each column. After she completes this task, Barbara needs to sort the data as requested by the Marketing Department; that is, first she needs to sort the data by city, and then by ZIP code, and then by company name. Because she needs to sort the data by more than one column, she uses the Sort dialog box.

Figure 7.11: Comma-delimited data converted to columns

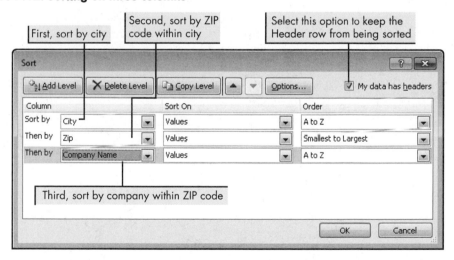

Each column contains data for one category

	A	B	C	D	E	F	G
1	65 Degrees	2 2nd Avenue	Wrangell	AK	99615	907-486-0233	
2	AA Billiards Sales & Service	24 2nd Avenue	Wasilla	AK	99501	907-278-0901	
3	Alaska Fly Outfitter	99 3rd Avenue	Wasilla	AK	99709	907-455-1006	
4	Alaska Hiking	101 Airport Way	Wasilla	AK	99503	907-272-1466	
5	Alaska Mountaineering Supply	104 Arctic Boulevard	Valdez	AK	99507	907-770-1542	
6	Alaska Outfitting Rentals	117 Arctic Boulevard	Valdez	AK	99901	907-225-1600	
7	Alaska SportMart	101 6th Avenue	Wasilla	AK	99507	907-346-1244	
8	Alaskan Experience Inc	139 Arena Avenue	Valdez	AK	99901	907-225-1750	
9	Alaskan Outfitters	171 Avenue Mall	Valdez	AK	99701	907-452-1811	
10	Anglerman's Inc	239 Business Boulevard	Soldotna	AK	99929	907-874-2229	
11	Anvil Outfitters	250 College Road	Soldotna	AK	99559	907-543-2290	
12	Apoc Design Inc	261 College Road	Soldotna	AK	99701	907-451-2300	

Each row contains data for one company

She clicks the Data tab, and then clicks the Sort button in the Sort & Filter group. Figure 7.12 shows the Sort dialog box with the City, ZIP code, and Company Name columns selected. Because Barbara added a header row to the worksheet, Excel automatically selects the Header row option button so that the header row is not included in the sort.

Figure 7.12: Sorting on three columns

First, sort by city

Second, sort by ZIP code within city

Select this option to keep the Header row from being sorted

Column	Sort On	Order
Sort by — City	Values	A to Z
Then by — Zip	Values	Smallest to Largest
Then by — Company Name	Values	A to Z

Third, sort by company within ZIP code

After clicking the OK button, Barbara's worksheet looks like Figure 7.13. The rows are sorted in ascending order, first by city, then by ZIP code, and, finally, by company name.

Figure 7.13: Data sorted by city, then by ZIP code, then by company name

Header row is not sorted

	A	B	C	D	E	F	G
1	Company Name	Address	City	State	Zip	Phone	
2	Blue Sports Marketing	9209 Tongass Avenue	Anchorage	AK	99501	907-279-7272	
3	Fifth Avenue Outfitters	300A University Avenue South	Anchorage	AK	99501	907-276-7335	
4	Raven Sports	Upper Omalley Road	Anchorage	AK	99501	907-274-7372	
5	Sunshine Outfitters	West Northern Boulevard	Anchorage	AK	99501	907-929-7867	
6	Northerner Sport Shop	West 4th Avenue	Anchorage	AK	99503	907-272-7555	
7	Play It Over Sports	7900 Spenard Road	Anchorage	AK	99503	907-278-7057	
8	Snow Sports LLC	West 6th Avenue	Anchorage	AK	99503	907-272-7755	
9	Suburban Outfitters	Richardson	Anchorage	AK	99504	907-333-8600	
10	Glenn Ski & Sports	6330 South Cushman Street	Anchorage	AK	99507	907-349-6881	
11	Travers Realty	Yenlo Street	Anchorage	AK	99507	907-346-8438	
12	Southern Sports Authority	West Parks Highway	Anchorage	AK	99515	907-349-7665	
13	Bill's Total Sports	West 27th Avenue	Anchorage	AK	99518	907-522-8288	

Analyzing Data by Creating Subtotals

Barbara remembers that the Marketing Department needs a count of the number of retailers in each city and ZIP code, so she must be able to collapse and expand the data set. The **Subtotal command** creates summary reports that quickly organize data into categories with subtotal calculations, and lets you collapse and expand the level of detail in the report. The data must be sorted by the chosen category for this tool to work properly. Also, note that the Subtotal command is not available if you are working with an Excel table. To add subtotals to a table, you must convert it to a normal range of data.

How To

Use the Subtotal Command

1. Sort data that you want to summarize, by category, and then select a cell within this data.

2. Click the Data tab on the Ribbon, and then click the Subtotal button in the Outline group. The Subtotal dialog box opens. See Figure 7.14.

Figure 7.14: Subtotal dialog box

Subtotals by city

Counts the number of values

Subtotals will appear in the Zip code column

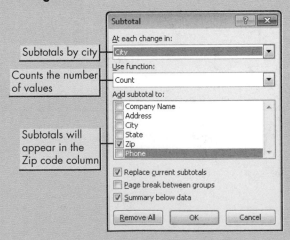

3. In the At each change in box, select the category by which to group the data.

4. In the Use function box, select the aggregate function to use in the summary.

5. In the Add subtotal to box, select the column in which to place the subtotal.

6. Click to select the Replace current subtotals, Page break between groups, and Summary below data check boxes as necessary to replace any existing subtotals in the worksheet, print groups on separate pages, and create summaries.

7. Click the OK button.

Barbara uses the Subtotal command to create a subtotal. The Subtotal command creates an outline along the left side of the worksheet that you can use to expand or collapse the data by a specific category—in this case, by city. Clicking the 1 button collapses the data set so that only the totals are shown, clicking the 2 button expands the data set to display only the subtotals (see Figure 7.15), and clicking the 3 button expands the data set to show each row included in the subtotals. Her worksheet now includes a summary row for each group of cities that calculates the number of retailers in each city. She saves her file and sends this information to the Marketing Department so it can easily identify those areas of the state where the most retailers are located.

Figure 7.15: Subtotals by city

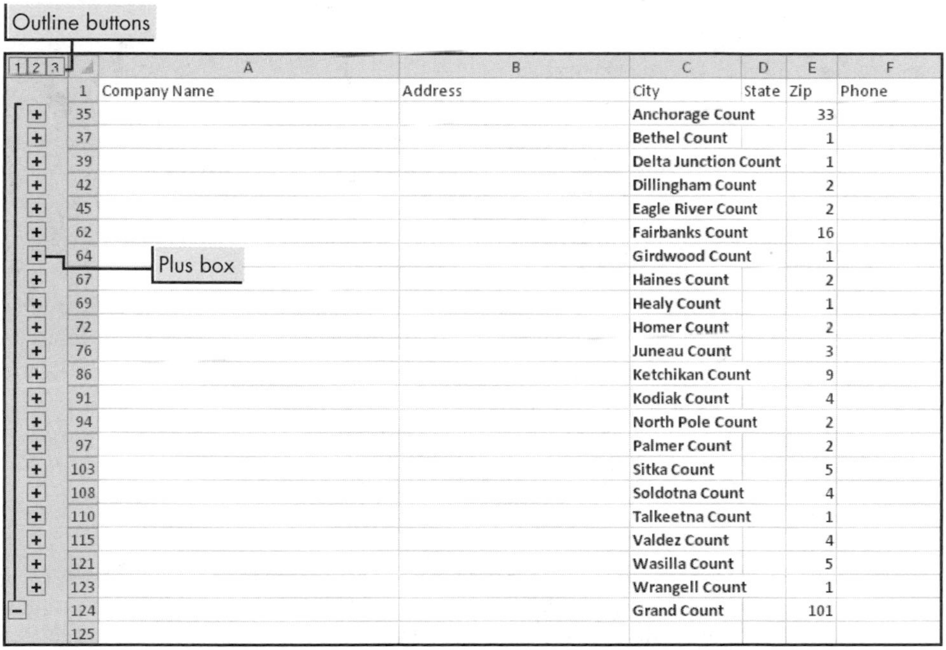

One limitation of the Subtotal command is that it works only with one category and one subtotal calculation at a time. However, you can change the category by opening the Subtotal dialog box again and changing the At each change in, Use function, and Add subtotal to values. The data is grouped by common elements within the chosen category and you can expand or collapse individual groups by clicking the plus or minus boxes to the left of the row numbers shown in Figure 7.15. You can select entire hierarchy levels using the numbers in the upper-left corner of the worksheet.

To remove the subtotals from a worksheet, click the Subtotal button in the Outline group on the Data tab, and then click the Remove All button in the Subtotal dialog box.

Creating and Working with an Excel Table

Barbara has provided information on the number of retailers in each city to the Marketing Department. She wants to be able to answer more questions like this without having to resort the data as required by the Subtotal command. She removes the subtotals from her worksheet so she can work with an Excel table.

Barbara's worksheet data is stored in a table structure in which the rows are independent and contain data organized into fields. Barbara's worksheet includes labels in the first row, and each retailer's information appears in a single row. Each column contains the same category of information in each row. For example, in column A, all values are company names. Barbara's worksheet is really just a simple database of information about retailers of sporting goods that are located in a specific geographic area. This arrangement of data is sometimes called a **flat-file database** because the data is stored in one table (or, in this case, the data is stored in one worksheet).

One issue that can come up when working with data in a table structure is that you can easily move cells of data to other areas in the worksheet. This flexibility often causes problems when sorting and filtering data because you risk omitting a column or row from the selection and compromising the integrity of the data. Another potential issue involves how you select data for sorting. If you select a single cell or column of data, Excel will open the Sort Warning dialog box to give you the opportunity to select all of your data. If you select multiple columns of data and leave a column out, there is no warning. For example, if you select the first five columns of data (company name, address, city, state, and ZIP code) and sort these rows, the values in the phone number column wouldn't be sorted with the rest of the data. The result would be a data set in which the phone numbers do not match the company name and address information.

When you are working in a worksheet that contains a table of information, as is the case with Barbara's worksheet, you can use the Excel table tools to work with all of the data in the table as a *unit* instead of as a *collection of individual cells*. An **Excel table** is a range of cells that you formalize as a single unit of data. When working with an Excel table, you should insert empty columns and rows around the table to segregate it from any other data in the worksheet. (The exception is a table that begins in column A; in this case, you do not need to insert a blank column to the left of the first column of data.) When you sort or filter data in an Excel table, the data in the columns of each row automatically remains intact, thereby protecting the integrity of the data.

Best Practice

Deciding When to Use an Excel Table

When you consider the enormous calculating power that Excel offers, it might surprise you to know that many users rely on Excel for list management. Many of the tables created in Excel would work equally well or better if they were managed using a database, but often users are more familiar with spreadsheets than databases. The flexibility of Excel lets the user "play" with the data and work out an organizational structure and supporting calculations that would require an expert's level of understanding to accomplish in a database. Creating an Excel table often bridges the gap between spreadsheets and simple databases. The database features of the Excel table protect the structure of the data, preventing the accidental deletion of rows or columns. The Excel table also adds many features that aren't available in an unstructured list of data, such as validation, sorting, and filtering, all of which can help you manage any set of related data. It is a good idea to use an Excel table to manage large amounts of data when your database skills are not sufficient to use a database to manage the same data.

Creating an Excel table lets you add some simple database functionality to a worksheet, but an Excel table has two limitations that you should understand. First, the maximum number of rows and columns in a worksheet limits the number of records and fields you can have in your table to 1,048,576 rows and 16,384 columns. The second, more important limitation is the fact that Excel must load the entire workbook into memory when you open it, which can lead to performance problems with very large tables.

Barbara decides to organize the data in her worksheet as an Excel table. She selects any cell in the worksheet, and then she clicks the Table button in the Tables group on the Insert tab on the Ribbon to open the Create Table dialog box. Excel automatically detects the table range surrounding the cell that was clicked in the worksheet, which is why it is useful to separate table data by a blank row or column if the spreadsheet also contains data you don't want included in the table.

How To

Create an Excel Table

1. Click any cell in the data that you want to format as an Excel table.
2. Click the Insert tab on the Ribbon, and then click the Table button in the Tables group. The Create Table dialog box opens, as shown in Figure 7.16. Be certain that the correct data set appears in the dialog box; if necessary, you can edit the range by typing new data or dragging a different range in the worksheet. If the table contains a header row, make sure that the My table has headers check box is selected.

Figure 7.16: Create Table dialog box

Range for the
Excel table

3. Click the OK button.

Barbara created the Excel table shown in Figure 7.17. An Excel table is formatted with alternating light and dark banded rows enclosed with white borders, and list arrows appear in each cell in the header row. Clicking within an Excel table displays the contextual Table Tools Design tab on the Ribbon. This contextual tab presents a number of options for managing and formatting Excel tables.

Figure 7.17: Excel table

Contextual Table Tools tab

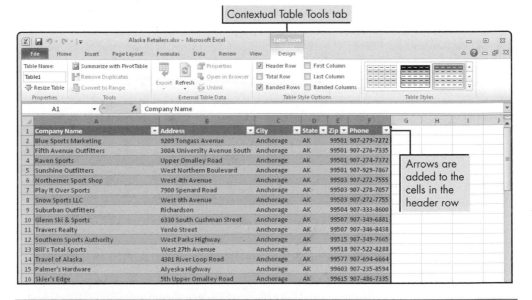

Arrows are added to the cells in the header row

Sorting an Excel Table

Sorting is done differently when your data is stored in an Excel table. When data is not in an Excel table, you simply select any cell in the range of data you want to sort, and then click the Sort & Filter button in the Editing group on the Home tab, or use the Sort button in the Sort & Filter group on the Data tab, as described earlier. If data is stored in an Excel table, you only need to select one cell in the column you want to sort and Excel automatically determines the borders of the data set and sorts the table accordingly, keeping the integrity of each row as it sorts.

To sort the table by a specific column, you click the filter arrow in the header row for that column. (You could also use the Sort Ascending or Sort Descending buttons in the Sort & Filter group.) If you want to sort by more than one column, you can use the Sort dialog box to sort by up to 64 columns.

Tables are a great way to keep data organized in record sets by row. As long as all of your cells refer to other cells in the same row, sorting has no impact on your formulas. If your formulas refer to cells in other rows, however, you might lose the cell references when you change the order of the data. If you use absolute cell referencing, however, there is no impact.

Filtering an Excel Table

When you create an Excel table, arrows appear in the header row for each column when the AutoFilter feature is enabled. (This feature is on by default; if you need to enable it, click the Filter button in the Sort & Filter group on the Data tab.) The **AutoFilter** feature lets you display data based on criteria you specify. When you click a filter arrow in the header row, you can sort the records in ascending or descending order, display all records, display the top 10 records, display records containing a specific value that appears in the column, or create a custom filter.

Barbara needs to display the retailers for each city. Barbara already sorted the data using the City column and could scroll the worksheet to find all retailers located in a certain city, such as Fairbanks. Instead, she clicks the arrow for the City column, and then selects Fairbanks as the filter in the menu that opens (clicking the Select All check box deselects the selections for individual values). Figure 7.18 shows the worksheet after filtering the data to display only those rows with the value Fairbanks in the City column. Notice that the row numbers for the selected records remain the same and that Excel displays only the filtered data. The row numbers change color from black to blue, and the filter arrow changes for the City column to indicate that the data has been filtered.

Figure 7.18: Filtered data

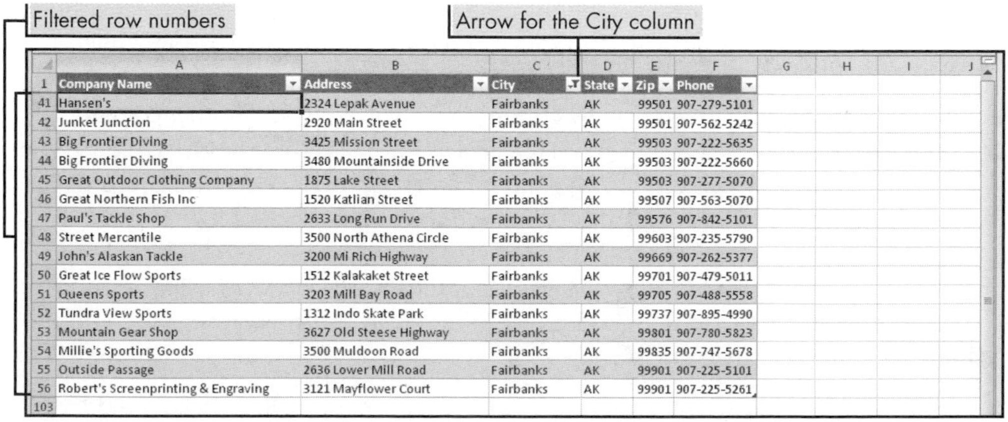

Table 7.2 describes the options available for filtering data. These options are context specific. For example, you will only have the option to use number filters on numeric values.

Table 7.2: AutoFilter options

AutoFilter Option	Description
Sort A to Z	Sorts the data in the column in ascending order.
Sort Z to A	Sorts the data in the column in descending order.
Sort by Color	If you have manually or conditionally formatted the background or font color of a range of cells, you can filter by these colors.
Clear Filter From	Removes any existing filters and displays all data in the column; restores the default (Select All) option.
Text Filters	Filters alphanumeric text by specific characters. Comparison operators include Equals, Does Not Equal, Begins With, Ends With, Contains, Does Not Contain, and Custom filters.
Number Filters	Filters numeric values using comparison operators such as Equals, Does Not Equal, Greater Than, Less Than, and Between. Some of the more powerful comparisons are the ability to rank the top or bottom number values and to only show those values that are above or below the average.
Date Filters	Filters date and time values using comparison operators such as Equals, Greater Than, or Less Than a specified date or time. You may also filter by a particular day, month, quarter, or year.
(Custom)	All of these filters include the option to filter the data using custom criteria that you specify. Use this option to find one or more rows that contain values that are equal to, do not equal, are greater than, are greater than or equal to, are less than, are less than or equal to, begin with, do not begin with, end with, do not end with, contain, or do not contain a specific value. Use the And or Or option and wildcards to filter data. For example, to find all retailers with the word *Outfitter* in their names, apply the custom filter "equals *Outfitter*" to the Company Name column. The asterisks at the beginning and end of the word *Outfitter* will find any phrase containing the word *Outfitter*.

If you need to perform calculations on the filtered data, you can display the Total row. The Total row lets you perform the following calculations for data in the Excel table: None, Average, Count, Count Numbers, Max, Min, Sum, Standard Deviation, Variance, and the ability to include more functions. You can display the Total row by placing a check mark beside Total Row in the Table Style Options group on the Design tab. Figure 7.19 shows the table with the Total row activated and the aggregate functions that are available.

You can filter data within filtered data by clicking the filter arrow for another column. For example, if you needed to select only those retailers in Fairbanks with the ZIP code 99501, you would click the list arrow for the ZIP code column, and then click 99501 in the menu. Based on the data, two records would be displayed in the Excel table.

To remove a filter from a column and display all of the data in the Excel table again, click the column's filter arrow, and then click Clear Filter From. An alternative way to do this is to click (Select All) in the same menu.

Figure 7.19: Total row added to an Excel table

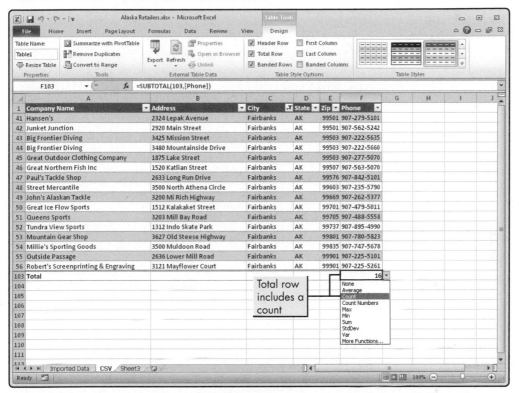

Adding Data to an Excel Table

When data is formatted as an Excel table, you can add new data in a variety of ways. If you wish to add a new blank column into the table, select a cell in the existing table just to the right of where the new column is to be inserted. Use the Insert button arrow in the Cells group on the Home tab; select Insert Table Columns to the Left. You can also insert a new blank row by choosing Insert Table Rows Above from the same menu. Selecting a cell in the last row of data in the table will open another option in the menu to Insert Table Row Below. Once the blank row or column is created, you can enter the data. You can enter existing values into the new row by right-clicking a cell, clicking Pick From Drop-down List on the shortcut menu, and then selecting the value to enter. This list is populated by the existing entries in the column.

Large amounts of data that are arranged under the same column headings can be added to the table by placing the data in the row below the existing table. A new row doesn't need to be inserted beforehand. Excel will automatically incorporate it into the table. This only works if there isn't a Total Row in the table. If there is a Total Row, you can select the last cell in the last row of the existing data and press the Tab key to create a new row.

Removing an Excel Table Definition

Data formatted as an Excel table can be returned or converted to a normal range very easily. Clicking within an Excel table opens the Design tab. Clicking the Convert to Range button in the Tools group removes the table definition. The only indication that the table has been converted to a normal range of data will be the absence of the filter arrows in each column heading. The data will retain the formatting of the former Excel table. Any desired changes can be applied by formatting the cells.

Steps To Success: Level 1

Barbara asks you to organize the data for sportswear retailers into an Excel table. The data is currently stored in a text file and is organized by state. You will begin by creating an Excel workbook and then pasting the data from the text file into a worksheet.

Complete the following:

1. Use Notepad (or another text editor) to open the text file named **Sportswr.txt** in the Chapter 7 folder, select all the data it contains, copy the data to the Clipboard, and then close Notepad.

2. Create a new workbook named **Sportswear Retailers.xlsx** and save it in the Chapter 7 folder. Paste the data you copied from the text file into a worksheet named **Imported Data**, starting in cell A1.

3. Create a list of comma-separated values from the data you pasted by concatenating the company name, street address, city, state, ZIP code, and phone number. Separate the name, street address, city, state, ZIP code, and phone number information with commas. Trim each text string in the concatenated value to remove all spaces except for spaces between words.

4. Copy and paste the concatenated information as a list of comma-separated values into a new worksheet named **CSV** in the Sportswear Retailers.xlsx workbook. Delete all invalid rows and columns that do not contain the comma-separated values.

5. Convert the comma-separated values into a structured list with the data for the company, street address, city, state, ZIP code, and phone number appearing in different cells of the worksheet. (*Hint*: Run the Convert Text to Columns Wizard twice to convert all of the data, being careful not to overwrite any existing data in the process. Be certain to remove any extra spaces remaining at the beginning or end of the data.)

6. Correct any errors in the data that were introduced during the conversion.

7. Add a header row with labels to describe the data in each column.

8. Change the data in the worksheet to an Excel table.

9. Sort the data by state, then by city, and then by company in ascending order.

10. Filter the results to display only those companies in Oregon and show the total number of companies in the state.

11. Save and close the Sportswear Retailers.xlsx workbook.

LEVEL 2

Analyzing Data Imported from a Database and Organizing Data with a PivotTable Report

Importing Data from a Database into Excel

The Marketing Department has been using the Excel list that Barbara created from the distributor's data to organize its efforts of contacting sporting goods retailers to maintain their relationships with TheZone and its products. The department is using Barbara's worksheet as a way to manage a simple database of information in a row-and-column format. Although this worksheet works well for the Marketing Department, Barbara is concerned about data integrity. She has been pushing for TheZone to use a database to store its data, but many of her colleagues are reluctant to change the existing systems, mostly because they are unfamiliar with how databases can simplify their work and ensure consistent and accurate data. Barbara has proposed the development of a prototype database as a way to demonstrate how TheZone can use a database in conjunction with spreadsheets to store, maintain, and analyze data. Barbara's managers have agreed to her idea and are especially interested in using a database to store information that they can export into Excel for later analysis. They agree that Barbara's proposal would protect the integrity of the data better than relying on just spreadsheets.

In any business, data is collected on a regular basis. Often, the key to a business's success is its ability to manage and organize this data into a usable format. A **database** is a set of related data that is stored in tables. In a database, a **table** is a collection of fields that describes a specific entity. For example, a table might store data about a company's products or its employees. A **field** is a single characteristic of the entity, such as a product ID number or an address. A set of fields that describes one product or person is called a **record**. A database is created by and defined in a **database management system (DBMS)**, which is a software program that creates and accesses the data in a database. Two examples of DBMSs are Microsoft Access and Oracle. DBMSs impose a great deal of structure on a data set. This structure makes it possible to find specific data very easily, but it can make analysis more difficult. The combination of Excel and a database is powerful. The database provides the structure to ensure that the right data is available and protected. The spreadsheet provides the analytical power and flexibility needed by most businesspeople.

7

Level 2

Most spreadsheets contain a combination of numeric and nonnumeric data. The nonnumeric data might take the form of labels that describe columns or rows, or it could be in the form of dates and times associated with the data in the spreadsheet. When nonnumeric data makes up most of the information in a spreadsheet, you should seriously consider using a database to organize the information. Databases are also used to store numeric data as well as nonnumeric data. Databases have the most advantages over spreadsheets when data is organized into a field/record structure and there is a large quantity of data. For example, in many companies, general ledger accounting data (which is primarily numeric in nature) is sometimes stored in a database and analyzed with a spreadsheet.

The same flexibility that makes Excel so powerful can lead to unintentional data corruption. One of the best ways to analyze text data is to sort it by categories, such as sorting a list of companies by company name. If you don't select all the data before sorting the rows, Excel might sort the company names but not the other data for each company, resulting in a list of alphabetical company names with incorrect address information. Although Excel warns you when you are about to sort data incorrectly, you can choose to ignore the warning and still sort the data incorrectly. This situation cannot happen in a database because all the field data is associated with a particular record.

Best Practice

Combining Spreadsheets and Databases

Importing information from a database table into a spreadsheet has some clear advantages. In a database, the data is protected from accidental changes, yet it is available for export into a spreadsheet for analysis. Database programs are also able to hold much larger and more complex data sets than Excel. Many people use Excel as a "quick-and-dirty" database because it is easy to enter data that might be better suited for a database into a workbook. Many DBMSs are called **relational database management systems** because the data is stored in tables that are related to each other through a common field in a process called **normalization**. By storing data in related tables in a normalized database, you can reduce data redundancy.

For example, consider a customer database that stores customer contact information and the details of each customer's purchases. In a database that contains only one table, each time a customer orders a product, a row is created in the table. Customers with multiple purchases might have different information stored about them in each record. In a relational database, the customer information is stored in a Customer table and the customer's purchases are stored in an Orders table. The Customer and Orders tables are linked with information in a common field that appears in both tables, such as a customer ID. In this case, the customer's information is only stored once, which reduces redundancy. Combining spreadsheets and databases is a good idea when you need to secure and protect the data but want to analyze it using a spreadsheet.

Barbara just received some sales data in a Microsoft Access database about sports apparel dealers and sales of TheZone products from the distributor. This database includes the number of orders and total sales of TheZone products for each retailer in the Pacific sales region. The database also includes the dates of each retailer's first and last order with the distributor. Barbara decides to use this database for her prototype system. She will import the appropriate data from the database into Excel. Barbara will then calculate how long a particular retailer has sold TheZone items and the length of time since its last order. This information will help the Marketing Department focus its efforts so that long-term customers and customers with recent orders are contacted first.

Importing an Access Table into Excel

The Access database contains one table with contact information for sports apparel retailers in the Pacific sales region. Barbara opened the database in Access and examined the contents of the Sports Apparel Retailers table. The table contains fields named CompanyName, StreetAddress, City, State, ZipCode, Phone, FirstOrderDate, LastOrderDate, NumberOfOrders, and TotalSales. She imports the data from the Sports Apparel Retailers table into a new Excel workbook named Sports Apparel Retailers.xlsx, as shown in Figure 7.20. The fields from the tables appear in columns in the worksheet. Each record in the database is one row in the worksheet.

Figure 7.20: Data imported from a database table

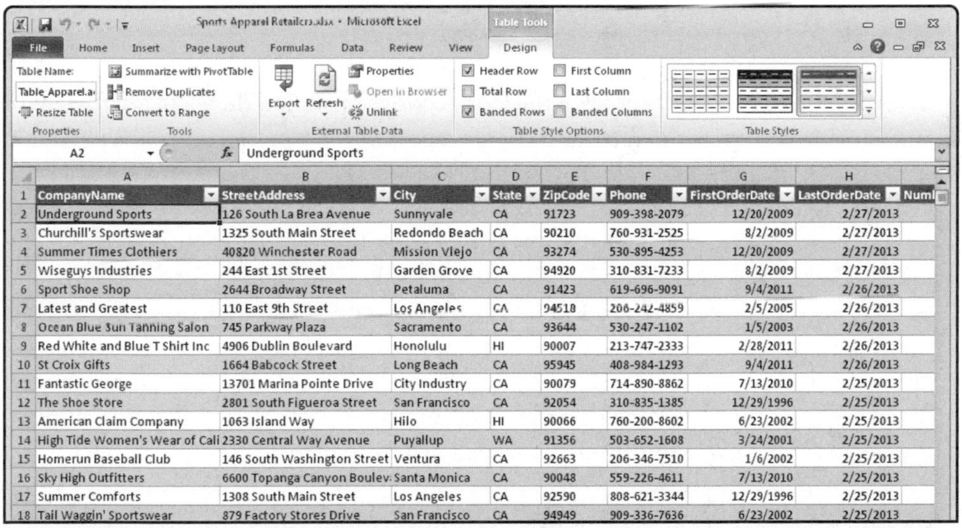

	CompanyName	StreetAddress	City	State	ZipCode	Phone	FirstOrderDate	LastOrderDate	Numl
2	Underground Sports	126 South La Brea Avenue	Sunnyvale	CA	91723	909-398-2079	12/20/2009	2/27/2013	
3	Churchill's Sportswear	1325 South Main Street	Redondo Beach	CA	90210	760-931-2525	8/2/2009	2/27/2013	
4	Summer Times Clothiers	40820 Winchester Road	Mission Viejo	CA	93274	530-895-4253	12/20/2009	2/27/2013	
5	Wiseguys Industries	244 East 1st Street	Garden Grove	CA	94920	310-831-7233	8/2/2009	2/27/2013	
6	Sport Shoe Shop	2644 Broadway Street	Petaluma	CA	91423	619-696-9091	9/4/2011	2/26/2013	
7	Latest and Greatest	110 East 9th Street	Los Angeles	CA	94518	206-242-4859	2/5/2005	2/26/2013	
8	Ocean Blue Sun Tanning Salon	745 Parkway Plaza	Sacramento	CA	93644	530-247-1102	1/5/2003	2/26/2013	
9	Red White and Blue T Shirt Inc	4906 Dublin Boulevard	Honolulu	HI	90007	213-747-2333	2/28/2011	2/26/2013	
10	St Croix Gifts	1664 Babcock Street	Long Beach	CA	95945	408-984-1293	9/4/2011	2/26/2013	
11	Fantastic George	13701 Marina Pointe Drive	City Industry	CA	90079	714-890-8862	7/13/2010	2/25/2013	
12	The Shoe Store	2801 South Figueroa Street	San Francisco	CA	92054	310-835-1385	12/29/1996	2/25/2013	
13	American Claim Company	1063 Island Way	Hilo	HI	90066	760-200-8602	6/23/2002	2/25/2013	
14	High Tide Women's Wear of Cali	2330 Central Way Avenue	Puyallup	WA	91356	503-652-1608	3/24/2001	2/25/2013	
15	Homerun Baseball Club	146 South Washington Street	Ventura	CA	92663	206-346-7510	1/6/2002	2/25/2013	
16	Sky High Outfitters	6600 Topanga Canyon Boulev	Santa Monica	CA	90048	559-226-4611	7/13/2010	2/25/2013	
17	Summer Comforts	1308 South Main Street	Los Angeles	CA	92590	808-621-3344	12/29/1996	2/25/2013	
18	Tail Waggin' Sportswear	879 Factory Stores Drive	San Francisco	CA	94949	909-336-7636	6/23/2002	2/25/2013	

How To

Import Data Stored in a Database Table into Excel

1. Open the workbook into which you want to import the database data, or open a new workbook.
2. Select the first blank cell where you want the data to appear, and then click the From Access button in the Get External Data group on the Data tab on the Ribbon. The Select Data Source dialog box opens.

3. Navigate to the database from which you will import the data, and then click the Open button. If the database you select contains more than one table, the Select Table dialog box opens. Click the table that contains the data you want to import, and then click the OK button. The Import Data dialog box opens, as shown in Figure 7.21.

Figure 7.21: Import Data dialog box

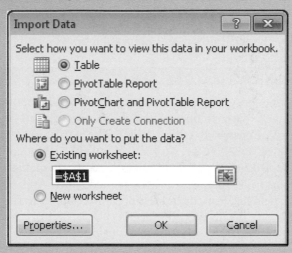

4. Click the Existing worksheet option button (if necessary), and then click the OK button.

Barbara can use the Refresh All button in the Connections group on the Data tab to update the imported data so that it contains the most current information from the database table from which it was imported. In other words, if someone adds or changes records in the Sports Apparel Retailers table in the Apparel database, clicking the Refresh All button in Excel makes those same changes in the worksheet. The Refresh All button refreshes the query and the data in the worksheet. Barbara imported all of the data in the Sports Apparel Retailers table in the Apparel database into the Sheet1 worksheet. Barbara also wants to demonstrate how to select specific data prior to importing it into Excel so her managers can see how this feature works. To accomplish this goal, Barbara needs to create a query. A **query** is a question that you ask a database. In response to a query, the database displays only those records that meet the criteria you specify in the query.

Using the Microsoft Query Wizard to Select Data from a Database

Excel includes a program called **Microsoft Query** that lets you create queries to select data from external sources, including Access, and import the query results into a worksheet. A simpler way to use Microsoft Query is to use the **Query Wizard**, which lets you choose your data source and select the database table and fields you want to import into a workbook. The Query Wizard prompts you to define any criteria for the data you want to import by selecting only rows that meet criteria that you specify.

The marketing representative for California needs a list of the retailers located only in California from the database, so Barbara needs to create a query to import only this data into Excel. The representative only wants the records for retailers whose last order date is January 1, 2012, or later. Barbara renames the Sheet2 worksheet as CA Data. Next, she starts the Query Wizard and selects the Sports Apparel Retailers table in the Apparel database as the data source. She selects all fields in the table and then applies a filter so that only those records with CA as the State value and dates equal to or later than 1/1/2012 as the LastOrderDate value are selected. Barbara also sets the options to sort by city, and then by last order date, in ascending order. She returns the results of her query to the CA Data worksheet, as shown in Figure 7.22.

Figure 7.22: Retailers in California

Records sorted by city and last order date in ascending order

Records selected with last order dates of 1/1/2012 and later

	A	B	C	D	E	F	G	H
1	CompanyName	StreetAddress	City	State	ZipCode	Phone	FirstOrderDate	LastOrderDate	Numb
2	Professional Times	3109 Imperial Avenue	Aiea	CA	90079	805-650-4300	6/5/2011 0:00	5/27/2012 0:00
3	R&R Sporting	4910 West Rosecrans Avenue Suite	Aiea	CA	90015	415-665-3394	12/16/2010 0:00	2/7/2013 0:00
4	City Sun Shop	14102 South Broadway	Albany	CA	90057	808-395-1808	3/12/2004 0:00	8/5/2012 0:00
5	Copeland's Fitness Store	10203 New Bedford Court	Albany	CA	90247	661-831-2602	3/17/2001 0:00	10/2/2012 0:00
6	North Shore Surf Shop	3500 South Meridian	Albany	CA	93722	805-238-3424	3/26/2006 0:00	1/12/2013 0:00
7	Jack's Sportswear	1440 South Anaheim Boulevard	Algona	CA	94520	909-820-2951	11/30/2009 0:00	6/14/2012 0:00
8	Baxter and Baxter	663 Pine Knot Avenue	Algona	CA	93010	909-788-2900	5/12/2009 0:00	7/6/2012 0:00
9	Susie's Factory Outlet	2612 South Croddy Way Suite I	Alpine	CA	90011	805-642-6530	7/23/2010 0:00	10/2/2012 0:00
10	One of a Kind Gifts	4071 North Valentine Avenue Suite	Alpine	CA	95678	541-967-8891	8/23/2009 0:00	2/13/2013 0:00
11	Just Beachy	1045 Oakwood Mall	Alpine	CA	93422	760-722-2676	6/11/2003 0:00	2/16/2013 0:00
12	Sweet Dream Designs	PO Box 1171	Alta Loma	CA	95020	707-668-6869	1/21/2010 0:00	3/2/2012 0:00
13	Professional Jersey Company	17639 Chatsworth	Alta Loma	CA	90247	909-885-7505	10/11/2002 0:00	12/22/2012 0:00
14	Pacific Surf CO	110 East 9th Street	Anacortes	CA	91950	808-886-1252	11/28/2008 0:00	4/25/2012 0:00
15	Pacific Connection Limited	4532 Crenshaw Blvd	Anacortes	CA	90058	808-593-5477	5/4/2010 0:00	6/1/2012 0:00
16	Big Guy Sportswear	461 South Fork Avenue Southwest	Anaheim	CA	91730	619-235-7246	7/9/2009 0:00	4/24/2012 0:00

How To

Use the Query Wizard to Import Data from Access

1. Open the worksheet into which you want to import the data.
2. Click the Data tab on the Ribbon, click the From Other Sources button in the Get External Data group, and then click From Microsoft Query, as shown in Figure 7.23. The Choose Data Source dialog box opens.
3. Click MS Access Database*, verify that the Use the Query Wizard to create/edit queries check box is selected, and then click the OK button. The Select Database dialog box opens.
4. Navigate to the Access database, click it to select it, and then click the OK button. The Query Wizard starts.
5. In the Query Wizard – Choose Columns dialog box, click the table that contains the data you want to import, and then click the plus box to the left of the table name to display the columns in the selected table. To select an individual column to be included in the query, click the column name in the Available tables and columns box, and then click the select single field button to add the column to the Columns in your query box. To add all fields to the query, click the table name in the Available tables and columns box, and then click the select all fields button to add the fields to the Columns in your query box. When you have selected the columns you want to include, click the Next button.

Figure 7.23: Importing data using Microsoft Query

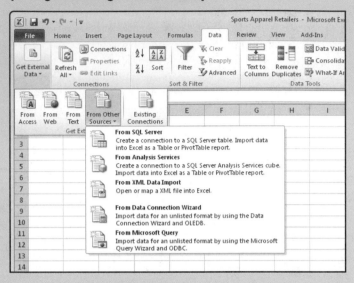

6. In the Query Wizard – Filter Data dialog box, click the column to filter and then select the appropriate filter for that column in the Only include rows where section of the dialog box. To include other filters in the query, click the arrow in the second row and define the next filter. Click the And option button to create an And query, or click the Or option button to create an Or query. See Figure 7.24. When you have finished creating the filters, click the Next button.

Figure 7.24: Query Wizard – Filter Data dialog box

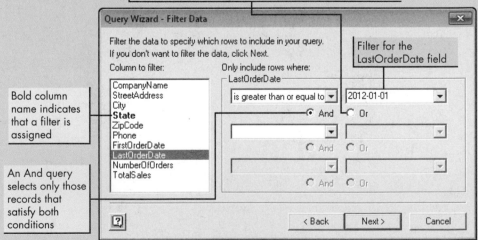

7. In the Query Wizard – Sort Order dialog box, click the Sort by arrow and select a column on which to sort. The default sort order is Ascending. You can specify up to three sorting options. When you have finished specifying the sort order, click the Next button.

8. In the Query Wizard – Finish dialog box, click the Return Data to Microsoft Office Excel option button, and then click the Finish button. The Import Data dialog box opens.

9. Verify that the Existing worksheet option button is selected, and then click the OK button. The query results are imported into the worksheet.

After using a query to import data, you can update the data by clicking the Refresh button in the External Table Data group on the Design tab. You can also change the query by right-clicking a cell in the table, clicking Table on the shortcut menu, and then clicking Edit Query. This starts the Query Wizard so you can change the data to select and display in the worksheet.

Making Calculations with Date and Time Data

The data shown in Figure 7.22 includes the date that each retailer in California began ordering TheZone products and the date of the last order by each retailer. Dates are represented by values in Excel. These values are not the same as using numbers in place of months as in the date 9/24/2010. Excel uses serial numbers to represent dates and times. Excel represents a date as the number of days since January 0, 1900: January 1, 1900 is represented as 1; January 2, 1900 is represented as 2; and so on. Excel also uses decimals to represent the time on a particular day. Each day is broken into decimal equivalents. For example, noon on January 1, 1900 is represented by the serial number 1.5; the whole number 1 is one day from January 0, 1900, and the decimal .5 represents noon (halfway through a 24-hour day, or 12 divided by 24). Excel further breaks down days into hours, minutes, and seconds by dividing the 24 hours in each day accordingly. Using serial numbers makes calculations involving dates and times very easy. To calculate the number of days between the dates in two cells, you just need to subtract one cell from the other.

Best Practice

Formatting Cells with Date and Time Calculations
When you create formulas referencing cells that contain dates and/or times, Excel sometimes formats the result as a date instead of as a number. If you need to calculate the number of days between dates stored in two cells and the result is a date instead of the number of days, select the cell, click the Home tab, and click the Number group dialog box launcher to open the Format Cells dialog box. Click the Number category, and then to show days in whole numbers, set the Decimal places option to 0. If you want to format the result as a serial number that indicates time, set the Decimal places option to the number of decimal places that you want to display.

The Marketing Department will use Barbara's data to prioritize the sales calls by geographic area, but it is also interested in prioritizing calls based on the length of time since the retailer last ordered TheZone products and the overall length of time each retailer has carried TheZone products. Barbara uses two functions to determine this information for the Marketing Department.

For the first request, the Marketing Department wants to know how many days have elapsed between the current date and the last order date. Barbara first adds today's date in cell M1 using the **TODAY function**. The TODAY function returns the current date's serial number (based on the computer's internal clock). The syntax for the TODAY function is:

$$\texttt{TODAY()}$$

The TODAY function requires no additional arguments, but the opening and closing parentheses are required.

Barbara adds the formula =$M$1−H2 in cell K2 in the CA Data worksheet to calculate the number of days between today's date (in cell M1) and the last order date. Because the order time is not important, she reformats the result as a number with zero decimal places. She adds the column heading "DaysSinceLastOrder" in cell K1 and copies the formula in cell K2 down the column. Because Barbara's formula includes the TODAY function, the current date according to the computer's internal clock is always used in the calculation, so the result is different depending on when the calculation occurs. Figure 7.25 shows the new column and current date.

Figure 7.25: Using the TODAY function

Number of days between the last order date and today | Today's date

	H	I	J	K	L	M	N
1	LastOrderDate	NumberOfOrders	TotalSales	DaysSinceLastOrder		6/2/2013	
2	5/27/2012 0:00	5	18895	371			
3	2/7/2013 0:00	63	274869	115			
4	8/5/2012 0:00	160	504160	301			
5	10/2/2012 0:00	405	1882035	243			
6	1/12/2013 0:00	109	106711	141			
7	6/14/2012 0:00	11	22110	353			
8	7/6/2012 0:00	57	78546	331			
9	10/2/2012 0:00	86	269094	243			
10	2/13/2013 0:00	67	160331	109			
11	2/16/2013 0:00	97	319809	106			
12	3/2/2012 0:00	36	115956	457			
13	12/22/2012 0:00	306	638928	162			
14	4/25/2012 0:00	110	188320	403			
15	6/1/2012 0:00	32	89344	366			
16	4/24/2012 0:00	12	17772	404			
17	5/16/2012 0:00	26	22776	382			
18	5/19/2012 0:00	313	1029457	379			

Barbara also needs to calculate the overall length of time that each retailer has ordered products from TheZone. To determine the length of each relationship, Barbara needs to subtract the number of days between today's date and the first order date. As she looks at the values in the FirstOrderDate column, she decides that determining the number of days between today's date and the first order date would yield very high numbers that would not be meaningful to the Marketing Department. For example, the retailer Just Beachy's first order date is 6/11/2003 and its last order date is 2/16/2013, which results in a length of over 3,500 days between order dates. Barbara decides that results using years would be more meaningful. She uses the **YEARFRAC function** to calculate the number of years between the two dates. The syntax for the YEARFRAC function is as follows:

```
YEARFRAC(start_date,end_date,basis)
```

In the YEARFRAC function, *start_date* is the date from which you want to start counting, *end_date* is the ending date, and *basis* is the argument that lets you establish the lengths of months and years. Using 1 for the basis calculates months and years with actual values. Using 0 as the basis calculates months using 30 days and years using 360 days. (Some people consider a standard month to be 30 days even though a month can have 28 to 31 days; using a 30-day month results in a year with 360 days. Most years have 365 days, except for leap years, which have 366 days.)

Barbara adds the column heading "RelationshipYears" in cell L1 and then adds the following formula in cell L2: =YEARFRAC(G2,H2,1). She wants to include fractional years, so she formats cell L2 as a number with two decimal places. Then, she copies the formula to the other cells in column L and the results appear in Figure 7.26.

Figure 7.26: Using the YEARFRAC function

Years between the first order date and the last order date

	FirstOrderDate	LastOrderDate	NumberOfOrders	TotalSales	DaysSinceLastOrder	RelationshipYears	6/2/2013
2	6/5/2011 0:00	5/27/2012 0:00	5	18895	371	0.98	
3	12/16/2010 0:00	2/7/2013 0:00	63	274869	115	2.15	
4	3/12/2004 0:00	8/5/2012 0:00	160	504160	301	8.40	
5	3/17/2001 0:00	10/2/2012 0:00	405	1882035	243	11.55	
6	3/26/2006 0:00	1/12/2013 0:00	109	106711	141	6.80	
7	11/30/2009 0:00	6/14/2012 0:00	11	22110	353	2.54	
8	5/12/2009 0:00	7/6/2012 0:00	57	78546	331	3.15	
9	7/23/2010 0:00	10/2/2012 0:00	86	269094	243	2.20	
10	8/23/2009 0:00	2/13/2013 0:00	67	160331	109	3.48	
11	6/11/2003 0:00	2/16/2013 0:00	97	319809	106	9.69	
12	1/21/2010 0:00	3/2/2012 0:00	36	115956	457	2.11	
13	10/11/2002 0:00	12/22/2012 0:00	306	638928	162	10.20	
14	11/28/2008 0:00	4/25/2012 0:00	110	188320	403	3.40	
15	5/4/2010 0:00	6/1/2012 0:00	32	89344	366	2.08	
16	7/9/2009 0:00	4/24/2012 0:00	12	17772	404	2.79	
17	7/30/2011 0:00	5/16/2012 0:00	26	22776	382	0.80	
18	9/27/2005 0:00	5/19/2012 0:00	313	1029457	379	6.64	
19	7/21/1999 0:00	6/19/2012 0:00	155	217000	348	12.91	
20	10/15/2008 0:00	8/6/2012 0:00	126	412524	300	3.81	

Table 7.3 lists and describes some other commonly used date and time functions.

Table 7.3: Date and time functions

Function Syntax	Description
DATE(year,month,day)	Returns the serial number of a particular date
DATEVALUE(date_text)	Converts a date in the form of text to a serial number
DAY(serial_number)	Converts a serial number to a day of the month
DAYS360(start_date,end_date,method)	Calculates the number of days between two dates based on a 360-day year
EDATE(start_date,months)	Returns the serial number of the date that is the indicated number of months before or after start_date
EOMONTH(start_date,months)	Returns the serial number of the last day of the month before or after a specified number of months
HOUR(serial_number)	Converts a serial number to an hour
MINUTE(serial_number)	Converts a serial number to a minute
MONTH(serial_number)	Converts a serial number to a month
NETWORKDAYS(start_date,end_date,holidays)	Returns the number of whole workdays (Monday through Friday, excluding dates identified as holidays) between two dates
NOW( )	Returns the serial number of the current date and time
SECOND(serial_number)	Converts a serial number to a second
TIME(hour,minute,second)	Returns a decimal number for a specific time
TIMEVALUE(time_text)	Returns a decimal number for a specific time that is represented by a text string
TODAY( )	Returns the serial number for today's date
WEEKDAY(serial_number,return_type)	Converts a serial number to a day of the week
WEEKNUM(serial_num,return_type)	Converts a serial number to a number representing where the week falls numerically in a year in which January 1 occurs in the first week of the year
WORKDAY(start_date,days,holidays)	Returns the serial number of the date before or after a specified number of workdays (Monday through Friday, excluding dates identified as holidays)
YEAR(serial_number)	Converts a serial number to a year
YEARFRAC(start_date,end_date,basis)	Returns the number of years between two dates as a fraction

Analyzing Data Using a PivotTable Report

Naturally, TheZone wants to keep all of the retailers serviced by the distributor that went out of business. However, even with Barbara's worksheets, it will be difficult for the Marketing Department to contact nearly 2,000 companies. After meeting with the Marketing Department, Barbara agrees to change her data analysis strategy to identify retailers that have ordered the most products from the TheZone. With this data, the Marketing Department can locate TheZone's best customers and concentrate its efforts on these businesses first. Barbara needs to determine the state with the most orders and the cities in each state with the highest sales. She needs to organize the data in different ways to produce meaningful reports for the Marketing Department. To produce these results, Barbara needs to create a PivotTable report.

A **PivotTable report** is an interactive report that lets you summarize and analyze a data set. You can use a PivotTable report to summarize selected fields from a list or data from an external source, such as a database. A unique feature of a PivotTable report is that its organization is somewhat dynamic. The PivotTable report can be "pivoted" to examine the data from various perspectives by rearranging its structure. Unlike any other table, you can change the data contained in a PivotTable report by simply dragging a column to a new location in the PivotTable report. You can transpose the columns and rows as needed for your analysis.

Best Practice

Deciding When to Use a PivotTable Report

PivotTables offer a unique way to analyze data that can come from a variety of sources. After creating a PivotTable report, you can easily rearrange its fields and change its data to analyze data from different perspectives. This ability to pivot summaries of the data by rows and columns is what gives this tool its name. PivotTables are best used to analyze data that can be summarized in multiple ways. One example is sales data that you need to summarize and analyze by month, quarter, and year, or by product line and sales region. A PivotTable allows the sales data to be easily rearranged to match the required analysis. Multiple worksheets containing the same data would be required to analyze this data without PivotTables.

Creating a PivotTable Report

Barbara decides that she needs to rename the worksheet containing the original data she imported from the Sports Apparel Retailers table in the Apparel database. A worksheet tab named Retailers will be much easier to find than one named Sheet1. After looking at both worksheets, she decides to use the more complete dataset in the Retailers worksheet for her PivotTable report. She selects the Retailers worksheet tab to display this data and clicks the Insert tab, and then clicks PivotTable in the Tables group to open the Create Pivot-Table dialog box, shown in Figure 7.27. Barbara selects the imported table from the Access file, Apparel.accdb.

Barbara selects the option to put the PivotTable report in a new worksheet. Because a PivotTable report usually analyzes a large data set, it is usually better to place it in a new worksheet. She then clicks the OK button.

Figure 7.28 shows the PivotTable report in a new worksheet. Notice the contextual PivotTable Tools tabs appear on the Ribbon and PivotTable Field List. Also, Barbara has renamed the worksheets that contain data to describe their contents.

Figure 7.27: Create PivotTable dialog box

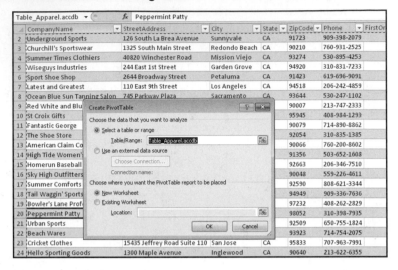

Figure 7.28: Layout of the PivotTable

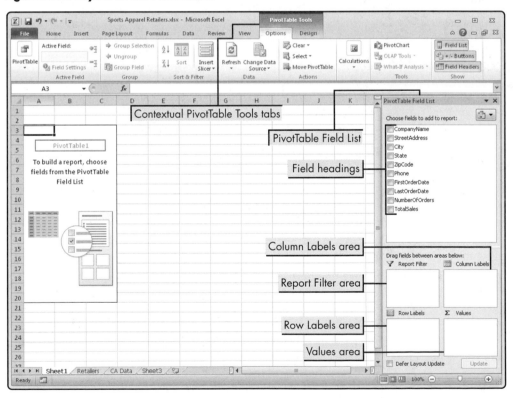

Analyzing Data Using the Row, Column, and Value Areas

When you create a PivotTable report, Excel opens the PivotTable Field List and the PivotTable Tools Options tab shown in Figure 7.28. (If you do not see this contextual tab, click inside the PivotTable area on the worksheet. If you do not see the PivotTable Field List, click the Field List button in the Show/Hide group on the PivotTable Tools Options tab.) The **PivotTable Field List** contains a list of fields in the data source you selected for the PivotTable report. Because you selected the data in the Retailers worksheet, the columns from that worksheet appear in the PivotTable Field List. To add data to the PivotTable report, you drag the field you want to summarize into one of the four areas in the lower portion of the PivotTable Field List: Report Filter area, Row Labels area, Column Labels area, or Values area. You can also click a field so Excel automatically adds it to the PivotTable in the order you selected. By default, fields containing numbers will be added to the Values area. Fields with other content will be added to the Row Labels area. You may then have to move these fields to other areas.

If you select a field from the PivotTable Field List and place it in the Report Filter area, you can display data in the PivotTable report grouped by the equivalent of pages. Placing a field in the Row Labels area displays data from that field in rows. Placing a field in the Column Labels area displays data from that field in columns. Placing a field in the Values area summarizes data from that field. The cell where a row and a column intersect represents a summary of the data on those two dimensions. When you place fields in either the Row Labels area or the Column Labels area, the PivotTable report displays all values of those fields. Clicking the arrow for a field lets you select either all field values or individual field values to display using a check box. The Values area is where you place the fields you want to summarize; this area usually includes field values rather than categories. You can rearrange fields in a PivotTable report by dragging them to any other location. You can also move fields to another area by clicking the field arrow and selecting the correct area. You can remove a field from the PivotTable report by dragging it out of the PivotTable report, or by removing the check mark from the check box in the Field List for that field.

Barbara starts setting up the PivotTable report by dragging the State field from the PivotTable Field List to the Row Labels area. When you drag a field over an area, the area is selected. When you drop the field in an area, the data from the field appears in the PivotTable report. Another way to add a field to a PivotTable report is to right-click the field in the PivotTable Field List, and then to select the area in which you want to drop the field from the shortcut menu.

Barbara then drags the TotalSales field to the Values area. The default field setting in the Values area is to calculate a sum of the items in this drop area by the categories in the Row Labels area or Column Labels area. Because Barbara did not place any fields in the Column Labels area, the PivotTable report displays the total sales by state, as shown in Figure 7.29.

Figure 7.29: Total sales by state

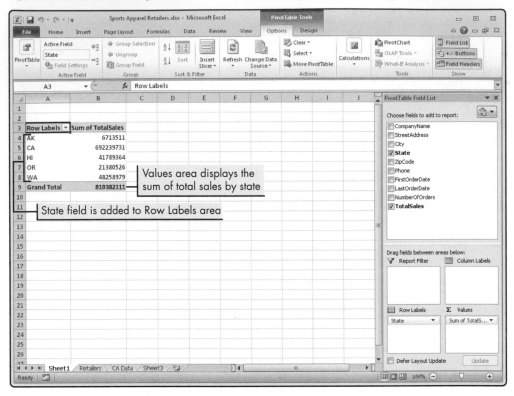

You can change the calculation used in the Values area by right-clicking a value in the Values area and then clicking Value Field Settings on the shortcut menu to open the Value Field Settings dialog box shown in Figure 7.30. By selecting a different calculation type in the Summarize value field by box, you can perform other calculations on the data, such as Count, Average, Max, and so on. You can also change the default name of the field by typing a new one in the Custom Name box. Clicking the Number Format button lets you change the number format of the values. In addition to changing the default name from Sum of TotalSales to Total Sales, Barbara changes the number format from General to Currency, so the values are displayed as currency. She also changes the default decimal places to zero to reduce the clutter on the spreadsheet.

Barbara also wants the PivotTable report to show the number of orders by state. You can place more than one value field in the Values area by dragging another field into the drop area, or by adding a check mark to the check box for the field in the PivotTable Field List. She selects the NumberOfOrders field by selecting the check box next to this field in the PivotTable Field List; this places it in the Values area. She opens the Value Field Settings dialog box and changes the number format to use a comma separator in values over 1,000 and zero decimal places. She then changes the default name from Sum of NumberOfOrders to Number of Orders. The PivotTable report changes to summarize the total sales and

Figure 7.30: Value Field Settings dialog box

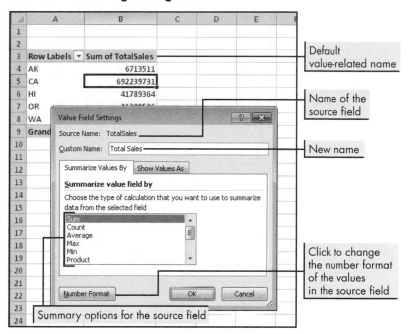

number of orders by state, in rows, as shown in Figure 7.31. When you organize the data by row, you can compare the states by the total sales and number of orders. This organization results in multiple value labels that indicate the sum of total sales and the number of orders for each state.

Figure 7.31: Total sales and number of orders by state (rows)

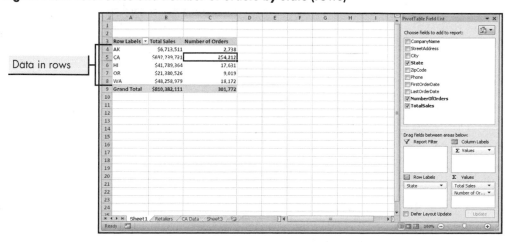

Barbara could have organized the data in columns, as shown in Figure 7.32, by moving the State field to the Column Labels area, moving the Values total to the Row Labels area, and keeping the Total Sales and Number Of Orders fields in the Values area. The location of the Values total determines whether the values are summarized by column or row. The PivotTable report displays the same information as shown in Figure 7.32, but the data is summarized in columns instead of in rows. This arrangement organizes the data by column and gives a slightly different perspective.

Figure 7.32: Total sales and number of orders by state (columns with labels)

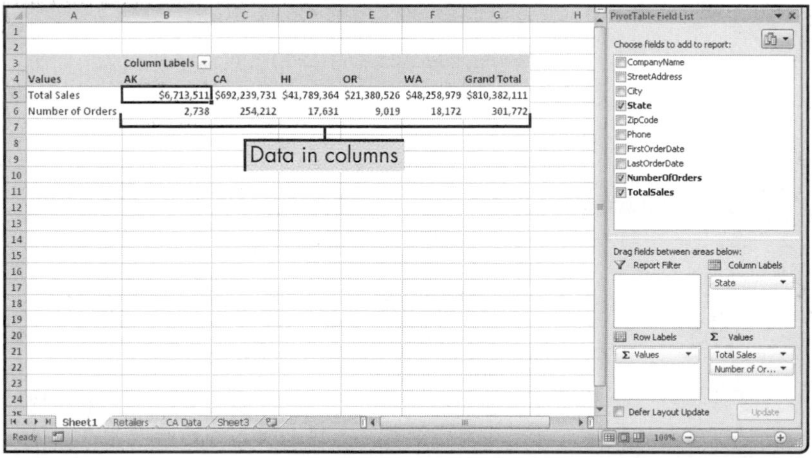

Adding Fields to the Report Filter Area

Barbara uses the PivotTable report and begins analyzing the data. She sees that California has the most orders and the highest total sales, followed by Washington, Hawaii, Oregon, and Alaska. Barbara wants to identify the cities in California that have the most retailers. She moves the State field to the Report Filter area, which organizes the data by the selected state. Then she places the City field in the Row Labels area and moves the Values total from the Row Labels area to the Column Labels area. Barbara would like to know how many retailers are in each city, so she adds the CompanyName field to the PivotTable report by placing a check mark next to this field in the PivotTable Field List. Because this field contains text, Excel assumes that it will be used as a label and inserts the field into the Row Labels area. Barbara wants to use this field to count the number of retailers in each city, so she drags it to the Values area, where it is summarized by count. Barbara changes the default name from Count of CompanyName to Number of Retailers and changes the format to use a comma separator in values over 1,000 and zero decimal places.

The data in the Pivot Table report is now sorted alphabetically by city name for all states. Because Barbara wants to identify the cities in California with the highest sales, she clicks the arrow in the Report Filter area, clicks CA in the list, and then clicks the OK button. She selects a cell in the Total Sales column, and then clicks the Sort button in the Sort & Filter group on the PivotTable Tools Options tab. In the Sort By Value dialog box, Barbara clicks the Largest to Smallest option and then clicks the OK button. Figure 7.33 shows that Los Angeles is the city with the highest sales. The Marketing Department can use this data to focus its efforts on contacting stores in the top California markets.

Figure 7.33: Cities in California with the highest sales

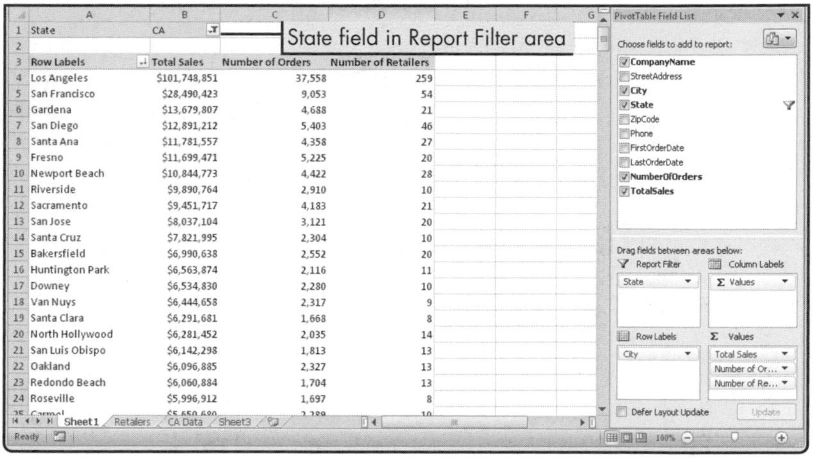

To view the cities with the most sales in another state, click the Filter button on the State label in the Report Filter field of the PivotTable Field List, and select another state. Another way to examine the data would be to sort the Number of Retailers column in Largest to Smallest order. To view the data for all states, click (All) instead of a particular state. When you sort the data in largest-to-smallest order, you see the cities with the most retailers for the region.

Using Slicers to Filter PivotTable Data

Barbara examines her PivotTable and decides that she would still like to be able to apply a filter to examine the data for a particular city or retailer. In a previous step, she placed the State field in the Report Filter field and selected CA. This filtered the data in the PivotTable report to include only those values from California. Barbara could also filter the PivotTable report by the City column label to show only the values for a particular city. The only indication that a PivotTable report has been filtered is a small icon next to the label. This small icon can be easily overlooked that the data has been filtered and can lead to the wrong conclusions and decisions. Excel 2010 provides a new feature that allows you to filter a data set by the current values of a field. The field values are turned into buttons in the PivotTable report. These buttons are grouped into an object called a **slicer**.

How To

Add a Slicer to a PivotTable Report

1. Click the Insert Slicer button in the Sort & Filter group on the PivotTable Tools Options tab on the Ribbon. The Insert Slicers dialog box opens. See Figure 7.34.

Figure 7.34: Insert Slicers dialog box

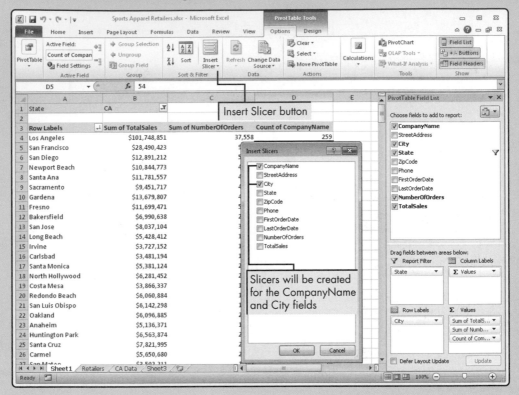

2. Select the check box for the PivotTable field for which you want a slicer created. You can select as many fields as you want.

3. Click the OK button. A slicer is created for each selected field.

Barbara creates slicers for the CompanyName and City fields. Barbara selects the city of Los Gatos using the City slicer, as shown in Figure 7.35. This filters the data in the PivotTable report to display only those values from this city. Notice that there are only three active buttons in the CompanyName slicer. All other buttons are grayed out. The active buttons in a slicer will change as the PivotTable report is filtered. For example, changing the state in the Report Filter field will change the active cities and company names in the slicers.

Barbara is satisfied with the results of her PivotTable report. She can now provide information on total sales, the number of retailers, and the number of orders by the cities in each state. She can also use slicers to filter this data down to a particular city or retailer. Before she saves her work, she clears the filter for Los Gatos and renames the worksheet tab as Sales by City.

Figure 7.35: Active vs. inactive slicer buttons

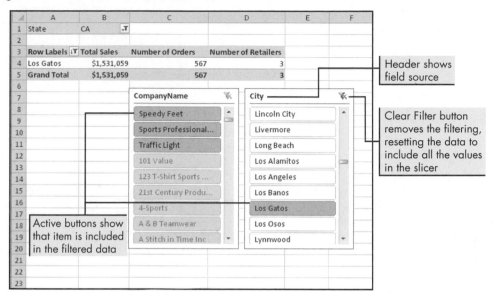

Barbara wants to examine when retailers in the Pacific sales region last ordered products carried by TheZone. She sets up another PivotTable report with Count of CompanyName in the Values area and State in the Report Filter area. She then adds the LastOrderDate field to the Row Labels area. The result is a very busy PivotTable report with a row for every date included in the LastOrderDate field. Obviously, Barbara needs to look at this data by month or perhaps even by quarter.

Because you can use a PivotTable report to analyze large amounts of data, you might need to summarize the data into groups. For example, if one of your fields contains date data, you can summarize values into periods, such as months, quarters, or years, to arrange records into groups instead of listing individual dates in the range. You can also summarize data by creating a group of days, such as 0 to 30 days, 31 to 60 days, and so on. You can do the same thing with numeric data.

How To

Group Data in a PivotTable Report

1. Drag the field that contains the values you want to group into the PivotTable report.

2. Click the field and then click the Group Selection button in the Group group on the PivotTable Tools Options tab on the Ribbon. If the data you are grouping contains date values, the Grouping dialog box shown in Figure 7.36 opens. When the Auto feature is enabled, the Starting at value is set to the first date in the range and the Ending at value is set to the last date in the range. Use the By box to select the desired grouping.

Figure 7.36: Grouping dialog box for date data

If the data you are grouping contains numeric values, the Starting at value is set to the lowest value in the range and the Ending at value is set to the highest value in the range. To change the starting or ending value, select the value in the box, and then type a new value. Set the By value to the range you want to group.

3. Click the OK button.

To remove an existing group from a PivotTable report, click the field in the PivotTable report that contains the group, and then click the Ungroup button in the Group group on the Options tab.

Barbara groups the LastOrderDate row labels by year and then by month. She also adds City to the Report Filter area under the State entry. She uses the Value Field Settings dialog box to change the custom name Count of CompanyName to Number of Last Orders. She names the worksheet Last Orders. The PivotTable report shown in Figure 7.37 allows her to examine the data for a single city—Los Angeles, in this case—which will make it easier to target stores that haven't ordered from TheZone in a while.

Barbara wants to see which 15 stores from Los Angeles last ordered from the distributor in March 2012. She double-clicks the cell showing 15 for that month. Double-clicking a cell drills down into the data on which the PivotTable report is based and creates a new worksheet, as shown in Figure 7.38. The data in this worksheet is the original data that matches the filters in the PivotTable. In this example, the 15 records have a State value of CA, a City value of Los Angeles, and a LastOrderDate value of March 2012. Clicking any value cell in a PivotTable report results in a new worksheet showing the original data used to build that cell. This function should be used sparingly because the data doesn't indicate the matching PivotTable entry. Multiple worksheets named Sheet4, Sheet5, or whatever the next available new worksheet number is can be very confusing. You can easily forget on what the drill-down data was based. Once you create a drill down, you should label it so you understand what it is showing. In this case, Barbara names the worksheet as Drill Down LA 3-12.

Figure 7.37: Row labels grouped by year and month

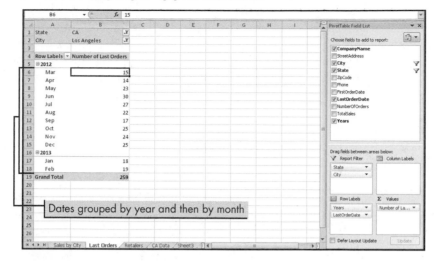

Dates grouped by year and then by month

Figure 7.38: Drill down for Los Angeles, March 2012

	CompanyName	StreetAddress	City	State	ZipCode	Phone	FirstOrderDate	LastOrderDate	NumberOfOrders	TotalSales
2	Beyond Denim Sto	340 Southwest M	Los Angel	CA	90815	502-652-1	5/31/2010	3/2/2012	41	49487
3	Khaki's Beverly Ce	83 Fortune Drive	Los Angel	CA	93274	310-652-4	12/25/2004	3/2/2012	51	61812
4	Blue Wave of Calif	238 Bellevue Squ	Los Angel	CA	96817	925-779-6	5/11/2007	3/4/2012	208	501696
5	Forum Sports	122 Los Cerritos N	Los Angel	CA	90292	805-773-9	12/17/2008	3/5/2012	116	502396
6	Four Paws Sportwe	20527 Yorba Linda	Los Angel	CA	97501	805-481-3	7/7/2011	3/8/2012	16	28902
7	La Rue Designer Cl	540 San Pablo Ave	Los Angel	CA	92707	310-323-3	10/31/2010	3/9/2012	38	117800
8	Blessed Enterprise	2403 Commercial	Los Angel	CA	90015	323-298-6	10/15/2005	3/9/2012	244	494100
9	Guatemala Fashio	4730 Franklin Bou	Los Angel	CA	93704	323-732-2	11/20/2005	3/10/2012	45	26730
10	Best Sportswear In	139 South Market	Los Angel	CA	91406	213-747-1	5/8/2009	3/13/2012	57	54207
11	Bill's Times	2108 Chestnut Str	Los Angel	CA	90255	760-253-6	5/31/2009	3/14/2012	67	251384
12	Sports Gear	1287 South Park V	Los Angel	CA	99801	760-341-1	3/14/2011	3/16/2012	10	29600
13	Aztec Sportswear	59 Throckmorton	Los Angel	CA	94102	323-766-4	5/22/2011	3/17/2012	10	32280
14	Fashion Fabulous S	17280 Northeast	Los Angel	CA	94109	559-229-8	7/23/2001	3/20/2012	54	41742
15	Bay Sportswear	357 Georgia Aven	Los Angel	CA	93551	310-456-4	9/12/2008	3/22/2012	71	57723
16	SET Leisure Inc	2550 Somersville	Los Angel	CA	95219	808-886-2	9/26/2007	3/30/2012	208	939536

Drill-down data for March 2012

Evaluating Data Using a PivotChart Report

Just like its chart counterpart, a **PivotChart report** represents source data as a graphic. The easiest way to create a PivotChart report is to use an existing PivotTable report as the source data. To create a PivotChart report using existing data from a PivotTable report, you just click the PivotChart button in the Tools group on the PivotTable Tools Options tab; this adds a PivotChart to the worksheet that contains the PivotChart report. After creating it, you can move the chart to a separate worksheet using the Move Chart button in the Location group on the contextual PivotChart Tools Design tab on the Ribbon. Unlike a regular chart, you can change the layout and data displayed in a PivotChart report by moving fields in addition to changing the chart type.

A PivotChart report includes series, axes, and data markers, just like a regular chart. A PivotChart report also includes the Report Filter field, a Legend field, an Axis field, and a Values field. The Report Filter field functions like the Report Filter area in a PivotTable report, in that it lets you filter data by specific values in a field. The Values field functions like the Values area in a PivotTable report, in that it is the field in the data source that includes the data to summarize. The Legend field provides the series of data for the chart. The Axis field is a field that contains the individual categories for the data points in the chart by combining the data in the Row labels and Column labels areas in the PivotTable report. Buttons to control the displayed data in these fields can be activated using the Field buttons button in the Show/Hide group on the PivotChart Tools Analyze tab.

Barbara created the PivotChart report shown in Figure 7.39 from the existing PivotTable report on the Last Orders worksheet. The PivotChart report shows how many Los Angeles retailers had their last order in each month.

Figure 7.39: PivotChart report showing the number of last orders for Los Angeles, CA

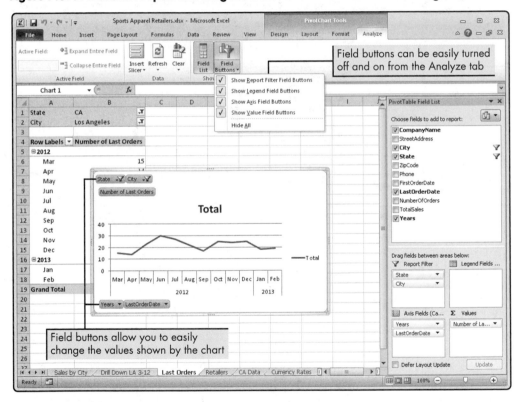

Most of the options available for regular charts are also available for PivotChart reports. For example, clicking the Change Chart Type button in the Type group on the PivotChart Tools Design tab lets you change the chart type. The PivotChart Tools Layout tab allows you to make more changes to a PivotChart's appearance.

How To

Create a PivotChart Report Using a PivotTable Report

1. Click the PivotTable report to select it.

2. Click the PivotChart button in the Tools group on the PivotTable Tools Options tab on the Ribbon.

Because a PivotTable report usually summarizes a large amount of data, you might need to experiment with different chart types or filter the data to find an effective way to present it visually. Barbara can also change the PivotChart report to remove fields from the chart, rearrange the chart's fields, and add fields to the chart just like in a PivotTable report.

Importing Information from the Web into Excel

TheZone has been looking for ways to expand its market by working with international distributors. Because some of these distributors provide their estimates in foreign currencies, Barbara spends a lot of time finding resources on the Internet that convert foreign currencies into U.S. dollars.

Excel 2010 offers a way to retrieve data from Web pages using a Web query. A **Web query** is an automated method for retrieving information from a Web page without having to copy and paste it into an application. Excel includes several external data sources saved as Web queries that you can use to import currency rates, investor indexes, and stock quotes from MSN MoneyCentral Investor. Figure 7.40 shows the Investor Currency Rates in a new workbook. Because this data source is a Web page that MoneyCentral updates on a regular basis, the data is refreshed each time Barbara opens the workbook. Barbara can use this information to get currency exchange rate information for approximately 50 countries around the world.

7

Level 2

Figure 7.40: Currency rates imported from MSN MoneyCentral Investor

	A	B	C	D	E
1	--> -->				
2	**Currency Rates Provided by MSN Money**				
3	Click here to visit MSN Money				
4					
5	**Name**	**In US$**	**Per US$**		
6	Argentine Peso to US Dollar	0.26123	3.828		
7	Australian Dollar to US Dollar	0.88449	1.131		
8	Bahraini Dinar to US Dollar	2.6498	0.377		
9	Bolivian Boliviano to US Dollar	0.14225	7.03		
10	Brazilian Real to US Dollar	0.52997	1.887		
11	British Pound to US Dollar	1.5982	0.626		
12	Canadian Dollar to US Dollar	0.93441	1.07		
13	Chile Peso to US Dollar	0.00191	524.2		
14	Chinese Yuan to US Dollar	0.14631	6.835		
15	Colombian Peso to US Dollar	0.0005	1989		
16	Czech Koruna to US Dollar	0.05285	18.923		
17	Danish Krone to US Dollar	0.18622	5.37		
18	Euro to US Dollar	1.386	0.722		
19	Egyptian Pound* to US Dollar	0.18304	5.463		
20	Hong Kong Dollar to US Dollar	0.12878	7.765		
21	Hungarian Forint to US Dollar	0.00511	195.7		
22	Indian Rupee to US Dollar	0.02164	46.22		
23	Indonesia Rupiah to US Dollar	0.00011	9355		
24	Japanese Yen to US Dollar	0.01107	90.3		
25	Jordanian Dinar to US Dollar	1.4096	0.709		
26	Kenyan Shilling to US Dollar	0.01316	75.97		

The data shown changes frequently

How To

Use a Saved Web Query to Import Data into a Worksheet

1. Open a new workbook or select the cell into which you want to import the data.
2. Click the Existing Connections button on the Data tab on the Ribbon. The Existing Connections dialog box, shown in Figure 7.41, opens and displays a list of saved Web queries (your list of Web queries might differ).
3. If necessary, browse to the folder that contains the Web query you want to use.
4. Click the Web query you want to use, and then click the Open button. The Import Data dialog box opens.
5. Click the option button for putting the data in the existing worksheet or a new worksheet, and then click the OK button.

Figure 7.41: Existing Connections dialog box

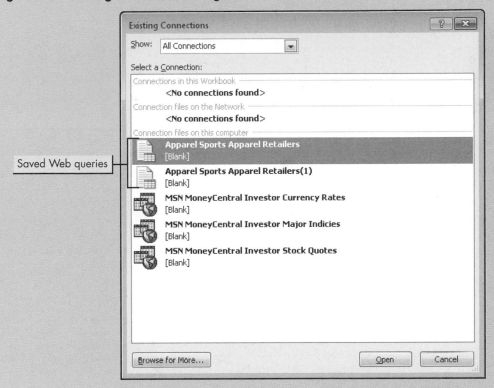

Saved Web queries

Steps To Success: Level 2

Barbara received some additional data from the distributor that she needs to analyze and give to the Marketing Department. The data is stored in an Access database. The data includes the company name, address, phone number, first order date, and last order date for each retailer located in the Pacific Northwest. There is a field that identifies the total number of orders placed by each retailer for TheZone products. The distributor's database also includes total sales by month, from January 2012 through March 2013. Some of the records in the database are for sales from retailers in British Columbia, Canada, and the sales amounts are reported in Canadian dollars. Barbara wants to use a Web query to convert the Canadian dollar amounts into U.S. dollars so she can learn how to use a Web query, but also so all of the sales figures will be in U.S. dollars. Because currency exchange rates change daily, Barbara realizes that the conversion amounts will not reflect the actual values at the time of the sales, but this quick conversion will be fine for her current data analysis needs.

Complete the following:

1. Create a new workbook and save it as **Pacific Sales.xlsx** in the Chapter 7 folder.

2. Import the data contained in the Pacific Region table of the **Pacific.accdb** Access database located in the Chapter 7 folder into a worksheet named **Pacific Region**.

3. Sort the data first by state/province, then by city, and then by company name in ascending order.

4. Use a Web query to import currency conversion rates from the appropriate MSN MoneyCentral Investor Web page into a worksheet named **Currency**.

5. In the Pacific Region worksheet, create an IF statement in cell Y2 to convert the sales amounts for companies in British Columbia, Canada, into U.S. dollars. For U.S. companies, display the U.S. dollar amount. (Hint: Use the In US$ amount in the Currency worksheet for Canada to convert Canadian dollars to U.S. dollars.) Format the result as currency. Copy the IF statement down column Y and then to the range Z2:AM2333. Copy the column labels from the original financial data into these new columns. To indicate that you have adjusted the data in these columns, type (**adj.**) at the end of each label.

6. Calculate the total sales since January 2012 for each company in a column labeled **AdjustedSales**. Format the result as currency.

7. Hide the original columns containing financial information to allow the data to be updated from the original database table.

8. Assuming a report date of 4/1/2013, calculate the number of days since each company has placed an order with TheZone in a column named **Days Since Last Order**. Format the values with zero decimal places.

9. Calculate the number of fractional years that each company has been ordering from TheZone in a column named **Relationship (Years)**. Format the values with two decimal places.

10. Create a PivotTable report from the data in the Pacific Region worksheet in a worksheet named **PivotTable Report**.

11. Add the AdjustedSales field to the Values area and format its values as currency.

12. Add the Days Since Last Order field to the Row Labels area of the PivotTable report. After adding the Days Since Last Order field to the PivotTable report, group records in this field into groups of 100, starting with the value 0.

13. Add the StateProv field to the Column Labels area, and then add the CompanyName field to the Values area to count the number of companies in each state.

14. Use the Value Field Settings dialog box to customize the field names in the PivotTable report as **Adjusted Sales** and **Number of Companies**.

15. Save and close the Pacific Sales.xlsx workbook.

LEVEL 3
Importing and Exporting XML Data

Understanding Markup Languages and XML

A computer's ability to store data in one medium and reproduce it many times in other media was the foundation for the theory that the information or content of a document could exist separately from the formatting of the document. A markup language is the link between the content in a document and the instructions for formatting that content. A **markup language** uses a set of tags to distinguish different elements in a document and uses attributes to define those elements further.

A markup language that you might already be familiar with is **HTML**, or **Hypertext Markup Language**, which is the markup language that creates Web pages (also called HTML documents). In HTML, you embed tags in the document to describe how to format its content. When a Web browser reads an HTML document, it uses the tags to format text according to a set of predefined descriptions of those tags. For example, when a browser reads the <b> and </b> HTML tags in a Web page, the browser formats the text between those tags as bold because the <b> and </b> tags are used to define bold text. Most Web browsers, regardless of the operating system on which they are installed, read and interpret the HTML tags in the same way, making HTML very effective at defining document content for a variety of computers.

The most significant markup language created for text was **Standard Generalized Markup Language (SGML)**, which was created in 1986 after eight years of development. SGML provides structure for a document by dividing it into elements (pieces), such as title, paragraph, text, name, part number, and so on. The markup language identifies these elements so that any program that interprets SGML can understand them. SGML also uses a **document type definition (DTD)** that identifies all the elements in a document and their structural relationships. The DTD contains information that identifies the tags used in the markup language and defines how they are related to each other. The DTD also describes which tags can be nested in other tags. SGML is a powerful and complex markup language that also allows the definition of other markup languages. HTML is defined as an SGML document type. HTML combines the text markup abilities of SGML with hypertext that links together Web pages. HTML uses predefined markup elements (called tags) to control the appearance of content in a Web page. The tags do not describe the content and are defined by a standards body that is fairly slow to change.

XML is the acronym for **Extensible Markup Language**. XML is a fairly recent innovation created through the efforts of the **World Wide Web Consortium (W3C)** (go to www.w3.org for more information). The W3C was created in 1994 with the goal of leading the World Wide Web to its full potential. The W3C has approximately 350 member organizations that develop common protocols to promote the Web's evolution and ensure its interoperability. The XML specification is part of that goal. XML was originally developed to meet the needs of large-scale electronic publishing efforts, but it has been playing an increasingly important role in describing and exchanging data.

XML was designed to combine the markup power of SGML with the ease of use of HTML. The result is a language that defines the structure and rules for creating markup elements—in fact, this flexibility is what the term extensible in Extensible Markup Language means. In a way, the XML standard just provides the grammatical rules and the alphabet. A user can apply the standard to data in any way that makes sense. XML is increasingly being used as an enterprise data format for the transfer of information between different applications. XML stores information in a nonproprietary data format. Many programs can read XML documents, which makes it possible to read the data using a variety of applications. Most programs store data in a proprietary binary format, which can result in an organization becoming locked into a particular solution. Translating data from one format to another can be a very expensive task.

Barbara is also part of a team that is exploring how to use XML to improve the company's business processes. After a discussion with the team about how spreadsheets and databases create a powerful combination for analyzing data, she fielded a question about how to use XML data in spreadsheets. Barbara agrees to report back to the team about the potential of using XML at TheZone. As part of her research, Barbara will convert some existing data into XML format to learn more about using XML.

XML Documents

XML documents are user-defined documents in which the user develops a DTD or schema that defines the elements contained in a document and descriptions of how those elements are related to each other. Because you can define elements in XML, it makes sense to make them as meaningful as possible. Instead of identifying a paragraph of text in a document as a paragraph, you can define individual types of paragraphs based on the content they will contain. For example, an XML document for TheZone might include elements that store data about a shoe as follows:

```
<shoe>
 <shoe_ID>SH-1987</shoe_ID>
 <shoe_name>Running shoe</shoe_name>
 <description>Men's size 11, white</description>
</shoe>
```

This code sample shows how you can combine data with metadata. **Metadata** is data that describes other data. You can think of it as data about data, but don't think too hard about that. XML uses angle brackets <> to separate the markup from the data. The end of a particular element is represented by a forward slash </>. In this code example, the metadata is combined with the content using XML. Because they are nested within the <shoe> and </shoe> elements, shoe_ID, shoe_name, and description describe one shoe sold by TheZone. XML adds meaning to content by providing a description of the data through user-defined elements and a hierarchical structure that shows the relationship of one data element to another. At first, this system might seem very simple and obvious, but much like a language, the real power isn't in the ability to write and speak—it is in the ability to have others read and understand what you say. The potential of XML to transform business lies in the ability for business partners to share both data and meaning in a nonproprietary format.

Best Practice

7

Level 3

Using XML Data in Excel

With Excel 2010, workbooks are saved in an XML file format that is modular in nature. The information in the workbook is divided into parts or modules of XML data, non-XML data such as charts and images, and relationship data that defines how each of the parts fits together. These modules are bundled together into a single file using ZIP technologies. Some benefits of the XML file format include smaller file sizes (files are automatically compressed), improved file recovery, safer documents (malicious code can be more easily separated), and easier integration. This last point is important because XML is quickly becoming a common output format for many enterprise data systems. As a result, native support of XML makes it possible for Excel to act as a front-end system for these larger data systems. For example, an employee might use Excel to manage travel receipts and then use XML to submit the travel claim information in the format required by the company for processing. It is a good idea to use XML data when the data is used by a variety of systems that can read and process data stored in this format.

Analyzing XML Data with Excel

As with other types of external data, the first step in analyzing XML data in Excel is to import the data into a worksheet. The import method you use depends on the data. For a simple XML document, you usually will import all of the data elements by importing the entire XML document as a table. For more complex XML documents with many data elements, you might be interested in only a few elements. In this case, you would use the XML Source task pane to map the elements you need to columns in a list. You can also export XML data that is added to or edited in Excel as a "well-formed" XML document for distribution that conforms to the XML specification put forward by the World Wide Web Consortium. The term well-formed is commonly used in the XML community to describe an XML document that is properly structured and that meets established rules and guidelines for how data is described and defined using XML. In addition, you can use XML schemas to validate the contents of an XML file. This ability is one of the best features of XML in an enterprise setting. One of the most time-consuming activities in any data analysis step is data cleansing—the process of fixing or removing incorrect data.

Importing XML Data as an XML Table

Barbara used Notepad to create a small XML document using data from the Sports Apparel Retailers table in the Apparel database. The XML document defines the data and includes two records. Because she wants the imported information to be inserted as an XML table, Barbara must include the data for at least two records. XML files with repeating elements (that is, multiple records of the same data) are imported into Excel in an XML table format and the element names appear as column headings. XML files with nonrepeating elements are imported as individual cells. Barbara's apparel XML file can be easily viewed using a Web browser as shown in Figure 7.42.

In Barbara's XML file, the <sports_apparel> element is the document's **root element**. An XML document can have only one root element, and all other elements are nested within the root element. She created the <retailer> element to contain the data for one record by nesting it in elements that describe the data. The elements between the <retailer> and </retailer> elements will become the column headings in the Excel table. The hierarchical structure clearly identifies which elements are related.

Figure 7.42: XML document with two records

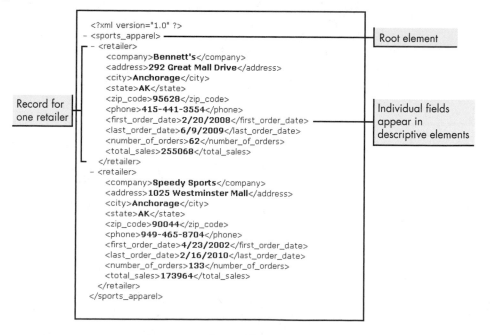

484

When you import XML data into a worksheet, Excel can create a schema based on the contents of the file being imported if the XML document does not already contain a schema. A **schema** is a set of validation rules for an XML document. The schema describes the elements in the document and how they are structured or related to each other. You can use a schema to create very complex validation rules by defining the data type and valid values for an element. Schemas are useful for establishing a set of standards as a way for organizations to share data. The schema acts like a dictionary that defines the permissible words and their meanings for a transaction.

Barbara imports her XML document into a worksheet. The content appears in the worksheet in an XML table, as shown in Figure 7.43. An **XML table** is similar in appearance and functionality to an Excel table, but the data in an XML table is mapped to XML elements. Each column in an XML table represents an XML element in the XML document. Barbara right-clicks a cell in the XML table, points to XML on the shortcut menu, and then selects XML Source. This opens the XML Source task pane, allowing Barbara to view the schema that Excel generated from the source data in the XML document. Because Barbara's XML document did not contain a schema, Excel created the one shown in the XML Source task pane in Figure 7.43.

When you add a schema to a workbook, Excel generates an **XML map** to create mapped ranges of data, and define the relationships between these ranges and the elements in the XML schema. Excel uses the XML map to relate the data to the elements when importing and exporting XML data. A workbook can contain many XML maps, but an XML map can contain only one root element. The sports_apparel XML map in Figure 7.43 shows the hierarchy of the XML document and the elements that contain data.

Figure 7.43: XML table in a worksheet

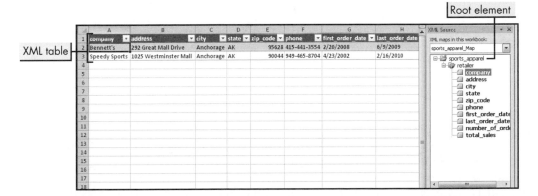

How To

Import an XML Document as an XML Table
1. Open the worksheet into which you want to import the data.
2. Select the first blank cell where you want the imported data to appear, click the From Other

Sources button in the Get External Data group on the Data tab on the Ribbon, and then select From XML Data Import. The Select Data Source dialog box opens.

3. Browse to the folder that contains the XML document you want to import.

4. Click the XML document, and then click the Open button. If the XML document does not refer to a schema, a message box opens to tell you that Excel will create a schema based on the XML source data.

5. Click the OK button to close the message box. The Import Data dialog box opens.

6. Click the option button to import the data in the existing worksheet or in a new worksheet, and then click the OK button to import the data.

The XML data in the XML table shown in Figure 7.43 functions just like the data in an Excel table. You can sort, filter, and analyze the data in the same way. The process for adding a new row to an XML table differs slightly; you use the handle in the lower-right cell of the XML table to increase the size of the table. You can then type or copy values into the cells. If you later export this data as XML data, any new rows you add will appear in the correct elements in the XML document that Excel creates. You can add new columns of data to the XML table, but these new columns will not be exported because new columns are not part of the XML map or schema.

Adding an XML Map to a Workbook

Another method for importing XML data into Excel is using the XML Source task pane. You can import a schema into a workbook or have Excel generate a schema or XML map from an existing XML document without importing any data. After you create the XML map in the workbook, you can use it to import individual data elements as columns in an XML table. You can use an XML map when you are importing a large, complex XML document that contains more elements than you need for your analysis. To import data using an XML map, open the XML Source task pane, and then click the XML Maps button. Figure 7.44 shows the XML Maps dialog box for Barbara's workbook.

At the moment there is only one XML map, named sports_apparel_Map, defined in the workbook. In her efforts to learn more about using XML, Barbara has been able to import a sample XML file with data into her workbook. Now she would like to try importing just the XML map without the data. Barbara has another sample XML file named Reps.xml with contact information for two sales reps. She decides to only import a portion of the XML elements in this file into her worksheet to see what happens to the XML file when an element is left out. She adds a map of the Reps.xml file to her workbook using the XML Maps dialog box. Adding the XML map allows Barbara to add individual XML elements to her worksheet by dragging the elements from the XML Source task pane to the chosen cell. Figure 7.45 shows Barbara's worksheet after adding the rep_info XML map to the workbook and adding XML elements to her worksheet. Notice that she added six of the seven fields from the rep_info XML map to the worksheet.

Figure 7.44: XML Maps dialog box

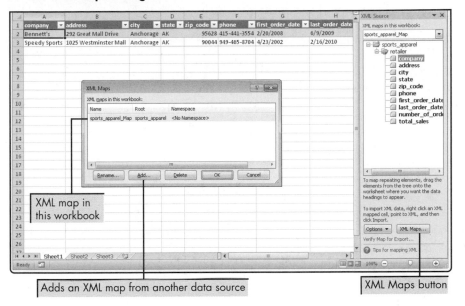

Adds an XML map from another data source   XML Maps button

Figure 7.45: New XML map added to a workbook

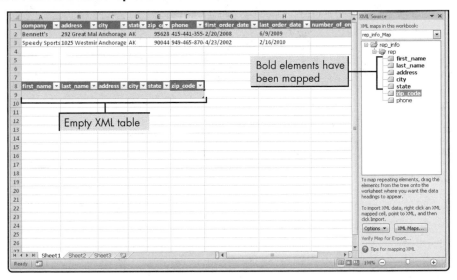

Another way to open the XML Map dialog box is through the Source button in the XML group on the Developer tab. The Developer tab is not displayed on the Ribbon by default. You can add the Developer tab using the Excel Options dialog box.

How To

Display the Developer Tab
1. Click the File tab on the Ribbon, and then click the Options command. The Excel Options dialog box opens.
2. Select the Customize Ribbon category, add a check mark to the Developer tab for the Main Tabs selection of the Customize the Ribbon box.
3. Click the OK button.

How To

Add an XML Map to a Workbook
1. Open the worksheet into which you want to import the data.
2. Click the Developer tab on the Ribbon, and then select the Source button in the XML group to open the XML Source task pane. You can also open the XML Source task pane by right-clicking any cell in an existing XML table, selecting XML on the shortcut menu, and then clicking XML Source on the shortcut menu.
3. Click the XML Maps button on the XML Source task pane. The XML Maps dialog box opens.
4. Click the Add button. The Select XML Source dialog box opens.
5. Navigate to the folder that contains the XML document, click the XML document to select it, and then click the Open button.
6. If the XML document does not refer to a schema, a message box opens to tell you that Excel will create a schema based on the XML source data. Click the OK button to acknowledge the message and close the message box.
7. Click the OK button in the XML Maps dialog box.

Because the data elements are being imported using an XML map, only the element names appear in the worksheet. To import the data from these elements into the worksheet, click the Refresh button in the External Table Data group on the Design tab. Figure 7.46 shows the worksheet after Barbara refreshes the data. The information for the two sales reps in the XML file has been added to the worksheet.

You can change or delete the data in a cell in an XML table just as you would a cell in any worksheet. However, because the columns of data in the XML table are mapped from a schema, deleting an entire column or XML element is a little different. You can remove mapped elements from an XML table in a worksheet by right-clicking the element you want to remove, pointing to Delete on the shortcut menu, and then clicking Table Columns. You can add rows of data to an XML table much like you can to an Excel table. Any data you enter in the row below an XML table will be added to the table. Barbara is able to add information for sales reps Lisa White and Jonathon Plocher to the XML table by inserting their information in the two rows below the table.

Figure 7.46: XML data added to an XML table

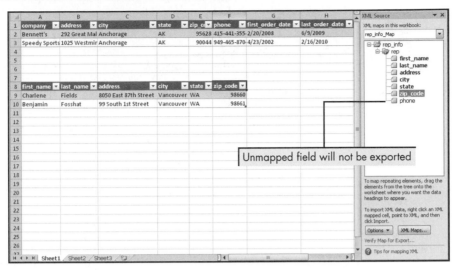

Exporting XML Data

Now that Barbara has successfully added content to the XML table, she wants to be certain that this new data is included in any exported XML file. She right-clicks a cell in the XML table, points to XML on the shortcut menu, and then selects Export to open the Export XML dialog box. She then exports the XML information to a new file named Reps1.xml. You can also open the Export XML dialog box using the Export button in the XML group on the Developer tab.

How To

Export an XML Table to an XML Document

1. Click the XML table to select it.

2. Click the Developer tab on the Ribbon, and then select the Export button in the XML group to open the Export XML dialog box. You can also right-click a cell in the XML table to display the shortcut menu, point to XML, and then select Export to open the Export XML dialog box.

3. Type a filename in the File name box, and then click the Export button.

Barbara's exported XML document is shown in Figure 7.47. Excel only exported the data and elements in the XML table; notice that the phone element is not included in the exported file. You need to be careful when you export an XML file because only the elements in the XML table are exported, and not the elements from the XML map.

Figure 7.47: Exported data in an XML document

One of the most difficult issues with any new data format is deciding which data to convert. XML is a free, nonproprietary format, but the labor used to convert information is not. One of Barbara's concerns is how to convert information that TheZone has already stored in Excel workbooks into well-formed XML documents. She has discovered a lot of information about how to import existing XML documents into Excel, but not much about how to export Excel data to XML. She wants to convert the data stored in the company's Excel workbooks to XML so the entire enterprise can share it. She found a way to use XML maps and Excel tables to do this conversion fairly simply.

Excel table data is organized in rows and columns. Each row defines a record and each column defines a field within a group of records. XML documents are organized in a running tabular form with each element occupying one line. The prospect of writing code that would take the rows in an Excel table, add the appropriate XML element tags, and then copy the result to a tabular format doesn't appeal to Barbara. She wants to convert the list of sports apparel retailers stored in an Excel worksheet into an XML table. She begins by creating a new workbook named XML-Apparel.xlsx.

Barbara imports the XML map from the Apparel.xml document she created earlier to load the elements from the Apparel.xml document into the XML Source task pane. Now, Barbara can map all the elements from the XML document into the worksheet at once.

How To

Map All Elements from an Existing XML Map to a Worksheet

1. Select the worksheet cell into which you want to paste the elements.

2. Right-click the root element of the XML map in the XML Source task pane, and then click Map element on the shortcut menu. The Map XML Elements dialog box opens and indicates the range into which you will paste the elements.

3. Click the OK button to close the Map XML Elements dialog box and to paste the elements into the worksheet.

Now, Barbara's worksheet contains the XML elements in an empty XML table. She can open the Sports Apparel Retailers.xlsx workbook, select all the rows that contain data about retailers, and copy this data to the Clipboard. Then, she can click the first cell in the blank row of the XML table and paste the copied data into the XML table. Figure 7.48 shows the pasted data.

Now that all of the retailer data is in the XML table, Barbara can export the XML table to an XML document so that all of the records are saved in an XML document with the same structure as the two original records that she used to create the XML map. Barbara clicks the Export button in the XML group on the Developer tab, enters a filename in the Export XML dialog box, and then clicks the Export button. The data is converted to an XML document that can be used in any application that supports XML data. Barbara plans to use this procedure to convert other data into XML documents.

Figure 7.48: XML table of sports apparel retailers

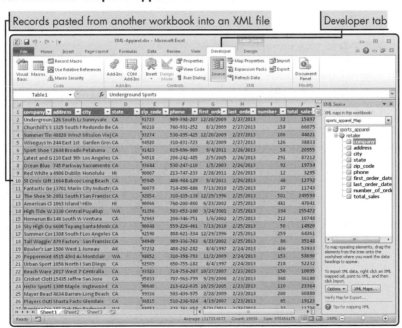

Steps To Success: Level 3

TheZone often partners with its larger customers on special projects to promote sales of TheZone products. One recently finished promotion was a gift certificate drawing with Above and Beyond Outfitters Inc. Customers from a variety of Above and Beyond stores purchased special TheZone products and filled out information cards for the chance to win certificates ranging in value from $25 to $75. You have a workbook containing the names and addresses of the winners along with the amounts of the gift certificates. You need to convert this information into an XML document that can be used to generate the personalized gift certificates.

Complete the following:

1. Open the **Promo.xlsx** workbook in the Chapter 7 folder, and then save it as **Above and Beyond Promotion.xlsx**.

2. Sort the information in ascending order by entry number.

3. Start Notepad, and then create an XML document using the following XML structure. Add the first two records in the workbook to the XML document. When you are finished, save the XML document as **XML-Promo.xml** in the Chapter 7 folder, and then close Notepad.

```
<?xml version="1.0" ?>
<promotion-456AB345-5>
    <entry_information>
        <entry_number></entry_number>
        <last_name></last_name>
        <first_name></first_name>
        <address></address>
        <city></city>
        <state></state>
        <zip_code></zip_code>
        <phone></phone>
        <amount></amount>
    </entry_information><entry_information>
        <entry_number></entry_number>
        <last_name></last_name>
        <first_name></first_name>
        <address></address>
        <city></city>
        <state></state>
        <zip_code></zip_code>
        <phone></phone>
```

```
    <amount></amount>
  </entry_information>
</promotion-456AB345-5> 4.
```

4. Import the **XML-Promo.xml** document into the workbook as an XML map.

5. On a new worksheet named **XML Promo**, map the elements from the XML map into the range A1:I1, and then refresh the XML data.

TROUBLESHOOTING: In order to complete this step, you must create a sample XML file with repeating elements. Using an XML file with only one set of entry information will only allow you to map the elements to the worksheet as individual cells instead of as an XML table. When you import an XML file with at least two sets of elements, Excel creates a schema that allows multiple instances of those elements. XML files without repeating elements will map to the spreadsheet as individual cells.

6. Copy rows 2 through 846 from the Gift Certificate Promotion worksheet, and then paste them into the XML table in the XML Promo worksheet.

7. Save the Above and Beyond Promotion.xlsx workbook, and then export the information in the XML Promo worksheet as an XML document named **Promotion-456AB345-5.xml** in the Chapter 7 folder.

8. Close the Above and Beyond Promotion.xlsx workbook.

7

Level 3

Chapter Summary

This chapter presented the different ways to import data from another source into Excel for analysis. In Level 1, you learned how to import data stored in a text file into Excel, and how to use the CONCATENATE, TRIM, RIGHT, and FIND functions to combine multiple text strings into a single text string, to trim unnecessary spaces from a text string, to find and extract characters from a text string, and to find specific characters in a text string. You also learned how to transform delimited data into rows and columns of data that you can sort and filter using the tools available in Excel. Finally, you learned how to create subtotals to analyze data and how to create and work with data stored in an Excel list.

In Level 2, you learned how to import data stored in a database into Excel, and about the advantages of using a database to store data that can be exported to Excel for analysis. You used the Query Wizard to select specific records in a database and import them into Excel. You also learned how Excel stores and works with dates and times, and uses dates in calculations to determine the number of days and years between two dates. You learned how to create and use a PivotTable and PivotChart to summarize and analyze data stored in a worksheet in a variety of ways. Finally, you used a Web query to import information from the Web into an Excel worksheet so that you can use it in calculations.

In Level 3, you learned about different markup languages, including XML. You saw how to use an existing XML document to import an XML map into a workbook, and how to map XML elements into a worksheet. You learned how to import data into an XML table and how to export data to an XML document. For very large data sets, Excel provides a very quickandeasy way to import and export XML data that can be used by other applications.

Conceptual Review

1. List and describe the steps you would take to create a structured list of data from a text file that contains values stored on separate lines.

2. Why should you remove unnecessary spaces from data imported from another source? How do you remove unnecessary spaces from a text string?

3. How do the FIND and SEARCH functions work, and how are they different?

4. What options are available for parsing data when you use the Convert Text to Columns Wizard?

5. What are the advantages and disadvantages of using the Subtotal tool to analyze data?

6. What is the difference between an unstructured list and an Excel list?

7. List and describe the six available options when using the AutoFilter feature in an Excel Table.

8. What is the primary advantage of storing data in a database and importing that data into Excel?

9. Explain the steps you must take to import data stored in an Access database into Excel.

10. What is the Query Wizard and when would you use it?

11. How does Excel store date and time values?

12. What are the arguments for the YEARFRAC function? What are the possible values for calculating months and years using this function?

13. When should you use a PivotTable report to analyze data?

14. List and describe the four areas of a PivotTable report.

15. Not including currency exchange rate data, what other types of Web queries might be useful to a business using Excel for data analysis?

16. List and describe the differences and similarities between HTML and XML.

17. Describe the steps you would take to import XML data as an XML table in Excel.

18. How do you import an XML map into a workbook and map its elements into the worksheet?

19. What advantages exist for businesses to create ways to import, export, and use XML data in their daily operations?

Case Problems

Level 1 – Importing and Analyzing Data for Johnson Equipment

Johnson Equipment, the medium-sized laboratory equipment manufacturing company where you work, is in the process of acquiring Sloan Manufacturing, a smaller equipment manufacturer in the same industry. Because operations between your company and Sloan overlap, you need to merge the data from the new company with similar data for your company. The text file you received from Sloan contains categories, product numbers, and product descriptions, in addition to the on-hand quantity for each product and the number of products produced during each month of the past year. You need to add prefixes to the category names so the data will match the existing data that your company uses. Then, you will use Excel to organize and summarize the data.

Accounting

Complete the following:

1. Use Notepad (or another text editor) to open the text file named **Sloan.txt** from the Chapter 7 folder, select all the data it contains, copy the data to the Clipboard, and then close Notepad.

2. Create a new workbook named **Johnson-Sloan.xlsx**, and save it in the Chapter 7 folder. Paste the data you copied from the text file into a worksheet named **Imported Data**.

3. Convert the information in the worksheet into columns.

4. Sort the data by category and then by product number in ascending order.

5. Use the CONCATENATE function to add the appropriate prefix and a dash to each category using the following list. For example, the Analyzer category would begin with **600**, followed by a dash and the category name (600-Analyzer).

Category	Prefix		Category	Prefix
Analyzer	600		Evaporators	619
Autoclave	601		Fermentors	621
Balances	603		Furnace	623
Bath	605		Gas Chromatographs	625
Biohood	607		Glove Boxes	627
Cell Disrupters	609		Microscopes	629
Cell Harvesters	611		Reactors	631
Centrifuges	613		Spectrophotometers	633
Chromatography	615		Ultrasonic Cleaners	635
Desiccators	617			

6. Change the data set into an Excel table.

7. Use the Total row to calculate the number of units on hand and the number of units produced in each month. Then add a new column named **Total** to the right of the December column that calculates the number of units produced for the year for each part.

8. Display the top 20 items based on the values in the Total column to show the parts with the highest production by month.

9. Save and close the Johnson-Sloan.xlsx workbook.

Level 2 – Analyzing Manager Performance at Home Station

You are a regional manager for Home Station, a national chain of home renovation stores. You are analyzing the weekly sales data for one of the retail stores located in Austin, Texas. The sales data is reported by department and manager. The Austin store manager wants to rotate the department managers in each of the store's departments so each manager becomes more familiar with the entire store's operations. You have been assigned the task of determining the impact of rotating the managers on store sales. You will import the sales data from a database into Excel and then create a PivotTable report to summarize the quarterly sales by department and by manager.

Sales

Complete the following:

1. Create a new Excel workbook and save it as **Home Station-Austin.xlsx** in the Chapter 7 folder.

2. Import the information from the Sales table in the **Sales.accdb** database in the Chapter 7 folder into a worksheet named **Sales**.

3. Create a PivotTable report using the data in the Sales worksheet and place the PivotTable report in a new worksheet named **Austin**.

4. Use the PivotTable report to analyze the sales by department. Change the number format of the sales data to currency and sort the sales so that the department with the highest sales appears first. Print the worksheet.

5. Rearrange the fields in the PivotTable report to analyze department sales by quarter. Which department had the highest quarterly sales and in which quarter did it occur? (Hint: Use the Date field to summarize the dates by quarter.)

6. Add the Manager field to the PivotTable report to analyze each department's quarterly sales performance by manager. Which manager had the highest sales for each department? In which quarter did the manager's highest sales occur?

7. Rearrange the fields in the PivotTable report to analyze each manager's quarterly sales performance by department. Which department resulted in the highest sales for each manager? In which quarter did the highest sales occur?

8. Based on the data collected, which manager would you choose to manage each department on a long-term basis? Support your recommendations with data from the PivotTable report.

9. Save and close the Home Station-Austin.xlsx workbook.

Level 3 – Creating a Loan Application and Amortization Schedule for CKG Auto

Finance

CKG Auto's Financial Department has asked you to finish developing an Excel workbook that it plans to use to analyze automotive credit application data stored in individual XML documents. The workbook is based on an existing credit analysis spreadsheet. The workbook will be used to calculate loan payment information and create a loan amortization schedule for customers purchasing new and used vehicles from dealerships that provide financing options through CKG Auto. The Smith.xml file contains sample data that you will import into the spreadsheet to test the workbook.

Complete the following:

1. Open the **Credit.xlsx** file from the Chapter 7 folder, and then save it as **Automotive Credit Application.xlsx**.

2. Use the XML Source task pane to create an XML map using the **Smith.xml** file in the Chapter 7 folder.

3. Map the elements in the XML Source task pane to the appropriate cells in the worksheet by dragging them from the XML Source task pane and dropping them into the appropriate cells in the worksheet.

4. Use the Developer tab to map and import the appropriate elements from the Smith.xml document to the blank cells for the Application Information, Loan Details, and Vehicle information sections in the Automotive Credit Application worksheet.

5. Insert the appropriate function and/or formula to calculate the monthly car payment in cell B13.

6. Prepare an amortization schedule based on the information imported from the XML document.

7. Save and close the Automotive Credit Application.xlsx workbook.

SAM: Skills Assessment Manager

For current SAM information, including versions and content details, visit SAM
Central (http://samcentral.course.com). If you have a SAM user profile, you
may have access to hands-on instruction, practice, and assessment of the skills
covered in this chapter. Since various versions of SAM are supported throughout
the life of this text, check with your instructor for the correct instructions and
URL/Web site for accessing assignments.

7

Chapter Exercises

Using Data Tables and Excel Scenarios for What-If Analysis
Marketing: Analyzing the Profitability and Pricing Policies of a Potential Product

"The only place where success comes before work is a dictionary."
—Vidal Sassoon

LEARNING OBJECTIVES

Level 1
Conduct break-even analyses
Conduct sensitivity analyses
Create, format, and interpret one-variable data tables
Create, format, and interpret two-variable data tables

Level 2
Understand and plan scenarios
Use the SUMPRODUCT function
Create, edit, and delete scenarios using Scenario Manager
Create and interpret scenario reports

Level 3
Prepare worksheets for simulations using data tables
Run simulations using data tables
Conduct statistical analysis of simulation results
Interpret simulation results

TOOLS/FUNCTIONS COVERED IN THIS CHAPTER

AVERAGE
Data tables
MAX
MIN
RAND
Scenario Manager
STDEV.S
SUMPRODUCT
VLOOKUP

Chapter Introduction

To solve some of the business problems presented in this book, you have used **what-if analysis**, a process of changing values to see how those changes affect the outcome of formulas in an Excel worksheet. What-if analysis allows you to see *what* output results *if* the values of various input assumptions change.

At its most basic level, what-if analysis involves asking a question about a worksheet, such as "What if the revenue of the swimwear product line increased by $10,000 per month?" Then, you can change the appropriate data in a worksheet cell and observe how the other values in the workbook change, such as those showing profit.

In this chapter, you will use other Excel tools that help you perform what-if analyses: data tables and the Scenario Manager. You will use a data table when you want to ask a what-if question involving a range of values. As you change the values in the data table, you will observe how that affects the results of formulas in the worksheet. Data tables let you perform many calculations at once and then compare the results of these variations on a single worksheet.

The **Scenario Manager** also allows you to consolidate multiple what-if models in one worksheet. You can switch between the scenarios to see how various sets of assumptions affect the results of your calculations.

Although data tables and scenarios are ideal for showing the results of the interaction of a number of variables, analyzing which results are more likely than others depends on your knowledge of your business and market. You can use two-variable data tables to base a what-if analysis on realistic, but not actual, data. Doing so is often called running a simulation. For example, you can run a simulation to help analyze the expected profitability of a company, given various product sales prices and estimated probabilities of product demand.

Case Scenario

TheZone is investigating a new swimwear product line for its Apparel division. Recent advances in fabric technology and aerodynamic styling have resulted in bodysuits that are highly prized by competitive swimmers. TheZone's sales staff reports that customers are requesting these high-tech bodysuits. Before TheZone commits to manufacturing the suits, Richard Rayburn, vice president of marketing, wants to evaluate the profitability outlook of the product he plans to call the TZSwimSkin. His analysis will include break-even and sensitivity analyses that will help TheZone set its pricing policies for the product. He also wants to evaluate marketing plans proposed for TheZone's current swimwear line. To determine which marketing plan will produce the best results for TheZone, he'll

Marketing

compare the plans using a variety of assumptions. Finally, Richard will analyze sales price options for a new swimwear product based on probabilities that demand for the product will range from high to low.

LEVEL 1
Using Data Tables to Perform Break-Even and Sensitivity Analyses

Conducting Break-Even and Sensitivity Analyses

Break-even analysis is a type of what-if analysis that concentrates on an activity at or around the point at which a product breaks even—in other words, the point at which the expenses of creating and selling the product are equal to the revenue it produces, or where the profit is $0. For example, suppose the TZSwimSkin product line has $60,000 of fixed costs—the costs of payroll, research and development, administration, and other expenses that TheZone pays no matter how many swimsuits it sells. In addition, each TZSwimSkin product has $20 of variable costs—the costs of raw materials, direct labor, and other expenses that change in proportion to the number of swimsuits sold. Figure 8.1 shows that the more swimsuits TheZone sells, the more its variable costs increase, while its fixed costs stay constant.

Figure 8.1: Comparing costs and sales

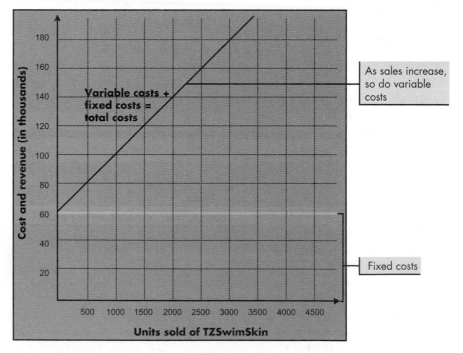

You can use this chart to determine the break-even point—the point at which revenue equals expenses. To do so, you plot another line that shows total revenue, which is calculated by multiplying the sales price by the number of units sold. If TheZone sells 2,000 TZSwimSkins for $70 each, for example, the company will generate $140,000 in total revenue. Figure 8.2 adds a line to the costs and sales chart that plots the growth of revenue.

Figure 8.2: Break-even point

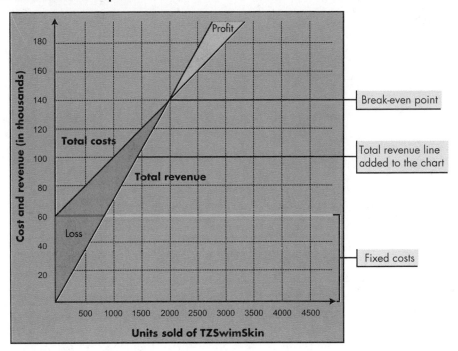

The point at which the total revenue line crosses the total costs line is the break-even point. In this case, TheZone needs to sell 2,000 TZSwimSkins at $70 each before that product begins to make a profit. Richard also knows that the Apparel division needs to spend $140,000 on costs before it starts profiting from the outlay made for the TZSwimSkins. Richard can then test the market to determine whether $70 is a competitive price. If not, he can adjust his break-even analysis to account for a higher or lower price per suit.

Sensitivity analysis is another type of what-if analysis that attempts to examine how sensitive the results of an analysis are to changes in the assumptions. Because what-if analysis usually involves many estimates and other projections, sensitivity analysis helps managers learn how tolerant the projected results are of changes in those estimates and assumptions. For example, a sensitivity analysis asks, "How much will projected profits change if the cost of goods sold per unit changes by $1? By $2?" Figure 8.3 shows a bar chart created from a simple profit sensitivity analysis that shows how sensitive profits are to sales price, variable costs, and fixed costs. As expected, sales price has the most positive effect on profit. The analysis also reveals that variable costs have the most negative effect on profit.

Figure 8.3: Simple sensitivity analysis

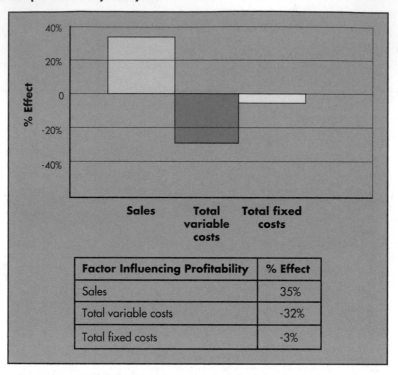

Factor Influencing Profitability	% Effect
Sales	35%
Total variable costs	-32%
Total fixed costs	-3%

Analyzing What-If Results with Data Tables

A **data table** is a range of cells containing values and formulas. When you change the values, the data table shows you how those changes affect the results from the formulas. Data tables allow you to organize and present the results of multiple what-if analyses. Because you can compare the results of many calculations in data tables, they can be very useful when performing break-even and sensitivity analyses.

Excel can be used to create two types of data tables: one-variable data tables and two-variable data tables. Both types have **input cells**, which are the cells containing values that can vary. They also have **result cells**, which contain formulas that involve the input cells in their calculations in some way. A **one-variable data table** has only one input cell and can have many result cells. Use a one-variable data table to see how different interest rates affect a loan payment, for example. In contrast, a **two-variable data table** has two input cells, but only one result cell. Use a two-variable data table to see how two factors—different interest rates and loan terms—affect a loan payment, for example.

Richard wants to create a worksheet to help evaluate the potential profitability of the TZSwimSkin product. He is particularly interested in a break-even and sensitivity analysis that will help him and other managers decide whether to add this product to the swimwear product line and to set pricing policies if they do.

Preparing a Worksheet for Data Tables

A data table depends on values and formulas used in a worksheet and must appear on the same worksheet that contains this data. You must structure the worksheet so it uses input cells that contain values you want to modify in a what-if analysis. It also should use result cells containing formulas that calculate the values you want to analyze. Figure 8.4 shows a one-variable data table that illustrates how revenue, expenses, and income vary if the number of units sold varies from 500 to 2,000.

Figure 8.4: Input and result cells

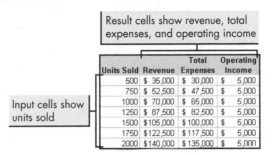

Result cells show revenue, total expenses, and operating income

Input cells show units sold

Units Sold	Revenue	Total Expenses	Operating Income
500	$ 35,000	$ 30,000	$ 5,000
750	$ 52,500	$ 47,500	$ 5,000
1000	$ 70,000	$ 65,000	$ 5,000
1250	$ 87,500	$ 82,500	$ 5,000
1500	$105,000	$100,000	$ 5,000
1750	$122,500	$117,500	$ 5,000
2000	$140,000	$135,000	$ 5,000

Richard's first task is to perform a break-even analysis on the TZSwimSkin product. To do so, he will combine information developed by a variety of TheZone's managers into a single worksheet.

At this point, the Sales Department estimates that it could sell about **3,000** units of the TZSwimSkin product at a selling price of $129.95 per unit if TheZone spends $75,000 on marketing the new product. Richard collects estimates of cost and expense data as follows:

- Cost of goods sold (COGS): $75.75 per unit
- Distribution expenses: $5.00 per unit
- Total marginal payroll expense: $52,000
- Total marginal overhead expense: $18,000

Richard decides to ignore the effects of income taxes because they introduce another level of estimates into an analysis already full of "best guesses."

Best Practice

Understanding What-If Analysis and Income Taxes
There is no right answer to the question of whether the effect of income taxes should be considered when performing what-if analysis. Income taxes are a real expense to companies: Because of the vagaries of and discrepancies between the federal and state income tax codes and the Financial Accounting Standards Board (FASB) accounting standards, income tax expense on Income Statements for publicly traded companies and the amount of income tax actually paid are two different numbers. Thus, if a company decides to use income tax expense as a factor in analyses, it must then decide whether to use rules based on

8

Level 1

Generally Accepted Accounting Principles (GAAP), tax-basis rules, or some other method when computing the effects.

Instead of attempting to compute the actual amount of the GAAP-basis or tax-basis tax effects on numbers, which are only estimates, many companies decide to use their marginal tax rate in their what-if analysis. This can be a simple and consistent way to include tax effects into a what-if analysis.

In short, taxes are an expense, but companies treat them differently in their analyses. You can omit taxes from your estimates or use your company's marginal tax rate.

Richard has developed a workbook for the swimwear line containing a worksheet named SwimSkin Projections, shown in Figure 8.5, which includes the assumptions and projections for the TZSwimSkin product. The Assumptions section of the worksheet consists of the input cells with their current data values, whereas the Projections section contains the result cells with their values computed by formulas. The income projections are presented in a contribution-margin format. A **contribution margin** is calculated by subtracting variable expenses from sales and represents the amount of revenue that contributes to covering the fixed expenses of a company. Contribution margins are widely used in analysis, especially when evaluating the profitability of sales alternatives and performing break-even analysis.

Figure 8.5: Input and result cells on the SwimSkin Projections worksheet

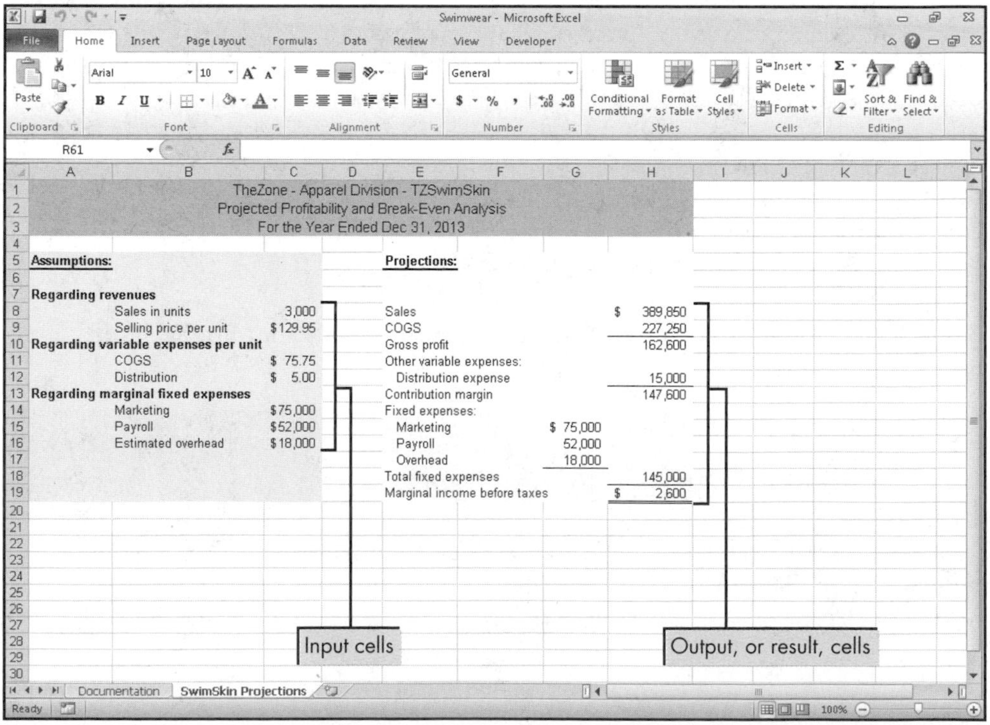

Figure 8.6 shows the formulas used in the SwimSkin Projections worksheet. These formulas calculate the results that Richard wants to analyze.

Figure 8.6: Formulas used in the income projections

	D	E	F	G	H	I
4						
5		Projections:				
6						
7						
8		Sales		=C8*C9		
9		COGS		=C8*C11		
10		Gross profit		=H8-H9		
11		Other variable expenses:				
12		Distribution expense		=C8*C12		
13		Contribution margin		=H10-H12		
14		Fixed expenses:				
15		Marketing	=C14			
16		Payroll	=C15			
17		Overhead	=C16			
18		Total fixed expenses		=SUM(G15:G17)		
19		Marginal income before taxes		=H13-H18		
20						
21						
22						

The SwimSkin Projections worksheet shows that, if all the estimates are correct, the TZSwimSkin will increase the company's profits by a modest $2,600 (the marginal income before taxes value in cell H19). That's not bad for a new product line. What if the Sales Department's estimate of the number of units sold is incorrect, however? What if the projected number of swimmers who want to wear bodysuit swimwear is too optimistic? Richard can answer these questions by recalculating the projections based on a new unit sales figure of 1,500, for example. As shown in Figure 8.7, that would result in a marginal net loss to the company of $71,200.

Figure 8.7: Projections based on 1,500 units sold

Units sold reduced to 1,500

$71,200 loss for TheZone

Richard could conduct a what-if analysis by continuing to change the unit sales input value and then viewing the updated worksheet. He could either note the various combinations of input values and results, or print each updated worksheet to compare the various analyses. To save time and effort, however, he can condense these tasks into one step by using a data table to conduct many analyses and see a summary of the results on the worksheet.

Varying One Value in a What-If Analysis

Recall that one-variable data tables allow you to compare results calculated from changes made to one input value. For example, in Richard's analysis, he can vary the number of units sold to see how this affects profits and other Income Statement results. Specifically, Richard is interested in what the sales revenue, gross profit, contribution margin, and income before taxes would be if the number of units sold varied from 500 to 5,000, in increments of 500 units. Because a one-variable data table allows only one input value to vary, all the cost and expense estimates must remain constant while unit sales change.

Creating a data table in Excel involves two major steps:

1. Set up the structure for the data table.

2. Instruct Excel about how the data table's structure relates to the input section of the worksheet.

How To

Create a One-Variable Data Table

1. On a worksheet that contains the input and result cells you want to analyze, type the list of values that you want to substitute in the input cell down one column or across one row.

2. If the data table is column-oriented, type the first formula that refers to the input cell (either directly or indirectly) in the row above the first value and one cell to the right of the column of values. See Figure 8.8. Type any additional formulas to the right of the first formula.

Figure 8.8: Setting up a column-oriented one-variable data table

If the data table is row-oriented, type the first formula that refers to an output cell of interest in the column to the left of the first value and one cell below the row of values. See Figure 8.9. Type any additional formulas below the first formula.

Figure 8.9: Setting up a row-oriented one-variable data table

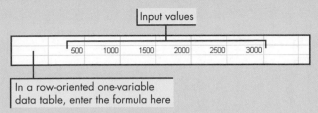

3. Select the data table, that is, the range of cells that contains the formulas and the values that you want to substitute.
4. On the Data tab on the Ribbon, click the What-If Analysis button in the Data Tools group, and then click Data Table.
5. In a column-oriented data table, enter the reference to the input cell in the Column input cell box. In a row-oriented data table, enter the reference to the input cell in the Row input cell box.
6. Click the OK button.

Setting Up a One-Variable Data Table's Structure

Creating the structure for a data table involves creating the set of input values you want to use in a what-if analysis and indicating the results you want to see in the data table. In a one-variable data table, you enter possible values for the single input variable in the first row or column of the data table. The corresponding results appear in the subsequent rows or columns.

Recall that Richard is interested in what the sales revenue, gross profit, contribution margin, and income before taxes would be if the number of units sold varied from 500 to 5,000. Thus, the structure for Richard's one-variable data table will include the input values of 500 to 5,000 in increments of 500, and formulas that refer to the cells that calculate the sales revenue, gross profit, contribution margin (abbreviated CM in the worksheet), and income before taxes. Formulas in the worksheet's Projections section use the units sold input cell in calculating their results. Therefore, by having the data table's formulas refer to cells in the Projections section of the worksheet, they are indirectly referring to the input cells.

Figure 8.10 shows the structure for Richard's data table. Because the data table contains formulas that refer to cells in the Projections section, the current values from the output cells of interest are displayed along the top row of the data table.

As Richard reviews the table structure, he becomes concerned that the values appearing in row 6 will confuse some people. The values in row 6 only reflect the values in the corresponding cells of the Projections section, but they could easily be misinterpreted. However, he can't simply remove the output formulas from the table because Excel needs them to calculate the table results. Instead, Richard can use a Custom number format to display a label in a worksheet even when the cell contains a value or a formula. Richard decides to apply Custom number formats to cells K6:N6, setting those cells to display column

8

Level 1

Figure 8.10: Setting up a column-oriented data table in the Swimwear worksheet

=H8 =H10 =H13 =H19

	C	D	E	F	G	H	I	J	K	L	M	N	O
4													
5			Projections:										
6									$194,925	81,300	73,800	$(71,200)	
7								500					
8	1,500		Sales			$194,925		1000					
9	$129.95		COGS			113,625		1500					
10			Gross profit			81,300		2000					
11	$ 75.75		Other variable expenses:					2500					
12	$ 5.00		Distribution expense			7,500		3000					
13			Contribution margin			73,800		3500					
14	$75,000		Fixed expenses:					4000					
15	$52,000		Marketing		$ 75,000			4500					
16	$18,000		Payroll		52,000			5000					
17			Overhead		18,000								
18			Total fixed expenses			145,000							
19			Marginal income before taxes			$ (71,200)							
20													
21													

Values that relate to cell C8 (unit sales), arranged in a column

These cells must remain blank—Excel calculates these values when it creates the data table

Results will be replaced with labels that identify the data

headings instead of the formulas. Excel still has access to the formulas it needs, but worksheet users can refer to the textual column headings to interpret the data table easily.

How To

Hide Formulas by Applying Custom Number Formats to Cells

1. Select the cell to format.
2. On the Home tab on the Ribbon, click the Number group dialog box launcher.
3. Click the Number tab in the Format Cells dialog box, if necessary.
4. Click Custom in the Category box.
5. Delete the format code in the Type box, and then enter the desired label in the Type box as a text string. Text strings must be enclosed in quotation marks. If the underlying formula might return a negative result, type the text string twice with the two instances separated by a semicolon (;) to ensure that the text will not appear with a minus sign (–) preceding it.
6. Click the OK button.

Completing a One-Variable Data Table

Now that Richard has set up the data table's structure and added column labels, he is ready to complete the data table. First, he selects the range that includes the input values, formulas, and eventual result cells, range J6:N16, as shown in Figure 8.11.

Next, Richard must specify how he structured the selected data table; in other words, whether the input cells are arranged in a column or row. He must also specify which input cell in the worksheet relates to the values in the data table, which in this case is cell C8. He

Figure 8.11: Selecting the data table

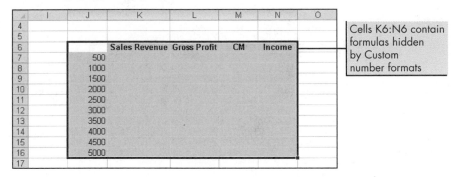

Cells K6:N6 contain formulas hidden by Custom number formats

opens the Data Table dialog box, shown in Figure 8.12, by clicking the Data tab on the Ribbon, clicking the What-If Analysis button in the Data Tools group, and then clicking the Data Table command.

Figure 8.12: Data Table dialog box

The input values in the data table are arranged in a column, so Richard clicks in the Column input cell box. They represent unit sales, which corresponds to the input cell (cell C8) in the Assumptions section. Richard enters $C$8 in the Column input cell box, as shown in Figure 8.13.

Figure 8.13: Specifying the input cell in the Data Table dialog box

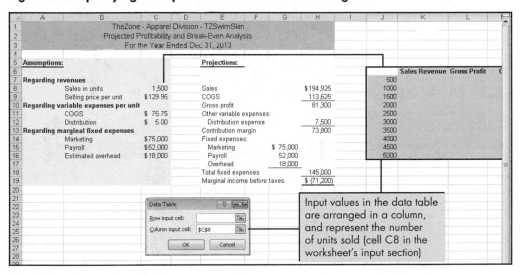

Input values in the data table are arranged in a column, and represent the number of units sold (cell C8 in the worksheet's input section)

When Richard clicks the OK button, Excel completes the data table. See Figure 8.14.

Figure 8.14: Completed data table

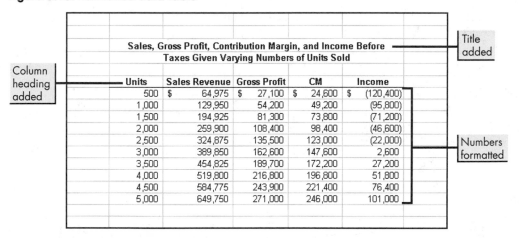

	Sales Revenue	Gross Profit	CM	Income
500	64975	27100	24600	-120400
1000	129950	54200	49200	-95800
1500	194925	81300	73800	-71200
2000	259900	108400	98400	-46600
2500	324875	135500	123000	-22000
3000	389850	162600	147600	2600
3500	454825	189700	172200	27200
4000	519800	216800	196800	51800
4500	584775	243900	221400	76400
5000	649750	271000	246000	101000

Approximation of break-even point

Excel calculates these values

Richard reviews the table, adds an appropriate title, and formats the numbers in the first row of results to include dollar signs. He also adjusts other formatting to make the data table more meaningful and accessible. See Figure 8.15.

Figure 8.15: Formatted data table

Column heading added   Title added   Numbers formatted

Units	Sales Revenue	Gross Profit	CM	Income
500	$ 64,975	$ 27,100	$ 24,600	$ (120,400)
1,000	129,950	54,200	49,200	(95,800)
1,500	194,925	81,300	73,800	(71,200)
2,000	259,900	108,400	98,400	(46,600)
2,500	324,875	135,500	123,000	(22,000)
3,000	389,850	162,600	147,600	2,600
3,500	454,825	189,700	172,200	27,200
4,000	519,800	216,800	196,800	51,800
4,500	584,775	243,900	221,400	76,400
5,000	649,750	271,000	246,000	101,000

Sales, Gross Profit, Contribution Margin, and Income Before Taxes Given Varying Numbers of Units Sold

Interpreting One-Variable Data Tables

From the one-variable data table, you can see that the break-even point (where profit is $0) occurs somewhere between 2,500 and 3,000 units of sales. If Richard used a smaller increment in specifying units sold, he could calculate the break-even point more precisely, but that would require a larger data table. Because he is working with estimates and projections, a range of results is usually sufficient when performing a rough break-even analysis. As Figure 8.16 shows, break-even revenues for the TZSwimSkin are between $324,875 and $389,850. This assumes that all the cost and expense data conforms to the assumptions in the SwimSkin Projections worksheet. Remember that a one-variable data table allows only one input assumption to vary, and Richard chose to vary unit sales from 500 to 5,000.

Figure 8.16: Completed SwimSkin Projections worksheet

	A	B	C	D	E	F	G	H	I
1			TheZone - Apparel Division - TZSwimSkin						
2			Projected Profitability and Break-Even Analysis						
3			For the Year Ended Dec 31, 2013						
4									
5	Assumptions:				Projections:				
6									
7	Regarding revenues								
8		Sales in units	1,500		Sales			$194,925	
9		Selling price per unit	$129.95		COGS			113,625	
10	Regarding variable expenses per unit				Gross profit			81,300	
11		COGS	$ 75.75		Other variable expenses:				
12		Distribution	$ 5.00		Distribution expense			7,500	
13	Regarding marginal fixed expenses				Contribution margin			73,800	
14		Marketing	$75,000		Fixed expenses:				
15		Payroll	$52,000		Marketing		$ 75,000		
16		Estimated overhead	$18,000		Payroll		52,000		
17					Overhead		18,000		
18					Total fixed expenses			145,000	
19					Marginal income before taxes			$ (71,200)	
20									
21									

Input section of the worksheet   Output section of the worksheet

Units	Sales Revenue	Gross Profit	CM	Income
	Sales, Gross Profit, Contribution Margin, and Income Before Taxes Given Varying Numbers of Units Sold			
500	$ 64,975	$ 27,100	$ 24,600	$ (120,400)
1,000	129,950	54,200	49,200	(95,800)
1,500	194,925	81,300	73,800	(71,200)
2,000	259,900	108,400	98,400	(46,600)
2,500	324,875	135,500	123,000	(22,000)
3,000	389,850	162,600	147,600	2,600
3,500	454,825	189,700	172,200	27,200
4,000	519,800	216,800	196,800	51,800
4,500	584,775	243,900	221,400	76,400
5,000	649,750	271,000	246,000	101,000

The data table shows that given the current assumptions, the break-even point is between these two data points

Richard can also find general profitability information about the TZSwimSkin product in the data table. For example, if the number of units sold is 4,000, sales revenue would be $519,800, gross profit would be $216,800, contribution margin would be $196,800, and income before taxes would be $51,800.

To conduct a sensitivity analysis, Richard can ask, "How would the break-even point and profitability estimates change if an estimate about one or more other assumptions changes?" You can easily perform this type of what-if analysis in a data table because it recalculates results when an assumption value changes in an input cell. For example, suppose the estimate of the COGS per unit changes from $75.75 to $95.00, and the estimated marketing expense is cut from $75,000 to $60,000. When Richard changes those values in the Assumptions section, Excel recalculates the data table. Figure 8.17 shows the results.

Figure 8.17: Changing assumptions in the SwimSkin Projections worksheet

	A	B	C	D	E	F	G	H	I
1			TheZone - Apparel Division - TZSwimSkin						
2			Projected Profitability and Break-Even Analysis						
3			For the Year Ended Dec 31, 2013						
4									
5	Assumptions:				Projections:				
6									
7	Regarding revenues								
8		Sales in units	1,500		Sales			$194,925	
9		Selling price per unit	$129.95		COGS			142,500	
10	Regarding variable expenses per unit				Gross profit			52,425	
11		COGS	$ 95.00		Other variable expenses:				
12		Distribution	$ 5.00		Distribution expense			7,500	
13	Regarding marginal fixed expenses				Contribution margin			44,925	
14		Marketing	$60,000		Fixed expenses:				
15		Payroll	$52,000		Marketing		$ 60,000		
16		Estimated overhead	$18,000		Payroll		52,000		
17					Overhead		18,000		
18					Total fixed expenses			130,000	
19					Marginal income before taxes			$ (85,075)	
20									
21									

COGS changed from $75.75 to $95.00

Marketing changed from $75,000 to $60,000

Sales, Gross Profit, Contribution Margin, and Income Before Taxes Given Varying Numbers of Units Sold				
Units	Sales Revenue	Gross Profit	CM	Income
500	$ 64,975	$ 17,475	$ 14,975	$ (115,025)
1,000	129,950	34,950	29,950	(100,050)
1,500	194,925	52,425	44,925	(85,075)
2,000	259,900	69,900	59,900	(70,100)
2,500	324,875	87,375	74,875	(55,125)
3,000	389,850	104,850	89,850	(40,150)
3,500	454,825	122,325	104,825	(25,175)
4,000	519,800	139,800	119,800	(10,200)
4,500	584,775	157,275	134,775	4,775
5,000	649,750	174,750	149,750	19,750

New assumption values move the break-even point to here

The break-even point has increased to between 4,000 and 4,500 units, which is a substantial increase in the break-even quantity. This shows that the profitability projections are relatively sensitive to changes in the cost and expense assumptions. This is useful for Richard and other managers to consider when deciding whether to continue plans for the TZSwimSkin product. Because Richard knows that unit sales are most likely to be around 3,000, he changes unit sales to 3,000, and then restores the other input figures in the Assumptions section to their original values.

Richard thinks the one-variable data table will provide a variety of useful information to TheZone's top management to help them decide whether to adopt the TZSwimSkin product.

Varying Two Values in a What-If Analysis

Richard just learned that the sales price for the TZSwimSkin will depend on its cost to TheZone, and that the Purchasing Department still hasn't calculated the cost per unit. Richard decides to develop a worksheet that shows the profitability effects of various interactions between the TZSwimSkin's selling price and cost of goods sold per unit. He could use a combination of the one-variable data table he created in the SwimSkin Projections worksheet and basic what-if analysis to find those results, but creating a two-variable data table would be more effective.

In a two-variable data table, you can vary the values of two input variables, but show the results for only one output value. The two input variables that Richard will vary are selling price and COGS per unit, and the result will be income before taxes.

As with one-variable data tables, to create a two-variable data table, you must first set up the structure for the data table. Then you indicate how the data table's structure relates to the input section of the worksheet. A two-variable data table has two lists of input values and one formula that refers to the two different input cells.

How To

Create a Two-Variable Data Table

1. On a worksheet that contains the input and result cells you want to analyze, type a formula that refers to the two input cells (either directly or indirectly).

2. Type one list of input values in the same column below the formula.

3. Type a second list of input values in the same row to the right of the formula. See Figure 8.18.

Figure 8.18: Setting up a two-variable data table

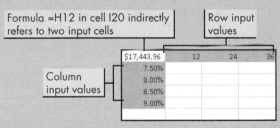

4. Select the data table, that is, the range of cells that contains the formula and the values that you want to substitute.

5. On the Data tab on the Ribbon, click What-If Analysis in the Data Tools group, and then click Data Table.

6. In the Row input cell box, enter the reference to the input cell for the input values in the row.

7. In the Column input cell box, enter the reference to the input cell for the input values in the column.

8. Click the OK button.

Setting Up a Two-Variable Data Table's Structure

Recall that creating the structure for a data table involves creating the set of input values you want to use in your what-if analysis, and then indicating the results you want to see in the data table. In a two-variable data table, you use two sets of values for two input variables, but unlike a one-variable data table, you display only the values of a single result cell. You use a two-variable data table to determine how two values affect a single output. Keep in mind that the input cells contain values and result cells show the results of formulas.

For example, suppose you are thinking of selling a product for $125 or $150, and you want to see how much revenue you'll generate if you sell 500, 750, 1,000, and so on, up to 2,000 units. You can create a two-variable data table to calculate revenue when the product sells for $125 or for $150. In Figure 8.19, the two unit sales prices, $125 and $150, are one set of input values. The seven units sold values are the other set of input values. The remaining cells show the result for each pair of input values. For example, if unit sales are 500 and the unit price is $125, the result, or revenue generated, is $62,500.

Figure 8.19: Result cells in a two-variable data table

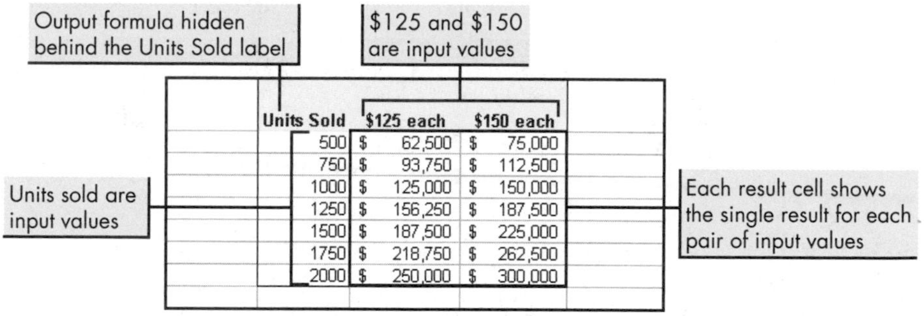

You must structure a two-variable data table so that the input values are perpendicular to each other and the table's output formula is located in the intersection of the two sets of input variables, as shown in Figure 8.19.

TheZone's Sales Department estimates that it could sell about 3,000 TZSwimSkins if $75,000 is spent on marketing the new product. Richard can add those estimates to the input section of the SwimSkin Projections worksheet. He also wants to conduct a sensitivity analysis to determine how profit is affected by selling prices that range from $99.95 to $149.95 with an increment of $10.00, and a COGS per unit of $49.75 to $109.75 with an increment of $5.00. The structure of Richard's two-variable data table will include the two sets of sales price and COGS per unit values, arranged perpendicular to each other. (It doesn't matter which set of input values you place in a column and which set you place in a row, as long as the table results can be understood by worksheet users.) He includes the output formula for the data table at the intersection of the two sets of input values. To calculate profitability, the output formula references the income before taxes cell in the worksheet's output section (cell H19).

The structure for Richard's two-variable data table is shown in Figure 8.20. As you can see from the figure, because the structure of the data table contains a formula that refers to the Marginal income before taxes cell in the worksheet's output section, the current value of that output cell is displayed at the intersection of the two sets of input values. All of the values in row 23 are selling prices amounts, so Richard adds a "Sales Prices" label to identify those values.

Figure 8.20: Setting up a two-variable data table in the SwimSkin Projections worksheet

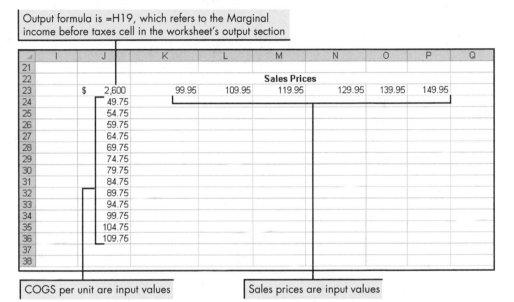

Output formula is =H19, which refers to the Marginal income before taxes cell in the worksheet's output section

	I	J	K	L	M	N	O	P	Q
21									
22					**Sales Prices**				
23		$ 2,600	99.95	109.95	119.95	129.95	139.95	149.95	
24		49.75							
25		54.75							
26		59.75							
27		64.75							
28		69.75							
29		74.75							
30		79.75							
31		84.75							
32		89.75							
33		94.75							
34		99.75							
35		104.75							
36		109.76							
37									
38									

COGS per unit are input values   Sales prices are input values

Completing a Two-Variable Data Table

Now that the data table's structure has been set up, Richard is ready to instruct Excel on how to complete the data table. In preparation for executing the command to complete the data table, Richard first selects the range that will constitute the completed data table, J23:P36.

Next, he clicks the Data tab, clicks the What-If Analysis button in the Data Tools group, and then clicks Data Table to open the Data Table dialog box. As with one-variable data tables, Richard must specify how the data table is structured and which cells in the worksheet's input section relate to the table's values. He specifies that the input values arranged in a row (the selling price) relate to cell C9, and the input values arranged in a column (COGS per unit) relate to cell C11. See Figure 8.21.

Richard clicks the OK button, and Excel completes the data table. The result is shown in Figure 8.22.

Figure 8.21: Selecting the two-variable data table

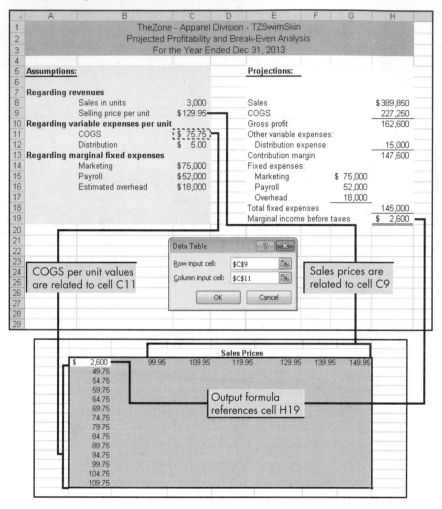

Figure 8.22: Completed two-variable data table

	I	J	K	L	M	N	O	P	Q
22					Sales Prices				
23		$ 2,600	99.95	109.95	119.95	129.95	139.95	149.95	
24		49.75	-9400	20600	50600	80600	110600	140600	
25		54.75	-24400	5600	35600	65600	95600	125600	
26		59.75	-39400	-9400	20600	50600	80600	110600	
27		64.75	-54400	-24400	5600	35600	65600	95600	
28		69.75	-69400	-39400	-9400	20600	50600	80600	
29		74.75	-84400	-54400	-24400	5600	35600	65600	
30		79.75	-99400	-69400	-39400	-9400	20600	50600	
31		84.75	-114400	-84400	-54400	-24400	5600	35600	
32		89.75	-129400	-99400	-69400	-39400	-9400	20600	
33		94.75	-144400	-114400	-84400	-54400	-24400	5600	
34		99.75	-159400	-129400	-99400	-69400	-39400	-9400	
35		104.75	-174400	-144400	-114400	-84400	-54400	-24400	
36		109.75	-189400	-159400	-129400	-99400	-69400	-39400	

He reviews the table, adds an appropriate title and borders, and applies other formats to make the worksheet more visually appealing and easy to understand. See Figure 8.23.

Figure 8.23: Formatted two-variable data table

Title added   Border added

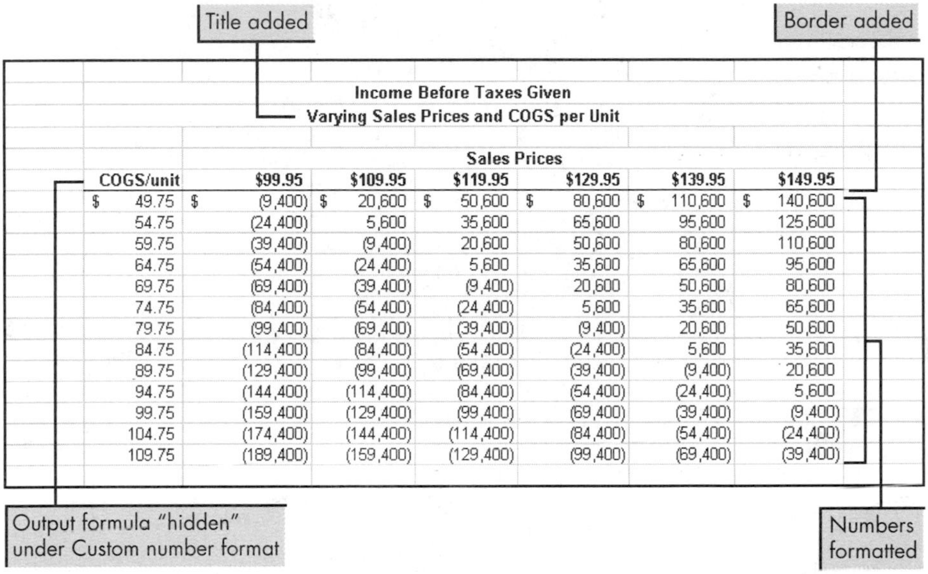

Income Before Taxes Given
Varying Sales Prices and COGS per Unit

		Sales Prices					
COGS/unit	**$99.95**	**$109.95**	**$119.95**	**$129.95**	**$139.95**	**$149.95**
$ 49.75	$ (9,400)	$ 20,600	$ 50,600	$ 80,600	$ 110,600	$ 140,600
54.75	(24,400)	5,600	35,600	65,600	95,600	125,600
59.75	(39,400)	(9,400)	20,600	50,600	80,600	110,600
64.75	(54,400)	(24,400)	5,600	35,600	65,600	95,600
69.75	(69,400)	(39,400)	(9,400)	20,600	50,600	80,600
74.75	(84,400)	(54,400)	(24,400)	5,600	35,600	65,600
79.75	(99,400)	(69,400)	(39,400)	(9,400)	20,600	50,600
84.75	(114,400)	(84,400)	(54,400)	(24,400)	5,600	35,600
89.75	(129,400)	(99,400)	(69,400)	(39,400)	(9,400)	20,600
94.75	(144,400)	(114,400)	(84,400)	(54,400)	(24,400)	5,600
99.75	(159,400)	(129,400)	(99,400)	(69,400)	(39,400)	(9,400)
104.75	(174,400)	(144,400)	(114,400)	(84,400)	(54,400)	(24,400)
109.75	(189,400)	(159,400)	(129,400)	(99,400)	(69,400)	(39,400)

Output formula "hidden" under Custom number format   Numbers formatted

Interpreting Two-Variable Data Tables

Interpreting a two-variable data table is similar to interpreting a one-variable data table. As shown in Figure 8.24, assuming TheZone sells 3,000 TZSwimSkins at $129.95 each, it will be profitable if the COGS per unit is $74.75 or less, assuming all the assumptions are true. Similarly, if the swimsuits had a COGS per unit of $94.75, TheZone would have to sell 3,000 suits at $149.95 each to earn income before taxes of $5,600.

Figure 8.24: Using the two-variable data table to conduct a sensitivity analysis

	A	B	C	D	E	F	G	H	I
1			TheZone - Apparel Division - TZSwimSkin						
2			Projected Profitability and Break-Even Analysis						
3			For the Year Ended Dec 31, 2013						
4									
5	Assumptions:				Projections:				
6									
7	Regarding revenues								
8		Sales in units	3,000		Sales			$389,850	
9		Selling price per unit	$129.95		COGS			227,250	
10	Regarding variable expenses per unit				Gross profit			162,600	
11		COGS	$ 75.75		Other variable expenses:				
12		Distribution	$ 5.00		Distribution expense			15,000	
13	Regarding marginal fixed expenses				Contribution margin			147,600	
14		Marketing	$75,000		Fixed expenses:				
15		Payroll	$52,000		Marketing		$ 75,000		
16		Estimated overhead	$18,000		Payroll		52,000		
17					Overhead		18,000		
18					Total fixed expenses			145,000	
19					Marginal income before taxes			$ 2,600	
20									
21									

If TheZone sells 3,000 TZSwimSkins at $129.95 each, it will
be profitable when the COGS unit price is $74.75 or less

				Income Before Taxes Given				
				Varying Sales Prices and COGS per Unit				
					Sales Prices			
COGS/unit	$99.95	$109.95	$119.95	$129.95	$139.95	$149.95
$ 49.75	$ (9,400)	$ 20,600	$ 50,600	$ 80,600	$ 110,600	$ 140,600
54.75	(24,400)	5,600	35,600	65,600	95,600	125,600
59.75	(39,400)	(9,400)	20,600	50,600	80,600	110,600
64.75	(54,400)	(24,400)	5,600	35,600	65,600	95,600
69.75	(69,400)	(39,400)	(9,400)	20,600	50,600	80,600
74.75	(84,400)	(54,400)	(24,400)	5,600	35,600	65,600
79.75	(99,400)	(69,400)	(39,400)	(9,400)	20,600	50,600
84.75	(114,400)	(84,400)	(54,400)	(24,400)	5,600	35,600
89.75	(129,400)	(99,400)	(69,400)	(39,400)	(9,400)	20,600
94.75	(144,400)	(114,400)	(84,400)	(54,400)	(24,400)	5,600
99.75	(159,400)	(129,400)	(99,400)	(69,400)	(39,400)	(9,400)
104.75	(174,400)	(144,400)	(114,400)	(84,400)	(54,400)	(24,400)
109.75	(189,400)	(159,400)	(129,400)	(99,400)	(69,400)	(39,400)

What if TheZone sells 2,000 suits instead of 3,000? What would happen to its profits
then? Because the number of units sold is not one of the two independent variables in the
data table, Richard can change the units sold value in the worksheet's input section, and
Excel will recalculate the data tables. As Figure 8.25 shows, the two-variable data table
now presents a much larger area of losses. If TheZone sells only 2,000 TZSwimSkins, it
would have to charge at least $129.95 each to earn a profit, and then only if the suits had
a cost per unit of $49.75 or less.

Figure 8.25: Sensitivity analysis when unit sales is 2,000

	A	B	C	D	E	F	G	H	I
1			TheZone - Apparel Division - TZSwimSkin						
2			Projected Profitability and Break-Even Analysis						
3			For the Year Ended Dec 31, 2013						
4									
5	Assumptions:				Projections:				
6									
7	Regarding revenues								
8		Sales in units	2,000		Sales			$259,900	
9		Selling price per unit	$129.95		COGS			151,500	
10	Regarding variable expenses per unit				Gross profit			108,400	
11		COGS	$ 75.75		Other variable expenses:				
12		Distribution	$ 5.00		Distribution expense			10,000	
13	Regarding marginal fixed expenses				Contribution margin			98,400	
14		Marketing	$75,000		Fixed expenses:				
15		Payroll	$52,000		Marketing		$ 75,000		
16		Estimated overhead	$18,000		Payroll		52,000		
17					Overhead		18,000		
18					Total fixed expenses			145,000	
19					Marginal income before taxes			$ (46,600)	
20									
21									

If TheZone sells only 2,000 TZSwimSkins at $129.95 each, it will be profitable when the COGS per unit is $49.75 or less

Income Before Taxes Given Varying Sales Prices and COGS per Unit

-COGS/unit	$99.95	$109.95	$119.95	$129.95	$139.95	$149.95
$ 49.75	(54,600)	(34,600)	(14,600)	5,400	25,400	45,400
54.75	(64,600)	(44,600)	(24,600)	(4,600)	15,400	35,400
59.75	(74,600)	(54,600)	(34,600)	(14,600)	5,400	25,400
64.75	(84,600)	(64,600)	(44,600)	(24,600)	(4,600)	15,400
69.75	(94,600)	(74,600)	(54,600)	(34,600)	(14,600)	5,400
74.75	(104,600)	(84,600)	(64,600)	(44,600)	(24,600)	(4,600)
79.75	(114,600)	(94,600)	(74,600)	(54,600)	(34,600)	(14,600)
84.75	(124,600)	(104,600)	(84,600)	(64,600)	(44,600)	(24,600)
89.75	(134,600)	(114,600)	(94,600)	(74,600)	(54,600)	(34,600)
94.75	(144,600)	(124,600)	(104,600)	(84,600)	(64,600)	(44,600)
99.75	(154,600)	(134,600)	(114,600)	(94,600)	(74,600)	(54,600)
104.75	(164,600)	(144,600)	(124,600)	(104,600)	(84,600)	(64,600)
109.75	(174,600)	(154,600)	(134,600)	(114,600)	(94,600)	(74,600)

In addition to break-even information about the interaction of various selling prices and costs per unit, Richard's data tables also show how sensitive the profit potential of the TZSwimSkin product is to $10 changes in price and $5 changes in COGS per unit.

Steps To Success: Level 1

Richard and other managers agree that the TZSwimSkin product is promising. Richard wants to conduct another profitability analysis with more sophisticated sales and marketing data. The Marketing Department has conducted research and determined the likely sales volume at various levels of marketing expenditures. Richard has started to create a revised break-even and sensitivity analysis in a workbook named TZSwimSkin, which contains input assumptions and an output section in the form of an Income Statement, as shown in Figure 8.26.

Figure 8.26: TZSwimSkin workbook

Richard asks you to finish the analysis by creating a one-variable data table to show the effects of the marketing expenditure levels on sales, gross profit, contribution margin, and marginal income before taxes. He also asks you to create a two-variable data table that shows the effects of the interaction of various marketing expenditures and sales prices on income before taxes. Complete the following:

1. Open the workbook named **TZSwimSkin.xlsx** located in the Chapter 8 folder, and save it with the name **TZSwimSkin Analysis.xlsx**.

2. Switch to the TZSwimSkin worksheet. Below the Projections section of the worksheet, create the structure for the one-variable data table. The table's input values should be marketing expenses of $25,000 to $125,000 in increments of $25,000. The table's output formulas should refer to the sales, gross profit, contribution margin, and marginal income before taxes results cells.

3. Complete the one-variable data table using the Data Table dialog box. Relate the table's input values to the marketing expense cell in the worksheet's input section.

4. Add headings and format the data table so it is appealing and professional.

5. A few rows below the one-variable data table, create the structure for the two-variable data table. One set of the table's input values should be marketing expenses of $25,000 to $125,000 in increments of $25,000. The other set of the table's input values should be sales prices of $99.95 to $149.95 in increments of $5.00. The table's output formula should refer to the marginal income before taxes cell.

6. Complete the two-variable data table using the Data Table dialog box. Relate the table's input values to the marketing expense cell and the selling price cell in the worksheet's input section.

7. Add headings and format the data table so it is appealing and professional.

8. Save and close the TZSwimSkin Analysis.xlsx workbook.

LEVEL 2
Using Scenarios to Perform What-If Analysis

Comparing the Results of Complex Analyses

You use data tables when you want to conduct a what-if analysis involving one or two input cells. Data tables help you answer questions such as, "If I change the unit price, how does that affect gross profit?" or "If I vary the unit price and the cost of goods sold, how does that affect income before taxes?" Some business problems, however, involve more than two input values that can vary. For example, suppose you want to compare three break-even analyses: a worst-case break-even analysis that shows the effects of lowering the unit price and decreasing projected unit sales, a likely break-even analysis that shows the effects of maintaining the current unit price and projecting realistic unit sales, and a best-case break-even analysis that shows the effects of increasing the unit price and exceeding sales expectations. You could create three different data tables by varying the unit price and sales projection values, but that would involve generating and printing each data table to compare the analyses. Instead, you can use the Scenario Manager to perform a what-if analysis with more than two input cells.

A **scenario** is a set of values stored in a worksheet that describes different situations, such as worst-case, likely case, and best-case scenarios. You use the Scenario Manager to define and save these sets of values as scenarios, and then you view and change them as necessary to produce and compare different results. To compare scenarios, you can create a summary report that lists the scenarios side by side or in a PivotTable.

To create a scenario, you plan the input data you want to use and the type of results, or output, you want to achieve. Next, you prepare a worksheet by adjusting its layout, if necessary, and naming the input and output cells or ranges. Finally, you create the scenario by naming it and then entering data into the Scenario Manager. After that, you can also generate a scenario summary report or PivotTable report.

Planning Scenarios

To set up a scenario, you create or use a worksheet that contains sets of input and output cells, as you do with data tables. For example, in a worksheet listing sales assumptions and projections, the assumptions are input cells and the projections are output cells.

Scenarios are best created using *sets* of input value assumptions, such as best-case, likely case, and worst-case outcomes. You could also group assumptions about future results around other factors, such as planned spending in a particular area. For example, to consider the results of future spending on marketing and advertising options, you can create sets of input values for a full media blitz, direct mail campaign, coupon campaign, and increased TV ads. You should plan these sets of input values before you enter data and formulas in a worksheet.

The Scenario Manager refers to the input cells (as they are called in data tables) as the **changing cells**, because these are the cells that you want to change as you switch from one scenario to another. The output cells are called the **result cells**. The Scenario Manager requires that the changing cells be on the same worksheet as the result cells for each individual scenario; a scenario cannot span worksheets.

Preparing the Inputs

As with data tables, Excel allows you to run scenarios only on worksheets that have well-structured input and output sections, with the output section depending on the input section through the use of formulas.

After analyzing income projections for TZSwimSkin, Richard Rayburn is working on a projected Income Statement for TheZone's existing swimwear, which includes men's racers, men's trunks, women's one-piece racers, and women's two-piece suits. He wants to evaluate the projected results of increased marketing campaigns for the swimsuit lines. In the Swimwear worksheet, he organizes assumptions in one section and includes the formulas for projections in another section, as shown in Figure 8.27.

This analysis worksheet is based on current sales and cost data, and projections from the sales and marketing staff. As shown in Figure 8.27, the number of units sold for each of the four swimsuit style categories appears in cells C8:F8. These numbers are based on last year's sales, rounded to the nearest thousand. The current sales price, cost of goods sold per unit, and distribution cost per unit (including processing and shipping costs) are also shown for each category of swimsuit.

Figure 8.27: Swimwear worksheet showing income projections for four types of swimwear

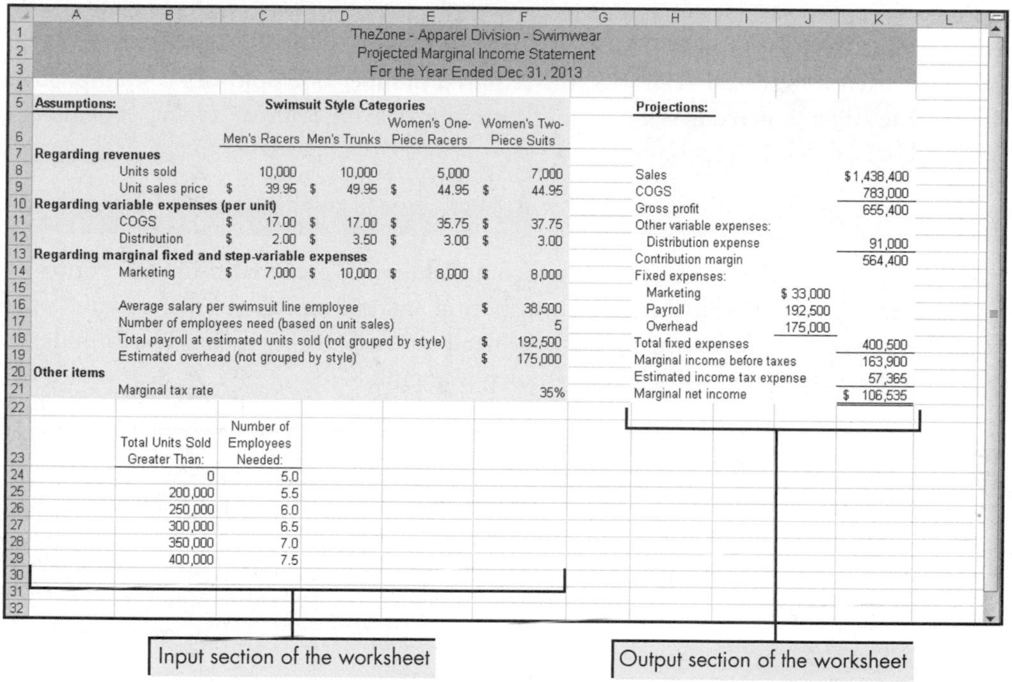

Input section of the worksheet

Output section of the worksheet

Row 14 of the worksheet contains last year's marketing expense for each swimsuit category. Each swimsuit category has its own marketing plan because each category has a different primary target market. Although all swimsuit styles are sold to sporting goods retailers, the men's trunks are sold in discount and lower-end retailers, men's and women's racers are sold to specialty sporting goods stores, and women's two-piece suits are sold primarily in mid- to upper-level retail outlets.

The estimated overhead expense for the swimsuit product category ($175,000) is shown in cell F19. TheZone is currently in the 35% marginal income tax bracket, so Richard will calculate marginal income tax expense based on that rate, as shown in cell F21.

The payroll expense estimate is more complicated. At last year's sales volume, the apparel operations manager estimated that it took the equivalent of five employees to produce the swimsuits and process their sales. The operations manager forecasts that if total swimsuit sales reach 200,000 units, the equivalent of one additional half-time employee will be needed to handle the workload. The operations manager has also forecasted that for each additional 50,000 units sold, the equivalent of one half-time employee will be needed. This step-variable relationship is reflected in the table shown in cells B23:C29. A **step-variable relationship** means that the cost does not vary directly with the number of units, but varies as the units reach steps of quantities.

Cell F17 contains a formula that computes the number of employees needed for the designated level of units: =VLOOKUP(SUM(C8:F8),B23:C29,2). This formula looks up the needed number of employees in the table based on the total number of units sold. To estimate the payroll expense in cell F18, the required number of employees is multiplied by the average salary (entered in cell F16, and currently showing last year's value). Chapter 5 covers the VLOOKUP function in detail.

Preparing the Outputs

The output section of the worksheet is an Income Statement prepared using the contribution margin format. Recall that the contribution margin represents the amount of revenue that can contribute toward covering the fixed expenses of a company. The formulas in the output section of the worksheet are shown in Figure 8.28.

Figure 8.28: Formulas used for the swimwear projections

Most of the output calculations in the worksheet involve basic formulas. Some use the SUMPRODUCT function to calculate the total sales revenue and each variable expense. The SUMPRODUCT function is very useful when you want to sum a series of products (the results of a multiplication task), as long as the ranges involved are parallel to each other in the worksheet. (Chapter 9 covers the SUMPRODUCT function in more detail.)

The formula in cell K8 is =SUMPRODUCT(C8:F8,C9:F9). This formula multiplies cell C8 (men's racers sold) by cell C9 (unit price of men's racers), cell D8 (men's trunks sold) by D9 (unit price of men's trunks), cell E8 (women's one-piece suits sold) by E9 (unit price of women's one-piece suits), and cell F8 (women's two-piece suits sold) by F9 (unit price of women's two-piece suits); then sums the results of these calculations to display the total sales. A similar method is used to calculate the total cost of goods sold and distribution expense.

Setting Up a Scenario

Now that you understand how the worksheet is constructed, you are ready to plan the scenarios. Recall that Richard created the worksheet to evaluate the projected results of increased marketing campaigns for the swimsuit line. Based on the market research, staff in the Sales and Marketing Departments have estimated the data shown in Table 8.1, assuming the sales prices stay the same as in the past year.

Table 8.1: Marketing and sales estimates for swimsuits

	Swimsuit Style Categories			
	Men's Racers	Men's Trunks	Women's One-Piece Racers	Women's Two-Piece Suits
Option 1: Discount				
If marketing expense is	$5,000	$10,000	$4,000	$4,000
Then units sold will be	6,000	15,000	3,000	4,000
Option 2: College				
If marketing expense is	$1,000	$3,500	$3,500	$4,500
Then units sold will be	12,500	6,000	3,500	4,500
Option 3: High End				
If marketing expense is	$5,000	$6,000	$5,000	$5,000
Then units sold will be	6,500	6,000	5,000	5,000
Option 4: Balanced				
If marketing expense is	$7,500	$7,500	$5,000	$5,000
Then units sold will be	11,500	12,500	8,000	9,000

As you can see, Option 1 concentrates on marketing the men's trunks that are sold primarily in discount and lower-level retailers. Option 2 examines expanding the men's and women's racers market in college outlets where marketing costs tend to be quite low. Option 3 focuses on increasing the presence of the suits in the high-end retailer market with relatively modest marketing expenditures. Option 4 considers expanding the market for all four styles. Notice there is some carryover from increased marketing focused on one style to sales of other styles.

The purchasing staff indicates that because of TheZone's long-term contracts with suppliers, the cost of inventory and distribution expense per unit will stay the same next year. The human resources staff estimates that the average salary for swimsuit-line employees will increase to $39,100. Overhead is expected to remain at $175,000 for the coming year. No change in the marginal tax rate is expected.

Richard now has all the information needed to plan the scenarios. He wants to compare the results of maintaining the current marketing plan to the four options proposed by the sales and marketing staff. Richard will create five scenarios: one for the current marketing plan and one for each of the four proposed marketing plan options.

Technically, the number of scenarios you can create is limited only by your computer's memory, but scenario reports can include data from only the first 251 scenarios. As a practical matter, however, you will likely want to limit the number of scenarios to that which a person can reasonably be expected to be able to process and evaluate.

Preparing a Worksheet for Scenarios

Richard needs to create five scenarios in the Swimwear worksheet. To do so, he needs to determine the changing cells in the worksheet. In other words, which input assumptions does he want to vary from one option to another?

Excel allows up to 32 changing cells in each scenario. Richard refers back to Table 8.1, which shows the units sold and marketing expense for each of the swimsuit styles. These are the input values that change under the various options, and will be the changing cells in his scenarios.

Best Practice

Determining Scenario Changing Cells

When you have many input assumptions that will vary in each scenario, it is sometimes easier to first identify the cells in the input section that will *not* change in the scenarios, thereby determining the scenarios' changing cells through a process of elimination. For example, if the sales prices, costs of goods sold, and distribution expenses per unit will not change from one scenario to another, those input cells will not be changing cells in the scenarios. If the number of needed employees and payroll expense are determined by formulas, they will not be changing cells when creating the scenarios. In fact, cells that contain formulas should *never* be specified as changing cells in scenarios because the formulas will be destroyed as the scenarios are built.

Richard considers whether the average salary input item is a changing cell. Although the average salary will change to $39,100 next year, it will not vary from that number for any of the five scenario options. Thus, after Richard changes the value in cell F16 from $38,500 to $39,100, that input cell will require no other changes.

Although it would not be completely incorrect to include cell F16 as a changing cell when building the scenarios, it would be less efficient. Suppose the average salary estimate changes again from $39,100 to $40,000. If Richard includes cell F16 as a changing cell for his scenarios, he would have to modify each of the five scenarios so that they include $40,000 as the average salary value. On the other hand, by omitting F16 as a changing cell, he would only have to type the new $40,000 estimate once in F16 to reflect the change in the estimate. Accordingly, he does not plan to use F16 as a changing cell.

Before you start creating scenarios, you can name the input and result cells you plan to use in the scenario. Using cell names can make the process of creating the scenarios and using them easier. Using descriptive names can also make your scenario reports easier to understand and use.

A **range name**, also called a **defined name**, can refer to a cell, range of cells, formula, or constant value in Excel. Names can be up to 255 characters long, but cannot include spaces or punctuation marks other than periods or underscores. Defined names that are the same as cell references, such as *Q3*, *Qtr4*, and *USA1*, are not allowed.

All defined names have a **scope**, which specifies the location in which the name is valid. A defined name can have a scope for the entire workbook (also referred to as the **global level**) or for just one worksheet (also referred to as the **local level**). Each defined name must be unique within its scope, but a defined name can be used outside its scope if it is *qualified*, which means if its original scope is identified in its reference. For example, if a cell with the defined name of *Sales_Price* has a scope that is local to the worksheet named Quarter1, it can be qualified to be used outside the Quarter1 worksheet by using the cell address Quarter1!Sales_Price when referring to it.

To create defined names with a local or global scope, you can use the Define Name command or the Create from Selection command in the Defined Names group on the Formulas tab on the Ribbon. Another method is to use the Name Box in the Formula Bar.

Richard decides to apply the names to the changing and result cells listed in Table 8.2.

Table 8.2: Applying names to the changing and result cells in the Swimwear worksheet

Changing or Result Cell Address	Defined Name
C8	RacersSold
D8	TrunksSold
E8	WOneSold
F8	WTwoSold
C14	RacersMktgExp
D14	TrunksMktgExp
E14	WOneMktgExp
F14	WTwoMktgExp
K8	SalesRevenue
K10	GrossProfit
K13	ContributionMargin
J16	PayrollExpense
K19	IncomeBeforeTaxes
K21	NetIncome

Best Practice

Applying Names to Cells and Ranges

To indicate the start and end of words in defined names, you can use a mix of uppercase and lowercase letters without spaces, as in MenTrunksUnitsSold, or you can include underscore (_) or period (.) characters in the names, as in Men_Trunks_Units_Sold or Men.Trunks.Units.Sold. Although Excel does not consider case when evaluating cell names (that is, Excel considers UnitsSold and unitssold to be the same name), the use of case differences in cell names can make them easier to read and interpret.

Use defined names that are fairly short but meaningful. Short names make it easier to work with the Scenario Manager dialog boxes. However, make sure the names are still meaningful to anyone using the workbook.

You can edit or delete defined names using the Name Manager dialog box.

How To

Delete One or More Defined Names

1. Click the Formulas tab on the Ribbon, and then in the Defined Names group, click the Name Manager button.
2. Select one or more names to be deleted.
3. Click the Delete button, and then click the OK button to confirm the deletion.
4. Click the Close button.

How To

Edit a Defined Name

1. Click the Formulas tab on the Ribbon, and then in the Defined Names group, click the Name Manager button.
2. Select the name to be edited.
3. If you want to change only the address to which the name applies, change the information in the Refers to box as desired, and click the Commit button to save the changes.
4. If you want to change the name itself, click the Edit button, type the new name, update the address in the Refers to box, if necessary, and click the OK button.
5. Repeat Steps 2 through 4 until all desired changes are made.
6. Click the Close button.

Adding Scenarios to a Worksheet

After Richard applies names to the worksheet's input cells, he is ready to create the scenarios in the Swimwear worksheet.

How To

Create a Scenario

1. On the Data tab on the Ribbon, click What-If Analysis in the Data Tools group, and then click Scenario Manager. See Figure 8.29.

Figure 8.29: Scenario Manager dialog box

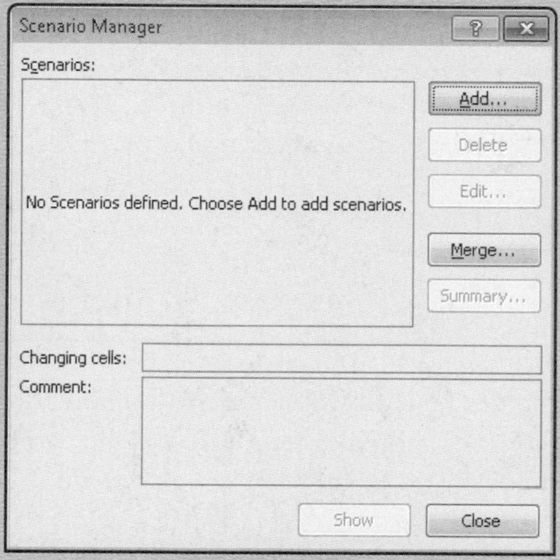

2. Click the Add button. The Add Scenario dialog box opens.

3. In the Scenario name box, type a name for the scenario.

4. In the Changing cells box, enter the references for the cells that you want to change in the scenario.

5. If desired, insert a comment in the Comment box describing the scenario.

6. Under Protection, select the options that you want.

7. Click the OK button. The Scenario Values dialog box opens.

8. Enter values for each changing cell in the scenario.

9. Click the OK button to create the scenario.

10. Repeat Steps 2 through 9 for each additional scenario you want to create.

11. Click the OK button.

You use the Scenario Manager to add a scenario. Richard opens the Scenario Manager by clicking the Data tab, clicking the What-If analysis button in the Data Tools group, and then clicking Scenario Manager. He clicks the Add button to add a new scenario to the workbook. The Add Scenario dialog box opens, as shown in Figure 8.30.

Figure 8.30: Add Scenario dialog box

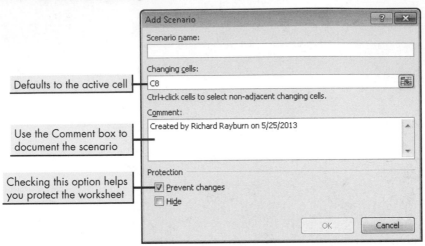

Defaults to the active cell

Use the Comment box to document the scenario

Checking this option helps you protect the worksheet

Each scenario must have a name. Richard will name the five scenarios Continued Marketing, Discount, College, High End, and Balanced. He types the name for the first scenario, Continued Marketing, in the Scenario name box.

Best Practice

Naming Scenarios

Although you can use generic names such as Option 1, Option 2, and Option 3 for your scenarios, you should use more descriptive names because they appear on any scenario summary reports you create and print. Using meaningful names for the individual scenarios makes the scenario reports easier to interpret.

Scenario names can contain up to 255 characters, including spaces. However, only the first 35 characters of the scenario name appear in the Scenario Manager list. Long scenario names also create wide columns on scenario reports. As a practical matter, it is best to keep scenario names concise, while still meaningful.

In addition, be certain you conform to the naming policies in your organization. Some organizations discourage the use of abbreviations in scenario names so that the associated reports contain formal labels. Other organizations encourage the use of abbreviations, as long as they are not open to misinterpretation, to conserve report space.

Next, Richard indicates the scenario's changing cells in the Changing cells box, which in this case are C8:F8, C14:F14. Richard also adds scenario documentation to the Comment box. Figure 8.31 shows the initial setup of the Continued Marketing scenario.

Figure 8.31: Setting up the Continued Marketing scenario

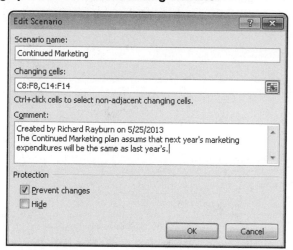

He clicks the OK button to open the Scenario Values dialog box shown in Figure 8.32, where he then enters the specific assumptions for the changing cells.

Figure 8.32: Scenario Values dialog box

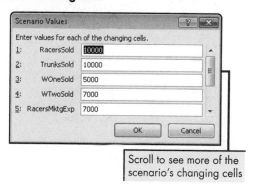

After entering the first scenario's values, Richard clicks the Add button to add the next scenario, and repeats the steps for the next four scenarios, using the data in Table 8.1. The Scenario Manager dialog box lists all of the scenarios, as shown in Figure 8.33.

Viewing and Analyzing Scenarios

To view a scenario in the worksheet, click the scenario name in the Scenario Manager dialog box, and then click the Show button. You can then click the Close button to close the Scenario Manager and view the worksheet. Figure 8.34 shows the projected Income Statement for the Continued Marketing scenario, which assumes the same marketing expenditures and units sold for each type of TheZone's swimsuits will continue into the future.

Figure 8.33: Scenario Manager dialog box with five scenarios

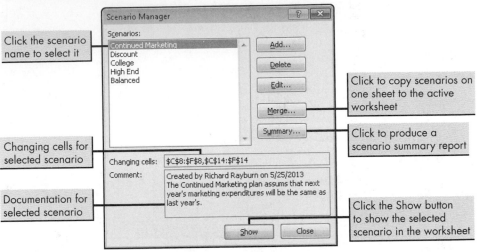

Figure 8.34: Continued Marketing scenario

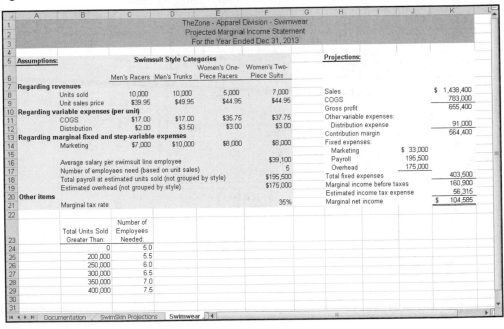

Excel automatically changed the values in the input cells and indicates that the swimwear line will produce about a $104,585 profit in 2013 if TheZone continues its current marketing plan. Richard wants to see how this compares with the other plans, so he opens and studies each one. Figure 8.35 shows the other four scenarios.

Figure 8.35: The four new scenarios

Discount scenario

	A	B	C	D	E	F	G	H	I	J	K	L
1					TheZone - Apparel Division - Swimwear							
2					Projected Marginal Income Statement							
3					For the Year Ended Dec 31, 2013							
4												
5	Assumptions:		Swimsuit Style Categories					Projections:				
6			Men's Racers	Men's Trunks	Women's One-Piece Racers	Women's Two-Piece Suits						
7	Regarding revenues											
8		Units sold	6,000	15,000	3,000	4,000		Sales			$ 1,303,600	
9		Unit sales price	$39.95	$49.95	$44.95	$44.95		COGS			615,250	
10	Regarding variable expenses (per unit)							Gross profit			688,350	
11		COGS	$17.00	$17.00	$35.75	$37.75		Other variable expenses:				
12		Distribution	$2.00	$3.50	$3.00	$3.00		Distribution expense			85,500	
13	Regarding marginal fixed and step-variable expenses							Contribution margin			602,850	
14		Marketing	$5,000	$10,000	$4,000	$4,000		Fixed expenses:				
15								Marketing		$ 23,000		
16		Average salary per swimsuit line employee				$39,100		Payroll		195,500		
17		Number of employees need (based on unit sales)				5		Overhead		175,000		
18		Total payroll at estimated units sold (not grouped by style)				$195,500		Total fixed expenses			393,500	
19		Estimated overhead (not grouped by style)				$175,000		Marginal income before taxes			209,350	
20	Other items							Estimated income tax expense			73,273	
21		Marginal tax rate				35%		Marginal net income			$ 136,078	
22												
23		Total Units Sold Greater Than:	Number of Employees Needed:									
24		0	5.0									
25		200,000	5.5									
26		250,000	6.0									
27		300,000	6.5									
28		350,000	7.0									
29		400,000	7.5									
30												
31												

Documentation / SwimSkin Projections / **Swimwear**

College scenario

	A	B	C	D	E	F	G	H	I	J	K	L
1					TheZone - Apparel Division - Swimwear							
2					Projected Marginal Income Statement							
3					For the Year Ended Dec 31, 2013							
4												
5	Assumptions:		Swimsuit Style Categories					Projections:				
6			Men's Racers	Men's Trunks	Women's One-Piece Racers	Women's Two-Piece Suits						
7	Regarding revenues											
8		Units sold	12,500	6,000	3,500	4,500		Sales			$ 1,158,675	
9		Unit sales price	$39.95	$49.95	$44.95	$44.95		COGS			609,500	
10	Regarding variable expenses (per unit)							Gross profit			549,175	
11		COGS	$17.00	$17.00	$35.75	$37.75		Other variable expenses:				
12		Distribution	$2.00	$3.50	$3.00	$3.00		Distribution expense			70,000	
13	Regarding marginal fixed and step-variable expenses							Contribution margin			479,175	
14		Marketing	$1,000	$3,500	$3,500	$4,500		Fixed expenses:				
15								Marketing		$ 12,500		
16		Average salary per swimsuit line employee				$39,100		Payroll		195,500		
17		Number of employees need (based on unit sales)				5		Overhead		175,000		
18		Total payroll at estimated units sold (not grouped by style)				$195,500		Total fixed expenses			383,000	
19		Estimated overhead (not grouped by style)				$175,000		Marginal income before taxes			96,175	
20	Other items							Estimated income tax expense			33,661	
21		Marginal tax rate				35%		Marginal net income			$ 62,514	
22												
23		Total Units Sold Greater Than:	Number of Employees Needed:									
24		0	5.0									
25		200,000	5.5									
26		250,000	6.0									
27		300,000	6.5									
28		350,000	7.0									
29		400,000	7.5									
30												
31												

Documentation / SwimSkin Projections / **Swimwear**

8

Level 2

Figure 8.35: The four new scenarios (cont.)

High End scenario

Balanced scenario

The Discount scenario, which focuses on men's trunks sold to discount retailers, produces around $136,078 in profit, about $30,000 more than the current marketing plan would produce. However, Richard has assumed that he can cut costs in the Discount scenario, which might not be possible. The College scenario only produces around $62,514 in profit, but its expenses may be more reasonable than those used in the Discount scenario.

When Richard examines the High End scenario, he is surprised to discover that TheZone would suffer a loss of over $17,000 if it follows that marketing plan. The Marketing Department does not think it can realistically sell many suits at higher prices. Finally, Richard compares the Balanced scenario, which increases marketing efforts for all four types of swimwear, with the other scenarios. This scenario produces a $195,618 profit, the highest among the four, and uses what are considered to be quite realistic assumptions.

Editing and Deleting Scenarios

After you create a scenario, you can use the Scenario Manager dialog box to change its values to extend your what-if analysis. For example, you can vary your assumptions and then show the new results in the scenario. Note that you can change values, but not the defined names for cells and ranges in the Scenario Manager dialog box. When you change the values, the scenario results are updated to reflect the new information.

Richard wants to modify the Discount scenario to use more realistic expense projections. Also, he wants to account for heavy competition in the discount market among other swimwear manufacturers. He'll adjust the optimistic sales values so that they are more realistic, and modify the expenses so they match those used in the Continued Marketing scenario.

How To

Edit Scenarios

1. On the Data tab on the Ribbon, click the What-If Analysis button in the Data Tools group, and then click Scenario Manager.
2. Click the desired scenario name in the Scenarios box.
3. Click the Edit button.
4. Make any desired changes to the scenario name, changing cells, and/or comments, and then click the OK button.
5. Make any desired changes to the changing cell values, and then click the OK button.
6. Click the Show button to display the results of the edited scenario, and then click the Close button.

Richard modifies the Discount scenario, entering 8,000 as the number of men's trunks sold. He also reduces the marketing expense for men's trunks to $6,000. The Discount scenario contains the new values shown in Figure 8.36.

Figure 8.36: Modified Discount scenario

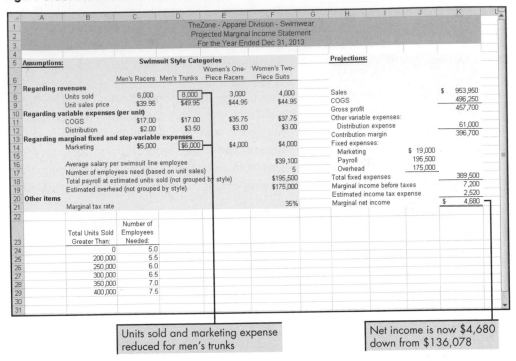

Units sold and marketing expense reduced for men's trunks

Net income is now $4,680 down from $136,078

Richard is concerned that a drop in sales volume caused by increased competition in the discount market could cut profits by about $131,000. He will discuss his findings with other managers and suggest that the discount market is risky for TheZone.

When he re-examines the High End scenario, he realizes that strategy is not realistic for TheZone. The cost of marketing is too high to justify the marginal net income. He deletes the High End scenario and saves the other four to discuss with the other managers.

How To

Delete Scenarios

1. On the Data tab on the Ribbon, click the What-If Analysis button in the Data Tools group, and then click Scenario Manager.
2. Click the desired scenario name in the Scenarios box.
3. Click the Delete button.
4. Click the Close button.

Richard feels that the Balanced scenario outlines the best approach for TheZone's marketing effort for the swimwear line. He plans to meet with other managers to discuss his findings. Before he does so, however, he wants to generate a report showing the scenarios. Then he can distribute it in the monthly marketing meeting to facilitate discussion.

Generating Scenario Reports

You can use the Scenario Manager to create two types of scenario reports: a scenario summary and a scenario PivotTable. You set up and print both types of scenario reports from the Scenario Manager dialog box by clicking the Summary button to open the Scenario Summary dialog box, as shown in Figure 8.37.

Figure 8.37: Scenario Summary dialog box

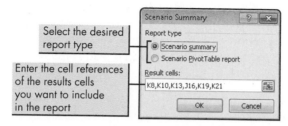

Select the desired report type

Enter the cell references of the results cells you want to include in the report

Before printing a scenario report, you indicate which result cells are of interest to you. Recall that the result cells come from the output area of your worksheet. Richard wants to include sales revenue, gross profit, contribution margin, payroll expense, income before taxes, and net income information for each of the four types of swimsuits—these are the result cells. He also wants to include the units sold and marketing expense information for each type—these are the changing cells.

Creating Scenario Summaries

When you create a scenario summary report, Excel generates it as a new worksheet in the workbook. Instead of listing all the cells on the SwimSkin Projections worksheet, the scenario summary report shows the values for all changing cells and for all indicated result cells for every scenario. See Figure 8.38.

Figure 8.38: Scenario Summary report

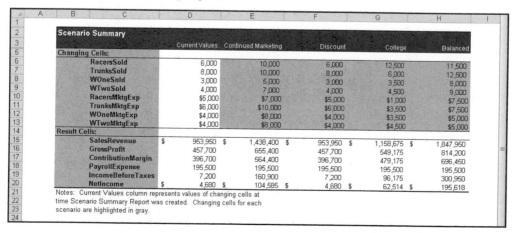

Note that the changing cells and result cells are listed by the names Richard gave them when he created the scenarios. The Current Values column represents the values of the changing cells when the report was created, and the other four columns show the four scenarios. In this report, the Current Values column (column D) contains the same information as column F, which shows the Discount scenario. Because the Current Values column does not contain unique information, Richard decides to hide column D.

The tabular format of the scenario summary report makes it easy to compare the results of the scenarios. In addition, Excel automatically shades the changing cell values and the cell names, which is convenient when you plan to distribute the report to others. Richard can provide this report to other managers, directing their attention to the Net-Income row, which clearly shows that the Balanced plan is the most profitable given the current assumptions.

Best Practice

Enhancing Scenario Summary Reports

Scenario summary reports are created with *Scenario Summary* as the worksheet title. Using a more specific title usually helps readers identify the type of information the report contains. For example, you could use a title such as *Summary of Marketing Options* or *Projected Net Income for Swimwear*.

Also, you should examine the number formats in a scenario summary report. Except for background color, each cell in the report uses the formatting of the scenario setup worksheet cell from which it originates. In other words, if a changing cell on the scenario setup worksheet uses the Accounting number format, the value of the corresponding changing cell is also formatted using the Accounting number format. Check the number formats in a scenario summary report in case they are appropriate for the setup worksheet, but not for the scenario summary report.

Recall that the row labels in a scenario summary report come from the cell names you applied to the changing and result cells on the scenario setup worksheet. Some organizations prefer to use more formal row labels, such as those that do not use abbreviations or those that include spaces between words. Other organizations want the row labels to match the cell names exactly.

Finally, you should review the scenario summary report to see if any formatting features can make the report more understandable. As with any worksheet, you want to use formatting to transform the scenario summary report from raw data into information.

Richard also wants to create another type of report—one that lists the four marketing options, and then summarizes the sales revenue, gross profit, contribution margin, payroll expense, income before taxes, and net income information for each option. He can generate this information by creating a scenario PivotTable report.

Creating Scenario PivotTable Reports

Recall from Chapter 7 that a PivotTable report is an interactive table that groups and summarizes information in a concise format so you can easily analyze the information. A PivotTable extracts, organizes, and summarizes data so you can analyze it by making comparisons, detecting patterns and relationships, and recognizing trends. Although a PivotTable usually summarizes information from a worksheet into different categories using functions such as COUNT, AVERAGE, and MAX, a scenario PivotTable lets you summarize the result cells from a scenario. In addition, because a PivotTable is interactive, you can change the view of the data to see more or fewer details.

You can also summarize a scenario by creating a PivotChart report. After you create a PivotTable report, you can analyze the information in a different form by generating an associated PivotChart, which contains the same elements as a regular Excel chart. The PivotTable and PivotChart can help you thoroughly analyze and interpret the results of your scenarios.

How To

Create a Scenario PivotTable Report

1. On the Data tab on the Ribbon, click What-If Analysis in the Data Tools group, and then click Scenario Manager.
2. Click the Summary button.
3. Click the Scenario PivotTable report option button.
4. In the Result cells box, enter the references for the output cells of interest. Separate multiple references with commas.
5. Click the OK button.

Richard returns to the Swimwear worksheet, which contains the swimwear scenarios, and then generates a scenario PivotTable report, as shown in Figure 8.39.

Figure 8.39: Scenario PivotTable report

Row Labels	SalesRevenue	GrossProfit	ContributionMargin	PayrollExpense	IncomeBeforeTaxes	NetIncome
Balanced	1847950	814200	696450	195500	300950	195617.5
College	1158675	549175	479175	195500	96175	62513.75
Continued Marketing	1438400	655400	564400	195500	160900	104585
Discount	953950	457700	396700	195500	7200	4680

($C$8:$F$8,$C$14:$F$14 by (All))

This PivotTable report lists the name of each scenario—the marketing options—in column A, and then summarizes the result cells in columns B to G. As in the scenario summary report, the PivotTable report confirms that the Balanced marketing plan should result in the largest increase in marginal profits for TheZone. In addition, the report makes it clear that the proposed marketing plans can increase the company's profits more than continuing the current marketing plan would. Richard will make it part of his recommendation that, if TheZone cannot afford to finance the increased marketing expenditures required for the Balanced marketing plan, implementing any of the other less-expensive options will also increase the company's marginal profits.

Richard examines the PivotTable report and wonders if editing the report would make it clearer to others. As you learned in Chapter 7, you can change the view of information in a PivotTable report just by dragging the field names around. In this case, Richard can rotate the report by listing the names of each calculation in column A instead of the marketing options. The results cells would then be summarized in columns B to E. In this way, you pivot that table's rows and columns to vary the summaries of the information.

Richard can also change the amount of detail shown. For example, he turns off some check boxes in the PivotTable Field List to show only some results, such as SalesRevenue, GrossProfit, ContributionMargin, and NetIncome. Also, because in its current form the field in the Report Filter box doesn't actually allow for any filtering of data, Richard removes it by dragging the field out of the Report Filter box. See Figure 8.40.

Figure 8.40: Reducing the amount of detail in a PivotTable report

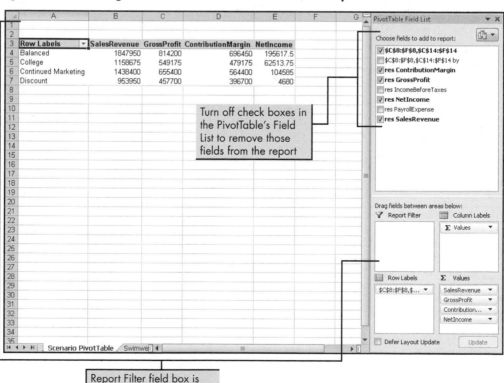

Next, Richard wants to make this PivotTable report easier to read and analyze, so he will edit the report's labels and formats. For example, he wants to replace the default heading in cell A3 with a more meaningful label, add a heading in cell B2, and include spaces in the column headings to make them appear more professional. These PivotTable heading labels can be edited just like any other labels that have been entered into cells. He inserts spaces between the words in cells B3:E3, changes the text in A3 to *Marketing Options*, and adds the text *Projections* in cell B2. He also applies Accounting number formats, both with and without dollar signs and without decimal places, to the cells containing values. The formatted report is shown in Figure 8.41.

Figure 8.41: Formatted scenario PivotTable report

	A	B	C	D	E	F
1						
2		Projections				
3	Marketing Options ▾	Sales Revenue	Gross Profit	Contribution Margin	Net Income	
4	Balanced	$ 1,847,950	$ 814,200	$ 696,450	$ 195,618	
5	College	1,158,675	549,175	479,175	62,514	
6	Continued Marketing	1,438,400	655,400	564,400	104,585	
7	Discount	953,950	457,700	396,700	4,680	
8						
9						
10						

Now Richard wants to generate a PivotChart so he can examine this information in a graphical form.

Creating Scenario PivotChart Reports

After creating a scenario PivotTable report, you can use it to create a PivotChart. In the Scenario PivotTable worksheet, Richard selects a cell within the PivotTable, clicks the contextual PivotTable Tools Options tab on the Ribbon, and then clicks the PivotChart button in the Tools group to open the Insert Chart dialog box. Richard accepts the Clustered Column chart layout and moves the chart to a new worksheet. After he adds a title, hides the field buttons, and formats the value axis, Richard's PivotChart appears as shown in Figure 8.42.

Figure 8.42: PivotChart report

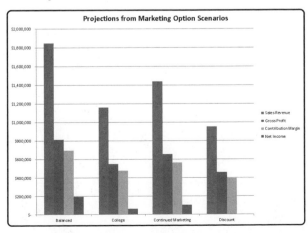

8
Level 2

The PivotChart clearly shows that the Balanced marketing plan produces the best results, and the Discount plan produces the worst results. It also shows that, although the Continued Marketing plan shows a substantial sales revenue increase over the College plan, the difference between the net incomes in the two plans is not nearly as significant.

Richard saves the workbook and plans to distribute the scenario reports and PivotChart to other managers for discussion.

Steps To Success: Level 2

TheZone's managers are impressed with the marketing plan analysis Richard did for the swimwear products. They now want something similar for swimwear accessories, which are grouped into three categories. Team accessories include goggles, duffel bags, towels, and other products that display a team name and logo. Competition accessories include items such as stopwatches, lane markers, and judging forms. Casual accessories include goggles, towels, flippers, and other products for all swimmers. These product categories should also be included in the four marketing options.

Richard has started a workbook in which to complete the analysis, as shown in Figure 8.43.

Figure 8.43: Swim Accessories worksheet

The Swim Accessories worksheet contains input assumption data that Richard has obtained from various departments in the company. He doesn't have time to complete the workbook, so he has asked you to do so for him. Complete the following:

1. Open the workbook named **SwimAcc.xlsx** located in the Chapter 8 folder, and save it with the name **Accessories Marketing.xlsx**.

2. Switch to the **Swim Accessories** worksheet. In cell J8, write a formula using the SUMPRODUCT function that will compute the total sales revenue.

3. In cell J9, enter a formula using the SUMPRODUCT function that will compute the total cost of goods sold. In cell J12, write a formula using the SUMPRODUCT function that will compute the distribution expense.

4. Apply names to the scenarios' changing cells, as shown in Table 8.3.

Table 8.3: Names for Changing Cells

Changing Cell	Name
C8	TeamUnitSales
D8	CompetitionUnitSales
E8	CasualUnitSales
C14	TeamMktgExp
D14	CompetitionMktgExp
E14	CasualMktgExp

5. Create four scenarios named **Continued Marketing**, **Discount**, **College**, and **Balanced**. The Continued Marketing scenario should consist of the worksheet's current values for units sold and marketing expense. The data for the other three options is shown in Table 8.4.

Table 8.4: Data for additional Scenarios

	Swimwear Accessories		
	Team	Competition	Casual
Discount plan:			
If Marketing expense is	$100,000	$50,000	$40,000
Then Units sold will be	13,000	5,000	4,000
College plan:			
If Marketing expense is	$35,000	$100,000	$40,000
Then Units sold will be	6000	12,500	4500
Balanced plan:			
If Marketing expense is	$35,000	$50,000	$45,000
Then Units sold will be	6000	6500	5000

6. Create a scenario summary report that shows the gross profit, contribution margin, income before taxes, and net income for all of the scenarios. Be certain to name the result cells appropriately before creating the report.

7. Create a scenario PivotTable report that shows the gross profit, contribution margin, income before taxes, and net income for all of the scenarios.

8. Format the scenario PivotTable report so it has a more professional appearance.

9. Create a PivotChart report in a stacked column format based on the PivotTable report.

10. Save and close the Accessories Marketing.xlsx workbook.

LEVEL 3

Using Excel's Data Tables to Create a Simulation

Understanding Simulation in Business

Scenarios and data tables can be powerful tools that provide useful information to managers performing what-if analysis. Although data tables are ideal for showing the results of the interaction of a number of variables, analyzing which results are more likely than others depends on your knowledge of your company's business and market. However, you can use two-variable data tables to produce simulated results that show how probable each result is. **Simulated results** are those that are based on realistic, but not actual, data. Businesses often work with simulated data and results when they are starting a new operation, expanding into a new market, or dealing with any other situation in which no real data is available. Instead of using historical or current data, you can use probable data in data tables, and then produce simulated results.

Some Excel functions help you create and compare simulated results. You can use the RAND and VLOOKUP functions to simulate and weight simulated results, which determine the probability of the results. You can also create a two-variable data table that contains probable data and generates simulated results.

After meeting with other managers, Richard wants to analyze sales price options for the new TZSwimSkin product. He wants to analyze the sales price options for the new swimwear product based on probabilities that demand for the product will range from high to low. Because this is a new product, he will use probable sales prices, not historical or current sales prices. The results he produces will, therefore, be simulated results. To determine which prices are more likely to produce profits than others, he will use the VLOOKUP and RAND functions.

Preparing a Worksheet for a Simulation Using a Data Table

To create the simulation, Richard adds a Probabilities worksheet to the Swimwear workbook. He created this worksheet based upon new information he received about the TZSwimSkin product. The Purchasing Department projects that the cost of TZSwimSkins to TheZone will likely be $69.75 per unit. After conducting more market research, the marketing staff generated information, including probabilities, associated with expected sales of the TZSwimSkin. See Figure 8.44.

As in Richard's other worksheets, the calculations in the output section are based on the data in the input section. Cells A22:B28 contain probability data. The Income Statement currently shows no sales revenue or cost of goods sold because the Assumptions section does not include a number of units sold value. This value will be generated as part of the simulation by calculating the **cumulative probability distribution**. In financial statistics, a probability distribution assigns a probability to every interval of numbers. In practical terms, suppose you forecast that a product's profit could range from –$50 to $25 per unit. You might want to know what percentage of these forecasted profits is less than zero. The cumulative probability distribution could calculate that there's a 5% chance that profits will be less than zero.

Richard plans to create a cumulative probability distribution table for the unit sales so he can randomly simulate sales ranging from 1,000 to 5,000 units. This distribution table will be used by a VLOOKUP function to calculate the simulated unit sales values.

Figure 8.44: Probabilities worksheet

Recall from Chapter 5 that the VLOOKUP function compares a lookup value to the first column of a lookup table, and returns the corresponding value in a designated column of the lookup table. In this case, the lookup function will compare a randomly generated decimal number between 0 and 1 to the cumulative probabilities of the unit sales figures, and then return the corresponding unit sales value. In this manner, the unit sales input value will randomly simulate potential sales in units, weighted according to their estimated probabilities of occurrence.

To use the VLOOKUP function, the cumulative estimated probabilities of the unit sales figures must be in the first column of the lookup table. The second column of the lookup table must contain the corresponding unit sales projections. Richard creates the unit sales lookup table shown in Figure 8.45. The values he uses are those that the Marketing and Purchasing Departments consider reasonable estimates.

Figure 8.45: Lookup table added to the Probabilities worksheet

	A	B	C	D	E
20					
21	Unit Sales Probabilities			Unit Sales Distribution Table	
22	Units	Individual Probability		Cumulative Probability	Related Units
23	1,000	25%		0	1,000
24	2,000	40%		25%	2,000
25	3,000	20%		65%	3,000
26	4,000	10%		85%	4,000
27	5,000	5%		95%	5,000
28		100%			
29					
30					

Lookup table

	A	B	C	D	E
20					
21	Unit Sales Probabilities			Unit Sales Distribution Table	
22	Units	Individual Probability		Cumulative Probability	Related Units
23	1000	0.25		0	=A23
24	2000	0.4		=D23+B23	=A24
25	3000	0.2		=D24+B24	=A25
26	4000	0.1		=D25+B25	=A26
27	5000	0.05		=D26+B26	=A27
28		=SUM(B23:B27)			
29					
30					
31					

Formulas for lookup table

The lookup table itself occupies cells D22:E27. The cumulative percentages are in the first column of the lookup table, and the corresponding unit sales projections are in the second column of the table. The Cumulative Probability column (column D) is based on the data in the Unit Sales Probabilities table, which shows that 25% of the time, TheZone will sell 1,000 units; 40% of the time, it will sell 2,000 units; 20% of the time, it will sell 3,000 units; 10% of the time, it will sell 4,000 units; and 5% of the time, it will sell 5,000 units. There is a 100% chance the demand will be one of these values.

The RAND function generates a number between 0 and 1. Richard uses the Cumulative Probability column to divide the space between 0 and 1 into lengths that match the individual probabilities of each number of units being demanded. If the random number is between 0 and 0.25, the demand used in the calculation is 1,000. If the random number is between 0.25 and 0.65, the demand is 2,000, and so on.

Richard now needs to write the RAND function that will compute the random number, and then write the VLOOKUP function that will return the simulated unit sales based on the random number. You can see the resulting worksheet in Figure 8.46. Since the unit sales quantity will be determined using the random number, your results will likely not match the exact results shown in Figure 8.46.

Figure 8.46: VLOOKUP and RAND formulas added to the worksheet

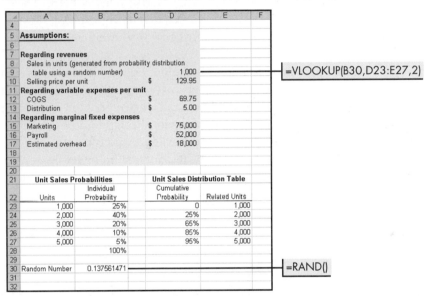

Again, the VLOOKUP function in cell D9 compares the random number to the first column of the lookup table and returns the corresponding unit sales value from the second column of the lookup table.

Developing a Simulation with a Two-Variable Data Table

Now that the input section of the worksheet is complete with a formula to return the simulated unit sales values, Richard is ready to create the two-variable data table that will compute the simulated output.

The data table is supposed to simulate the output of the interaction between probable unit sales and various selling prices. Richard will use the same set of selling price input values that he did in the previous two-variable data table, namely $99.95 to $149.95 by $10.00 increments. He knows that, statistically, 100 iterations are enough to generate realistic results.

Structuring a Two-Variable Data Table for a Simulation

Recall that when setting up a two-variable data table, it must be structured so that the two sets of input values are perpendicular to each other, and the table's output formula is located at the intersection of the two sets of input variables.

Because Richard is evaluating the profitability of the interaction between the unit sales and sales prices, you might expect that he would arrange sets of input values for unit sales and sales prices perpendicular to each other in a worksheet and that he would use a formula that refers to the marginal income before taxes cell (J19) in the worksheet's output section at the intersection of those two sets of input values. (Refer back to Figure 8.43.) This would be correct if he were creating a regular two-variable data table. In this case, however, he will use the data table to run a simulation, so the structure is a bit different.

When using a two-variable data table to run a simulation, one set of input values in the data table's structure *must* be a sequence of numbers that represents the number of iterations of the simulation. Only one spot remains in the table's structure for the set of input values. Richard used the RAND and VLOOKUP functions to randomize the number of units sold for the simulation because those functions will provide the set of input values for the number of units sold during the simulation. Because the unit sales figures are randomly generated, that leaves Richard with the values for the sales prices that need to be placed in the data table's structure. Accordingly, the structure for Richard's data table appears in Figure 8.47.

Figure 8.47: Setting up the two-variable data table for a simulation

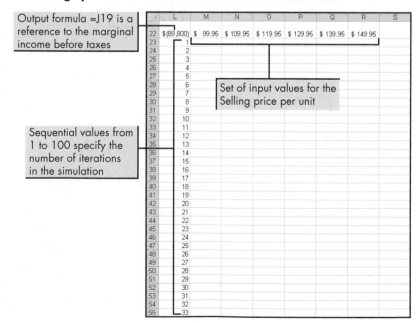

Completing a Two-Variable Data Table for a Simulation

Just as you need to alter the structure of a data table when using it to run a simulation, so do you need to alter the completion of the table. You still need to highlight the entire table range (L22:R122, in this case) and then tell Excel to which input cells the sets of input values relate. However, one set of input values in the table's structure doesn't relate to a real input item, but to the iteration sequence. To correctly perform the simulation, *the iteration values are directed to any empty cell in the worksheet.*

Because the input values arranged in the top row of the data table represent selling prices, the row input cell is related to cell D10, which shows the selling price per unit. Because the input values arranged down the column in the table represent simulation iterations instead of input values, the column input cell is related to any blank cell, such as G21, as shown in Figure 8.48.

Figure 8.48: Specifying the row and column input cells for a simulation

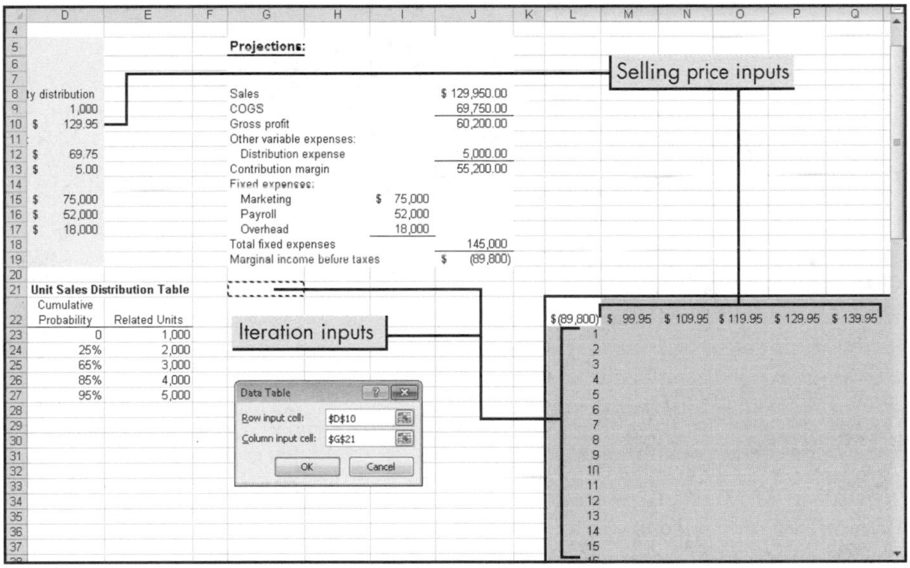

Richard runs the simulation by having Excel complete the table, which it does by filling it with the simulated profitability results. Richard then adds a title and heading, and formats the data. See Figure 8.49.

Note that RAND, a random number generating function, is used as part of the table's structure, albeit indirectly. Furthermore, the RAND function and the data table are automatically recalculated every time a change is made to any of the worksheet's contents. By default, the data table's values are, therefore, randomly recalculated every time the data changes. Because two-variable data tables used in simulations can be quite large, recalculating can take a few minutes. To avoid this delay, you can turn off the automatic recalculation of data tables separate from the automatic recalculation of all other workbook

Figure 8.49: Results of a simulation

	Iterations	$ 99.95	$ 109.95	$ 119.95	$ 129.95	$ 139.95	$ 149.95
18							
19		Simulated Income Before Taxes Given Various Selling Prices					
20							
21		Selling Prices					
22							
23	1	(119,800.00)	(4,200.00)	(54,600.00)	(89,800.00)	50,600.00	5,400.00
24	2	(69,400.00)	(74,600.00)	(9,400.00)	(89,800.00)	(14,600.00)	80,600.00
25	3	(94,600.00)	(74,600.00)	(9,400.00)	(34,600.00)	50,600.00	5,400.00
26	4	(94,600.00)	(74,600.00)	(54,600.00)	131,000.00	(14,600.00)	80,600.00
27	5	(69,400.00)	(74,600.00)	(9,400.00)	20,600.00	(14,600.00)	(69,800.00)
28	6	(44,200.00)	(74,600.00)	(99,800.00)	(34,600.00)	115,800.00	(69,800.00)
29	7	(44,200.00)	(109,800.00)	(9,400.00)	(34,600.00)	(79,800.00)	5,400.00
30	8	(69,400.00)	(4,200.00)	35,800.00	(89,800.00)	115,800.00	80,600.00
31	9	(119,800.00)	(4,200.00)	(9,400.00)	(89,800.00)	(79,800.00)	(69,800.00)
32	10	(69,400.00)	(74,600.00)	(54,600.00)	(34,600.00)	(79,800.00)	(69,800.00)
33	11	(119,800.00)	(39,400.00)	(54,600.00)	20,600.00	(79,800.00)	80,600.00
34	12	(119,800.00)	(39,400.00)	(9,400.00)	20,600.00	(14,600.00)	5,400.00
35	13	(19,000.00)	(39,400.00)	(99,800.00)	20,600.00	(14,600.00)	(69,800.00)
36	14	(94,600.00)	(74,600.00)	(54,600.00)	75,800.00	50,600.00	5,400.00
37	15	(94,600.00)	(109,800.00)	(54,600.00)	(34,600.00)	(14,600.00)	5,400.00
38	16	(94,600.00)	(109,800.00)	(9,400.00)	(34,600.00)	(14,600.00)	(69,800.00)
39	17	(119,800.00)	(109,800.00)	(54,600.00)	75,800.00	(79,800.00)	155,800.00
40	18	(94,600.00)	(74,600.00)	(54,600.00)	75,800.00	(14,600.00)	155,800.00
41	19	(94,600.00)	(109,800.00)	(54,600.00)	20,600.00	50,600.00	(69,800.00)
42	20	(69,400.00)	(109,800.00)	(54,600.00)	(89,800.00)	50,600.00	(69,800.00)
43	21	(44,200.00)	(39,400.00)	(54,600.00)	(34,600.00)	(14,600.00)	80,600.00
44	22	(94,600.00)	(74,600.00)	(9,400.00)	(34,600.00)	(14,600.00)	155,800.00
45	23	(69,400.00)	(39,400.00)	81,000.00	(34,600.00)	(79,800.00)	231,000.00
46	24	(44,200.00)	(74,600.00)	(54,600.00)	(89,800.00)	(79,800.00)	155,800.00
47	25	(19,000.00)	(74,600.00)	(99,800.00)	(34,600.00)	(79,800.00)	231,000.00

formulas. To do so, click the Formulas tab, and in the Calculation group, click the Calculation Options button, and then click the Automatic Except for Data Tables option to turn on this setting.

As shown in Figure 8.50, if you have disabled the automatic recalculation of data tables in a workbook, you can click the Calculate Sheet button in the Calculation group to recalculate the entire worksheet, or click the Calculate Now button (or press F9) to recalculate the entire workbook.

Figure 8.50: Controlling Calculation Options

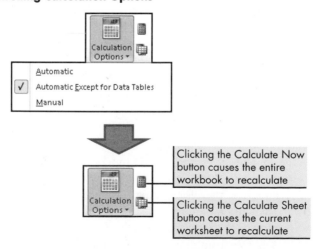

Calculating Simulation Statistics

One hundred rows of simulated profitability data can be difficult to interpret directly. When using data tables to run a simulation, it is usually best to calculate some statistics about the data and to base your analysis on those statistics, not the raw data itself.

Richard realizes that the most basic statistics are often the best because they are the easiest to understand and, thus, the most readily interpreted. Accordingly, he decides to calculate the average, maximum, and minimum simulated profit, and the standard deviation of the simulated profits for each selling price option. The added section, complete with headings and formatting, is shown in Figure 8.51.

Figure 8.51: Adding simulation statistics to the worksheet

	K	L	M	N	O	P	Q	R	S
6									
7			Simulated Profitability Statistics Given Various Selling Prices						
8									
9					Selling Prices				
10			$99.95	$109.95	$119.95	$129.95	$139.95	$149.95	
11		Average income	$ (85,675.00)	$ (69,466.67)	$ (28,233.33)	$ (8,150.00)	$ (7,808.33)	$ 32,033.33	
12		Standard deviation	27,255.28	37,723.05	49,191.17	63,388.87	57,440.88	93,706.21	
13		Maximum income	(19,000.00)	31,000.00	81,000.00	131,000.00	115,800.00	231,000.00	
14		Minimum income	(119,800.00)	(109,800.00)	(99,800.00)	(89,800.00)	(79,800.00)	(69,800.00)	
15									
16									
17									
18									
19			Simulated Income Before Taxes Given Various Selling Prices						
20									
21					Selling Prices				
22		Iterations $	99.95 $	109.95 $	119.95 $	129.95 $	139.95 $	149.95	
23		1	(119,800.00)	(4,200.00)	(54,600.00)	(89,800.00)	50,600.00	5,400.00	
24		2	(69,400.00)	(74,600.00)	(9,400.00)	(89,800.00)	(14,600.00)	80,600.00	
25		3	(94,600.00)	(74,600.00)	(9,400.00)	(34,600.00)	50,600.00	5,400.00	
26		4	(94,600.00)	(74,600.00)	(54,600.00)	131,000.00	(14,600.00)	80,600.00	
27		5	(69,400.00)	(74,600.00)	(9,400.00)	20,600.00	(14,600.00)	(69,800.00)	
28		6	(44,200.00)	(74,600.00)	(99,800.00)	(34,600.00)	115,800.00	(69,800.00)	
29		7	(44,200.00)	(109,800.00)	(9,400.00)	(34,600.00)	(79,800.00)	5,400.00	
30		8	(69,400.00)	(4,200.00)	35,800.00	(89,800.00)	115,800.00	80,600.00	
31		9	(119,800.00)	(4,200.00)	(9,400.00)	(89,800.00)	(79,000.00)	(69,800.00)	
32		10	(69,400.00)	(74,600.00)	(54,600.00)	(34,600.00)	(79,800.00)	(69,800.00)	
33		11	(119,800.00)	(39,400.00)	(54,600.00)	20,600.00	(79,800.00)	80,600.00	
34		12	(119,800.00)	(39,400.00)	(9,400.00)	20,600.00	(14,600.00)	5,400.00	
35		13	(19,000.00)	(39,400.00)	(99,800.00)	20,600.00	(14,600.00)	(69,800.00)	

The formulas view of the worksheet section is shown in Figure 8.52.

The figure also shows the table's output formula in cell L22 and the TABLE functions that Excel used to fill the table with the simulated profitability data. Excel inserted the TABLE functions as it filled in the table with data. You can see that they contain arguments that refer to the input cells you specified in the Data Table dialog box. The TABLE function is used only by Excel when creating data tables; it is not generally available for use. In other words, workbook users cannot write TABLE functions as they can other functions.

8

Level 3

Figure 8.52: Viewing simulation formulas

	L	M	N	O	P	Q	R
6							
7				Simulated Profitability Statistics Given Various Selling Prices			
8							
9				Selling Prices			
10		99.95	109.95	119.95	129.95	139.95	149.95
11	Average income	=AVERAGE(M23:M122)	=AVERAGE(N23:N122)	=AVERAGE(O23:O122)	=AVERAGE(P23:P122)	=AVERAGE(Q23:Q122)	=AVERAGE(R23:R122)
12	Standard deviation	=STDEV.S(M23:M122)	=STDEV.S(N23:N122)	=STDEV.S(O23:O122)	=STDEV.S(P23:P122)	=STDEV.S(Q23:Q122)	=STDEV.S(R23:R122)
13	Maximum income	=MAX(M23:M122)	=MAX(N23:N122)	=MAX(O23:O122)	=MAX(P23:P122)	=MAX(Q23:Q122)	=MAX(R23:R122)
14	Minimum income	=MIN(M23:M122)	=MIN(N23:N122)	=MIN(O23:O122)	=MIN(P23:P122)	=MIN(Q23:Q122)	=MIN(R23:R122)
15							
16							
17							
18							
19				Simulated Income Before Taxes Given Various Selling Prices			
20							
21				Selling Prices			
22	=J19	99.95	109.95	119.95	129.95	139.95	149.95
23	1	=TABLE(D10,G21)	=TABLE(D10,G21)	=TABLE(D10,G21)	=TABLE(D10,G21)	=TABLE(D10,G21)	=TABLE(D10,G21)
24	2	=TABLE(D10,G21)	=TABLE(D10,G21)	=TABLE(D10,G21)	=TABLE(D10,G21)	=TABLE(D10,G21)	=TABLE(D10,G21)
25	3	=TABLE(D10,G21)	=TABLE(D10,G21)	=TABLE(D10,G21)	=TABLE(D10,G21)	=TABLE(D10,G21)	=TABLE(D10,G21)
26	4	=TABLE(D10,G21)	=TABLE(D10,G21)	=TABLE(D10,G21)	=TABLE(D10,G21)	=TABLE(D10,G21)	=TABLE(D10,G21)
27	5	=TABLE(D10,G21)	=TABLE(D10,G21)	=TABLE(D10,G21)	=TABLE(D10,G21)	=TABLE(D10,G21)	=TABLE(D10,G21)
28	6	=TABLE(D10,G21)	=TABLE(D10,G21)	=TABLE(D10,G21)	=TABLE(D10,G21)	=TABLE(D10,G21)	=TABLE(D10,G21)
29	7	=TABLE(D10,G21)	=TABLE(D10,G21)	=TABLE(D10,G21)	=TABLE(D10,G21)	=TABLE(D10,G21)	=TABLE(D10,G21)
30	8	=TABLE(D10,G21)	=TABLE(D10,G21)	=TABLE(D10,G21)	=TABLE(D10,G21)	=TABLE(D10,G21)	=TABLE(D10,G21)
31	9	=TABLE(D10,G21)	=TABLE(D10,G21)	=TABLE(D10,G21)	=TABLE(D10,G21)	=TABLE(D10,G21)	=TABLE(D10,G21)
32	10	=TABLE(D10,G21)	=TABLE(D10,G21)	=TABLE(D10,G21)	=TABLE(D10,G21)	=TABLE(D10,G21)	=TABLE(D10,G21)
33	11	=TABLE(D10,G21)	=TABLE(D10,G21)	=TABLE(D10,G21)	=TABLE(D10,G21)	=TABLE(D10,G21)	=TABLE(D10,G21)
34	12	=TABLE(D10,G21)	=TABLE(D10,G21)	=TABLE(D10,G21)	=TABLE(D10,G21)	=TABLE(D10,G21)	=TABLE(D10,G21)
35	13	=TABLE(D10,G21)	=TABLE(D10,G21)	=TABLE(D10,G21)	=TABLE(D10,G21)	=TABLE(D10,G21)	=TABLE(D10,G21)

PivotChart | Scenario PivotTable | Swimwear | **Probabilities**

Interpreting Simulation Results

Richard could have guessed that the highest selling price, $149.95, would result in the best profitability numbers for TheZone, which is clearly borne out by the simulated results statistical summary. Did he waste his time creating and running the simulation?

Considering the realities of setting sales prices for new products, not really. Companies might choose to set a lower sales price when they first start to sell a product to gain market share ahead of their competitors, hoping to make up the profits in the future. On the other hand, if a company expects its competitors to follow a new product into the market quickly, a company might want to make as much profit as it can in the early period when there is little competition, expecting that it will have to reduce its markup on the product in future years. By performing the simulation and computing statistics on the simulated results, Richard has now quantified the profitability differences of the selling prices, and can make a more informed decision about what type of pricing strategy to follow.

Steps To Success: Level 3

TheZone's Sales Department has determined that no matter what the marketing expenditures, the unit product mix among the four styles of swimsuits remains relatively constant, with the men's racers sales about equal to the men's trunks sales, the women's one-piece sales being approximately 50% of the men's trunks sales, and the women's two-piece sales being approximately 70% of the men's trunks sales. By determining the probability of different sales volumes for the men's trunks, you can determine estimates of the sales of the other swimsuit styles.

In addition, TheZone has decided that its general policy will be to set the selling price of the men's racers $7 over the selling price of the other three types of suits. TheZone's marketing staff has conducted market research to determine the relative probability of various sales levels for the men's trunks.

Richard wants to evaluate the profitability of future price increases for the swimsuits line via a simulation. He has started a workbook named Sim that will contain the simulation and its results. Richard has gathered all the data needed for the assumptions section of the worksheet, and used an Income Statement format to model the profitability results, but he needs your help to set up and run the simulation. Complete the following:

1. Open the workbook named **Sim.xlsx** located in the Chapter 8 folder, and save it with the name **Swimsuits Simulation.xlsx**.

2. In the Swimsuits worksheet, to the right of the cells that contain the individual probabilities for the various men's racers style sales figures, create a cumulative probability distribution table for the unit sales estimates. The cumulative probabilities must be in the first column of the table so the lookup function you create in Step 4 works properly. Add informative headings and basic formatting to the distribution table so it has a more professional appearance.

3. In a cell close to the distribution tables, use the RAND function to add a randomly generated value to the worksheet.

4. Write a VLOOKUP function in cell C8 that looks up the random number you generated with the RAND function in Step 3 in the cumulative probability distribution lookup table you created in Step 2 and returns the corresponding unit sales figure.

5. Create the structure for a two-variable data table that will run a simulation to calculate the income before taxes given various units sold and men's trunks selling prices of $39.95 to $59.95 by increments of $5.00. The default value of 100 iterations of the simulation is sufficient. (*Hint*: Remember that when using a two-variable data table to run a simulation, one set of input values in the data table's structure must be a sequence of numbers that represents the number of iterations of the simulation. Because the number of units sold is determined via the RAND and VLOOKUP functions, the range of selling prices is the only "real" set of input values included in the data table's structure.)

6. Instruct Excel to complete the data table. (*Hint*: Remember that when using a data table to run a simulation, the real set of input values is directed to the input section of the worksheet and the iteration values are directed to any empty cell in the worksheet.) Add informative headings and basic formatting to the data table so it has a more professional appearance.

7. Use the AVERAGE, STDEV.S, MAX, and MIN functions to create a range in the worksheet that summarizes the simulation's profitability results for each sales price. Add informative headings and basic formatting to the summary range so it has a more professional appearance.

8. Save and close the Swimsuits Simulation.xlsx workbook.

Chapter Summary

This chapter introduced Excel scenarios and data tables for use in simulations and other types of what-if analyses. Basically, what-if analysis allows you to see what output would result if the value of various input assumptions changed.

In Level 1, you used data tables for what-if analysis. One-variable data tables allow you to use multiple output formulas to show the results that come from one set of input values. Two-variable data tables allow you to use one output formula to show the results of the interaction of two different sets of input values. When setting up the structure of a one-variable data table, you must enter the set of input values perpendicular to the set of output formulas with no value or formula located in the upper, leftmost cell of the data table, which is at the intersection of the set of input values and the set of output formulas . When setting up the structure of a two-variable data table, you must set up the two sets of input values perpendicular to each other, and the output formula must be in the cell at the intersection of the two sets of input values. After you set up the data table's structure, you specify how Excel should complete the table by indicating to which cells in the worksheet's input section the table's input values relate.

In Level 2, you were introduced to Excel Scenarios, which allow you to save a number of sets of different input values, referred to as changing cells, and switch between the scenarios to see the results of these different sets of assumptions in the worksheet. In addition, your selected results of the scenarios can be shown on scenario summary reports or scenario PivotTables and PivotCharts. You also used the SUMPRODUCT function to sum the products of multiplication operations

In Level 3, you learned how to use two-variable data tables to run simulations of data models. In this case, one set of input values is replaced with a sequence of numbers that determines the number of iterations of the simulation that are run. Because one set of input values is replaced by an iteration sequence, the replaced input variable must be determined by some other means, usually related to a random number generating function, such as RAND. When specifying how to complete a two-variable data table used to run a simulation, the sequence of iteration numbers is referred to an empty cell instead of a cell in the worksheet's input section, as is the real set of input values. Because a large quantity of simulated data is often difficult to interpret directly, some method of classifying or aggregating the data, such as the use of statistical functions, can help facilitate the interpretation process related to simulated data.

Conceptual Review

1. Compare break-even analysis and sensitivity analysis.

2. How does a data table help you perform what-if analysis?

3. What is the difference between a one-variable data table and a two-variable data table? When would you use each type of data table?

4. What are the two major steps involved in creating a data table in Excel?

5. In a two-variable data table, what do the first column and first row of the table contain?

6. When should you create a scenario instead of a data table? Give an example of a business situation that could best be analyzed with scenarios.

7. Why are defined names important when you create scenarios?

8. What types of reports can you create for scenarios? Which type shows results only?

9. What type of what-if question can a simulation answer?

10. Explain how you must vary the setup of a two-variable data table to run a simulation via the table.

Case Problems

Level 1 – Estimating Travel Expenses for Customers of Executive Transport, Inc.

Executive Transport, Inc., is a company that rents cars, vans, and limos to a wide range of customers. Customers frequently call Executive Transport's sales staff to receive quotes for rental expenses. As gas prices have been climbing over the last few years, customers have become more conscious of fuel efficiency and its impact on their total cost of transportation. As a service to its customers, Executive Transport has modified its Quotes workbook to include information on its cars' gas mileage and an estimate of the gas expense related to customers' planned trips. All that remains to be added to the workbook is information specific to each of the car types, and a more detailed analysis of the interaction between gas prices and total cost of transportation, and the gas mileage of cars and its impact on the total cost of transportation. Complete the following:

Sales

1. Open the workbook named **Quotes.xlsx** located in the Chapter 8 folder, and save it as **Transport Quotes.xlsx**.

2. Examine the Analysis worksheet, and apply appropriate names to cells D17:D20.

3. Set up the structure of a one-variable data table on the Analysis worksheet that shows the car charge, mileage charge, gas expense, and total transportation expense given changes in the average price of gas from $2.20 to $3.80 by increments of $0.20.

4. Instruct Excel to complete the one-variable data table.

   TROUBLESHOOTING: In order to complete the one-variable data table successfully, be sure to select the correct data table range. If you instruct Excel to complete an incorrect range, you cannot just delete any "extra" results that might have appeared at the bottom or right of the intended data table area. When you try to do so, you will receive the "Cannot change part of a data table" error message. You cannot delete only some results from a filled-in data table; you must delete *all* results values from a one-variable data table if you want to delete any results.

5. Add headings and basic formatting to the data table so it has a more professional appearance.

6. A few rows below the one-variable data table, create the structure for a two-variable data table that shows the total projected transportation expense given the interaction between average gas prices from $2.20 to $3.80 by increments of $0.20 and miles per gallon from 18 to 28 by increments of 2 miles per gallon.

7. Instruct Excel to complete the two-variable data table.

8. Add headings and some basic formatting to the data table so it has a more professional appearance.

9. Save and close the Transport Quotes.xlsx workbook.

Level 2 – Evaluating Expansion Financing Options for Granite City Books

Finance

Granite City Books is planning a $2.5 million expansion of its facilities. It needs to evaluate its options for financing the expansion. The company's bank might not allow it to obtain more long-term debt financing if its debt-to-equity ratio gets too high. Alternatively, common stockholders might be displeased if their ownership rights become diluted by issuing a substantial amount of preferred stock, or even additional common stock if it's not issued on a pro rata basis. A workbook has been started that contains a basic Balance Sheet, solvency, and capital structure ratio data. Your task is to create scenarios for each financing alternative and prepare reports that Granite City Books' bank and management can use to compare the various financing alternatives. Complete the following:

1. Open the workbook named **Granite.xlsx** located in the Chapter 8 folder, and save it as **Granite City Expansion.xlsx** in the same location.

2. In the Options worksheet, apply appropriate names to the worksheet's scenario changing cells as described in Table 8.5.

Table 8.5: Descriptions of the changing cells

Changing Cell	Description
F9	Change in assets
F12	Change in long-term debt
F14	Change in the dollar amount of common stock issued
F15	Change in the dollar amount of preferred stock issued

3. Create four scenarios in the Options worksheet using the scenario names and changing cell values shown in Table 8.6.

Table 8.6: Data for the four scenarios

Changing Cell	Long-Term Debt Financing	Common Stock Financing	Preferred Stock Financing	Balanced Financing
F9	2,500	2,500	2,500	2,500
F12	2,500	0	0	1,000
F14	0	2,500	0	750
F15	0	0	2,500	750

4. Based on the information in Table 8.7, apply appropriate names to the worksheet's result cells.

Table 8.7: Descriptions of the result cells

Cell	Description
F13	Change in total liabilities
F17	Change in total equity
G21	Debt-to-equity ratio
G24	Long-term-debt-to-common-equity ratio
G25	Preferred stock ratio

5. Create a professional-looking scenario summary report that shows all the result cells listed in Table 8.7.

8

Chapter Exercises

6. Create a professional-looking scenario PivotTable that shows the last three result cells listed in Table 8.7. Also generate a PivotChart based on the PivotTable.

7. Save and close the Granite City Expansion.xlsx workbook.

Level 3 – Analyzing Health Insurance Plan Options for CKG Auto

Human Resources

CKG Auto has traditionally paid 75% of the premiums for its employees' health insurance. Like many companies, CKG is reevaluating this employee benefit as health insurance premiums have increased at a rate much higher than the general rate of inflation. CKG is evaluating all of its options with regard to health insurance. The company has received quotes from insurance companies for three different health plans: a co-pay plan, a low-deductible plan, and a high-deductible plan. In addition, it is considering instituting a self-insurance health plan, under which the employees pay a quasi-premium and co-pay directly to CKG, and in turn, CKG pays the employees' health claims, just as an insurance company would.

CKG's human resources staff has started a workbook that contains data about the cash effects of the options for purchasing health insurance plans and the proposed self-insurance plan based on CKG's employees' past health insurance participation and claim history. You have been asked to finish the worksheet, complete with scenarios under which CKG pays different percentages of employees' health insurance premiums, and a simulation estimating the cash effects of the self-insurance plan. Complete the following:

1. Open the workbook named **CKGHealth.xlsx** located in the Chapter 8 folder, and save it as **CKG Health Insurance.xlsx**.

2. In the Self-InsuranceSim worksheet, create two cumulative probability distribution tables: one for the co-pay events and one for the dollar value of claims.

3. Add a randomly generated value somewhere in the worksheet.

4. In cells D12 and D13, use the appropriate functions to return a number of co-pay events and a dollar value of claims based on a random entry from the cumulative distribution tables.

5. Set up a data table that will run a simulation to calculate the net cash paid for employee health coverage given various numbers of co-pay events, dollar value of claims, and monthly premiums paid by employees of $50 to $130 by increments of $10. CKG Auto's management has decided that 100 iterations of the simulation are sufficient.

6. Instruct Excel to complete the data table. Add informative headings and formatting so the table has a more professional appearance.

7. Use the AVERAGE, STDEV.S, MAX, and MIN functions to create a range in the worksheet that summarizes the simulation's net cash effects for each monthly premium value.

8. Add informative headings and formatting to the summary range so it has a more professional appearance.

9. Save and close the CKG Health Insurance.xlsx workbook.

SAM: Skills Assessment Manager

For current SAM information, including versions and content details, visit SAM Central (http://samcentral.course.com). If you have a SAM user profile, you may have access to hands-on instruction, practice, and assessment of the skills covered in this chapter. Since various versions of SAM are supported throughout the life of this text, check with your instructor for the correct instructions and URL/Web site for accessing assignments.

Enhancing Decision Making with Solver

Operations Management: Developing Solver Models to Allocate Production and Transportation Resources

"Good management is the art of making problems so interesting and their solutions so constructive that everyone wants to get to work and deal with them."
—Paul Hawken

Chapter Introduction

In Chapters 2 and 8, you learned how to use Goal Seek to change the value in a specified cell until the desired result is returned by the formula. Although Goal Seek only lets you change one cell, it can be quite useful at times. A much more powerful alternative to Goal Seek is the **Solver** add-in. Although you can use Solver in the same manner as Goal Seek to find the required inputs to return a specific result, its ability to maximize or minimize the results of a formula is much more powerful. You can set up complex business models in a worksheet and use Solver to determine the optimal set of decision inputs to meet an objective, such as minimizing costs or maximizing profits. Because you can use Solver to answer very complex questions, it is an excellent tool for determining the best way to apply resources to a particular problem. Determining the best allocation of resources, such as people, money, or materials, is frequently one of the most difficult decisions that managers face.

Case Scenario

TheZone is in the process of introducing the TZAdvantage, a new tennis racquet that incorporates nanotechnology into the production process. The TZAdvantage tennis racquet is constructed using a unique combination of carbon, graphite, and Kevlar fibers. The Kevlar fibers are modified at the molecular level to give them tiny "barbed fingers" that help the fibers bond with each other during the manufacturing process, resulting in a racquet that is much stronger and more stable than any model the company has previously offered. The TZAdvantage is being manufactured in two models: TZAdvantage Model I is designed for beginning and intermediate players, and TZAdvantage Model II is designed for advanced players.

Operations Management

Beth Mallory is an operations manager working on the product development team. Beth's job is to analyze a variety of situations associated with the TZAdvantage product launch, including production planning and distribution of the new racquets to the company's distribution centers. One immediate task is how to best spend TheZone's budget of $10,000 for special tournament versions of the TZAdvantage racquets as part of a promotion for a Pro-Am tennis tournament that TheZone is sponsoring next month. The tournament racquets will be given to key guests and players in the tournament. TheZone will manufacture its regular production run of TZAdvantage racquets to meet the product launch delivery schedule that is scheduled for the following month. TheZone must accomplish the production run of tournament racquets without setting back the scheduled production of the regular racquets. Beth also must develop a distribution plan to schedule shipments of the finished racquets to the company's distribution centers to meet demand for advance orders from retailers. After finishing her work with the production of the TZAdvantage racquets, Beth is also responsible for awarding three transportation contracts to various shipping companies that will distribute the racquets and other TheZone products to retailers.

LEVEL 1
Solving Product Mix Questions Using Goal Seek and Solver

The Other Side of What-If Analysis

Companies set goals using research that analyzes the choices or options that identify the decisions they need to make and the best potential outcomes. The method you use to narrow the available options for a problem so you can choose the best potential outcome is an analytical process known as **optimization** in the field of management science. You must answer three questions before using optimization to solve a problem:

• How many resources are there and how many are needed?
• How many resources does each decision variable consume?
• How much does each decision variable contribute to the objective?

For example, consider the problem that a baker might have: How many and which products should he or she prepare for the next day's sales? The baker's primary goal might be to maximize revenue. The decision variables in this case are how many of each product to prepare. Some products will generate more revenue than others but might use more resources. Each product will require a different number and amount of resources to produce. The resources in this example include ingredients, labor, and baking time. The combination of products sold determines how much revenue the baker generates. Each product contributes to the goal of increasing the baker's revenue, but there is an optimal combination of products that he or she can prepare to use the available resources and generate the maximum amount of revenue.

Beth's first optimization task is to determine the best way to allocate the $10,000 production budget for the tournament racquets. Beth created the worksheet shown in Figure 9.1, which shows the cost estimates for producing the tournament racquets. The Model II racquet costs $28.00 per racquet to produce and the Model I racquet, which is much simpler to produce, costs $18.00 per racquet to produce. These costs include labor and material costs as well as an allocation of the overhead costs at the plant that produces the racquets. Beth must consider many more factors when planning the production of these racquets. However, for her preliminary analysis, Beth will allocate resources using only the costs to produce the racquets. After conducting her preliminary analysis on how to best allocate the resources to produce the maximum number of racquets, Beth will further refine her calculations to ensure that there are enough raw materials in inventory to produce the racquets.

The Marketing Department has allocated $10,000 to produce the tournament versions of both racquets and wants to give away at least 150 racquets of each model, for a total of at least 300 racquets. The plant's one-time setup cost for each racquet appears in the

Figure 9.1: Production Plan worksheet for the tournament racquets

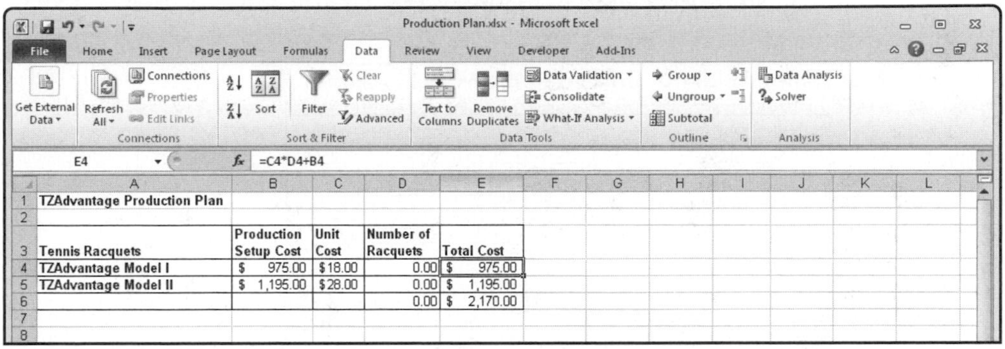

Production Setup Cost column in Beth's worksheet. The setup costs include costs associated with setting up the machinery to produce the racquets, such as changing out fixtures, obtaining new inventory supplies, and moving out the inventory associated with the previous production run. The Unit Cost column identifies the production cost for each racquet produced. The Number of Racquets column identifies the number of each model to produce, and the Total Cost column calculates the cost of producing the specified number of racquets.

In her worksheet, Beth could type values into cells D4 and D5 to try to divide the budget between the two models in such a way as to maximize the total number of racquets produced while staying within the overall production budget. She could change the number of racquets produced (cells D4:D5) until the total amount spent on racquets is approximately equal to $10,000. By manually estimating the number of racquets produced, Beth would perform a manual what-if analysis. Instead of finding the results that occur when different inputs are used, Beth can use this approach to find the combination of inputs that result in the desired answer. However, inserting the values manually isn't a very efficient way to find the values that result in the desired answer. Excel provides two tools to help solve this problem—Goal Seek and Solver.

Performing What-If Analysis Using Goal Seek

Beth decides not to enter values manually. Instead, she has decided to use Goal Seek to make the calculations automatically and to divide the production budget equally between the two models. In Chapter 2, you learned that Goal Seek lets you specify the desired value in a cell and the cell that should be changed to reach that goal. For the TZAdvantage Model I, Beth can specify one half of the total budget, or $5,000, as the desired goal in cell E4 and specify cell D4 as the value to change in the formula in cell E4 to arrive at the number of racquets to produce. In this case, Goal Seek determines that producing 223.61 Model I racquets, including the production setup cost, results in a total cost of exactly $5,000, as shown in Figure 9.2. Beth knows that she cannot produce 223.61 racquets, but decides to continue using Goal Seek to evenly divide the budget between the two models, and to delay the rounding problem until she is finished.

Figure 9.2: Goal Seek solution for producing the Model I racquet

Beth repeats this process in cell E5 to arrive at the final solution. Goal Seek shows that she can produce 223.61 TZAdvantage Model I racquets for $5,000 and 135.89 TZAdvantage Model II racquets for $5,000, for a total of 359.5 racquets and $10,000. She rounds the number of racquets produced down to 223 and 135, respectively, and the total cost is $9,964 to produce 358 racquets.

After viewing Beth's worksheet, Nick Staples, the product manager for TZAdvantage, wants to ensure that at least 300 racquets are available for the promotion, with at least 150 Model I and Model II racquets each. Nick and Beth also discuss the limited inventory of some of the fibers used in the manufacturing process. Nick asks Beth to verify that enough raw material inventories are in stock to produce the tournament racquets, but he doesn't want the regular production schedule to slip because of the promotion. Beth checks the stock of raw fiber inventories to ensure that sufficient inventories of carbon, graphite, and Kevlar fibers are available to produce the tournament racquets. Beth was able to use Goal Seek to find single answers very easily. However, these new requirements mean that she must compare the two production quantities simultaneously with the available inventory—a task that is beyond the capability of Goal Seek. Beth could use a manual what-if process to find the right production combination to meet Nick's new requirements, but she would need many formulas to try all of the different input combinations. Beth decides to use another Excel tool, Solver, to make her calculations.

Creating a Solver Model

Solver is similar to Goal Seek in that it lets you specify what you want to occur in a particular cell by letting Excel change the values of one or more related cells. Goal Seek is limited to changing values in a single cell to reach a goal in another related cell. This related cell is known as the objective cell in Solver. With Solver, you can change the values in as many as 200 cells at one time to reach a goal in the **objective cell** (which in earlier versions of

Excel was called the target cell). Solver changes the values in the **variable cells** (also known as **decision variables**) to maximize, minimize, or set the objective cell to a specific value. Solver also lets you establish **constraints** that restrict the values that are entered into the variable, or changing, cells. The combination of a spreadsheet model with the objective cell, variable cells, and constraints that are used to solve the problem is called a **Solver model**.

There are three required parameters when running a Solver model: the objective cell that you want to maximize, minimize, or set to a specific value; the variable cell(s) that Solver uses to produce the desired results in the objective cell; and the constraint(s) that limit how to solve the problem. Any Solver solution requires a well-organized spreadsheet that links the variable cells with the objective cell and links the known facts about the problem with the objective cell. Solver inserts values in the variable cells until the value of the objective cell has reached the specified goal. At the same time that Solver is inserting values into the variable cells, it examines the constraints to ensure that the solution satisfies them. You can use Solver to determine how to allocate resources, such as people, budgets, or inventories, in such a way as to achieve the greatest benefits.

Beth decides to use Solver to find the optimal number of tournament racquets to produce within the given constraints. She sets up the problem's known facts in the worksheet shown in Figure 9.3. She names this worksheet "Maximize Racquets" to indicate that its calculations maximize the number of tournament racquets to produce.

Figure 9.3: Worksheet to maximize the number of tournament racquets produced

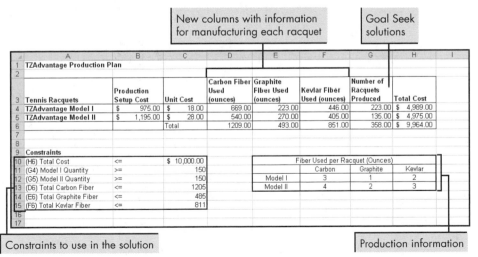

Beth's worksheet includes information about the available resources and how many resources are needed. The resources in this problem are the $10,000 production budget and the available amount of raw materials (carbon, graphite, and Kevlar fibers). Second, Beth needs to know how many resources each decision variable consumes. The decision variables in this problem are how many of each racquet to produce. The total cost of producing each racquet (cells H4:H5) represents the cost of each decision variable. The total ounces of fiber used (cells D6:F6) represent the raw material resources that the decision variables consume. The amount of fibers used to produce each racquet equals the amount for the model and fiber (cells F12:H13) multiplied by the number of racquets produced. Third, Beth needs to know how much each decision variable contributes to the solution. The total in cell G6 represents the number of racquets produced.

Beth needs to add the objective cell, the variable cells, and the constraints to the Solver Parameters dialog box. In this case, the objective is to maximize the total number of racquets produced by varying the number of each model produced. The number of racquets Beth can produce from each model is limited by the following constraints from the product manager:

- Do not exceed the $10,000 budget.
- Produce at least 150 TZAdvantage Model I racquets.
- Produce at least 150 TZAdvantage Model II racquets.
- Do not exceed the available amounts of carbon, graphite, and Kevlar fibers in inventory.

Notice that Beth's worksheet identifies these constraints in cells A10:C15. By including the constraints and cell references in a constraints table in her worksheet, Beth has a record of them for later use and also has a data-entry reference when she sets up Solver.

Solver lets you create a mathematical model of a business scenario. You can base the constraints that limit the value of a particular cell in the Solver model on company policies or on physical limits. *Policy constraints* are often based on company history and, to some extent, inertia. One example of the difference between these constraint types might be a transportation problem that determines the optimal route for delivery trucks to use on their routes. The size of the truck is a *physical limit;* a constraint that only fully loaded trucks make deliveries is an example of a policy limit. Another example is restricting the number of gallons of milk that a customer can buy at a sale price (a policy limit) versus the actual inventory of milk available in the store (a physical limit).

Nick established a policy constraint when deciding that Beth's solution must produce at least 150 models of each tournament racquet. You can use Solver to identify the impact of policy constraints and how changes in policies can affect the bottom line. The physical constraint in this problem is the amount of carbon, graphite, and Kevlar fibers that are available for production.

Beth wants to use Solver but notices that it isn't available on the Ribbon. She needs to load the add-in using the Excel Options dialog box. After you load the Solver Add-in, the Solver command is available in the Analysis group on the Data tab on the Ribbon.

How To

Load the Solver Add-In

1. Click the File tab on the Ribbon, and then click the Options command in the navigation bar. The Excel Options dialog box opens.

2. Select the Add-Ins category, click the Manage arrow, and then click Excel Add-ins.

3. Click the Go button. The Add-Ins dialog box opens, as shown in Figure 9.4.

Figure 9.4: Add-Ins dialog box

4. Click the check box next to the Solver Add-in, and then click the OK button.

5. If a message appears indicating Excel cannot run the add-in because the feature isn't installed, click the Yes button to install it.

Note: If a full installation of Microsoft Excel 2010 was not originally performed and the Solver Add-in is not available, you may need your original software to run a custom installation of this feature.

To start Solver, Beth clicks the Solver button in the Analysis group on the Data tab. The Solver Parameters dialog box opens, as shown in Figure 9.5. The default solving method when the Solver Parameters dialog box opens is GRG Nonlinear. The production plan contains no nonlinear formulas or arrangement, so Beth changes the solving method to Simplex LP.

Figure 9.5: Solver Parameters dialog box

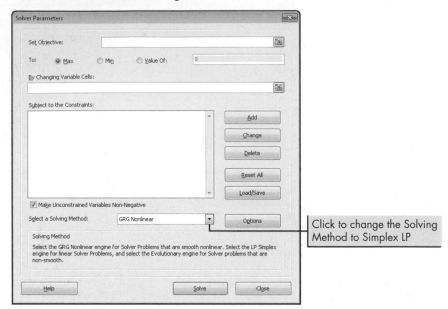

Click to change the Solving Method to Simplex LP

Best Practice

Using Solver with Nonlinear Functions

An Excel worksheet looks like a piece of paper on the screen; it is designed to resemble a ledger book that is used in accounting. The cells in a worksheet usually display combinations of text or numbers; the math that generates the answers is not visible in the worksheet itself. The model you create when using Solver is mathematical. The objective function or formula that you use in the objective cell can be either linear or nonlinear. The production plan for TZAdvantage racquets uses a linear function. A **linear function** results when a decision variable is multiplied by a constant, such as price. When you plot a linear function in a chart, the result is a straight line, thus the term linear. When you cannot describe a function in linear terms, it is called a **nonlinear function**. When you graph a nonlinear function on two dimensions, it results in a curve, not a straight line. An example of a nonlinear function is the relationship between the price of an item and the demand for that item. As the price of the item increases, the demand for the item might decrease. Because demand varies as a function of price, calculating the revenue (price multiplied by demand) for an item means that you are multiplying price by a function of price. The result is a nonlinear function or a curve.

It is more difficult to use Solver with nonlinear functions. You might encounter a situation in which Solver creates different answers depending on the starting values in the variable cells. Imagine hiking on a twisty, wooded mountain trail that climbs and then suddenly levels off or even starts to descend. You might think that you have reached the highest point on the trail when the trail starts to level off, but around the bend the trail starts to climb again. If your objective is to reach the highest point on the trail, you might assume that you have maximized your objective of reaching the highest point and then turn around and head back down the trail. Solver can do the same thing with nonlinear objective functions. Solver tries out values and discovers that it has reached a maximum or minimum value, depending on the objective, and stops. Solver might assume that it has reached a global maximum or minimum when it has actually reached a local maximum or minimum.

The new version of Solver in Excel 2010 includes the GRG (Generalized Reduced Gradient) nonlinear solving method for smooth nonlinear problems. One of the options for this method is to use multiple starting points. Entering a variety of starting points ensures that the answer that Solver reports is actually the optimal solution.

Beth enters the parameters for the problem to solve. First, she clicks the Set Objective box, and then she clicks cell G6, which contains a formula to calculate the total number of Model I and Model II racquets to produce. Excel changes the cell reference G6 to an absolute cell reference ($G$6) to preserve the link to that cell in the event of any future changes to the worksheet.

If we were to write the contents of cell G6 as a mathematical formula where the number of racquets produced (Z) is represented by the variables Q1 and Q2, the resulting formula is:

$$\text{Maximize } Z = Q1 + Q2$$

This formula is an **objective function**, a mathematical formula that relates the decision variables or variable cells to the desired outcome, which in this case is to maximize the total number of racquets produced. Although Excel does the math for you so that all you see is the result, the mathematical formula is still present. Understanding the math Excel uses to solve business problems is an important part of understanding the result. The result of this objective function becomes the objective cell. In this case, the objective cell (G6) contains a SUM function that adds the results of cells G4 (Q1) and G5 (Q2).

Next, Beth needs to specify whether Solver should maximize, minimize, or set the objective cell to a certain value by selecting the Max (maximum), Min (minimum), or Value Of option button. If she selects the Value Of option button, she also must enter a specific value in the Value Of input box. Usually, you need to maximize items such as revenue or profit and minimize items such as expenses or losses. In this case, Beth needs to maximize the number of total racquets produced to get the most from the allocated production budget, so she ensures that the Max option button is selected.

Next, Beth needs to specify the decision variables, or the cells that Solver will change to find a solution, in the By Changing Variable Cells box. She clicks the By Changing Variable Cells box, and then selects the cells in the range G4:G5 in the worksheet; this range represents the number of Model I and Model II racquets produced. Solver will change the values in these cells as it seeks to maximize the value in the objective cell (G6). Obviously, the variable cells must influence the result in the objective cell or Solver will not be able to reach a solution.

Finally, Beth needs to specify the constraints, or limitations, to use when generating the solution. Because she added the constraints to the worksheet, it is easy to identify and enter them. She clicks the Add button in the Solver Parameters dialog box to open the Add Constraint dialog box shown in Figure 9.6. Each constraint contains a cell reference to a cell in the worksheet, a comparison operator, and a cell reference or a constraint value. The five comparison operators you can use in Solver are less than or equal to (<=), equal to (=), greater than or equal to (>=), integer (int), binary (bin), and different (dif). The int operator restricts the cell value to a whole number, the bin operator restricts the value to 0 or 1, and the dif operator is a new type of integer constraint used to ensure a permutation of distinct values.

Beth's first constraint is that the total cost (cell H6) cannot exceed $10,000. She clicks cell H6 to add it to the Cell Reference box. As the name suggests, the Cell Reference box only accepts cell references; you cannot enter values in this input box. The less than or equal to (<=) comparison operator is the default operator and the one that she needs to use because the value in this cell must be less than or equal to $10,000 to stay within the allocated production budget. To select another comparison operator, she would click the arrow. Finally, Beth clicks the Constraint box and then clicks cell C10 in the worksheet, which contains the constraint value for the production budget, as shown in Figure 9.6.

The Constraint box can contain values, references to cells that contain those values, or even formulas. Beth could have typed 10000 in the Constraint box, but chooses instead to use a cell reference that contains the value 10,000 so that changes are easier to make later if the product manager increases or decreases the budget. After entering the information for the first constraint, Beth clicks the OK button to return to the Solver Parameters dialog box. The constraint now appears in the Subject to the Constraints box, as shown in Figure 9.7.

Beth clicks the Add button to create the second constraint, which ensures that at least 150 Model I racquets are produced ($G$4 >= $C$11). This time she clicks the Add button in the Add Constraint dialog box to allow her to enter the next constraint without returning to the Solver Parameters dialog box. The next constraint ensures that at least 150 Model II racquets are produced ($G$5 >= $C$12). Because Solver is a mathematical model, there is nothing to keep it from producing negative quantities of racquets to make an inventory last longer. Solver might calculate a solution using a negative quantity of racquets unless you include a constraint that prevents Solver from using a negative value in the variable cells. It might be favorable to permit the use of negative values in a Solver model in some situations, but TheZone can produce only a positive quantity of tennis racquets. Beth addresses the issue of a negative quantity by specifying that the number of racquets produced must be greater than or equal to 150. There is no need to set up a specific constraint

Figure 9.6: Add Constraint dialog box with first constraint added

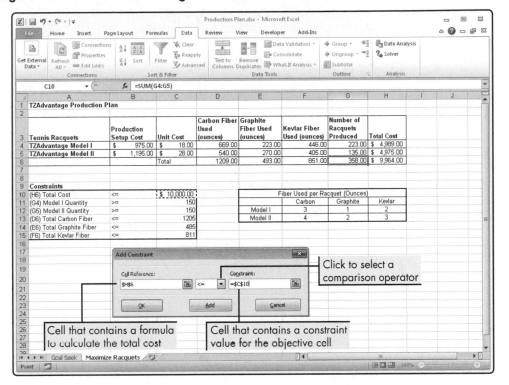

Figure 9.7: First constraint added to the Solver Parameters dialog box

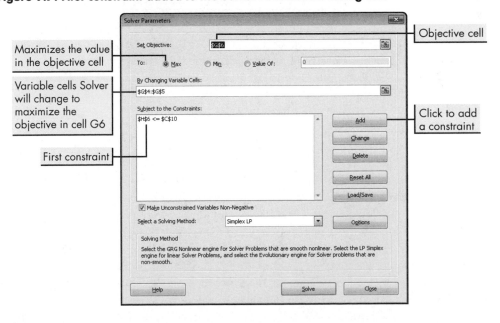

just to make a variable positive. This is handled by the default check in the Make Unconstrained Variables Non-Negative check box under the list of constraints in the Solver Parameters dialog box. Of course, this can be unselected if a situation arises where negative values are appropriate to the model.

Beth uses the Add Constraint dialog box to add the three remaining constraints that indicate the maximum amounts (in ounces) of carbon, graphite, and Kevlar fibers available for production (cells D6:F6 cannot exceed the amounts in cells C13:C15). She clicks the OK button, and the completed Solver Parameters dialog box appears in Figure 9.8.

Figure 9.8: Completed Solver Parameters dialog box

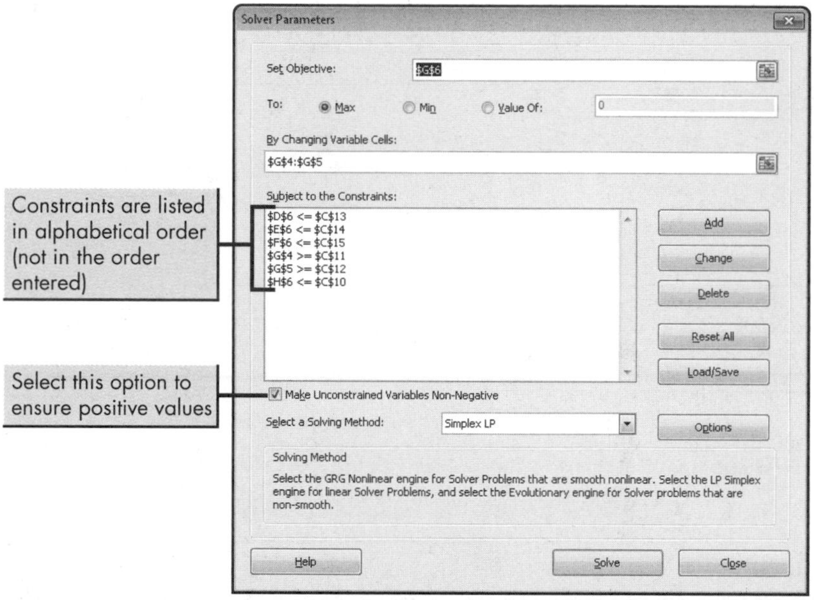

Best Practice

Creating a Constraints Table to Organize a Solver Model

Although you can enter constraints directly into the Solver Parameters dialog box without creating a constraints table in your worksheet, creating a constraints table in the worksheet is a much better way of organizing your Solver models. Optimization problems using Solver can have up to 200 variable cells. Complex problems with this many variable cells can have numerous constraints. Constraints that are entered into the Add Constraint dialog box are stored in Solver and are only visible when you open the Solver Parameters dialog box, but you can see only 13 constraints at a time in this way. Creating a constraints table in the worksheet—with the description of the constraint, the comparison operator used, and the constraint value entered into a cell—organizes the constraints and makes them visible in the worksheet at any time without the limitation of having to open the Solver Parameters dialog box and scroll the constraints to view them. Having a cell in the worksheet that contains the constraint value makes it possible for you to refer to each constraint value as a cell reference in the Add Constraint dialog box. You can use cell references in the Constraint box of the Add Constraint dialog box instead of entering a specific value. Changing a constraint value is much easier with this approach because you can change the values in the constraints table as necessary without having to edit them individually in the Change Constraint dialog box. After changing one or more values in your constraints table, you must click the Solve button in the Solver Parameters dialog box to "resolve" the problem because Solver is not included in the automatic recalculation that Excel performs when you change a cell in a worksheet.

Beth clicks the Solve button. Solver either displays a solution or determines that a solution is not feasible, and then opens the Solver Results dialog box shown in Figure 9.9 to indicate the status of the results. In Beth's worksheet, Solver finds a solution.

Figure 9.9: Solver Results dialog box and solution

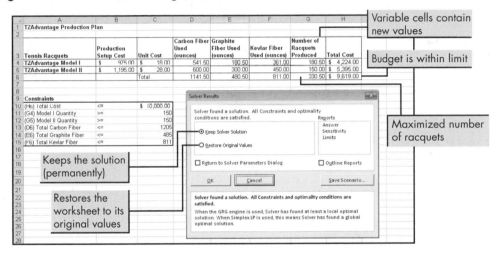

Beth can save the solution by clicking the Keep Solver Solution option button and then clicking the OK button. If she keeps the Solver solution, the original values are lost and she cannot recover them unless she previously saved them. If the solution isn't what she wanted, she can return the worksheet to its original values by clicking the Restore Original Values option button. The constraints that Beth added to the Solver Parameters dialog box are saved with the worksheet and she can run them again or change them by opening the Solver Parameters dialog box.

How To

Use Solver to Find a Solution
1. Click the Solver button in the Analysis group on the Data tab on the Ribbon. The Solver Parameters dialog box opens.
2. Enter the cell reference for the objective cell, which is the cell you want to maximize, minimize,

or set to a certain value in the Set Objective box. If you want to set the objective cell to a specific value, enter the value in the Value Of box.

3. Use the By Changing Variable Cells box to identify the cells that Solver can change to arrive at the solution.

4. Click the Add button to add constraints to limit the changes Solver makes to the values in the variable cells.

5. Click the Solve button.

Adding or Changing a Constraint in a Solver Model

The results show that the optimal solution is to produce 180.5 Model I racquets and 150 Model II racquets. This combination results in a total of 330.5 racquets produced at a total cost of $9,619.00. Beth immediately sees a problem—she has produced a fractional number of Model I racquets. The plant cannot produce one-half of a racquet, so Beth needs to add a constraint to use integers in the variable cells. At first glance, it appears that rounding the values in the variable cells would solve this problem; but rounding might cause additional problems in some situations. Beth clicks the Restore Original Values option button in the Solver Results dialog box, and then she clicks the OK button to close it and return to the original values in the worksheet. Beth updates the constraints section in her worksheet, and then uses the Add Constraint dialog box to add a new constraint so that cells G4:G5 will contain only integers. Figure 9.10 shows these revisions.

Figure 9.10: New constraint added to the Solver model

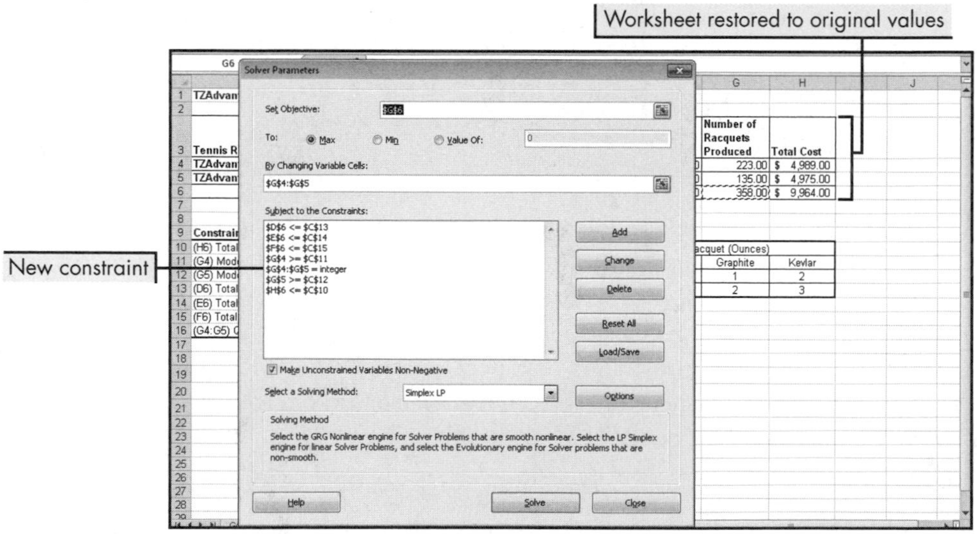

Best Practice

Requiring Integer Constraints

One of the options available when assigning constraints to a Solver model is to include the integer operator (int). You might be tempted to include this constraint automatically when a value in your Solver model is expressed as a whole number. For example, you can purchase fractional gallons of fuel, but not fractional doughnuts. Using the integer constraint significantly adds to the computational complexity of a Solver model; very large Solver models run noticeably slower when they include integer constraints because Solver uses a different solution method (called integer programming) when a model includes integer constraints. When creating a Solver model, it is a good idea to run the model without an integer constraint first, and then add it later if necessary.

Beth clicks the Solve button and Solver calculates the solution using integers in the variable cells (G4:G5), as shown in Figure 9.11. The integer constraint changes the results to produce 180 Model I racquets and 150 Model II racquets for $9,610.00.

Figure 9.11: Revised solution using integers in the variable cells

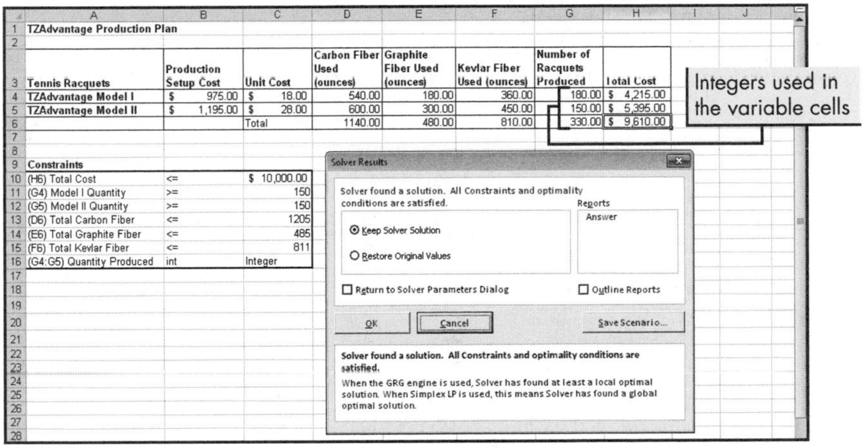

How To

Add, Change, and Delete a Constraint in Solver

1. Click the Solver button in the Analysis group on the Data tab on the Ribbon. The Solver Parameters dialog box opens and displays the existing constraints for the solution.

2. To add a constraint, click the Add button to open the Add Constraint dialog box, in which you must select a cell reference for the constraint, the comparison operator, and the cell reference or value to use. When possible, use cell references for constraints so that the Solver model changes as you update your worksheet. Click the Add button in the Add Constraint dialog box to create additional constraints, or click the OK button to return to the Solver Parameters dialog box.

3. To change an existing constraint, click the constraint that you want to change, and then click the Change button to open the Change Constraint dialog box. Change the cell reference, comparison operator, or constraint value or cell as necessary, and then click the OK button to return to the Solver Parameters dialog box.

4. To delete an existing constraint, click the constraint that you want to delete, and then click the Delete button. The constraint is deleted from the Solver Parameters dialog box.

5. Click the Solve button to find a solution, use the Solver Results dialog box to keep the Solver solution or restore the worksheet to its original values, and then click the OK button.

6. If the changes to the Solver model are too extensive, click the Reset All button in the Solver Parameters dialog box to clear all of the existing constraints from the Solver Parameters dialog box.

Beth's solution is acceptable. Before continuing, she decides to save this solution as a scenario so she can refer to it later if necessary.

Saving a Solver Solution as a Scenario

Beth wants to document her solution before making it permanent, so she saves the solution as a scenario. A **scenario** saves the result of a Solver model so that you can load it later. Scenarios are useful when you need to refer to the result of a previous Solver model so you can compare it with another model's results. Beth clicks the Save Scenario button in the Solver Results dialog box to open the Save Scenario dialog box. She enters the name "Pro-Am Production" in the Scenario Name box, as shown in Figure 9.12, and then clicks the OK button. Then she clicks the Keep Solver Solution option button and the OK button in the Solver Results dialog box to make the changes in her worksheet permanent.

Figure 9.12: Save Scenario dialog box

Beth just received an update from the plant's inventory manager; he was able to locate another five pounds (80 ounces) of Kevlar fibers that can be used without disrupting the regular production run. The additional Kevlar fibers will change the number of tournament racquets that TheZone can produce. Because Beth saved her current solution as a scenario, it will be easy for her to compare the impact of the additional Kevlar fibers with the objective of maximizing the number of racquets produced.

Beth changes cell C15 in the constraints table in the worksheet from 811 to 891 to reflect the additional 80 ounces of available Kevlar fibers. She runs Solver again to determine the impact of the additional Kevlar fibers on the number of racquets produced. The additional Kevlar fibers increase the number of Model I racquets from 180 to 185. She saves this solution as a scenario named "Pro-Am Production 891 Kevlar Ounces", and then chooses the option to keep the Solver solution. If Beth needs to view her previous solution (in which there were 811 ounces of Kevlar fiber), she can click the What-If Analysis button in the Data Tools group on the Data tab, and then click Scenario Manager to open the Scenario Manager dialog box shown in Figure 9.13. To view a previously saved scenario, Beth would select it in the Scenarios box, and then click the Show button to update the worksheet with the data saved in the scenario.

Figure 9.13: Scenario Manager dialog box

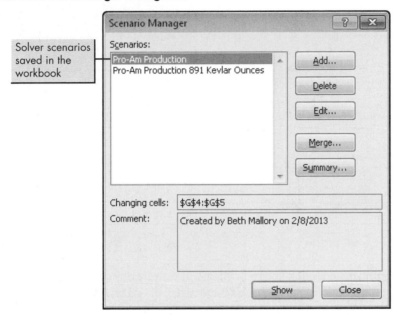

Beth has produced a feasible solution, so now she needs to document it for the product manager and the product development team.

Analyzing Data Using a Solver Report

When Solver produces an acceptable solution to the problem you identified, you can use the Keep Solver Solution option button in the Solver Results dialog box to permanently change the values in the worksheet to reflect the solution. You can also create a report that documents and describes the solution, and identifies the constraints that affected the results. Solver can produce three different reports: answer, sensitivity, and limits. Of the three reports, the answer report is the most frequently used and most useful report for business users. The sensitivity and limits reports are mostly used to analyze the mathematical results of a Solver model, and are used by more experienced users. In addition, the sensitivity and limits reports are not available when the model has integer constraints.

Beth already closed the Solver Results dialog box when she chose the option to keep the Solver solution. She opens the Solver Parameters dialog box again, clicks the Solve button, and then clicks the Answer option in the Reports box (Figure 9.11). When Beth clicks the OK button in the Solver Results dialog box, Excel creates an answer report in a new worksheet, as shown in Figure 9.14. (The new worksheet is named Answer Report 1, because this is the first answer report created in this workbook.)

Figure 9.14: Solver answer report

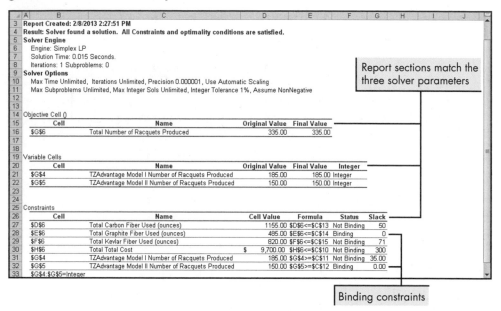

Report sections match the three solver parameters

Binding constraints

The answer report includes detailed information about the objective cell, variable cells, and constraints used in the Solver model. The Objective Cell (Max) section includes the objective cell reference and name (which is generated from the worksheet's labels), the original value in the cell, and the final value in the cell. The Variable Cells section includes the cell reference, name, original value, and final value of the variable cells in the worksheet. Notice that the names of the variable cells are the combinations of the labels in columns A and G. The Constraints section contains the cell reference, name, cell value, and formula for cells that have constraints. In addition, two more columns include the status and slack for each constraint. A **binding** status indicates that the constraint has a final value that is equal to the value of the constraint. A **not binding** status indicates that the constraint does not have a final value that is equal to the value of the constraint. You can use the status information to identify the constraint(s) that affected the solution. In Beth's Solver model, the constraint that prevented more racquets from being produced is the fact that the graphite fibers were completely used, as indicated by the binding status for this constraint. If Beth can add more graphite fibers to the product mix, she might be able to produce more tennis racquets. When a constraint is binding, the slack column is set to 0 because the constraint equals the final value. When the status is not binding, the slack column indicates the difference between the final value and the constraint.

Steps To Success: Level 1

John Pinot is the marketing manager who is heading up the magazine promotion for the TZAdvantage tennis racquets. John already worked with a graphic artist and copy editor to produce the full-page color ad for the campaign. John will use the same ad in each of five magazines that he has selected as representing the primary target audience. John prepared a spreadsheet that includes each magazine's circulation (the number of distributed copies) and ad cost per issue (the cost of placing one full-page ad in one issue of the magazine). John's spreadsheet also indicates how many issues each magazine produces yearly: monthly magazines produce 12 issues and bimonthly magazines produce six issues.

John asks you to determine the best way to place ads in each magazine to achieve his primary goal of reaching at least 10 million readers in one year while minimizing the total cost. You need to calculate the total audience reached for each magazine (circulation multiplied by the number of issues in which the ads are placed) and the total cost (the ad cost per issue multiplied by the number of issues in which the ad appears) for running the specified number of ads in each magazine. John's final requirement is that you must place the ad in at least two issues of each magazine during the promotion.

Complete the following:

1. Open the **Magazine.xlsx** workbook from the Chapter 9 folder, and then save it as **MagazineAds.xlsx**.

2. Insert the appropriate formulas in cells F4:F8 to calculate the audience (circulation multiplied by the ad placement) for each magazine.

3. Insert the appropriate formulas in cells G4:G8 to calculate the total cost (ad cost per issue multiplied by the ad placement) for running the specified number of ads in each magazine.

4. Insert formulas in cells E9, F9, and G9 to calculate the total number of issues in which the ad will appear (ad placement), the total audience, and the total cost of the magazine ad campaign.

5. In the constraints table, specify the constraints that John has provided and any other necessary constraints. After determining the objective cell, the variable cells, and the constraints, use Solver to specify your inputs.

6. Use Solver to calculate your solution and then evaluate your solution. If necessary, add, change, or delete constraints and rerun Solver to produce a feasible solution.

7. Save your solution as a scenario named **Minimize Cost**, and then produce an answer report.

8. John just gave you some new information to include in your solution. He has replaced Magazine 3 with a magazine that has a bimonthly circulation, and he wants you to recalculate the promotion with this new information. Make the appropriate changes to your Solver model, use Solver to calculate a new solution, save your solution as a scenario named **Reduced Issues**, and then produce an answer report.

9. John wants the gross audience for the entire promotion to be more than 14 million readers. Without changing any of the constraints in your Solver model, explain your reasoning as to why the magazine promotion can or cannot support a gross audience of more than 14 million readers. If you determine that the promotion cannot support a total audience of this size, which constraint(s) will impede or bind the goal of increasing the gross audience, and why?

10. Save and close the MagazineAds.xlsx workbook.

LEVEL 2
Enhancing the Production Plan with Solver

Adding Time Variables to the Production Plan

Now that Beth has determined the best use of inventory and budgetary resources for producing the tournament racquets for the Pro-Am promotion, she turns her attention to determining how this special order of racquets will fit into the production schedule at the plants that will manufacture the TZAdvantage racquets that TheZone will send to its distributors and then to retailers for sale.

Three plants, located in Seattle, Indianapolis, and Boston, will produce the regular racquets in the normal production run. After talking with the Indianapolis plant manager, Bob Jensen, Beth learns that the Indianapolis plant can schedule production time this month to produce the tournament racquets. Producing each racquet requires two production steps—a molding operation and a finishing operation. Bob can schedule 70 hours of molding time and 100 hours of finishing time for the production of the tournament racquets. Each racquet requires a specific amount of molding time to cast the outer frame of the racquet, and a specific amount of finishing time to apply the grip and to string the racquet. For the TZAdvantage Model I racquet, the molding time is 12 minutes (0.20 hours) per racquet and the finishing time is also 12 minutes (0.20 hours) per racquet. For the TZAdvantage Model II racquet, the molding time is 12 minutes (0.20 hours) and the finishing time is 30 minutes (0.50 hours). Beth needs to change her production plan to include the additional constraints (available molding and finishing times) to determine the production quantity for both racquets that maximizes the number of racquets produced while staying within the established time limits as well as inventory and budget constraints.

Adding Formulas and Constraints to the Solver Model

Without any limits or constraints on the production run, the number of Model I and Model II racquets could be any positive value. However, Beth needs to limit the number of racquets produced based on the total budget available, the amount of raw materials available, and the molding and finishing times available at the Indianapolis plant. Beth's previous Solver model includes constraints that restrict the total cost to $10,000 and restrict the number of racquets produced based on the amount of carbon, graphite, and Kevlar fibers available to produce the racquets. Now, she needs to add the additional constraints to her worksheet so that the total molding time (70 hours) and finishing time (100 hours) available to produce the racquets are incorporated into the Solver model. Beth creates a copy of the Maximize Racquets worksheet, renames the copy as "Maximize Racquets and Times", and then includes the new constraints in the constraints table and in the Solver model. She adds two new columns to the worksheet to calculate the molding time and finishing time per racquet, and adds formulas to cells G6 and H6 to calculate the total molding and finishing times for all racquets. Beth's worksheet appears in Figure 9.15.

Figure 9.15: New constraints added to the worksheet

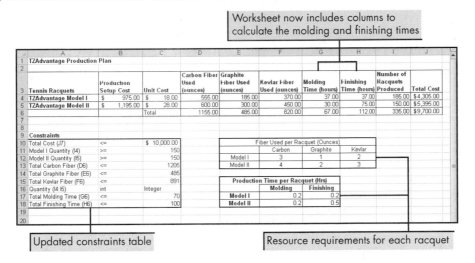

Worksheet now includes columns to calculate the molding and finishing times

Updated constraints table

Resource requirements for each racquet

Beth opens the Solver Parameters dialog box and adds the two new constraints (molding time and finishing time) using the Add Constraint dialog box. Because she has added more decision variables to the Solver model, she decides to test her worksheet using simple values before running Solver to ensure that her formulas and their expected results are correct. She clicks the Close button to close the Solver Parameters dialog box, and then enters the value 1 in cells I4 and I5 to simulate the production of one racquet for each model. Beth's worksheet appears in Figure 9.16.

Beth carefully checks the results in each cell to ensure that the formulas return the correct values. If the formulas do not return the correct values, you can fix the errors before running Solver. If the Solver model contains errors in formulas or cell references, Solver might not be able to generate a feasible solution—or worse, Solver might generate an incorrect solution.

Figure 9.16: Worksheet with test values

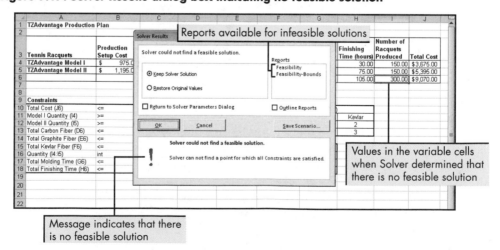

	A	B	C	D	E	F	G	H	I	J
1	TZAdvantage Production Plan									
2										
3	Tennis Racquets	Production Setup Cost	Unit Cost	Carbon Fiber Used (ounces)	Graphite Fiber Used (ounces)	Kevlar Fiber Used (ounces)	Molding Time (hours)	Finishing Time (hours)	Number of Racquets Produced	Total Cost
4	TZAdvantage Model I	$ 975.00	$ 18.00	3.00	1.00	2.00	0.20	0.20	1.00	$ 993.00
5	TZAdvantage Model II	$ 1,195.00	$ 28.00	4.00	2.00	3.00	0.20	0.50	1.00	$1,223.00
6			Total	7.00	3.00	5.00	0.40	0.70	2.00	$2,216.00
7										
8										
9	Constraints									
10	Total Cost (J6)	<=	$ 10,000.00			Fiber Used per Racquet (Ounces)				
11	Model I Quantity (I4)	>=	150				Carbon	Graphite	Kevlar	
12	Model II Quantity (I5)	>=	150		Model I	3	1	2		
13	Total Carbon Fiber (D6)	<=	1205		Model II	4	2	3		
14	Total Graphite Fiber (E6)	<=	485							
15	Total Kevlar Fiber (F6)	<=	891			Production Time per Racquet (Hrs)				
16	Quantity (I4:I5)	int	Integer				Molding	Finishing		
17	Total Molding Time (G6)	<=	70		Model I	0.2	0.2			
18	Total Finishing Time (H6)	<=	100		Model II	0.2	0.5			
19										
20										

Produce one Model I racquet

Produce one Model II racquet

Beth's worksheet is working correctly, so now she is ready to use Solver to find the combination of Model I and Model II production quantities that maximize the total number of racquets produced while staying within the resource limits defined by the constraints. She opens the Solver Parameters dialog box and clicks the Solve button to generate a solution. The Solver Results dialog box indicates that Solver could not find a feasible solution. Because the Solver model includes integer constraints, the Solve Without Integer Constraints option is provided. Beth selects this option and clicks the OK button to rerun the model, ignoring the integer constraints. The Solver Results dialog box, shown in Figure 9.17, still indicates that Solver could not find a feasible solution. Because Solver could not find a feasible solution, your options now are to produce either a Feasibility Report or a Feasibility-Bounds Report. Beth selects the Feasibility Report and chooses the option to keep the Solver solution so she can examine the worksheet from the point at which Solver stopped attempting to find a solution.

Figure 9.17: Solver Results dialog box indicating no feasible solution

Reports available for infeasible solutions

Solver Results

Solver could not find a feasible solution.

Reports
- Feasibility
- Feasibility-Bounds

⦿ Keep Solver Solution

○ Restore Original Values

☐ Return to Solver Parameters Dialog   ☐ Outline Reports

OK   Cancel   Save Scenario...

Solver could not find a feasible solution.

Solver can not find a point for which all Constraints are satisfied.

Values in the variable cells when Solver determined that there is no feasible solution

Message indicates that there is no feasible solution

The Feasibility Report, shown in Figure 9.18, indicates that the total finishing time in cell H6 had a value of 105. The Slack value of –5 indicates that the cell requires five more units over the limit set by the constraint of 100 units in cell C18. As Beth compares the Feasibility Report with the values in the infeasible Solver solution, she notices that when Solver stopped working, the total finishing time in cell H6 (105 hours) exceeds the limit set by the constraint (100 hours). The number of racquets in cells I4:I5 are both at the specified minimum value of 150 racquets, the fiber inventories are all below the specified limits, and the total cost is below the $10,000 limit. Beth interprets these results and determines that the requirement to produce at least 150 of each racquet type will require more finishing time than is available.

Figure 9.18: Solver Results Feasibility Report

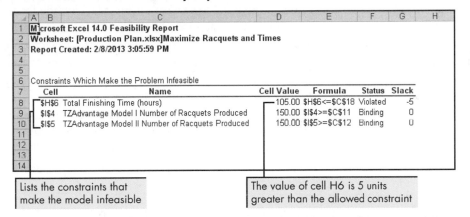

Lists the constraints that make the model infeasible

The value of cell H6 is 5 units greater than the allowed constraint

Troubleshooting an Infeasible Solution

Constraints are usually the source of the problem when Solver cannot find a feasible solution. Constraints are the boundaries that define the feasible solution area. An **infeasible solution** results when Solver cannot produce a combination of decision variables that satisfies all of the constraints. When this situation occurs, Solver displays a message to tell you that it could not find a feasible solution. In this case, you should keep the Solver solution, select the Feasibility Report option, and then examine the Solver model and the constraints to determine the reason for the infeasible solution.

How To

Troubleshoot an Infeasible Solution

1. Correct any data-entry errors in the Solver Parameters dialog box. Compare the constraints listed in the Solver Parameters dialog box with the constraints table you created in your worksheet. Verify that your cell references are correct and that you selected the correct operators.
2. Review the Feasibility Report for constraints with a violated status. Try loosening these constraint values by the slack value for each suspected problem. Loosening a criterion with a greater than or equal to operator decreases values. Loosening a criterion with a less than or equal to operator increases values. Loosening the criteria values expands the solution area.

3. Review the constraints to see if a policy constraint is the cause of the infeasibility. Policy constraints with minimum or maximum limits are a good place to look for causes of infeasibility.

After you have identified the criteria that prevent the solution from being feasible, you have two choices: You can do nothing and declare that there is no solution to the problem, or you can adjust the constraints to create a feasible solution. In the case of a policy constraint, you can attempt to change the constraint. In the case of a physical constraint, you might not have many options.

Troubleshooting an Unbounded Solution

If you try to solve a problem in which there are no constraints or too few constraints, the solution is unbounded. An **unbounded solution** occurs in situations in which the feasible solution is unrestrained or unlimited on some dimension. In the case of a maximization problem, Solver can increase the values in the variable cells and drive the objective cell higher. By default, Solver attempts to solve a problem 100 times before it stops working and determines that there is no feasible solution. (To change the number of times Solver attempts to solve a problem, click the Options button in the Solver Parameters dialog box, change the value in the Iterations box, and then click the OK button.) If Solver attempts the maximum number of iterations without the objective cell converging to an answer, the assumption is that the solution is unbounded. In this case, the Solver Results dialog box indicates that the Objective cell values do not converge, as shown in Figure 9.19. In this case, you must add constraints to create a feasible solution.

Figure 9.19: Solver Results dialog box indicating an unbounded solution

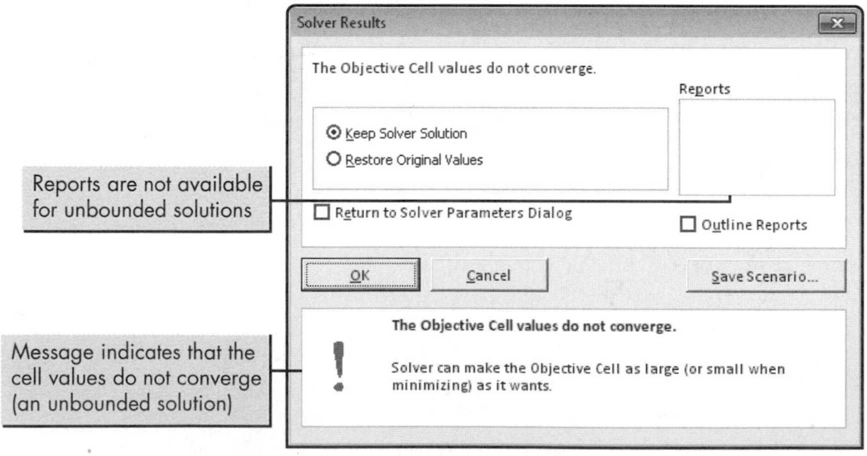

Identifying a Feasible Solution

Beth clicks the OK button in the Solver Results dialog box to keep the values in the worksheet at the point that Solver stopped working. She inserts some sample values in the worksheet to calculate the production cost and how many resources are used. For example, producing 200 Model I racquets and 100 Model II racquets costs $8,570 and consumes 60 hours of molding time and 90 hours of finishing time. This situation, which is identified as Sample 1 in Table 9.1, leaves $1,430 of the budget, 10 hours of available molding time, and 10 hours of available finishing time unused. These unused resources are called slack. The optimal solution maximizes the number of racquets produced while staying within the limits of the constraints. If all of the constraints, which represent the availability of resources, have slack values, the solution isn't the optimal solution that maximizes the available resources.

Beth inserts some more values in the worksheet's variable cells to determine the impact on the molding and finishing times. Her second sample, identified as Sample 2 in Table 9.1, produces 500 Model I and 250 Model II racquets. This solution is significantly outside the feasible solution area because its cost is $8,170 above the budget, and it requires an additional 80 hours of molding time and 125 hours of finishing time. The third sample, which shows that Solver stopped working, produces 150 racquets each for Model I and Model II racquets. This solution has 10 hours of slack in the total molding time, but uses five additional hours of finishing time, which consumes more resources than are available. The constraint that limits the finishing time to 100 hours is the one that prohibited Solver from finding a feasible solution.

Table 9.1: Three sample production runs of the tournament racquets

	Model I	Model II	Total	Constraint	Slack
Sample 1					
Number Produced	200	100			
Production Cost	$18.00	$28.00	$8570.00	$10,000.00	$1430.00
Molding Time	0.20	0.20	60.00	70.00	10.00
Finishing Time	0.20	0.50	90.00	100.00	10.00
Sample 2					
Number Produced	500	250			
Production Cost	$18.00	28.00	18,170.00	$10,000.00	($8170.00)
Molding Time	0.20	0.20	150.00	70.00	(80.00)
Finishing Time	0.20	0.50	225.00	100.00	(125.00)
Sample 3					
Number Produced	150	150			
Production Cost	$18.00	$28.00	$9070.00	$10,000.00	$930.00
Molding Time	0.20	0.20	60.00	70.00	10.00
Finishing Time	0.20	0.50	105.00	100.00	(5.00)

9

Level 2

Visualizing the Constraints in a Solver Model

When there are two variable values in an optimization model, you can use graphs to better illustrate what makes a solution feasible. You can use a two-dimensional X Y Scatter chart to illustrate how the molding and finishing time constraints affect the number of racquets that can be produced. For the Model I and Model II racquets, each racquet requires 0.20 hours of molding time, and the total molding time for all racquets cannot exceed 70 hours. The mathematical model of the resulting constraint for molding time is as follows:

```
Required molding time =
(0.20 * (Model I quantity)) + (0.20 * (Model II quantity))
```

The available molding time for the tournament racquets is 70 hours, so you can write the constraint as the following mathematical formula:

```
0.20 * Q1 + 0.20*Q2 <= 70
```

The chart shown in Figure 9.20 shows Model I racquets on the y-axis and Model II racquets on the x-axis. If you produce 350 Model I racquets and 0 Model II racquets (350, 0), you will consume exactly 70 hours of molding time. Because the Model II racquet requires the same amount of molding time, producing 0 Model I racquets and 350 Model II racquets (0, 350) also consumes exactly 70 hours of molding time. When you plot these situations in a line chart, the shaded area below the line represents all combinations of the number of Model I racquets (Q1) and Model II racquets (Q2) that consume less than 70 hours of molding time. The line represents all combinations of Model I and Model II racquets that consume exactly 70 hours of molding time.

Figure 9.20: Visual representation of the molding time constraint

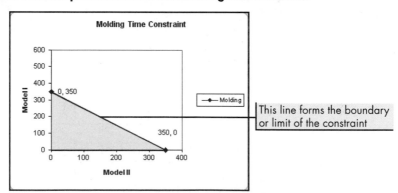

In Figure 9.20, the points on the line represent the boundary of the constraint; that is, these combinations of producing Model I and Model II racquets use the full capacity of the molding time (70 hours total). These two points are calculated by setting the production quantity of Model I to 0 and calculating the number of Model II units that could be produced, and then setting the production quantity of Model II to 0 and calculating the number of Model I units that could be produced. Any quantities outside the shaded area will require more resources than are available in the Molding Department, resulting in an infeasible solution with the given constraints.

In addition to the molding time, each Model I racquet requires 0.20 hours of finishing time and each Model II racquet requires 0.50 hours of finishing time. The mathematical model of the resulting constraint for finishing time is:

<pre>
            Required finishing time =
 (0.20 * (Model I quantity)) + (0.50 * (Model II quantity))
</pre>

The available finishing time for the tournament racquets is 100 hours, so you can write the constraint as the following mathematical formula:

<pre>
        0.20 * Q1 + 0.50*Q2 <= 100
</pre>

Producing 0 Model I racquets and 200 Model II racquets (0, 500) consumes exactly 100 hours of finishing time; producing 500 Model I racquets and 0 Model II racquets (200, 0) also consumes exactly 100 hours of finishing time. Every combination of Model I (Q1) and Model II (Q2) racquets on the line shown in Figure 9.21 consumes exactly 100 hours of finishing time. The shaded area below the line represents all the combinations of the number of Model I racquets and Model II racquets that consume fewer than 100 hours of finishing time. All points on the line represent the boundary of the constraint and use the full capacity of the finishing time (100 hours). Any quantities outside the shaded area will require more resources than are available in the Finishing Department, resulting in an infeasible solution with the given constraints.

Figure 9.21: Visual representation of the finishing time constraint

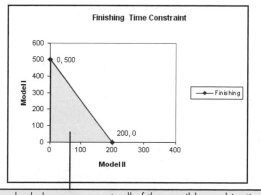

Combining the molding and finishing time constraints results in the line chart shown in Figure 9.22. The intersection of the line for all possible combinations of racquets that use exactly 70 hours of molding time with the line for all possible combinations of racquets that use exactly 100 hours of finishing time defines the optimal solution to the problem. The shaded area below the intersection of these two lines represents the feasible solution area; any area outside the intersection of these two lines represents an infeasible solution area.

Figure 9.22: Visual representation of three possible solutions

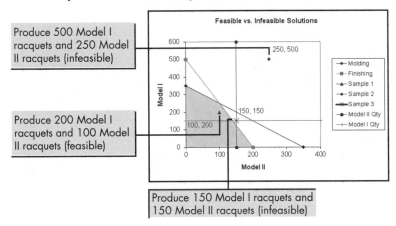

TheZone set the minimum production of Model I and Model II racquets to 150 each. As shown in Figure 9.22, the point at which 150 racquets of each model are produced is outside the feasible solution area. There is no feasible solution area that meets all the constraints of the problem, and this is why Solver could not find a solution. In this case, Beth does not have an error in her worksheet or in her Solver model—she just created a problem that has no feasible solution. No combination of variable cells can satisfy all the constraints in her Solver model. At this point, Beth must identify the constraints that caused the infeasibility and look for ways to loosen the constraints to create a feasible solution. Solver stopped at 150 racquets for each model because of the constraint requiring the production of a minimum of 150 racquets for each model. The chart clearly shows that the solution is infeasible because producing at least 150 Model I and 150 Model II racquets is outside the feasible solution area.

Finding an Optimal Solution

At this point, Beth has two options. She can talk with the product manager about reducing the constraint of producing a minimum number of racquets for each model, or she can ask the Indianapolis plant manager to increase the available molding and finishing times to make the minimum number of racquets. Unless one of these constraints is loosened, there is no feasible solution to this problem.

Beth discussed the results of her analysis with both the product manager and the plant manager. The plant manager was not able to allocate any more finishing time to the production of the tournament racquets without affecting the production of the regular racquets, so increasing the production time in the plant is not an option. However, Nick was willing to change the constraint of producing 150 racquets for each model. He asks Beth to produce at least 150 of the TZAdvantage Model II racquets and use the remainder of the resources to produce as many Model I racquets as possible. In effect, this means the constraint on the Model I racquet is no longer needed.

Beth changes her Solver model to remove the constraint. She was tempted to modify the constraint to ensure the company produces 0 or more Model I racquets (to prevent Solver from producing a negative number of racquets). She remembered that this is handled by the default check in the Make Unconstrained Variables Non-Negative check box under the list of constraints in the Solver Parameters dialog box. She runs Solver again, and this time Solver finds an optimal solution that maximizes the total number of racquets produced while satisfying all of the constraints. Beth creates the answer report shown in Figure 9.23 to document her solution. The answer report shows that the binding constraints were the number of hours of finishing time available in the Indianapolis plant and the constraint to create at least 150 of the Model II racquets. Beth can use the answer report to identify the constraints that prevented the production of additional racquets by examining the slack status for each constraint.

Figure 9.23: Answer report for the new solution

Solver Engine
Engine: Simplex LP
Solution Time: 0.016 Seconds.
Iterations: 1 Subproblems: 0
Solver Options
Max Time 100 sec, Iterations 100, Precision 0.000001
Max Subproblems Unlimited, Max Integer Sols Unlimited, Integer Tolerance 5%, Assume NonNegative

Objective Cell (Max)

Cell	Name	Original Value	Final Value
$I$6	Total Number of Racquets Produced	275.00	275.00

Variable Cells

Cell	Name	Original Value	Final Value	Integer
$I$4	TZAdvantage Model I Number of Racquets Produced	125.00	125.00	Integer
$I$5	TZAdvantage Model II Number of Racquets Produced	150.00	150.00	Integer

Constraints

Cell	Name	Cell Value	Formula	Status	Slack
$F$6	Total Kevlar Fiber Used (ounces)	700.00	$F$6<=$C$15	Not Binding	191
$E$6	Total Graphite Fiber Used (ounces)	425.00	$E$6<=$C$14	Not Binding	60
$D$6	Total Carbon Fiber Used (ounces)	975.00	$D$6<=$C$13	Not Binding	230
$G$6	Total Molding Time (hours)	55.00	$G$6<=$C$17	Not Binding	15
$H$6	Total Finishing Time (hours)	100.00	$H$6<=$C$18	Binding	0
$J$6	Total Total Cost	$ 8,620.00	$J$6<=$C$10	Not Binding	1380
$I$5	TZAdvantage Model II Number of Racquets Produced	150.00	$I$5>=$C$12	Binding	0.00
$I$4:$I$5=Integer					

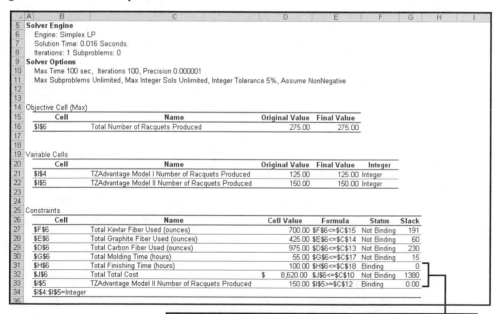

The minimum requirement for Model II racquets and the finishing time are the binding constraints in the case

Steps To Success: Level 2

The Marketing Department has allocated a $225,000 budget for the radio promotion that it has planned as part of the product launch for TZAdvantage. The Marketing Department has provided you with a worksheet that shows the cost estimates for producing and placing radio ads with the three major radio networks that the marketing manager plans to use. The one-time cost of each ad appears in the Production Cost column. The AQH Persons column identifies the average number of people listening to each network during any 15 minutes. The Cost per Ad column indicates the cost of running an ad once on each network. The Number of Ads column identifies the number of times that the ad will run on the network, and the Total Cost column shows the cost of running the specified number of ads. The Gross Impressions column is the product of multiplying the AQH Persons value by the Number of Ads value, and indicates the potential reach of the ad. Gross impressions represent the number of times an ad is heard during a promotion without regard to duplication. Your goal is to maximize the number of gross impressions by varying the number of ads purchased from each radio network. The number of ads you can purchase from each network is limited by the following requirements:

- Do not exceed the $225,000 budget.
- Achieve at least 15,000,000 gross impressions.
- Purchase at least 50 ads from each network.
- There are no more than 100 ads available on each network.

Complete the following:

1. Open the **Radio.xlsx** workbook from the Chapter 9 folder, and then save it as **RadioAds.xlsx**.

2. Enter the appropriate formulas in the Radio worksheet to calculate the gross impressions for each radio network.

3. Enter the appropriate formulas to calculate the total cost for running the specified number of ads on each network.

4. Insert formulas in cells E7, F7, and G7 to calculate the total number of ads in the campaign, the total gross impressions, and the total cost for the radio campaign.

5. Insert formulas in cells H4:H6 to calculate the percentage of ads placed on each network.

6. Create a constraints table that identifies the constraints that you must use in your solution. After determining the objective cell, the variable cells, and the constraints, use the Solver Parameters dialog box to specify your inputs.

7. Use Solver to calculate your solution and then evaluate your solution. If necessary, add, change, or delete constraints and rerun Solver to produce a feasible solution. Balance the need to stay at or under the budget with the desire to reach a level of at least 15,000,000 gross impressions.

8. Produce an answer report for your solution.

9. The marketing manager just gave you some new information about the radio promotion. The advertising managers from two of the three radio networks have limited the number of units (advertising spots) available to no more than 40 ads per client for Radio Network 2 and no more than 50 ads per client for Radio Network 3 during the time in which TheZone wants to run its promotion. The manager raised the limit on Radio Network 1 ads to no more than 125. Save your first Solver model as a scenario named **50 Ads per Network**, and then change your Solver model and find a new solution that limits the number of ads for the second and third networks accordingly. Save the scenario as **Limited Ads** and keep your Solver solution.

10. Which constraint(s) are binding? Explain your findings, and then recommend some changes that might create a better solution.

11. Save and close the RadioAds.xlsx workbook.

LEVEL 3
Managing Transportation Problems with Solver

Developing a Distribution Plan Using Solver

With the successful completion of the Pro-Am tournament, Beth can turn her attention to helping the plant managers find the best way to distribute the TZAdvantage racquets that they have already produced and packaged for distribution to retailers across the country. Every business that produces goods or relies on the transportation of goods must determine the best way to ship those goods in the most efficient way to move them from a source to a destination to meet some demand. When a transportation problem involves multiple shipping costs between different sources and destinations, supply and demand issues, and constraints that limit how to ship those goods, you can use Solver to determine the most efficient and cost-effective way to ship those goods. Because transportation problems involve many variables, you must set up the worksheet that contains the data and the Solver model very carefully.

Beth needs to create a distribution plan for transporting the regular shipments of TZAdvantage racquets between the plants where they are produced and the distribution centers that send them to retailers. As is the case with most transportation problems, Beth must balance supply and demand at a minimum cost, with contingencies for situations in which the demand for the racquets is greater than the supply and vice versa. TheZone has three manufacturing plants that are located in Seattle, Indianapolis, and Boston. The racquets are sent from these plants to eight distribution centers that are located in Atlanta, Baltimore, Boise, Chicago, Dallas, Denver, New York, and San Diego. After arriving at the distribution centers, the racquets are shipped to retailers for sale to the public.

Because of TheZone's successful Pro-Am tournament and promotional campaigns, the initial demand for the TZAdvantage racquets from retailers across the country has been very high. To reduce transportation costs, TheZone normally ships goods from the plants to the closest distribution centers, which then ship the goods to retailers in the area. Because demand is high, management at TheZone has decided to ship the TZAdvantage racquets from any of the plants to meet demand at the distribution centers, while still attempting to minimize shipping costs. In this situation, management wants to ship the racquets from any plant to any distribution center to fill orders from retailers. Although this new policy might result in higher shipping costs, TheZone will be able to fulfill orders to retailers and ensure a successful product launch of TZAdvantage.

Setting Up a Worksheet for the Distribution Plan

Beth's first task is to collect information about the number of cases of TZAdvantage racquets that are ready to ship from the plants in Seattle, Indianapolis, and Boston to the eight distribution centers. After talking with the plant managers, she learns that the Seattle plant is ready to ship 500 cases, the Indianapolis plant is ready to ship 475 cases, and the Boston plant is ready to ship 325 cases. Each case holds 50 tennis racquets that have been packaged for the retail market.

Beth also identified the demand for racquets at each distribution center and the cost to ship one case from each plant to each of the eight distribution centers. These decision variables are shown in Table 9.2.

Table 9.2: Demand and shipping costs for TZAdvantage racquets

Distribution Center	Demand (Cases)	Shipping Costs (per Case)		
		Seattle	Indianapolis	Boston
Atlanta	125	$108.95	$21.50	$27.15
Baltimore	187	$116.45	$25.40	$47.90
Boise	64	$20.25	$78.15	$65.55
Dallas	313	$84.00	$38.40	$13.90
Denver	50	$50.85	$50.00	$33.95
Chicago	163	$86.65	$7.95	$26.20
New York	250	$120.20	$32.15	$55.70
San Diego	125	$53.10	$89.30	$67.95

Beth has identified the availability of the racquets, the demand for the racquets, and the costs of sending the racquets to the distribution centers. TheZone can ship only products that are in stock at the plants, and the shipments must meet the demand at each distribution center. Beth creates the worksheet shown in Figure 9.24 with the plants listed in columns and the distribution centers listed in rows. The cost of shipping one case to a particular distribution center is represented by the value at the intersection of the distribution center's row and the plant's column. For example, it costs $108.95 to ship one case from the Seattle plant to the Atlanta distribution center (cell C5). Beth needs to minimize the total shipping costs (in the objective cell, J13) that are calculated using the number of cases shipped (in the variable cells, F5:H12), so she creates her worksheet to calculate both the shipping costs and how many cases are shipped to each distribution center. She also tracks the remaining inventory at each plant in cells F16:I16.

Figure 9.24: Distribution plan worksheet for TZAdvantage racquets

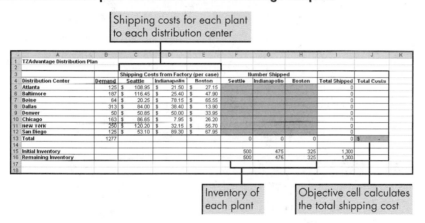

Because each of the three plants can ship cases to any of the eight distribution centers, 24 possible combinations of plants and distribution centers exist. Arranging the shipping costs and variable cells into two identical ranges with the same pattern of cells is the most effective way to set up this model. The shipping costs per case are located in the range C5:E12, and the numbers of cases shipped are in the range F5:H12. Beth needs to compute the cost of shipping one case from each plant to each distribution center. The objective function uses the shipping costs, and N represents the number of cases shipped. Multiplying the number of cases (N) by the shipping costs represents the total cost (Z) of shipments on a particular route between a plant and a distribution center as follows:

$$
\begin{aligned}
\text{Minimize } Z = \\
\$108.95 * N1 + \$116.45 * N2 + \$20.25 * N3 + \$84.00 * N4 + \$50.85 * N5 \\
+ \$86.65 * N6 + \$120.20 * N7 + \$53.10 * N8 + \$21.50 * N9 + \$25.40 * N10 \\
+ \$78.15 * N11 + \$38.40 * N12 + \$50.00 * N13 + \$7.95 * N14 + \$32.15 * N15 \\
+ \$89.30 * N16 + \$27.15 * N17 + \$47.90 * N18 + \$65.55 * N19 + \$13.90 * N20 \\
+ \$33.95 * N21 + \$26.20 * N22 + \$55.70 * N23 + \$67.95 * N24
\end{aligned}
$$

Beth would need to enter this objective function in the objective cell, replace the shipping costs with cell references, and replace the N values with the number of cases shipped. Instead of entering this complicated formula, Beth decides to use the SUMPRODUCT function, which sums a series of products (the result of a multiplication task) in ranges of identical sizes, called **arrays,** that are arranged in the same orientation to each other in a worksheet. Beth can use the SUMPRODUCT function (discussed in Chapter 8) to multiply the values according to their positions in both ranges and then add the results to obtain the total shipping cost. Beth already set up her worksheet correctly so that the arrays are the same size, shape, and orientation. She adds the following SUMPRODUCT function to cell J5 to compute the total shipping costs for the number of cases shipped (F5:H5) from each of the three plants (C5:E5) to the distribution center in Atlanta:

`=SUMPRODUCT(C5:E5,F5:H5)`

To check her worksheet and ensure that this formula is correct, Beth enters "2" in each cell in range F5:H5 to represent the cost of shipping two cases from each plant in Seattle, Indianapolis, and Boston to the distribution center in Atlanta, as shown in Figure 9.25.

Figure 9.25: Worksheet with test values for the SUMPRODUCT function

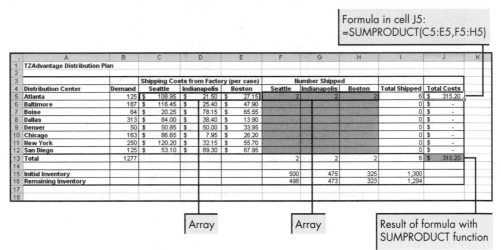

The SUMPRODUCT function in cell J5 produces the result as follows:

```
Total Cost (J5) = (C5 * F5) + (D5 * G5) + (E5 * H5)
Total Cost = ($108.95 * 2) + ($21.50 * 2) + ($27.15 * 2)
Total Cost = $315.20
```

Beth's worksheet also includes formulas in cells F16:H16 to compute the remaining inventory at each plant as the cases are shipped to the distribution centers. If two cases are shipped from each plant, 498 cases will remain in Seattle (F16), 473 cases will remain in Indianapolis (G16), and 323 cases will remain in Boston (H16). Beth adds these formulas to calculate the remaining inventories at the three plants to ensure that the demand at each distribution center is met and to prevent the plants from shipping more cases than they have in stock.

Beth copies the SUMPRODUCT function in cell J5 into cells J6:J12 and clears her test values from cells F5:H5. Now, she is ready to set up the Solver model to determine the best way to ship products from the plants and to meet the demand at each distribution center. Beth creates a constraints table in her worksheet to manage the constraints for this problem. She sets up her Solver model as follows:

- Cell J13 (the objective cell) totals the shipping costs for all distribution centers. Beth minimizes the objective cell to find the lowest cost for meeting the demand.
- The cells in the range F5:H12 (the variable cells) contain the number of cases shipped from each plant to the distribution centers. Because the plants cannot ship partial cases or negative quantities, Beth adds constraints so that values in the variable cells must be integers and must be greater than or equal to 0.
- The total number of cases shipped to each distribution center must be greater than or equal to the demand at each distribution center. The layout that Beth has created allows her to enter multiple constraints at once. Selecting the range of shipments to each distribution center in cells I5:I12 and then the range of demand values in cells B5:B12 is much easier than selecting individual cells.

Beth enters the constraints into the Solver model using the information in her constraints table. She clicks the Solve button in the Solver Parameters dialog box, and the Solver Results dialog box indicates that Solver found a solution, as shown in Figure 9.26.

Figure 9.26: Evaluating a feasible solution that doesn't work

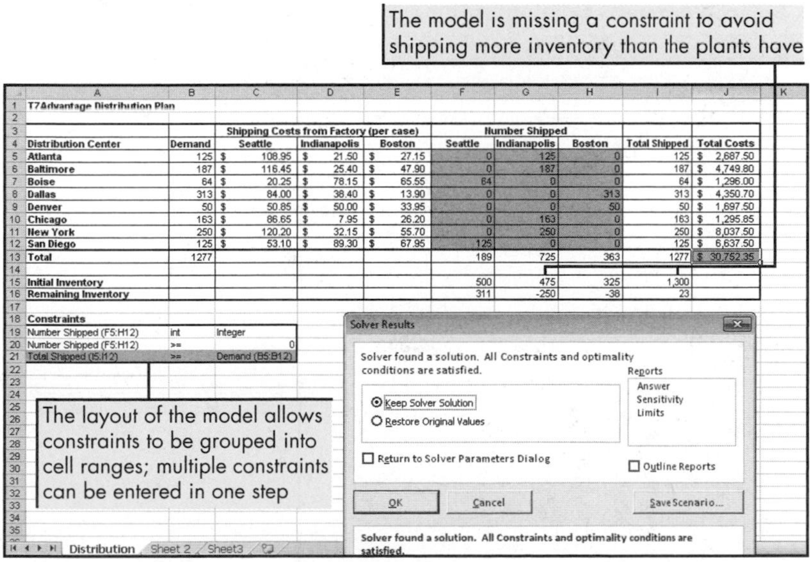

The model is missing a constraint to avoid shipping more inventory than the plants have

The layout of the model allows constraints to be grouped into cell ranges; multiple constraints can be entered in one step

Beth's Solver solution fulfills the demand for cases at each distribution center and the total number of cases shipped. However, as Beth examines the number of cases remaining in inventory at the three plants, she notices that her solution has created a negative inventory at the Indianapolis and Boston plants. Beth realizes that she omitted a constraint to ensure that the number of cases shipped from each plant does not exceed the initial inventory at each plant.

Beth also needs to change the demand value for the San Diego distribution center, which just increased its request from 125 to 175 cases. Before proceeding, Beth wants to save her Solver model so she can return to it later, if necessary.

Saving a Solver Model

Before changing the Solver parameters to troubleshoot a problem in a Solver model, you might want to save it as a baseline so you can return to it later if necessary. You can copy the worksheet and solution to a new worksheet for troubleshooting, which gives you the freedom to change anything necessary to locate the problem without destroying the existing Solver model. A better option is to save the worksheet and the Solver model in a blank section of the worksheet. Saving a Solver model is different from saving a Solver scenario, which saves only the result of a Solver model. Saving a Solver model saves the Solver parameters that were used in the Solver model so you can load them later if necessary.

Beth clicks the OK button in the Solver Results dialog box, and then she zooms the worksheet to 80% of its original size so she can view a blank range of cells to the right of her data. She selects cell L3, a cell in an empty column of her worksheet. She clicks Solver in the Analysis group on the Data tab, and then clicks the Load/Save button in the Solver Parameters dialog box shown in Figure 9.27.

Figure 9.27: Solver Parameters dialog box

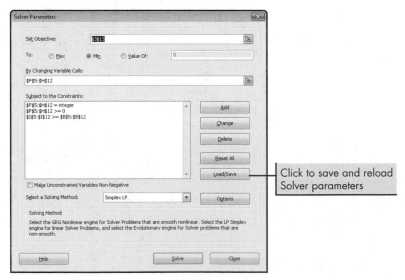

Beth clicks the Load/Save button and opens the Load/Save Model dialog box. The input box displays the currently selected cell as shown in Figure 9.28. The dialog box also indicates how many cells are required to save a particular Solver model. The variation is based on the number of constraints in the model.

Figure 9.28: Load/Save Model dialog box

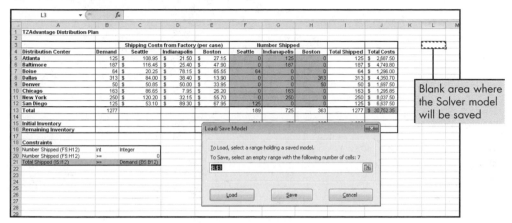

For this example, Beth needs to save the model in a blank area of the worksheet with a column of seven empty cells available to contain the model information. She confirms that cell L3 has six empty cells below it and clicks the Save button. The cells in the range L3:L9 now contain the saved Solver model, as shown in Figure 9.29.

Figure 9.29: Solver model saved to cells L3:L9

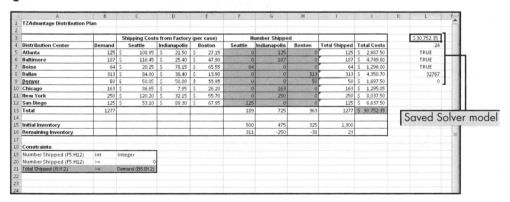

The MIN function in cell L3 shows that the value in the objective cell (J13) is being minimized. Cell L4 contains a count function of the Solver model's variable cells. The values in the range L5:L7 indicate the values for the constraints. A value of TRUE indicates a satisfied constraint; a value of FALSE indicates a constraint that could not be satisfied. The last two cells (L8 and L9) store the option settings for this Solver model.

Save and Load a Solver Model

Save a Solver Model

1. To save a Solver model, click the Solver button in the Analysis group on the Data tab on the Ribbon. The Solver Parameters dialog box opens.
2. Click the Load/Save button in the Solver Parameters dialog box. The Load/Save Model dialog box opens.
3. Select an empty range in the worksheet with the number of cells listed in the dialog box.
4. Click the Save button to close the Load/Save Model dialog box and to save the model in the worksheet.
5. Click the Close button to close the Solver Parameters dialog box.

Load a Solver Model

1. To load a Solver model, click the Solver button in the Analysis group on the Data tab on the Ribbon. The Solver Parameters dialog box opens.
2. Click the Load/Save button in the Solver Parameters dialog box. The Load/Save Model dialog box opens.
3. Select the range in the worksheet that contains the saved Solver model, and then click the Load button.
4. To replace the current model or merge the new model with the current model, click the Replace button or the Merge button. You can click the Cancel button to stop this process.
5. Click the Close button to close the Solver Parameters dialog box, or click the Solve button to run Solver with the loaded Solver model.

Beth clicks the OK button to close the Solver Options dialog box, and then closes the Solver Parameters dialog box. She increases the demand value for San Diego (cell B12) from 125 to 175. Then, she updates her constraints table to include the new constraint that the remaining inventory must be greater than or equal to 0. Finally, she adds this new constraint to the Solver model. Beth clicks the Solve button to solve for a solution; however, the Solver Results dialog box shows that Solver cannot find a feasible solution. Beth selects the Feasibility Report in the Solver Results dialog box and clicks the OK button. When Beth examines the report, she sees that there isn't enough material to satisfy demand—San Diego is short by 27 units (Figure 9.30).

The constraints in Beth's model must meet the demand from each distribution center, but the plants cannot ship more cases than they have in inventory. As a result, there is no feasible solution area that satisfies all of the constraints. (Remember the chart used in Level 2 to graph an infeasible solution. In this case, the principle is the same, but the number of decision variables makes it impossible to graph this problem because you would need a chart with 24 axes.) Beth needs to change her model so that it can produce a feasible solution with a shortage that doesn't violate the demand criteria. At first, she is tempted to change her model by arbitrarily reducing one or more of the distribution center demand

Figure 9.30: Infeasible solution where demand exceeds supply

	Cell	Name	Cell Value	Formula	Status	Slack
1		Microsoft Excel 14.0 Feasibility Report				
2		Worksheet: [@Dist Plan L3-fig 9-30.xlsx]Distribution				
3		Report Created: 3/18/2013 3:31:11 PM				
6		Constraints Which Make the Problem Infeasible				
8	$F$16	Remaining Inventory Seattle	0	$F$16>=0	Binding	0
9	$G$16	Remaining Inventory Indianapolis	0	$G$16>=0	Binding	0
10	$H$16	Remaining Inventory Boston	0	$H$16>=0	Binding	0
11	$I$5	Atlanta Total Shipped	125	$I$5>=$B$5	Binding	0
12	$I$6	Baltimore Total Shipped	187	$I$6>=$B$6	Binding	0
13	$I$7	Boise Total Shipped	64	$I$7>=$B$7	Binding	0
14	$I$8	Dallas Total Shipped	313	$I$8>=$B$8	Binding	0
15	$I$9	Denver Total Shipped	50	$I$9>=$B$9	Binding	0
16	$I$10	Chicago Total Shipped	163	$I$10>=$B$10	Binding	0
17	$I$11	New York Total Shipped	250	$I$11>=$B$11	Binding	0
18	$I$12	San Diego Total Shipped	148	$I$12>=$B$12	Violated	-27

This constraint prevented a feasible solution

Inventory is short by 27 units

values. However, after careful consideration, she decides that adding an arbitrary constraint to her Solver model and thereby forcing a solution might result in a solution that might not be the best one possible, even under a shortage condition.

Using Solver When Demand Exceeds Supply

Beth built her model on the assumption that the company's supply of tennis racquets will meet or exceed demand. Even when demand exceeds supply, you can still use Solver to find an optimal solution. With the increased demand at the San Diego distribution center, the inventory of TZAdvantage racquets is 27 cases fewer than the total demand. This shortage condition means that TheZone must choose which distribution center(s) will not receive enough cases to fill their orders.

The best way for Beth to deal with the shortage situation in her transportation model is to create an "empty" plant with an initial inventory that matches the shortage of 27 cases. (She can adjust the inventory at the empty plant as necessary to match the overall shortage.) The inventory at the empty plant makes it possible for Solver to create a feasible solution for a problem that does not have a feasible solution area.

Beth clicks the OK button to close the Solver Results dialog box, and then opens it again and saves the model in column O so she can load it later if necessary. Next, she adds columns for shipping costs and the number of cases "shipped" by the empty plant to the worksheet, and updates her constraints table. Because there won't be any shipping costs at the empty plant, Beth sets the shipping costs in this column to 0. In addition, because there are no shipping costs from the empty plant, she does not need to update the SUMPRODUCT functions in cells L5:L12 to include the empty plant's shipping costs in the total cost calculations. She sets the initial inventory at the empty plant to 27 cases (cell

J15), and then updates the formulas in the Total Shipped column to include the shipments from the empty plant.

Beth also changes her Solver model so the variable cells include the number of cases shipped from the empty plant. In addition, she modifies her constraints to include these new cells representing the number of cases shipped from the empty plant. When she runs Solver, the number of cases shipped from the empty plant will identify which distribution centers will receive "short" orders and not enough cases to meet their demand. Figure 9.31 shows Beth's solution.

The empty plant's value of 27 cases for the New York distribution center means that this distribution center's order will be short 27 cases. If this shortage is unacceptable to the New York distribution center, Beth could add additional constraints to limit shipments from the empty plant to a lower number, so the orders are short at several distribution centers instead of just one. For now, however, the shortage for the New York center is acceptable, so Beth generates an answer report to document her solution.

Figure 9.31: Feasible solution created by using an "empty" plant

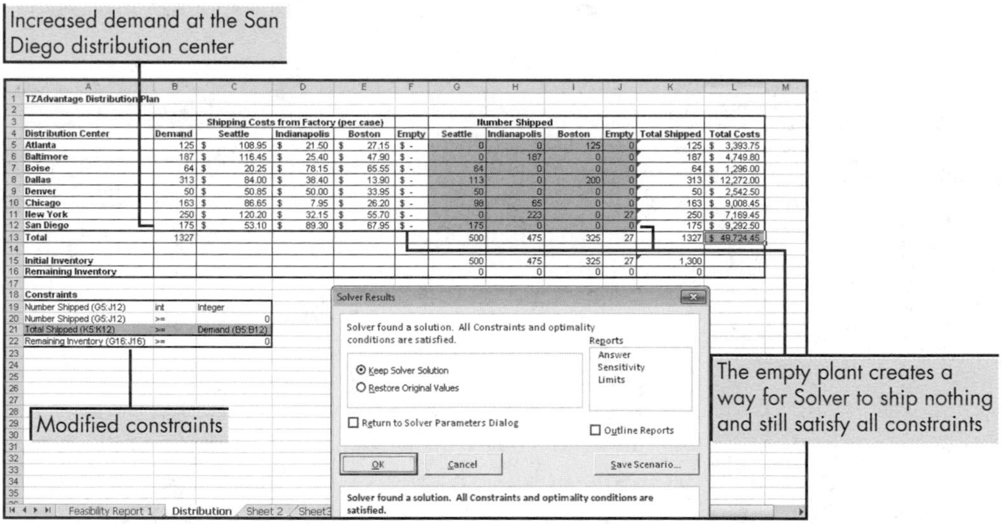

Best Practice

Saving Solver Models

When you copy a worksheet that contains a Solver model, the Solver model is not saved with the new worksheet unless you save it as a model in a blank area of the worksheet and load the Solver model into the new worksheet. Sometimes, you might need to save several Solver models in a worksheet to track your progress in solving a specific problem. It is a good idea to use labels in the worksheet to identify which Solver model is stored in the different ranges of the worksheet. Without labels, it might be difficult to determine which saved Solver model appears in the different ranges.

Assigning Contracts by Using Binary Constraints

As a part of her work with product distribution and transportation planning, Beth needs to assign three long-term shipping contracts to trucking companies. After a long review process, TheZone has selected the three trucking companies it wants to use. Each trucking company has submitted bids for each contract. TheZone established a policy constraint in which it will award one contract to each trucking company. TheZone wants to minimize the total contract costs when awarding contracts. Table 9.3 shows the bid amounts for each contract by the three trucking companies.

Table 9.3: Contract bids by company

Company	Contracts		
	1	2	3
McPhearson Inc.	$100,000.00	$140,000.00	$85,000.00
Oldham Company	$60,000.00	$175,000.00	$60,000.00
Kozworth Inc.	$70,000.00	$130,000.00	$25,000.00

Beth first considers each contract separately, before she looks at the overall picture. Beth attempts to minimize the costs for each project without considering the impact on the other contracts. She decides to award the first contract to Oldham Company for $60,000 because Oldham offered the lowest bid. Using the same objective of awarding contracts based on the lowest bid, she awards the second contract to Kozworth Inc. When awarding the third contract, Beth realizes that the lowest bid is again by Kozworth; but she cannot award more than one contract to any trucking company, so she awards the third contract to the only remaining trucking company, McPhearson Inc. Beth has met the requirement of awarding one contract to each trucking company, but she has not minimized the total cost to TheZone. In addition, if she assigns the third contract first, her solution will be different because Kozworth has the lowest bid. Beth's manual process of elimination won't reach an optimal solution.

Beth can treat this situation as an assignment problem. An **assignment problem** is an optimization problem in which there is a one-to-one relationship between a resource and an assignment or job. For example, one machine in a plant might be assigned to one job. The machine cannot begin a second job until it finishes the first job. Instead of a machine, the resource might be one employee doing one task.

Beth begins her work by setting up the worksheet shown in Figure 9.32, which includes the contract information from Table 9.3. The contract bid amounts in cells B5:D7 are the costs that will be multiplied by the contract assignments in cells E5:G7, which are also the variable cells. Beth adds a binary constraint to the variable cells (E5:G7); Solver will use the value 1 to award a contract and the value 0 to indicate that the contract was not awarded. Beth's worksheet calculates the total cost in the objective cell (H9) using the

SUMPRODUCT function: =SUMPRODUCT(B5:D7,E5:G7). Beth adds constraints so each trucking company is awarded only one contract and each contract has only one trucking company assigned to it. The total number of assignments for each trucking company (cells H5:H7) and the number of assignments for each contract (cells E8:G8) must equal 1. Solver finds a feasible solution that awards one contract to each trucking company at the lowest possible cost as shown in Figure 9.32.

Figure 9.32: Shipping contracts worksheet

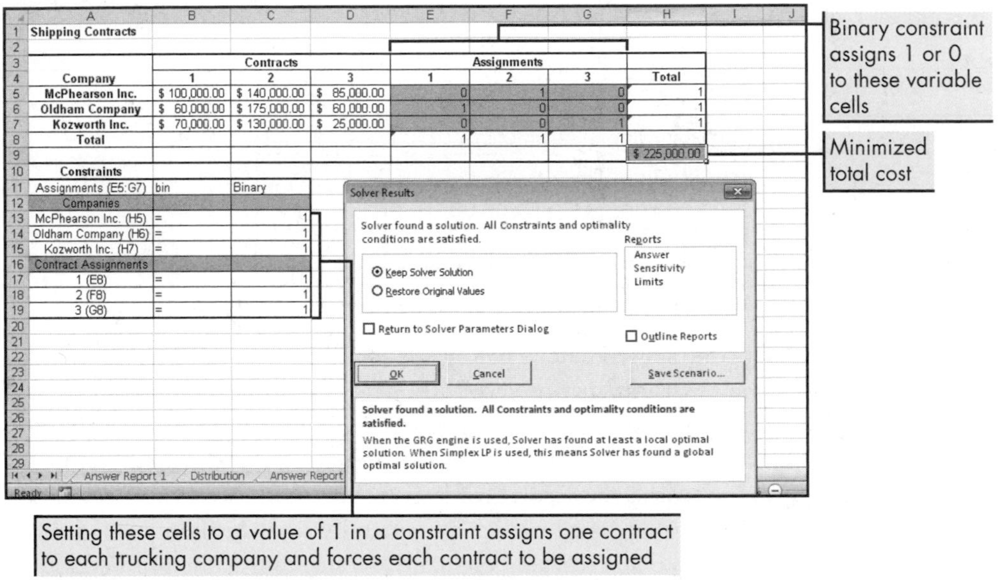

Binary constraint assigns 1 or 0 to these variable cells

Minimized total cost

Setting these cells to a value of 1 in a constraint assigns one contract to each trucking company and forces each contract to be assigned

Beth creates an answer report to document her solution, which minimizes the cost and assigns one contract to each trucking company.

Evaluating Assignment Problems with Too Many Resources

Beth's previous problem involved an equal number of contracts to award and trucking companies to assign to them, and Solver found a feasible solution that awarded contracts based on minimizing the total cost. TheZone wants to try to lower the total cost even further and asks Beth to include two additional trucking companies and their bids on the three contracts to see if she can reduce the total cost. Beth adds the new trucking companies and their bids to her worksheet, updates the formulas in cells E10:G10 and the SUMPRODUCT function in cell H11 to include the new rows, and then updates the constraints table in her worksheet. She updates the Solver parameters for the new problem and runs Solver. An infeasible solution results, as shown in Figure 9.33.

Figure 9.33: Infeasible solution caused by constraints

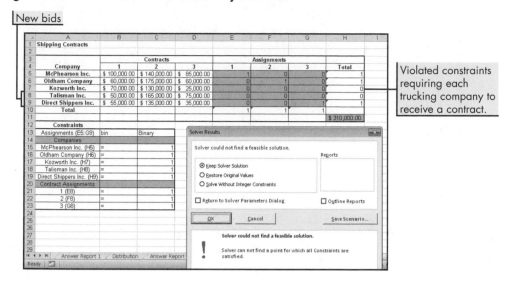

New bids

Violated constraints requiring each trucking company to receive a contract.

The constraint that each company should receive a contract causes the infeasible solution because Solver cannot satisfy the constraint to make cells H7 and H8 equal to 1. Beth needs to minimize the total costs using five trucking companies but she can award only three contracts. Much like the distribution plan in which an empty plant accounted for the short shipments, Beth can create an empty assignment to deal with the extra trucking companies. She has two choices for changing her Solver model: She can create two empty assignments or one contract that requires two trucking companies. Beth chooses the second option and changes her worksheet to include an empty contract column and an empty assignment column. She updates the formulas in column J and in row 10, and then she updates her constraints table to indicate that the empty contract must have two trucking companies because there are two extra trucking companies in her problem. (If she had four extra trucking companies, the empty contract would require four trucking companies.) Her changes make the number of assignments equal to the number of contracts so Solver can find a feasible solution while still minimizing the total cost. The trucking companies assigned to the empty contract will be the ones that are not awarded any "real" contract.

Beth updates the Solver parameters so that cell I10 must equal 2. In this case, Solver finds a solution, as shown in Figure 9.34.

McPhearson Inc. and Oldham Company have empty assignments, so TheZone will not award contracts to these trucking companies. The other three trucking companies are awarded the contracts for a total cost of $210,000. The additional bids from the new trucking companies lowered the total cost by $15,000. Beth generates an answer report of her findings so that the contracts can be awarded.

9

Level 3

Figure 9.34: Feasible solution created by using an empty assignment

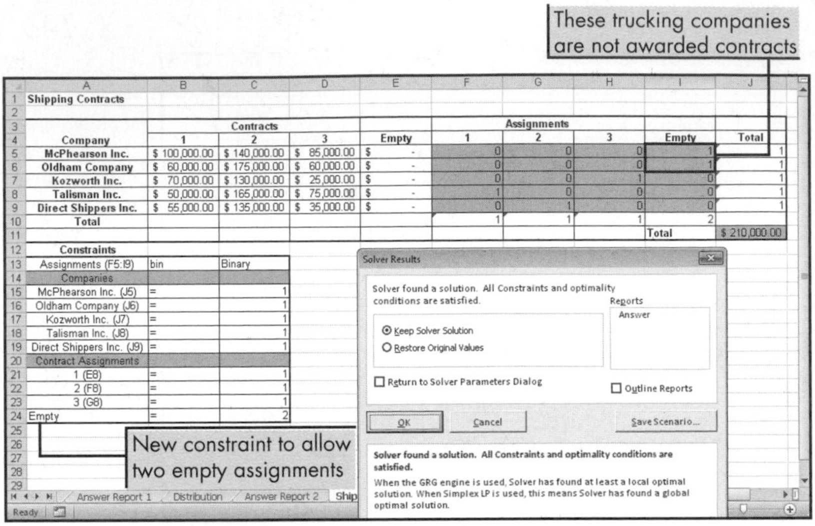

These trucking companies are not awarded contracts

New constraint to allow two empty assignments

Steps To Success: Level 3

One of TheZone's overseas partners is manufacturing a new racquetball racquet for distribution and sale in the United States. You need to create a distribution plan for shipping cases of racquets from the port into which they are shipped to the eight distribution centers located in the United States. The first shipments will arrive into the ports of San Francisco and Los Angeles next week. There are 3,750 cases of racquets loaded on each ship, and each case holds 50 racquets. Your job is to find the least expensive way to distribute the racquets based on the current demand from retailers to the distribution centers. Your solution must meet the demand at each distribution center and no cases can remain on the ships, so any additional cases or racquets must be stored at one or more distribution centers.

Complete the following:

1. Open the **Racquet.xlsx** workbook from the Chapter 9 folder, and then save it as **Racquet Distribution.xlsx**.

2. Use the SUMPRODUCT function in formulas that calculate the cost of shipping the cases from each port (San Francisco and Los Angeles) to each distribution center.

3. Determine the constraints for your solution, and then create a constraints table in the worksheet.

4. Add the constraints you identified to the Solver model, and then run Solver. Were there any remaining cases of racquets? If there were, where were they shipped and why?

5. Produce an answer report for your solution.

6. The ships arrived into the ports of San Francisco and Los Angeles, but there were only 3,500 cases of racquets on each ship instead of 3,750 as originally planned. Save your Solver model to an empty range in the worksheet.

7. Create a copy of the Distribution Plan worksheet and then rename the copy using the worksheet name **Shortage**. Load the saved Solver model into the Shortage worksheet, and then modify your worksheet and Solver model to deal with this shortage.

8. Run the Solver model and create an answer report. Which distribution center(s) will receive incomplete orders? Why did Solver select these distribution center(s) to receive short orders?

9. Save and close the Racquet Distribution.xlsx workbook.

Chapter Summary

This chapter presented different ways to solve problems that include decision variables and goals. In Level 1, you used Goal Seek to change the value in one cell by finding the optimal value to include in a related cell. Because Goal Seek is limited to one input and one outcome, you also learned how to use Solver to manage multiple inputs to maximize or minimize the value in an objective cell. The Solver add-in is a very powerful tool that lets you set up a goal (objective cell) to maximize or minimize the result or to arrive at a specific value. Solver can change the values in up to 200 cells to arrive at the desired value in the objective cell, to help you arrive at the optimal goal.

In Level 2, you learned how to change an existing Solver model to include additional decision variables to produce a solution with multiple constraints. You examined the ways to change an infeasible solution into a feasible solution by adjusting the constraints used to define a solution, and by creating empty columns to deal with supply shortages. You also learned about policy constraints and physical constraints, and examined the different ways in which these constraints affect the solution. Finally, you learned about unbounded solutions and ways to avoid them.

In Level 3, you used binary constraints in a Solver model to solve assignment problems in which there is a one-to-one relationship between decision variables. You also learned how to use empty assignments in situations in which there is a disproportionate number of variables. Finally, you learned how to save and load a Solver model.

9

Chapter Exercises

Conceptual Review

1. What are the limitations of using Goal Seek?

2. How many changing variable cells can you use in a Solver model?

3. What are the three required parameters of a Solver model and what do they represent?

4. What are two advantages of creating a constraints table in a worksheet that includes a Solver model?

5. What is the advantage of linking the constraints in the Solver Parameters dialog box to values in a constraints table in the worksheet?

6. What is the difference between a policy constraint and a physical constraint? Give one example of each type of constraint.

7. What is an objective function?

8. What are the five comparison operators that you can use in Solver?

9. When should you include integer constraints in a Solver model? What is the disadvantage of using an integer constraint?

10. What is a scenario in Solver?

11. What are the types of Solver reports? What information is described in an answer report? What is the difference between a binding status and a not binding status? What is slack?

12. What is an infeasible solution? What steps can you take to attempt to change an infeasible solution into a feasible solution?

13. What is an unbounded solution?

14. What is the difference between a linear function and a nonlinear function?

15. What requirements exist for cells in arrays when you use the SUMPRODUCT function?

16. Describe how the SUMPRODUCT function works.

17. Describe the steps for saving a Solver model. What is the advantage of saving a Solver model?

18. What is an assignment problem?

19. How does the binary comparison operator work?

Case Problems

Level 1 – Creating a Production Plan for ATC Inc.

ATC Inc. is a manufacturing company that produces industrial valves. As the operations manager, you need to determine the production schedule for manufacturing three valves in the new 102 Series, which is used in oil refineries. Producing the 102 Series valves is a three-part process. During the casting phase, the body of the valve and some of the attaching pieces are created; during the machining phase, the casting surfaces are finished and the inner valve flange is created; and during the final phase, the valves are assembled and inspected.

Operations Management

The plant manager provided you with a workbook that contains the production times for each production phase, and the unit cost and list price for each 102 Series valve. The plant manager also told you that your time is limited to 500 hours in the Casting Department, 500 hours in the Machining Department, and 100 hours in the Final Assembly Department. The workbook also includes the setup costs associated with a production run for each valve; you must account for these costs in the profit amounts for each valve.

Based on historical demand for these valves, the company has a policy that any single valve in the 102 Series should constitute at least 10% of the production run and that no single valve should constitute more than 50% of the total production time. Your goal is to maximize the total profit of producing these valves while not exceeding the time available in each department.

Complete the following:

1. Open the **ATCValve.xlsx** workbook from the Chapter 9 folder, and then save it as **ATCValve Production.xlsx**.

2. Add formulas to the worksheet to calculate the total production time for casting, machining, and final assembly. Enter a mathematical formula in the objective cell, and then enter formulas to link the objective cell with the variable cells. Add test values to the variable cells to ensure that your worksheet is set up correctly and produces the expected results.

3. Create a constraints table in the worksheet that identifies the constraints in this problem.

4. Use Solver to determine the optimal combination of valves to build to maximize profit.

5. Produce an answer report of your solution. Which constraints could you modify to maximize the total profit?

6. Save your solution as **Scenario 1**.

7. Modify the constraints in your constraints table and in Solver that you determined would further improve the solution, and then run Solver again. Save this scenario as **Scenario 2**.

8. Produce an answer report of your revised solution. Did your solution accomplish the goals you identified in Step 5? What other changes can you recommend to maximize the total profit?

9. Save and close the ATCValve Production.xlsx workbook.

Level 2 – Managing Purchases for Brightstar Toy Company

Accounting

Brightstar Toy Company, a national toy store, is planning a huge promotion for Power Blocks action figures during the upcoming holiday season. As the company's purchasing manager, your job is to determine the best way to purchase these toys from the manufacturer at the lowest price.

After contacting the Power Blocks manufacturer, you learned that volume discounts and discounts for preseason orders are available on the Power Blocks product line. You need to determine the best product mix based on the following information. The Power Blocks Urban Adventure set is the first item that most people will buy. Customers can also purchase the optional Turbo Action kit, which can be attached to the Power Blocks Urban Adventure set. Another companion set, the Outdoor set, has an optional Camping kit that customers can purchase separately.

The marketing director for Brightstar, Betty Wright, wants to allocate the purchasing budget of $100,000 among the four toys. Because the Turbo Action kit and the Camping kit are accessories, Betty wants to buy at least half as many kits as sets, but the total number of kits cannot exceed the number of sets. Betty also wants to purchase at least 5,000 units of each set.

Because you are purchasing the Power Blocks toys early, you must consider the cost of storing the toys in the Brightstar warehouse until the holiday sales season begins. Your workbook includes the retail price for each toy, the unit cost from Power Blocks, and the storage cost for storing the toys until you can send them to retailers. Your objective is to maximize the profit on all four toys.

Complete the following:

1. Open the **Power.xlsx** workbook from the Chapter 9 folder, and then save it as **Power Blocks.xlsx**.

2. Add formulas to the worksheet to calculate the gross revenue (number purchased multiplied by the retail price), the total unit cost (unit cost multiplied by the number purchased), the total storage cost (storage cost per unit multiplied by the number purchased), the total cost (total unit cost plus total storage cost), and the profit (gross revenue minus the total cost).

3. Enter a mathematical formula in the objective cell, and then check that formulas entered in Step 2 link the objective cell with the variable cells. Add test values to the variable cells to ensure that your worksheet is set up correctly and produces the expected results.

4. Create a constraints table in the worksheet that identifies the constraints in this problem.

5. Use Solver to determine the best way to purchase the Power Blocks sets and kits, and maximize the profit.

6. Produce a Feasibility Report to troubleshoot the solution to determine how the cost and quantity constraints caused the solution to be infeasible. Betty tells you that she cannot increase the available budget and asks you to change the constraints to maximize the profit. However, she asks you to keep the constraint to purchase more sets than kits, and to purchase at least 5,000 total of Power Blocks Urban Adventure sets and Power Blocks Outdoor sets.

   TROUBLESHOOTING: In order to complete this step, you must run the Solver model again without the integer constraints. This is the only way to produce a Feasibility Report.

7. Save your Solver model as a scenario named **Purchase Plan 1**, update your constraints table and the Solver model with your changes, and then run Solver again. If necessary, adjust your constraints until you find a feasible solution.

8. Produce an answer report of your final solution. Use the answer report to recommend any additional changes that might maximize the total profit.

9. Save and close the Power Blocks.xlsx workbook.

**Human
Resources**

Level 3 – Assigning Specialists to Teams at CKG Auto

In the CKG Auto Racing Division, your group builds specialized versions of CKG's Puma sports car for the amateur racing circuit. The operations manager for the racing division, Bob Mather, wants you to identify the most effective way to assign automotive specialists to the three major assembly areas for the Puma: engine/transmission, suspension, and body/frame. Each assembly area requires a two-person team and there are six people whom Bob can use on the three teams. After evaluating each team member, Bob assigned a skill level for each of the three assembly areas. The skill levels normally range from 1 to 100 and represent qualifications, training, and experience. Because the cars in the racing division are high-performance vehicles, the skill of the team members is very high, with no team member scoring less than 71 in any area. Bob asks you to assign two team members each to the three assembly areas so that each team member's skills are maximized. The skill levels are maximized by computing the sum of the skill levels of the individual team members in each area.

Complete the following:

1. Open the **Puma.xlsx** workbook from the Chapter 9 folder, and then save it as **Puma Assembly.xlsx**.

2. Add formulas to the worksheet to calculate the number of people assigned to an assembly area and the number of assignments for each person. Complete the worksheet to allow Solver to select the top two team members for each team based on the skill levels of each team member.

3. Enter a mathematical formula in the objective cell, and then enter formulas to link the objective cell with the variable cells. Add test values to the variable cells to ensure that your worksheet is set up correctly and produces the expected results.

4. Create a constraints table in the worksheet that identifies the constraints in this problem.

5. Use Solver to determine the best way to assign team members to the three assembly area teams while maximizing the skill levels of each team member and team. When you find a feasible solution, create an answer report.

6. Bob wants to see if adding another of his top team members to the mix will increase the skill level of any of the teams in the racing division. Save your Solver model in a blank area of the worksheet, and then create a copy of the Assembly Area Teams worksheet and name it **Assembly Area Teams — Revised**. Load the saved Solver model into the new worksheet, and then add **Ned Hall** to your worksheet with the following skill levels: Engine/Transmission: **97**, Suspension: **94**, and Body/Frame: **92**.

7. Use Solver to determine whether Ned should replace one of the existing team members; and if so, identify which team member Ned should replace. When you find a feasible solution, create an answer report.

8. Save and close the Puma Assembly.xlsx workbook.

SAM: Skills Assessment Manager

For current SAM information, including versions and content details, visit SAM Central (http://samcentral.course.com). If you have a SAM user profile, you may have access to hands-on instruction, practice, and assessment of the skills covered in this chapter. Since various versions of SAM are supported throughout the life of this text, check with your instructor for the correct instructions and URL/Web site for accessing assignments.

Troubleshooting Workbooks and Creating Excel Applications
Accounting: Creating Automated Income Statements

"For every failure, there's an alternative course of action. You just have to find it. When you come to a roadblock, take a detour."
—Mary Kay Ash

LEARNING OBJECTIVES

Level 1

Plan an Excel application
Control data-entry errors
Protect workbooks
Document workbooks

Level 2

Audit formulas for accuracy and validity
Evaluate and trace formula errors
Identify, analyze, and correct errors
Set error-checking options

Level 3

Plan and record macros
Run and test macros
Add macro buttons to a worksheet
Edit macros using the Visual Basic Editor

TOOLS COVERED IN THIS CHAPTER

Comments
Data validation
Formula auditing
Macro recorder
Visual Basic Editor
Worksheet and workbook protection

Chapter Introduction

In previous chapters of this book, you created workbooks designed to help solve business problems. In this chapter, you will create a workbook that can specifically function as an **information system**, a system that is used to collect, organize, and process data, and to communicate and distribute the results in a coordinated manner. Many workbooks are designed to help managers solve problems and make decisions related to product pricing strategies, salesperson bonuses, and capital budgeting, for example. Such a workbook is a decision support system (or DSS), a type of information system that helps managers model business situations, especially through what-if analysis.

A DSS created in a workbook might have errors that can affect the results under certain circumstances. These kinds of errors can include data-entry errors common in all kinds of information systems, and problems with formulas and calculations. Designers of DSS workbooks need to troubleshoot their systems as thoroughly as developers troubleshoot other types of information systems.

In this chapter, you will learn how to minimize data-entry errors in Excel workbooks. You will also learn how to document workbooks and troubleshoot worksheet errors. Finally, you will learn how to automate tasks to further enhance the usefulness and reliability of workbooks.

10

Case Scenario

Kiola Taylor is a financial analyst for TheZone and is working closely with the Apparel Division to develop annual income projections for individual products within product lines, such as outerwear, custom clothing, swimwear, and accessories. A former intern created a preliminary worksheet containing projections for TheZone's sports sunglasses, which are part of the accessories product line. Kiola plans to start with this worksheet and develop a projected Income Statement for the sunglasses product. She will add worksheets that contain historical sales data, budgets for sales, costs of goods sold (COGS), and administrative expenses, and a sheet that explains how to use the workbook efficiently and effectively. When it is completed, Kiola will distribute the workbook to product managers so they can prepare income projections for all of TheZone's products, using her workbook as a model.

Accounting

Kiola wants the workbooks for each type of product to be as uniform and error-free as possible. She plans to develop an automated Excel application that guides the product managers to provide accurate information and is easy to work with, even for novice Excel users.

LEVEL 1

Preparing Error-Free Workbooks

Planning an Excel Application

An Excel **application** is a workbook that you design so that others can use it in a relatively error-free manner. An Excel application is usually a DSS, a tool that helps managers or other workbook users make decisions or solve problems. In general, an Excel application supports your decisions by allowing you to perform what-if analysis and other types of data analysis to model business situations.

Because you design an Excel application to be used by others, it typically provides an easy-to-use interface that assists users as they work. This interface can include custom buttons that users click to perform certain tasks, clearly written documentation, and instructions for entering data and performing calculations. To guide users to enter accurate data, Excel applications control the type of values users enter and where they can enter them.

Kiola has a plan for transforming the projected income workbook a former intern created into an Excel application. The workbook currently includes a Projected Income worksheet that summarizes the assumptions and projections for the sunglasses products. Kiola will add a worksheet that shows the sales history for sunglasses during the past three years, and she will not allow users to change that historical data. She will also add other worksheets that provide budgets for sales, COGS, and administrative expenses. After troubleshooting these worksheets, she will refine the projected Income Statement by using the data from these budgets. To document the workbook, Kiola will add a sheet explaining the purpose of the workbook and how to use it. She will also add a button to the Projected Income worksheet that users can click to print the formulas. Figure 10.1 shows Kiola's plan for the Sunglasses workbook.

Kiola wants to make the workbook as error-free and easy to use as possible. She will take advantage of Excel tools that control the data users enter and provide instructions for using the workbook.

Figure 10.1: Plan for the Sunglasses workbook

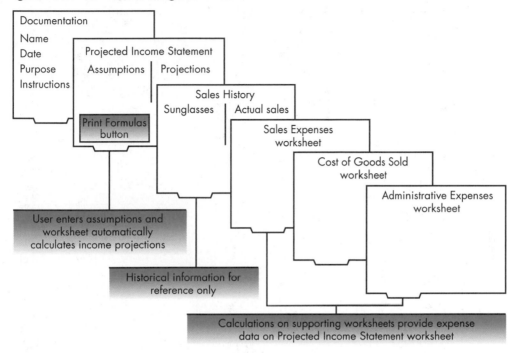

Controlling Data-Entry Errors

To help minimize the errors users make as they enter data into worksheets, Excel provides a **data validation** tool. You use this tool to create rules that define what data is valid in a particular cell. A **validation rule** can specify the type of data that is appropriate, such as whole numbers, decimal numbers, dates, times, or text. A validation rule can also specify a range of acceptable values, such as those between 1 and 100, or those in a particular list of values. To help prevent a user from entering data that doesn't satisfy the validation rule for a cell, you can display an **input message** that identifies the kind of data the user should enter. To guide users who do enter invalid data, you can display an **error alert**, a message box that displays a message of varying severity.

Kiola starts revising the Sunglasses workbook by reviewing the Income Statement that the intern created for TheZone's sunglasses products, as shown in Figure 10.2.

Columns A and B in the Projected Income worksheet include the assumptions that will affect the net income, which is basically calculated as follows:

```
Revenue - COGS - Other Expenses = Net Income
```

Figure 10.2: Projected Income worksheet in the Sunglasses workbook

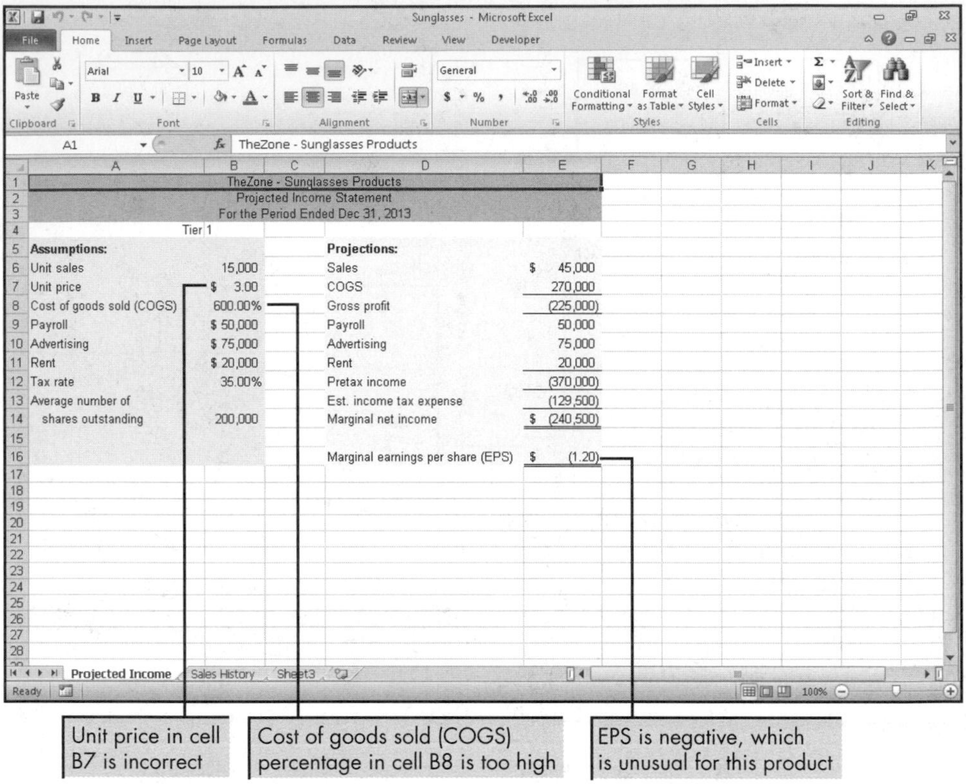

Unit price in cell B7 is incorrect

Cost of goods sold (COGS) percentage in cell B8 is too high

EPS is negative, which is unusual for this product

The assumptions include the number of sunglasses sold (unit sales) and their average unit price. COGS is the cost of purchasing raw materials and manufacturing the finished sunglasses that have been sold, and is included in this Income Statement as a percentage of the sales price. Major expenses are payroll, advertising, rent, and taxes. The average number of shares—referring to common stock outstanding—is provided by the Accounting Department, to be used to calculate earnings per share (EPS).

Columns D and E compute the projections based on these formulas:

- Sales = Unit sales (cell B6) * Unit price (cell B7)
- COGS = Sales (cell E6) * Cost of goods sold percentage (cell B8)
- Gross profit = Sales (cell E6) – COGS (cell E7)
- Pretax income = Gross profit (cell E8) – Expenses (cells E9:E11)
- Estimated income tax expense = Pretax income (cell E12) * Tax rate (cell B12)
- Net income = Pretax income (cell E12) – Estimated income tax expense (cell E13)
- Earnings per share = Marginal net income (cell E14) / Average number of common shares outstanding (cell B14)

EPS is the amount of profit that has been earned by each averaged share, which is a measure of the earning power of the product. Kiola notices that in this Income Statement, the EPS is a negative value. As much as TheZone plans for profits, losses are entirely possible, so a negative EPS is not impossible. However, Kiola knows that the sunglasses products have always been profitable, so she checks the assumptions. The unit sales figure in cell B6 seems accurate, but the unit price in cell B7 does not. In addition, the COGS percentage value in cell B8 is too high. Kiola is certain she has identified two data-entry errors, and uses the data validation tool to prevent these types of errors from happening in the future.

Validating Data Using the Data Validation Tool

To help users enter correct values in a worksheet, you can use the data validation tool to ensure that data entered in a cell meets specified criteria. To determine these criteria, you build on what you already know about your products or services. For example, Kiola knows that the $3.00 value in cell B7 of the Projected Income worksheet is not correct—TheZone's sunglasses are sports glasses with specialized lenses that reduce glare and prevent injury. They fall into three types: Tier 1 sunglasses average $30.00 each, Tier 2 average $50.00, and Tier 3 average $75.00. Failing to include a zero is a common data-entry error, which reinforces Kiola's suspicion that the intern intended to enter "30" in cell B7, not "3."

Another common data-entry error is to include an extra 0 with a value. Kiola notices this error in cell B8—the value in cell B8 should probably be 60%, not 600%. To achieve a profit, COGS should always be less than the sales price or, in other words, less than 100%. The COGS percentage value should, therefore, be between 0% and 100%, or a decimal number between 0 and 1.

In the Projected Income worksheet, the data-entry errors affect the assumptions, meaning that they can also dramatically affect the projections. Recall that the total sales value in cell E6 is calculated by multiplying unit sales in cell B6 by the unit price in cell B7. If the unit price in cell B7 should be 10 times higher, the sales value in cell E6 should also be 10 times higher. Because many of the other projections in cells E7:E16 depend on the value in cell E6, they are also incorrect. Furthermore, the COGS percentage value in cell B8 is used to project the COGS dollar amount in cell E7, which also affects profit. Clearly, the common data-entry errors made in cells B7 and B8 create inaccuracies in the entire worksheet.

Kiola decides to create two validation rules:

- Unit price in cell B7 must be 30, 50, or 75.
- COGS percentage in cell B8 must be a decimal value between 0 and 1.

Kiola will provide another way to reduce the chance of data-entry errors—an input message that appears when a user clicks a cell. To prevent users from storing inaccurate data in the worksheet, she will also include an error alert message.

10

Level 1

Using the data validation tool to control data entry involves three basic steps:

1. Set up the data validation rule.

2. Create the input message.

3. Specify the error alert style and message.

You access the data validation tool by clicking the Data tab on the Ribbon, and then clicking the Data Validation button in the Data Tools group to open the Data Validation dialog box. This dialog box contains three tabs—Settings, Input Message, and Error Alert—and these tabs provide the options for the three-step process for using data validation in a workbook.

Setting Up a Data Validation Rule

Kiola needs to set up a rule for cell B7, the cell containing the unit price. She will specify that the value in cell B7 can be only 30, 50, or 75. She also will set up a validation rule for cell B8, specifying that it can only contain a decimal value between 0 and 1.

How To

Create a Data Validation Rule

1. Click the cell for which you want to specify a validation rule.
2. Click the Data tab on the Ribbon, and then click the Data Validation button in the Data Tools group. The Data Validation dialog box opens.
3. Click the Settings tab, if necessary. See Figure 10.3.

Figure 10.3: Data Validation dialog box

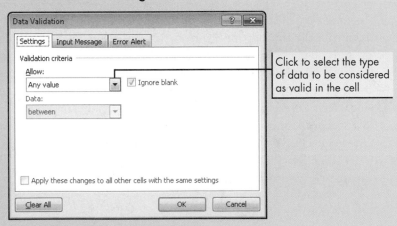

Click to select the type of data to be considered as valid in the cell

4. Click the Allow arrow, and then select the type of data allowed in the cell. The dialog box displays options appropriate to the type of data selected.
5. Enter the validation rule using the available options.
6. Click the OK button.

The options in the Allow box determine the types of values users can enter in the selected cell. Table 10.1 lists and describes these options.

Table 10.1: Data validation rules

Allow Box Options	Description
Any value	No restrictions on data. This is the default setting for cells.
Whole number	Data is restricted to values that are whole numbers only.
Decimal	Data is restricted to values that can be expressed with any number of decimal places.
List	Data is restricted to labels or numbers that must be chosen from a list. The valid data can be specified in the Data Validation dialog box as a list of values separated by commas, or by referring to a cell range that contains the appropriate data.
Date	Data is restricted to date values.
Time	Data is restricted to time values.
Text length	Data is restricted to labels of a specified length.
Custom	Data is restricted as defined by a formula, an expression, or a calculation in another cell.

To create the data validation rule for cell B7, Kiola opens the Data Validation dialog box, selects List in the Allow box, and then types "30, 50, 75" as the acceptable values, as shown in Figure 10.4.

Figure 10.4: Specifying the validation rule for cell B7

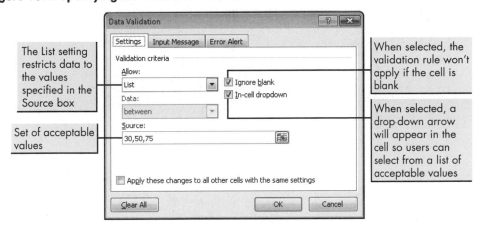

To create the data validation rule for cell B8, Kiola selects the Decimal option in the Allow box, and then specifies that the decimal value is between 0 and 1, as shown in Figure 10.5.

Now, Excel accepts only the values 30, 50, or 75 in cell B7, and only decimal values between 0 and 1 in cell B8. However, when users of this worksheet try to enter data in these cells, they won't know they contain validation rules unless you create an input message for each cell.

Figure 10.5: Specifying the validation rule for cell B8

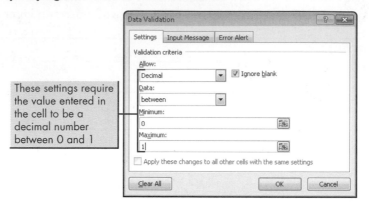

These settings require the value entered in the cell to be a decimal number between 0 and 1

Creating an Input Message

Displaying an input message when a user clicks a cell is a helpful way to let the user know what type of data to enter in the cell. By default, input messages appear as comments next to the cell when the cell is selected. You can use input messages even for cells that allow any data values to be entered in them.

How To

Create an Input Message

1. Click the cell for which you want to specify an input message.
2. On the Data tab on the Ribbon, click the Data Validation button in the Data Tools group. The Data Validation dialog box opens.
3. Click the Input Message tab.
4. Verify that the Show input message when cell is selected check box is selected.
5. Enter a title and text for the input message. See Figure 10.6.

Figure 10.6: Input Message tab in the Data Validation dialog box

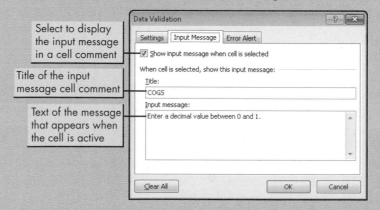

Select to display the input message in a cell comment

Title of the input message cell comment

Text of the message that appears when the cell is active

6. Click the OK button.

Kiola includes an input message for cell B7 that reminds users to enter 30, 50, or 75 as the unit price, and another input message for cell B8 that instructs users to enter a decimal number between 0 and 1. The input message for cell B7 is shown in Figure 10.7.

Figure 10.7: Input message for cell B7

Now users will see the input messages for cells B7 and B8 when one of those cells is the active cell. However, users can ignore the input message and try to enter 100 in cell B7 or 2 in cell B8. To reinforce the validation rule, you can set up an error alert message for a cell.

Specifying an Alert Style and Message

In addition to displaying a helpful message that appears before users enter data, you can also display an error alert message in a message box if users enter data that violates the cell's validation rule. You can use one of three error alert styles for a cell: Stop, Warning, or Information. Table 10.2 lists and describes these styles.

Table 10.2: Error alert messages

Error Alert Style	Description
Stop	The entry is incorrect and must be canceled or corrected before continuing. This is the default setting.
Warning	The entry does not conform to the validation rule, and can be canceled, corrected, or accepted. If accepted, the entry overrides the validation rule for the cell.
Information	The entry does not conform to the data validation rules, and is either accepted or canceled.

You use the Error Alert tab in the Data Validation dialog box to specify error alert styles and messages.

How To

Specify an Error Alert Style and Message

1. Click the cell for which you want to create an error message.

2. Click the Data tab on the Ribbon, and then click Data Validation in the Data Tools group. The Data Validation dialog box opens.

3. Click the Error Alert tab.

4. Make sure the Show error alert after invalid data is entered check box is selected.

5. Click the Style arrow, and then select Stop, Warning, or Information.

6. Enter a title and text for the error message. See Figure 10.8.

Figure 10.8: Setting an error alert

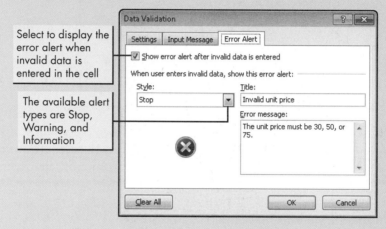

Select to display the error alert when invalid data is entered in the cell

The available alert types are Stop, Warning, and Information

7. Click the OK button.

Kiola specifies Stop style error messages for cells B7 and B8. Now, Excel prohibits users from entering invalid data in those cells.

Best Practice

Using the Data Validation Tool Effectively

The validation rule is the part of the data validation tool that restricts the data entry. If you set up the validation rule only, all future data entry to that cell is restricted to the values you have specified. However, using only a validation rule without an input message or error alert message can frustrate users of the worksheet. Be certain to include input messages and error alert messages to train new users and guide more experienced users to enter correct data.

Note that the data validation tool restricts data being entered, not data already stored in the worksheet. Excel provides a different tool that identifies invalid data already stored in a worksheet.

Circling Invalid Data

Whereas the data validation tool prevents data-entry errors, another tool can identify these errors. You click the Circle Invalid Data command on the Data Validation menu to find and mark cells containing data that does not meet validation criteria.

How To

Circle Invalid Data

1. Click the Data tab on the Ribbon, click the Data Validation button arrow in the Data Tools group, and then click Circle Invalid Data on the menu. Circles then appear around any cells containing data that violates their specified data validation rule.

2. To remove the circle around a cell, enter valid data in the cell.

3. To hide all circles, click the Data Validation button arrow, and then click Clear Validation Circles on the menu.

Kiola uses the Circle Invalid Data command on the Data Validation menu to identify the data that does not meet the validation rules she specified in the Projected Income worksheet, as shown in Figure 10.9.

Figure 10.9: Circling invalid data

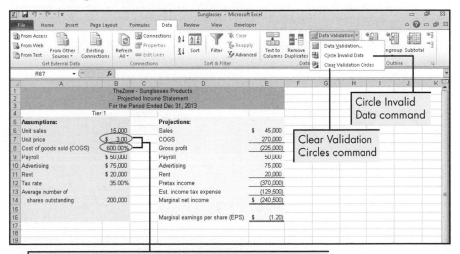

Red circles appear to indicate the values in cells B7 and B8 do not meet the data validation criteria for those cells

Kiola changes the value in cell B7 to 30 and the value in cell B8 to 60, which automatically removes the circles from around those cells, and she then scans the rest of the assumption values to verify they are correct.

Now that she has created data validation rules to help prevent errors, Kiola also wants to limit access to certain parts of the workbook.

Protecting Workbooks

In addition to typing an incorrect entry, workbook users can cause errors in a worksheet by accidentally deleting a value or other information that shouldn't be deleted. They can also create problems if they change formulas or insert new ones. To prevent these types of errors, you can protect portions or all of a workbook, which lets you control the changes users can make to a workbook. For example, you can protect a workbook in the following ways:

- Lock cells so that users cannot change their contents
- Hide cells so that users cannot see them
- Restrict actions users can perform on specified portions of specified worksheets
- Prevent a worksheet from being deleted from a workbook

Best Practice

Selecting an Appropriate Level of Protection in Excel

You can use up to three levels of security and protection to control who can access and change your Excel data:

- **Worksheet protection**—Protect the contents of a worksheet to prevent anyone from changing, moving, or deleting its data. Be certain the cells you want to protect are locked, unlock the cells you want users to be able to access, and then use the Protect Sheet dialog box to select the actions users can still take after worksheet protection is enabled. Specifying a password that users must enter before unprotecting the worksheet is optional. This level of password protection is not designed to secure confidential information in Excel, but only to prevent others from viewing or making changes to your data.

- **Workbook protection**—Protect a workbook to prevent anyone from inserting, deleting, or renaming worksheets or from changing the size and position of the worksheet window. Use the Protect Workbook dialog box to protect the worksheet structure or its windows. As with worksheet protection, specifying a password that users enter before they remove protection from a workbook is optional.

- **File protection**—Protect your entire workbook file with a password for optimal security. Securing a file means only authorized users can open a workbook and use its data. While the Save As dialog box is open, you can protect a file by clicking the Tools button, clicking General Options, and then using the General Options dialog box to specify a password that users must enter to open and view a workbook file; this password helps you prevent unauthorized users from viewing your workbook. You can also use this dialog box to specify another password users must enter to modify the file; this password allows you to prevent unauthorized users from editing your workbook.

For optimal password security, Microsoft recommends that you always assign a password to open and view a file. Users who also have permission to modify data should then enter a second password.

Kiola wants to prohibit users from changing the formulas in the Projected Income worksheet, while allowing them to change values such as unit sales and unit price. She also has imported a worksheet named Sales History, which contains sales information for sunglasses for the last year, as shown in Figure 10.10.

Figure 10.10: Sales History worksheet

Other product managers do not need to see the names of the salespeople

	A	B	C	D	E	F	G
1		TheZone - Sunglasses Products					
2		Sales History					
3		For the Period Ended Dec 31, 2013					
4							
5	Product	Salesperson	Qtr 1	Qtr 2	Qtr 3	Qtr 4	
6	XLS Racing Goggles	ANTON		$709.02			
7	Univisor Sports 333	BERGS	$315.12				
8	SkiOptics 730	BOLID				$1,181.70	
9	K-Twenty	BOTTM	$1,181.70				
10	Litton Q30	ERNSH	$1,134.43			$2,633.22	
11	Bascom Optics	GODOS		$283.61			
12	GlareFree 225	HUNGC	$63.02				
13	Eton High Bend	PICCO		$1,575.60	$945.36		
14	Univisor Sports 333	RATTC		$598.73			
15	XLS Racing Goggles	REGGC				$748.41	
16	Bascom Optics	SAVEA			$3,939.00	$797.65	
17	Litton Q30	SEVES		$886.28			
18	Litton Q30	WHITC				$787.80	
19	Univisor Sports 333	ALFKI				$80.80	
20	K-Twenty	BOTTM				$202.00	
21	Bascom Optics	ERNSH				$181.80	
22	Litton Q30	LINOD	$549.44				
23	Univisor Sports 333	QUICK		$606.00			
24	XLS racing goggles	VAFFE			$141.40		
25	GlareFree 225	ANTON		$167.26			
26	GlareFree 225	BERGS		$929.20			
27	Bascom Optics	BONAP		$250.88	$529.64		
28	Bascom Optics	BOTTM	$556.76				
29	Univisor Sports 333	BSBEV	$148.47				
30	XLS Racing Goggles	FRANS				$18.58	
31	XLS Racing Goggles	HILAA		$92.92	$1,115.04		
32	Univisor Sports 333	LAZYK	$148.47				
33							

10

Level 1

The product managers only need to see some of this information, such as the product names and sales amounts for the products they manage. They don't need access to the salespersons' names. Kiola plans to hide the information the product managers don't need to see so they can focus on pertinent data. She also wants to protect the workbook itself so that no one can delete a worksheet.

Locking and Unlocking Cells

Protecting the contents of a worksheet is a two-step process, similar to protecting the contents of a car. To protect the contents of your car, you must first have working locks on your doors, and then you must engage the locks so that no one can access your car. In a worksheet, you use the Locked property of a cell to determine whether users can change the data in that cell. To engage the Locked property of the cells, you protect the worksheet.

By default, every cell in a worksheet has a lock on it—that is, it is formatted with the Locked property. However, users can change the data and formulas in any cell if the worksheet is unprotected, which is the default setting. In other words, although every cell starts out with a lock on it, those locks are not engaged until the worksheet is protected. Once you protect the worksheet, users cannot change any data or formulas in any locked cell. To allow users to edit some cells while preventing them from changing others, you unlock— that is, you must clear the Locked property from the cells you want users to be able to access—and then you can protect the worksheet. Doing so allows users to change the contents of unlocked cells, but not the contents of locked cells, on the protected worksheet.

How To

Unlock Cells
1. Select the cell or range of cells you want to unlock.
2. Right-click the selection and then click Format Cells on the shortcut menu. The Format Cells dialog box opens.
3. Click the Protection tab. See Figure 10.11.

Figure 10.11: Unlocking cells

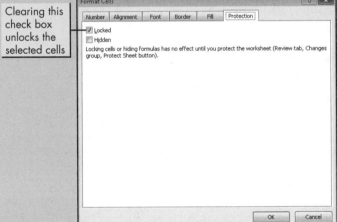

Clearing this check box unlocks the selected cells

4. Click the Locked box to remove the check mark.
5. Click the OK button.

In the Projected Income worksheet, Kiola wants to allow users to change the assumption values, but not the projection formulas. She unlocks the cells in the B6:B14 range.

Protecting a Worksheet

After you unlock cells to allow users to enter data in those cells, you can protect the worksheet so that users cannot change the contents of the rest of the cells, which are locked by default. Furthermore, as you protect a worksheet, you can specify what users can do in the worksheet. For example, users might be able to format cells, whether locked or unlocked, but only enter data in unlocked cells.

You can also specify that users enter a password before they remove protection from a worksheet. The password is case sensitive, so *NorthStar* is considered a different password than *northstar*.

How To

Protect and Unprotect a Worksheet

1. Unlock the cells that you don't want to protect.
2. Click the Review tab on the Ribbon, and then click the Protect Sheet button in the Changes group. The Protect Sheet dialog box opens. See Figure 10.12.

Figure 10.12: Protect Sheet dialog box

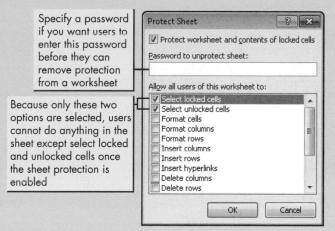

Specify a password if you want users to enter this password before they can remove protection from a worksheet

Because only these two options are selected, users cannot do anything in the sheet except select locked and unlocked cells once the sheet protection is enabled

3. Make sure the Protect worksheet and contents of locked cells check box is selected.
4. If you want to require users to enter a password before unprotecting the worksheet, enter the password in the Password to unprotect sheet box.
5. Select the actions that users can perform in the protected worksheet.
6. Click the OK button.
7. To unprotect the worksheet and allow users to access all the cells, click the Unprotect Sheet button in the Changes group on the Review tab.

10

Level 1

Kiola enables worksheet protection, and then tests the Projected Income worksheet by attempting to edit a formula in the Projections column. Excel displays a message box indicating that the cell is protected and cannot be modified. To disable worksheet protection and allow changes to the contents of all cells again, Kiola can unprotect the worksheet. She will also enable worksheet protection for the Sales History sheet. Users will not be able to change the contents of any cell in this worksheet because all of its cells have remained locked and the sheet will be protected. Before protecting the Sales History sheet, however, Kiola wants to hide the Salesperson column.

Hiding and Displaying Rows and Columns

If you do not want others to view data in a worksheet, but want to retain the information, you can hide rows or columns. Hiding a row or column does not affect the data or any formulas that reference a hidden cell. When you need to work with hidden data, you can redisplay it.

How To

Hide and Display Rows or Columns
1. Select the rows or columns you want to hide.
2. Right-click the selection, and then click Hide on the shortcut menu.
3. To display a hidden row or rows, select the headings of the rows that border the hidden row range. Similarly, to display a hidden column or columns, select the headings of the columns that border the hidden columns.
4. Right-click the selection, and then click Unhide on the shortcut menu.

In the Sales History worksheet, Kiola hides column B, which contains the names of salespeople, as shown in Figure 10.13. Then she protects the Sales History worksheet so users can view but not change its data.

Protecting a Workbook

Now that Kiola has protected the contents of the worksheets in the Sunglasses workbook, she wants to protect the worksheets themselves. If you want to prohibit workbook users from adding, renaming, or deleting worksheets in the workbook, you can enable workbook protection. When you protect a workbook, you can secure the workbook structure or its windows. Protecting the structure means users cannot insert, delete, or rename worksheets. Protecting windows means that the Excel windows are the same size and in the same position each time the workbook opens.

Figure 10.13: Worksheet with hidden column

To display column B again, select columns A and C contiguously, right-click the selection, and then click Unhide

	A	C	D	E	F	G
1		TheZone - Sunglasses Products				
2		Sales History				
3		For the Period Ended Dec 31, 2013				
4						
5	Product	Qtr 1	Qtr 2	Qtr 3	Qtr 4	
6	XLS Racing Goggles		$709.02			
7	Univisor Sports 333	$315.12				
8	SkiOptics 730				$1,181.70	
9	K-Twenty	$1,181.70				
10	Litton Q30	$1,134.43			$2,633.22	
11	Bascom Optics		$283.61			
12	GlareFree 225	$63.02				
13	Eton High Bend		$1,575.60	$945.36		
14	Univisor Sports 333		$598.73			
15	XLS Racing Goggles				$748.41	
16	Bascom Optics			$3,939.00	$797.65	
17	Litton Q30		$886.28			
18	Litton Q30				$787.80	
19	Univisor Sports 333				$60.60	
20	K-Twenty				$202.00	
21	Bascom Optics				$181.80	
22	Litton Q30	$549.44				
23	Univisor Sports 333		$606.00			
24	XLS racing goggles			$141.40		
25	GlareFree 225		$167.26			
26	GlareFree 225		$929.20			
27	Bascom Optics		$250.88	$529.64		
28	Bascom Optics	$556.76				
29	Univisor Sports 333	$148.47				
30	XLS Racing Goggles				$18.58	
31	XLS Racing Goggles		$92.92	$1,115.04		
32	Univisor Sports 333	$148.47				
33						

10

Level 1

How To

Protect and Unprotect a Workbook

1. Click the Review tab on the Ribbon, and then click the Protect Workbook button in the Changes group to open the Protect Structure and Windows dialog box. See Figure 10.14.

Figure 10.14: Protect Structure and Windows dialog box

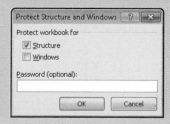

2. Select the check boxes to indicate whether you want to protect the workbook structure, windows, or both.

3. If you want to require users to enter a password before unprotecting the workbook, enter the password.

4. Click the OK button.

5. To unprotect a workbook, click the Protect Workbook button in the Changes group on the Review tab, and then deselect the necessary check boxes.

As with worksheet protection, you can specify that users enter a case-sensitive password before they remove protection from a workbook.

Creating Effective Passwords

Whether you are using a password to protect a worksheet, workbook, or file, be certain to use effective passwords, which are passwords that are easy for you to remember but difficult for others to guess. Excel passwords in general can contain letters, numbers, spaces, and symbols, and are case sensitive, meaning you must type uppercase and lowercase letters correctly when you set and use a password. An effective password contains at least eight characters and combines uppercase and lowercase letters, numbers, and symbols, such as kT913!tZ.

Use effective passwords that you can remember easily so you don't have to write them down. If this is not possible, store a copy of the password in a safe place, out of plain view. Be certain that you remember the passwords that you set; without them, you cannot unprotect the protected worksheet or workbook, or access the protected file.

To be certain that no one can delete or otherwise modify the worksheets in the Sunglasses workbook, Kiola protects the workbook structure. She tests this setting by right-clicking the Projected Income tab; the Insert, Delete, Rename, Move or Copy, Tab Color, Hide, and Unhide commands are dimmed, meaning that the commands to modify the worksheet structure are not available.

Kiola's next task is to add a new worksheet to the Sunglasses workbook. This will be a documentation worksheet that provides information about the content and purpose of the workbook, and includes instructions for entering assumptions. Kiola unprotects the Sunglasses workbook so she can add the new sheet.

Documenting Workbooks

A documentation worksheet usually contains the workbook title, the creation date, the name of the person who created the workbook, and any other information that describes the purpose and content of the workbook. This type of documentation worksheet is sufficient for most workbooks, but an Excel application requires more extensive documentation because it is designed to be used by others. Furthermore, as companies grow and their information systems become more complex, they usually develop structured documentation guidelines; the documentation worksheet can fulfill some of the goals in these guidelines.

Documentation refers to all the records that describe how and why a system has been developed and how it should be used. Documentation can be descriptions of the system, checklists, flowcharts, and other hard-copy documents, as well as notations built into the system itself. In addition to basic information that identifies the workbook author, date created, and purpose, the following types of documentation are helpful in an Excel application:

- Step-by-step instructions for entering data and performing needed calculations
- Notes or comments that identify the source of data, such as another workbook, a database, or a Web page
- Notes or comments that define terms, explain calculations, and describe assumptions

Thorough, well-written documentation is a tremendous timesaver. For example, if you are updating a workbook, even one that you created, sufficient documentation can indicate the purpose and approach of the worksheets and the form of the calculations, relieving you of the task of examining data and formulas to understand or recall how they work.

Documentation of workbooks used to calculate values that appear on formal financial statements or relate to contracts or other types of covenants is especially important. Auditors, lenders, and others outside an organization frequently need to verify calculations as part of larger compliance work. For example, if you work for a publicly traded company, it is regulated by the Securities and Exchange Commission (SEC) and is subject to an annual financial statement audit. If workbooks are properly documented, the external auditor or other compliance official can usually verify the workbooks' calculations on a sample basis instead of testing the workbooks' results more strenuously. This can reduce a company's compliance costs substantially.

Besides including documentation within a workbook, you can also print workbook information such as the documentation worksheet and a copy of the workbook's formulas. Cell formula printouts also serve as a backup for workbooks. If the workbook becomes corrupted or unavailable for some reason, it can be re-created based on its hard-copy documentation. Obviously, you should keep workbook documentation up to date so that if a workbook needs to be reconstructed, the documentation reflects its most recent state.

10

Level 1

How To

Print Worksheet Formulas

1. Display formulas in your worksheet by clicking the Formulas tab on the Ribbon, and then clicking the Show Formulas button in the Formula Auditing group (or by pressing Ctrl+`).

2. Click the File tab on the Ribbon to display Backstage view, and then click the Print tab.

3. Select the desired print options.

4. Click the Print button.

Best Practice

Selecting Print Options When Printing Worksheet Formulas

When printing worksheet formulas, especially for the purposes of documentation, it is very helpful to set the print options to print the row and column headings. Having the column letters and row numbers printed on the top and left side of the formula printout allows readers to easily see which cells contain each formula, and to which cell each formula refers as part of its calculation. You can set these printing options on the Page Layout tab on the Ribbon. Click the Print check box under Headings in the Sheet Options group.

It is also best to include the workbook's filename, worksheet name, and date on cell formula printouts that are used for documentation. The worksheet's header and footer are handy locations for this kind of information.

Providing a Thorough Documentation Worksheet

TheZone has recently established a policy of thoroughly documenting its financial data. Excel workbooks in particular must include a documentation sheet that answers the basic questions of who, what, when, where, why, and how: Who created the workbook? What are its contents? When was it created? Where do the data and calculations come from? Why was the workbook created? How should it be used?

With this in mind, Kiola adds a worksheet named Documentation to the Sunglasses workbook. She includes the basic workbook information specified by TheZone's policy, and adds a description of the assumptions used to project income. She also decides to add instructions to the Projected Income worksheet to guide users to enter appropriate assumptions and then analyze the projections. See Figure 10.15.

Figure 10.15: Documentation worksheet

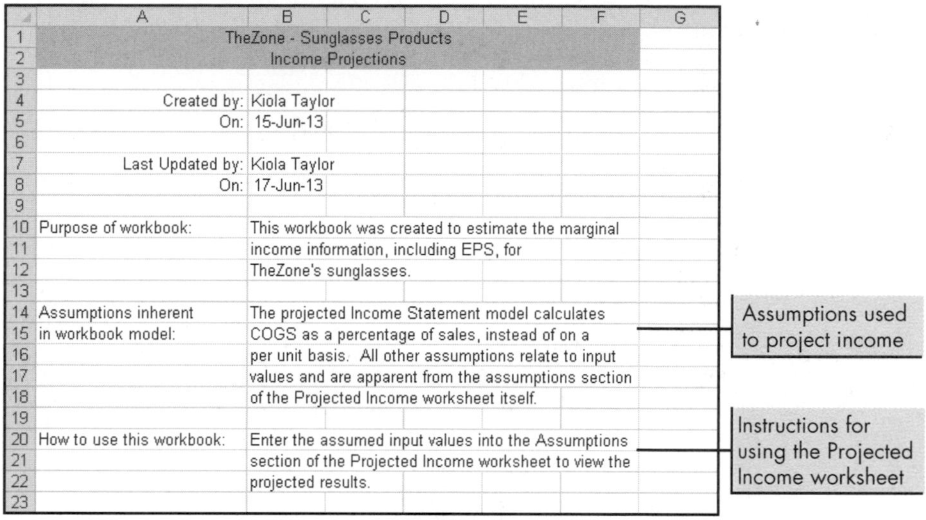

She also wants to include information that describes or defines particular cells, such as COGS in cell B8, or that identifies the source of the data, such as the average number of shares in cell B14. To do this, Kiola will add comments to the worksheet.

Including Comments in a Worksheet

A **comment** is a note that you attach to a cell, separate from other cell content. Comments are especially useful to display short blocks of text, such as a brief explanation of a formula or a reminder such as "Totals are calculated automatically."

Cells with comments have red indicator triangles in the upper-right corner. You point to a cell with an indicator to display its comment, as shown in Figure 10.16. (*Note*: Figures shown throughout this chapter do not reflect the actual colors of the different elements as they appear in the Excel window.) You can also use the buttons in the Comments group on the Review tab on the Ribbon to read each comment in a workbook in sequence.

Kiola unprotects the Projected Income worksheet and adds a comment to cell B14 to define what the average number of shares outstanding assumption value is used for.

10

Level 1

Figure 10.16: Using a comment as documentation

	A	B	C	D	E	F
1			TheZone - Sunglasses Products			
2			Projected Income Statement			
3			For the Period Ended Dec 31, 2013			
4		Tier 1				
5	Assumptions:			Projections:		
6	Unit sales	15,000		Sales	$ 450,000	
7	Unit price	$ 30.00		COGS	270,000	
8	Cost of goods sold (COGS)	60.00%		Gross profit	180,000	
9	Payroll	$ 50,000		Payroll	50,000	
10	Advertising	$ 75,000		Advertising	75,000	
11	Rent	$ 20,000		Rent	20,000	
12	Tax rate	35.00%		Pretax income	35,000	
13	Average number of			expense	12,250	
14	shares outstanding	200,000		ome	$ 22,750	
15						
16				s per share (EPS)	$ 0.11	
17						
18						
19						

Kiola Taylor: Average number of shares outstanding is used to compute EPS.

Comment attached to cell B14

How To

Add a Comment to a Cell

1. Click the cell to which you want to add a comment.

2. Right-click the cell, and click Insert Comment on the shortcut menu.

3. Type the text that you want to appear in the comment, and then click outside the comment box.

In an Excel application, you can ensure that cells containing documentation comments are locked, and then protect the worksheet so that users cannot inadvertently delete or edit a comment. Kiola reprotects the Projected Income worksheet. She also protects the Documentation worksheet and reengages the workbook protection.

Kiola has now created validation rules to help prevent data-entry errors, and set up and enabled protection so that users cannot delete or change important information. Does that mean that there are now no errors in the workbook? No, not necessarily. Another common class of workbook problems involves formulas, which can cause calculation errors. In Level 2, you will learn how to identify and solve problems with worksheet formulas.

Steps To Success: Level 1

Kiola has another workbook that the former intern prepared to show the projected income for helmets, also part of the accessories product line. Figure 10.17 shows the Projected Income worksheet in the Helmets workbook.

Figure 10.17: Projected Income worksheet for the Helmets product line

	A	B	C	D	E	F
1				TheZone - Helmets Products		
2				Projected Income Statement		
3				For the Period Ended Dec 31, 2013		
4		Tier 1				
5	Assumptions:			Projections:		
6	Unit sales	12,000		Sales	$ 48,000	
7	Unit price	$ 4.00		COGS	240,000	
8	Cost of goods sold (COGS)	500.00%		Gross profit	(192,000)	
9	Payroll	$50,000		Payroll	50,000	
10	Advertising	$75,000		Advertising	75,000	
11	Rent	$ 20,000		Rent	20,000	
12	Tax rate	35.00%		Pretax income	(337,000)	
13	Average number of			Est. income tax expense	(117,950)	
14	shares outstanding	200,000		Marginal net income	$ (219,050)	
15						
16				Marginal earnings per share (EPS)	$ (1.10)	
17						
18						

As in the Sunglasses workbook, columns A and B contain the assumptions, whereas columns D and E contain the projections. To prepare this workbook so that TheZone's product managers can use it, use the data validation and protection tools to help prevent data-entry errors. Also provide adequate documentation. Complete the following:

1. Open the workbook named **Helmets.xlsx** located in the Chapter 10 folder, and then save it as **Helmet Projections.xlsx**.

2. In the Projected Income worksheet, apply a validation rule to cell B7 that limits unit prices to values between $20.00 and $99.99. Create an appropriate input message and Warning style error alert.

3. Apply a validation rule to cell B8 that limits the COGS percentage to values between 0 and 1. Create an appropriate input message and Warning style error alert.

4. Apply a validation rule to cells B9:B11 that limits the expense estimates to whole numbers greater than or equal to $0. Create appropriate input messages and Stop style error alerts.

5. Apply a validation rule to cell B12 that limits the tax rate percentage to decimal number values between 0.1 and 0.5. Create an appropriate input message and Warning style error alert.

6. Apply a validation rule to cell B14 that limits the average shares outstanding to whole numbers greater than or equal to 50,000. Create an appropriate input message and Stop style error alert.

7. Use the Circle Invalid Data feature to identify existing data entry errors. Correct the errors assuming they are simply errors of the "incorrect number of zeros" type.

10

Level 1

8. Include a comment for cell E7 that defines COGS and a comment for cell E16 that defines earnings per share.

9. Remove the Locked property from cells B6:B14.

10. Turn on worksheet protection. Do not specify a protection password.

11. Switch to the Documentation sheet and enter *your name* and the *current date* in the appropriate cells. Include text that explains the purpose of the workbook and how to use it.

12. Turn on worksheet protection. Do not specify a protection password.

13. Turn on workbook protection. Do not specify a protection password.

14. Save and close the Helmet Projections.xlsx workbook.

LEVEL 2
Preventing Errors in Formulas

Auditing Formulas

Some problems with workbooks are more obvious than others. As you learned in Chapter 1, if an error message appears in a cell, something is clearly wrong in the worksheet, and the error message that appears can identify or provide hints about the error. For example, when #DIV/0! appears in a cell, you know that a formula is trying to divide by the value 0, which cannot be done. This kind of error message can be caused by a data-entry error (entering a 0 value in a cell that should not contain a 0), or by an inaccurate formula. Other error messages—such as #NAME?—are always due to an error in a formula, such as an invalid range name or invalid function name.

In Chapter 1, you examined erroneous cell formulas and determined how to fix them so they would no longer display an error message. In this chapter, you will learn how to take advantage of more sophisticated Excel tools that help you find and respond to formula errors. First, you will address error messages caused by problems with the formulas in the workbook. In some cases, the inaccurate formula could have originally been constructed incorrectly. In other cases, deleting cells or a range name could render an accurate formula invalid. You will also learn how to audit formulas, including those that have been entered incorrectly and those that are inappropriate for the data or task.

In the projected Income Statement that Kiola is developing for TheZone's sunglasses, she wants to account for expenses more precisely. She currently lists payroll, advertising, and rent, but she wants to eliminate these entries and replace them with more precise selling expenses, such as salaries, commissions, travel, and advertising, and administrative expenses, such as insurance, taxes, and depreciation. She develops preliminary versions of two worksheets—one includes the first-quarter budget of expenses related to sunglasses sales, and another includes the first-quarter budget of administrative expenses. To save time, she copied formulas from other budget worksheets. When she entered the sales expense budget numbers, error indicators appeared. She needs to audit the formulas to identify and solve these problems. Then, she can update the projected Income Statement so it contains precise and accurate information.

Using the Formula Auditing Tools

Chapter 1 explained how to respond to worksheet errors that Excel flags with a green error-indicator triangle in the upper-left corner of a cell, or by displaying an error message that begins with a pound sign (#)—such as #NAME?—for unrecognized text in a formula. You can respond to these errors in the following ways:

- **Fix obvious errors**—If an error message indicates an obvious error, such as ####, you can immediately fix the problem, such as by widening the column to display the complete value in the cell.
- **Use the Error Alert button**—If a cell contains an error-indicator triangle in its upper-left corner, you can click the cell to display the Error Alert button. Click this button to see a list of possible problems and solutions.
- **Examine the formula**—Click the cell containing an error message, and then examine the formula in the Formula Bar. (You can also press the keyboard combination Ctrl+` (grave accent) to display the formula in the problematic cell and all the other cells in the worksheet.) If you double-click the cell, Excel displays color-coded borders around related cells, as shown in Figure 10.18. (*Note*: Figures shown throughout this chapter do not reflect the actual colors of the different elements as they appear in the Excel window.) Common formula errors include using incorrect cell references, problems with mathematical order of precedence, and using a value as text. (These types of errors are described in Chapter 1.)

Figure 10.18: Formula with color-coded cell references and related cell borders

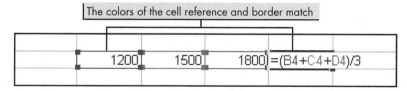

If these approaches don't solve the problem, you can use the Excel **formula auditing** tools that help you troubleshoot formula problems by letting you review the structure and behavior of a formula. Excel groups these tools in the Formula Auditing group on the Formulas tab on the Ribbon, as shown in Figure 10.19.

Figure 10.19: Formula Auditing group on the Formulas tab

Table 10.3 describes each button in the Formula Auditing group.

Table 10.3: Formula Auditing

Button	Description
Trace Precedents	Displays tracer arrows that indicate which cells affect the value of the currently selected cell
Trace Dependents	Displays tracer arrows that indicate which cells are affected by the value of the currently selected cell
Remove Arrows	Removes all displayed tracer arrows
Remove Arrows menu	Provides options to remove all tracer arrows, or just precedent or dependent tracer arrows
Show Formulas	Toggles between displaying formulas or results of formulas in the worksheet
Error Checking	Checks for errors in the worksheet
Error Checking menu	Provides access to the Error Checking, Trace Error, and Circular References tools, when appropriate
Trace Error	Traces errors in the active cell
Circular References	Allows you to step through a set of cells that directly or indirectly refer to themselves
Evaluate Formula	Displays the different parts of a nested formula evaluated in the order in which the formula is calculated
Watch Window	Allows you to keep track of cell properties, such as name, value, and formula, even if the cell is out of view

Many tools in the Formula Auditing group display **tracer arrows** on your worksheet to show which cells are related to the active cell. Tracer arrows show a path to precedent cells and dependent cells. A **precedent cell** contains a value that is used in a formula. For example, if cell D2 is the active cell and it contains a formula such as =B7*C2, precedent tracer arrows would point from cells B7 and C7 to cell D2. A **dependent cell** uses the value in the active cell in its formula's calculation. If cell B7 is the active cell, for example, a dependent tracer arrow would point from cell B7 to cell D2. Tracer arrows are normally blue, but are displayed in red if a precedent or dependent cell contains an error message.

Tracing and Solving Formula Errors

Kiola begins working with her new budgets by examining the Selling Expenses worksheet, as shown in Figure 10.20. The obvious place to start is with the cells that contain error messages; those clearly indicate a problem.

Figure 10.20: Selling Expenses worksheet

Error messages indicate problems

	A	B	C	D	E	F	G	H	I	J	K	L
1			Sunglasses Products -- Budgeted Selling Expenses for 2013									
2				January			February			March		
3	Type	Rate	Fixed	Variable	Total	Fixed	Variable	Total	Fixed	Variable	Total	
4	Salaries		$ 3,000		$ 3,000	$ 3,000		$ 3,000	$ 3,000		$ 3,000	
5	Commissions	3%	-	2,925	2,925	-	3,094	3,094	none	3,287	#VALUE!	
6	Travel	2%	-	1,950	1,950	-	2,063	2,063	none	2,191	#VALUE!	
7	Advertising	1%	-	975	975	-	1,031	1,031	none	1,096	#VALUE!	
8	Depreciation		1,000		1,000	1,000		1,000	1,000		$ 1,000	
9	Miscellaneous		800		800	800		800	800		$ 800	
10	Total selling expenses		#NAME?	$ 5,851	$ 10,651	$ 4,800	$ 6,188	$ 10,988	$ 4,800	$ 6,574	#VALUE!	
11												
12	Statistics											
13	Average monthly expense		#VALUE!									
14	Max expense		#VALUE!									
15	Min expense		#VALUE!									
16												
17												

Green triangles in the upper-left corners of cells indicate possible problems or errors

Kiola clicks cell C10, which contains a #NAME? error. Next, she displays the Formulas tab and then clicks the Error Checking button in the Formula Auditing group to open the Error Checking dialog box shown in Figure 10.21.

Figure 10.21: Error Checking dialog box

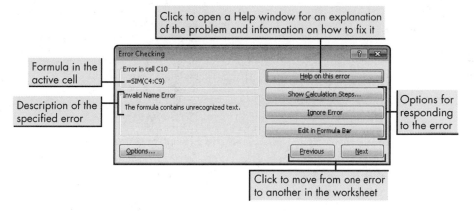

Click to open a Help window for an explanation of the problem and information on how to fix it

Formula in the active cell

Description of the specified error

Options for responding to the error

Click to move from one error to another in the worksheet

The Error Checking dialog box indicates that the error in cell C10 is caused by a word in the formula that Excel doesn't recognize. Excel assumes that any text in a formula is either a command word, such as a function name, or a reference to a cell, such as a named range. The only exception to this is when text is surrounded by quotation marks; in that case, it is treated as a text string. In cell C10, because Excel doesn't recognize the text "SIM" as either a command word or a named range, it displays the #NAME? error message in the cell. It is clear that the SUM function command word was misspelled. Kiola clicks the Edit in Formula Bar button, fixes the typo in the command word, and presses the Enter key to confirm the change. The value 4,800 appears in C10, which is the correct sum of cells C4:C9.

10

Level 2

Now, Kiola closes the Error Checking dialog box and turns her attention to the other errors identified in the Selling Expenses worksheet.

Tracing Errors

The Selling Expenses worksheet contains #VALUE! errors in cells C13:C15, K5:K7, and K10, indicating that each of those cells' formulas refers to a value that is an incorrect operand or argument type. When multiple cells contain the same error message, business analysis and understanding the purpose of a worksheet can often help solve the problem. In this case, the Selling Expenses worksheet calculates monthly totals for fixed selling expenses, such as salaries and depreciation, and variable selling expenses, such as commissions and travel. It displays these monthly totals in cells E10, H10, and K10. Cell K10 should sum the selling expenses for March. It might display an error message because its formula is constructed incorrectly and does not sum the appropriate values.

However, when Kiola examines the formula in the active cell (K10), she finds that it is =SUM(K4:K9). This is correct: the total selling expenses for March should sum the values in cells K4:K9. She decides to use the Formula Auditing tools to trace the error.

How To

Trace Errors
1. Click the cell displaying an error.
2. Click the Formulas tab on the Ribbon, and then click the Error Checking button arrow in the Formula Auditing group.
3. Click the Trace Error command.
4. Examine the possible sources of the error as shown by the tracer arrows.
5. Correct the source of the error.

With K10 selected as the active cell, Kiola clicks the Error Checking button arrow in the Formula Auditing group, and then clicks the Trace Error command. Two tracer arrows appear, as shown in Figure 10.22.

Blue or red tracer arrows point to precedent cells that provide data for the active cell. Red tracer arrows indicate when a precedent cell contains an error. In the Selling Expenses worksheet, a red arrow points from cell K5 to cell K10, showing that cell K5 contains an error. The small solid circles on the blue tracer arrow indicate that cells I5, J5, and K5 are also precedent cells for cell K10—their values are used in the =SUM(K4:K9) formula in cell K10.

Kiola clicks cell K6, which also contains a #VALUE! error, and then clicks the Trace Error command on the Error Checking menu. She does the same for the error in cell K7. The previous tracer arrows remain on the worksheet as she adds the tracer arrows for each subsequent active cell. See Figure 10.23.

Figure 10.22: Tracing the error in cell K10

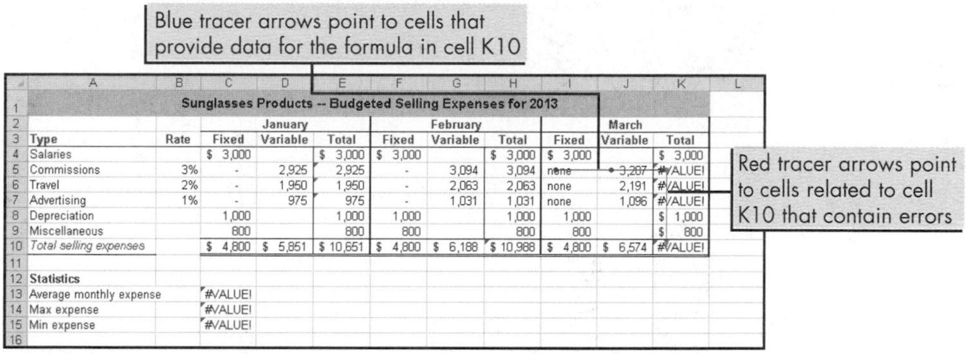

Blue tracer arrows point to cells that provide data for the formula in cell K10

Red tracer arrows point to cells related to cell K10 that contain errors

Figure 10.23: Continuing to trace errors

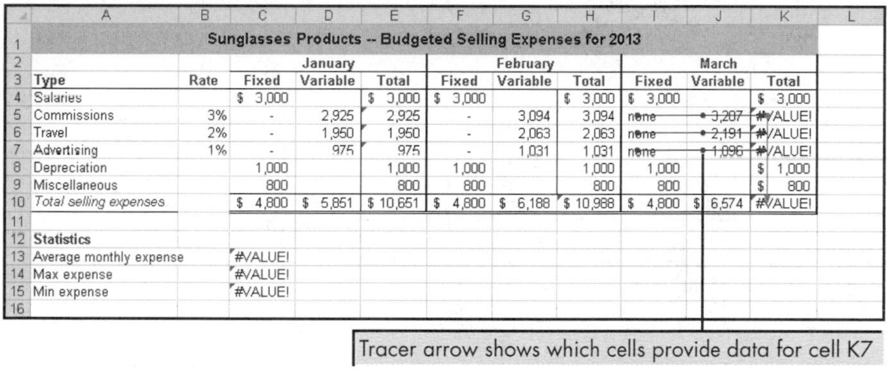

Tracer arrow shows which cells provide data for cell K7

Now Kiola knows that the #VALUE! errors in column K are all related to each other. She uses the Error Alert button to identify and correct the errors.

Identifying and Correcting Errors

The tracer arrows indicate that the #VALUE! error in cell K10 involves cells I5:K7. An Error Alert button also appears on the tracer arrows. This button can be helpful in identifying the error and solving the problem. Like the Error Checking dialog box, it names the type of error and lets you access the Excel Help tool or edit the formula in the Formula Bar. Kiola clicks the Error Alert button, and then clicks Help on this error. The Microsoft Excel Help window opens with information related to the #VALUE! error. See Figure 10.24.

Kiola reads the possible causes, focusing on the one that begins "One or more cells that are included in a formula contain text." Cells I5:I7 contain the word "none" instead of a numeric value, and the formulas in cells K5:K10 expect to use numeric values in their formulas. She edits the contents of cells I5:I7 so that they contain zeroes instead of the word, which fixes the #VALUE! errors, and then she removes the tracer arrows. See Figure 10.25.

10

Level 2

Figure 10.24: Help information for a #VALUE! error

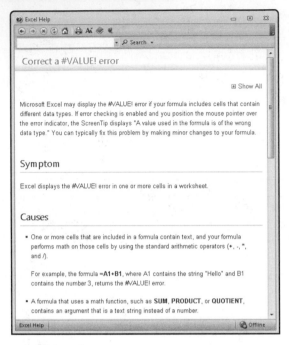

Figure 10.25: Fixing the #VALUE! errors

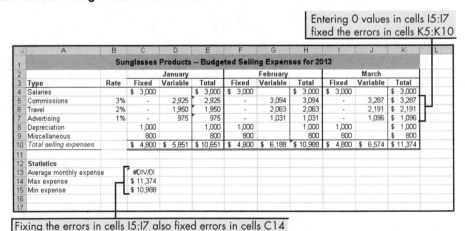

Entering 0 values in cells I5:I7 fixed the errors in cells K5:K10

Fixing the errors in cells I5:I7 also fixed errors in cells C14 and C15, but also revealed a new error in cell C13

Correcting the errors in cells I5:I7 solved not only the problems in cells K5:K7 and K10, but also the problems in cells C14 and C15, which display the maximum and minimum expenses, respectively. Correcting the #VALUE! errors also unexpectedly revealed a new error, the #DIV/0! error in cell C13.

Best Practice

Relying on Business Knowledge

As you audit a worksheet, let your common sense and business knowledge guide you to identify and diagnose errors. For example, if a sales worksheet shows total sales of $3 billion for a product with a unit price of $30.00, you should recognize that the sales total of $3 billion is unreasonable, even if the formula is correct. To achieve $3 billion in sales, TheZone would have had to sell 100 million sunglasses at $30.00 each, meaning half of the U.S. population bought TheZone sunglasses, which is not reasonable. You should also audit the formulas in worksheets to ensure they conform to standard accounting calculations. For example, EPS is calculated by dividing net income by the average number of shares of stock outstanding. If you are auditing an Income Statement, verify that the EPS formula references the cells that contain the net income and the average number of shares outstanding. It is often helpful to list important but less commonly known formulas on the documentation worksheet.

Tracing Precedent Cells

Kiola is familiar with the #DIV/0! error, and knows that it means the formula in cell C13 is trying to divide a value by 0. She decides to use the Trace Precedents tool in the Formula Auditing group to identify the precedent cells for the formula in cell C13. If one of those cells has the value of 0, she has probably identified the problem.

How To

Trace Precedent Cells

1. Click the cell displaying an error or containing a formula you want to trace.
2. Click the Formulas tab on the Ribbon, and then click the Trace Precedents button in the Formula Auditing group to display tracer arrows pointing to the formula's precedent cells.

When Kiola selects cell C13 and clicks the Trace Precedents button in the Formula Auditing group, tracer arrows point to cells B10, E10, H10, and K10, as shown in Figure 10.26.

Figure 10.26: Tracing the precedents to cell C13

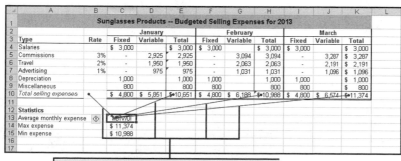

Tracer arrows show the precedents for cell C13

Cells E10, H10, and K10 contain values, but cell B10 is a blank cell, which evaluates as the value 0 in a formula involving division. Cell C13 is supposed to show the average monthly expense, so it should sum the values in cells E10, H10, and K10 and divide the result by 3, not by the value in cell B10. Kiola corrects the formula so it becomes =(E10+H10+K10)/3. The tracer arrows associated with cell C13 automatically disappear when the error message disappears from the cell. See Figure 10.27.

Figure 10.27: Fixing the #DIV/0! error

Cell C13 now contains the correct formula

	A	B	C	D	E	F	G	H	I	J	K	L
	C13			fx	=(E10+H10+K10)/3							
1				Sunglasses Products -- Budgeted Selling Expenses for 2013								
2			January			February			March			
3	Type	Rate	Fixed	Variable	Total	Fixed	Variable	Total	Fixed	Variable	Total	
4	Salaries		$ 3,000		$ 3,000	$ 3,000		$ 3,000	$ 3,000		$ 3,000	
5	Commissions	3%	-	2,925	2,925	-	3,094	3,094	-	3,287	$ 3,287	
6	Travel	2%	-	1,950	1,950	-	2,063	2,063	-	2,191	$ 2,191	
7	Advertising	1%	-	975	975	-	1,031	1,031	-	1,096	$ 1,096	
8	Depreciation		1,000		1,000	1,000		1,000	1,000		$ 1,000	
9	Miscellaneous		800		800	800		800	800		$ 800	
10	Total selling expenses		$ 4,800	$ 5,851	$ 10,651	$ 4,800	$ 6,188	$ 10,988	$ 4,800	$ 6,574	$ 11,374	
11												
12	Statistics											
13	Average monthly expense		$ 11,004									
14	Max expense		$ 11,374									
15	Min expense		$ 10,988									
16												
17												

Error indicators remain in cells E5:E7 and H10

Cells E5:E7, which show the variable expenses for January, and cell H10, which shows the total selling expenses for February, appear with the small green triangles in their upper-left corners, which indicates that there might still be errors in them. Kiola clicks cell H10 and examines the formula, but doesn't recognize the problem. She also notices another possible error that Excel has not flagged. Cell C15 should show the minimum monthly expense, but shows $10,988, which is the expense total displayed in cell H10. The minimum monthly expense, however, is actually the $10,651 found in cell E10. Because cell C15 displays the value in cell H10, Kiola wants to see if they are correctly related. She decides to troubleshoot cell H10 by tracing which cells depend on the formula in cell H10. If they include cell C15, she might be able to solve both errors at once.

Tracing Dependent Cells

Recall that a dependent cell contains a formula that refers to other cells. When you trace dependent cells, you trace the components of a formula that references other cells.

How To

Trace Dependent Cells

1. Click the cell displaying a formula you want to trace.

2. Click the Formulas tab on the Ribbon, and then click the Trace Dependents button in the Formula Auditing group to display tracer arrows pointing to the formula's dependent cells.

Kiola clicks cell H10, and then clicks the Trace Dependents button in the Formula Auditing group. Tracer arrows appear, indicating which cells depend on the formula in cell H10, as shown in Figure 10.28.

Figure 10.28: Tracing dependents

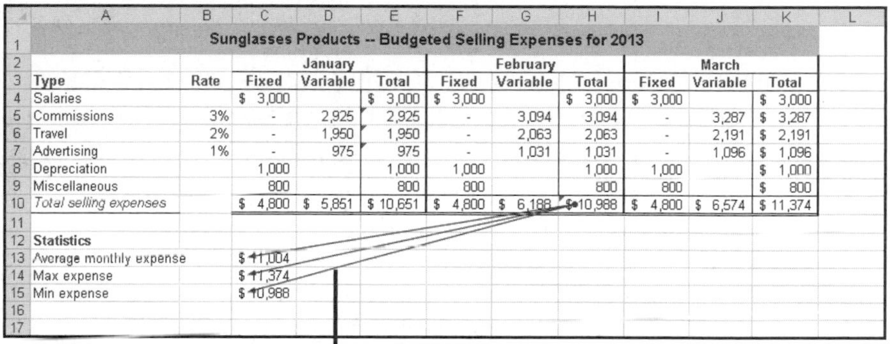

Blue tracer arrows show which cells depend on the value in cell H10

Using the Trace Dependents button confirms that cell C15, which contains an unflagged error, depends on the formula in cell H10. Kiola then removes the tracer arrows.

Kiola continues to diagnose the possible problem in cell H10 by pointing to the Error Alert button that appears to the left of the cell. A ScreenTip is displayed indicating that the formula in the active cell differs from the formulas in this area of the worksheet. Kiola double-clicks the cell to examine the formula and to see which cells the formula refers to directly. See Figure 10.29.

Figure 10.29: Diagnosing the problem in cell H10

	A	B	C	D	E	F	G	H	I	J	K	L
1			Sunglasses Products -- Budgeted Selling Expenses for 2013									
2				January			February			March		
3	Type	Rate	Fixed	Variable	Total	Fixed	Variable	Total	Fixed	Variable	Total	
4	Salaries		$ 3,000		$ 3,000	$ 3,000		$ 3,000	$ 3,000		$ 3,000	
5	Commissions	3%	-	2,925	2,925	-	3,094	3,094	-	3,287	$ 3,287	
6	Travel	2%	-	1,950	1,950	-	2,063	2,063	-	2,191	$ 2,191	
7	Advertising	1%	-	975	975	-	1,031	1,031	-	1,096	$ 1,096	
8	Depreciation		1,000		1,000	1,000		1,000	1,000		$ 1,000	
9	Miscellaneous		800		800	800		800	800		$ 800	
10	Total selling expenses		$ 4,800	$ 5,851	$ 10,651	$ 4,800	$ 6,188	=SUM(F10:G10)		$ 6,574	$ 11,374	
11												
12	Statistics											
13	Average monthly expense		$ 11,004									
14	Max expense		$ 11,374									
15	Min expense		$ 10,988									
16												
17												

Double-clicking cell H10 displays its formula in the cell and activates the Range Finder

The formula in cell H10 sums the values in the two cells to its left: cell F10, which contains the fixed selling expenses for February, and cell G10, which contains the variable selling expenses for February. Because cell H10 shows the total selling expenses for February, its formula is correct. Why does Excel flag cell H10 with an error indicator?

Kiola examines the worksheet more carefully, noting the formulas that calculate the total selling expenses for January in cell E10 and the total selling expenses for March in cell K10, as well as the other formulas in row 10 that total the fixed and variable expenses for each month. Each of those formulas sums the values in the cells *above* it. For example, recall that the formula in cell K10 sums K4:K9. Excel includes an error indicator in cell H10 because Excel recognizes from the structure of the worksheet that cell H10 has the same type of data surrounding it as do cells F10 and G10, but it contains a formula that uses different relationships than do the formulas in those cells. This is not truly an error because cell H10 uses a valid formula that calculates the correct value. However, because Kiola is distributing this workbook to others, she does not want them to be confused by the error indicator in cell H10. Instead of retyping the formula in cell H10, she decides to have Excel update the formula automatically. She clicks the Error Alert button, and then clicks Copy Formula from Left. Excel copies the formula from cell E10, which calculates the total sales expense for January by summing the values in cells E4:E9.

Now, Kiola checks cell C15, which should display the minimum monthly sales expense, to see if correcting the error in cell H10 solved the unflagged problem in cell C15. Unfortunately, cell C15 still displays the incorrect result. Kiola makes cell C15 the active cell so she can examine the formula, as shown in Figure 10.30.

Figure 10.30: Diagnosing the error in cell C15

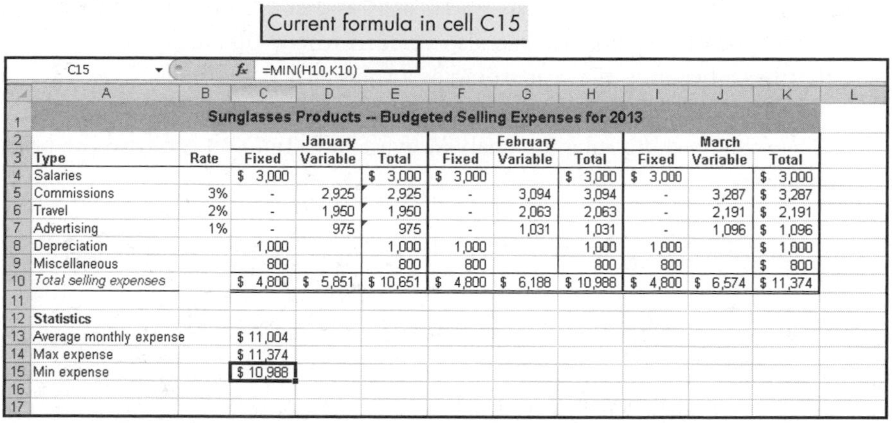

Current formula in cell C15

| C15 | | fx =MIN(H10,K10) | | | | | | | | | |

This problem turns out to be easy to solve—cell C15 should determine the minimum of the three values in cells E10, H10, and K10, but only refers to the values in cells H10 and K10. Kiola edits the formula so it becomes =MIN(E10, H10, K10), and cell C15 then shows the correct value: $10,651.

In the preceding two problems that Kiola solved, cell H10 was flagged with an error indicator, even though it did not contain a true error, and cell C15 was not flagged, even though it contained an error. Relying on the Excel formula auditing tools can result in both false positives and false negatives. **False positives** are items that are flagged as incorrect, but are, in fact, correct. **False negatives** are items that are, in fact, incorrect, but are not flagged as such. When you design an Excel workbook, you will know more about the real-life business situation being modeled in the workbook than Excel does. You must take advantage of your knowledge of the business processes and relationships in identifying and correcting errors, including false positives and false negatives. You can also fine-tune the errors that Excel flags on the Error Checking tab of the Excel Options dialog box.

Setting Error-Checking Options

Like a grammar checker, Excel uses certain rules to check for potential problems in formulas. For example, one rule checks for numbers stored as text, and another looks for values excluded from formulas that refer to adjacent cells.

This second example is the rule that is causing an error indicator to be displayed in cells E5:E7. The formulas in those cells correctly refer to the two cells to their immediate left, summing the fixed and variable expenses for each line item. For example, the formula in cell E5 sums the values in C5:D5. Because cell B5 contains a value (3%, the commission rate) but is excluded from the formula in cell E5, which references cells immediately adjacent to it, Excel suspects that B5 should be included in the range summed by the formula in E5. Since a workbook user can easily see that B5 contains a very different type of value—a percentage—than do cells C5 and D5, which contain dollar amounts, it is also easy to see that the error indicators in cells E5:E7 are another example of false positives on Excel's part. This type of false positive can also be seen when you are summing a column of numbers that has a heading of a year stored as a value.

Most of Excel's error-checking rules are enabled by default, but you can turn the rules on or off individually.

How To

Set Error-Checking Options
1. Click the File tab on the Ribbon, and then click the Options command to open the Excel Options dialog box.
2. Click the Formulas category. See Figure 10.31.

Figure 10.31: Error Checking options for formulas

Select to display green error indicators in cells

Select or clear the check boxes to specify which rules you want Excel's Error Checking feature to test

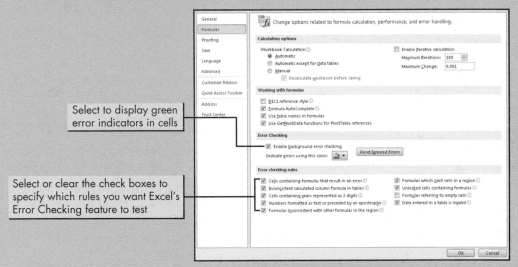

3. In the Error checking rules section, select a check box to enable a rule or clear a check box to disable the rule.
4. Click the OK button.

Kiola turns off the Formulas which omit cells in a region error checking rule by removing the check mark. Turning off this option eliminates the false positive error indicators in cells E5:E7 of her worksheet, and then she saves her file.

Using Test Data to Locate Errors

Another technique that can help you ferret out spreadsheet errors is the use of test data. **Test data** is input data for which you already know the results. By entering a variety of input data and comparing the results to output you have already calculated outside the worksheet, you can use what-if analysis to indirectly verify the validity of your worksheet. This technique is most powerful when you use a wide range of input test data, anticipating all possible real-world situations. In other words, testing data at the extreme limits of data's relevant range can provide the most powerful test of the worksheet's validity.

Remember to remove all sample data from the worksheet when you have finished testing. Otherwise, the same data can cause problems in the worksheet and produce invalid results, which is the exact opposite of the purpose it was meant to serve.

After troubleshooting a workbook by checking for data-entry errors and auditing formulas, you can continue to prepare an Excel application by automating tasks. When you are designing a workbook that others will use, you can make the application easy to work with and prevent errors by using macros, which are discussed in Level 3.

Steps To Success: Level 2

Kiola creates a Cost of Goods Sold worksheet for use in the Sunglasses workbook, and notices that it contains a few error messages and error indicators. Figure 10.32 shows the Cost of Goods Sold worksheet.

Figure 10.32: Cost of Goods Sold worksheet

	A	B	C	D	E
1	Sunglasses Products -- Budgeted Cost of Goods Sold for 2013				
2					
3		January	February	March	
4	Direct material	$24,053	$27,625	$30,240	
5	Direct labor	17,190	22,750	23,520	
6	Manufacturing overhead	18,000	19,055	19,356	
7	Total manufacturing cost	#NAME?	69,430	73,116	
8	Add: Beginning inventory	43,035	42,599	46,458	
9	Less: Ending inventory	42,599	46,458	48,198	
10	Cost of goods sold	#NAME?	#VALUE!	#VALUE!	
11					
12	Statistics				
13	Average monthly manufacturing cost	#NAME?			
14	Maximum monthly manufacturing cost	#NAME?			
15	Minimum monthly manufacturing cost	#NAME?			
16					
17					

10

This budget worksheet calculates the monthly total manufacturing cost of producing sunglasses by summing labor, materials, and overhead. It also records the costs of the beginning and ending sunglasses inventory for the month. It calculates COGS by subtracting the ending inventory cost from the beginning inventory cost and adding that to the total manufacturing cost—totaling the cost of the sunglasses TheZone could have sold, and subtracting the cost of the sunglasses TheZone didn't sell each month. Your task is to audit the worksheet and correct the problems. Complete the following:

1. Open the workbook named **COGS.xlsx** located in the Chapter 10 folder, and then save it as **COGS Budget.xlsx**.

2. Use the Error Checking dialog box to diagnose and fix the #NAME? error message in cell B7.

3. Use the Trace Error command on the Error Checking menu to trace the #VALUE! errors in cells C10 and D10. Diagnose and fix the error(s).

4. Make cell B14 the active cell, and then use the Error Alert button to view Help information about the error. Read the Help information, and then close the Microsoft Excel Help window.

5. Use the Trace Dependents tool in the Formula Auditing group to trace the error in cell B14.

6. Correct the error in cell B14 so it identifies the maximum manufacturing cost among the three months.

7. View and evaluate the worksheet formulas, which contain one more error. Correct the error.

8. Save and close the COGS Budget.xlsx workbook.

LEVEL 3
Automating Excel Tasks

Understanding and Using Macros

One way to make a workbook easier to use is to automate repetitive or difficult tasks. To do so, you can use a **macro**, a series of commands that you store and then run when you need to perform a task. For example, you can create a macro that displays the formulas in a workbook, prints the workbook in landscape orientation showing row and column headings and gridlines on the printout, then returns the page layout settings to normal, and redisplays the results of the formulas. To perform this task manually, you have to perform seven tasks: display the formulas; set the page setup orientation to landscape; set the sheet options to print gridlines; set the sheet options to print row and column headings; access the Print tab of Backstage view to print the worksheet; reset the page setup options; and redisplay the results of the formulas. If you create a macro to perform these steps, Excel can perform them more quickly and accurately than you can. In addition, you don't need to remember the various steps each time you want to print the formulas—they are stored as **Visual Basic for Applications (VBA)** commands in the macro, and are performed in sequence when you run the macro. You can create an Excel macro by using the **macro recorder** to record your keystrokes and mouse actions as you perform them, or you can write macros from scratch by entering VBA commands in the **Visual Basic Editor**.

Kiola wants to create a macro that prints the formulas in the Projected Income worksheet. She also wants to insert a button in the worksheet that users can click to run the macro. She will start by creating a basic macro.

To work with macros, the Developer tab must be displayed on the Ribbon. Thus, Kiola sets her Excel options to display that Ribbon tab.

How To

Display the Developer Tab on the Ribbon
1. Click the File tab on the Ribbon to display Backstage view.
2. Click the Options command. The Excel Options dialog box opens.
3. In the Customize Ribbon category, under Main tabs, select the Developer check box to add this tab to the Ribbon.
4. Click the OK button.

10

Level 3

Best Practice

Understanding Macro Security in Excel
When you are distributing Excel workbooks or receiving them from others, you need to be concerned about macro viruses. A virus is a program that is attached to a file and runs when you open the file. A virus can harm your computer by changing your program settings, for example, or deleting files on your hard disk. **Macro viruses** are viruses that are written and stored as macros attached to documents created in Office programs such as Excel, and run when you open the infected document. Accordingly, you should never allow a macro from an unknown source to run on your computer because it might contain a virus.

If you know a document came from a trustworthy source and contains only safe macros, you can store it in a **trusted location**, allowing any macros in it to run without being checked by the **Trust Center**'s security settings. A trusted location is usually a folder on your hard drive or shared network drive that has been designated by you or your network administrator as containing documents that always come from trustworthy sources.

Also, after you create and test a macro, you can attach a **digital certificate** to vouch for its authenticity. You can obtain a digital certificate from a commercial certification authority or, in some cases, from your system administrator. A digital certificate should contain a **digital signature**, which confirms that the signer created the macro and that the macro has not been changed since its digital certificate was created.

You control how Excel handles macros that are not stored in trusted locations by choosing one of the following macro settings in its Trust Center:

- **Disable all macros without notification**—Excel disables all macros and security alerts about macros in documents that are not stored in a trusted location.
- **Disable all macros with notification**—Excel disables all macros but retains security alerts about macros in documents that are not stored in a trusted location. This allows you to enable macros on a case-by-case basis. This is the default setting for macros.
- **Disable all macros except digitally signed macros**—This setting is the same as the Disable all macros with notification setting except that macros that are digitally signed can run if you have already identified the source as a trusted publisher.
- **Enable all macros**—Excel allows all macros to run. Because this setting makes your computer vulnerable to potentially malicious code, it is not recommended.

You use the Trust Center to choose these macro security settings. To open the Trust Center, click the Developer tab, then click the Macro Security button in the Code group.

As yet another layer of protection against malicious code, the default file format in Excel 2010 (.xlsx extension) does not support VBA code. To save and run a macro in an Excel workbook, it must be saved as a **macro-enabled workbook**, giving it an .xlsm extension.

Recording a Macro

New or casual Excel users usually prefer to create a macro using the macro recorder. This is an excellent choice for automating tasks that you perform using the keyboard or mouse. You can assign a macro to a shortcut key, which is a combination of keystrokes you press to run the macro, such as the keystroke combination Ctrl+Shift+P. When you want to run the macro, you press the keys to which the macro is assigned. For example, press Ctrl+Shift+P to run a macro that you recorded with that shortcut key specification. You can also run a macro using the Macro dialog box.

The first task that Kiola wants to automate in the Sunglasses workbook is documenting the workbook by printing its formulas. These documentation printouts will also benefit from the filename and date codes she has already put in the footers of the worksheets so that the users of the printouts know exactly what file the printout is helping to document, and when the documentation was last printed (which can give a rough indication of whether or not the documentation is up to date).

How To

Record a Macro

1. Click the Developer tab on the Ribbon, then click the Record Macro button in the Code group. The Record Macro dialog box opens. See Figure 10.33.

Figure 10.33: Record Macro dialog box

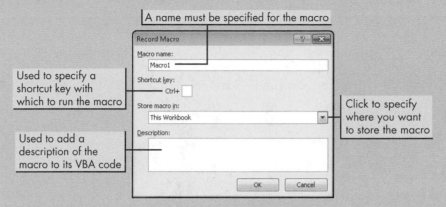

A name must be specified for the macro

Used to specify a shortcut key with which to run the macro

Used to add a description of the macro to its VBA code

Click to specify where you want to store the macro

2. In the Macro name box, enter a unique name for the macro. The name can contain up to 255 characters, including letters, numbers, and the underscore symbol. You cannot use spaces or special characters in a macro name.

3. Click the Store macro in arrow, and then select a location for the macro, such as the current workbook.

4. To assign the macro to a shortcut key, enter the key name in the Shortcut key box. You can also enter a description for the macro.

5. Click the OK button to start the macro recorder. The Stop Recording button replaces the Record Macro button in the Code group.

6. Perform the tasks you want to record.

7. Click the Stop Recording button in the Code group.

10

Level 3

Before recording the printing formulas macro, Kiola plans the steps:

1. On the Formulas tab on the Ribbon, click the Show Formulas button in the Formula Auditing group to display the worksheet formulas instead of the results of the formulas.

2. On the Page Layout tab on the Ribbon, click the Page Setup dialog box launcher.

3. In the Page Setup dialog box, click the Page tab, if it isn't already active.

4. Set the Orientation to Landscape.

5. Click the Sheet tab.

6. In the Print section of the Sheet tab, select the Gridlines and Row and column headings check boxes.

7. Click the Print button on the bottom of the Sheet tab to close the Page Setup dialog box and display the Print section of Backstage view.

8. Click the Print button.

9. On the Page Layout tab, click the Page Setup dialog box launcher.

10. On the Page tab of the Page Setup dialog box, reset the Orientation to Portrait.

11. On the Sheet tab, deselect the Gridlines and Row and column headings check boxes.

12. Close the Page Setup dialog box by clicking the OK button.

13. On the Formulas tab, click the Show Formulas button in the Formula Auditing group to redisplay the results of the formulas.

Kiola will save the macro in the current workbook for now. However, as she reviews the steps that she has planned, she realizes that if she decides to save the macro in her personal macro workbook at a later date, the macro would work for any worksheet in any workbook. This is because there are no cell- or worksheet-specific steps in the macro, such as entering data in cells or inserting text strings in a header or footer.

Kiola performs the planned steps carefully to test them on the Projected Income worksheet, and then she returns the worksheet to its original condition, without the formulas displayed and the specialized Page Layout settings, so she can perform the steps correctly. (For instance, if she did not return the worksheet to its original condition, performing the first step in her plan would turn *off* the display of the formulas.)

She records the macro, naming it PrintFormulas and assigning it to the Ctrl+Shift+P shortcut key combination. She also adds information about the macro to the Documentation worksheet, explaining how to run it. In addition, she saves the file as a macro-enabled workbook.

How To

Save an Excel file as a Macro-Enabled Workbook
1. Click the File tab of the Ribbon to display Backstage view.
2. Click the Save As command.
3. Choose Excel Macro-Enabled Workbook from the Save as type list.
4. Specify the desired location and filename for the workbook.
5. Click the Save button.

Running a Macro

After you record a macro, you can run it in two ways: press the shortcut key assigned to the macro, or use the Macro dialog box.

How To

Run a Recorded Macro

Press the shortcut key assigned to the macro.

OR

1. Click the Developer tab on the Ribbon, then click the Macros button in the Code group. The Macro dialog box opens. See Figure 10.34.

Figure 10.34: Macro dialog box

2. In the Macro name box, click the name of the macro you want to run.
3. Click the Run button.

Now Kiola wants to make it even easier for users to run the PrintFormulas macro. She will create a macro button that users can click to print the formulas in the Projected Income worksheet.

Creating a Macro Button

Besides using a shortcut key or the Macro dialog box, you can also run a macro by assigning it to a button that you place on a worksheet. You can use a standard button supplied on the Forms Control palette, and include a descriptive label on the button that clarifies what it does. Users can then click the button to run the associated macro.

How To

Create a Macro Button

1. Click the Developer tab on the Ribbon, then click the Insert button in the Controls group to display the Form Controls menu.
2. Click the Button (Form Control) button on the Form Controls menu, and then click and drag on the worksheet to draw the button, until it is the size and shape you want.
3. Release the mouse button. Excel assigns a default label to the button and opens the Assign Macro dialog box, shown in Figure 10.35.

Figure 10.35: Assign Macro dialog box

4. Click the macro you want to assign to the button, and then click the OK button.
5. Type a descriptive label on the button.
6. Click anywhere off the button.

Kiola creates a macro button for the PrintFormulas macro on the Projected Income worksheet and labels the button Print Formulas, as shown in Figure 10.36.

Figure 10.36: Print Formulas button on the Projected Income worksheet

	A	B	C	D	E	F
1			TheZone - Sunglasses Products			
2			Projected Income Statement			
3			For the Period Ended Dec 31, 2013			
4		Tier 1				
5	**Assumptions:**			**Projections:**		
6	Unit sales	15,000		Sales	$ 450,000	
7	Unit price	$ 30.00		COGS	270,000	
8	Cost of goods sold (COGS)	60.00%		Gross profit	180,000	
9	Payroll	$ 50,000		Payroll	50,000	
10	Advertising	$ 75,000		Advertising	75,000	
11	Rent	$ 20,000		Rent	20,000	
12	Tax rate	35.00%		Pretax income	35,000	
13	Average number of			Est. income tax expense	12,250	
14	shares outstanding	200,000		Marginal net income	$ 22,750	
15						
16				Marginal earnings per share (EPS)	$ 0.11	
17						

Print Formulas

The PrintFormulas macro is assigned to this button

Best Practice

Testing Macros

After you create a macro, you should run it to verify that it runs correctly. If you over-looked a step, or the macro has an unexpected result, you can correct the macro in the following ways:

- Record the macro again using the same macro name and shortcut key (if appropriate).
- Delete the macro by opening the Macro dialog box, clicking the macro you want to delete, and then clicking the Delete button. Then record the macro again.
- Run the macro one step at a time by opening the Macro dialog box, clicking the macro you want to correct, and then clicking the Step Into button. After you identify the step causing the problems, record the macro again.

Kiola tests the macro button and is delighted that it works correctly. However, she can see the macro open and close dialog boxes as it runs, and she thinks this will be distracting for users. She knows that re-recording the macro will not solve this problem. Instead, she needs to edit the macro using the Visual Basic Editor.

Editing a Macro in the Visual Basic Editor

Recall that all Excel macros, including the ones you record, consist of VBA code. When Excel runs a macro, it performs the actions specified by the VBA code. To view the code of a macro, you open the Visual Basic Editor, a separate program that works with Excel and other Microsoft Office applications and lets you work with VBA code.

How To

Edit a Macro

1. Click the Developer tab on the Ribbon, click the Macros button in the Code group. The Macro dialog box opens.

2. Click the name of the macro you want to edit, and then click the Edit button. The Visual Basic Editor window opens, as shown in Figure 10.37.

Figure 10.37: Visual Basic Editor window

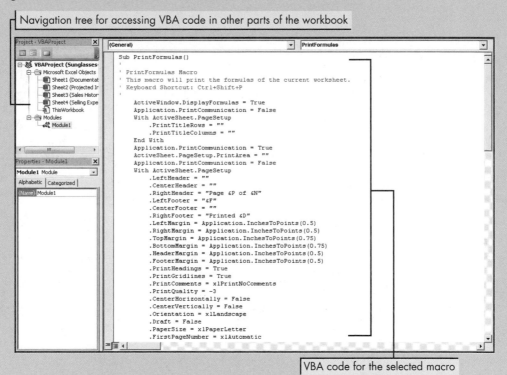

Navigation tree for accessing VBA code in other parts of the workbook

VBA code for the selected macro

3. Edit the macro code.

4. Click File on the menu bar, and then click Close and Return to Microsoft Excel.

Kiola needs to use the VBA Screen Updating command to control the Excel screen-updating feature and show or hide any actions that run in the macro. When she hides the actions, they are still performed, but not displayed in the Excel window. She will use the Screen Updating command to hide the dialog boxes that the PrintFormulas macro opens and closes as it runs.

Understanding VBA Basics

Kiola starts by viewing the VBA code for the PrintFormulas macro, as shown in Figure 10.38.

Figure 10.38: Beginning of code for the PrintFormulas macro

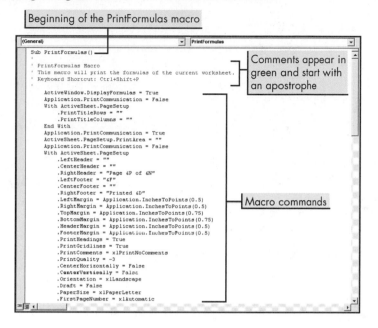

The VBA code lists all of the actions Kiola performed when she recorded the PrintFormulas macro. VBA calls macros **sub procedures** and starts each sub procedure name with *Sub*, followed by its descriptive name and a pair of parentheses, as in Sub PrintFormulas( ).

Following the sub procedure name are comments, which appear in green and start with an apostrophe ('). The apostrophe indicates to VBA that it can ignore these lines of text— they do not contain commands that Excel should perform. In macro code, the comment text includes the description entered in the Record New Macro dialog box.

Following the comments are the VBA commands the macro performs. Some commands are easy to decipher, even if you are not a VBA programmer. For example, in Figure 10.38, *ActiveWindow.DisplayFormulas = True* means "In the active window, display the formulas (set the DisplayFormulas property to true)."

The words *End Sub* indicate the end of the sub procedure, or the macro. (This is not shown in Figure 10.38 because it only shows the beginning of the PrintFormulas macro, but you can see it in the upcoming Figure 10.39.)

Best Practice

Learning VBA

The Visual Basic Editor has a comprehensive collection of Help information, including command references, explanations of programming concepts, and instructions for performing common tasks in VBA.

Before you work in the Visual Basic Editor on your own, consult with a VBA programmer or other expert. Refer to the Visual Basic Editor Help information frequently. A good place to start is the Visual Basic How Do I topics in the Help table of contents. In the Visual Basic Editor window, click Help on the menu bar, and then click Microsoft Visual Basic for Applications Help. The Visual Basic Help dialog box opens. Click the How Do I item and explore the various topics.

Writing a Macro Command

To control the screen-updating feature in Excel, Kiola inserts two commands into the PrintFormulas sub procedure:

- **Application.ScreenUpdating = False**—This command turns off the screen-updating feature so that Excel does not display any dialog boxes or other new windows, hiding the results of the actions that the macro performs.
- **Application.ScreenUpdating = True**—After turning off the screen-updating feature, Kiola needs to insert this command to turn the feature back on so that Excel displays the final results of the PrintFormulas macro.

Kiola inserts the first command (Application.ScreenUpdating = False) on the line after the Sub PrintFormulas() statement. If the command is inserted elsewhere in the macro, Excel will show some of the macro actions that it performs. Then Kiola inserts the second command (Application.ScreenUpdating = True) on the line before the End Sub statement so that Excel will again update the screen normally when the macro is finished running. See Figure 10.39.

Kiola saves her changes to the PrintFormulas command and then closes the Visual Basic Editor window by clicking File on the menu bar and then clicking Close and Return to Microsoft Excel. She tests the PrintFormulas macro by clicking the macro button on the Projected Income worksheet, and discovers that the screen updates are hidden and the macro runs a bit faster.

Kiola makes a final check of the Documentation sheet and other sheets in the Sunglasses workbook, and being satisfied by what she sees, saves the file one last time as a macro-enabled workbook. See Figure 10.40.

Figure 10.39: New commands in the PrintFormulas macro

```
Sub PrintFormulas()
Application.ScreenUpdating = False
'
' PrintFormulas Macro
' This macro will print the formulas of the current worksheet.
' Keyboard Shortcut: Ctrl+Shift+P
'
    ActiveWindow.DisplayFormulas = True
    Application.PrintCommunication = False
    With ActiveSheet.PageSetup
        .PrintTitleRows = ""
        .PrintTitleColumns = ""
    End With
    Application.PrintCommunication = True
    ActiveSheet.PageSetup.PrintArea = ""
    Application.PrintCommunication = False
    With ActiveSheet.PageSetup
        .LeftHeader = ""
        .CenterHeader = ""
        .RightHeader = "Page &P of &N"
        .LeftFooter = "&F"
        .CenterFooter = ""
        .RightFooter = "Printed &D"
        .LeftMargin = Application.InchesToPoints(0.5)
        .RightMargin = Application.InchesToPoints(0.5)
        .TopMargin = Application.InchesToPoints(0.75)
        .BottomMargin = Application.InchesToPoints(0.75)
        .HeaderMargin = Application.InchesToPoints(0.5)
        .FooterMargin = Application.InchesToPoints(0.5)
        .PrintHeadings = True
        .PrintGridlines = True
        .PrintComments = xlPrintNoComments
        .PrintQuality = -3
        .CenterHorizontally = False
        .CenterVertically = False
        .Orientation = xlLandscape
        .Draft = False
        .PaperSize = xlPaperLetter
```

New command inserted in the PrintFormulas macro to turn off Screen Updating while macro is running

```
        .HeaderMargin = Application.InchesToPoints(0.5)
        .FooterMargin = Application.InchesToPoints(0.5)
        .PrintHeadings = False
        .PrintGridlines = False
        .PrintComments = xlPrintNoComments
        .PrintQuality = -3
        .CenterHorizontally = False
        .CenterVertically = False
        .Orientation = xlPortrait
        .Draft = False
        .PaperSize = xlPaperLetter
        .FirstPageNumber = xlAutomatic
        .Order = xlDownThenOver
        .BlackAndWhite = False
        .Zoom = 100
        .PrintErrors = xlPrintErrorsDisplayed
        .OddAndEvenPagesHeaderFooter = False
        .DifferentFirstPageHeaderFooter = False
        .ScaleWithDocHeaderFooter = True
        .AlignMarginsHeaderFooter = True
        .EvenPage.LeftHeader.Text = ""
        .EvenPage.CenterHeader.Text = ""
        .EvenPage.RightHeader.Text = ""
        .EvenPage.LeftFooter.Text = ""
        .EvenPage.CenterFooter.Text = ""
        .EvenPage.RightFooter.Text = ""
        .FirstPage.LeftHeader.Text = ""
        .FirstPage.CenterHeader.Text = ""
        .FirstPage.RightHeader.Text = ""
        .FirstPage.LeftFooter.Text = ""
        .FirstPage.CenterFooter.Text = ""
        .FirstPage.RightFooter.Text = ""
    End With
    Application.PrintCommunication = True
    ActiveWindow.DisplayFormulas = False
    Application.ScreenUpdating = True
End Sub
```

New command inserted in the PrintFormulas macro to turn Screen Updating back on when macro is finished running

10

Level 3

Figure 10.40: Final Projected Income worksheet and Sunglasses macro-enabled workbook

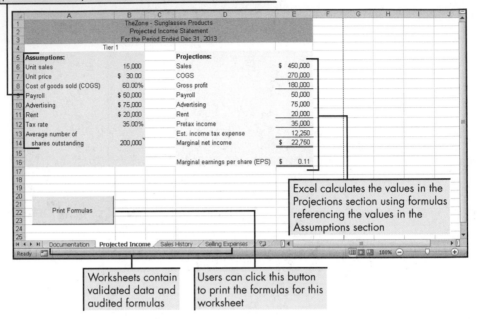

Validation settings and documentation comments help prevent data entry errors in cells in the Assumptions section

Excel calculates the values in the Projections section using formulas referencing the values in the Assumptions section

Worksheets contain validated data and audited formulas

Users can click this button to print the formulas for this worksheet

Steps To Success: Level 3

Kiola wants to add a macro button to the Documentation worksheet that allows users to print the sheet with a footer that shows the filename and the current date. Your task is to plan and record the macro and then assign it to a button on the Documentation worksheet. Complete the following:

1. Open the workbook named **PrintDoc.xlsx** located in the Chapter 10 folder, and save it as the macro-enabled workbook **Print Documentation.xlsm**.

   TROUBLESHOOTING: In order to complete this step, the macro settings on your computer must be enabled. If you receive a Security Warning saying macros have been disabled or the file can't be saved as a macro-enabled workbook, open the Trust Center to check the macro security settings. If you don't have access to the Trust Center, contact your instructor or computer support person for assistance.

2. Plan a macro that performs the following steps: opens the Page Setup dialog box, creates a custom header with the filename in the right section, creates a customer footer with the current date in the right section, prints the Documentation worksheet in landscape orientation, and then returns the page settings to their original state.

3. Record the macro, naming it **PrintDocumentation**, and saving it in the current workbook. Assign the macro to the Ctrl+Shift+P shortcut key combination. Enter a description for the macro.

4. Run the macro to test it. If it doesn't perform all the tasks you planned, rerecord the macro using the same name.

5. Add a macro button on the Documentation worksheet with the label **Print**.

6. Save the workbook, and then test the macro button.

7. Use the Visual Basic Editor window to insert the **Application.ScreenUpdating = False** command to turn off the screen-updating feature at the start of the macro. Also, insert the **Application.ScreenUpdating = True** command to turn the feature back on at the end of the macro.

8. Save the VBA code, close the Visual Basic Editor window, and then test your changes to the PrintDocumentation macro.

9. Save and close the Print Documentation.xlsm workbook.

Chapter Summary

This chapter explored creating an Excel application that functions as a decision support system. In Level 1, you planned an Excel application that others can use. You validated data entry and protected a workbook. You also provided thorough documentation for users, including a documentation worksheet and cell comments.

In Level 2, you audited formulas and evaluated error messages in cells using the Excel formula auditing tools to trace and correct errors. In Level 3, you automated a workbook by creating and running a macro. You made the macro easy to use by assigning it to a button that users can click to run the macro. Finally, you worked in the Visual Basic Editor window to edit a macro so that it runs more effectively.

10

Chapter Exercises

Conceptual Review

1. What is a decision support system?

2. How does an Excel application differ from other types of Excel workbooks?

3. What is a data validation rule? When should you create one?

4. What is the difference between an input message and an error alert in the context of Excel data validation?

5. What style of error alert prevents a user from storing an invalid entry in a worksheet?

6. Explain the two basic steps you must perform to protect the contents of a worksheet.

7. What does it mean to protect the structure of a workbook?

8. Describe two ways to document a workbook.

9. Before using the tools in the Formula Auditing group on the Formulas tab, what three troubleshooting tasks can you perform to audit formulas?

10. Explain the difference between precedent and dependent cells.

11. What are false positives and false negatives, and which are harder to detect in worksheets?

12. What is a macro? How could you use one in an Excel workbook?

13. Identify three ways to run a macro in Excel.

14. What is VBA?

15. Under what circumstances would you work in the Visual Basic Editor window?

16. What is the major difference between an Excel workbook with an .xlsx filename extension and an .xlsm extension?

Case Problems

Level 1 – Troubleshooting Formulas and Data Entry in a Payroll Data Workbook for Irene's Scrapbooking World

Similar to other small businesses, Irene's Scrapbooking World outsources the processing of its payroll to its accounting firm. Twice per month, Irene Watson, the owner of Irene's Scrapbooking World, creates a workbook that contains her employees' payroll information to send to the accounting firm of Wipson & Lynn, LLP. Wipson & Lynn then uses that information to prepare the paychecks for the employees and calculate Irene's Scrapbooking World's payroll liabilities to the government and other entities, and to prepare its payroll-related reports, such as the Federal 941 forms.

Human Resources

Wipson & Lynn charges Irene based on the number of paychecks it processes for her company. A number of Irene's payroll-related workbooks have contained data-entry errors that the firm's personnel had to fix before it could process the payroll. Wipson & Lynn also charges Irene for the time it takes to track down and fix those errors.

Irene has asked you to use the Excel data validation and protection tools to troubleshoot the current payroll workbook and set up the workbook to help prevent errors from occurring in the future.

Complete the following steps:

1. Open the workbook named **Payroll.xlsx** located in the Chapter 10 folder, and then save it as **Scrapbooking Payroll.xlsx**.

2. On the Documentation sheet, insert *your name* and the *current date* in the appropriate cells. Review the documentation information.

3. Swtich to the Payroll Register worksheet. Set up an appropriate validation rule, input message, and error alert for the Tax Status data in cells C7:C15.

4. Set up an appropriate validation rule, input message, and error alert for the Allowances data in cells D7:D15. (*Hint*: Employees can take 0 or more withholding allowances.)

5. Set up an appropriate validation rule, input message, and error alert for the Insurance Plan data in cells E7:E15. (*Hint*: The valid health plan options are stored in cells K22:K24.)

6. Set up appropriate validation rules, input messages, and error alerts for at least one other range of data in the Payroll Register worksheet.

7. Identify and correct all data that does not meet the validation settings you created in Steps 3 through 6.

10

Chapter Exercises

8. Determine which cells contain data that changes regularly. Then change the cells' properties so that users can edit this data when the worksheet is protected.

9. Enable worksheet protection. Do not specify a password.

10. Print the Payroll Register worksheet.

11. Save and close the Scrapbooking Payroll.xlsx workbook.

Level 2 – Troubleshooting Formulas in a Job Invoicing Workbook for David's Computer Repair

Accounting

David Green has been performing computer consulting services for family, friends, and neighbors for a number of years. He has decided to use an Excel workbook to create a template for a sales invoice. David's idea is that he will enter the data for each job in a few cells on a worksheet. This data will be inserted in an invoice in another portion of the worksheet, which he can then print and send to the customer as a bill.

As a new user of Excel, David has asked for your help in identifying and correcting errors in the invoice area of his worksheet. In addition, he asks for your help in creating some basic documentation for the workbook so that others can use it.

Complete the following steps:

1. Open the workbook named **Repair.xlsx** located in the Chapter 10 folder, and then save it as **Repair Invoicing.xlsx**.

2. On the Documentation sheet, insert *your name* and the *current date* in the appropriate cells.

3. On the Job Invoicing worksheet, use the Formula Auditing tools to identify and fix errors in the formulas of the Customer Invoice section of the Job Invoicing worksheet. Evaluate whether all flagged errors indicate true errors or false positives. Fix the flagged errors that are truly errors. Also look for any false negative errors in the invoice's formulas.

   Use the following explanations for the calculations as you troubleshoot the worksheet:

   • The Invoice Date should be a formula that displays the current date.
   • The total labor charge is computed by multiplying the number of hours spent on the job by the labor charge per hour.
   • Sales tax is computed by multiplying a sales amount by the sales tax rates. Sales tax is computed separately for labor and parts because they have different sales tax rates.
   • The total invoice amount due from the customer is the sum of the total charges for parts, labor, and the sales tax items.

4. Save the Repair Invoicing.xlsx workbook.

5. Enter the following job data and view the resulting invoice:

- Job date: **2/17/13**
- Customer name: **Ian Hancock**
- Total hours spent on job: **2.5**
- Charge per hour: **$60**
- Total parts for the job: **$19.95**

6. On the Documentation sheet, explain the purpose of the workbook, assumptions in the workbook, and instructions for using the workbook.

7. Print the worksheets in the Repair Invoicing workbook, and then save and close it.

Level 3 – Projected Sales and Commissions for CKG Auto

You are working in CKG Auto's Sales Department as an analyst. The sales manager, Leroy Mason, wants to automate the worksheet he uses to calculate monthly sales commissions so that others can use it. CKG Auto pays each salesperson a base salary plus a commission of 6.5% on each sale. Leroy asks for your help in ensuring users enter valid data and do not change or delete the sales data the workbook already contains. He also wants to include a chart comparing the total sales of each salesperson.

Sales

10

Complete the following:

1. Open the workbook named **Sales.xlsx** located in the Chapter 10 folder, and then save it as the macro-enabled workbook **June Sales.xlsm**.

2. On the Documentation worksheet, enter *your name* and the *current date* in the appropriate cells.

3. Examine the SalesEntryForm worksheet and correct its formula error. Enter test data to learn how the worksheet interacts with the Sales&CommissionList worksheet. Based on what you learn and your knowledge of CKG Auto and its sales policies, create data validation rules as appropriate for the SalesEntryForm worksheet.

4. In the Sales&CommissionList worksheet, create formulas in column E that determine the total sales for each salesperson.

5. Create a macro that places a bar chart on a new sheet in the workbook. The bar chart should compare the sales totals achieved by each salesperson that month without showing the salespersons' names.

6. Assign the macro to a button on the Sales&CommissionList worksheet.

7. Edit the macro so that the screen does not flash when the macro runs.

8. On the Documentation worksheet, explain how to use the workbook.

9. Create another macro that prints two copies of the Documentation worksheet in landscape orientation with the filename in the right section of the footer.

10. Edit the macro so that only one copy of the Documentation worksheet prints.

11. Test the macro to ensure it works correctly.

12. Protect the worksheets and workbook so that users cannot change their data or organization.

13. Save and close the June Sales.xlsm workbook.

SAM: Skills Assessment Manager

For current SAM information, including versions and content details, visit SAM Central (http://samcentral.course.com). If you have a SAM user profile, you may have access to hands-on instruction, practice, and assessment of the skills covered in this chapter. Since various versions of SAM are supported throughout the life of this text, check with your instructor for the correct instructions and URL/Web site for accessing assignments.

10

Chapter Exercises

Glossary

A

absolute cell referencing A cell reference that does not change when copied to another location in the workbook. To indicate that a cell reference is absolute, a dollar sign ($) precedes both the column reference and row reference of a cell address; for example, $B$2.

Accounting Number Format A number formatting option that displays the dollar sign ($) at the left edge of the cell, commas, and two decimal places for the numeric values, with a column of values aligned on the decimal point. Negative values are inside parentheses.

active cell The selected cell of a worksheet.

algorithm A rule that governs how a function works. An algorithm is a systematic set of procedures that the computer always steps through to calculate the results of a function.

amortization table A schedule detailing the payments of a financial transaction and the remaining principal in each period.

analysis The process of collecting, organizing, and otherwise transforming data into information that can be used to support decision making.

AND function The function that determines if the Boolean values in a list are all TRUE. If such is the case, a TRUE value is returned.

annual percentage rate (APR) A percentage rate charged, taking into account any additional borrower fees.

annual percentage yield (APY) An equivalent interest rate based on simple interest, including the effects of compounding.

application A workbook designed so that others can use it in a relatively error-free manner. An Excel application is usually a decision support system.

area chart A chart that displays trends over time or by category. Values are indicated by the filled areas below the lines.

argument A function input. For example, the ROUND function contains two arguments—a value and the number of decimal places, as follows: =ROUND(2.22,0).

array A specific arrangement of cells in a range. For example, a range of cells two wide by three high could be referred to as a 2×3 array.

assignment problem An optimization problem in which there is a one-to-one relationship between a resource and an assignment or job. For example, one machine in a plant might be assigned to one job. The machine cannot begin a second job until it finishes the first job.

AutoFilter An Excel table feature that displays arrows in the header row for each column for sorting and filtering the data in the column. This feature is enabled by default.

AutoSum A feature that automatically inserts a SUM function (or an AVERAGE, MIN, MAX, or COUNT function—if selected from the drop-down list). This feature automatically inserts a range based on the relative location of the cell versus adjacent data.

AVERAGE function The function that determines the arithmetic mean of the values in a defined range. Blank cells are ignored.

B

Backstage view A view that provides access to file-level features, such as creating new files, opening existing files, saving files, printing files, and closing files, as well as the most common program options.

balloon payment A final payment (additional amount) due at the end of a loan term.

binding A term that indicates the constraint has a final value that is equal to the value of the constraint; the constraint limits, or binds, the solution of the Solver model.

Boolean logical functions The AND, OR, and NOT functions that operate on Boolean logical values and return a Boolean logical value.

Boolean value A TRUE or FALSE value.

break-even analysis A type of what-if analysis that concentrates on an activity at or around the point at which a product breaks even—in other words, the point at which the expenses of creating and selling the product are equal to the revenue it produces, or the point at which the profit is $0.

bubble chart A chart that compares sets of three values. Values are indicated by the size of the bubbles (filled circles) and by position on the x-axis and y-axis.

C

calculated value A value that is the result of an Excel formula.

cash flow The money flow into and out of a financial entity.

cell The intersection of a row and column. Each cell is named according to the column and row where it's located. For example, the cell at the intersection of column G and row 5 is cell G5.

cell range Cell references separated by a colon that designate a range of cells. Ranges are used in function arguments to define the cells on which to operate. Ranges can be one-dimensional, along a row or column; two-dimensional, a block of rows and columns; or span multiple worksheets (for example, A1:A10, A1:Z1, Cost:Price!B3).

chart title The descriptive text that identifies the chart's contents.

CHOOSE function The function that returns a value or a range for up to 29 different values.

cleansing A step in which any data corruption is identified and corrected, if possible. Corrupt data is missing some element or is incorrect in some way. Corruption can be caused by data loss because of computer problems, but is often caused by human error.

column chart A chart that compares values across categories in a vertical orientation. Values are indicated by the height of the columns.

comma-delimited file A text file format that separates the values in each record with commas as delimiters. The term "delimiter" refers to the

character used to separate the values. Data stored in this way is also called comma-separated values (CSV).

comma-separated values (CSV) A text file format that separates the values in each record with commas as delimiters. The term "delimiter" refers to the character used to separate the values.

comment A note that you attach to a cell, separate from other cell content, and that usually displays short blocks of text, such as a brief explanation of a formula or a reminder.

Compatibility functions A new Excel 2010 category of functions that provides more consistent function names used in spreadsheet programs.

compound interest The interest that is calculated by including any previously earned/owed interest.

concatenate The process of combining separate strings of characters into a single string.

CONCATENATE function The function that can be used to combine up to 255 strings into one text string.

conditional formatting The formatting that is automatically applied if a set of specified criteria is met.

constraints In a Solver model, the conditions that restrict the values that are entered into the variable cells.

contribution margin A financial value calculated by subtracting variable expenses from sales, and representing the amount of revenue that contributes to covering the fixed expenses of a company.

COUNT function The function that counts the number of numeric and/or Boolean values in a range. Text values and empty cells are ignored.

COUNTA function The function that counts the number of numeric and/or Boolean or text values in a range. Empty cells are ignored.

COUNTIF function The function that counts the number of elements in a range that meet specific criteria.

CUMIPMT function The function that calculates the accumulated value of the interest portion of the period payments of a financial transaction between two specified periods.

CUMPRINC function The function that calculates the accumulated value of the principal portion of the period payments of a financial transaction between two specified periods.

custom An available option when splitting data points between charts in a Pie of Pie or Bar of Pie chart type. With this option, you can drag individual pie segments between the two charts so you can include exactly the segments you want in the main pie chart and the second chart, or plot.

custom number format An Excel formatting tool that allows you to customize the number format of a cell, including alignment in the cell, display of symbols such as $, display of negative values, and so on.

D

dashboard A business intelligence software package feature that display performance indicators in a fashion similar to the instrument panel in a car's dashboard. A dashboard usually features a set of charts that summarize several sets of data graphically.

data The term that can include words, images, numbers, or even sounds.

data gathering The process of identifying sources and obtaining data.

data labels Additional information on a chart about a data point or value.

data markers A graphical representation on a chart of data in a data series.

data points The points in a data series at which the x-axis and y-axis values intersect.

data series The related data points that are plotted on the chart; each data series on a chart has a unique color or pattern and is identified in the chart legend.

data set A group of related data.

data table A range of cells containing values and formulas. When you change the values, the data table shows you how those changes affect the results of the formulas.

data validation An Excel tool that allows you to create rules that define what data is valid in a particular cell.

database An organized collection of related data that is stored in tables.

database management system (DBMS) A system that creates and defines a database; a software program that creates and accesses the data in a database.

decision making The process of choosing among various options.

decision support system (DSS) A type of information system that helps decision makers model business scenarios, especially through what-if analysis.

decision variable The value in a cell that Solver changes to maximize, minimize, or set the objective cell to a specific value. Also known as variable cell.

defined name A name that refers to a cell, range of cells, formula, or constant value in Excel. Defined names can be up to 255 characters long, but cannot include spaces or punctuation marks other than periods or underscores. Defined names which are the same as cell references, such as "Q1," are not allowed.

dependent cell A cell that uses the value in the active cell in its formula.

depreciation A process of allocating the cost of an asset less its salvage value over its useful life.

digital certificate An electronic certification attached to a file or macro to vouch for its authenticity.

digital signature The part of a digital certificate that confirms that the signer created the file or macro and that it has not been changed since its digital certificate was created.

discount rate The rate at which cash flows are discounted. Usually, this rate reflects current interest rates and the relative risk of the cash flows being evaluated. Also known as the hurdle rate or rate of return.

document type definition (DTD) A document that contains information that identifies the elements used in the markup language and how they are related to each other.

documentation The record that describes how and why a system has been developed and how it should be used.

double-declining balance A method that computes the depreciation at an accelerated rate. Depreciation is highest in the first period and decreases in successive periods.

doughnut chart A chart that compares the contribution each value in multiple numeric data series makes to the whole, or 100%. Values are indicated by the size of the doughnut segments.

down payment An amount of money paid up front in a financial transaction that is not part of the loan amount.

E

error alert A message box that displays a message of varying severity depending on the data entry or other errors you make.

Excel program button A button, located to the left of the Quick Access Toolbar, that displays a menu with the standard window sizing features.

Excel table An Excel table is a range of cells that you formalize as a single unit of data.

Extensible Markup Language (XML) A programming language that combines the markup power of SGML with the ease of use of HTML, provided through the efforts of the W3C.

F

FALSE The Boolean value FALSE, as differentiated from the text label "False."

false negative A value or formula that is incorrect, but is not flagged as an error.

false positive A value or formula that is flagged as incorrect, but is, in fact, correct.

field A single characteristic of a table entity, such as a product ID number or an address.

File tab A tab on the Ribbon that provides access to commonly used commands, such as Save, Open, Print, and Close, as well as to tabs, including Recent, New, and Help. Clicking these commands or tabs opens the related options in Backstage view. This tab replaces the 2007 Office button.

file protection A type of security that protects an entire workbook file with a password for optimal security, allowing only authorized users to open a workbook and use its data.

filtering A step that involves temporarily hiding data that is not useful or necessary for the analysis.

FIND function The function that returns the starting position of one text value within another text value. The function is case sensitive.

fixed-declining balance A method that returns the depreciation of an asset for a specified period of time.

flat-file database The data stored in rows and columns in one worksheet or table.

formula An equation written in Excel syntax that performs a calculation. Formulas always begin with an equal sign (=) and can contain combinations of operators, operands, and functions, for example, = 2+B2*SUM(A1:A5).

formula auditing A set of tools in Excel that help you find and respond to formula errors.

freezing panes A technique that divides the worksheet into separate vertical and/or horizontal sections. The top and/or left sections are "frozen" in place so they remain in view while you scroll the bottom and/or right sections.

function A predefined formula that performs a calculation. Functions begin with an equal sign (=), followed by the function name and a list of arguments enclosed in parentheses. The arguments must be in a specified order.

FV function The function that calculates the future or ending value of a financial transaction. The FV function contains arguments for the number of periods (nper), periodic rate, periodic payment amount (pmt), and present value (pv) of the financial transaction.

G

Goal Seek An Excel tool that determines the value of a single input to obtain a specified output.

H

header row A row at the top of the worksheet containing labels that identify the data contained in each column.

HLOOKUP function The function that looks up a value stored in the first row of a horizontal lookup table and retrieves data stored in the same column of a subsequent row.

horizontal lookup table A lookup table in which data is stored in rows instead of columns.

hurdle rate The rate at which cash flows are discounted. Usually, this rate reflects current interest rates and the relative risk of the cash flows being evaluated. Also known as the discount rate or rate of return.

Hypertext Markup Language (HTML) A markup language that creates Web pages (also called HTML documents). In HTML, you embed tags in the document to describe how to format its content. When a Web browser reads an HTML document, the browser uses the tags to format text according to a set of predefined descriptions of those tags.

I

IF function The logical function that evaluates a logical test (True or False) and applies different outcomes depending upon if the logical test evaluates to True (value_if_true) or to False (value_if_false).

IFERROR function The function that combines aspects of the IF function and the ISERROR function to simplify error checking.

INDEX function The function that retrieves data from multidimensional tables.

infeasible solution The result when Solver cannot determine the combination of decision variables that satisfy all of the constraints identified in the Solver model.

information Data that is organized in some meaningful way.

input cell In a data table, a cell that contains a value that can vary.

input message A message that identifies the kind of data you should enter in a particular worksheet cell.

inputs The values and text labels that are directly entered into cells.

interest A user fee paid for the use of money, usually charged by the lender as a percent of the value borrowed over a specified period of time.

internal rate of return (IRR) A rate at which a set of cash flows has an NPV (net present value) of $0.

IPMT function The function that calculates the value of the interest portion of a loan payment based on the original loan amount, periodic interest rate, and payment number.

IRR function The function that calculates the internal rate of return at which discounted cash flows in and out are equal.

IS functions A category of functions, including ISBLANK and ISNUMBER, that test a value or cell reference, and then return a TRUE or FALSE value depending on the results.

K

key data The data that you want to look up when using a lookup function.

KeyTips Access keys for commands or tabs displayed when you press the Alt key.

knowledge workers The people who work with and develop knowledge. Data and information are their raw material. Knowledge workers use this raw material to analyze a particular situation and evaluate a course of action.

L

LARGE function The function that displays kth largest element of a data set. K is the position from the largest value.

LEFT function The function that extracts characters from the beginning or "left side" of a text string.

legend A box that identifies the patterns or colors assigned to the data series in a chart.

line chart A chart that displays trends over time or by category. Values are indicated by the height of the lines.

linear function A function that results when a decision variable is multiplied by a constant, such as price. When you plot a linear function in a chart, the result is a straight line, thus the term linear.

local scope A worksheet in which a defined (range) name is valid.

LOOKUP function The function that looks up the greatest value that does not exceed a specified value anywhere in a table or range, whether it is organized in a vertical or horizontal orientation.

lookup table A data list that categorizes values you want to retrieve.

M

macro A series of commands that are stored and can be run to perform a task.

macro-enabled workbook An Excel workbook for which macro security settings have been specified in the Trust Center.

macro recorder An Excel tool that allows you to create macros by recording keystrokes and mouse actions as you perform them.

macro virus A virus found in a macro that is attached to a document created in a Microsoft Office program, such as Excel, and that runs when you open the infected document.

markup language A link between the content in a document and the instructions for formatting that content. A markup language uses a set of tags to distinguish different elements in a document and uses attributes to define those elements further.

MATCH function The function that returns the relative position (such as 1, 2, or 3) of a matched value in a list.

MAX function The function that determines the maximum value in the defined range. Blank cells are ignored.

mean The arithmetic average of a data set.

median A middle value of a data set in which there is an equal number of values both higher and lower than the median.

MEDIAN function The function that returns the median of the given numbers, which is the number in the middle of a set of numbers; that is, half the numbers have values that are greater than the median, and half have values that are less than the median.

metadata Data that describes other data.

Microsoft Query A Microsoft Office program that lets you create queries to select data from external sources, including Microsoft Access, and import the query results into a worksheet.

MIN function The function that determines the minimum value in the defined range. Blank cells are ignored.

mixed cell reference A cell reference that has both a relative and absolute component—for example, $B2 when copied always keeps column B

(absolute component) but varies the row. B$2 when copied varies the column but not the row.

mode The most common arithmetic value found in a data set.

MODE.SNGL function The function that returns the most frequently occurring value in a range of data.

moving average A term that is used when the average is recalculated each period over a set number of previous periods in a chart. For example, a 30-day moving average calculates the average for the last 30 days—moving the average along the chart. Varying degrees of smoothing are achieved by changing the length of the moving average.

N

negative cash flow The monies paid from a person/institution; cash that is paid out.

nesting A process of placing one formula inside another formula. For example, –ROUND (AVERAGE(B2:B10), 0) nests an AVERAGE function within a ROUND function. The AVERAGE function is evaluated first and then the results are used as the first argument of the ROUND function.

net present value (NPV) A method of discounting cash flows to the present value based on a selected discount rate. A positive NPV for a cash flow indicates that an investment will add value to the investor.

none of construct A combination of Boolean logical functions that test if none of the elements of a list contain a TRUE value for specified criteria.

nonlinear function A function that cannot be described in linear terms. When you graph a nonlinear function on two dimensions, it results in a curve, not a straight line.

normal distribution A data set that has an equal number of values, equally spaced both above and below the median value.

normalization A process of storing data in related tables to reduce data redundancy.

not binding The term that indicates that a constraint in a Solver model does not have a final value that is equal to the value of the constraint.

NOT function The function that changes the Boolean value TRUE to FALSE and the Boolean value FALSE to TRUE.

NPER function The function that calculates the duration of a financial transaction as expressed by the number of equal periods. The NPER function contains arguments for the periodic rate, periodic payment amount (pmt), present value (pv), and future value (fv) of the financial transaction.

NPV function The function that evaluates the hurdle rate and the series of cash flow values and automatically calculates the discounted value.

numeric values Numbers such as integers and real numbers—1, 2, 3.3, 6.75, and so on.

O

objective cell The cell in Solver that you can change to reach a goal. In earlier versions of Excel, this was called the target cell.

objective function A mathematical formula that relates the decision variables or variable cells in a Solver model to the desired outcome in the objective cell.

one-variable data table A type of data table that has only one input cell and many result cells.

only construct A combination of Boolean logical functions that test if only certain elements of a list have a TRUE value for specified criteria and that none of the other elements of a list contain a TRUE value for that criteria.

optimization An analytical process used to narrow the available options for a problem so you can choose the best potential outcome.

OR function The function that determines if at least one item from a list of Boolean values is TRUE. If such is the case, a TRUE value is returned.

outputs The information generated as a result of data inputs and formulas.

P

payback period The number of periods (years) it will take to pay back an original investment.

percent value An available option when splitting data points between charts in a Pie of Pie or Bar of Pie chart type. This option allows you to select a cut-off point by percentage, rather than value,

and assign all the percentages below that point to the second plot.

pie chart A chart that compares the contribution each value in a single numeric data series makes to the whole, or 100%. Values are indicated by the size of the pie slices.

PivotChart report An analysis tool that represents PivotTable source data as a graphic. A PivotChart report includes series, axes, and data markers, just as a regular chart does.

PivotTable Field List A list of fields in the data source selected for a PivotTable report.

PivotTable report An interactive report that lets you summarize and analyze a data set. You can use a PivotTable report to summarize selected fields from a list of data from an external source, such as a database.

PMT function The function that calculates the periodic payment of a financial transaction. This payment is assumed to be paid in equal periodic installments. The PMT function contains arguments for the periodic rate, number of periods (nper), present value (pv), and future value (fv) of the financial transaction.

position An available option when splitting data points between charts in a pie of pie or bar of pie chart type. Data is directed to the secondary chart based on the relative position in the range.

positive cash flow The monies paid to a person/institution; cash that is received.

PPMT function The function that calculates the value of the principal portion of a loan payment based on the original loan amount, periodic interest rate, and payment number.

precedent cell A cell that contains a value that is used in the formula in the current cell.

precise value The number of decimal places stored, not necessarily displayed. For example, the value 0.3 might be displayed in a cell, but the precise value stored might be 0.333333333333333. Excel can store up to 15 significant digits for a value.

pre-processing A process of manipulating data into the needed format.

principal The value of a loan or investment.

problem A term that can be considered in two ways: as a question to be answered or as an obstacle or difficulty that prevents you from reaching some goal.

pseudocode A kind of shorthand for a formula that shows the structure of a formula without the syntactical details.

PV function The function that calculates the initial value of a financial transaction. The PV function contains arguments for the number of periods (nper), periodic rate, periodic payment amount (pmt), and future value (fv) of the financial transaction.

Q

query A question that you ask a database. In response to a query, the database displays only those records that meet the criteria you specify in the query.

Query Wizard A wizard that lets you choose a data source and select the database table and fields you want to import into a workbook. The Query Wizard prompts you to define any criteria for the data you want to import by selecting only rows that meet criteria that you specify.

R

radar chart A chart that displays changes in values relative to a center point and is named for their resemblance to the plots on radar screens as they scan a 360-degree circle. Values radiate from the center of the chart in a way that can be compared to radar screen plots, showing the distance of an object from the radar in the center. The categories are represented by lines that radiate out from the center.

RAND function The function that generates a random number (real number) between 0 and 1.

RANDBETWEEN function The function that generates a random integer between two values.

range name A name given to a cell, range of cells, formula, or constant value in Excel. Also called a defined name.

RANK function The function that gives the relative position of a value in a data set.

RANK.EQ function The function that calculates or ranks a value from a given list and then counts the

number of entries either above or below the value in question.

rate of return The rate at which cash flows are discounted. Usually, this rate reflects current interest rates and the relative risk of the cash flows being evaluated. Also known as the hurdle rate or discount rate.

RATE function The function that calculates the periodic interest rate of a financial transaction. The RATE function contains arguments for the number of periods (nper), periodic payment amount (pmt), present value (pv), and future value (fv) of the financial transaction.

record A set of fields that are related, such as the information that describes one customer for a business.

Reference and Lookup functions A category of functions that can look up or reference data stored in a table.

relational database management system Another term for a database management system (DBMS) when the data is stored in tables that relate to each other through a common field.

relational expression A formula containing a relational operator that compares two values and returns a Boolean logical value (TRUE/FALSE).

relational operator An operator that compares two values: > greater than; >= greater than or equal to; < less than; <= less than or equal to; = equal to; <> not equal to.

relative cell referencing A cell reference that, when copied from one location to another, automatically changes relative to the location to which it is being moved. For example, if a formula containing relative cell references is being copied one row down and two columns to the right, the formula adjusts each cell reference by one row down and two columns to the right.

result cell A cell in a data table containing a formula that involves input cells in its calculations. In Scenario Manager, these are output cells. In a data table, a cell containing a formula that involves the input cells in its calculation.

RIGHT function The function that returns the final character or characters in a text string, based on the number of characters specified.

return on investment (ROI) The ratio of profits to initial investment.

root element The element in an XML document within which all other elements are nested. An XML document can have only one root element.

ROUND function The function that rounds a value to the specified number of digits. This function changes not only the display of the value, but also the precision stored.

S

scenario A set of values stored in a worksheet that describes different situations, such as worst-case, likely case, and best-case scenarios, or the result of a Solver model, that is saved in a worksheet so you can load and review it later.

Scenario Manager A tool in Excel that allows you to create, edit, and summarize scenario models.

schema A set of validation rules for an XML document. The schema describes the elements in the document and how they are structured or related to each other. You can use a schema to create very complex validation rules by defining the data type and valid values for an element.

scope The location in which the defined (range) name is valid. A defined name valid in an entire workbook has global scope. A defined name valid in a worksheet has local scope.

SEARCH function The function that returns the starting position of one text value within another text value in the same manner as the FIND function, but the SEARCH function is not case sensitive.

sensitivity analysis A type of what-if analysis that attempts to examine how sensitive the results of an analysis are to changes in the assumptions.

simple interest The interest that is calculated without including any previously earned/owed interest.

simulated results The results that are based on realistic, but not actual, data.

simulation An analytical method that creates artificially generated data to imitate real data.

slicer A PivotTable feature that groups filtered data sets into button-like objects.

SMALL function The function that displays the *k*th smallest element of a data set. *K* is the position from the largest value.

SNL function The function that calculates depreciation using the straight line method.

Solver An Excel add-in program used for optimization. You can set up complex business models in a worksheet and use Solver to determine the optimal set of decision inputs to meet an objective, such as minimizing costs or maximizing profits. Because you can use Solver to answer very complex questions about allocation and optimization, it is an excellent tool for determining the best way to apply resources to a particular problem.

Solver model The combination of the objective cell, variable cells, and constraints that are used to solve a problem.

sparklines Small word-sized charts or graphics are embedded within the words, numbers, and images they represent in a worksheet, making multiple comparisons of trends and patterns much easier.

split An Excel tool that divides the worksheet into separate vertical and/or horizontal sections.

standard deviation A measure of how widely a data set varies from the arithmetic mean.

Standard General Markup Language (SGML) A markup language that provides structure for a document by dividing it into elements (pieces), such as title, paragraph, text, name, part number, and so on. The markup language identifies these elements so that any program that interprets SGML can understand them.

statistics A subset of mathematics that is applied to understanding observed data.

STDEV.S function The function that estimates standard deviation based on a sample, ignoring logical values and text.

step-variable relationship A relationship that shows how an expense does not vary directly with the number of units produced, but varies as the units reach steps of quantities.

stock chart A chart that displays stock price and volume trends over time. Plotted values can include volume, opening price, highest price, lowest price, and closing price.

straight line depreciation A method that allocates the asset's useful life evenly over a specified time period.

sub procedure A list of statements in Visual Basic for Applications used to perform actions, such as with an Excel macro.

Subtotal command An Excel command that you use to create summary reports that quickly organize data into categories with subtotal calculations and lets you collapse and expand the level of detail in the report.

SUM function The function that adds a list of adjacent and/or non-adjacent cell references, constants, and/or cell ranges, for example, =SUM(A1:A10,B7,3).

SUMIF function The function that sums specific elements of a data set if a corresponding value meets specific criteria.

SUMPRODUCT function The function used to sum a series of products.

sum of the year digits A method of depreciation in which the cost allocation is apportioned based on a declining fractional amount of the asset's life.

surface chart A chart that displays value trends in three dimensions. Values are indicated by areas with colors or patterns on the surface of the chart.

syntax The specific format of a function, including the function name and the order of the arguments in the function.

T

table A collection of fields that describe a specific entity. For example, a table might store data about a company's products or its employees.

test data The input data for which you already know the results and use to verify the results in a worksheet.

text label The textual information that appears in a worksheet.

TODAY function The function that returns the current date's serial number (based on the computer's internal clock).

tracer arrows Arrows that show precedent cells and are dependent on a worksheet.

trendline A line in a chart that graphically illustrates trends in the data using a statistical technique known as regression.

TRIM function The function that removes all spaces in a text string except for the single spaces between words.

TRUE The Boolean value TRUE, as differentiated from the text label "True."

Trust Center An Excel dialog box in which you set security and privacy options for Excel and other Microsoft Office applications. Provides options for setting security for macros that are not stored in trusted locations.

trusted location A folder on a hard drive or shared network drive that has been designated by you or your network administrator as containing documents that always come from trustworthy sources.

two-dimensional table A lookup table in which data is stored at the intersection of a column and row.

two-variable data table A type of data table that has two input cells, but only one result cell.

U

unbounded solution A solution that occurs in a Solver model in which the feasible solution is unrestrained or unlimited on some dimension; there is no limit to what can be inserted in the variable cells.

V

validation rule A rule that specifies the type of data that is appropriate in a particular worksheet cell.

value An available option when splitting data points between charts in a Pie of Pie or Bar of Pie chart type. This option allows you to select a cut-off point that assigns all the values below that point to the second plot.

variable cell A cell in which Solver changes the values to maximize, minimize, or set the objective cell to a specific value. Also known as a decision variable.

variable-declining balance A method of depreciation that returns the cost allocation of an asset for any period specified, including partial periods, using the double-declining balance method or some other method specified.

Visual Basic Editor The application used to edit VBA code in Excel and other Microsoft Office document macros.

Visual Basic for Applications (VBA) A programming code used to create and store macros in Microsoft Office documents.

VLOOKUP function The function that looks up a value stored in the first column of a vertical lookup table and retrieves data stored in the same row of a subsequent column.

W

Web query An automated method for retrieving information from a Web page without having to copy and paste it into an application.

what-if analysis A process of changing values to see how those changes affect the outcome of formulas in an Excel worksheet.

wildcard A symbol that can be used as part of criteria in a text string in which the wildcard can be substituted for another character or set of characters. For example, an asterisk (*) specifies that any number of characters can be substituted, and a question mark (?) specifies that a single character can be substituted.

workbook An Excel file that contains one or more worksheets.

workbook protection A type of security that protects a workbook by preventing users from inserting, deleting, or renaming worksheets or from changing the size and position of the worksheet window.

worksheet An Excel spreadsheet; a single two-dimensional sheet organized into rows (identified by row numbers 1, 2, etc.) and columns (identified by column letters A, B...Z; AB...). An Excel 2007 worksheet contains a maximum of 16,384 columns and 1,048,576 rows.

worksheet protection A type of security that protects a worksheet by preventing users from changing, moving, or deleting its data.

World Wide Web Consortium (W3C) The organization that was created in 1994 with the goal of leading the World Wide Web to its full potential. The W3C has approximately 350 member organizations that develop common protocols to promote the Web's evolution and ensure its interoperability.

X

X Y (Scatter) chart A chart that compares pairs of numeric values on the x- and y-axes with the data points plotted proportionally to the values on the x-axis; can also be used to display a functional relationship, such as y=mx+b. Values are indicated by the position of the data points.

x-axis The horizontal axis on which categories are plotted in a chart.

x-axis labels The labels that identify the categories plotted on the x-axis.

XML (Extensible Markup Language) A markup language that was designed to combine the markup power of SGML with the ease of use of HTML. The result is a language that defines the structure and rules for creating markup elements. XML is increasingly being used as an enterprise data format for the transfer of information between different applications.

XML map A map generated by Excel to create mapped ranges of data and define the relationships between these ranges and the elements in the XML schema. Excel uses the XML map to relate the data to the elements when importing and exporting XML data.

XML table A table that is similar in appearance and functionality to an Excel table, but the data in an XML table is mapped to XML elements. Each column in an XML table represents an XML element in the XML document.

Y

y-axis The vertical axis on which data values are plotted in a chart.

y-axis labels The labels that identify the data values plotted on the y-axis.

YEARFRAC function The function that calculates the number of years between two dates.

Index

Note: Boldface indicates location of definition.